Essentials of
Business Law

Fifth Edition

Ewan MacIntyre

Senior Lecturer
Nottingham Law School
Nottingham Trent University

PEARSON

Harlow, England • London • New York • Bos on • San Francisco • Toronto • Sydney
Auckland • Singapore • Hong Kong • Tokyo • Seoul • Taipei • New Delhi
Cape Town • São Paulo • Mexico City • Madrid • Amsterdam • Munich • Paris • Milan

PEARSON EDUCATION LIMITED

Edinburgh Gate
Harlow CM20 2JE
United Kingdom
Tel: +44 (0)1279 623623
Fax: +44 (0)1279 431059
Web: www.pearson.com/uk

First published 2007 (print)
Second edition published 2009 (print)
Third edition published 2011 (print)
Fourth edition published 2013 (print and electronic)
Fifth edition published 2015 (print and electronic)

ISBN: 978-1-292-08270-7 (print)
978-1-292-08272-1 (PDF)
978-1-292-08273-8 (eText)

British Library Cataloguing-in-Publication Data
A catalogue record for the print edition is available from the British Library

Library of Congress Cataloging-in-Publication Data
MacIntyre, Ewan, author.
  Essentials of business law / Ewan MacIntyre, Senior Lecturer, Nottingham Law School,
Nottingham Trent University. -- Fifth edition.
    pages cm
  Includes index.
  ISBN 978-1-292-08270-7
  1. Commercial law--England. 2. Commercial law--Wales. I. Title.
  KD1629.6.M33 2015
  346.4207--dc23
                                                          2014048762

10 9 8 7 6 5 4 3 2 1
16 15 14 13

Print edition typeset in 9.5/12 pt ITC Charter by 35
Printed by Ashford Colour Press Ltd, Gosport

NOTE THAT ANY PAGE CROSS REFERENCES REFER TO THE PRINT EDITION

Brief contents

Contents

mylawchamber
unrivalled support for legal education

Join over 5,000 law students succeeding with MyLawChamber

Visit **www.mylawchamber.co.uk/macintyreessentials** to access a wealth of tools to help you develop and test your knowledge of business law, strengthening your understanding so you can excel.

 The Pearson eText is a fully searchable, interactive version of *Essentials of Business Law*. You can make notes in it, highlight it, bookmark it, even link to online sources – helping you get more out of studying and revision. The Pearson eText is linked to the learning tools you'll find in MyLawChamber.

- Interactive multiple-choice questions to test your understanding of each topic
- Practice exam questions with guidance to hone your exam technique
- Weblinks to help you read more widely around the subject and really impress your lecturers
- Glossary to use as a quick reference for legal terms and definitions
- Glossary flashcards to test yourself on legal terms and definitions
- Legal newsfeed to help you read more widely, stay right up to date with the law and impress examiners
- Legal updates to help you stay up to date with the law and impress examiners

 Case Navigator provides in-depth analysis of the leading cases in business law, improving your case-reading skills and understanding of how the law is applied.

 Explore the world of Virtual Lawyer and develop your skills in answering legal problem questions as you apply your knowledge of the law to a range of interactive scenarios.

Use the access card at the back of the book to activate MyLawChamber. Online purchase is also available at **www.mylawchamber.co.uk/register**.

Lecturers *Teach your course, your way.*

MyLawChamber is a powerful teaching tool which you can use to assess your students, and improve their understanding.

 Make the interactive Pearson eText a 'live' teaching resource by annotating with your own commentary, links to external sources, critique, or updates to the law and share with your students.

 PEARSON mytest Set quizzes and mini-assessments using the bank of over 900 multiple-choice questions to gauge your students' understanding.

 Use Case Navigator, a case reading resource we offer in conjunction with LexisNexis, to assign student seminar work.

- Virtual Lawyer is an engaging way to help your students develop their problem-solving skills through scenario-based learning
- PowerPoint slides with visual support in explaining legal concepts
- Instructor's Manual including ideas for seminars and assessment with handouts for use in class

For information about teaching support materials, please contact your local Pearson sales consultant or visit **www.mylawchamber.co.uk**.
The regularly maintained mylawchamber premium site provides the following features:

- Search tool to help locate specific items of content.
- Online help and support to assist with website usage and troubleshooting.

Case Navigator access is included with your MyLawChamber registration. The LexisNexis element of Case Navigator is only available to those who currently subscribe to LexisNexis Butterworths online.

Preface

My aim in writing this text is to give a clear account of the areas of law which affect businesses. It differs from other texts in that it contains the following distinguishing features.

- Over 90 comprehensive diagrams.
- A detailed study skills section.
- An extensive glossary of terms used.
- A comprehensive website, containing nearly 300 additional questions.

Before saying a little more about these distinguishing features, I would like to make it plain that they are not intended as alternatives to the main text. The main text could stand alone without these additional features. However, it is hoped that the additional features will reinforce the main text.

I have included over 90 figures, consisting mainly of flowcharts and tables. These figures have been developed from diagrams which I use when teaching. Having started with a few obvious diagrams, I found that my students were frequently asking whether a diagram could recap new material covered. I hope very much that the figures aid comprehension. They are not intended as a substitute for the written text, but to supplement it, either by giving an overview of a topic about to be covered or by recapping one already explained.

I have also included a fairly lengthy study skills section. This runs to several thousand words and concentrates mainly on two matters. First, it explains, in a legal context, the skills which students might be expected to show in their assessments. Then it shows how these skills can be put to use in answering a problem style of question. The problem question used to demonstrate this relates to offer and acceptance of a contract because this is a topic studied early on in most business law courses. For those readers whose course does not cover this topic, or whose course covers it later on, I would recommend reading the relevant pages on offer and acceptance before reading the material on study skills. I hope that the study skills section will help readers to achieve higher grades and also reveal how creatively and interestingly a problem question can be answered. Above all, I hope that the section will dispel the myth that law assessments are about learning vast amounts of law and then reproducing them.

The glossary explains the meaning of some 400 words or phrases. I hope that it will prove useful to readers and enable them quickly to discover the meaning of some of the legal words used in this book.

The final feature of this book is its accompanying website. This website is very large, containing 280 additional questions which supplement the Practice Questions in the text. Answers to the website questions are provided on the site. The website also contains flash-cards of 90 of the most important cases featured in the text. These should prove a very useful revision aid, in that a user of the website will be able to click on the name of a case and bring up a brief summary of the decision. A final feature of the website is that it contains a simple set of company accounts, along with brief questions and answers which enable readers to understand them. Almost all businesses have the making of a profit as their major objective and I thought that it would be useful for readers to see what a balance sheet and a profit and loss account actually look like.

The opening chapter of this text deals with the legal system and the settlement of legal disputes. The part of this chapter which deals with the sources of English law should help readers to understand the substantive law covered in later chapters. Four chapters on the law of contract come next and these are followed by two chapters on closely related subjects, agency and sale of goods. Two chapters on tort come next. The first of these deals with the tort of negligence and with torts related to negligence. The next chapter deals with torts which are not related to negligence. The following three chapters examine closely the law relating to companies, partnerships and limited liability partnerships. Any business carried on by two or more people must trade in one of these three ways. Two chapters on employment law come next. The first of these deals with the contract of employment and the rights of a dismissed employee. The second deals with discrimination and health and safety. The next chapter deals with trade descriptions and misleading price indications. The penultimate chapter deals with credit and types of business property, and the final chapter covers the resolution of business disputes.

Finally, I would like to thank my good friend Eddie Fox for the company accounts which feature on the website.

Table of cases

Case Navigator provides in-depth analysis of the leading cases in business law, improving your case-reading skills and understanding of how the law is applied.

Visit **www.mylawchamber.co.uk/macintyreessentials** to access unique online support:

- **Direct deep links** to the core cases in **business** law
- **Short introductions** provide guidance on what you should look out for while reading the case
- **Questions** help you to test your understanding of the case, and provide feedback on what you should have grasped
- **Summaries** contextualise the case and point you to further reading so that you are fully prepared for seminars and discussions

Case Navigator cases are highlighted **in bold** below.

Case Navigator access is included with your MyLawChamber registration. The LexisNexis element of Case Navigator is only available to those who currently subscribe to LexisNexis Butterworths online.

Case Navigator cases are highlighted in **bold**

Table of statutes

International Legislation

Table of statutory instruments

Table of European legislation

Study skills

Get organised from the start

When you start your course, decide how much time you can afford to devote to your study of each subject. Be realistic when doing this. There will be a lot to learn and that is why your time must be managed as effectively as possible. Listen to your lecturers, who will explain what is expected of you. Having made your decision to devote a certain amount of time per week to a particular subject, stick to what you have decided. If it will help, draw up a weekly chart and tick off each period of study when you complete it. You should attend all your lectures and tutorials, and should always read the pages of this book which are recommended by your lecturer. Steady work throughout the year is the key to success.

Take advantage of what your lecturer tells you

Many lecturers set and mark their students' assessments. Even if the assessment is externally set and marked, your lecturer is likely to have experience of past assessments and to know what the examiners are looking for. Take advantage of this. If you are told that something is not in your syllabus, don't waste time on it. If you are told that something is particularly important, make sure you know it well. If you are told to go away and read something up, make sure that you do so, and if you are told to read certain pages of this text, make sure that you read them. You may be told to read this text after you have been taught, so as to reinforce learning. Or you may be told to read it beforehand, so that you can apply what you have read in the classroom. Either way, it is essential that you do the reading.

After the lecture/tutorial

It is tempting to file your notes away until revision time, as soon as the class is over. You probably understood the ground that was covered and therefore assumed that it would easily be remembered later. However, it is an excellent idea to go over what was covered within 24 hours. This need not take too long. You should check that all the points were understood, and if any were not understood you should clear them up with the help of your notes and this text. Make more notes as you do this. Give these notes a separate heading, something like 'Follow up notes'. These additional notes should always indicate which aspects of the class seemed important. They should also condense your notes, to give you an overview of the lecture.

In many cases your lecturer will be setting your exam or coursework. If a particular area or topic is flagged up as important, it is more likely to be assessed than one which was not. Even if your assessment is externally set, your lecturer is likely to know which areas are the most important, and thus most likely to be tested. Fifteen minutes should be plenty to go over a one-hour class. Each 15 minutes spent doing this is likely to be worth far more time than an extra 15 minutes of later revision just before the exam.

Answering questions

What skills are you expected to show?

In 1956 Benjamin Bloom categorised the skills which students are likely to be required to display when being assessed. These skills are shown in the following figure. Each skill in the pyramid builds upon the one beneath it.

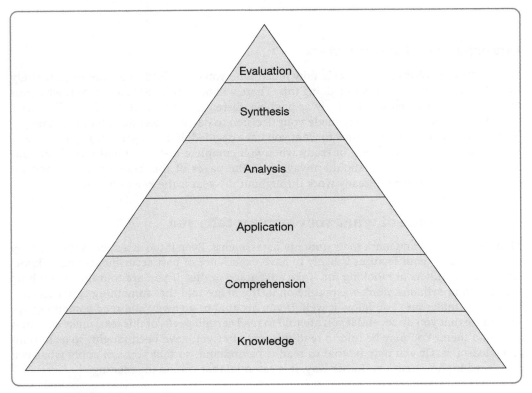

Figure 1 Study skills

Before deciding which skills you might be required to demonstrate, a brief explanation of the skills, in a legal context, needs to be made.

Knowledge, on its own, is not nearly as important as many students think. On the one hand, knowledge is essential because without knowledge none of the other skills are possible. But mere knowledge is unlikely to score highly in a traditional law assessment. Most assessments require comprehension, analysis and application. An exam question *might* require mere knowledge by asking something such as, '*List the terms implied by the Sale of Goods Act 1979*'. But not many assessments are so limited. Far more likely is a question such as, '*Describe the terms implied by the Sale of Goods Act 1979 and analyse the extent to which they adequately protect consumers*'. This is a very different question. It requires knowledge, of course, but it also requires the higher level skills. It is these later skills which gain the higher marks. In 'open book' exams especially, mere knowledge is likely to be worth very little.

Comprehension cannot be shown without knowledge. Some questions do require just knowledge and comprehension, for example, '*Explain the effect of the Contracts (Rights of*

Third Parties) Act 1999'. However, you should make sure that this is all the question requires. For example, if the question had said, *'Consider the extent to which the Contracts (Rights of Third Parties) Act 1999 has changed the law relating to privity of contract'*, most of the marks would be gained for application, for showing how the Act would have changed the pre-Act cases such as **Tweddle v Atkinson (1831)** (Chapter 2).

Application of the law is very commonly required by a legal question. There is little point in knowing and understanding the law if you cannot apply it. The typical legal problem question, which sets out some facts and then asks you to advise the parties, always requires application of the law. It is not enough to show that you understand the relevant area of law, although some credit is likely to be given for this; you must then apply the law to advise the parties. These problem questions frequently also allow you to demonstrate analysis, synthesis and evaluation, as we shall see below when we consider how to answer such a question. However, this is not always true. When there is only one relevant case, and where it is obviously applicable, mere application of that case is all that is required.

Analysis of the law occurs when you recognise patterns and hidden meanings. You break the law down into component parts, differentiating and distinguishing ideas. For example, you might explain how one case (**Adams v Lindsell (1818)** in Chapter 2) introduced the postal rule on acceptance of contracts, and how another case (**Holwell Securities Ltd v Hughes (1974)**, Chapter 2) limited its application. Having made such an analysis of the law, you could apply it to a problem question.

Synthesis is the gathering of knowledge from several areas to generalise, predict and draw conclusions. Precisely the skill required to deal with the more complex problem questions!

Evaluation of the law requires you to compare ideas and make choices. It is a useful skill in answering problem questions. For example, in a problem question on offer and acceptance, you might need to evaluate the applicability of **Adams v Lindsell** and **Holwell Securities Ltd v Hughes**. Evaluation is often asked for in essays, for example, *'Consider the extent to which the Unfair Terms in Consumer Contracts Regulations 1999 add to the protection of consumers conferred by the Unfair Contract Terms Act 1977'*. When you evaluate you are giving your own opinion, realising that there are no absolutely right and wrong answers. However, it is not pure opinion which is required. You must demonstrate the lower level skills described above in order to give some justification for your opinion.

So when you look at past assessments, try to work out which skills are required. Then make sure that you demonstrate these skills. Do not introduce the higher level skills if they are not expected of you in a particular question. For example, the very simple question *'List the terms implied by the Sale of Goods Act 1979'* is looking only for knowledge. No extra marks will be gained for evaluating the effectiveness of the terms. It must be said that such a question would be more suitable to a test than to an exam. The point here is that you should see what skills the question requires and then make sure that you demonstrate those skills.

Answering problem questions

Almost all law exams have some problem questions, such as the Practice Questions in this text. These questions require application of the law rather than mere reproduction of legal principles.

You should always make a plan before you answer a problem question. Read the question thoroughly a couple of times, perhaps underlining important words or phrases. Problem questions can be lengthy, but the examiner will have taken this into account and allowed time for thorough reading of the question. So don't panic or read through too hurriedly. Next, see what the question asks you to do. (This is usually spelt out in the first or the last sentence of the question.) Then identify the legal issues which the question raises. Finally, apply the relevant cases to the issues and reach a conclusion.

Chapter 2 Practice Question 2, reproduced here, can be used as an example.

> Acme Supastore advertised its 'price promise' heavily in the Nottown Evening News. This promise stated that Acme was the cheapest retailer in the city of Nottown and that it would guarantee that this was true. The advertisement stated, 'We are so confident that we are the cheapest in the area that we guarantee that you cannot buy a television anywhere in Nottown cheaper than from us. We also guarantee that if you buy any television from us and give us notice in writing that you could have bought it cheaper at any other retailer within five miles of our Supastore on the same day we will refund twice the difference in price. Offer to remain open for the month of December. Any claim to be received in writing within 5 days of purchase.' Belinda saw the advertisement and was per-suaded by it to buy a television from Acme Supastore for £299. The contract was made on Monday 3 December. On Saturday 8 December Belinda found that a neighbouring shop was selling an identical model of television for £289 and had been selling at this price for the past six months. Belinda immediately telephoned Acme Supastore to say that she was claiming her money back. She also posted a letter claiming her money back. The letter arrived on Monday 10 December. Acme Supastore are refusing to refund any of the purchase price. Advise Belinda as to whether or not any contract has been made.

The final sentence of the question tells you what you are required to do – advise Belinda as to whether or not a contract has been made. You should remember from your study of con-tract law that the requirements of a contract are an offer, an acceptance, an intention to create legal relations and consideration. So if these are all present a contract will exist. Notice that all the question asks you is whether or not a contract exists. It did not ask what remedies might be available if such a contract did exist and was breached. It might have done this, but it did not. So make sure you answer the question asked.

The first legal issue is whether the advertisement is an offer. So first define an offer as a proposal of a set of terms, made with the intention that both parties will be contractually bound if the proposed terms are accepted. Then you apply your legal knowledge in depth. The advertisement might be an invitation to treat. **Partridge v Crittenden (1968)** (see Chapter 2) established that most advertisements are not offers. If advertisements were classed as offers, problems with multiple acceptances and limited stock of goods would soon arise. The advertisement here, like the one in **Partridge v Crittenden**, uses the word 'offer'. However, this advertisement can be distinguished because it shows a much more definite willingness to be bound. Nor would possible multiple acceptances cause a problem here. There would be no need for Acme to hold unlimited stock. If many people accepted, Acme would need only to make multiple price refunds, which would probably be small. So the multiple acceptance issue would not indicate a lack of intention to make an offer.

You then compare the advertisement in the question to the one in **Carlill v The Carbolic Smoke Ball Company (1893)** (see Chapter 2), noting similarities and differences. (Analysis, evaluation and synthesis will be shown in a really good answer.) There is no need to reproduce all the facts of **Carlill's case**. You might point out that the advertisement in the question said that it was guaranteeing that what it said was true, and that this is similar to the Smoke Ball Company's advertisement, which said that money had been deposited in the bank to show that they meant what they said. You would explain that whether or not there is an intention to create legal relations is an objective test, and that in this commercial context it would be presumed that there was an intention unless there was evidence to suggest otherwise. Again, a comparison could be made with **Carlill's case**, where, as in the question, the advertisement was made in a commercial context. You might explain that, as in **Carlill's case**, the advertisement set out what action was required to accept the offer and that acceptance could be made only by performing the requested act. In both the question and **Carlill's case**, a valid acceptance could not be made by merely promising to perform the requested act. It is a feature of unilateral offers that acceptance can be made only by performing the act requested.

Next, you would consider whether the offer had been accepted within the deadline, noting that the terms of the offer ruled out the acceptance by telephone. The letter would have been within the deadline only if the postal rule applied. The rule should be explained and analysed, along with the limitations put upon it by **Holwell Securities Ltd v Hughes** (see Chapter 2). An analysis of this case would probably lead you to conclude that the postal rule would not apply, particularly as the advertisement in the question said that the acceptance had to be received before the deadline. In **Holwell Securities Ltd v Hughes** the Court of Appeal refused to apply the postal rule because the offer said that the acceptance had to be received to be effective.

Finally, we would explain that there could have been consideration from both parties. Acme's consideration would have been their promise to give the refund. Belinda's consideration would have been performing the act requested. You might think it a waste of time to mention consideration. It would be a waste of time to consider it at length. However, consideration is a requirement of a contract and you were asked to advise whether or not a contract existed. If you were absolutely certain that there was no valid acceptance, it might be all right to say that there was therefore no need to consider consideration. However, whether or not the postal rule would apply is not a matter of certainty. You might be wrong to say that it would not apply. If this was the case, consideration would be a part of the answer. If you reach a conclusion before the end of a question, which makes further investigation of the question unnecessary, you should conduct that further investigation anyway. It is most unlikely that a question has been set where the first line gives the answer and the rest of the question is irrelevant. For example, you might have decided that Acme's advertisement was definitely an invitation to treat. If this were true, then there could have been no contract. (Belinda would have made an offer which was not accepted.) So if you did decide that the advertisement was an invitation to treat, by all means say so. However, you should then explain that it might possibly have been an offer and go on to consider the rest of the question.

You should reach a conclusion when answering a problem question. However, your conclusion might be that it is uncertain how the cases would apply and that therefore there might or might not be a valid contract. Do not be afraid of such an answer. Often it is the only correct answer. If lawyers were always certain as to how the law applied, cases would never go to court.

Take care not to be on Belinda's side just because you have been asked to advise her. Belinda wants an objective view of the law. A lawyer who tells his or her client what they want to hear does the client no favours at all. The client may well take the case to court, lose the case when the judge gives an impartial decision, and then be saddled with huge costs. If the news is bad for Belinda, as it probably is, then tell her so.

Try to practise past problem questions, but make sure that these are from your exam, and that there is no indication that future questions will be different. It can be very helpful to do this with a friend, or maybe a couple of friends, and to make a bit of a game of it. Find some old questions and give yourselves about ten minutes to make a plan of your answer. Then go through the questions together, awarding points for applying relevant cases or for making good points. It is probably best to keep this light-hearted but perhaps to gently criticise each other (and yourself!) if you are missing things out.

Finally, a great technique is to get together a group of friends who all set a problem question for each other. First, you have to define the subject you are considering, perhaps formation of a contract. Then go over all the past questions. Then each try and set a similar question, along with a 'marking plan' showing how you would allocate a set number of marks (maybe 20). In the marking plan make sure that you list the skills which should be shown, analysis, application, etc. This will get you thinking like the examiner. It is hoped that it will show you that all of the questions have great similarities and that the same things tend to be important in most answers. Lecturers who set a lot of exams know that most questions on a particular topic are looking for the same issues, that the same cases tend to be important, and that it is very difficult to invent wholly original questions. By the time you have set each other questions in this way, the real exam questions should look a lot easier.

Using cases and statutes

Whenever you can, you should use cases and legislation as authority for statements of law. In the section above, on answering problem questions, we saw how **Carlill's case** might be used. Notice how different that use was from writing **Carlill's case** out at great length and then saying that the advertisement in the question is just the same and so **Carlill's case** will be applied. To do that not only wastes a lot of words but, worse, it also shows little application of the law. You have recognised that the case might apply, but you have not applied it convincingly. To apply the case well you will need to analyse it, and to evaluate arguments and ideas. As we have seen, these are the skills which score the highest marks.

If a Sale of Goods Act satisfactory quality question concerned a car sold by a taxi driver, you would want to apply **Stevenson *v* Rogers (1999)** (see Chapter 3). There would be no point in writing out all of the facts. You might say that **Stevenson *v* Rogers** established that, whenever a business sells anything, it does so in the course of a business for the purposes of s. 14(2) SGA. Better still, you might say that the taxi driver will have sold the car in the course of a business for the purposes of s. 14(2) SGA, because this is essentially the same as the fisherman in **Stevenson *v* Rogers** selling his boat. In each case what was sold was not what the business was in business to sell, but a business asset which allowed the business to be carried on.

As for sections of statutes, there is usually little point in reproducing them in full if you can briefly state their effect. They might be worth reproducing in full, however, if you are going to spend a lot of time analysing them. For example, if a large part of a question was concerned with whether or not a car was of satisfactory quality, you might reproduce the statutory definition of satisfactory quality in full, or at least fairly fully. You would do this only because you would then go on to analyse the various phrases in it, perhaps devoting a brief paragraph to each relevant phrase. Reproducing a statute is particularly likely to be a bad idea if you can take a statute book into the exam with you.

In this study skills section I have concentrated on how to answer legal questions. I hope that this will be useful to you. I also hope that you enjoy the subject and enjoy reading this text. Above all, I hope that you appreciate that the study of law is not a dry matter of learning facts and reproducing them. Some learning is necessary, but the true fascination of the subject lies in the endlessly different ways in which legal principles might apply to any given situation.

Last, I wish you good luck with your assessments. In doing so, I would like to remind you of the famous reply of Gary Player, the champion golfer, when he was accused of winning tournaments because he was lucky. He admitted that he was lucky, but said that the more he practised the luckier he seemed to get. So practise your study skills, put in the work and make yourself lucky!

1

The legal system

Introduction

An English trial is a peculiar process. The achievement of justice is not the main aim of the lawyers or of the judge. The lawyers are adversaries, arguing with every means at their disposal to win the case for the client they represent. If they exchanged clients, they would argue the opposing case with equal enthusiasm. The judge is not an inquisitor searching for truth and justice. He is there to apply the law, regardless of whether or not this leads to the fairest outcome. His job is to obey the rules and see that everyone else does the same.

Despite its adversarial nature, the English legal system seems to achieve justice as effectively as any other. Indeed, English business law, the subject of this text, is one of the United Kingdom's invisible exports. When two foreign businesses make a contract with each other, perhaps a German company buys goods from a Japanese company, it is common for a term of the contract to state that, in the event of a dispute, English law should apply.

Most people have little idea of how a lawyer argues a case. It is commonly assumed that the strongest argument in a lawyer's armoury is that a decision in favour of his or her client would be the fairest outcome to the case. In English law this is far from true.

Once the facts of a civil case have been established (and in many cases they are not even in dispute), the lawyers will try to persuade the judge that he or she is bound to decide in favour of their client, whether this is fair or not. The judge is, of course, in a superior position to the lawyers, being in charge of the proceedings. What is often not realised, however, is that judges are bound by very definite legal rules and that it is their duty to apply these rules, no matter how much they might wish not to do so.

These legal rules might well be contained in a statute, an Act of Parliament. Alternatively, they might be found in the growing body of European EU law. However, the heart of English law is the system of judicial precedent. As we shall see, the courts are arranged in a hierarchical structure and the system of precedent holds that judges in lower courts are bound to follow legal principles which were previously laid down in higher courts.

Most of the law examined in this text was made by judicial precedent rather than by statute. This is the case even though some of the areas of law have a strong statutory framework. Amongst other subjects, this book examines company law, partnership law and sale of goods law. The Companies Act 2006 provides the framework for company law, the Partnership Act 1890 for partnership law and the Sale of Goods Act 1979 for sale of goods law. These statutes are the basis of the law in the areas of law concerned. But, when studying company law, partnership law and sale of goods law, it is soon seen that the framework laid down by the various statutes is constantly refined by the process of judicial precedent. The higher-ranking courts make decisions as to how these statutes should be interpreted, and these decisions immediately become binding upon lower courts. In this way the law remains alive, constantly being refined and updated.

So, having seen that courts must follow legal rules, this chapter begins by considering where those rules are to be found.

Sources of law

Legislation

Legislation is the name given to law made by Parliament. It can either take the form of an Act of Parliament, such as the Sale of Goods Act 1979, or take the form of delegated legislation, such as the Unfair Terms in Consumer Contracts Regulations 1999. The difference lies in the way the legislation was created. To become a statute, a draft proposal of the legislation, known as a Bill, must pass through both Houses of Parliament and then gain the Royal Assent. Many Bills achieve this without significant alteration. Others have to be amended to gain parliamentary approval, and some Bills fail to become statutes at all. Once the Bill has received the Royal Assent, it becomes a statute which the courts must enforce.

Delegated legislation is passed in an abbreviated version of the procedure needed to pass a statute. Once delegated legislation has been passed, it ranks alongside a statute as a source of law which is superior to any precedent. The courts cannot declare a statute void, but they do have the power to declare delegated legislation void. However, this can be done only on the grounds that the delegated legislation tries to exercise powers greater than those conferred by the Act of Parliament which authorised the delegated legislation to be created.

Effect of legislation

A statute is the ultimate source of law. The theory of parliamentary sovereignty holds that the UK Parliament can pass any law which it wishes to pass and that no Parliament can bind later Parliaments in such a way as to limit their powers to legislate. In order to secure the UK's entry into what is now the European Union, Parliament had to pass the European Communities Act 1972. This statute accepted that in certain areas the UK had surrendered the right to legislate in a way which conflicted with European law. (European law is examined later in this chapter.) While the European Communities Act 1972 remains in force, Parliament is therefore no longer truly sovereign. However, parliamentary sovereignty is preserved, in theory at least, because Parliament still retains the power to pass a statute which would remove the limitations imposed by the European Communities Act. To pass such a statute would mean the UK leaving the European Union.

Judges may not consider the validity of statutes, and they are compelled to apply them. In **British Railways Board v Pickin (1974)**, for example, a person whose land had been compulsorily purchased under the British Railways Act 1968 tried to argue that the statute was invalid, on the grounds that Parliament had been fraudulently misled into passing it. The House of Lords, now the Supreme Court, ruled that such an argument could not be raised in any court.

Furthermore, statutes remain in force indefinitely or until they are repealed. A statute loses none of its authority merely because it lies dormant for many years. In **R v Duncan (1944)**, for example, a defendant was convicted of fortune-telling under the Witchcraft Act 1735, even though the statute had long since fallen into disuse.

A judge, then, must apply a statute, and in the vast majority of cases he or she will find no difficulty in doing so. However, some statutes are ambiguous. When faced with an ambiguous statute a judge must decide which of the two or more possible interpretations to apply.

Rules of statutory interpretation

Literal rule of statutory interpretation

The literal rule of statutory interpretation says that words in a statute should be given their ordinary, literal meaning, no matter how absurd the result. An example of this rule can be seen in **IRC _v_ Hinchy (1960)**, in which the House of Lords was considering the effect of the Income Tax Act 1952. Section 25 of the ITA stated that any tax avoider should pay a £20 fine and 'treble the tax which he ought to be charged under this Act'. Hinchy's lawyers argued that this meant a £20 fine and treble the amount of tax which had been avoided. Unfortunately for Hinchy, the House of Lords decided that the literal meaning of 'treble the tax which he ought to be charged under this Act' was that a tax avoider should pay a £20 fine and treble his whole tax bill for the year. The outcome of the case was that Hinchy had to pay £438, even though the amount he had avoided was only £14.

It is almost certain that the meaning applied by the House of Lords was not what Parliament had in mind when the Income Tax Act 1952 was passed. The statute was badly worded. The blame for this must lie with the parliamentary draftsmen. At the same time, however, it must be realised that they have a near impossible task. Skilled lawyers though these draftsmen are, they cannot possibly foresee every interpretation of the statutes they prepare. Once the statute has become law, every lawyer in the land might be looking for an interpretation which would suit his or her client. In **Hinchy's case** the Revenue lawyers, with typical ingenuity, spotted a literal meaning that had not been apparent before. They then managed to persuade the House of Lords judges that it was their duty to apply this meaning.

Judges who adhere to the literal rule approach do so in the belief that less harm is done by allowing a statute to operate in a way in which Parliament had not intended for a short time, until Parliament has time to pass another amending statute, than would be done by allowing the judges to take over the law-making role altogether, as they would be in danger of doing if they interpreted statutes in any way they saw fit.

The golden rule (or purposive approach)

Other judges, though, perhaps the majority, adopt the purposive approach to statutory interpretation. Using this approach, the judges give the words in a statute their ordinary, literal meaning as far as possible, but only to the extent that this would not produce an absurd result.

In **R _v_ Allen (1872)**, for example, the defendant's lawyers argued that although Allen had married two different women he could not be guilty of bigamy because the crime, as described in the Offences Against the Person Act 1861, was impossible to commit. Section 57 of the Act provides that 'whosoever, being married, shall marry any other person during the life of the former husband or wife', shall be guilty of bigamy. Allen's lawyers argued that this crime was impossible to commit because one of the qualifications for getting married is that you are not already married. Therefore, 'whosoever, being married, shall marry . . .' has already defined the impossible. They contended that the section should have read, 'whosoever, being married, shall _go through a ceremony of marriage_ during the life of the former husband or wife' shall be guilty of bigamy.

If the judges in this case had used the literal rule they might well have acquitted. Unfortunately for Allen, they used the purposive approach and convicted him. They decided that the literal approach would have produced an absurd result, that they had not the slightest doubt as to what Parliament had meant when it passed the statute, and that Allen was therefore plainly guilty.

It is never possible to say in advance which rule a court will adopt, although the golden rule is currently more in favour than the literal rule. It is also important to remember that the rules are guiding principles, rather than rules which must be obeyed. In **Maunsell v Olins (1975)** Lord Reid said: 'They are not rules in the ordinary sense of having some binding force. They are our servants, not our masters. They are aids to construction, presumptions or pointers. Not infrequently one "rule" points in one direction, another in a different direction. In each case we must look at all relevant circumstances and decide as a matter of judgment what weight to attach to any particular "rule".' In **Cusack v London Borough of Harrow (2013)** Lord Neuberger explained, 'In my view, canons [rules] of construction have a valuable part to play in interpretation, provided that they are treated as guidelines rather than railway lines, as servants rather than masters.'

The mischief rule

The mischief rule holds that the judge can take into account what 'mischief' the statute set out to remedy. In **Smith v Hughes (1960)**, the Lord Chief Justice, Lord Parker, had to consider whether prostitutes who were soliciting from balconies and from behind windows were soliciting 'in the street' within the meaning of s. 1 of the Street Offences Act 1959. Using the mischief rule, he had little difficulty in deciding that they were. The prostitutes were not literally soliciting 'in the street', but their behaviour was just the kind which the Act sought to prevent.

The Court of Appeal recently applied the mischief rule in **Wolman v Islington LBC (2007)**. A GLC bye-law made it a criminal offence to park a vehicle with one or more wheels 'on any part of' a pavement. The claimant, a barrister, parked his motorbike on a stand in such a way that its wheels were above the pavement but not actually on it. He therefore claimed not to have committed the offence. Applying the mischief rule, the Court of Appeal held that the offence was committed if one or more of the bike's wheels were either on or over the pavement. It must be remembered that the mischief rule is used only where there has plainly been a mistake in the writing of a statute. For example, in **Farstad Supply A/S v Enviroco Ltd (2011)** the Supreme Court thought it likely that a provision had been incorrectly omitted from a statute but refused to apply the mischief rule. Lord Collins said that the court could not be 'abundantly sure' the words had been omitted and so it could not read the missing words into the statute, as to do so would be 'an impermissible form of judicial legislation'.

Whichever rule the judges adopt, there is no doubt that, in theory, a statute is the strongest source of law. A lawyer who has a statute on his or her side holds the most powerful card in the game. The lawyer may appear to be inviting the judge to apply the statute, but in effect is ordering the judge to do so. However, we shall shortly see that in practice even the power of a statute can be subject to EU law or subject to another very important statute, the Human Rights Act 1998.

Minor rules

Other, less important, rules of statutory interpretation are applied by all judges. The *ejusdem generis* rule (of the same kind rule) holds that general words which follow specific words must be given the same type of meaning as the specific words. For example, the Betting Act 1853 prohibited betting in any 'house, office, room or other place'. In **Powell v Kempton Racecourse Company (1899)**, the court held that the Act did not apply to a racecourse. The specific words 'house, office, room' were all indoor places, and so the general words 'or other place' had to be interpreted as applying only to indoor places.

The rule *expressio unius est exclusio alterius* (to express one thing is to exclude another) holds that if there is a list of specific words, not followed by any general words, then the statute applies only to the specific words mentioned. For example, in **R v Inhabitants of Sedgeley (1831)**, a statute which raised taxes on 'lands, houses, tithes and coal mines' did not apply to other types of mines.

Until relatively recently, a judge interpreting a statute was not allowed to consider the speeches which MPs made when the statute was being debated. However, in **Pepper v Hart (1993)**, a landmark decision, the House of Lords held that *Hansard*, which records the debates in Parliament, could in some circumstances be consulted if this was the only way to solve an ambiguity.

Judicial precedent

As already mentioned, the doctrine of judicial precedent holds that judges in lower courts are absolutely bound to follow decisions previously made in higher courts.

The hierarchy of the courts

The court structure is examined in more depth in a later chapter. (See Figures 17.1, 17.2 and 17.3.) For the purposes of understanding the system of precedent, we need only to know that the courts are arranged in a hierarchical structure and that there are five levels in the hierarchy.

The Supreme Court

The Supreme Court is the highest court in Great Britain and Northern Ireland. It replaced the House of Lords on 1 October 2009, when the 11 Law Lords who used to sit in the House of Lords became the first Supreme Court justices. The court now has a full complement of 12 justices. The Supreme Court justices, five of whom sit in most cases, are not bound by any previous precedents. Furthermore, their decisions are binding on all courts beneath them. In practice, the Supreme Court justices do tend to follow their own previous decisions unless there is a good reason not to. Supreme Court justices also hear appeals from some Commonwealth countries. When they sit in this capacity, the justices are known as the Privy Council. Technically, decisions of the Privy Council are not binding on English courts, but in practice they are usually regarded as having the same authority as Supreme Court decisions. In some particularly important cases seven, or even nine, Supreme Court justices sit, rather than the usual number of five. Seven Law Lords sat in **Pepper v Hart (1993)**, the effect of which we have already considered. In 2008, nine Law Lords sat in a case to decide whether foreign nationals suspected of terrorism could be held in prison without trial. The Supreme Court has no power to overturn a statute.

The Court of Appeal

The Court of Appeal is the next rung down the ladder. Its decisions are binding on all lower courts. They are also binding on future sittings of the Court of Appeal. In **Young v Bristol Aeroplane Co Ltd (1944)** it was decided that the Court of Appeal could refuse to follow its own previous decisions in only three circumstances:

● First, where there were two conflicting earlier Court of Appeal decisions, it could decide which one to follow and which one to overrule.

● Second, if a previous Court of Appeal decision had later been overruled by the House of Lords (now the Supreme Court), the Court of Appeal should not follow it.

- Third, a previous Court of Appeal decision should not be followed if it was decided through lack of care, ignoring some statute or other higher-ranking authority such as a previously decided House of Lords (now the Supreme Court) case.

Although the principles set out apply to both the Civil and Criminal Divisions of the Court of Appeal, it is generally recognised that the Criminal Division has slightly wider powers to depart from its own previous decisions. It can do so where justice would otherwise be denied to an appellant.

In terms of precedent, the Court of Appeal is the most important court. The Supreme Court hears only about 100 cases a year. The Court of Appeal hears several thousand. However, the Supreme Court hears cases of greater public importance, and there is no doubt that its decisions have the greatest authority. Generally, the 38 Court of Appeal judges sit in courts of three judges. Sometimes there are five judges sitting, but this does not increase the extent to which the decision must be followed or give any greater power not to follow previous Court of Appeal decisions.

The Divisional Courts

There are three Divisional Courts of the High Court. These courts are appeal courts in which two or three High Court judges sit. Their decisions are binding on other Divisional Courts, subject to the **Young v Bristol Aeroplane Co Ltd** exceptions, and on all courts below. They are not binding on the Court of Appeal or the Supreme Court.

The High Court

Judges in the High Court are bound by decisions of the Supreme Court and the Court of Appeal. High Court decisions are binding upon all courts beneath the High Court. If there is only one judge sitting in a High Court case, the decision is not binding on other High Court judges. In a Divisional Court of the High Court more than one judge sits. The decisions of Divisional Courts are therefore binding on future sittings of the High Court.

Inferior courts

The decisions of inferior courts (the Crown Court, the county court and the magistrates' court) are not binding on any other courts. Judges sitting in these courts do not make precedents.

Figure 1.1 shows an overview of which courts bind which other courts.

The binding part of a case

The *ratio decidendi*, loosely translated from the Latin as 'the reason for the decision,' is the part of the case which is binding on other judges. It is the statement of law which the judge applied to the facts and which caused the case to be decided as it was. Despite the great length of most cases, the *ratio* is often quite simple. For example, the *ratio* of **Partridge v Crittenden (1968)** (the facts of which are set out in Chapter 2), might be that 'magazine advertisements, which describe goods and the price for which they will be sold, are not contractual offers but only invitations to treat'. As you will see when you consider the law of contract, this is a relatively straightforward statement of law.

Ultimately, the *ratio* of a case will be decided by future courts when they are considering whether or not they are bound by the case.

Partridge v Crittenden was decided by a Divisional Court of the High Court. It would not therefore be binding on the Supreme Court or on the Court of Appeal. However, later sittings of the High Court, as well as county courts, Crown Courts and magistrates' courts, would be

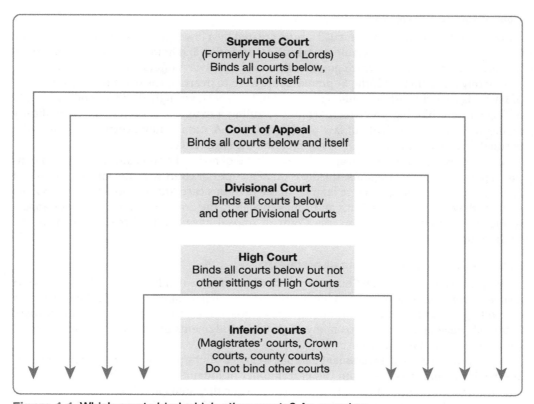

Figure 1.1 Which courts bind which other courts? An overview

compelled to follow it, unless they were confronted with a statute or higher-ranking precedent to the contrary.

Statements of law which did not form the basis of the decision are known as *obiter dicta* (other things said). Examples of *obiter dicta* can be found in most cases. For example, in **Partridge v Crittenden** Ashworth J said that the fact that the appellant's advertisement did not directly use the words 'offers for sale' made it less likely that Partridge was guilty of the crime with which he was charged – offering for sale a bramblefinch hen contrary to s. 6(1) of the Protection of Birds Act 1964. This statement of law is *obiter*, not *ratio*, because it was not the reason for deciding that Partridge was not guilty.

Obiter dicta are not binding on judges, no matter what court they were made in. However, if the judges in the Supreme Court all express the same *obiter*, then a lower court judge would almost certainly follow the *obiter* in the absence of a precedent which he or she was compelled to follow.

Courts which hear appeals (appellate courts) usually have more than one judge sitting. Fortunately, it is an odd number of judges rather than an even number. A majority of judges will therefore decide for one of the parties or for the other. If the decision is unanimous, for instance the Court of Appeal decides 3:0 for the defendant, then the *ratio* of the case can be found in the judgments of any of the three judges. If the court decides for the defendant 2:1, then the *ratio* must be found in the decisions of the two judges in the majority. The decision of the judge in the minority may be persuasive as *obiter*, but it cannot form a *ratio* which will bind future courts.

Overruling and reversing

A higher-ranking court can **overrule** a *ratio* created by a lower-ranking court. The Supreme Court, for example, could overrule **Partridge v Crittenden** and hold that magazine advertisements stating the price at which goods will be sold are always offers. (This is most unlikely, it is merely an example.) If the Supreme Court were to overrule the decision, then the *ratio* of **Partridge v Crittenden** would be deemed to have been wrongly decided, and so it could no longer be a binding precedent. When overruling a case, the superior court specifically names the case and the rule of law being overruled. A statute may overrule the *ratio* of a particular case, but the statute will not mention the case concerned.

Many cases are **reversed** on appeal. Reversing is of no legal significance. It merely means that a party who appeals against the decision of an inferior court wins the appeal. No rule of law is necessarily changed. For example, in the fictitious case **Smith v Jones**, let us assume that Smith wins in the High Court and Jones appeals to the Court of Appeal. If Jones's appeal is allowed, for whatever reason, the Court of Appeal have reversed the judgment of the High Court.

Disadvantages of the system of precedent

There are currently 108 High Court judges, 38 Court of Appeal judges and 12 Supreme Court justices. Every sentence of every judgment they make might contain a precedent which would be binding on future judges. It is an impossible task for anyone to be aware of all of these potential precedents. In fact, so many High Court judgments are made that most are not even reported in the Law Reports.

Law reporting is not a government task but is carried out by private firms. The law reporters are barristers and they weed out the vast number of judgments which they consider to be unimportant. Even so, as students become aware when they step into a law library, the system of precedent does mean that English law is very bulky. There are hundreds of thousands of precedents and it can be very hard for a lawyer to find the law he or she is looking for.

Precedent suffers from another disadvantage, and that is that bad decisions can live on for a very long time. Before 1966, a House of Lords decision was binding on all other courts, including future sittings of the House of Lords. If a bad decision was made, then it could be changed only by Parliament, which was generally far too busy to interfere unless grave injustice was being caused. Sometimes a superior court says, *obiter*, that it thinks a binding precedent should be changed. However, the court cannot change the precedent until it hears a case where such a change would be the *ratio* of that case. The court cannot choose to hear such a case, it has to wait for such a case to be brought before it.

These disadvantages of the system of precedent are thought to be outweighed by two major advantages.

Advantages of the system of precedent

The first advantage is that the device of **distinguishing** a case means that the system of precedent is not entirely rigid. A judge who is lower down the hierarchy can refuse to follow a precedent by distinguishing it on its facts. This means that the judge will say that the facts of the case he or she is considering are materially different from the facts of the case by which he or she appears to be bound. This device of distinguishing gives a degree of flexibility to the system of precedent. It allows judges to escape precedents which they consider inappropriate to the case in front of them. For example, if a county court judge strongly wanted to hold that a television advertisement was an offer to sell, it is possible that he or she might distinguish **Partridge v Crittenden** on the grounds that a television advertisement is materially different from an advertisement in a magazine. Similarly, a county court judge might distinguish **Partridge *v* Crittenden** if the wording of an advertisement suggested that a definite contractual offer had been made.

The second and more important advantage of precedent is that it causes high quality decisions to be applied in all courts. Judges in appellate courts have the time and the experience to make very good decisions, often on difficult or philosophical matters. These decisions can then be applied by much busier and less experienced lower court judges, who do not have to consider whether the legal principles behind the decisions are right or wrong.

Until recently, judges were chosen only from the ranks of barristers. Now solicitors too can become judges. The Bar is a career, rather like acting, which has extremes of success, and very many talented young people enter it. If a barrister gains promotion and becomes a circuit judge, he or she will sit in the Crown Court or the county court. This is an honour and an achievement. Even so, the judge will make no law. He or she will supervise proceedings, decide who wins civil cases, award damages and sentence criminals. However, no matter how brilliant the judge's analysis of the law might be, it will not form a precedent.

High Court judges are a different matter. They make the law of England from the very first case in which they sit. Every word of their reported judgments is open to scrutiny by the other judges, by lawyers and by academics. If they were not very able, this would soon be noticed.

Almost 50 judges are promoted beyond the High Court to the Supreme Court or Court of Appeal. These days it seems unthinkable that any but the very able should go this far.

It is not only on the grounds of ability that the Supreme Court ought to come to very high quality decisions. Unlike the lower court judges, the justices who sit in the Supreme Court do not decide a case there and then. They read the facts of the case, and hear the arguments of the barristers, and then reserve their judgment. They talk to each other informally to see whether there is a consensus of opinion. If there is a consensus, one of the judges is chosen to write the judgment. If there is no consensus, the minority will write their own dissenting judgments. In a particularly difficult case the process of writing the judgment can take a very long time.

The system of precedent has a further advantage in that it can lead to certainty as to what the law is. If an appellate court makes a clear decision on a particular matter, then lawyers will advise their clients that the law on the matter is settled, and that there is no point in pursuing a contrary argument.

Alternatives to the system of precedent

As already stated, most other countries do not use a system of precedent. France, which is fairly typical of European countries, has a codified system of law known as a civil law system. All of the civil law is contained in the Civil Code, which originated in the late eighteenth century.

French judges, who choose a career as a judge early on, do not feel compelled to interpret the Code according to previous decisions until those decisions have for some time unanimously interpreted the Code in the same way.

Scotland has a mixed legal system. It is based on the civil law system, but has strong common law influences. In Scotland the system of precedent is used, but a precedent does not have quite the same force as in England.

European Union Law

In 1952 the European Coal and Steel Community was set up with the object of preventing any European country from building up stockpiles of steel and coal, the raw materials needed to wage war. Following the success of this, the European Economic Community (EEC) came into existence in 1957. The six original Member States signed the Treaty of Rome. This used to be called the EC Treaty but is now called the Treaty on the Functioning of the European Union. These six original countries were Germany, France, Italy, Belgium, the Netherlands and Luxembourg. Part of the founding philosophy of the Community was to provide an appropriate response to the Soviet Bloc countries to the East. However, the motivation was also economic, in that there seemed to be obvious advantages to the creation of a free market in Europe. The EEC is now known as the European Union (EU). At the time of writing, there are 27 Member States, the original six having been joined by Austria, Bulgaria, Cyprus, the Czech Republic, Denmark, Estonia, Finland, Greece, Hungary, Ireland, Latvia, Lithuania, Malta, Poland, Portugal, Romania, the Slovak Republic, Slovenia, Spain, Sweden and the United Kingdom. Croatia, Macedonia, Serbia and Turkey are candidate countries, meaning that their application to join has been officially accepted by the European Council. Five other Balkan states are potential candidate countries.

The United Kingdom joined the EU in 1973. In order to be admitted as a member, the UK Parliament passed the European Communities Act 1972. This statute agreed that Community law should be directly effective in UK courts.

In 1986 the EU consisted of 12 Member States, all of whom signed the Single European Act. This Act was designed to remove all barriers to a single market by 1992. In addition, the Act introduced a system of qualified majority voting in the European Council, thereby reducing the power of any single State to block developments.

In 1992 the Treaty on European Union (the Maastricht Treaty), was signed by all 15 States which were at that time Member States. The Treaty was more of a statement of political intention than a statement of precise obligations. It proposed co-operation on matters other than purely economic matters, envisaging the creation of a European Union with the three following pillars: the European Community; a common foreign and security policy; and co-operation in the fields of justice and home affairs. The Treaty also envisaged that economic and monetary union would be achieved in three stages. However, the UK and Denmark opted out of the third stage. The UK also opted out of participation in the social chapter, which set out employment and social rights.

The Treaty of Amsterdam was signed in October 1997 and came into force in May 1999. This Treaty aimed for closer political co-operation between Member States. It incorporated much of the Justice and Home Affairs pillar into the original EC Treaty and gave Member States a greater power to veto proposals which would affect their vital national interests.

The Treaty of Lisbon was signed by all EU leaders in December 2007. However, it could not become effective until all Member States ratified it. In June 2008 Irish voters rejected the Treaty in a referendum. In October 2009, at the second time of asking, they voted in favour of the Treaty. The Treaty became effective in December 2009, although other EU countries have not asked their voters to ratify it by way of referendum.

The Treaty of Lisbon amended the existing treaties, incorporating them into a new treaty called the Treaty on the Functioning of the European Union. This has four main aims: to make the EU more democratic and transparent; to make it more efficient; to promote rights, values, freedom, solidarity and security; and to make the EU an actor on the global stage.

The first of these aims involves increasing the power of the European Parliament so that it will be placed on an equal footing with the Commission. As regards most EU legislation, the Parliament and the Commission will approve legislation using a co-decision procedure. A greater role in making EU law will be given to national parliaments in areas where they can achieve better results than the EU. A Citizens' Initiative will allow 1 million citizens from several Member States to ask the Commission to introduce new policies. The relationship between the EU and Member States will be clarified, and States which wish to do so will be allowed to withdraw from the EU.

Great efficiency will be achieved by extending qualified majority voting. From 2014, a qualified majority will be achieved if a dual majority of 55 per cent of Member States, and Member States representing 65 per cent of the EU's population, vote in favour. The EU Commission will be reduced in size and a new President of the European Council will be elected by national governments for a period of office lasting two and a half years. The European Council will be separate from the Council of Ministers, the leaders of which will continue to be elected on a six-month rotating basis. The European Council will not have legislative powers but will guide policy.

The promotion of rights, values, freedom, solidarity and security will be achieved by guaranteeing the principles set out in the Charter of Fundamental Rights, and by giving them legal force. This charter set out principles of human rights to be applied throughout the EU but at present it has no legal force. In addition, the EU will be given a greater role in fighting crime and preventing terrorism. The EU will be made a stronger actor on the global stage by creating a High Representative for Foreign Affairs and Security Policy, and by encouraging the EU to act as a single legal personality.

The provisions of the Treaty of Lisbon will be introduced gradually, and may take about ten years to become fully adopted.

The institutions of the EU

The original EEC Treaty set up four main institutions. These institutions are now known as: the Council of the European Communities; the European Commission; the European Parliament; and the Court of Justice of the European Union.

The Council of the European Communities

The Council of the European Communities, generally known as the Council, is not a permanent body. It consists at any given time of the President of the European Commission and one Minister from the government of each Member State. Which Government Ministers will constitute the Council of Ministers depends upon the nature of the measures which the Council is considering. For example, if the measures relate to agriculture, then it will be the relevant Ministers of Agriculture. Often the Council is made up of Heads of Government or the Member States' Foreign Ministers. Up to four times a year the Presidents or Prime Ministers of all of the countries along with the President of the European Commission, hold meetings as the 'European Council'. At these meetings overall EU policy is set and issues which could not be settled at a lower level are settled.

The Council is the main policy-making body of the EU. It passes legislation, coordinates EU policy, concludes international agreements, approves the EU budget and develops the EU Common Foreign and Security Policy. When the Council passes legislation, generally in conjunction with the European Parliament, it does so under a system of qualified majority voting. However, a Treaty might require unanimity for votes on certain matters, such as the common and foreign security policy, police and judicial cooperation in criminal matters, asylum and immigration policy, economic and social cohesion policy or taxation. Under this system each country is allocated a certain number of votes in relation to its population. The United Kingdom is one of four countries having the maximum of 29 votes. Malta has the fewest votes, with just three. There are 345 votes in total. A qualified majority is reached in two circumstances. First, if 255 (73.9 per cent) votes are in favour. This means that 91 votes can defeat a proposal and so at least four countries must vote against. Second, if a simple majority of Member States approve. However, if a matter which was not based on a proposal from the Commission is being voted upon, a two-thirds majority of Member States must approve. Additionally, any Member State can require confirmation that votes representing at least 62 per cent of the total population of the EU were in favour. If it is discovered that this figure was not reached, then the proposal voted upon will not be regarded as having been accepted.

Article 11 of the Treaty of Amsterdam gives effect to the Luxembourg Accord and allows any Member State to argue that unanimity, rather than a qualified majority vote, should be required on any particular proposal. When such an argument is raised, the Council will delay taking a vote in order to allow the dissenting State to gain the support of other Member States. However, if it is unsuccessful in this, the issues will in any event be resolved by a qualified majority vote.

The European Commission

Twenty-seven individual commissioners are appointed by the Member States to serve in a full-time capacity for a term of five years. When these commissioners act collectively they are known as the European Commission, which is generally abbreviated to the Commission. Each commissioner also has individual responsibility for a particular matter, such as agriculture. The Commission is supported by large executive and administrative systems. The commissioners are expected to act completely independently of their Member States, but in practice tend to guard the independence of their Member States. They are selected on political grounds, and all UK commissioners have previously played a leading role in UK politics.

The most powerful position in the EC is the President of the Commission. The President is the figurehead of the EC and has a strong political influence upon it. The Council selects the President and the appointment must then be approved by the European Parliament.

The Commission is involved in broad policy-making. It prepares specific proposals to be submitted to the Council. It also manages and implements EU policies and the EU budget, it acts jointly with the Court of Justice to enforce EU law and it acts as the EU's representative when dealing with other countries. It is politically accountable to the European Parliament, which can demand that the whole Commission resigns. Individual commissioners can be forced to resign if the President of the Commission demands this and the other commissioners agree. In addition to its major roles, the Commission also commissions research and prepares reports on matters which concern the Community and negotiates with non-Member States on these matters. It also prepares the draft Community budget.

The European Parliament

Members of the European Parliament (MEPs) are elected directly by Member States, using a system of proportional representation. Elections are held every five years. The UK elects 72 out of the 736 MEPs who make up the Parliament. The MEPs do not sit in blocks representing their Member States, but in blocks representing seven Europe-wide political groups. It is perhaps surprising that the European Parliament does not have the power to initiate and pass legislation on its own. Generally, the power to pass legislation is shared by the Parliament and the Council. One of the Parliament's most significant powers is to approve or amend the EC budget. The Commission prepares a draft budget, which is submitted to the Council and then to the Parliament. The Parliament must approve, amend or reject the budget within 45 days.

The Parliament must approve the Commission when it is first appointed and must also approve the new President. It must also approve the accounts of the Commission and new appointments to the Commission. Article 234 of the Treaty on the Functioning of the

European Union (TFEU) gives the Parliament the power to pass a vote of censure to dismiss the Commission. Such a vote must be passed by a two-thirds majority. In January 1999 a vote to remove the Commission on account of nepotism and corruption failed. Two hundred and thirty-two MEPs voted for removal, 293 voted against. However, the whole of the Commission resigned in March 1999, on publication of a report made by an investigative committee.

Initially the Parliament had few real powers. It had to be consulted about EC legislation but had no powers to block any legislation. The EU Parliament still does not have the power to legislate in the way that the UK Parliament has. It passes law by 'co-decision' with the Council. On many matters the Parliament and the Council have equal standing, but on others the Council has the power to legislate after consulting the Parliament. The Parliament also has the power to ask the Commission to put forward proposals for legislation.

The Court of Justice of the European Union

The Court of Justice of the European Union (CJEU), which sits in Luxembourg, is made up of 27 judges. These judges are assisted by advocates-general. The judges and advocates are appointed by common consent of the Member States and hold office for a six-year term which may be renewed.

The decisions of the court are signed by all the judges, without any indication that some may have dissented. It is comparatively rare for the full court to sit. Eighty per cent of cases are referred to one of the six chambers, where either three or five judges sit. The number of judges sitting is always odd, so that a majority decision can always be reached. The more important the issues involved, the greater the number of judges sitting. The judgments of the Court are available free on its website, but cases typically take between 18 months and two years to be heard.

The advocates-general must act with complete impartiality and independence, in open court, making reasoned submissions on cases brought before the Court. They do not therefore argue the case for one or other of the sides involved. Each case has an advocate-general assigned to it. The advocate-general makes a summary of the facts, an analysis of all the relevant Community law and a recommendation as to what the decision of the Court should be. The parties cannot comment on this and the judges deliberate upon it in secret. The Court has no obligation to agree with the advocate-general's recommendation.

When ready to vote, the most junior judges vote first and then the other judges vote in order of reverse seniority. The Court does not use a system of precedent: it can and does depart from its own previous decisions.

Certain matters may be referred to the Court of First Instance rather than to the CJEU. These matters tend to concern competition law or cases brought by private individuals. The Court of First Instance operates in a very similar way to the way in which the CJEU operates. There is an automatic right of appeal on a point of law from the Court of First Instance to the CJEU.

Jurisdiction of the CJEU

Apart from hearing appeals from the Court of First Instance, the CJEU has three separate areas of jurisdiction. First, it can express an authoritative opinion on EC law, if requested to do so by a national court, so that EU law is applied uniformly across the EU. Once the ruling has been made by the CJEU, the case returns to the court which asked for the ruling so that that court can apply the ruling. Article 267 TFEU allows a national court to request an authoritative ruling as to three types of matters: the interpretation of EU legislation; the validity and interpretation of acts of institutions of the Community; and on the interpretation of statutes of bodies established by an act of the Council, where those statutes so provide.

Any national court or tribunal may refer a matter within Article 267 to the CJEU if it thinks this necessary to give judgment. Most of the CJEU's work involves preliminary rulings. The ruling is sought by the court, not by the parties to the case. Although a national court has a discretion to seek a preliminary ruling, a court of final appeal has an obligation to do so where a relevant point of EU law is at issue and where there has been no previous interpretation of the point by the CJEU. However, there is no such obligation where the point is so obvious as not to require a ruling.

The second area of jurisdiction arises under Articles 263 and 264 TFEU, which allows the CJEU to review the legality of acts done by the European Parliament or other Community institutions. The CJEU can also review a community institution's failure to act. This review process is similar to the process of judicial review whereby the High Court ensures that the Government and others do not exceed their powers.

The third area of jurisdiction arises under Article 258, which allows the CJEU to bring actions against Member States to make sure that they fulfil their Community obligations. Article 259 allows Member States to take other Member States to the CJEU for failure to live up to their Treaty obligations.

Sources of EU law

Applicability and effect

In order to understand the effect of EU law, it is necessary to understand the distinction between the terms 'direct applicability' and 'direct effect'. If EU legislation is directly applicable, it automatically forms part of the domestic law of Member States, without those States needing to do anything to bring the law in. However, this would not necessarily mean that individuals could directly rely upon the legislation in the domestic courts of their own countries. In order for such reliance to be possible, the legislation would have to be capable of having direct effect. Where EU legislation has direct effect an individual can directly rely upon the legislation, either as a cause of action or as a defence, in the domestic courts of his or her country. The Articles of the Treaty on the Functioning of the European Union are always directly applicable, as are EU Regulations, but, as we have seen, this does not necessarily mean that they have direct effect.

No EU legislation can have direct effect unless it satisfies the criteria laid down by the Court of Justice in **Van Gend en Loos v Nederlands Administratie der Belastingen (1963)**. These criteria will be satisfied only if the legislation is sufficiently clear, precise and unconditional, and if the legislation intends to confer rights. Many Treaty Articles do not meet these criteria as they are mere statements of aspiration. Even if Community legislation does meet the **Van Gend** criteria, it may have only direct vertical effect, rather than direct horizontal effect. If it has direct vertical effect it can be invoked by an individual only against the State and against emanations of the State, such as health authorities. A provision which has direct horizontal effect can be invoked against other individuals as well as against the State and emanations of the State.

If an EU law does not have direct effect it might nevertheless have indirect effect. An indirectly effective EU law could not be enforced in national courts. However, these courts would be obliged to interpret their own national law, to the extent that this is possible, in such a way that it did not conflict with the indirectly effective EU law.

Treaty Articles

The Treaty on the Functioning of the European Union has over 350 Articles. These are directly applicable. Whether or not a Treaty Article has direct effect depends first upon whether it satisfies the criteria in **Van Gend**. As we have seen, some will not satisfy these criteria as they are merely statements of aspiration. Some of the Articles are much more significant than others. Article 157 TFEU requires Member States to ensure and subsequently maintain the application of the principle that men and women should receive equal pay for equal work, and the effect of this Article has been highly significant.

Some Treaty Articles, like Article 157, have both direct horizontal and vertical effect, others have only direct vertical effect. Whether or not they have direct horizontal effect will depend upon the wording of the Article and the interpretation of the Article by the CJEU. For example, Article 34 TFEU, which prohibits restrictions on the free movement of goods, only has direct vertical effect. It can therefore only be invoked by an individual against the State or against an emanation of the State. One private company could not invoke Article 34 against another private company which was not an emanation of the State.

Regulations

Regulations are binding in their entirety and are directly applicable in all Member States without any further implementation by Member States. Regulations have direct effect, sometimes both vertically and horizontally, providing the **Van Gend** criteria are satisfied. Even if these criteria are not satisfied, a Regulation may have **indirect effect**. This means that, although an individual cannot invoke the Regulation, the courts of Member States are bound to take account of it.

Directives

Directives, which are addressed to the governments of Member States, are not directly applicable. It is therefore left to each individual Member State to implement the objectives of the Directive in a way that is best suited to its own particular political and economic culture. All Directives are issued with an implementation date and Member States are under a duty to implement by this date. If the Directive is not implemented by the due date, the Commission has the power to take proceedings against the Member State in question.

Before the implementation date has been reached, Directives have no effect at all. However, in the **Wallonie ASBL case (1997)** the Court of Justice held that a Member State should not enact legislation or implement measures that significantly conflict with the objectives of a Directive that has yet to meet its implementation date. Generally, the UK Government will implement EC Directives by delegated legislation. Several statutory instruments which we consider in this book, such as the Commercial Agents (Council Directive) Regulations 1993, were enacted to give effect to Directives. (It is slightly confusing that these statutory instruments are usually called Regulations, given that EC Regulations are a quite different matter.) Once an EC Directive has been implemented by UK legislation then, obviously, an individual can invoke the domestic legislation against another individual. For example, the Commercial Agents (Council Directive) Regulations 1993 are regularly invoked by individuals against other individuals.

There can, however, be a problem if the UK Government either fails to implement a Directive at all, or does not implement the Directive properly. Once the implementation date has been reached, whether or not an unimplemented Directive has direct effect depends first upon whether the Directive satisfies the **Van Gend** criteria, and second upon the relationship between the parties involved. Where the parties to a legal action are in a vertical relationship (for example, patient and health authority), the Directive is capable of having direct effect. Where the parties are in a horizontal relationship (for example, a consumer suing a shop), the Directive does not have direct effect. In other words, Directives which should have been implemented are capable of having direct vertical effect, but not direct horizontal effect. (This can mean that a person employed by an emanation of the State, such as a worker in the NHS, might have more rights against his employer than a person employed by a person who is not an emanation of the State.) However, when dealing with a case between two individuals, the domestic courts are under a duty to try, as far as possible, to interpret the domestic legislation so as to give effect indirectly to the objectives of the Directive. In situations where it is not possible for the domestic court to give direct or indirect effect to an EC Directive, the remedy of last resort is for the aggrieved individual to sue the Member State for failure to implement. If found to be in breach, the Member State could be ordered to pay compensation to the aggrieved individual.

In **Francovich and Bonifaci *v* Republic of Italy (1993)** the CJEU held that an individual could be compensated on account of a Directive not having been implemented if certain criteria were satisfied. **Brasserie du Pêcheur SA *v* Germany (1996)** subsequently established that the three necessary criteria are as follows. First, the rule of law in question must confer rights upon individuals. Second, the breach must be sufficiently serious. Third, there must be a direct causal link between the breach and the damage.

The legal effect of the Treaties, Regulations and Directives is shown in Figure 1.2.

Decisions

Decisions are addressed to one or more Member States, to individuals or to institutions. They are binding in their entirety, without the need for implementation by Member States, but only on those to whom they were addressed. In practice, decisions are of little practical importance.

Recommendations and opinions

The Commission has the power to make recommendations and opinions. These have no binding legal force. However, where a Member State passes legislation to comply with a decision or an opinion, a national court may refer a case to the CJEU to see whether or not the decision or opinion applies and how it should be interpreted.

Supremacy of EU law

EU law can only be effective if it overrides national law. If every Member State were free to pass legislation which conflicted with EU legislation, the EU would be rendered ineffective. In **Costa *v* ENEL (1964)** the CJEU stated that the Treaty on Rome, as amended, had become an integral part of the legal systems of Member States and that the courts of Member States were bound to apply the Treaty. It also stated that Member States had, by signing the Treaty, limited their sovereign rights, within limited areas, and created a body of law which bound both their citizens and themselves. The case specifically decided that Italian legislation which was incompatible with Community law, and which had been passed after Italy had signed the Treaty, could have no effect.

In **R *v* Secretary of State for Transport, ex parte Factortame (No. 2) (1991)**, Spanish companies sought judicial review of the Merchant Shipping Act 1988, which they claimed breached two Articles of the EC Treaty. The companies asked for an injunction to suspend that part of the Act which was in breach of the relevant Treaty Article. The House of Lords held that injunctions could not be effective against the Crown and refused to grant the injunction. However, the case was referred to the CJEU, which held that UK limitations on the availability of remedies should be overruled and that the injunctions should be available. Subsequently, the House of Lords immediately suspended the operation of the offending part of the Act. A few years after **Factortame**, in **Equal Opportunities Commission *v* Secretary of State for Employment (1994)**, the House of Lords suspended the operation

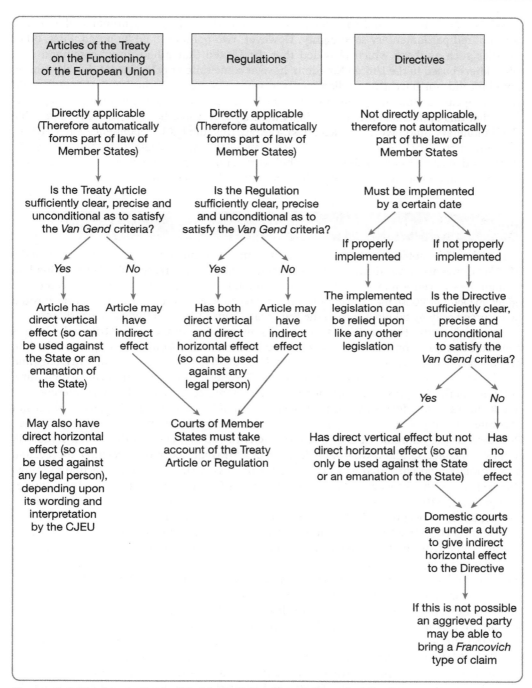

Figure 1.2 The legal effect of Treaty Acticles, Regulations and Decisions

of a section of employment legislation on the grounds that it was in breach of the EU Equal Treatment legislation. However, it should be noted that this power of UK courts to suspend conflicting domestic legislation will only be used sparingly in cases involving serious breaches of directly effective EU legislation.

Whilst the United Kingdom remains a member of the EU, it is arguable that it has surrendered parliamentary sovereignty. However, two points should be noted. First, other Treaties such as those which provided that the United States had direct command over US soldiers based in the United Kingdom, have at some time or other meant that the United Kingdom did not have true parliamentary sovereignty. Second, the UK Parliament could vote to repeal the European Communities Act 1972 and leave the EU. It must be said, however, that this option becomes increasingly unlikely and would become virtually impossible if full monetary union were ever achieved. Despite this, the UK Independence Party (UKIP) will run in the 2015 general election with leaving the EU as their main policy, and the Conservative Party has published a draft bill which states that if they win the 2015 election, a referendum on leaving the EU must be held before the end of 2017.

The Human Rights Act 1998

First, it should be noted that the European Convention on Human Rights is not a creation of the EU. The Convention was drawn up in 1950, before the EU was created. The United Kingdom ratified the Convention in 1951. Before the Human Rights Act 1998 (HRA 1998) came into effect, in October 2000, the Convention could not be directly enforced in the UK courts. It could be enforced only by taking a case to the European Court of Human Rights in Strasbourg.

Section 2 of the Human Rights Act 1998 now requires any court or tribunal which is considering a question which has arisen in connection with a Convention right to take into account any decision of the European Court of Human Rights. This court sits in Strasbourg and is quite separate from the Court of Justice of the European Union, which sits in Luxembourg. Section 2 of the Act preserves parliamentary sovereignty because the UK courts merely have to take into account decisions of the European Court of Human Rights. The UK courts are not absolutely bound by these decisions. This point was emphasised by Lord Phillips, the then President of the Supreme Court, in **R v Horncastle (2009)**. He said that when senior UK judges had concerns about whether a decision of a Strasbourg Court sufficiently appreciated or accommodated particular aspects of the UK process, a UK court could decline to follow the decision of the Strasbourg Court, giving reasons for this course of action. Lord Phillips thought that, if this happened, the Strasbourg Court would then be given the opportunity to reconsider the aspect of its decision which had caused the problem.

Section 3 HRA 1998 requires that all legislation is read and given effect in a way which is compatible with the Convention rights, but only in so far as it is possible to do this. Any precedent-making court has the power in any legal proceedings to make a declaration of incompatibility, stating that any legislation is incompatible with Convention rights. However, such a declaration would not invalidate the legislation in question. It would give the relevant minister the option to revoke or amend the legislation. The minister could, however, leave the incompatible legislation in place. If the European Court of Human Rights delivers an adverse ruling the relevant minister has the same powers to revoke, amend or leave in place the incompatible legislation. Any court can declare delegated legislation, but not statutes, invalid on the grounds of incompatibility. However, this is not the case if the parent Act, which authorised the legislation in question, provides that the legislation should prevail even if it is incompatible. Whenever a new Bill is introduced into Parliament, s. 19 HRA 1998 says that the relevant minister must make a statement to Parliament, before the second reading, declaring that the legislation either is compatible or is not. If the minister states that the legislation is incompatible, he or she must state that the Government intends to proceed with it anyway. The minister does not need to state the way in which the legislation is incompatible.

Section 6(1) HRA 1998 provides that it is unlawful for a public authority to act in a way which is inconsistent with a Convention right, unless the public authority could not have acted differently as a result of a UK Act of Parliament. This section will have a major effect on many UK businesses, as a public authority is defined as including persons whose functions are functions of a public nature. It follows that businesses such as private schools, private nursing homes and private security firms will all be regarded as public authorities for the purposes of the HRA 1998. If a public authority breaches a Convention right, a victim of the breach may bring legal proceedings against it for breach of a new public tort.

The rights conferred by the Convention are as follows:

- the right to life (Art. 2);
- the right not to be subjected to torture or inhumane or degrading punishment (Art. 3);
- the right not to be held in slavery or servitude or required to perform forced or compulsory labour (Art. 4);
- the right to liberty and security of the person (Art. 5);
- the right to a fair trial (Art. 6);
- the right not to be convicted of a criminal offence which was created after the act was committed (Art. 7);
- the right to respect for a person's private and family life, home and correspondence (Art. 8);
- the right to freedom of thought, conscience and religion (Art. 9);
- the right to freedom of expression (Art. 10);
- the right to freedom of peaceful assembly and to freedom of association with others (Art. 11);
- the right to marry and form a family (Art. 12);
- the right to have the Convention applied without discrimination (Art. 14).

Article 15 allows departure from the Convention in time of war. Articles 1 and 13 have not been incorporated into UK law.

The United Kingdom has also agreed to be bound by protocols, which give the right to peaceful enjoyment of possessions, and outlaw the death penalty.

Forty-seven States have signed the Convention on Human Rights and there are 47 judges in the plenary Court of Human Rights, one judge representing each State. This plenary court almost always delegates the hearing of complaints to Chambers. Each Chamber has seven judges plus an additional judge who represents the State against which the complaint is being made. The Chambers themselves set up Committees of three judges. These Committees sift through complaints and dismiss as soon as possible those which are completely unfounded. The European Court of Human Rights is very much a court of last resort. Article 35 of the Convention requires an applicant to the court to prove four things:

(1) that the complaint involves a breach of the Convention by a country which has ratified it;

(2) that the breach happened within that country's jurisdiction;

(3) that all domestic remedies have been exhausted; and

(4) the application has been made within six months of these being exhausted.

However, if domestic remedies are unsatisfactory, then the court can deem them to have been exhausted. The court cannot enforce its judgments but can order 'just satisfaction' amounting to the payment of compensation and costs. The court does not use a system of precedent. The Human Rights Act 1998 has already had a significant impact on many areas of UK law (see Figure 1.3). Both government ministers and senior judges who supported the passing of the HRA 1998 have recently said that it is being applied too widely, both by judges and those in official positions.

Civil law and criminal law

The distinction between civil and criminal liability is fundamental to English law. The courts themselves are divided into civil courts and criminal courts, and the two sets of courts have quite different purposes. The civil courts are designed to compensate people who have been injured by others. The criminal courts are designed to punish people who have committed a crime.

Table 1.1 shows the essential differences between civil and criminal law.

Despite the differences shown in Table 1.1, it is quite possible that the same wrongful act will give rise to both civil and criminal liability. For example, if a motorist injures a pedestrian by dangerous driving, then both a crime and a **tort** (a civil wrong) will have been committed.

The State might prosecute the driver for the crime of dangerous driving, and if the driver is found guilty he or she will be punished. The driver would probably be banned from driving, and might also be fined or imprisoned. The injured pedestrian might sue the driver in the civil courts for the tort of negligence. If the driver is found to have committed the tort, then he or she will have to pay damages to compensate for the pedestrian's injuries.

Table 1.1 The differences between civil and criminal law

	Criminal	Civil
Purpose of the case	To punish a wrongdoer	To compensate a person injured by an unlawful act
The parties	The state prosecutes a defendant, e.g. R v Smith	An individual (the claimant) sues an individual (the defendant), e.g. Smith v Jones
The outcome	The defendant is either acquitted or convicted	The claimant either wins the case or does not
The consequences	If convicted, the defendant will be sentenced	If the claimant wins, he or she will be awarded a remedy
The courts	The case will be tried in the magistrates' court or the Crown Court	The case will first be heard in either the county court or the High Court
The facts	Decided by the magistrates or by a jury	Decided by the judge
The law	Decided and applied by the judge or by the magistrates on the advice of the clerk to the court	Decided and applied by the judge
Burden and standard of proof	The prosecution must prove the defendant's guilt, beyond reasonable doubt	The claimant must prove his or her case on a balance of probabilities
Examples	Murder, theft, false trade descriptions, misleading price indications	Negligence, trespass, breach of contract, disputes as to ownership of property

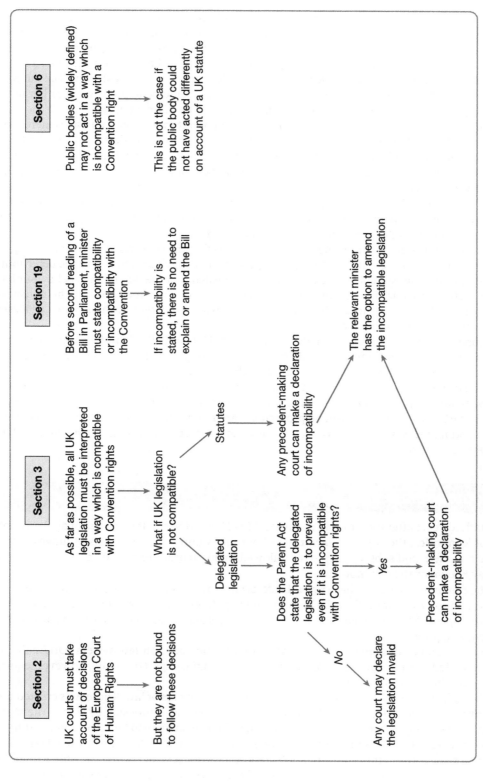

Figure 1.3 An outline of the effect of the Human Rights Act 1998

The different functions of the civil and criminal courts can be further demonstrated if we consider what would have happened if the driver's behaviour had been much worse.

Let us now assume that the driver was very drunk, driving very badly, and that the pedestrian was killed. Under the criminal law the driver would be charged with the more serious offences of causing death by reckless driving and of driving with excess alcohol. The purpose of charging the driver with these more serious offences would be to punish him or her more severely. If convicted, the driver would almost certainly be imprisoned.

However, the civil courts would not order the defendant to pay more damages merely on account of his or her behaviour having been worse. In fact, if the pedestrian was killed, the damages might well be less than if he or she had been badly injured. Damages payable to a pedestrian injured so badly that nursing care would be required for the rest of his or her life might well exceed £1 million. They would take account of the cost of the claimant's nursing care, as well as pain and suffering and loss of earnings. If the driver was killed instantly, no damages would be paid in respect of nursing care or pain and suffering. A pedestrian who was not injured at all could bring no claim for damages.

This example demonstrates the different purposes that the two sets of courts are trying to achieve. The criminal courts are designed to punish bad behaviour. The worse the behaviour, the greater the punishment. Once it has been established that the defendant's behaviour has been such as to incur civil liability, the civil courts are not concerned with the heinousness of the defendant's behaviour. They are concerned with the extent of the injuries or losses which the claimant has suffered.

Crimes which cause injury to a victim will also give rise to a civil action. However, 'victimless' crimes will not. Possessing a controlled drug, for example, is a crime, but the fact of the defendant's possessing the drug does not directly injure anyone else.

Most civil wrongs are not crimes. A person who breaks a contract or trespasses on another's property might well be sued, but will not have committed a crime. Notices on private land which state that 'trespassers will be prosecuted' are misstating the law. Trespassers commit a tort and might be sued for it. However, they generally do not commit a crime and so they cannot be prosecuted.

Common law and equity

A hundred years after the Norman conquest, King Henry II began the process of applying one set of legal rules, the common law, throughout the country. The decisions of judges began to be recorded, and subsequent judges followed them, in order to provide a uniform system of law known as the common law.

The common law grew to have several defects and, to counter these, people seeking a remedy could petition the Chancellor, the highest-ranking clergyman, to ask him to intercede. This justice dispensed by the Chancellor, and later by judges under the Chancellor's control, became known as equity.

Equity was not designed to be a rival system to the common law system. Originally, it was intended to supplement the common law, to fill in the gaps. Gradually, however, equity developed into a rival system.

The Judicature Acts 1873 and 1875 merged the two systems of law. These Acts created the modern court structure, designed to apply common law and equity side by side in the same courts. Even today, however, equity still has an influence on English law. The administration of law and equity was fused, but the separate rules of each branch of the law lived on.

From a student's point of view it is sufficient to say that certain matters are still 'equitable' and that there are two main consequences of this. First, certain remedies are equitable in nature and are therefore awarded only if the court considers it equitable to award them. Second, some relationships, such as the relationship between partners in a firm, are governed by equitable principles and therefore require very high standards of honesty and openness.

Features of the English legal system

The English legal system is unlike that of any other European country.

Antiquity and continuity

English law has evolved, without any major upheaval or interruption, over many hundreds of years. The last successful invasion of England occurred in 1066, when King William and his Normans conquered the country. King William did not impose Norman law on the conquered Anglo-Saxons, but allowed them to keep their own laws. These laws were not uniform throughout the kingdom. Anglo-Saxon law was based on custom, and in different parts of the country different customs prevailed.

In the second half of the twelfth century, one set of legal rules, known as 'the common law', began to be applied throughout England. Since that time, English law has evolved piecemeal. For this reason the English legal system retains a number of peculiarities and anomalies which find their origins in medieval England.

English law does not become inoperative merely because of the passage of time. When we study the law of contract we shall see that two ancient cases, **Pinnel's case (1602)** and **Lampleigh v Brathwaite (1615)**, are still important precedents. Although these cases have been refined and developed by subsequent cases, there would be no reason why a modern lawyer should not cite them in court. In the same way, statutes remain in force indefinitely or until they are repealed.

Occasionally, a litigant springs a major surprise by invoking an ancient law. In 1818 the defendant in **Ashford v Thornton (1818)**, who was accused of murder, claimed the right to have his case settled by battle. Trial by battle had been a method of resolving disputes shortly after the Norman Conquest (as described below) but had fallen into disuse before the end of the thirteenth century. In **Ashford v Thornton** the offer of trial by battle was declined and so the defendant was discharged. The Appeals of Murder Act 1819 was hurriedly passed. Until Parliament passed this Act, trial by battle still existed as a possible means of settling some types of legal disputes.

The adversarial system of trial

The English system of trial is adversarial. This means that the lawyers on either side are adversaries, who 'fight' each other in trying to win judgment for their clients. The judge supervises the battle between the lawyers, but does not take part. Recent reforms of the civil justice system now require the judge to manage the case rather than to leave this to the lawyers. The judge will therefore set timetables for the completion of certain stages of litigation and try to encourage cooperation on certain issues. Despite this judicial case management, a trial is still conducted on adversarial lines. Today the battle is metaphoric, but in the early Middle Ages many disputes were resolved with a trial by battle. The parties would fight each other, both armed with a leather shield and a staff, and it was thought that God would grant victory to the righteous litigant. If either of the parties was disabled, or too young, or too old, he could hire a champion to fight for him. This was no doubt considerably more entertaining than a modern trial, but eventually it came to be realised that it was not the best way to achieve justice. Lawyers replaced the champions. However, the idea of a battle survived, and a trial is still a battle between the lawyers, even if the shields and staves have given way to witnesses and precedents.

Most other European countries have an inquisitorial system of trial, where the judge is the inquisitor, determined to discover the truth. A French examining magistrate, for example, has enormous powers. He or she takes over the investigation of a criminal case from the police and can interrogate witnesses. He or she can also compel witnesses to give evidence and can surprise witnesses with other witnesses, hoping that the confrontation will point the finger of guilt.

When a French case reaches court, it is often all but decided. By contrast, no-one can ever be certain of the outcome of an English trial. The lawyers will fight each other on the day and either side might win. The judge should be disinterested in the outcome, merely ensuring that the lawyers fight by the rules.

Absence of a legal code

In most European countries the law has been codified. This means that the whole of the law on a particular subject, for example the law of property, can be found in one document or code. As we have seen in this chapter, the bulk of English law has been made by judges in individual cases.

Occasionally, Parliament codifies an area of law with a statute such as the Partnership Act 1890. Such an Act aims to take all the relevant case law on a particular subject and to codify it into one comprehensive statute. However, as we shall see, the vast majority of English law remains uncodified. Nor does Britain have a written constitution, as most other democratic countries have.

The law-making role of the judges

In most European countries the judges interpret the legal code. In doing this they do not themselves deliberately set out to create law. Earlier in this chapter, when we studied the doctrine of judicial precedent, we saw that the decisions of judges in the High Court, the Court of Appeal and the House of Lords must be followed by lower-ranking judges. So these senior judges are constantly creating the law.

Importance of procedure

In the Middle Ages a claim would fail if the correct court procedure was not rigidly adhered to, even if the substance of the claim was perfectly valid. To some extent this is still true today. If a litigant fails to follow the correct procedure, it is possible that his claim will be struck out. Recent reforms of the judicial process have attempted to reduce the importance of procedure. However, in cases which involve a substantial claim there is no doubt that procedure remains very important.

Absence of Roman law

The Romans occupied England from 55 BC to AD 430. Roman law was extremely sophisticated by the standards of its day. The other European countries which were part of the Roman Empire have retained elements of Roman law. However, English law has almost no Roman law influence, although Roman law is still taught as an academic subject at some English universities.

Other features

Two other features of the English legal system are worth mentioning. First, the legal profession is divided, lawyers being either barristers or solicitors. Second, in almost all criminal trials the innocence or guilt of the accused is decided by laymen, rather than by lawyers or judges. If the accused is tried in the Crown Court, it will be a jury which decides whether the accused is guilty. If the crime is tried in the magistrates' court, it is generally a bench of lay magistrates who make this decision.

The legal profession

Unlike other European countries, England has two different types of lawyers – barristers and solicitors. There are slightly over 15,500 practising barristers, about 35 per cent of whom are female and 11 per cent of whom are from ethnic minorities. The main job of barristers is to argue cases in court. However, the role of the practising barrister is much wider than merely acting as an advocate. Barristers spend a considerable amount of time giving written opinions, in which they state what they consider the law to be. They also draft statements of case, the formal documents which the parties must exchange before a case is heard in court. Barristers tend to specialise either in criminal law or in a particular branch of civil law. They have rights of audience in all civil and criminal courts. Until 1990, barristers had an exclusive right to be heard in the higher courts, but now some solicitors also have rights in such courts.

About 1,500 senior barristers are known as Queen's Counsel, and they generally appear in court with a junior barrister assisting them. Since June 2005 they have been appointed by a Queen's Counsel selection panel. Queen's Counsel, or QCs as they are usually known, can charge higher fees than other barristers, in recognition of their expertise.

Traditionally, barristers operate from chambers, which are offices where several barristers are allocated work by a barrister's clerk, who also negotiates the barrister's fees. Under the 'cab rank' rule a barrister, like a taxi, is supposed to provide his services to any client. Theoretically, therefore, any barrister is available to any client whose solicitor asks that the barrister should be engaged. This is not always true, as some barristers' fees are beyond the means of many clients and because barristers' clerks, who arrange what cases a barrister can take, are skilled at deflecting unwanted cases. It often happens that when a particular barrister has been engaged, he is not available when the case starts because another case in which he is appearing has not finished in time. The client is then allocated a different barrister. Many barristers do not practise, but work in industry or commerce or for local government or the Civil Service. Until recently barristers could be engaged only through a solicitor. However, members of the public are now allowed to instruct a barrister directly, without going through a solicitor. The Legal Services Act 2007 has allowed barristers and solicitors to work together in partnership.

There are about 130,000 practising solicitors, almost 12 per cent of whom are from ethnic minority groups. Almost 49 per cent of practising solicitors are women, a percentage which is increasing annually. Solicitors, many of whom work in very large partnerships, are the first point of contact for a client with a legal problem.

A solicitor in a one-person business should have a good idea of most areas of law and should know where more information could be found if needed. In the larger firms solicitors would tend to specialise in one particular area of law. Solicitors routinely give their clients legal advice, enter into correspondence on their behalf, draft wills, and draw up documents which transfer ownership of land.

Until 1990, solicitors were allowed to argue cases only in the magistrates' court and the county court. Now the barristers' monopoly right to appear in the Crown Court and appellate courts has been removed by statute, and solicitors who have gained the necessary advocacy qualifications can represent clients in any court. However, barristers still perform the vast bulk of advocacy work in these courts. Whereas solicitors have gained rights of audience since 1990, they have lost their monopoly rights to perform conveyancing and to obtain grants of probate. The Administration of Justice Act 1985 allowed licensed conveyancers to practise. It was widely predicted that this would be disastrous for many small firms of solicitors, but this does not seem to have been the case. However, the Legal Services Act 2007 has allowed non-lawyers to own law firms, and many have suggested that this will be very damaging to small high-street firms.

The Legal Services Act 2007

The Legal Services Act (LSA) received Royal Assent in 2007. However, it did not fully come into force until 2012. The Act sets up a new framework of regulation for legal services in England and Wales and is probably the most significant reform of legal services ever to have been made. Part 1 of the Act sets out the Act's eight regulatory objectives, namely:

(1) protecting and promoting the public interest;
(2) supporting the constitutional principle of the rule of law;
(3) improving access to justice;
(4) protecting and promoting the interests of consumers;
(5) promoting competition in the provision of services;
(6) encouraging an independent, strong, diverse and effective legal profession;
(7) increasing public understanding of the citizen's legal rights and duties; and
(8) promoting and maintaining adherence to the professional principles, which are set out in s. 1(3).

The professional principles set out in s. 1(3) require 'authorised persons', that is to say those who can offer 'reserved legal services', to act with independence, integrity and confidentiality; to maintain proper standards of work; to act in the best interests of clients; and to act in the best interests of justice when litigating in court.

Part 2 of the Act has created a Legal Services Board (LSB), which aims to maintain and develop standards relating to the legal profession. The LSB has a duty to promote the eight regulatory objectives set out in Part 1 of the Act, and to establish a Consumer Panel. It is independent from the Law Society and the Bar Council, with the Solicitors' Regulation Authority and the Bar Standards Board carrying out regulatory functions, these are now called 'front-line' legal regulators.

Part 3 of the Act sets out the 'reserved legal activities' which can be carried out only by lawyers. These matters are advocacy in court, formally conducting litigation, and charging for the preparation of probate papers. Other, minor, reserved legal activities can be carried out by notaries or commissioners for oaths.

Part 5 of the Act, which came into force in 2009, allows Legal Disciplinary Practices (LDPs) to be set up as companies, partnerships or limited liability partnerships. Within LDPs, solicitors can be in business with non-solicitor partners and non-lawyer managers. (However, managers must be solicitors, barristers, notaries, licensed conveyancers, legal executives, patent agents, trade mark agents or law costs draftsmen.) This allows expertise to be brought into a business, increasing its ability to provide a one-stop service to customers. It also allows non-solicitors to provide capital to businesses which provide legal services. As from September 2012, all LDPs with non-lawyer managers have needed to register as Alternative Business Structures (ABS).

In an ABS lawyers and those without legal qualifications can work together to provide both reserved legal activities and other services. In such businesses non-lawyers are able to exercise professional, management and ownership roles. As long as an ABS has been licensed by an approved licensing body, such as the Law Society, it can offer 'reserved legal activities', which need to be carried out by lawyers. However, any other activities can be carried out by those who are not legally qualified. It seems very likely that many non-traditional legal services providers will employ non-lawyers to carry out much of the background work which was traditionally carried out by lawyers. This has caused several distinguished commentators to fear that lawyers, if they are to be able to compete, will have to give up much of the work which they have traditionally done, or accept much reduced salaries for doing it. The legal services market is estimated to be worth about £19 billion annually. It seems very likely that banks, insurance companies and large retailers will try to take over a large share of the market. Lawyers will probably have to change their outlook and their business structures to compete effectively. However, it should be remembered that the LSA does not provide for complete deregulation of legal services providers. Any new ABS still needs to apply for a licence if any non-lawyer has a material interest in the ABS or is able to control it. A licence will be granted only to businesses which are competent to provide legal services. Furthermore, any non-lawyer who owns more than 10 per cent of an ABS is subject to a fitness-to-own test. It should also be remembered that the demise of the legal profession was widely predicted, not least by the profession itself, when in the late 1980s solicitors lost their monopoly rights to write wills and practise conveyancing. Such predictions have been proved spectacularly wrong.

The LSA 2007 is intended to allow non-lawyers to do much of the work currently done by lawyers and thereby to lead to innovation, price reductions and greater access to legal services. Following these changes, some businesses which have traditionally not provided legal services have decided to do so. However, this may not be as easy as is sometimes envisaged. For example, in April 2014 the Law Society Gazette reported that Co-operative Legal Services had suffered a £22m operating loss.

The judiciary

There are five main levels in the judicial hierarchy. Supreme Court Justices sit as judges in the Supreme Court. Lords Justices of Appeal sit in the Court of Appeal. There are currently 38 Lords Justices of Appeal and 12 Supreme Court justices. There are also 108 High Court judges, who sit in the High Court and sometimes in the Crown Court.

It is convenient to consider the judges who sit in the High Court, the Court of Appeal and the Supreme Court as distinct from judges who sit in lower courts. The High Court is generally not an appeal court. The Court of Appeal and Supreme Court do not try cases but only hear appeals. The further up the hierarchy the judge is sitting, the more importance he is likely to attach to the precedent which he is creating.

There are currently 680 circuit judges, who try criminal cases in the Crown Court and civil cases in the county court. In the Crown Court these circuit judges are assisted by some 1,300 part-time judges called recorders. In the county court they are assisted by around 450 district judges and 800 deputy district judges. Circuit judges and district judges do not create precedents. Their role is therefore confined to trying the cases which they hear. They supervise the proceedings in court, and in civil cases decide the facts of the case if they are in dispute and award damages and costs. In criminal cases in which a judge sits, the facts will be decided by the jury, but the judge will supervise the proceedings. He will also sum up the law to the jury, so that they can reach the correct verdict, and pass sentence if the accused is convicted.

Twenty-four per cent of judges are female and five and a half per cent are of minority ethnic origin. In the precedent-making courts the judges are almost exclusively white and male.

Ninety-seven per cent of all criminal cases are decided in the magistrates' court, rather than in the Crown Court. Most magistrates are lay magistrates, meaning that they are not legally qualified. However, there are currently 137 district judges (magistrates' court) and they are assisted by 143 deputies.

There are somewhere around 30,000 lay magistrates, who are not paid a salary. Although they are not legally qualified, upon appointment lay magistrates do receive training on matters such as decision-making, stereotyping and avoiding prejudice. Magistrates generally sit as a bench of three, and are advised about the law by the legally qualified clerk of the court. As well as deciding whether or not a person accused of a crime is granted bail, magistrates try cases, deciding whether an accused is innocent or guilty and passing sentence on those who are convicted. They also conduct committal proceedings when a defendant is sent for trial to the Crown Court. Lay magistrates must live or work in the area in which they serve, must have a good knowledge of the local community, must be of good character and have personal integrity. Generally, they must be between the ages of 27 and 65. Most people are eligible to become magistrates, but those in the police or the armed forces are not.

Judicial review

Judicial review is a legal procedure which allows the Administrative Court to examine whether a public law decision, or the exercise of discretionary power by a public body, is legal. The definition of public body includes government ministers and has been held to cover decisions of private bodies which make decisions that affect the public.

The court can grant one or more of the following remedies:

- an order that overrules the original decision;
- an order that forces the decision-maker to do something;
- an order which prevents a decision-maker from doing something which is not legal;
- state the legal position between the parties.

Judicial review has become increasingly important in recent years as the number of applications has increased dramatically. Businesses are increasingly either applying for judicial review or are subject to judicial review proceedings. A business might apply, for example, on the grounds that a decision taken by a government minister affects the running of the business.

Juries

In the Crown Court the jury decides whether the accused is guilty or not guilty. This decision is based on the judge's summing up, which explains the relevant law to the jury. It is therefore said that juries decide the facts of the case. A judge can direct a jury to acquit an accused, but cannot direct them to convict. Juries do not give an explanation for their decisions. If a jury acquits, an appeal cannot overturn this acquittal. This enables juries to bring in 'perverse acquittals' if they think that the circumstances of the case so demand.

Juries play little part in civil cases. The absolute right to trial by jury in the Crown Court for an indictable (serious) offence has also been breached. In March 2010 four men were convicted in the Crown Court of armed robbery, without a jury, because there were serious concerns about jury nobbling. Since then, two other trials for indictable offences have been earmarked for trial in the Crown Court without a jury. However, in the near future it is highly unlikely that more than a handful of such trials will be tried without a jury each year.

In the past few years problems have arisen because jurors have used the Internet to help them with their deliberations. In **R v Thompson and others (2010)** the Court of Appeal held that, at the beginning of a trial, jurors should be specifically told not to use the Internet but to base their verdict on the evidence presented to them in court. In June 2011 a juror who contacted via Facebook a defendant who had already been acquitted, thereby causing a multi-million pound drug trial to collapse, was jailed for eight months for contempt of court.

Essential points

- Legislation is the name given to law made by Parliament.
- The literal rule of statutory interpretation says that words in a statute should be given their ordinary, literal meaning, no matter how absurd the result.
- The golden rule gives the words in a statute their ordinary, literal meaning as far as possible, but only to the extent that this would not produce an absurd result.
- The mischief rule holds that the judge can take into account what 'mischief' the statute set out to remedy.
- The doctrine of judicial precedent holds that judges in lower courts are absolutely bound to follow decisions previously made in higher courts.
- The *ratio decidendi*, loosely translated from the Latin as 'the reason for the decision', is the part of the case which is binding on other judges.
- Statements of law which did not form the basis of the decision are known as *obiter dicta* (other things said).
- A higher-ranking court can overrule a *ratio* created by a lower-ranking court.
- The United Kingdom joined what is now the EU in 1973. In order to be admitted as a member, the UK Parliament passed the European Communities Act 1972. Under this statute the United Kingdom agreed to apply EU law in UK courts.
- The Human Rights Act 1998 requires that all legislation is read and given effect in a way which is compatible with the Convention rights, but only in so far as it is possible to do this.
- The English courts are divided into civil courts and criminal courts, and the two sets of courts have quite different purposes.
- The civil courts are designed to compensate people who have been injured by others. The criminal courts are designed to punish people who have committed a crime.
- Unlike other European countries, England has two different types of lawyers – barristers and solicitors.
- Judicial review is a legal procedure which allows the Administrative Court to examine whether a public law decision, or the exercise of discretionary power by a public body, is legal.
- In the Crown Court the jury decides whether the accused is guilty or not guilty.

Practice questions

1 What are the three main rules of statutory interpretation? What is the effect of these rules?

2 What is the effect of the *ejusdem generis* rule and the rule *expressio unius est exclusio alterius*?

3 What is meant by the doctrine of judicial precedent?

4 What are the five main levels of the courts, for the purposes of precedent?

5 What is meant by *ratio decidendi* and *obiter dicta*? What is the significance of the distinction? What is meant by overruling, reversing and distinguishing?

6 Find a case concerning the Human Rights Act 1998 either in a newspaper or on the Internet. Which articles of the Convention did the case concern? Describe the outcome of the case or, if it has not yet been decided, state what you think the outcome of the case might be.

7 Describe how the system of judicial precedent operates. Do you consider that the advantages of the system outweigh the disadvantages?

Task 1

Draw up a report for your employer, briefly explaining the following matters:

(a) The main rules of statutory interpretation.

(b) The way in which the system of judicial precedent operates.

(c) The ways in which EU law is created and the effect of EU law in the United Kingdom.

(d) The effect of the Human Rights Act 1998.

mylawchamber

Visit **www.mylawchamber.co.uk/macintyreessentials** to access tools to help you develop and test your knowledge of business law, including interactive multiple choice questions, practice exam questions with guidance, weblinks, glossary, glossary flashcards, legal newsfeed and legal updates.

mylawchamber
unrivalled support for legal education

2

Making a contract

Definition of a contract

A contract is a legally binding agreement. In order for a contract to be created, one of the parties must make an offer to the other party and the other party must accept this offer. Furthermore, the circumstances in which the offer and acceptance were made must indicate that the parties intended to enter into a legal relationship. A final requirement, which distinguishes contracts from gifts, is that the two contracting parties must both give some benefit (known as consideration) to the other. There are then four requirements of a contract. There must be an offer, an acceptance of that offer, an intention to create legal relations and consideration given by both parties. In this chapter we consider these four requirements, which are shown in Figure 2.1.

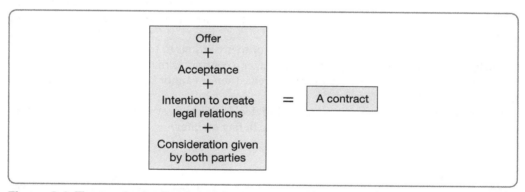

Offer
+
Acceptance
+
Intention to create
legal relations
+
Consideration given
by both parties

=

A contract

Figure 2.1 The requirements of a contract

Once a contract has been made, both sides will be bound to honour its terms or take the legal consequences. A party who does not stick to what was agreed in a contract is said to have breached the contract. Whenever one of the parties breaches a contract, legal remedies will be available to the other party.

Offer

A person who makes an offer is known as an offeror. A person to whom an offer is made is known as an offeree. An offer is made when an offeror proposes a set of terms to an offeree, with the intention that if the proposed terms are accepted they will create a binding contract between the two parties. By accepting the terms proposed, the offeree would also agree to become legally bound by them. This acceptance would therefore form a contract. As a contract is a legally binding agreement, neither an offer nor an acceptance should be made without a willingness to accept the legal consequences.

Neither the offer nor the acceptance need to be made in writing, or even in words. For example, when goods are sold at an auction a contract is formed even though both the offer and the acceptance are made by conduct. Each bidder makes an offer to buy the particular lot being auctioned by making a gesture which the auctioneer recognises as a bid. The auctioneer accepts the highest bid by banging the gavel on the table. At that moment the contract is created, even though both the offer and acceptance were made without the use of words.

Invitation to treat

It is important to make a distinction between an offer and an invitation to treat. An invitation to treat is not an offer. It is an invitation to negotiate or an invitation to make an offer.

An offer should not be made by a person who is not fully prepared to take the legal consequences of its being accepted. For example, I should not offer to sell you my car for £100 unless I am fully prepared to go through with the deal, because if you accept my offer, I will either have to go through with the contract which will have been created or take the legal consequences. A response to an invitation to treat, however, cannot result in a binding contract. It is quite safe for me to ask you how much you would give me for my car. You might name a price (thereby making an offer) but I would have no obligation to agree to the deal.

A court decides whether or not one of the parties has made an offer by looking objectively at what it thinks that both of the parties intended. All the circumstances of the case will be considered in reaching this decision.

Advertisements can amount either to offers or to invitations to treat. If an advertisement is an offer, then a person who accepts the offer makes a contract with the person who advertised. If an advertisement is only an invitation to treat, then it cannot be accepted in such a way that a contract is thereby formed.

In the following two cases the court had to decide whether or not an advertisement was merely an invitation to treat or whether it was in fact an offer.

 Partridge v Crittenden (1968)

The defendant had advertised bramblefinches in a magazine at £1.25 each. A customer sent the defendant £1.25 and a bramblefinch was sent to him. The defendant was charged with offering for sale a wild live bird, contrary to the Protection of Birds Act 1964.

Held The defendant was not guilty because his advertisement was an invitation to treat, not an offer. As the advertisement was not an offer, the defendant had not 'offered for sale' a wild bird. (The defendant had committed a different crime, selling a wild bird. However, he had not been charged with this offence.)

Comment This was a criminal case but it was decided upon a point of civil law. Several criminal offences are committed by offering goods for sale. Whether or not an offer has been made is decided by analysing the law of contract.

At first sight it seems as if the defendant in **Partridge v Crittenden** did make an offer. However, the court reasoned that this could not be the case. If the advertisement had been an offer, then the defendant would have had to supply a bird to everyone who wrote in accepting the offer. The defendant had only a limited supply of birds and so could not have intended that any number of customers would be supplied with one. Therefore, his advertisement was an invitation to treat, not an offer.

Although the vast majority of advertisements will amount to no more than invitations to treat, some advertisements do amount to offers. The following case shows that if all advertisements were only invitations to treat then this would lead to unfairness.

⚖ Carlill v The Carbolic Smoke Ball Co (1893) (Court of Appeal)

The defendants manufactured smoke balls. They claimed that the use of these smoke balls cured many illnesses and made it impossible to catch flu. A large advertising campaign stated that if anyone used a smoke ball correctly, but still caught flu, they would be paid £100 reward. One advertisement stated that the defendants had deposited £1,000 in a Regent Street bank to show that they meant what they said. The claimant, Mrs Carlill, was persuaded by this advertisement to buy a smoke ball. Despite using the smoke ball properly, she still caught flu. When Mrs Carlill claimed the £100 reward the defendants refused to pay, arguing that their advertisement was not an offer.

Held The advertisement was an offer of a unilateral contract (see below). The claimant had accepted this offer by using the smoke ball in the correct way and catching flu. She was therefore entitled to the £100 reward.

Comment If the advertisement had been held not to have been an offer, this would unfairly have allowed the Smoke Ball Company to break its promise. In reaching their decisions the Court of Appeal judges considered what the reasonable person would have made of the advertisement.

In **Carlill v The Carbolic Smoke Ball Co** the offer was made to the whole world. Offers are more usually made to just one person or to a limited number of people. Only a person to whom an offer was made, an offeree, can accept an offer. For example, an offeror might offer to sell a car very cheaply to one particular person, a friend. Only the person to whom the offer was made, the offeree, could accept the offer.

Offer of a unilateral contract

The vast majority of contracts are bilateral (two-sided) because both parties make a promise to the other. Let us assume, for example, that Martin phones John and asks whether or not he wants to buy a consignment of goods. John accepts the offer. This is a bilateral contract because both of the parties have made a promise to the other. Martin has promised to deliver and give ownership of the goods at the price agreed. John has promised to pay the price and take delivery of the goods. A bilateral contract such as this is made up of an exchange of promises. When one of the parties makes an offer of a unilateral contract, as happened in **Carlill v The Carbolic Smoke Ball Co**, only one promise is made. The party making the offer promises that *if* the offeree performs some specified act then the offeror promises to do something in return. The offeree makes no promises. The offeree either performs the specified act, thereby creating a contract, or does not. For example, in **Carlill v The Carbolic Smoke Ball Co** the Smoke Ball Co promised that if Mrs Carlill, or anyone else, properly used a smoke ball but still caught flu, they would be entitled to the £100 reward. Mrs Carlill did not promise to use a smoke ball and catch flu. Furthermore, she could not have accepted the offer by promising to do these things. The only way in which she could accept the offer was by doing the acts requested. Whenever a reward is offered, this is very likely to be the offer of a unilateral contract.

Goods in shops

Customers who buy goods in shops make contracts to buy those goods. In the following case the court had to analyse exactly when the offer and acceptance were made when goods were purchased in a self-service shop.

 Pharmaceutical Society (GB) v Boots Cash Chemists Ltd (1953) (Court of Appeal)

The Pharmacy and Poisons Act 1933 made it a criminal offence to sell listed drugs without a pharmacist being present. The defendants displayed listed drugs on a supermarket shelf in an area of their supermarket where no pharmacist was present. However, a pharmacist was present near the till. It therefore had to be decided *where* the drugs were sold, that is to say *where* the contract to sell the drugs was made. If the contract was made in the area of the supermarket where the drugs were displayed, then the defendants would have been guilty of the offence. If, however, the contract was made at the till, then the defendants would not have been guilty. The prosecution argued that the displayed drugs amounted to an offer and that this offer was accepted when customers put the drugs into their baskets.

Held The defendants were not guilty. The display of goods on supermarket shelves amounts only to an invitation to treat. A customer makes an offer to buy the goods displayed by selecting the goods and taking them to the till. The cashier can accept this offer by ringing up the price. However, the cashier has no obligation to accept the offer and can refuse to sell. So the defendants were not guilty of the offence because any contract to sell the listed drugs was made at the till and would therefore have been made in the presence of a pharmacist.

A display of goods in a shop window does not amount to an offer to sell the goods displayed. The display is only an invitation to treat.

 Fisher v Bell (1961)

The defendant was charged with offering for sale an offensive weapon, contrary to the Restriction of Offensive Weapons Act 1959. He had displayed a flick knife in his shop window and a ticket behind the knife had said, 'Ejector knife – 4 shillings'.

Held The defendant was not guilty. The display of the knife amounted only to an invitation to treat and not to an offer to sell. The defendant had not therefore 'offered for sale' the offensive weapon. Lord Parker said: 'the display of an article with a price on it in a shop window is merely an invitation to treat. It is in no sense an offer for sale the acceptance of which constitutes a contract. That is clearly the general law of the country.'

Acceptance

As we have already seen, a contract comes into existence as soon as an offer is validly accepted. Generally, the acceptance of an offer is regarded as complete only when it is received by the offeror, as the following case shows.

 Entores Ltd *v* Miles Far East Corporation (1955) (Court of Appeal)

The claimants, who were in London, telexed an offer to buy goods to the defendants, who were in Holland. (Telex is a form of near instantaneous communication, whereby a message typed in one place is received on a different typewriter in another place.) The defendants telexed acceptance of the offer back to the claimants. A dispute later arose and the defendants were sued on the contract in an English court. The defendants argued that the contract was made in Holland, not England, and that the English courts therefore did not have the jurisdiction to hear the case. This defence was based on the argument that the acceptance was effective as soon as it was typed out in Holland.

Held The acceptance only became effective once it was received. Therefore, the contract was made in England, where the acceptance was received, and so the English courts had jurisdiction to hear the case.

An acceptance cannot be made by doing and saying nothing, even if the offeror specifies that the acceptance should be made in this way. For example, in **Felthouse *v* Bindley (1862)** the claimant wanted to buy a horse from his nephew for £30.75. The claimant was fairly sure that his nephew would want to sell at this price. He therefore wrote a letter saying that if he heard no reply he would take it that the horse was sold at this price. The nephew wanted to sell at £30.75 and so he did not reply. Later, a dispute arose when an auctioneer sold the horse by mistake. The court held that there had been no acceptance and so there was no contract.

Although **Felthouse *v* Bindley** established that a person cannot accept an offer by doing and saying nothing, some businesses try to sell goods by sending them to people who have not requested them. They then follow this up with a letter demanding the return of the goods or payment for them.

Regulation 27A of the Consumer Protection from Unfair Trading Regulations 2008 provides that in cases of 'inertia selling' a consumer does not need to pay for goods supplied by a trader and may treat them as an unconditional gift. Inertia selling occurs when a trader sends unsolicited goods and demands payment for them, or asks the consumer to return them or keep them safe. The Regulations also make it a criminal offence to demand payment for unsolicited goods.

An acceptance can be made by conduct, as happens when goods are sold by auction. A court may decide that as soon as a person does an act which makes payment for goods or services inevitable, that act must be an acceptance (if no earlier act was acceptance). For example, in **Thornton *v* Shoe Lane Parking Ltd (1971)** (Court of Appeal) Lord Denning MR held that once a customer had driven into a multi-storey car park the contract had been concluded. By this time the customer was committed beyond being able to change his mind.

The postal rule

Whenever an acceptance is made by posting a letter, the possible effect of the postal rule has to be considered. If the rule applies, then the acceptance is effective when the letter is *posted*, not when it is received. The rule originated in the following case.

 Adams *v* Lindsell (1818)

On 2 September 1818 the defendants posted an offer to sell some wool to the claimant. The offer asked for a reply by return of post. The letter containing the offer was misdirected because it was not properly addressed. It therefore arrived on 5 September, whereas if it had not been misdirected it would have arrived on 3 September. The claimant posted a letter of acceptance by return of post. This letter arrived on 9 September. If the first letter had not been misdirected, a reply by return of post would have reached the defendants by 7 September. On 7 September the defendants sold the wool to someone else because they had not received a reply to their offer. The claimant sued for breach of contract.

Held The defendants were in breach of contract. The claimant's acceptance was effective on 5 September, as soon as it was posted.

The postal rule has been developed by subsequent cases. In **Household Fire Insurance Co *v* Grant (1879)** it was applied even when the letter of acceptance was permanently lost in the post. (The Court of Appeal accepted evidence that the letter of acceptance had been posted.) In **Henthorn *v* Fraser (1892)** the Court of Appeal held that the rule would apply whenever it could reasonably be expected that acceptance would be made by post, even if the offer was not made by post. However, in **Re London and Northern Bank (1900)** it was held that the rule could apply only if the letter of acceptance was properly posted. Handing it to a postman to post was held not to be good enough. A letter handed to a postman would be properly posted only when the postman actually did post it.

   In the following case the Court of Appeal reviewed the postal rule.

 Holwell Securities Ltd *v* Hughes (1974) (Court of Appeal)

On 19 October 1971, Dr Hughes gave the claimants an option to purchase his house for £45,000. This option amounted to an offer to sell and was to be exercisable 'by notice in writing' within six months. The claimants posted a letter of acceptance on 14 April 1972, but this letter was never delivered. After the option had expired the claimants sued for specific performance (a court order requiring Dr Hughes to honour the contract and sell the house to them. The nature of this remedy is explained in Chapter 5). The claimants argued that the postal rule applied and that a contract had therefore been made as soon as the letter of acceptance was posted.

Held There was no contract. The postal rule did not apply because the offer, by asking for 'notice in writing', had expressly stated that an acceptance had to reach the offeror. The postal rule would not apply where all the circumstances of the case indicated that the parties did not intend there to be a binding contract until an acceptance was actually received. Furthermore, the court stated that the rule would never apply where its application would produce 'manifest inconvenience and absurdity'.

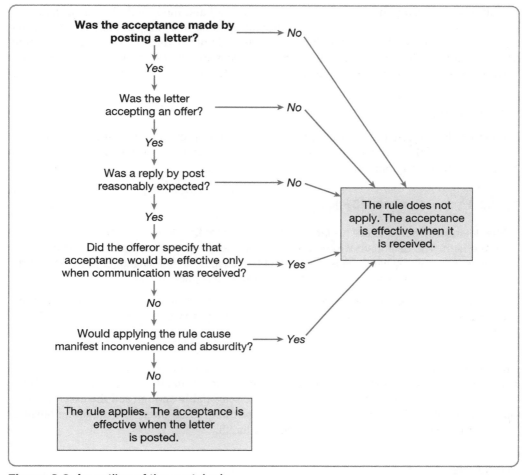

Figure 2.2 An outline of the postal rule

Despite the decision in **Holwell Securities Ltd *v* Hughes**, the postal rule is still very much alive and can still apply. It is, however, important to remember that the rule can apply only when *acceptance is made by posting a letter*. As we saw when considering **Entores Ltd *v* Miles Far East Corporation**, the rule does not apply to acceptance by telex. Nor will it apply to acceptance by any other means such as fax or email. The rule will never apply to revocation (withdrawal) of an offer, even when the revocation is made by posting a letter. The rule is confined to acceptance of an offer by posting a letter. An outline of the effect of the postal rule is shown in Figure 2.2.

Acceptance of the offer of a unilateral contract

We have seen that, the postal rule apart, an acceptance of a bilateral contract is effective when it is received rather than when it is sent. However, acceptance of an offer of a uni-lateral contract is effective as soon as the act requested is fully performed, even if the offeror does not yet know that the act has been performed. This can be demonstrated by considering the decision in **Carlill *v* The Carbolic Smoke Ball Co**. Mrs Carlill could not have accepted the offer by promising that she would buy a smoke ball and then catch flu. She accepted by actually doing these things. Furthermore, her acceptance was complete as soon as she had done the acts requested, even though the company did not yet know that she had done them. This was not unfair to the Smoke Ball Company. It made the offer and chose to make the reward payable when the acts requested were completed.

Counter offer

A counter offer rejects the offer to which it responds and replaces it with a different offer. Having rejected the original offer, an offeree who responded with a counter offer can no longer accept the original offer.

 Hyde *v* Wrench (1840)

The defendant offered to sell his farm to the claimant for £1,000. The claimant offered £950 for the farm. The defendant wrote to the claimant declining the counter offer of £950. The claimant immediately wrote back, saying that he accepted the original offer to sell the farm for £1,000. The defendant refused to sell the farm at this price.

Held There was no contract. The defendant's original offer had been revoked by the claimant's counter offer. The original offer had therefore ceased to exist and could not later be accepted.

The decision in this case makes good sense. If a business offers an asset for sale at a certain price and receives a counter offer, then the counter offer is in effect a refusal of the offer to sell. The business wishing to sell might therefore reasonably enough sell the asset to someone else. If the original offeree could then accept the original offer, and make the business liable for breach of contract, this would be very harsh.

Auctions

As we have seen, a lot at an auction is sold when the auctioneer's gavel hits the table. Before such an acceptance is made, any bid can be withdrawn. When a person makes a new bid, all previous bids lapse. As soon as the gavel hits the table, a contract is formed and the highest bidder has bought the lot which is up for sale. A bid can be withdrawn before the gavel falls, but not after the gavel has hit the table.

If an auction is advertised as being 'without reserve', this means that the auctioneer makes a definite promise that if the auction of any particular lot is commenced, that lot will be sold to the highest genuine bidder. This is the case no matter how low the highest genuine bid might be. Furthermore, the person who put the goods into the auction, the owner of the goods, cannot make a genuine bid. These principles are demonstrated by the following case.

 Barry *v* Davies (trading as Heathcote-Ball & Co) (2000) (Court of Appeal)

Two machines were put up for auction without reserve. The machines were each worth £14,000 and the auctioneer tried to get a bid of £5,000. The claimant bid £400 for the machines but the auctioneer refused to accept the bid.

Held The auctioneer was in breach of contract and the claimant was awarded damages of £27,600. (This was the difference between what the claimant had bid and the amount he would have had to pay to buy the machines elsewhere.) The auctioneer's promise that the machines would be sold without reserve was the offer of a unilateral contract, given in exchange for the claimant's attending the auction and making the highest bid.

The fact of advertising that an auction will take place 'without reserve' does not amount to a promise that the auction will actually take place, or that any goods will actually be included in the auction. For example, in **Harris *v* Nickerson (1873)** an auctioneer placed advertisements in London newspapers, stating that office furniture was to be sold by auction, without reserve, in Bury St Edmunds. Some of the furniture in question was not included in the auction. A dealer, who had travelled to the auction from London, sued the auctioneer on the grounds that he had wanted to buy the furniture which was not auctioned. It was held that the auctioneer had committed no breach of contract as the advertisement was just an invitation to treat.

It must be remembered that most auctions do allow reserves. At such auctions the auctioneer will take bids in the normal way but refuse to sell if the highest bid does not exceed the reserve. For example, when goods are auctioned on eBay there is often a reserve price below which the goods will not be sold.

Tenders

Goods can be either bought or sold by tender. This is perhaps best explained by considering an example. Let us assume that a business will need a very large quantity of a particular type of paper. The business might place an advertisement, asking for tenders to supply the paper needed. This advertisement could either be an offer or an invitation to treat, depending upon the words it used. If the advertisement merely asked for tenders to supply the paper, without anywhere including a statement that the lowest tender would definitely be accepted, then the advertisement would be just an invitation to treat. Those who responded by putting in tenders to supply the paper would be making offers. The business which asked for tenders could choose to accept one of these offers but would have no obligation to do so. It might accept the lowest offer, or any other offer, or just not accept any of the offers. However, if the advertisement stated that the tenderer who submitted the lowest price would definitely be awarded the contract to supply the paper, then the advertisement would amount to an offer of a unilateral contract. This offer could be accepted by submitting the lowest price.

'Referential tenders' refer to other tenders. In **Harvela Investments Ltd *v* Royal Trust Co of Canada Ltd (1986)** the House of Lords held that referential tenders can have no effect because to give them effect would destroy the whole idea behind fixed competitive tendering. The facts of the case were that two people had been invited to put in tenders to buy a parcel of shares and it was promised that the highest bid would get the shares. Both invitees put in a tender. One tender offered to pay $2,175,000. This tender was successful because the other tender, which had agreed to pay $101,000 more than any other tender, was held to be invalid.

Certainty of agreement

Even if an offer is accepted, a contract will be created only if the reasonable person could state with certainty exactly what it is that has been agreed.

The courts use the device of the reasonable person because this gives an objective view of what the parties intended. If the court looked at what the parties actually intended, the subjective views of the parties might well be of little benefit. (One of the parties would claim that the agreement was definite enough to be a contract; the other party would claim that it was not.)

In the following case the House of Lords had to decide whether or not a written agreement was sufficiently certain to amount to a contract.

 Scammel v Ouston (1941) (House of Lords)

A firm of furnishers agreed to take a van from the defendants. It was agreed that the price should be £288 and that £100 should be allowed against an old van which was traded in. The agreement then said: 'this order is given on the understanding that the balance of the purchase price can be had on hire-purchase terms over a period of two years.' The parties began to disagree. Later, the defendants refused to supply the van, arguing that there had never been an agreement which was certain enough to amount to a contract.

Held There was no contract. The agreement was not certain enough to amount to a contract because the reasonable person would not have known exactly what had been agreed.

A contract may contain a price variation clause, which allows the price to be adjusted to take account of matters such as a rise in the cost of raw materials. Such a term will not make the contract void for uncertainty, as long as the contract agrees a definite procedure for setting how the price will change.

Meaningless terms

It is not unusual for a written business contract to contain one or more meaningless terms. Such terms can be ignored and will not therefore invalidate the contract. For example, in **Nicolene Ltd v Simmonds (1953)** the defendants agreed to sell 3,000 tons of reinforced steel bars to the claimants. It was agreed that 'the usual conditions of acceptance apply'. There were no usual conditions of acceptance and the defendants therefore claimed that there was no enforceable contract. However, the Court of Appeal held that if the words were meaningless they could be ignored, leaving behind an enforceable contract.

Lord Denning explained that if a party to a contract could escape from it on account of having discovered a meaningless term, anyone who did not want to be bound by a contract could be found looking through it for a meaningless term which would provide an escape from liability.

When the parties have previously dealt with each other, their previous dealings might well indicate what has been agreed. For example, if in **Nicolene Ltd v Simmonds** the two parties had made similar contracts on several previous occasions, it might well have been certain what the usual conditions of acceptance were. The decision in **Scammel v Ouston** might also have been different if there had been previous dealings between the parties. If the furnishers had previously taken vans from the defendants on hire purchase terms, the words 'the balance of the purchase price can be had on hire-purchase terms over a period of two years' might have been sufficiently certain to mean that there would have been a binding contract.

Offer and acceptance when dealing with machines

It has become common for people to buy goods (or tickets which entitle them to services) from machines. At first sight this seems to cause considerable difficulty in finding the offer and the acceptance. The customer cannot make both the offer and the acceptance so the machine, on behalf of the supplier of the goods or services, must make either the offer or the acceptance.

In **Thornton *v* Shoe Lane Parking Ltd (1971)** (Court of Appeal) Lord Denning MR analysed the position when a customer is given a ticket by a machine. He concluded that the contract was completed not when the customer received the ticket, but as soon as the customer became irrevocably committed to the contract. In the case of a machine which did not have a coin refund this would be as soon as he put his money into the machine. He said:

> The customer pays his money and gets a ticket. He cannot refuse it. He cannot get his money back. He may protest to the machine, even swear at it. But it will remain unmoved. He is committed beyond recall. He was committed at the very moment when he put his money into the machine. The contract was concluded at that time. It can be translated into offer and acceptance in this way: the offer is made when the proprietor of the machine holds it out as being ready to receive the money. The acceptance is made when the customer puts his money into the slot.

Earlier in this chapter we considered **Entores Ltd *v* Miles Far East Corporation (1955)**, and saw that an acceptance by telex will generally be effective when it is received. However, difficulties with contracts concluded by machines may arise where the acceptance is received out of office hours or in the middle of the night. In **Brinkibon Ltd *v* Stahag Stahl und Stahlwarenhandelsgesellschaft GmbH (1983)** (House of Lords) Lord Wilberforce, dealing with communication by telex, made it plain that the courts will take a practical, flexible approach.

> The message may not reach, or be intended to reach, the designated recipient immediately: messages may be sent out of office hours, or at night, with the intention, or on the assumption, that they will be read at a later time. There may be some error or default at the recipient's end which prevents receipt at the time contemplated and believed in by the sender . . . And many other variations may occur. No universal rule can cover all such cases; they must be resolved by reference to the intentions of the parties, by sound business practice and in some cases by a judgment where the risks should lie.

It does seem fairly certain that if an acceptance by telex or fax is received during office hours it is effective when received and not when it is noticed. In **Brinkibon** Lord Fraser said: 'Once the message has been received on the offeror's telex machine, it is not unreasonable to treat it as delivered to the offeror, because it is his responsibility to arrange for prompt handling of messages within his own office.' Lord Fraser also made the point that the acceptor by telex can generally tell if his message has not been received, whereas the offeror would not know that an unsuccessful attempt had been made to send an acceptance.

Offer and acceptance made over the Internet

As yet there have been no significant decisions by the courts as to when a contract is concluded over the Internet. There are two main ways in which such a contract might be formed. First, a contract could be made by exchange of emails. Second, a customer might visit a website and buy goods or services described there.

The position where emails have been exchanged should be catered for by the common law rules already considered in this chapter. The courts will take an objective view of an email and consider whether it was an offer, an acceptance or an invitation to treat. An offer might or might not be of a unilateral contract. The difficulty most likely to arise will be deciding precisely when an acceptance by email is effective. The general principles laid down in relation to telex seem likely to be applied. However, email differs from communication by telex in that a person who sends an email does not immediately know whether or not it has been received. In some ways acceptance by email is more similar to acceptance by letter than to acceptance by telex. However, it seems very unlikely that the postal rule will apply. The approach of the courts has been to restrict the rule rather than to expand it. It seems much more likely that the statement of Lord Wilberforce in **Brinkibon**, set out above, will apply to acceptance by email. This statement does not provide a cast-iron answer applicable to all situations. It indicates that the court will be flexible and will look at the intentions of the parties, sound business practice and a judgment as to where the risks should lie.

In general, websites which describe goods and services and the prices at which they are available will be making invitations to treat rather than offers. This would be particularly true if the material on the website makes it plain that it is the customer who makes the offer and that his offer might or might not be accepted. The customer might make the offer by clicking on a button. Any acceptance would be effective when the customer was informed that his offer had been accepted. However, there is no reason why a website should not make the offer of a unilateral contract. If this were the case, then the contract would be concluded as soon as the customer had performed the stipulated act of acceptance (generally by clicking on an acceptance button).

As we have seen, the key question when dealing with the conclusion of contracts is the time when the acceptance is effective. The Electronic Commerce (EC Directive) Regulations 2002 are concerned with the formalities which must be complied with when a contract is concluded by electronic means. They do not deal, as such, with the time at which the contract is concluded. In any event (as we shall see in Chapter 5), the question is often of little relevance in consumer contracts because the Consumer Contracts (Information, Cancellation and Additional Charges) Regulations 2013 give consumers the right to cancel concluded distance contracts within 14 days. However, the Regulations give no such right to non-consumers.

Termination of offers

As soon as an offer is accepted, a contract is created. However, an offer which has been made might cease to exist in various ways, and once an offer has ceased to exist it can no longer be accepted.

Revocation

If an offer is revoked, it is called off by the offeror. Once an offer has been revoked it can no longer be accepted. A revocation is effective when it is received rather than when it is sent. We have already seen that acceptance of an offer is also effective when received. Therefore, cases involving revocation often amount to discovering which of the parties managed to communicate with the other first. Was the acceptance communicated before the revocation was communicated? If so, there will be a contract. Or was the revocation communicated before the acceptance was communicated? If so, there will be no contract. The following case provides an example of this type of dispute and also demonstrates that revocation can be communicated by an unauthorised third party, if he can be regarded as reliable.

Dickinson _v_ Dodds (1876)

On Wednesday 10 June the defendant wrote a letter to the claimant offering to sell his house. The letter stated that the offer would be kept open until 9 a.m. on Friday 12 June. On Thursday the defendant sold the house to a third party, Allen. Yet another person, Berry, found out about this and told the claimant. At 7 a.m. on Friday 12 June the claimant accepted the defendant's offer. The defendant told the claimant that he was too late to accept. The claimant sued for breach of contract.

Held There was no contract because the offer to sell had been revoked by Berry when he told the claimant that the house had been sold to Allen. Therefore, the offer no longer existed when the claimant attempted to accept it.

Comment It might seem unfair that the offer could be revoked before the deadline. This was allowed because no consideration was given in return for the promise to keep the offer open, that is to say nothing of any value was given in return. Consideration is examined later in this chapter.

The postal rule, which we examined earlier, has always been confined to acceptance of offers and has never applied to revocations. Revocations are always effective when received, whether sent by letter or not.

 Byrne & Co _v_ Van Tienhoven & Co (1880)

On 1 October 1879 the defendants, who carried on business in Cardiff, posted an offer to sell 1,000 boxes of tinplate to the claimants in New York. On 8 October the defendants posted a revocation of their offer. The defendants' offer was received by the claimants on 11 October and a telegram of acceptance was sent the same day. On 20 October the defendants' letter of revocation reached the claimants.

Held A good contract came into existence on 11 October. The revocation was not effective until it was received on 20 October.

An offer of a unilateral contract can be revoked before the offeree has begun to accept it. If the offer was made to the whole world by means of an advertisement it can be revoked in two ways: first, by direct communication with an offeree; second, by another advertisement likely to reach the same audience as the advertisement which made the original offer. However, it is not possible to revoke the offer of a unilateral contract once the offeree has begun to perform the act which was requested as acceptance.

In **Errington _v_ Errington & Woods (1952)**, for example, a man bought a house for £750, taking out a mortgage of £500. He promised his daughter-in-law that if she paid all of the mortgage instalments, she could have the house when the mortgage was paid off. This unilateral offer could not be revoked once the daughter-in-law started to pay the mortgage instalments as they became due. In **Daulia Ltd _v_ Four Millbank Nominees (1978)** Goff LJ confirmed this approach, saying: 'Until [the offeree starts to perform] the offeror can revoke the whole thing, but once the offeree has embarked on performance it is too late for the offeror to revoke his offer.'

Refusal

If an offeree refuses an offer, then, as far as that offeree is concerned, the offer is terminated and cannot later be accepted. We saw earlier, when we considered **Hyde *v* Wrench**, that a counter offer is regarded as a refusal of the original offer and that it therefore ends it. Difficulties may arise in distinguishing a counter offer from a request for more information about the offer. As a request for more information does not imply a rejection of the offer, it does not terminate it. For example, in **Stevenson, Jacques & Co *v* McLean (1880)** the defendant offered to sell a quantity of iron at £2 a ton. The offeree asked if he could have credit. The defendant did not reply, but instead sold the iron to a third party. Then the offeree accepted the offer to sell at £2 a ton. The defendant was in breach of contract because the offeree had only made a request for more information. Unlike a counter offer, this request did not revoke the original offer.

Lapse of time

If a time limit is put on an offer, then the offer will end when the time limit expires. However, even where there is a time limit, the offeror can revoke the offer before the expiry time (unless some consideration was given for keeping the offer open). We saw an example of this in **Dickinson *v* Dodds**. When no time limit is placed upon an offer, it will remain open for a reasonable time. The amount of time which is reasonable will depend upon all the circumstances of the case. If, for example, a business made two offers, one to sell a boatload of ripe fruit and the other to sell a lorry, the offers would not remain open for the same length of time.

Subject to contract

Houses and land are often said to be sold 'subject to contract'. It has become established that this means that no contract has yet been concluded. This principle is not confined to contracts for the sale of land and houses. If goods are sold 'subject to contract', then a court would be likely to infer that no definite contract had yet been concluded.

Condition not fulfilled

An offeror might expressly or impliedly state that an offer is to remain open only until a certain condition is fulfilled. For example, when an offer to buy goods is made, it is implied that the offer will lapse if the goods are damaged before acceptance.

Alternatively, it might be agreed that a contract will become operative only if a condition is fulfilled. If A and B make a contract of sale, and agree that C will fix the price, this agreement is sufficiently certain to amount to a contract. However, if C refuses to fix a price, then the agreement will be avoided.

Battle of the forms

We shall see later (in Chapter 3) that many businesses use their standard terms and conditions when buying or selling goods. This can cause difficulties when both the buyer and the seller of goods insist that a contract is made upon their own particular standard terms. If the parties refuse to agree whose terms are to apply, then there will be no contract. If the parties do agree, so that a contract is formed and the goods are sold and delivered, a court might need to discover which set of terms was agreed to. This would be done by applying the ordinary principles of offer and acceptance, as the following case demonstrates.

Butler Machine Tool Co Ltd *v* Ex-Cell-O Corporation Ltd (1979) (Court of Appeal)

On 23 May the claimants offered to sell a machine to the defendants. This offer was made on the claimants' standard terms and conditions, which said that they were to prevail over any terms and conditions contained in the buyer's order. On 27 May the defendants ordered a machine. This order said that it was made on the defendants' terms and conditions. The claimants' terms and conditions contained a price variation clause whereas the defendants' terms and conditions did not. The defendants' terms and conditions contained a tear-off slip at the bottom of the order. This said: 'We accept your order on the Terms and Conditions stated thereon.' On 5 June the claimants signed this slip and returned it to the defendants. They also added that the order 'is being entered in accordance with our revised quotation of 23 May'. After the machine had been delivered the claimants argued that their terms and conditions prevailed and that they were entitled to an additional £2,892 under their price variation clause.

Held The claimants were not entitled to the extra money. The price variation clause did not apply as the contract was made on the defendants' terms and conditions. On 23 May the claimants made an offer. On 27 May the defendants made a counter offer. On 5 June the claimants accepted this counter offer when they signed the acknowledgement slip and returned it to the defendants.

Comment In **Tekdata Interconnections Ltd *v* Amphenol Ltd [2009]** the Court of Appeal held that in a 'battle of the forms' case the party who fired the last shot would generally win, but that his would not always be the case. The question would always depend upon what the parties must be taken, objectively, to have intended when the contract was made. This should be determined, objectively, on the basis of a proper interpretation of the documents.

Intention to create legal relations

The acceptance of an offer will create a contract only if the offeror and offeree *appeared to intend* to create a legally binding agreement. It is therefore said that it is a requirement of a contract that there must be an intention to create legal relations. This requirement can be demonstrated by considering an example. Let us assume that one motor dealer says to another, 'I've got to sell that Ford Ka you were interested in. If you want it, you can have it for £5,500', and that the other motor dealer replies, 'Thanks a lot. I'll definitely take it.' If this conversation took place in a business context, for example if the dealers were speaking on the phone during office hours, then there would be a contract. All of the circumstances would indicate that by making the offer and the acceptance the parties did intend to enter into a legally binding agreement. However, if the offer and acceptance were made jokingly, for example in a pub as part of a long-standing joke between the parties, then there would be no contract. The circumstances would indicate that the parties did not intend to enter into a legal relationship.

In deciding whether or not there was an intention to create legal relations, the court takes an *objective* view of the parties' intentions. The court does not ask what the parties actually intended, but looks at what they appeared to the reasonable person to intend.

Agreements made in a business or commercial context

If an agreement is made in a business or a commercial context, there is a presumption that the parties did intend to make a contract. As this is only a presumption, it is not a cast-iron rule but only a starting point. It will therefore be up to the party who is claiming that there was no intention to create legal relations to introduce evidence to rebut the presumption (to show that it was not correct). It might be possible to do this, but if the presumption is not rebutted then there will be a contract.

In **Esso Petroleum Ltd v Commissioners of Customs and Excise (1976)** Esso advertised that they would give a World Cup coin to any motorist who bought at least four gallons of petrol at an Esso garage. (The coins showed the images of one of the England players taking part in the 1970 World Cup.) For tax reasons it became necessary to know whether or not the coins were supplied under a contract. The House of Lords held that there was an intention to create legal relations and so there was a contract to supply the coins.

In the **Esso** case the advertisement made a definite promise which motorists were entitled to believe would be kept. Many claims made in advertisements, such as that a particular type of beer refreshes the parts that other beers cannot reach, are regarded as mere 'sales puffs'. These sales puffs do not make any definite binding promise and are not intended to be taken seriously. They are either obviously untrue or incapable of being proved true or false. So even though sales puffs are made in a commercial context, the reasonable person would not think that they were intended to be legally binding.

It is quite possible to make an agreement, even a business agreement, on the understanding that it will have no legal effect at all. In such cases there will be no contract because the parties will have shown that they did not intend to create legal relations.

Agreements made in a social or domestic context

Social agreements are made between friends. Domestic agreements are made between the members of a family. When either a social or a domestic agreement is made, the courts begin with the presumption that the parties do not intend to make a contract. A party who claims that such an agreement is a contract will need to introduce evidence to show that this is what both parties intended. This may well be possible. For example, if friends or family members contributed money to buy a lottery ticket, a court would almost certainly decide that they intended that any prize should be shared. In **Wilson and another v Burnett (2007)** the Court of Appeal considered whether or not three friends had made a contract to share a bingo prize of over £100,000. On the evidence, the Court of Appeal agreed with the trial judge that they had not. May LJ gave the only judgment and said that the case depended upon whether the friends had made a sufficiently certain binding agreement. He was prepared to accept that this might have happened, but said there would always be 'intrinsic problems . . . on the question of whether a necessarily casual conversation could be elevated into an agreement binding and enforceable in law.'

The approach which a court will take is shown in Figure 2.3.

Figure 2.3 Intention to create legal relations

Consideration

A contract is a bargain under which each party must give some benefit, known as consideration, to the other. The consideration of one party is given in return for the consideration of the other. For example, let us assume that I visit a garage and agree to buy a new car for £9,999. A contract has been made. My consideration is the promise to pay £9,999 to the garage. The garage's consideration is its promise to pass ownership of the car to me. In bilateral contracts, such as the one used in this example, the consideration of both parties consists of a promise to do something. The one promise is given in return for the other.

In unilateral contracts the consideration of only one of the parties consists of a promise to do something. The consideration of the other party consists of actually performing the act requested by the promisor. For example, if I offered a £100 reward to anyone who found my lost dog, and you found the dog, a unilateral contract would have been created. My consideration would have been the promise to pay the reward. Your consideration would have been the act of finding the dog.

If only one of the parties gives some consideration, then a contract will not be created. Instead, any agreement will be a gift. So if a garage offered to give me a car for nothing, and I accepted this offer, there would be no contract. The garage would have provided some consideration to me, by promising to give me the car. But I would have provided no consideration to the garage because I would not have promised anything in return. Therefore, there would be no contract and the garage would not have to give me the car.

Later in this chapter we shall see that the promise of a gift is not enforceable unless the promise was made by a deed. When an agreement is made by a deed, it is enforceable as a specialty contract even if no consideration was received by one of the parties.

Consideration can be defined as a benefit given by one party or a loss suffered by the other. Usually, consideration is both a benefit to one party and a loss to the other. For example, if I buy a car from a garage, the garage's promise to give me ownership of the car is a benefit to me and a loss to the garage. Conversely, my promise to pay the money is a benefit to the garage and a loss to me.

Executed, executory and past consideration

Executory consideration consists of a promise to do something in the future. The consideration is called executory because when the contract is made the promisor has not yet performed (executed) his consideration. If we examine a typical bilateral contract, for example **Nicolene Ltd v Simmonds** (earlier in the chapter), we see that the consideration of both parties was executory. The defendants promised that they would deliver the 3,000 tons of steel bars, and the claimants promised that they would pay the price.

   Executed consideration occurs when one of the parties makes the offer or the acceptance in such a way that he has completely fulfilled his liability under the contract. The only contractual liability remaining is that of the other party. A seller of goods, for example, might ask the buyer to send cash with his order. If the buyer does this, then his consideration is executed. Executed consideration is found in the acceptance of unilateral offers, where the acceptance is made by performing some action rather than by promising to do something in the future. For example, in **Carlill v The Carbolic Smoke Ball Company** Mrs Carlill's consideration was executed. She did not promise to use a smoke ball and catch flu, she just did it. The consideration of the smoke ball company, being a promise, was executory.

   It is not possible to give as consideration a promise to do some act which has already been done. **Past consideration** is no consideration. This seems sensible enough, because to promise to do something which has already been done is to promise nothing at all. For example, in **Re McArdle (1951)** the claimant lived in a house which she did not own, and spent a considerable amount of money on having the house repaired. The owners had not asked her to do this. After the claimant had done this, the owners of the house signed an agreement to pay the claimant £488 in consideration of her having had the repairs done. The owners did not have to pay. When the promise to pay was made the claimant had already had the repairs done.

   Despite the rule that past consideration is no consideration, a past act can be good consideration if two conditions are satisfied. First, the other party must have requested that the act be performed. Second, both parties must at the time of the contract have contemplated that payment would be made. The following case provides an example.

⚖ **Lampleigh v Brathwaite (1615)**

The defendant had killed another man and needed to get a pardon from the King. He asked the claimant to get him a pardon. The claimant managed, at considerable personal expense, to obtain the necessary pardon. Upon hearing that the pardon had been granted, the defendant agreed to pay the claimant £100 for what he had done. Later, the defendant grew less grateful and refused to pay. The claimant sued for breach of contract.

Held The defendant had to pay the £100. Both of the conditions were satisfied. First, the defendant had asked the claimant to get the pardon. Second, both parties had contemplated that the claimant would be paid for his services.

Comment This case demonstrates the principle that a past act can amount to good consideration if the two conditions are satisfied. The amount of money payable would now be governed by s. 15(1) of the Supply of Goods and Services Act 1982. Section 15(1) implies a term that where the price of a service supplied under a contract is not fixed by the parties, a reasonable price will be paid.

Sufficiency and adequacy

A well-known principle of the law of contract holds that consideration must be sufficient but does not need to be adequate. At first sight this can seem puzzling, as in everyday language the words 'sufficient' and 'adequate' have a very similar meaning. However, in the context of the law of contract the two words have quite different meanings:

● By saying that consideration must be *sufficient* it is meant that consideration must be of some recognisable value, however small.

● By saying that consideration does not need to be *adequate* it is meant that consideration does not have to be of the same value as the other party's consideration.

An example demonstrates what is meant. If I agree to buy a new television from a shop for its ordinary selling price of £299.99, then my consideration, like that of the shop, is sufficient and adequate. My consideration is sufficient because it has some recognisable value. It is adequate because my promise to pay the money is worth much the same as the shop's promise to give me ownership of the television. If the shop and I had agreed that I could have the television for £1, then my consideration would have been sufficient but would not have been adequate. That is to say, my promise to pay £1 would have been worth something, but would not have been worth as much as I was getting in return. However, a contract would still have been formed, because consideration does not need to be adequate. If the shop had agreed to give me the television for nothing, then no contract would have been formed. I would not have given any consideration to the shop in return for the promise to give me ownership of the television. The shop would therefore not need to give me the television, unless its promise to do so had been made in a deed.

There are two main reasons why the law is not concerned with the adequacy of consideration. The first is that it is not always possible to say what something is worth. A thing is worth what someone will give for it, and this will depend on all of the circumstances. The second reason is that a business which makes bad contracts should not be allowed to escape from these contracts.

The performance of a trivial act can amount to good consideration as long as it confers an economic benefit on the other party. For example, in **Chappell & Co v The Nestlé Co Ltd (1959)** the defendants advertised that they would 'give away' records to members of the public who sent in 7.5p, which was one-fifth of the usual price, and three chocolate bar wrappers. For copyright reasons it became necessary to know whether or not the sending in of the wrappers was part of the customers' consideration. The House of Lords held that it was. Customers who sent in 7.5p without the wrappers would not have received a record. The principle in this case is important. As consideration does not need to be adequate, a trivial act could be given as consideration in any contract, as long as it conferred an economic benefit on the other party. In **Chappell & Co v The Nestlé Co Ltd** the defendants benefited through the publicity generated.

Performing an existing duty

Sometimes, a person claims to have given as consideration a promise to perform an existing duty. Whether or not such a promise amounts to good consideration depends upon how the duty arose in the first place. Three possibilities must be considered: first, that the duty arose under the general law of the land; second, that the duty arose under a previous contract with a third party; third, that the duty arose under a previous contract with the same person.

The duty arose under the general law

It is not good consideration to promise to perform a duty which is imposed by the general law of the land.

 Collins *v* Godefroy (1831)

The claimant was subpoenaed to attend a trial and give evidence. This means that he had a legal duty to attend the trial, this duty having arisen under the general law. The defendant agreed to pay the claimant six guineas (£6.30) if he actually did attend the trial.

Held The claimant was not entitled to the payment of any money. He could not give as consideration his promise to attend the trial. The general law of the land already obliged him to do this.

However, it is good consideration to promise to *exceed* a duty which has arisen under the general law of the land.

 Glasbrook Bros *v* Glamorgan County Council (1925) (House of Lords)

During a strike by coal miners the police were doing their best to protect collieries. The defendants asked the police to provide extra protection for their colliery, by stationing policemen on the colliery premises. The police superintendent in charge said that this would not be necessary. However, 100 policemen were stationed on the colliery premises when the defendants agreed to pay the wages of these policemen. After the strike the defendants refused to pay the £2,300 bill for the policemen's wages, arguing that the police had provided no consideration.

Held The defendants had to pay the £2,300. The police had a duty to protect property under the general law of the land. However, the extra protection provided was in excess of that which the police were obliged to provide under the general law of the land. Providing the extra protection therefore amounted to good consideration for the promise to pay the policemen's wages.

The duty arose under a previous contract with a different person

The same consideration can be given to two different people, so that two contracts are validly created. The following case provides an example.

 Shadwell *v* Shadwell (1860)

The claimant was engaged to marry Ellen Nicholl. In those days, such an engagement amounted to a contract. If the claimant had breached the contract, by not marrying Ellen Nicholl, then she could have sued him. The claimant's uncle was pleased that the marriage was going to take place, and agreed that after it had he would pay the claimant £150 a year until the claimant's income as a barrister amounted to £630 a year. This agreement was to last for the whole of the uncle's life. The uncle died 18 years after the marriage had taken place. He had paid the full allowance for 12 of the 18 years and part of the allowance for one year. The claimant sued for the amounts of the allowance which had not been paid.

Held The claimant was entitled to the allowance which had not been paid. He had already made a contract with Ellen Nicholl that he would marry her. However, he was entitled to give exactly the same consideration (marrying Ellen Nicholl) in a separate contract with his uncle.

Comment A modern example of this principle can be seen in **New Zealand Shipping Co v A. M. Satterthwaite & Co (1974)** (Privy Council). A business which had agreed with a shipowner that it would unload a ship (contract 1) could give the same promise to unload the ship to the owner of the goods on the ship (contract 2).

The duty arose under a previous contract with the same person

Until recently it was not possible to create two contracts by giving the same person the same consideration twice. The following case established this principle.

 Stilk *v* Myrick (1809)

The claimant signed a contract, agreeing to be a sailor on a ship for wages of £5 a month. The ship had a crew of only eleven men. When two of the crew deserted, the captain promised the remaining nine that if they continued with the voyage, as they had originally agreed to do, they could have the wages of the two deserters shared amongst them. The claimant and the other eight remaining crew agreed to this and completed the voyage. However, the captain refused to pay any more than the £5 a month originally agreed. The claimant sued for his share of the extra money which had been promised.

Held The men were not entitled to the extra money which they had been promised. At the start of the voyage they had promised the captain that they would do their duty in return for £5 a month. They could not later give the captain the same promise as consideration for a new contract.

Comment It might be thought that the nine remaining crew were doing more than they had originally agreed. However, the court thought that they had agreed to do whatever was necessary to complete the voyage. Lord Ellenborough said: 'They had sold all their services till the voyage be completed.'

The facts of **Hartley *v* Ponsonby (1857)** were very similar, except that half of the crew had deserted. To carry on with half a crew would have been dangerous. It was held that the sailors who agreed to continue the voyage were entitled to the extra payment which the captain had promised. They were regarded as having exceeded their duty because they had not originally agreed to work on a dangerous ship.

In the following case the Court of Appeal again considered this area of the law.

Williams *v* Roffey Bros Ltd (1990) (Court of Appeal)

The defendants had contracted to refurbish a block of flats. They subcontracted the carpentry work to the claimant, who was to be paid £20,000 for doing the carpentry on 27 flats. Soon after starting work, the claimant realised that he had priced the job too low. He told the defendants that he would not be able to afford to finish the job if he were not paid more. If all the work on the flats was not finished on time the defendants would have become liable to pay huge damages to the owner of the block of flats. The defendants were so concerned about this that they agreed to pay the claimant an extra £575 per flat if he carried on and did the carpentry work as originally agreed. Happy with this agreement, the claimant carried on with the work. The claimant was not paid the extra money which he had been promised and so he sued for breach of contract.

Held The defendants were in breach of contract, and so had to pay the extra £575 per flat which they had agreed to pay. By agreeing to complete the carpentry work on time, the claimant had conferred a benefit on the defendants. This was the case even though he had already agreed with the defendants that he would do this work at the original contract price. By agreeing to do the work in return for the extra payment, the claimant had enabled the defendants to avoid paying the damages to the owner of the flats and had saved them the trouble of finding a different carpenter. This was a benefit to the defendants. Therefore, the claimant had provided fresh consideration for the defendants' promise to pay the extra £575 per flat.

In **Williams *v* Roffey Bros Ltd** the Court of Appeal claimed to have refined **Stilk *v* Myrick**, rather than to have overruled it. However, it is not easy to see how the two cases differ in principle. It is of some relevance that there was no such concept as economic duress when **Stilk *v* Myrick** was decided. If there had been, it seems likely that the contract would have been voidable because the sailors pushed the captain into the agreement in such a way that he did not really agree to it. **Williams *v* Roffey Bros Ltd** was different, in that it was the defendants who suggested the extra payment. Economic duress is considered in a later chapter (Chapter 4).

The following table shows the extent to which a promise to perform an existing duty can amount to good consideration.

Table 2.1 Whether a promise to perform an existing duty amounts to consideration

Extent to which duty was promised to be performed How duty arose	Promise to perform the duty	Promise to exceed the duty
Under the general law	No consideration	Good consideration
Under a previous contract with the same person	Maybe consideration **Stilk *v* Myrick** – no (but consider economic duress) **Williams *v* Roffey** – possibly yes	Good consideration
Under a previous contract with a third party	Good consideration	Good consideration

Settling out of court

A dispute is settled out of court when a person agrees not to pursue a legal action in return for the payment of a sum of money. By way of example, let us assume that Sajjid has been injured in an accident and has a claim against Tom. It is possible that if Sajjid and Tom cannot agree on the correct amount of compensation, the dispute will go to court. It is much more likely that Sajjid will take an amount of money offered by Tom, and in return will promise never to bring any legal claim against Tom in respect of the accident. If such an agreement were made, the dispute would have been settled out of court. (Sajjid and Tom would generally make such an agreement through their solicitors.) Once made, such an agreement would be binding upon both of the parties because it is a contract. The consideration of Tom would consist of paying the sum of money agreed. The consideration of Sajjid would consist of promising not to sue. Most legal disputes are settled out of court. It is obviously good public policy that, once a dispute has been finally settled, it cannot be reopened.

Part payment of a debt

If one person owes a sum of money to another, the debt can be extinguished in two ways. First, obviously enough, the debt is extinguished if the debtor pays the sum owing in full. Second, the debt is extinguished if the debtor and creditor agree that the creditor will take anything other than money instead of the amount owing. For example, if Harry owes Bill £10,000, the debt can be extinguished either by Harry paying the full £10,000 or by Harry and Bill agreeing that Bill should take Harry's car in full settlement of the debt. If Harry and Bill do agree that Bill should take the car in full settlement of the debt, the court would not be concerned with how much the car was actually worth. As we have seen, the courts are not concerned with the adequacy of consideration. So no matter what Harry's car might be worth, the full debt would be extinguished.

Difficulties arise where the parties agree that the creditor should take a sum of money which is less than the amount owing, in full settlement of the debt. Let us assume, for example, that Harry owes Bill £10,000 and that Bill agrees that if Harry pays £9,000 the debt will be extinguished and Bill will never ask for the rest of the money. **Pinnel's Case (1602)** held that a lesser sum of money cannot be consideration for a greater sum owed. Bill would therefore be able to sue Harry for the balance of £1,000, even though he had promised that he would not do this. The promise which Bill gave does not create a contract because no consideration was received in return for it. The promise made by Harry, to pay £9,000 in full settlement of the debt, could not be consideration to extinguish the whole debt of £10,000 because a lesser sum cannot be consideration for a greater sum owed. In this area the law does seem to be concerned with the adequacy of the consideration. It is saying that £9,000 is not enough consideration for a debt of £10,000. The reason for this is that the only thing which can always be given a definite monetary value is money itself. In extreme circumstances, a pen, a bicycle or a car might be worth £10,000. However, in no circumstances could £9,000 be worth £10,000. The decision in **Pinnel's Case** was directly approved by the House of Lords in the following case.

 Foakes v Beer (1884) (House of Lords)

Mrs Beer had successfully sued Dr Foakes, who had been ordered to pay her £2,090 damages. Dr Foakes was unable to pay all of this immediately. Mrs Beer agreed in writing that if Dr Foakes paid the full amount by instalments she would not 'take any proceedings whatever' on the judgment in her favour. Dr Foakes paid the full amount in instalments, as he had agreed to do. Mrs Beer then sued him for £360 interest. (Interest is always payable on a court judgment which is paid in instalments.)

Held Dr Foakes had to pay the £360 interest. A lesser sum of money cannot be consideration for a greater sum owed. Therefore, £2,090 payable by instalments without interest (the lesser sum) could not be consideration for £2,090 payable by instalments with interest (the greater sum owed).

Comment **Foakes v Beer** is an important case because in it the House of Lords directly approved the decision in **Pinnel's Case**. As House of Lords decisions are binding upon all other courts, the decision gave great strength to the rule that a lesser sum of money cannot be consideration for a greater sum owed.

Despite the decision in **Foakes v Beer**, the rule that a lesser sum of money cannot be consideration for a greater sum owed has always been subject to some exceptions:

- If the creditor agrees to take anything else instead of, or as well as, a lesser sum of money, then the debt is extinguished.
- If the creditor asks for a lesser sum to be paid before the debt is actually due, then the debtor's paying the lesser sum early can amount to good consideration.
- If the creditor requests that a lesser sum be paid in a different place, perhaps a different country, then the debtor's agreeing to this could possibly amount to good consideration.
- If there is a dispute as to the amount owed, and the creditor agrees to settle for less than he thinks he is owed, this agreement will be binding. (The parties will have settled out of court.)
- Another possible exception, promissory estoppel, is considered below.

Promissory estoppel

The concept of promissory estoppel arose in the following case.

Central London Property Trust Ltd *v* High Trees House Ltd (1947) (the High Trees Case)

In 1937 the defendants took a lease on a block of flats in London at a rent of £2,500 a year. During the Second World War (1939–45), many people moved away from London as it was being bombed. In 1940 the defendants found that they could not sublet the flats and could not therefore pay the claimants the full rent. The claimants accepted that this was the position and agreed that the defendants should pay a reduced rent of £1,250 a year. It was not agreed for how long the reduced rent should be paid. In 1945 the defendants were once again able to fully sublet the flats. However, the defendants were still paying a rent of only £1,250 a year. In September 1945 the claimants sued for the full rent in the future and the full rent from the time when the flats had once again become fully sublet.

Held The claimants were entitled to the full rent both in the future and from the date on which the flats had become fully sublet.

The decision in the **High Trees Case** was not particularly surprising. However, the judge who heard the case, Denning J, caused considerable controversy by saying that, if the claimants had asked for the full rent for the years when the flats were not fully sublet, they would not have got it. This statement is at odds with the decision in **Pinnel's Case** (i.e. that a lesser sum of money cannot be consideration for a greater sum owed). Denning's theory became known as promissory estoppel. It said that if a person made a promise, and the person to whom it was made was intended to rely on the promise and did rely on it, then the promise would be binding. This would be the case even if no consideration was given in return for the promise. However, promissory estoppel will apply only if the following four conditions are satisfied:

(1) There must have been an existing legal relationship between the parties.
(2) The promisor must have intended to enter into legal relations, by promising not to insist on his strict legal rights.
(3) The promisor must have known that the promisee would act upon this promise.
(4) The promisee must actually have acted upon the promise.

If the claimants in the **High Trees Case** had sued for the full rent for the years when the flats were not fully sublet, the four conditions would have been satisfied. According to Denning J, the claimants would therefore have been defeated by promissory estoppel.

Three further points about promissory estoppel must be made. First it is 'a shield not a sword' and this means that it can only be used as a defence. A claimant cannot use promissory estoppel to sue somebody with. Therefore, the decision in **Stilk v Myrick** would not be changed by promissory estoppel. In order to get their extra money, the sailors needed to sue the captain for it.

Second, there is no certainty as to whether promissory estoppel acts so as to permanently extinguish the right to sue, or whether it merely suspends the right to sue until reasonable notice of the intention to reintroduce the right to sue has been given. It is probably the case that where there is a continuing obligation it merely suspends the right to sue, unless the claimant indicated that he was permanently giving up his rights, but where there is a one-off obligation, such as to pay a debt, promissory estoppel could possibly extinguish the right to sue. However, in **Re Selectmove (1995)** the Court of Appeal held that it was bound by **Foakes v Beer**, which was still good law, and that part payment of a debt could not amount to good consideration.

Finally, it is certain that promissory estoppel is an equitable doctrine. It will therefore only act so as to prevent a claimant from breaking a promise where it would be inequitable (unfair) of the claimant to break the promise. In the following case promissory estoppel did not apply because it was not inequitable for the claimants to break the promise to accept a lesser sum of money.

 D & C Builders v Rees (1966) (Court of Appeal)

The claimants were a small firm of builders. The defendant owed the claimants £482 for work which the claimants had properly done. The defendant's wife knew that the claimants were very short of money. She told them that they would have to accept £300 in full settlement of the debt or they would be paid nothing. She knew that if the claimants refused to accept this, and sued for the full amount, they would be bankrupt before the case came to court. The claimants reluctantly agreed to take the £300, in full settlement of the debt. Once they had received this money, the claimants sued for the remaining £182.

Held The claimants were entitled to the remaining £182. **Foakes v Beer** applied and the lesser sum of money could not be satisfaction for the greater sum owed. The defendant could not use promissory estoppel as a defence. It was not inequitable for the claimants to break their promise to accept £300 in full settlement of the debt because they had been pressurised into making this promise.

Comment Since this case, the law on economic duress has changed a great deal. If such a case were to arise today the agreement to accept the lesser sum of money would be voidable for economic duress. (See Chapter 4.)

An outline of the requirements of promissory estoppel is set out in Figure 2.4. However, it must be remembered that the doctrine is surrounded by considerable uncertainty.

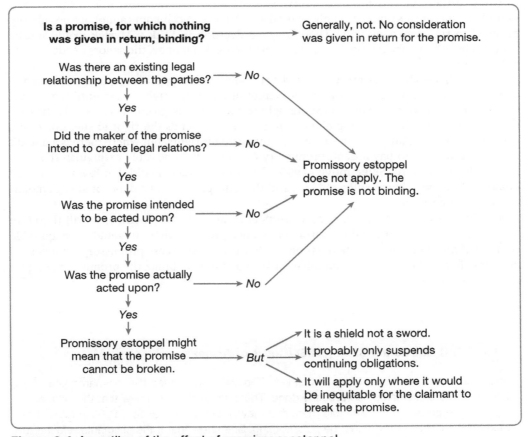

Figure 2.4 An outline of the effect of promissory estoppel

Privity of contract

The doctrine of privity of contract holds that a contract is private between the parties who made it. Anyone who did not make the contract cannot sue on the contract or be sued on it. The Contracts (Rights of Third Parties) Act 1999 has created an exception to the privity rule. However, privity is perhaps best understood if it is considered before the effect of the 1999 Act is considered. The following case provides a classic example of the privity rule.

 Tweddle *v* Atkinson (1831)

William Guy and John Tweddle made a contract with each other that William Guy would pay the claimant £200 and in return John Tweddle would pay the claimant £100. The claimant was the son of John Tweddle, who was marrying the daughter of William Guy. The contract between William Guy and John Tweddle said that the claimant should be able to sue either of them to enforce the contract. John Tweddle paid the money he had promised to pay but William Guy died before paying the money he had promised. The claimant sued William Guy's personal representatives to make them pay. The personal representatives took over William Guy's affairs and would have had exactly the same obligation to pay as William Guy would have had.

Held The claimant could not sue on the contract because he did not make the contract.

The privity rule was affirmed by the House of Lords in the following case.

 Dunlop Pneumatic Tyre Co Ltd *v* Selfridge & Co Ltd (1915) (House of Lords)

Dunlop sold car tyres to Dew & Co, who were dealers in motor accessories. In return for being given a 10 per cent discount on the price, Dew & Co agreed that they would obtain a written undertaking from any person to whom they resold the tyres that the tyres would not be sold below a certain price. Dew & Co resold the tyres to Selfridge & Co. Dew & Co gave Selfridge & Co a discount on the price of the tyres in return for the written agreement not to resell below the agreed price. Selfridge & Co resold the tyres below the agreed price and Dunlop sued them on the written agreement not to do this.

Held Dunlop could not sue Selfridge on the agreement as there was no contract between them. Dunlop had given no consideration to Selfridge & Co in return for the promise not to sell below the agreed price. The discount which Selfridge & Co had been given in return for their agreement had been given by Dew & Co and not by Dunlop.

Figure 2.5 shows how privity operated in **Tweddle *v* Atkinson** and **Dunlop Pneumatic Tyre Co Ltd *v* Selfridge & Co Ltd**.

Privity could cause particular injustice when one person bought unsafe goods or services on behalf of another. The following case provides an example.

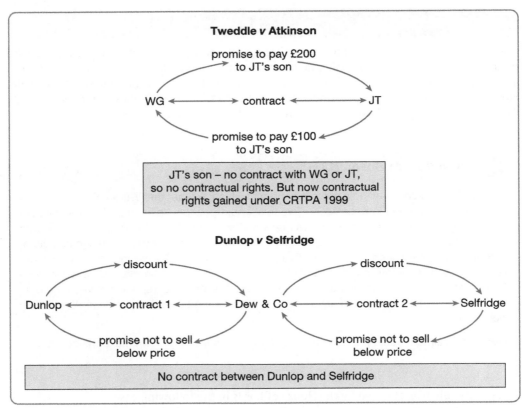

Figure 2.5 Tweddle *v* Atkinson and Dunlop Pneumatic Tyre Co Ltd *v* Selfridge & Co

---

⚖️ **Daniels and Daniels *v* R White & Sons Ltd and Tarbard (1938)**

Mr Daniels bought a bottle of lemonade. Both Mr and Mrs Daniels drank the lemonade, which was contaminated with carbolic acid. They were both injured by this and both sued the manufacturers of the lemonade for the tort of negligence. Mr Daniels also sued the retailer of the lemonade for breach of contract.

Held The manufacturers were not liable for the tort of negligence. They showed that they operated a 'fool proof' system and so it could not be proved that they had failed to take reasonable care. Mr Daniels succeeded in his claim for breach of contract. The retailer had to pay damages to compensate Mr Daniels for his injuries, but did not have to pay damages in respect of Mrs Daniels's injuries. The damages for breach of contract were only to compensate for the loss caused to Mr Daniels. Mrs Daniels could not sue the retailer for breach of contract because she had no contract with the retailer.

Comment If the case were to arise today, Mrs Daniels would succeed against the manufacturers under the Consumer Protection Act 1987 Part 1, which is considered in Chapter 8. However, this does not affect the contractual liability of the retailer.

In **Jackson *v* Horizon Holidays Ltd (1975)** the Court of Appeal allowed a husband who had booked a holiday for himself and his wife to recover substantial damages for both himself and his wife when the holiday proved to be disastrous. The House of Lords later commented that this decision was correct and suggested that some contracts, such as those to provide holidays or to book a taxi, call for special treatment. As regards package holidays, the Package Travel, Package Holidays and Package Tours Regulations 1992 now provide that damages can be awarded to holidaymakers who do not get the holiday contracted for, even if they did not themselves make the contract. However, these Regulations are confined to package holidays and do not change the principles of the general law of contract.

The Contracts (Rights of Third Parties) Act 1999

The Contracts (Rights of Third Parties) Act 1999 has changed the privity rule but not abolished it. The Act provides that a third party can in two circumstances sue on a contract which he or she did not make:

(1) A third party can sue on the contract if the contract expressly provided that he should be able to sue. (The s. 1(1)(a) route.)

For example, a man might buy a car for his son and the contract might state that if the car was not of satisfactory quality the son could sue the seller on the contract. (**Tweddle v Atkinson** would now therefore be differently decided.)

(2) A third party can sue on the contract if the contract intended to confer a benefit on the third party. (The s. 1(1)(b) route.)

However, the s. 1(1)(b) route does not apply if the other party to the contract can show that the parties to the contract did not intend the contract to be enforceable by the third party.

Section 1(3) requires that the third party must be expressly identified in the contract by name, as a member of a class or as answering a particular description. This is the case for both routes. Express identification by name needs no explanation. Express identification by class could arise in many ways: for example, if a contractual provision was made for the benefit of all the members of a particular club, or for the benefit of the contracting party's brothers and sisters. Express identification of the third party as his or her answering a particular description could also arise in many ways: for example, if a contractual provision was made for the benefit of 'my youngest brother' or for the benefit of the Sheriff of Nottingham. Applying the Act to **Daniels v White and Tarbard**, we can see that the Act would not have allowed Mrs Daniels to sue on the contract with the retailer unless Mr Daniels had expressly identified Mrs Daniels as a person for whose benefit the contract was being made.

When a benefit is conferred on a third party by the Act, the third party gets any remedy which would have been available to him if he had made the contract. The third party can also avail himself of exclusion or limitation clauses. Any rights conferred on the third party are additional to rights conferred on the person who made the contract. However, s. 5 protects the promisor from double liability.

If a party to the contract has any defences arising from the contract, these are as available against the third party as they would have been available against the other party to the contract.

Example

A contract is made between Bert and Chas. Bert is to sell 50 bicycles to Chas, and a term of the contract provides that Chas should pay the price to Dan. Bert delivers only 30 bicycles to Chas. Chas accepts the 30 bicycles. Chas will not need to pay the whole contract price to Dan, but will need to pay only the price of 30 bicycles.

The promisor (in the above example Chas) will also have available defences, rights of set-off and counterclaims which did not arise in connection with the contract, if these would have been available against the third party if the third party had been a party to the contract.

> **Example**
>
> Bert agrees to sell 50 bicycles to Chas. A term of the contract provides that Chas is to pay the price of £5,000 to Dan. Bert delivers 50 bicycles to Chas. Dan owes £1,000 to Chas in connection with a contract made last month. Chas is entitled to set-off the £1,000 and pay Dan only £4,000.

Figure 2.6 gives an overview of the Contracts (Rights of Third Parties) Act 1999.

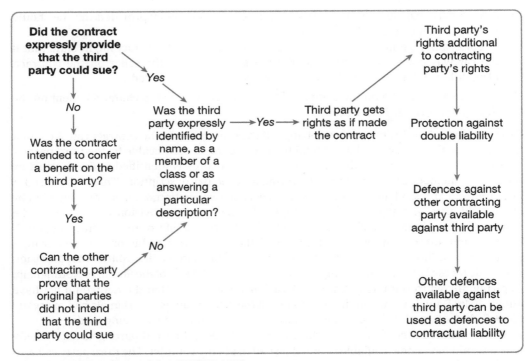

Figure 2.6 The effect of the CRTPA 1999

Formalities

In general, contracts can be created without the need for any special formalities. The types of contracts which can be made only if certain formalities are observed are as follows.

Contracts which must be made by a deed

A conveyance of a legal estate in land must be made by a deed. Also, a lease of land of over three years' duration must be made by a deed or no legal estate will be created.

Earlier in this chapter we saw that gifts are not contracts and that the promise of a gift is not enforceable as a contract. However, if a gift is made by a deed it is enforceable as a contract. This is because the act of making the deed is regarded as providing the required consideration.

Deeds must be made in writing and must be signed by the maker of the deed in the presence of a witness. The witness must sign the deed to indicate having witnessed the signature of the maker of the deed. The deed must also indicate that it is intended to be a deed. This can be done if the deed states that it is signed as a deed by the maker in the presence of the witness. For example: 'This document is signed as a deed by Jane Smith in the presence of Mary McGuire.'

Later (in Chapter 5), we shall see that the Limitation Act 1980 provides that the right to sue on a simple contract is lost after six years have passed from the time when the right to sue arose. When a contract is made by a deed, this time limit is increased to 12 years after the right to sue arose.

Contracts which must be in writing

Contracts to sell or dispose of an interest in land must be made in writing. The written contract must incorporate all the terms of the contract in one document, or in both contracts where contracts are exchanged, and must be signed by both of the parties. If these formalities are not complied with, the contract will be void and therefore of no effect. There is, however, one exception. A lease of land for a period of three years or less will be valid if made orally, as long as the lease takes effect immediately.

Regulated consumer credit agreements cannot be enforced unless they were made in writing and unless the other requirements of the Consumer Credit Act 1974 have been complied with. An agreement is a regulated consumer credit agreement whenever an individual (who can be in business, but cannot be a company) is provided with credit.

Contracts which must be evidenced in writing

Contracts of guarantee must be evidenced in writing, and signed by the person giving the guarantee, or they will be unenforceable. When a contract of guarantee is made, one person agrees to undertake secondary liability to settle the debts or liabilities of another person. Although the contract under which the guarantee is given needs to be evidenced in writing, the contract which created the debt which is being guaranteed does not. An example might make this more clear.

Let us assume that Paint Ltd agrees to buy a new van from a garage for £10,000 and that Sarah guarantees to pay the price if Paint Ltd should fail to do so. The contract under which Paint Ltd buys the van does not need to be in writing nor evidenced in writing. However, the contract under which Sarah guarantees to pay the price if Paint Ltd should fail to do so does need to be evidenced in writing.

A contract which is evidenced in writing does not need to be a written contract as such. However, there must be some written evidence that the contract has been made. This written evidence, which might for example be in a letter or a note, must be signed by the person giving the guarantee and must contain all the material terms of the contract of guarantee.

Minors

A person who is capable of making contracts is said to have capacity to make contracts. Adults have full contractual capacity, but special rules apply to minors (persons who are under the age of 18). Contracts made by minors might be either valid, voidable or void, depending upon the type of contract made.

Valid contracts

Section 3 of the Sale of Goods Act 1979 provides that minors must pay a reasonable price for necessary goods sold and delivered to them. They must also pay a reasonable price for necessary services supplied. Therefore, contracts to supply minors with either necessary goods or necessary services are valid contracts. Goods are regarded as necessary if they are suitable to the minor's position in life and are actually required by him. This obviously varies from person to person. It is worth noticing that the amount which minors must pay is a reasonable price, which might not always be the same as the price agreed in the contract.

A minor can also validly make a contract of employment, as long as the contract is beneficial overall to the minor.

Voidable contracts

Contracts which impose a continuing liability on a minor are voidable by the minor. This means that the contracts are valid, except that the minor has the option to avoid the contract (call the contract off). (The way in which a voidable contract can be avoided is considered in Chapter 4.) A minor who is to avoid these types of voidable contracts must do so either before reaching the age of 18 or within a reasonable time of having reached the age of 18. The main types of contracts voidable by a minor are contracts of partnership, contracts to buy shares and contracts to take a lease of property.

Void contracts

Minors are not bound by contracts to buy unnecessary goods or services. A minor who makes such a contract may be entitled to regain any money paid under the contract, but only if the minor has not received any benefit under the contract. Nor are minors bound by contracts to borrow money. For this reason it would be most unusual for a bank or other commercial lender to lend money to a minor unless repayment of the loan was guaranteed by an adult. Agreements by the minor to repay the loan will be of no effect if they were made before the minor had reached the age of 18. Agreements to repay which were made after the minor had reached the age of 18 will compel the minor to repay the loan. If a minor acquires property under an unenforceable contract, s. 3(1) of the Minors' Contracts Act 1987 allows a court to order the minor to give the property back to the supplier. This remedy is available at the court's discretion and would not be applied if the minor had paid for the property.

Essential points

- A contract is a legally binding agreement.
- A contract is formed when an offer is accepted.
- An invitation to treat is not an offer, but an invitation to negotiate or an invitation to make an offer.

- As soon as an acceptance of an offer is received, a contract is created.
- If the postal rule applies, an acceptance made by posting a letter is effective when it is posted.
- An offer of a unilateral contract can be accepted only by performing the act requested.
- A counter offer is not an acceptance and revokes the original offer.
- A contract can be created only if the reasonable person could state with certainty exactly what it is that has been agreed.
- An offer which has been revoked cannot be accepted.
- Revocation of an offer is effective when it is received. (The postal rule never applies to revocations.)
- A contract will only be created if the parties appeared to intend to create a legal relationship.
- Consideration consists of a right given to one party, or a loss or detriment suffered by another.
- A past act cannot be given as consideration.
- Most contracts do not need to be made in writing.
- Minors (persons under 18) are bound by contracts to buy necessary goods or services.
- Minors must pay a reasonable price for necessary goods or services which they have contracted to buy, if the goods or services are supplied to them.
- If minors make contracts to buy goods or services which were not necessary, the contract will be void.

Practice questions

1   On 10 July Ace Ltd posted an offer to sell a consignment of 1,000 widgets to Brian, a retailer. The offer said that the price was £10,000 and that the offer would remain open until 31 July. On 12 July Brian telephoned Ace Ltd and asked whether he would be allowed three months' credit. Ace Ltd's manager replied that payment would have to be made in cash, upon delivery. On 29 July Ace Ltd sold the consignment of widgets to a third party, Charles. On 30 July Brian posted a letter accepting Ace Ltd's offer. This letter arrived on 1 August. Upon opening the letter, Ace Ltd's manager telephoned Brian and told him that the consignment of widgets had been sold and that further similar widgets were not available. Advise the parties as to whether or not a contract has been created.

2   Acme Supastore advertised its 'price promise' heavily in the Nottown Evening News. This promise stated that Acme was the cheapest retailer in the city of Nottown and that it would guarantee that this was true. The advertisement stated: 'We are so confident that we are the cheapest in the area that we guarantee that you cannot buy a television anywhere in Nottown cheaper than from us. We also guarantee that if you buy any television from us and give us notice in writing that you could have bought it cheaper

at any other retailer within five miles of our Supastore on the same day, we will refund twice the difference in price. Offer to remain open for the month of December. Any claim to be received in writing within 5 days of purchase.' Belinda saw the advertisement and was persuaded by it to buy a television from Acme Supastore for £299. The contract was made on Monday 3 December. On Friday 7 December Belinda found that a neighbouring shop was selling an identical model of television for £289 and had been selling at this price for the past six months. Belinda immediately telephoned Acme Supastore to say that she was claiming her money back. She also posted a letter claiming her money back. The letter arrived on Monday 10 December. Acme Supastore are refusing to refund any of the purchase price. Advise Belinda as to whether or not any contract has been made.

3 A large department store advertised its January sale on a local radio station and in a local newspaper. The advertisement said that the first customer to enter the store when it opened on 2 January would be able to buy a new video recorder for just £1. The advertisement showed the model of video recorder which could be bought. Joanne decides to try to be the first in the department store so that she can buy the video recorder. She camps outside the shop at midday on 1 January, relieved to see that nobody else is yet queuing. At 7 a.m. on 2 January the manager of the department store tells Joanne that the offer has been called off. Joanne refuses to accept this. At 8 a.m. the manager shows Joanne an advertisement in the morning edition of the local newspaper. This advertisement says that the offer has been called off. Again, Joanne refuses to leave. When the department store opens, at 9 a.m., Joanne enters the shop and tells the manager that she is the first customer and that she is buying the video recorder for £1. The manager refuses to accept the money and says that the video recorder is only available at its usual price of £299.99. Advise Joanne as to whether or not a contract has been created.

4 **Brogden v Metropolitan Railway Co (1877)** concerned a dispute between a coal merchant and a railway company. The House of Lords had to decide whether a contract existed and if so, what the terms of the contract were. The facts of the case can be set out as the following four statements.

(a) After the railway company had taken coal from Brogden for many years, the company sent Brogden a written agreement which set out the position as regards future supplies of coal.

(b) Brogden altered the written agreement, then signed it and sent it back to the company.

(c) The company filed the agreement in a drawer, leaving it there for two years.

(d) Brogden delivered coal, which the company had ordered, in accordance with the altered agreement.

Each of the four statements above amounts to one of the following: an offer; an invitation to treat; an acceptance; a revocation; a counter offer; a contract; or nothing at all. Decide which of these matters each of the statements amounts to. (In reaching your decision you should apply at least three of the cases which we have considered in this chapter.)

5 A company which deals in gold and jewellery employs two private security guards to guard the premises each night. The security guards are both self-employed, providing their services under two separate contracts. One night, one of the security guards

phones in to say that he will not be able to work for the rest of the week, as he is ill. The company tells the other security guard that he must work single-handed for the remainder of the week. The security guard manages to do this, although it involves a certain amount of extra work. At the end of the week the company tells the security guard who worked alone that he will be paid double wages for the week. Now the company has changed its mind and pays the guard only his normal amount. Advise the security guard as to whether or not he will be entitled to the extra amount promised.

6   With reference to decided cases, explain the difference between an offer and an invitation to treat. Why does the distinction matter?

Task 2

A friend of yours, Rory, works as self-employed painter and decorator. Rory has heard that materials can often be bought more cheaply at auction or by tender than from wholesalers. Rory has asked you to write a brief report, indicating the following matters:

(a) The way in which a contract is made by the process of offer and acceptance.

(b) How an offer differs from an invitation to treat.

(c) How the offer and acceptance are made when goods are bought at auction.

(d) How the offer and acceptance are made when goods are bought by tender.

(e) The extent to which offers can be withdrawn after they have been made.

(f) What is meant by an intention to create legal relations.

(g) What is meant by consideration.

(h) Whether all contracts can be made without the need for writing.

mylawchamber

Visit **www.mylawchamber.co.uk/macintyreessentials** to access tools to help you develop and test your knowledge of business law, including interactive multiple choice questions, practice exam questions with guidance, weblinks, glossary, glossary flashcards, legal newsfeed and legal updates.

Use **Case Navigator** to read in full some of the key cases referenced in this chapter with commentary and questions:

Carlill v The Carbolic Smoke Ball Co (1893)

Pharmaceutical Society (GB) v Boots Cash Chemists Ltd (1953)

Williams v Roffey Bros Ltd (1990)

Central London Property Trust Ltd v High Trees House Ltd (1947)

3

The terms of the contract

The terms of a contract define the obligations which the parties to the contract have undertaken. This chapter begins by examining the ways in which terms can arise, and explains the difference between express and implied terms. Next the different types of terms are considered. Breach of some types of terms gives the injured party the right to terminate the contract, whereas breach of other types does not. Breach of any term always gives a right to sue for damages.

Exclusion clauses are terms which attempt to exclude liability for breach of contract or for breach of a tortious duty of care. This chapter concludes by considering the special rules which apply to exclusion clauses.

Nature of terms

A contract is made up of terms. All of the promises which the contract contains, whether they were made expressly or impliedly, will be terms. If any of these promises are not kept, one or more terms of the contract will have been breached. The injured party will then always have a remedy for breach of contract.

Terms can find their way into contracts in one of two ways: they can be expressed, in either speech or writing, or they can be implied. Express terms are actually agreed by the parties in words. Implied terms are implied either by the court (on the grounds of the presumed intention of the parties) or by a statute. Figure 3.1 shows the ways in which terms arise.

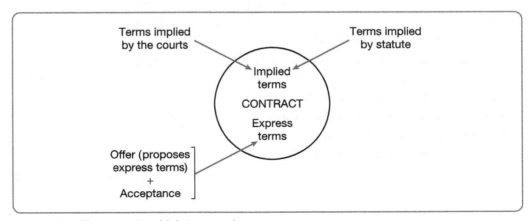

Figure 3.1 The ways in which terms arise

Express terms

A contract is formed when an offer is accepted. The offeror proposes a set of terms. If the offer is accepted by the offeree, these proposed terms become legally binding as the terms of the contract. Oral contracts usually contain very few express terms. Written contracts, especially business contracts, usually contain far more. If there is any conflict between an express term and an implied term the express term will prevail, unless the implied term is a statutory one which cannot be changed. (See later in the chapter.)

Terms implied by the courts

The courts have the power to imply terms into contracts. Despite having this power, the courts have always made it plain that they are not prepared to make a contract for the parties. The courts will imply a term on only two grounds. First, that it was so obviously intended to be a part of the contract that the parties felt no need to mention it. Second, that the term must be implied as a matter of law.

Terms based on intentions of the parties

 The Moorcock (1889) (Court of Appeal)

A jetty owner made a contract which allowed a shipowner to moor his ship at the jetty. Both parties knew that the ship would be grounded at low tide. When the ship did touch the ground it was damaged because there was a ridge of rock beneath the mud. The shipowner asked the court to imply a term that the jetty owner had taken reasonable care to ensure that the jetty was a safe place to unload a ship.

Held The term was implied by the court. The jetty owner had breached the term and was therefore in breach of contract. It was obviously intended by both parties that the mooring should be safe.

Care must be taken when looking for terms implied by the courts, as the courts do not imply them freely.

Lord Pearson said in **Trollope *v* NWRHB (1973)**:

> An unexpressed term can be implied if and only if the court finds the parties must have intended that term to form part of their contract . . . it is not enough for the court to find that such a term would have been adopted by the parties as reasonable men if it had been suggested to them . . . it must have been a term which went without saying, a term necessary to give business efficacy to the contract.

If the courts were prepared to imply terms freely, they would move towards making a contract for the parties rather than giving effect to what the parties had themselves agreed.

Customary terms

Terms may be implied by the courts on the grounds that they are customary in a particular trade, customary in a particular locality or customary between the parties.

Many trades have customs, and these customs will be implied into contracts made within the context of those trades. In the bakery trade, for example, a dozen used to mean 13, and a baker who sold 20 dozen loaves would be deemed to have sold 260, not 240.

In a similar way, customs of a particular locality will be implied into contracts made in that locality. A term can become customary between the parties to the contract if they regularly make contracts which include such a term.

In **Kendall v Lillico (1969)** the parties had often dealt with each other. Whenever an oral contract was made, the same 'sold note' containing a large number of terms was always sent the following day. The House of Lords held that the terms in the 'sold note' had become customary between the parties and were therefore incorporated into an oral contract which was made. However, the course of dealing must be well established. In **Hollier v Rambler Motors Ltd (1972)** the claimant had signed the same exclusion clause three or four times in the previous five years when he had had his car repaired at the defendant's garage. The car was damaged while being repaired under a contract made orally. The garage tried to rely on their exclusion clause but the court held that they could not do so. The exclusion clause was not incorporated into the oral contract. Salmon LJ said: 'I am bound to say that, for my part, I do not know of any other case in which it has been decided or even argued that a term could be implied into an oral contract on the strength of a course of dealing (if it can be so called) which consisted at the most of three or four transactions over a period of five years.'

Terms implied as a matter of law

The courts imply terms into particular types of contracts as a matter of law. These terms are not implied because the parties must have intended them to be a part of the contract; they are implied because, as a matter of law, such terms are always implied into the type of contract in question. For example, in **Liverpool City Council v Irwin (1977)** the House of Lords implied a term that the landlord of a block of flats would keep the flats in reasonable repair and reasonably usable. This term was implied because such a term would be implied generally into contracts between landlord and tenant.

Later it will be seen that certain terms are implied generally into contracts of employment (see Chapter 13).

Exclusion of implied terms

Later in this chapter we shall see that the terms implied by statutes can never be excluded in consumer cases and can be excluded in non-consumer cases only where this is reasonable. However, terms implied by the court on the basis that they are customary, or are what the parties obviously intended, can always be excluded by an express term.

Types of terms

If any term is breached the injured party will always have a remedy for breach of contract. The nature of that remedy will depend upon what type of term was breached.

Conditions and warranties

Traditionally, all terms could be classified as being either conditions or warranties.

A condition is a term which seemed vitally important when the contract was made (a term which went 'to the root of the contract'). If a condition is breached, then the injured party can terminate the contract and claim damages.

A warranty is a term which did not seem vitally important when the contract was made (a term which did not go 'to the root of the contract'). If a warranty is breached, the injured

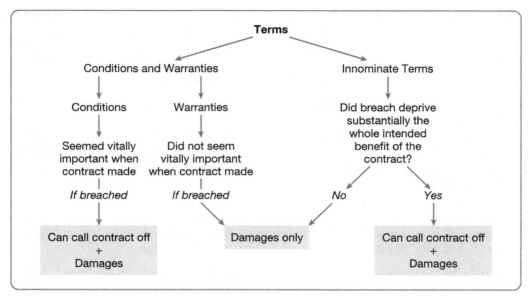

Figure 3.2 Types of terms

party can claim damages but cannot treat the contract as terminated. Figure 3.2 shows an outline of the different types of terms.

> **Example**
>
> Packaging Ltd bought 1,000 cardboard boxes from Box Ltd. A term of the contract provided that the boxes would weigh a certain amount. This term is breached because the boxes do not weigh the correct amount. If the term was a condition, Packaging can terminate the contract. If they did terminate, they could reject all of the boxes, refuse to pay for the boxes, and claim damages. If the term was a warranty, Packaging cannot terminate the contract. So they could not reject the boxes, or refuse to pay the price, but they could claim damages. Even if the term was a condition, Packaging could treat it as a warranty if they chose to do this. So Packaging Ltd would not be compelled to reject the boxes if the term was a condition. The important point to note is that they could do this if they wanted to.

It might be thought that the right to terminate a contract is of little importance if damages are always available. However, the right to terminate can be very important when one of the parties has made what has turned out to be an ongoing bad bargain.

Innominate terms

In the **Hong Kong Fir Case (1962)** the Court of Appeal invented a new category of term, the innominate or intermediate term. In deciding whether or not breach of such a term gives the injured party the right to terminate the contract, the court does not consider how important the term seemed when the contract was made. Instead, the court asks whether or not the breach deprived the injured party of substantially the whole benefit of the contract. If the breach did do this, the injured party can treat the contract as terminated and claim damages. If the breach did not do this, the injured party can claim damages but cannot treat the contract as terminated. Innominate terms have not replaced conditions and warranties. Some terms can now be classed as conditions or warranties; others are innominate terms.

There may be some uncertainty as to whether a court will classify a particular term as either a condition, a warranty or an innominate term. Generally, the position is as follows.

- A statute, such as the Sale of Goods Act 1979, or a rule of law might establish that a term is a condition or a warranty.
- The parties themselves might agree that certain terms will or will not give the right to terminate if they are breached. The court will give effect to such an agreement. However, the mere labelling of a term as a condition or a warranty will not of itself be enough to indicate such an agreement.
- If no term of the contract or rule of law stipulates that a particular term will or will not allow termination, the courts will regard the term as an innominate term. Breach of such a term will allow the injured party to terminate the contract only if the breach deprived the injured party of substantially the whole benefit of the contract.

It should also be remembered that damages will always be available for any breach of contract, whether the injured party has the right to terminate the contract or not. The subject of damages is considered later (see Chapter 5).

Terms implied by statute

Terms are currently implied into contracts by three statutes: the Sale of Goods Act 1979; the Supply of Goods (Implied Terms) Act 1973; and the Supply of Goods and Services Act 1982. The terms which these statutes imply are inserted into certain types of contracts without the parties needing to agree to them. Indeed, as we shall see, in consumer contracts the terms can be implied even if the parties expressly agree that they should not be.

The Sale of Goods Act 1979

When the Consumer Rights Act 2015 (CRA 2015) comes into force the Sale of Goods Act 1979 (SGA 1979) implied terms will no longer apply to contracts under which a trader supplies goods to a consumer. Instead, the CRA 2015 will apply similar terms, and additional terms, into such consumer contracts. The remedies available if these terms are breached are not the same as the remedies available if a SGA 1979 implied term is breached. The CRA 2015 is considered later in this chapter, where the definitions of 'trader' and 'consumer' are discussed. The SGA 1979 implied terms will continue to apply to non-consumer contracts.

The Sale of Goods Act 1893 was the first statute to imply terms into contracts. The 1893 Act has been replaced by the SGA 1979. The implied terms contained in the SGA 1979 are virtually identical to those contained in the original 1893 Act. The terms implied by the other two statutes, the Supply of Goods (Implied Terms) Act 1973 (SGITA 1973) and the Supply of Goods and Services Act 1982 (SGSA 1982), are also very closely modelled on the terms implied by the Sale of Goods Acts 1893 and 1979. Almost all of the case law on statutory implied terms is concerned with terms implied by the Sale of Goods Acts. We therefore consider the terms implied by the Sale of Goods Act 1979 before we consider the terms implied by the SGITA 1973 and the SGSA 1982.

Scope of the Sale of Goods Act 1979

The SGA 1979 applies only to contracts of sale of goods. Such contracts are defined by s. 2(1) of the Act:

> A contract of sale of goods is a contract by which the seller transfers or agrees to transfer the property in goods to the buyer for a money consideration, called the price.

Reading s. 2(1), we can see that a sale occurs when a buyer pays money in return for ownership of goods. It does not matter whether the buyer pays cash, by cheque or by credit card. A free gift, however, where the buyer pays no money, cannot be a sale. Nor is it a sale where goods are bartered (exchanged) for other goods.

Note also that the seller must transfer the property in goods (ownership of the goods) to the buyer. This requirement rules out contracts to hire or to lease, where possession of the goods is transferred but ownership is not.

As long as there is a definite commitment to pass ownership in return for money, either immediately or in the future, it does not matter that the money is paid later or that ownership is transferred later. If the contract agrees that the property in the goods should be transferred at some future date, or when some condition has been satisfied, then this is an agreement to sell goods rather than a sale of goods. Agreements to sell goods are governed by the SGA 1979 and become sales of goods when the time elapses or the condition is fulfilled. For example, a merchant might agree to sell 100 tons of wheat of a certain type, to be delivered on 1 August next year. This is an agreement to sell goods and is governed by the SGA 1979. On 1 August next year the agreement becomes a sale of goods.

Meaning of goods

Section 61(1) of the SGA 1979 defines goods as 'all personal chattels other than things in action'.

A personal chattel is a physical thing which can be touched and moved, for example a car, a cup or a computer. Land and houses cannot be moved and are real property rather than personal chattels.

A thing in action is a right which can be enforced only by suing (taking legal action). A guarantee, for example, is a thing in action. A guarantee may be written on a piece of paper but the paper is not the property. The property is the right which the guarantee gives and, ultimately, that right can only be enforced by suing the person who gave it. Debts and intellectual property rights are other examples of things in action.

If software is supplied on a disk, or contained in a product, then the disk or product will be regarded by the SGA 1979 as goods. However, if software is downloaded on to a computer then this transaction would not be covered by the SGA. However, when the CRA 2015 comes into force it will cover all forms of 'digital content', such as downloaded software, as well as goods or services.

The terms implied by the Sale of Goods Act 1979

Sections 12–15 of the SGA 1979 contain five major **implied terms**, all of which are conditions. These terms do not need to be mentioned by the buyer or the seller, as the Act will automatically imply them into contracts of sale of goods. The five conditions implied by the SGA 1979 are as follows.

(1) Section 12(1) implies a condition that the seller has *the right to sell the goods*.

(2) Section 13(1) implies a condition that the goods *will correspond with any description by which they were sold*.

(3) Section 14(2) implies a condition that the goods are of *satisfactory quality*.

(4) Section 14(3) implies a condition that the goods are *fit for the buyer's purpose*.

(5) Section 15(2) implies a condition that where goods are sold by sample *the bulk will correspond with the sample*.

The terms implied by ss. 14(2) and (3) are implied only into sales of goods which are made in the course of a business. The other terms are implied into all contracts of sale of goods.

These implied terms are vitally important and each one must be examined closely.

The right to sell (s. 12(1))

Section 12(1) of the SGA 1979 provides that unless the circumstances show a different intention:

> There is an implied [condition] on the part of the seller that in the case of a sale he has a right to sell the goods, and in the case of an agreement to sell he will have such a right at the time when the property is to pass.

This term, like the others, is a condition. As we have seen, when a condition is breached the injured party can treat the contract as terminated and also claim damages. If a seller breaches a condition and the buyer chooses therefore to treat the contract as terminated, the buyer will get all of the purchase price back.

⚖ Rowland *v* Divall (1923) (Court of Appeal)

A thief stole a car from its owner and sold the car to the defendant. The claimant, a motor dealer, bought the car from the defendant for £334. The claimant did the car up and sold it to a customer for £400. On discovering that the car was stolen, the police took it from the customer and returned it to its original owner. The customer complained to the claimant who returned his £400. The claimant asked the defendant for the return of the £334 he had paid. The defendant refused to pay, saying that he had no idea that the car was stolen.

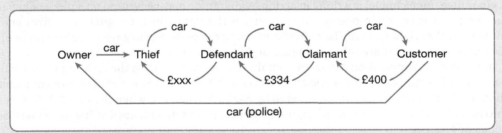

Figure 3.3 Rowland *v* Divall

Held The claimant got all of his money back. Section 12(1) provides that the seller must have the right to sell, and when the defendant sold the car to the claimant he did not have this right because he did not own the car. The thief never owned the car. He therefore could not pass ownership to the defendant, who could not pass ownership to the claimant, etc. None of the parties except the original owner ever had the right to sell the car.

Atkin LJ held: 'It seems to me that in this case there has been a total failure of consideration, that is to say that the buyer has not got any part of that for which he paid the purchase price. He paid the money in order that he might get the property, and he has not got it.'

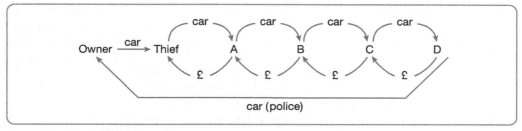

Figure 3.4 Who is the loser?

Where there is a chain of innocent sellers, the loser will generally be the person who bought from the thief, as in **Rowland v Divall**. Of course, this person could successfully sue the thief, but in practical terms this would probably be a waste of money as it is most unlikely that the thief could be found and would have the money to pay when the case reached court.

However, if any of the the sellers in the chain has become insolvent, then the person who bought from that seller will be the one with no practical remedy.

For example, let us assume that a thief has stolen a car from its owner and then sold the car to A, who sold it to B, who sold it to C, who sold it to D. As can be seen from Figure 3.4, A will be the loser.

But now let us further assume that B has become insolvent. D can recover from C, but C cannot recover from B. Nor can C leapfrog B and sue A – there is no contract between the two of them.

Section 12(2) implies two warranties. First, that the goods are free from encumbrances, meaning that no-one has a mortgage or charge over the goods. Second, that no person will interfere with the buyer's right to enjoy quiet possession of the goods. This term would be important if the seller owned the goods sold and had the right to sell them, but the buyer was later prevented from using the goods because a third party had acquired a property right, such as a patent, in the goods. The term will not be implied if the seller reveals before the sale that the buyer will not enjoy quiet possession of the goods. As we have seen, when a warranty is breached the injured party can claim damages for breach of contract, but cannot treat the contract as terminated.

Correspondence with description (s. 13(1))

Section 13 of the SGA 1979 provides that:

> Where there is a contract for the sale of goods by description, there is an implied [condition] that the goods will correspond with the description.

A seller has no obligation to describe the goods sold. Furthermore, the fact that the seller has made a description does not necessarily mean that the goods were sold by that description so as to bring in s. 13.

Several hurdles must be overcome before s. 13 is satisfied. First, there must actually have been a description of the goods. Second, the description must have been intended to be a term of the contract. Section 13 will not apply if the description was intended to be a representation or intended to have no legal effect. Third, the goods must have been sold by reference to the description. So it must have been reasonably intended that the buyer would rely on the description. For example, in **Harlingdon & Leinster Enterprises Ltd v Christopher Hull Fine Art Ltd (1991)** the Court of Appeal held that two paintings had not been sold by description. The paintings had been described as being by a German expressionist called Munter. The buyer was an expert in German expressionist painting, but the seller had made it plain that he was not. In fact, the paintings were fakes and were worth only 1 per cent of the price which the buyer paid. Section 13(1) provided no help to the buyer. The paintings were not sold by description because the description was not an important term of the contract on which the buyer relied. The buyer did not rely on the term, he relied on his own expertise. However, when unascertained goods are sold in a commercial context, it is presumed that the buyer does rely on any description of them. **Unascertained goods** are identified *only* by description, so that any goods matching the description can be supplied under the contract. They are contrasted with **specific goods**, which are identified and agreed upon, before the contract is made, as the particular goods which must be supplied. (For further detail, and an example of the two types of goods, see Chapter 7.) Finally, the description must be a substantial ingredient in the identity of the thing being sold, so that it identifies the commercial characteristics of the goods which are being bought. However, when unascertained goods are sold in bulk, it is likely that s. 13 will require exact correspondence with all aspects of the description.

 Arcos Ltd v EA Ronaasen & Son (1933) (House of Lords)

The seller contracted to sell a quantity of wooden staves which were to be used for making cement barrels. The goods were unascertained. The staves had been described as 'half an inch thick'. Ninety per cent of the staves were between half an inch and five-eighths of an inch, but 10 per cent were over five-eighths of an inch. The buyer rejected all of the staves, even though they were perfectly fit for making cement barrels. He did this because the market price of such staves had dropped.

Held Section 13(1) was breached because the staves did not correspond with the description by which they were sold. The buyer could therefore treat the contract as terminated and was entitled to all of his money back.

Comment This case differs from **Harlingdon & Leinster Enterprises Ltd v Christopher Hull Fine Art Ltd** in that the contract was for the sale of unascertained goods and so the buyer had to rely on the seller's description. In **Harlingdon** the goods were specific and the buyer did not rely on the seller's description.

Since s. 13 can apply only where the description is a term of the contract, the real significance of s. 13 is that it makes the term a condition, rather than a warranty or an innominate term. So breach of s. 13 will always give the buyer a right to terminate the contract and get his money back (subject to ss. 15A and 35 considered below). Breach of a warranty would not give this right and breach of an innominate term might not.

Having decided that a sale was made by description, we then need to examine how closely the description must be adhered to. A rule expressed in Latin, *de minimis non curat lex* (the law is not concerned with trifles) has always been a general principle of the common law. The effect of the rule here is that if the failure to match the description was very trivial the seller will not breach s. 13(1). However, the following case shows that where goods are sold by description in a commercial context the description must be very closely adhered to.

Re Moore & Co and Landauer & Co (1921) (Court of Appeal)

A consignment of 3,100 tins of peaches was sold. The goods were to be shipped from Australia to a buyer in London. The buyer rejected the consignment on the grounds that whereas the peaches had been described as packed 30 tins to a case, about half of the tins were packed 24 to a case instead of 30. The correct number of tins were delivered.

Held The buyer could reject all of the tins. Section 13(1) had been breached because the goods did not correspond with the description by which they had been sold.

Comment The principle in this case, that where unascertained goods are sold in a commercial context then any description is likely to be within s. 13, has not changed. However, s. 15A would now force the buyer to treat the breach of condition as a breach of warranty. Therefore, he could not terminate the contract if the case were to arise today, but could only claim damages. (Section 15A is considered later in this chapter, after all of the statutory implied terms have been considered.)

Section 13(2) provides that goods can be sold by both sample and description. If they are, they must correspond with both the description and the sample. Section 13(3) provides that goods can still be sold by description even if, being exposed for sale or hire, they are selected by the buyer. So the fact that a buyer chooses goods, perhaps in a supermarket for example, will not prevent the goods from having been sold by description.

Figure 3.5 shows how s. 13 operates.

Quality and fitness in business sales (s. 14)

Section 14(2) of the SGA 1979 implies a term that goods sold in the course of a business are of satisfactory quality.

Section 14(3) of the SGA 1979 implies a term that goods sold in the course of a business are reasonably fit for the buyer's purpose.

Business sales

The terms as to satisfactory quality and fitness for purpose are implied only where goods are sold in the course of a business. Neither section will apply where goods are sold by a private seller. The following case considered the circumstances in which goods are sold in the course of a business.

 Stevenson *v* Rogers (1999) (Court of Appeal)

The defendant had been in business as a fisherman for 20 years. He sold an old fishing boat when he wanted to buy a new one. The boat he sold, which was not of satisfactory quality, was not being used as part of the stock in trade of the business at the time of sale. The defendant argued that no term as to satisfactory quality should be implied as the boat was not sold in the course of a business.

Held The boat was sold in the course of the defendant's business. For the purposes of s. 14 of the SGA 1979, the words 'in the course of a business' should be taken at face value. Section 14 applies to any sale made by a business, even if what is sold is not the stock in trade which the business exists in order to sell. Even a one-off sale by the business is a sale in the course of a business. However, purely private sales which are made outside the limits of the business would not be made in the course of a business.

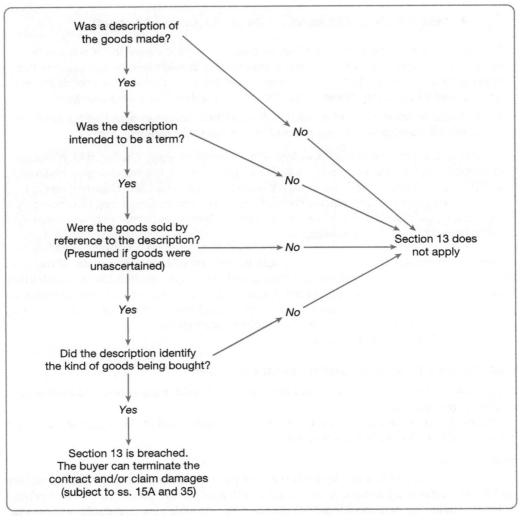

Figure 3.5 Section 13 SGA 1979

Satisfactory quality (s. 14(2))

Section 14(2) of the SGA 1979 provides that:

> Where the seller sells goods in the course of a business, there is an implied [condition] that the goods supplied under the contract are of satisfactory quality.

Circumstances in which s. 14(2) will not be implied

Even where goods are sold in the course of a business, s. 14(2C) indicates that the term as to satisfactory quality will not be implied in two circumstances:

(1) It will not apply as regards defects which were specifically pointed out to the buyer before the contract was made.

(2) Where the buyer examines the goods before buying them, it will not apply as regards defects which *that examination* ought to have revealed.

If a defect is specifically pointed out to the buyer, then that particular defect cannot make the goods unsatisfactory. This is the case even if the defect proves to be more serious than the buyer imagined.

 Bartlett *v* Sidney Marcus Ltd (1965) (Court of Appeal)

A dealer sold a second-hand car and pointed out to the buyer that the car had a defective clutch. The buyer negotiated a reduced price to take account of the defect. Repairing the clutch cost far more than the buyer had anticipated, and he claimed to reject the car under s. 14(2).

Held The defect had been pointed out to the buyer and so it did not cause s. 14(2) to have been breached.

A buyer has no obligation to examine goods before buying them. If, however, the buyer does examine the goods, the goods cannot be rendered unsatisfactory on account of defects which that examination ought to have revealed. However, even the most glaringly obvious defects will make the goods unsatisfactory if the buyer chooses not to examine the goods.

Meaning of satisfactory quality

This requirement that the goods supplied under the contract must be of satisfactory quality is relatively recent. The Sale of Goods Act 1979 was amended in 1995. Before the amendment, the 1979 Act implied a term that goods sold in the course of a business had to be of merchantable quality. However, the meaning of merchantable quality had become unclear, and so the requirement was changed to one of satisfactory quality. Section 14(2A) of the SGA 1979 now provides the following definition of satisfactory quality.

> Goods are of satisfactory quality if they meet the standard that a reasonable person would regard as satisfactory, taking account of any description of the goods, the price (if relevant) and all the other relevant circumstances.

We should note three things about this definition. First, the standard required is objective, being that which a reasonable person would regard as satisfactory. Second, any description of the goods may be taken into account. (There is no requirement here that the goods are sold by description, as there was in the case of s. 13(1).) Third, any other relevant circumstances, which may include the price, can be taken into account. It is also worth noticing that it is not only the goods sold which must be of satisfactory quality. Section 14(2) requires that 'the goods supplied under the contract' must be of satisfactory quality and this would include any packaging.

Section 14(2B) lists five factors which can be taken into account in assessing the quality of the goods.

> For the purposes of this Act, the quality of goods includes their state and condition and the following (among others) are in appropriate cases aspects of the quality of the goods—
>
> (a) fitness for all the purposes for which goods of the kind in question are commonly supplied,
>
> (b) appearance and finish,
>
> (c) freedom from minor defects,
>
> (d) safety, and
>
> (e) durability.

It is important not to get carried away with s. 14(2B). The five matters listed are not absolute requirements of quality. They are *aspects of quality in appropriate cases*.

> ### Example
>
> A car which has been written off in an accident is sold by a business for scrap. The car will be of satisfactory quality even though it might be unfit to be driven, badly battered and completely unsafe. Taking into account the description, the price and all the other relevant circumstances, the reasonable person would regard such a car as being of satisfactory quality.

The liability imposed on the seller by s. 14(2) is strict and does not depend upon the seller having been at fault. Shops which sell defective goods will breach s. 14(2) even if the goods were sold in packaging which prevented the defect from being discovered.

In **Darren Egan *v* Motor Services (Bath) Ltd (2007)** Lady Justice Ward, giving the only significant judgment of the Court of Appeal, considered the extent to which a minor defect would make an expensive new car of unsatisfactory quality. She said,

> . . . it seems to me unlikely that a buyer will be entitled to reject goods simply because he can point to a minor defect. He must also persuade the judge that a reasonable person would think that the minor defect was of sufficient consequence to make the goods unsatisfactory. Of course, if a car is not handling correctly, one would expect any reasonable person to say that it is not of satisfactory quality . . . But the mere fact that a setting is outside the manufacturer's specification will not neces- sarily render the vehicle objectively unsatisfactory. The reasonable person may think that the minor defect is of no consequence.

In **Thain *v* Anniesland Trade Centre 1997** a Scottish court held that durability was not an appropriate aspect of quality when a five- or six-year-old Renault 19, which had done 80,000 miles, was bought for slightly under 30 per cent of the price of a new model. Within two weeks of purchase the car's gear box developed a fault which soon made the car undriveable. The court was satisfied that this fault had not been present when the car was bought. It held that the car was of satisfactory quality. Durability was not a quality which a reasonable person would have expected of this particular car.

In the following case the Court of Appeal considered whether a new motor home was of unsatisfactory quality because it was, technically, too wide to be legally driven on UK roads.

> ### Bramhill *v* Edwards (2004) (Court of Appeal)
>
> E was a specialist dealer in motor homes imported from the USA. He imported a 'Dolphin' motor home which was 102 inches wide. Vehicles over 100 inches wide cannot legally be used on the UK roads, although insurance companies are prepared to insure them. B and his wife were enthusiasts who knew that vehicles over 100 inches wide could not legally be used. They saw the Dolphin at a show in Malvern where E was displaying it. Shortly afterwards, after living in the Dolphin for a few days, B bought it for £61,000. B had ample opportunity to measure the width of the Dolphin before purchasing it but there was no evidence that he actually did this. After some seven months using the vehicle, B measured it and found it to be 102 inches wide. B complained to E about this. E said that the width would not cause a problem and B continued to use the Dolphin. After another four months B complained to E that he thought he had bought a 100-inch wide vehicle, not an illegal 102-inch wide one. Two months later B asked E to take the Dolphin back in part exchange for one of two other vehicles, one of which was also 102 inches wide. When these requests were refused he sued E.

Held B had not proved that s. 14(2A) had been breached on account of the vehicle being too wide. There was plenty of evidence that the authorities turned a blind eye to the use of vehicles which were 102 inches wide and enthusiasts for such vehicles knew this. Consequently, B had not proved, on a balance of probabilities, that a reasonable person would regard the vehicle as unsatisfactory.

Comment Auld LJ gave the only judgment. When considering the excessive width of the vehicle, he said that the test of satisfactory quality was an objective test which focused on the attitude of the reasonable person. However, he went on to say that this meant the reasonable person in the position of the buyer with the buyer's knowledge, and that it would not be appropriate to consider a reasonable third-party observer who was not acquainted with the background of the transaction. '*The reasonable buyer must be attributed with knowledge of all background facts . . . such facts in this case would include that: . . . a significant number of vehicles of greater width than permitted in this country were in use on its roads; and the authorities were turning a blind eye to that illegal use.*' Recognising that there were arguments both for and against a reasonable person thinking that the Dolphin was of satisfactory quality, Auld LJ held that B had failed to prove that the reasonable person would think that the Dolphin was not of satisfactory quality. B had therefore not discharged his obligation to prove his case on a balance of probabilities.

Public statements on the specific characteristics of the goods

Section 14(2D) provides that where the buyer deals as a consumer, the relevant circumstances in s. 14(2A) include any public statements on the specific characteristics of the goods made about them by the seller, the producer or his representatives, particularly in advertising or labelling. (Producer means the manufacturer of the goods, or the person who imported them into the EU or a person who put his own name, trade mark or other distinctive mark on the goods.) So if a car manufacturer advertised that a certain model of car did 45 miles per gallon, a customer who bought such a car new from a garage, and found that it did not achieve this mileage, might be able to claim that the car was not of satisfactory quality. However, s. 14(2E) provides that a public statement is not by virtue of s. 14(2D) to be considered a relevant circumstance if the seller can show one of three things:

(1) that at the time of the contract the seller was not, and could not reasonably have been, aware of the statement; or

(2) that the statement had been withdrawn in public or corrected in public before the contract was made; or

(3) that the consumer's decision to buy the goods could not have been influenced by the statement.

The circumstances in which a buyer deals as a consumer are considered below, in relation to the Unfair Contract Terms Act 1977 (see later in the chapter). It will be seen there that a company can deal as a consumer when buying goods.

Figure 3.6 gives an overview of the circumstances in which s. 14 will apply.

Fitness for purpose (s. 14(3))

Section 14(3) of the SGA 1979 states that if the buyer expressly or impliedly makes known to the seller any particular purpose for which the goods are being bought, then there is an

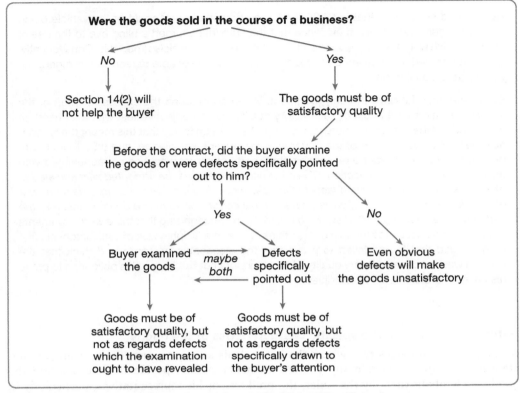

Figure 3.6 The circumstances in which s. 14(2) SGA 1979 will apply

implied condition that the goods are reasonably fit for that purpose. This is the case whether or not the purpose made known by the buyer is the purpose for which goods of that particular type are commonly supplied.

However, s. 14(3) will not apply if the circumstances show either that:

● the buyer does not rely on the skill and judgement of the seller; or

● it was unreasonable for the buyer to rely on the skill and judgement of the seller.

The following example shows how s. 14(3) might operate.

Example

Hannah visits a shop and buys a cake. Before buying the cake, Hannah asks the seller whether or not the cake contains nuts, explaining that she is allergic to nuts. The seller says that it does not. Relying on this, Hannah buys the cake and eats it. Hannah is made ill by the cake, because it did contain nuts. Section 14(3) will have been breached even though there was nothing wrong with the general quality of the cake.

If the purpose for which goods are to be used is perfectly obvious, then the buyer does not need to state the purpose. The terms as to satisfactory quality and fitness for the buyer's purpose will both be implied.

Grant *v* Australian Knitting Mills Ltd (1936) (Privy Council)

A customer who bought a pair of underpants from a shop contracted dermatitis because a chemical used in the manufacture of the underpants had not been rinsed out properly. The customer sued under s. 14(3), as well as under s. 14(2), because the purpose for which he bought the underpants was perfectly obvious.

Held The buyer won under both sections.

The term in s. 14(3) will not protect a buyer who does not make known, expressly or impliedly, the particular purpose for which the goods are bought.

 Griffiths *v* Peter Conway Ltd (1939) (Court of Appeal)

A customer with abnormally sensitive skin contracted dermatitis from a tweed coat which she bought from a shop. The coat would not have affected most people.

Held The shop were not liable under s. 14(2) because there was nothing wrong with the coat. The shop were not liable under s. 14(3) because the customer had not made her condition known.

When defective goods are bought for their usual purpose, it is common for the buyer to sue under both s. 14(2) and s. 14(3), as **Grant *v* Australian Knitting Mills** demonstrates. However, the terms are not implied in identical circumstances. Section 14(2) applies even if the buyer did not make any purpose known to the seller or rely in any way on the seller's skill and judgement. However, s. 14(2) does not apply where the buyer examined the goods and ought to have noticed a defect. Nor does it apply where the defect was specifically pointed out to the buyer. Section 14(3) applies only where the buyer makes a particular purpose known to the seller and relies on the skill and judgement of the seller (although both of these matters can be done impliedly). It can apply even as regards defects which the buyer noticed or which were specifically pointed out. (If, for example, the seller wrongly said that the defect would cause the buyer no problems.)

Figure 3.7 shows how s. 14(3) operates.

Sale by sample (s. 15)

Section 15 provides that if goods are sold by sample the following two conditions are implied:

(1) the bulk of the goods must correspond with the sample in quality; and
(2) the bulk must be free from hidden defects, which would render the goods unsatisfactory, if these defects would not be discovered on a reasonable examination of the sample.

These two terms are implied into all sales by sample, even those which were not made in the course of a business. The first term is similar to sale by description, with the sample acting as the description. The buyer should look at the sample to assess the quality of the goods, knowing that the bulk must be of the same quality. The second term is similar to s. 14(2). However, s. 14(2) does not require the buyer to examine the goods. A sample is there to be examined, so s. 15 regards the buyer as having examined the sample. If the bulk of the goods

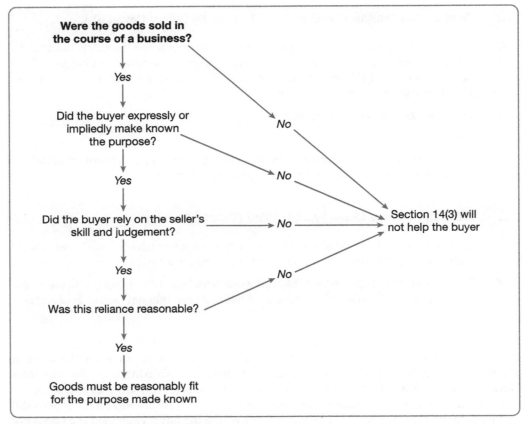

Figure 3.7 Section 14(3) SGA 1979

contain a defect which renders the goods of unsatisfactory quality, the outcome will depend upon whether this defect would have been apparent on a reasonable examination of the sample. If the defect would have been apparent, then neither s. 14(2) nor s. 15 will have been breached. This is the case even if the buyer did not examine the sample or notice the defect. If the defect would not have been apparent, then s. 15 will have been breached.

⚖ Godley *v* Perry (1960)

A six-year-old boy bought a catapult which snapped in use and caused the boy to lose an eye. The boy sued the shopkeeper under s. 14(2) and won. The shopkeeper sued the wholesaler under s. 15 because, before buying the catapults, he had tested a sample catapult by pulling back the elastic, and this sample had not snapped.

Held The shopkeeper won under s. 15. The defect was not apparent on a reasonable examination of the sample.

If a sale is made by both sample and description, the bulk of the goods must correspond with both the sample and the description. For example, in **Nichol v Godts (1854)** oil was sold by sample and was also described as 'foreign rape seed oil'. The goods not only had to correspond with the sample but also had to correspond with the description.

The Supply of Goods (Implied Terms) Act 1973

When the Consumer Rights Act 2015 comes into force the terms implied by the SGITA 1973 will no longer apply to contracts made between traders and consumers. Instead, the CRA 2015 will apply similar terms, and additional terms, into such consumer contracts. The remedies available if these terms are breached are not the same as the remedies available if a SGITA 1973 implied term is breached. The CRA 2015 is considered later in this chapter, where the definitions of 'trader' and 'consumer' are discussed. The SGITA 1973 implied terms will continue to apply to non-consumer contracts.

As we have seen, the terms implied by the Sale of Goods Act have given excellent protection to buyers of goods since 1893. However, for many years people who acquired goods under contracts which could not be classed as contracts of sale of goods had to rely on case law for protection.

In the 1970s Parliament passed two statutes which extended the Sale of Goods Act implied terms into other types of contract.

The first of these statutes was the Supply of Goods (Implied Terms) Act 1973 (SGITA 1973), which extended the implied terms into contracts of hire-purchase. The terms implied, which are virtually identical to the terms implied by ss. 12–15 of the Sale of Goods Act 1979, are contained in the following sections.

Section 8	Right to pass ownership
Section 9	Correspondence with description
Section 10(1)	Satisfactory quality (business contracts only)
Section 10(2)	Fitness for purpose (business contracts only)
Section 11	Correspondence with sample

A contract of **hire-purchase** is one whereby a customer agrees to hire goods for a certain period, and is given an option to purchase the goods for a small sum at the end of that period.

Example

Mr Smith takes a fridge on hire-purchase from a shop. The fridge would have cost £350 to buy, but Mr Smith takes it on hire-purchase for three years at £17 a month. Until the final payment is made, Mr Smith is merely hiring the fridge. The last payment he makes will include a nominal purchase price and when Mr Smith makes the final payment he then buys the fridge.

The SGITA 1973 implies terms as to the right to pass ownership, description, quality, fitness and sample as soon as the hire-purchase agreement begins.

Section 10, which implies the terms as to satisfactory quality and fitness for the hirer's purpose, applies only if the owner of the goods makes the hire-purchase agreement in the course of a business. The other sections apply to all contracts of hire-purchase. In almost all hire-purchase agreements the owner will make the agreement in the course of a business.

The Supply of Goods and Services Act 1982

When the Consumer Rights Act 2015 comes into force, the terms implied by the SGSA 1982 will no longer apply to contracts made between traders and consumers. Instead, the CRA 2015 will apply similar terms, and additional terms, into such consumer contracts. The remedies available if these terms are breached are not the same as the remedies available if a SGSA 1982 implied term is breached. The CRA 2015 is considered later in this chapter, where the definitions of 'trader' and 'consumer' are discussed. The SGSA 1982 implied terms will continue to apply to non-consumer contracts.

Part I of the Act

Part I of the Supply of Goods and Services Act 1982 (SGSA 1982) implies terms equivalent to the terms in the SGA 1979 into two types of contracts. First, the terms are implied into contracts for the transfer of property in goods. Second, the terms are implied into contracts of hire. The terms are implied by the following sections.

Contracts for the transfer of property in goods

Section 2	Right to transfer the property
Section 3	Correspondence with description
Section 4(2)	Satisfactory quality (business contracts only)
Section 4(3)	Fitness for purpose (business contracts only)
Section 5	Correspondence with sample

A contract will be a contract for the transfer of property in goods if it is any contract which involves the passing of ownership of goods (except a contract of sale of goods or a contract of hire-purchase). It would therefore include contracts under which goods are bartered for other goods. It would also cover the supply of goods in a contract under which services are supplied. For example, it would cover the supply of oil when a car is serviced.

Contracts of hire

Section 7	Right to hire
Section 8	Correspondence with description
Section 9(2)	Satisfactory quality (business contracts only)
Section 9(3)	Fitness for purpose (business contracts only)
Section 10	Correspondence with sample

Table 3.1 shows the terms implied by the SGA 1979, SGITA 1973 and SGSA.

Table 3.1 The terms implied by SGA 1979, SGITA 1973 and SGSA 1982

Type of contract / Term implied	Sale of goods	Hire-purchase	Transfer of property in goods	Hire
Right to sell	SGA 1979 s. 12(1)	SGITA 1973 s. 8	SGSA 1982 s. 2	SGSA 1982 s. 7
Quiet possession and freedom from encumbrances	SGA 1979 s. 12(2)	SGITA 1973 s. 8	SGSA 1982 s. 2	SGSA 1982 s. 7
Correspondence with description	SGA 1979 s. 13	SGITA 1973 s. 9	SGSA 1982 s. 3	SGSA 1982 s. 8
Satisfactory quality in business sales	SGA 1979 s. 14(2)	SGITA 1973 s. 10(2)	SGSA 1982 s. 4(2)	SGSA 1982 s. 9(2)
Fitness for purpose in business sales	SGA 1979 s. 14(3)	SGITA 1973 s. 10(3)	SGSA 1982 s. 4(3)	SGSA 1982 s. 9(3)
Correspondence with sample	SGA 1979 s. 15	SGITA 1973 s. 11	SGSA 1982 s. 5	SGSA 1982 s. 10

Under a contract of hire, a hirer is given temporary possession of goods but not ownership, by the owner of the goods.

Part II of the Act

Part II of the Supply of Goods and Services Act 1982 implies three terms into contracts under which a service is supplied. These terms are as follows:

Section 13   Reasonable care and skill (business services only)
Section 14   Reasonable time (business services only)
Section 15   Reasonable price

Reasonable care and skill (s. 13)

SGSA 1982 s. 13 provides that:

> In a contract for the supply of a service where the supplier is acting in the course of a business, there is an implied term that the supplier will carry out the service with reasonable care and skill.

First, it is important to note that this term will be implied only where the service is supplied in the course of a business. Second, and very important, it must be realised that this term does not impose strict liability. It imposes a tort standard of reasonable care and skill. For example, in **Thake and another *v* Maurice (1986)** a patient sued a surgeon who had carried out a vasectomy which did not have the desired effect. The surgeon was not liable because he had used reasonable care and skill. (The effect of a very few vasectomies can be reversed naturally.) If the surgeon had guaranteed that the vasectomy would be successful, then he would have been liable. In the absence of such a guarantee, however, s. 13 implies a term only that the provider of a service in the course of a business will use reasonable care and skill.

The test of whether the service provided was carried out with reasonable care and skill is objective, not subjective. A person who professes to have a certain level of skill must show the level of skill which the reasonable person would expect. Professionals, such as solicitors and accountants, and tradesmen, such as plumbers and roofers, would be expected to show the level of skill which is normal in that profession or trade. The government has indicated that a new Consumer Rights Act, passed in 2015, will give effect to an EU directive, the Consumer Rights Directive. Under the new Act, the standard required when a business provides a service to a consumer will be made closer to the Sale of Goods Act s. 14 requirements of satisfactory quality and fitness for purpose. As regards some types of service there will be a statutory guarantee of the quality of the service, with statutory remedies if this quality is not met.

It is also important to realise that a contract can still be a contract for the supply of a service even though it is a contract under which possession of goods or ownership of goods is transferred.

Example

A contract is made under which a motorist buys new tyres, to be fitted by the garage. This is both a contract of sale of goods and a contract for the supply of a service. In such cases two sets of terms are implied. Sections 14(2) and 14(3) of the Sale of Goods Act 1979 imply terms as to satisfactory quality and fitness for purpose. Section 13 of the Supply of Goods and Services Act 1982 implies a term that the service is carried out using reasonable care and skill. So if the tyres fitted were worn at the time of sale, the buyer would sue under SGA 1979 s. 14(2) because the tyres were not of satisfactory quality. If the tyres were fitted badly and came off the car, causing the driver to be injured, the driver would sue under SGSA 1982 s. 13 because the tyres were not fitted with reasonable care and skill. If the contract had merely been to service the car, this would not have been a sale of goods but would have been a contract to supply a service. If the service was performed negligently, liability would arise under s. 13 SGSA 1982. However, if through no fault of the garage the oil put into the engine was not of satisfactory quality, then the buyer would sue under SGSA 1982 s. 4(2).

Reasonable time of performance (s. 14)

Section 14 SGSA 1982 applies only to services which are supplied in the course of business. It provides that if no time for completion of the service was either expressly or impliedly fixed, then the service should be performed within a reasonable time. The length of a reasonable time will depend upon all the circumstances of the case.

Reasonable price (s. 15)

Section 15 SGSA 1982 provides that if no price for a service was expressly or impliedly fixed, then the customer should pay a reasonable price. This section applies to all services, whether supplied in the course of a business or not.

The status of the statutory implied terms

When the Consumer Rights Act 2015 comes into force the terms which it implies will no longer be classified as conditions, warranties or innominate terms. Instead, a different set of remedies will be available, as explained later in this chapter. The CRA 2015 will apply only to contracts made between traders and consumers. As regards other contracts, the CRA 2015 will not change the law.

The term contained in s. 12(1) of the Sale of Goods Act 1979 is always a condition. If this term is breached, the buyer is always therefore entitled to treat the contract as terminated and/or claim damages. The term is a condition because if the seller does not have the right to sell, this amounts to a total failure of consideration. The corresponding terms contained in the SGITA 1973 s. 8 and the SGSA 1982 ss. 2 and 7 are also always conditions.

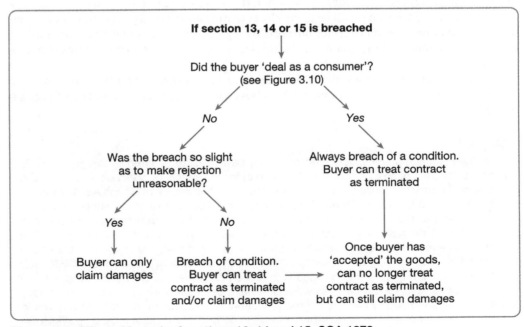

Figure 3.8 Effect of breach of sections 13, 14 and 15, SGA 1979

The term contained in s. 12(2) of the Sale of Goods Act 1979 is a warranty. If this term is breached, the buyer will therefore be able to claim damages but will not be entitled to treat the contract as terminated. The corresponding terms in the SGITA 1973 and the SGSA 1982 are also always warranties.

The terms contained in ss. 13–15 of the Sale of Goods Act 1979 are conditions. So are the corresponding terms in the SGITA 1973 ss. 9–11 and the SGSA 1982 ss. 3–5 and 8–10. Where the person buying or acquiring the goods is a consumer, all of these terms are always conditions. However, s. 15A of the Sale of Goods Act 1979 (and corresponding terms in the SGITA 1973 and in the SGSA 1982) provides that a buyer who does not deal as a consumer cannot treat the contract as terminated where breach of one of these implied terms is so slight that it would be unreasonable to allow the buyer to treat the contract as terminated. Instead, the buyer must treat the breach of condition as a breach of warranty and therefore cannot terminate the contract but can still claim damages. Section 15A does not apply if the parties showed an intention that the person acquiring the goods should be able to treat the contract as terminated even where the breach was so slight as to make this unreasonable.

> **Example**
>
> A car dealer bought a new car from a car manufacturer and sold the car on to a consumer. The car had a very slight defect, which was just enough to mean that it was not of satisfactory quality, both when the manufacturer sold it and when the dealer sold it. Section 14(2) of the SGA 1979 has therefore been breached as regards both sales. The consumer can treat this breach as breach of a condition and will be entitled to reject the car and treat the contract as terminated (as well as to claim damages). The car dealer will not be able to treat the contract as terminated if the breach is so slight as to make this unreasonable. As he did not deal as a consumer when buying the car, s. 15A requires him to treat the breach of condition as a breach of warranty. So the car dealer will not be able to reject the car, but will be able to claim damages for breach of warranty. The car dealer would therefore be likely to repair the car, or have it repaired, and then claim damages from the manufacturer. These damages might reflect the cost of the repair and any profit which the dealer lost as a result of the sale to the consumer falling through.

Section 15A applies only where the buyer does not 'deal as a consumer'. The SGA 1979, like the SGITA 1973 and the SGSA 1982, decides whether or not a person is dealing as a consumer by applying the definition set out in s. 12 of the Unfair Contract Terms Act 1977. This definition is complex and is considered later in this chapter, where a flow chart shows how the section should be applied.

The Sale of Goods Act 1979 s. 11(4) makes one further important rule. It provides that where a seller of goods breaches a condition, a buyer who has 'accepted' the goods must treat the breach of condition as a breach of warranty. Therefore, such a buyer cannot terminate the contract but can still claim damages. Acceptance by the buyer has a technical meaning (which is examined in detail in Chapter 7). Here it is enough to say that a buyer will be deemed by s. 35 to have accepted the goods if he:

- keeps them for more than a reasonable time without rejecting them; or
- indicates acceptance of them; or
- does an act which is inconsistent with the seller continuing to own the goods.

Additional rights of the buyer in consumer cases

The law set out below will be contained in the Consumer Rights Act 2015 when it comes into force.

The Sale and Supply of Goods to Consumers Regulations 2002 amended the SGA 1979 by adding ss. 48A–48F. These new sections confer significant new rights on buyers who deal as consumers when the goods bought do not conform to the contract of sale. Before considering the new rights in detail, it is important to note that the new rights are additional to any other rights which the consumer might have. They do not replace the statutory implied terms or any other remedies which might exist.

The circumstances in which the new rights apply

Two requirements must be satisfied before the new rights will apply:

(1) The buyer must have dealt as a consumer.

(2) The goods bought must fail to conform to the contract of sale at the time of delivery.

For the purposes of ss. 48A–48F, the definition of dealing as a consumer set out in the Unfair Contract Terms Act 1977 (UCTA 1977) is applied. This definition, which is complex, is considered later in this chapter in relation to the UCTA 1977. Figure 3.10 gives an overview of how the definition should be approached.

Section 48F provides that the goods do not conform to the contract of sale if either an express term of the contract is breached or if one of the statutory terms implied by ss. 13–15 of the SGA 1979 is breached. Furthermore, s. 48A(3) provides that if the goods fail to conform to the contract within six months of the date of delivery, they are to be presumed not to have conformed on the date of delivery. Section 48A(4) allows this presumption to be overturned if:

- it is established that the goods did conform to the contract at the date of delivery; or
- the presumption is incompatible with the nature of the goods or the nature of the lack of conformity.

The hierarchy of rights

Once it has been established that the buyer dealt as a consumer, and that the goods did not conform to the contract at the time of delivery, the buyer acquires a hierarchy of rights. The two primary remedies of the buyer are to have the goods repaired or replaced. The two secondary remedies are to gain a reduction of the price or to rescind the contract.

Section 48B allows the buyer to require the seller to either repair or replace the goods. It also requires the seller to carry out the repair or replacement within a reasonable time and without causing significant inconvenience to the buyer. The seller has to bear any costs in doing this, including the costs of labour, materials and postage. However, a buyer cannot insist on repair or replacement if the remedy requested would be disproportionate in relation to one of the other three remedies. A remedy is disproportionate if the costs which it imposes on the seller are unreasonable, taking into account:

- the value which the goods would have if they did conform to the contract of sale;
- the significance of the lack of conformity; and
- whether the other remedy could be effected without significant inconvenience to the buyer.

For example, if a consumer bought a very cheap digital watch which did not work at all, repair of the watch would be disproportionate in relation to rescinding the contract or taking a replacement watch. Where the buyer does request repair or replacement of the goods, s. 48D requires the seller to be given a reasonable time to perform the remedy requested. Until this reasonable time has passed, the buyer cannot ask for any other remedy, whether the remedy arose under ss. 48A–48F or in some other way.

Section 48C deals with the secondary remedies; that is to say it deals with requiring the seller to reduce the contract price by an appropriate amount and with rescission of the contract. In this context, rescinding the contract means treating it as if it had never been made and claiming the return of the contract price. However, this amount can be reduced to take account of any use of the goods which the buyer has had. These two remedies are regarded as secondary because they cannot be claimed as of right, but only in two circumstances. The first circumstance is that the buyer cannot require repair or replacement because both of these remedies are impossible or are disproportionate in relation to one of the secondary remedies. The second circumstance is that the buyer has required the seller to repair or replace the goods but the seller has not done so within a reasonable time and without significant inconvenience to the buyer.

Section 48E gives the court additional powers when a claim is made by a buyer under ss. 48A–48F. The court can order the seller to specifically perform an obligation to repair or replace the goods as requested by the buyer. If the buyer requests one of the remedies set out in the new sections, the court can instead award a different one of these remedies if it decides that the other remedy is more appropriate. The court also has the power to adjust any of the new remedies on such terms and conditions as it sees fit, perhaps by ordering that damages also be paid.

Earlier in this chapter we saw that a buyer who has 'accepted' goods can no longer reject those goods for breach of a condition. We also saw that s. 35 SGA deems a buyer to have accepted goods in three circumstances: first, where the buyer indicates to the seller that the goods are accepted; second, where the buyer does any act which is inconsistent with the seller still owning the goods (such as consuming the goods); and third, where the buyer keeps the goods for more than a reasonable time without letting the seller know that the goods are rejected. It seems probable that ss. 48A–48F will be most useful to a buyer who cannot reject for breach of a condition on account of having accepted the goods. Figure 3.9 shows an outline of the additional rights of the consumers which are conferred by SGA ss. 48A–F.

Example

Mary, a teacher, bought a new radio from a shop in January. Mary did not use the radio until she went on holiday in May. She then found that the radio did not work properly because it could not pick up FM. Despite this problem, Mary continued to use the radio to listen to AM stations. Section 14(2) SGA would have been breached if Mary could prove that the radio was not of satisfactory quality when she bought it. However, as Mary kept the radio for more than a reasonable time without rejecting it, she would be too late to reject under s. 14(2). (She could, of course, still claim damages for the breach of s. 14(2).) Mary dealt as a consumer and the radio did not conform to the contract of sale. (As the radio did not conform to the contract within six months of the date of delivery, it is presumed that it did not conform to the contract at the date of delivery.) Mary's primary remedies under ss. 48A–48F would be to have the radio either repaired or replaced. Mary could choose which remedy she wanted. If the shop did not give Mary the remedy which she asked for within a reasonable time, and without causing significant inconvenience to her, then Mary could require one of the secondary remedies, rescission of the contract or a reduction of the price. Rescission of the contract would seem to be the more appropriate remedy. Mary would then be entitled to get the purchase price back, but perhaps not the whole of the price if the court deducted an amount to take account of any use of the radio which Mary had had.

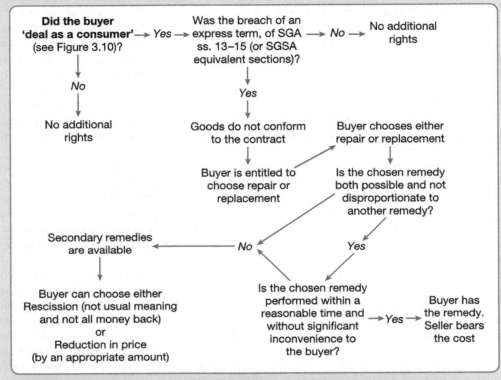

Figure 3.9 **The additional rights of consumers conferred by SGA ss. 48A–48F**

The Supply of Goods and Services Act 1982 was amended at the same time as the SGA 1979. Amendments which are virtually identical to those made to the SGA 1979 were made to the SGSA 1982, in so far as it relates to contracts for the transfer of goods. Goods do not conform to the contract if an express term is breached or if any of the statutory implied terms as to description, satisfactory quality, fitness for purpose or correspondence with sample are breached. In addition, if installation forms part of the contract the goods do not conform to the contract if they are not installed properly. The consumer is given the same hierarchical rights as those given by ss. 48A–48F of the SGA.

The Consumer Rights Act 2015

When the Consumer Rights Act 2015 comes into force it will amend the statutory rights of consumers who buy goods, services or software. The Act applies only to consumer contracts, that is to say contracts under which a consumer deals with a trader. It does not change the law as it relates to non-consumer contracts. Its definition of a consumer therefore becomes vitally important. If a non-consumer buys goods, services or software then the existing law, explained earlier in this chapter, will apply. The statutory implied terms which benefit non-consumers will continue to be contained in the SGA 1979, the SGITA 1973 and the SGSA 1982. However, the SGA 1979 will be amended so that its rules on acceptance (ss. 11 and 35–36), the statutory implied terms (ss. 12–15) and the additional rights of consumer buyers (ss. 48A–F) will be repealed **as regards consumer contracts only**, and replaced by the CRA. It is possible that section numbers will change as the Bill progresses through parliament. However, it is unlikely that the content of the Bill will be changed significantly.

The CRA definitions

The CRA implies terms into 'consumer contracts' for the supply of goods, digital content and services and to 'mixed contracts', under which a trader supplies or agrees to supply to a consumer a combination of goods, digital content or services.

A 'trader' is defined by s. 2(2) as 'a person acting (personally or through an agent) for purposes relating to that person's trade, business, craft or profession'. The definition of a 'consumer' replaces the UCTA 1977 and SGA 1979 concept of a person 'dealing as a consumer'. Section 2(3) defines a consumer as 'an individual [therefore not a company or a LLP] acting for purposes that are wholly or mainly outside that individual's trade, business, craft or profession.' 'Digital content' is defined by s. 2(9) as data which are produced and supplied in digital form.

The statutory terms applicable to goods

The CRA implies identical terms into contracts of sale, hire, hire-purchase and barter. So it does not require a consumer to classify the type of contract under which the goods were supplied, and then to proceed to the relevant legislation, as the previous law did. Section 2(8) defines 'goods' as any tangible, moveable items.

Section 9 requires the goods to be of satisfactory quality. Section 10 requires that they be fit for any particular purpose made known to the trader. Section 11 requires that they should match any description by which they were supplied. Section 13 requires that if they were supplied by sample they should correspond with the sample. Section 17(1) implies a term that the trader has the right to sell or transfer the goods. Sections 17(2) to (6) imply terms that the goods are free from any charge or encumbrance not made known to the consumer and that the consumer will enjoy quiet possession of the goods. These terms are the direct equivalent of ss. 12–15 SGA 1979, although the order in which they appear in the CRA has changed. Case law applicable to ss. 12–15 SGA will therefore be applicable to the CRA. However, the terms are not classified by the CRA as conditions or warranties. Instead, if the implied terms are breached the goods are generally regarded as not conforming to the contract and new remedies are set out, as considered below.

Section 14 introduces a term that the goods should match a model which has been seen or examined, unless differences between the model and the goods supplied are brought to the consumer's attention before the contract is made.

Section 15 provides that if the goods supplied are also to be installed but the goods are not installed with reasonable care and skill then the goods are to be regarded as not conforming to the contract.

Section 16 provides that if the goods, which would otherwise conform to the contract, include digital content which does not conform to the contract then the goods themselves will be regarded as not conforming to the contract.

Section 12(1) provides that when Article 5 or 6 of the Consumer Rights Directive requires the trader to provide information to the consumer before the contract becomes binding, this information is to be treated as a term of the contract, unless it is information about the main characteristics of the goods. (Articles 5 and 6 are considered below.)

Consumer's remedies in respect of non-conforming goods

Goods do not conform to the contract if ss. 9, 10, 11, 13, 14, 15 or 16 are breached. They may also fail to conform if they do not conform to requirements which are stated in the contract. If the goods fail to conform on account of ss. 9–16 being breached then ss. 20–24 give the consumer the following remedies: the short-term right to reject; the right to repair or replacement; or (if repair or replacement are not possible or do not deal with the fault) the right to a price reduction or the right to finally reject. If only some of the goods fail to conform to the contract the short-term right to reject and the final right to reject can be total or partial. If it is partial then s.21 allows the consumer to reject some or all of the non-conforming goods. These remedies are considered below. The following table shows when the various remedies are available.

Statutory right breached	Remedies
Satisfactory quality (s. 9)	Short-term right to reject (ss. 20 and 22) Repair or replacement (s. 23) Possibly, price reduction or final right to reject (s. 24)
Fitness for purpose (s. 10)	Short-term right to reject (ss. 20 and 22) Repair or replacement (s. 23) Possibly, price reduction or final right to reject (s. 24)
Correspondence with description (s. 11)	Short-term right to reject (ss. 20 and 22) Repair or replacement (s. 23) Possibly, price reduction or final right to reject (s. 24)
Conformity with CRD information (s. 12)	Recover costs incurred up to amount of price paid.
Correspondence with sample (s. 13)	Short-term right to reject (ss. 20 and 22) Repair or replacement (s. 23) Possibly, price reduction or final right to reject (s. 24)
Correspondence with model (s. 14)	Short-term right to reject (ss. 20 and 22) Repair or replacement (s. 23) Possibly, price reduction or final right to reject (s. 24)
Goods not installed with reasonable care and skill (s. 15)	Repair or replacement (s. 23) Price reduction or final right to reject (ss. 20 and 24)
Goods not conforming because digital content does not conform (s. 16)	Short-term right to reject (ss. 20 and 22) Repair or replacement (s. 23) Possibly, price reduction or final right to reject (s. 24)
The right to sell (s. 17(1))	The right to reject (s. 20)
Freedom from charge or encumbrance and right to quiet possession (s. 17(2) to (6))	No statutory remedies but can claim damages

Figure 3.10 Remedies under CRA 2015

The right to reject

Section 20 provides that the right to reject allows the consumer to reject the goods, treat the contract as at an end and to receive a refund from the trader. Section 20 then goes on to distinguish a short-term right to reject, which is subject to ss. 22, and a final right to reject, which is subject to s. 24. Under the short-term right to reject, the consumer is entitled to a full refund of the price, whereas under the final right to reject, a deduction can be made by the trader to take account of any use of the goods which the consumer has had.

Section 22 provides that a consumer can lose the short-term right to reject by failing to reject within the time limit. Any agreement that the short-term right to reject would be lost before the time limit has passed is not binding on the consumer. The time limit is 30 days, beginning with the day after ownership (or possession in the case of hire or hire-purchase) has been transferred, and the goods have been delivered and the contract has been completed. But if the goods can reasonably be expected to perish within a shorter period then the time limit is that shorter period. If repair or replacement are requested then the time limit for short-term rejection stops running for a 'waiting period'. The time limit for short-term rejection of goods is then seven days after the waiting period ends or the original period for rejecting the goods, plus the waiting period, if this is longer. The waiting period begins with the day the consumer requests or agrees to the repair or the replacement and the waiting period ends with the day on which the consumer receives goods supplied by the trader in response to the request or agreement for repair or replacement.

The rights to repair or replacement, price reduction and final rejection

The rights relating to repair or replacement, price reduction and final rejection are available if the goods do not conform to the contract at the time of delivery to the consumer. If the right of final reduction is exercised then the consumer's refund can be reduced to take account of any use had of the goods. However, no deduction can be made if the final right to reject is exercised in the first six months, unless the goods consist of a motor vehicle. Section 24(10) sets out a presumption that if the goods do not conform to the contract within six months of delivery then they did not conform on the date of delivery. As regards these four rights, the 30-day time limit does not apply. The rules relating to the four rights are substantially the same as those previously set out in ss. 48A–F of the SGA 1979, considered earlier in this chapter on pages 94–7. So the 'primary' remedies of repair or replacement are available whenever the goods do not conform to the contract, and the consumer can choose which one he wants. The 'secondary' remedies of price reduction and final rejection are not available as of right. They are available only if the consumer cannot require repair or replacement because these remedies are impossible or disproportionate in relation to one of the other remedies, or if the consumer has requested repair or replacement and the trader is in breach of his obligation to perform the remedy requested within a reasonable time and without significant inconvenience to the consumer. However, as regards the 'secondary' remedies, that is to say price reduction or final rejection, there is an additional right to claim either of these remedies if after one repair or replacement of the goods they still do not conform to the contract.

If s. 17(1) (the right to sell) is breached then the only statutory remedy is the right of final rejection. If the warranties set out in s. 17(2)–(6) are breached then there are no statutory remedies but only a common law right to damages. None of the remedies prevent a consumer from seeking damages.

Comparison of CRA 2015 remedies with remedies available under SGA 1979

The implied terms set out in ss. 12–15 SGA 1979 are conditions. If they are breached then, subject to the rules on acceptance set out in s. 35 SGA, the buyer has a right to reject the goods and receive a full refund of the price. If the right to reject is lost, or is not exercised, then the only other right generally available is the right to damages. The CRA 2015 sets out five rights which are available if the goods do not conform to the contract on account of the equivalent implied terms being breached. The right of short-term rejection entitles the consumer to a full refund of the price and is therefore equivalent to the SGA 1979 right to reject the goods for breach of condition. The other four rights conferred by the CRA 2015 (repair, replacement, price reduction and final rejection without a full price refund) will have no equivalent in the amended SGA 1979. These rights are available if ss. 9–17 are breached, as shown in Figure 3.10 above.

Liability that cannot be excluded or restricted

Section 31 provides that a term of a contract for the supply of goods cannot exclude or restrict the trader's liability arising under ss. 9–17. However, in the case of contracts of hire only, it is possible for a trader to contract out of the s. 17 requirement that the trader has the right to transfer possession of the goods, but this is subject to a requirement for contract terms to be fair.

The terms implied into a contract to provide digital content

Digital content is defined by s. 2(9) as data which are produced and supplied in digital form. So this would include, for example, software, downloaded music, computer games or 'apps'. The CRA applies to contracts under which a trader provides or agrees to provide digital content to a consumer, either for a price or free with goods or services or other digital content for which the consumer pays a price.

Section 35 requires the digital content to be of satisfactory quality; s. 36 requires it to be fit for any particular purpose made known to the trader; and s. 37 requires it to correspond with any description by which it was sold. The detail of these implied terms is similar to that in the corresponding terms relating to goods. If the terms contained in ss. 35–37 are breached then the digital content is regarded as not conforming to the contract and ss. 43–45 set out the three remedies available: the 'primary' remedies of the right to repair or replacement; and the 'secondary' remedy of a price reduction. Price reduction is available only if repair or replacement is impossible, or disproportionate in relation to repair or replacement, or has been requested by the consumer but the trader is in breach of his requirement to perform the remedy requested within a reasonable time and without causing significant inconvenience to the consumer. The three remedies, and the circumstances in which they are available, have already been examined above in relation to goods. However, there is no right to reject the digital content unless it forms part of goods or unless the trader did not have the right to supply it. This is because it is impractical to return digital content. However, if goods are supplied with digital content which fails to conform to the contract then the goods themselves do not conform to the contract, as explained in s. 16 above, and there would then be a right to reject the goods. As is the case with goods, if the digital content does not conform within six months of the date on which it was provided then it is presumed that it did not conform when it was provided.

Section 38 is the equivalent of s. 12 considered above. It provides that if the trader is required to provide the consumer with any other information under the Consumer Contracts (Information, Cancellation and Additional Charges) Regulations 2013 this information is to be treated as a term of the contract. (The Regulations are considered later in this chapter.) If s. 38 is breached the consumer has a right to a price reduction.

Statutory right breached	Remedies
Satisfactory quality (s. 35)	Repair or replacement (s. 44) Possibly, price reduction (s. 45)
Fitness for purpose (s. 36)	Repair or replacement (s. 44) Possibly, price reduction (s. 45)
Correspondence with description (s. 37)	Repair or replacement (s. 44) Possibly, price reduction (s. 45)
Pre-contractual information (s. 38)	Price reduction
Right to provide content (s. 42)	Right to a full price refund (s. 46)
Damage to other digital content (s. 47)	Damages to value of cost of replacing device or digital content damaged (s. 47)

Figure 3.11 Remedies relating to digital content under CRA 2015

Section 42 includes a term that the trader has the right to provide digital content. If this term is breached the consumer has a right to a full refund of the price under s. 46, with no corresponding duty to return or delete the digital content. There is no allowance for use of the digital content which the consumer might have had. However, if some digital content was provided without a breach of s. 42 then there is no right to a refund as regards that part of the digital content. So if a consumer bought a collection of downloadable films, and the trader did not have the right to provide one of them, then there would be a full refund only as regards that one. Generally, a trader does not pass ownership of digital content but provides a limited right to use it.

Section 47 allows a consumer to claim compensation if digital content supplied by a trader damages a device or other digital content belonging to the consumer and the damage is of a kind which would not have occurred if the trader had exercised reasonable care and skill. However, the payment is limited to the cost of replacing the device or digital content that is damaged. This section is intended to give the consumer a remedy without having to sue in the tort of negligence. However, if a claim greater than that allowed by s. 47 is made then an action in negligence would still be necessary. Figure 3.11 summarises the remedies available if the terms relating to digital content are breached.

Section 48 prevents exclusion or restriction of the terms relating to digital content.

Terms implied into a contract to provide a service

Sections 50, 52 and 53 imply terms into contracts under which a trader agrees to provide a service to a consumer. The terms implied by ss. 13–15 SGSA 1982, which were considered earlier in this chapter, continue to apply where a trader supplies a service to a non-consumer. Section 50 requires a service provided by a trader to be performed with reasonable care and skill. Section 52 provides that a reasonable price is to be paid, if no price was fixed. Section 53 requires the service to be performed within a reasonable time, if no time for performance was fixed. Section 51 provides that information about the service provided by the trader is to be treated as an express term of the contract, if it was taken into account by the consumer when deciding to enter into the contract, or when making any decision about the service after entering into the contract. This changes the existing law in that previously many such statements would merely have been representations. Section 51 also provides that if the trader is required to provide the consumer with any other information under the Consumer Contracts (Information, Cancellation and Additional Charges) Regulations 2013 this information is to be treated as a term of the contract. (The Regulations are considered later in this chapter.)

Remedies in respect of non-conforming services

A service does not conform to the contract if s. 50 or s. 51 is breached. In addition to any rights set out in the contract, the consumer then has a right to request repeat performance under s. 56 or, in some circumstances the right to a price reduction under s. 57. If the trader is in breach of s. 51 but the term in question does not relate to the service, or if the trader is in breach of s. 53, then s. 57 gives the consumer the right to a price reduction. In addition to the statutory remedies the consumer may seek any other remedies which are available under the common law.

The s. 56 right to a repeat performance is described as the right to require the trader to perform the service again, to the extent necessary to complete its performance in conformity with the contract. If the consumer requests this then the trader must repeat the performance within a reasonable time and without causing significant inconvenience to the consumer and to pay any necessary costs in doing this. However, a consumer cannot require repeat performance if repeating performance in conformity with the contract is impossible.

A price reduction is the right to require the trader to reduce the price by an appropriate amount. Where a customer has the right to both a price reduction and repeat performance, repeat performance is the default remedy. When a consumer has both remedies a price reduction will be available only if repeat performance is impossible, or if the consumer has required repeat performance but the trader is in breach of his requirement to do it within a reasonable time and without causing significant inconvenience to the consumer.

Section 58 provides that it is not possible to contract out of ss. 50–53 so as to exclude or restrict liability. However, disputes can be referred to arbitration. Figure 3.12 shows an outline of the remedies available.

Damages and specific performance

The remedies available under the Act do not prevent the consumer from also seeking damages or specific performance.

Statutory right breached	Remedies
Performance with reasonable care and skill (s. 50)	Repeat performance (s. 56) Possibly, price reduction (s. 57)
Performance within a reasonable time (s. 53)	Price reduction (s. 57)
Not performed according to information which was supplied, or which legislation required to be supplied, to the consumer (s. 51)	Repeat performance (s. 56) Possibly, price reduction (s. 57)
If no price agreed, reasonable price to be paid (s. 52)	If applicable, price payable is a reasonable price (s. 57)

Figure 3.12 Remedies in respect of non-conforming services.

The information required by Articles 5 and 6 of the Consumer Rights Directive 2011/83/EU (CRD)

This Directive was implemented into UK law in 2013. As well as making changes to distance and off-premises contracts, Articles 5 and 6 require traders to supply information to consumers with whom they contract. As we have seen, several sections of the CRA provide that this information is to be treated as a term of the consumer contract.

Article 5

Article 5 paragraph 1 requires the trader to supply the following information if the contract is not a distance or off-premises contract: (a) the main characteristics of the goods; (b) the identity of the trader, such as trading name, the geographical address at which the trader is established and the trader's telephone number; (c) the total price of the goods or services inclusive of taxes, freight, delivery or postal charges; (d) the arrangements for payment, delivery and performance; the time by which the trader undertakes to deliver or perform; and the trader's compliant handling policy; (e) a reminder of the existence of a legal guarantee of conformity for goods and, where applicable, the existence and conditions of after-sales services and commercial guarantees; (f) the duration of the contract, where applicable, or, if the contract is of indeterminate duration or is to be extended automatically, the conditions for terminating the contract; (g) where applicable, the functionality of digital content, including appropriate technical protection measures; and (h) where applicable, any relevant interoperability of hardware and software that the trader is aware of or can reasonably be expected to have been aware of. The information in para. 1 does not need to be supplied to contracts which involve day-to-day transactions and which are performed immediately at the time of their conclusion, for example where a customer buys groceries in a shop.

Article 6

In addition to the information which Article 5 requires to be supplied, Article 6 requires the following information, which is to be regarded as forming part of the contract, to be supplied in distance and off-premises contracts: the cost of using the means of distance communication for the conclusion of the contract where the cost is calculated other than at the basic rate; where applicable, that the consumer will have to bear the cost of returning the goods in case of withdrawal; and, for distance contracts, if the goods cannot by their nature normally be returned by post, the cost of returning the goods.

Consumer guarantees

When the Consumer Rights Act 2015 comes into force the Sale and Supply of Goods to Consumers Regulations 2002 (SSGCR 2002) will be repealed, as their provisions will be incorporated into the CRA 2015.

The SSGCR 2002 brought in rules which apply to consumer guarantees. There is no need for a guarantee to be given when goods are sold. However, Regulation 15(1) provides that where goods are sold or otherwise supplied to a consumer, and a consumer guarantee is given, the guarantee takes effect as a contractual obligation under the conditions set out in the guarantee and associated advertising. So the guarantee and associated advertising become terms of the contract. Before the Regulations came into force, there was considerable doubt as to whether or not a consumer could enforce a guarantee.

A 'consumer' is here defined as a natural person (and therefore not a company) who is acting for purposes outside his trade, business or profession. It should be noticed that this EU definition of a consumer is quite different from the SGA 1979 and UCTA 1977 definition of 'dealing as a consumer'. A 'consumer guarantee' is defined as any undertaking to a consumer, given without extra charge by a person acting in the course of his business, to reimburse the price paid or to replace or handle consumer goods in any way if they do not meet the specifications set out in the guarantee or in the relevant advertising. This definition takes account of the fact that many guarantees do not offer to refund the price. They might merely agree to repair the goods and might require the consumer to pay costs such as postage and packing. So when goods bought by a consumer are defective, the primary remedy will be under s. 14(2) of the SGA 1979. However, a guarantee will be useful if the goods were of satisfactory quality when delivered but have become defective within the guarantee period, or if the consumer cannot reject the goods on account of having accepted them. The Regulations do not apply to contracts to provide services. They do apply to contracts to supply goods, whether the supply is by way of sale, lease, hire or hire-purchase.

Regulation 15(2) requires that the guarantee is written in plain, intelligible English and that it contains a statement that the consumer has statutory rights which are not affected by the guarantee. It also requires the guarantee to set out the essential particulars necessary for making claims, including the length of the guarantee period, the name and address of the guarantor and the countries in which the guarantee is effective. If the consumer requests a copy of the guarantee from either the retailer or the person giving the guarantee, then a copy must be supplied in writing. Trading standards officers can apply for injunctions to enforce the Regulations.

Exclusion clauses

Exclusion clauses, or exemption clauses as they are sometimes known, are clauses which try to exclude or limit one party's liability. Usually, the liability in question will have arisen as a result of an express or implied term of a contract. However, exclusion clauses can go further and can exclude other types of liability, such as liability arising in tort.

We shall see that Parliament has restricted the effect of exclusion clauses. The following case demonstrates how unfairly exclusion clauses could operate before Parliament intervened.

 L'Estrange v Graucob (1934) (Court of Appeal)

A café owner bought a cigarette vending machine and signed a sales agreement which she did not read. A term of this agreement which was 'in regrettably small print but quite legible', said that the machine did not need to work and that all statutory implied terms were not to apply. The machine did not work. The café owner sued to get her money back, claiming that s. 14(2) of the Sale of Goods Act had been breached.

Held The café owner failed, even though s. 14(2) of the Sale of Goods Act had clearly been breached. The claimant had signed the agreement and so she was bound by it.

Because of the unfairness of such cases, Parliament felt the necessity to intervene. In 1977 it passed the Unfair Contract Terms Act (UCTA 1977). We shall examine UCTA 1977 later in this chapter. When faced with an exclusion clause, however, the first step is to consider whether the exclusion clause was a term of the contract. If the clause was not a term of the contract, then it would not have any effect anyway, and it would not be necessary to consider the Act.

Is the exclusion clause a term of the contract?

It is always necessary when considering the effect of an exclusion clause in a contract to first decide whether or not the clause was a term of the contract. As we saw in **L'Estrange v Graucob**, a person who signs a document will be bound by its contents. Written, signed documents therefore present little difficulty in deciding whether or not an exclusion clause was a term of the contract. However, a person who misrepresents the effect of an exclusion clause may not be able to rely on it, even if the other party does sign the document which contains the clause. An example can be seen in **Curtis v Chemical Cleaning and Dyeing Co Ltd (1951)**, in which a customer who took her wedding dress to a dry cleaners was asked to sign a 'receipt'. The customer asked what it said and was told that it just covered liability for damage to beads and sequins. She signed the document, which in fact excluded all liability on the part of the dry cleaners. The wedding dress was badly stained and the dry cleaners tried to rely on their exclusion clause. The Court of Appeal held that they could not do so because they had misrepresented the effect of the clause.

If an exclusion clause is contained in a document, such as a train ticket, which the reasonable person would think was a part of the contract, then the term will be binding. If the clause was contained in a document, such as a receipt, which the reasonable person would not think contained the terms of the contract, then the clause will not be binding. Sometimes what the reasonable person would have thought is obvious enough. In other cases it can be very hard to tell.

 Chapelton v Barry UDC (1940) (Court of Appeal)

The claimant hired a deck chair for 2d (1p). When he sat in the chair it collapsed and he was injured. The hirers of the chair relied on an exclusion clause, which said that they were not liable for any accident or damage resulting from the hire of the deck chair. This clause had been printed on a slip of paper which the attendant issued to hirers of the chairs. It was possible to sit on a chair for an hour or two before the attendant took the money and issued the slip.

Held The clause was not a part of the contract because it was contained in a mere receipt. The reasonable person would not have expected the terms of the contract to be contained in such a receipt.

This case must be contrasted with **Thompson v London, Midland and Scottish Railway Co (1930)**, in which the Court of Appeal held that a train passenger who could not read was bound by an exclusion clause in the railway's timetables. The ticket was for a cheap excursion, and was said to be available subject to the company's timetable and regulations. The timetable was not free but was available to be purchased. It contained an exclusion clause. It was held that the passenger had been given reasonable notice of the exclusion clause.

An exclusion clause will be effective only if it was agreed as a term of the contract, or if reasonable notice of it was given before the contract was made. A term cannot later be put into a contract which has already been made.

Olley v Marlborough Court Hotel Ltd (1949) (Court of Appeal)

A married couple booked into a hotel for one week and paid their bill in advance. During their stay at the hotel the wife's fur coat was stolen from their room. The hotel denied liability because a notice in their room said that the hotel were not liable for lost or stolen property, unless it had been handed in to reception for safe custody.

Held The notice was too late to be effective. The contract was made when the couple booked into the hotel.

 Thornton v Shoe Lane Parking Ltd (1971) (Court of Appeal)

The claimant was badly injured in the defendants' car park, the accident being partly caused by the defendants' negligence. The claimant had driven into the car park and passed a notice at the entrance which said that cars were parked at the owner's risk. When the claimant stopped at a red light he was issued with a ticket. The ticket said on it that it was issued subject to notices displayed inside the car park. These notices, which could only be read once fully inside the car park, said that the defendants were not liable for damage to goods or for injuries to customers. The defendants denied liability for the claimant's injuries, saying that the conditions displayed inside the car park were a part of the contract.

Held The notices inside the car park were not a part of the contract. By the time the claimant had been given the ticket which referred to these notices the contract had been made. (The contract was made either at the time the claimant had put his money into the machine or when he drove past the point at which he could no longer change his mind about entering the car park.)

Earlier in this chapter we saw that a term can be implied into a contract because of a course of dealing between the parties. We considered **Kendall v Lillico**, in which the House of Lords held that an exclusion clause was a part of an oral contract. This was because the parties had often made similar oral contracts, and on each occasion the seller had sent a 'sold note' which always contained exactly the same terms. All the terms in the sold note, including several exclusion clauses, were therefore implied into the oral contract. We also saw that terms can be implied on the basis that they are customary in a particular trade or industry. **British Crane Hire Corpn Ltd v Ipswich Plant Hire Ltd (1975)** provides an example. The claimants needed a crane in a hurry and made an oral contract to hire one from the defendants. This contract was made subject to all the terms in the 'Contractors' Plant Association Form' because both sides knew that whenever cranes were hired they were hired subject to the terms contained in this form.

Does the exclusion clause cover the breach which occurred?

An exclusion clause will not exclude liability for a breach of contract unless the court is satisfied that the wording of the clause has this effect. When considering the effect of exclusion clauses the courts interpret them *contra preferentum* (against the wishes) of the party who wants to rely on them. So the wording will need to clearly exclude liability or it will not do so.

Only if the court does decide that the exclusion clause was a term of the contract and that it excluded liability for the loss which arose will it be necessary to move on to consider the effect of the Unfair Contracts Terms Act 1977 and the Unfair Terms in Consumer Contracts Regulations 1999.

The Unfair Contract Terms Act 1977

When the Consumer Rights Act 2015 comes into force, the provisions of the UCTA 1977 which protect consumers will be replaced by provisions in the CRA 2015. The ways in which the CRA 2015 protects consumers against unfair contract terms and notices is explained towards the end of this chapter.

Contracts covered by the Act

The important sections of UCTA 1977 apply only to business liability. This is defined by s. 1 of the Act as liability which arises:

- from things done or to be done by a person in the course of a business; or
- from the occupation of premises used for the business purposes of the occupier.

So, in general, a person who is not in business will not be subject to the Act. However, s. 12(1) SGA 1979 (the implied term as to the right to sell) can never be excluded. Nor can the corresponding terms in SGITA 1973 and SGSA 1982. Furthermore, a person who is not in business will be subject to s. 6 UCTA 1977, the effect of which is explained below.

The effect of the Act

Section 2 – Excluding liability arising from negligence

Section 2(1) provides that no contract term can exclude liability for death or personal injury arising from negligence.

Section 2(2) provides that liability for other types of loss or damage arising from negligence, such as damage to goods, can be excluded if the term excluding liability was reasonable.

(Schedule 2 to the Act and s. 11 define what reasonable means, and we will look at these later in this chapter.)

 Smith v Eric S Bush (1989) (House of Lords)

The claimant applied to a building society for a mortgage to buy a house. The building society employed the defendants to make a survey of the house. The claimant paid £40 to the building society, who agreed to supply her with a copy of the report. A disclaimer said that neither the building society nor the surveyors would be liable for any inaccuracies. The report itself also carried a similar disclaimer. The report said that the house was worth £16,000 and that no major building work was necessary. Eighteen months later the chimneys fell through the roof because a chimney breast had been removed without proper supports being fitted. The claimant sued the defendants for negligence.

Held The defendants were liable to the claimant in the tort of negligence. The disclaimer which excluded liability had to be reasonable under UCTA s. 2(2). It was not reasonable and so it did not apply.

Comment If the claimant had been killed or injured by the falling chimneys, then s. 2(1) UCTA 1977 would have applied. It would not have been possible for any term to exclude liability for the death or injury if it was caused by negligence. It would not therefore have been necessary to consider whether or not any term which tried to do so was reasonable.

Earlier in this chapter we examined s. 13 SGSA 1982. It provides that where a service is supplied in the course of a business, a term is implied that the service is supplied using reasonable care and skill. Whenever s. 13 SGSA 1982 is breached, the UCTA 1977 regards this as negligence. Therefore, s. 2 UCTA 1977 will determine the extent to which liability for breach of s. 13 SGSA 1982 can be excluded, if it can be excluded at all.

Section 3 – Liability arising in contract

Section 3 protects two classes of people who make a contract:

(1) those who 'deal as a consumer'; and

(2) those who deal on the other party's written standard terms.

Before considering what protection s. 3 offers, we should be clear about exactly who is protected.

The Act makes a very important distinction between a person who deals 'as a consumer' and a person who does not.

Section 12(1) UCTA defines dealing as a consumer by saying that a person deals as a consumer if:

● he neither makes the contract in the course of a business nor holds himself out as doing so; and

● the seller does make the contract in the course of a business.

Unfortunately, the words 'in the course of a business' do not have the same meaning here as they have in s. 14 SGA 1979. When we considered s. 14, earlier in this chapter, we saw that **Stevenson v Rogers** held that whenever a business sells anything it does so in the course of a business, for the purposes of s. 14 SGA. When considering the meaning of the words 'in the course of a business' in s. 12 UCTA 1977, the test set out in **R & B Customs Brokers Ltd v United Dominions Trust Ltd (1988)** must be used. This test allows a business to buy goods without buying them 'in the course of a business'. It regards a buyer as acting in the course of a business only if the contract is an integral part of the business. The case also explains what this means. A purchase by a business will be made as an integral part of the business in only three circumstances:

(1) If the goods the business bought are the type of goods which the business is in business to sell. For example, if a car dealer buys a car this contract will be an integral part of the business and so the dealer will not deal as a consumer.

(2) If the goods are not the type of goods the business usually sells, but they were bought with the intention of selling them at a profit. For example, if a car dealer bought a yacht, intending to sell it at a profit.

(3) If the goods are the type of goods which the business buys fairly regularly. For example, if a car dealer bought petrol to be used in demonstration cars.

It does seem unfortunate that the words 'in the course of a business' have different meanings, depending upon whether they are used in s. 14 SGA or s. 12 UCTA. However, in **Feldaroll Foundry plc v Hermes Leasing (London) Ltd (2004)** the Court of Appeal confirmed that this was the case.

If the buyer is a company, then a further requirement is added by s. 12(1)(c) UCTA. This requirement is that the goods supplied under the contract must be of a type ordinarily supplied for private use or consumption. In **R & B Customs Brokers** this condition was satisfied when an import and export company bought a car. If the company had bought a

JCB digging machine, then it could not have dealt as a consumer because this is not a type of goods which are ordinarily used for private use or consumption. A JCB is a type of goods ordinarily bought only for business use.

Figure 3.13 shows how to decide whether or not a person deals as a consumer for the purposes of UCTA 1977. Since the SGA 1979 uses the UCTA definition of dealing as a consumer, the figure also applies to the SGA. We have already seen that s. 15A SGA applies only where the buyer deals as a consumer. We have also seen that the new remedies in SGA ss. 48A–48F apply only where a buyer deals as a consumer.

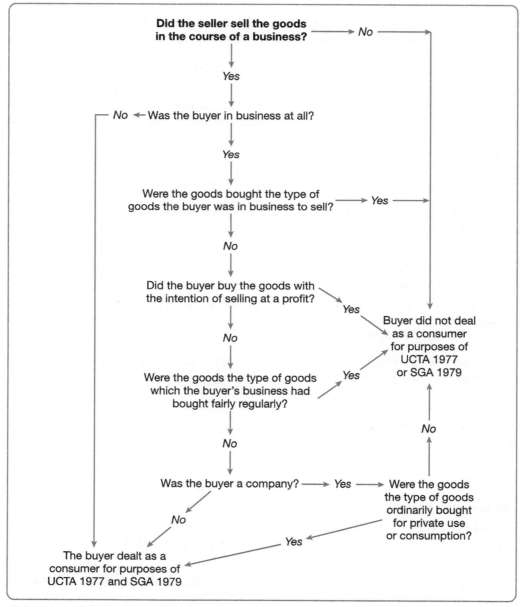

Figure 3.13 Did the buyer deal as a consumer for purposes of UCTA and SGA?

A person deals on the other party's written standard terms when the same written terms are used whenever the business deals with this person or whenever it deals with customers generally. Matters such as the price and quantity may of course be different. Contracts to hire tools or cars are usually made on standard terms, as are terms referred to on bus or train tickets.

Having decided that a person is either dealing as a consumer or dealing on the other party's written standard terms, the protection given by s. 3 is as follows:

- an exclusion clause cannot protect a party against liability for breach of contract unless this is reasonable; and

- an exclusion clause cannot protect a party who fails to perform the contract at all, or who performs in a manner different from what was reasonably expected, unless this is reasonable.

Sections 6 and 7 – Exclusion of statutory implied terms

Sections 6 and 7 of the Unfair Contract Terms Act 1977 deals with exclusion of liability for breach of the terms implied by ss. 12–15 SGA 1979 and the corresponding terms implied by the SGITA 1973 and the SGSA 1982. These implied terms were considered earlier in this chapter.

Sections 6 and 7 UCTA 1977 provide that no term can exclude liability for breach of the implied term as to the right to sell, contained in s. 12(1) SGA 1979. Nor can any term exclude liability for breach of the corresponding terms contained in the SGITA 1973 or the SGSA 1982.

The terms implied by ss. 13–15 of the Sale of Goods Act 1979 (and the corresponding terms implied by the SGITA 1973 and the SGSA 1982) are treated differently. As regards these terms, ss. 6 and 7 UCTA 1977 make two rules.

(1) If the buyer deals as a consumer, none of the statutory implied terms can be excluded by any contract term.

(2) If the buyer does not deal as a consumer, the statutory implied terms can be excluded, but only to the extent that the term which does exclude them satisfies the UCTA 1977's requirement of reasonableness.

One further point should be noted. A person who buys at an auction or by tender is never to be regarded as dealing as a consumer.

Section 8 – Excluding liability for misrepresentations

Section 8 UCTA 1977 provides that no term can restrict liability for misrepresentation, unless the term satisfies the requirement of reasonableness.

The effect of UCTA 1977 is undoubtedly rather complex. Figure 3.14 might make it more easily understood.

The meaning of reasonableness

Most of the sections of the UCTA 1977 which we have considered do allow an exclusion clause to be effective if the clause satisfies the Act's requirement of reasonableness.

Section 11 says that the requirement is satisfied if:

> the term shall have been a fair and reasonable one to be included having regard to the circumstances which were, or ought reasonably to have been, known to or in the contemplation of the parties when the contract was made.

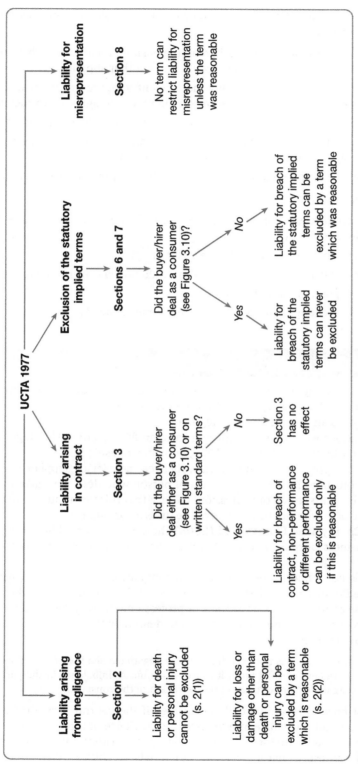

Figure 3.14 The effect of UCTA 1977

Schedule 2 to the Act says that regard must be had to the following, in deciding whether or not a term was reasonable:

(1) The relative strength of the parties' bargaining position relative to each other, which will include whether or not the customer could find another supplier.

(2) Whether the customer was given any inducement to agree to the term, or could have made a similar contract with a different supplier without agreeing to such a term.

(3) Whether the customer knew or ought to have known that the term existed.

(4) If the term excludes liability unless some condition is complied with, whether or not it was reasonably practicable to comply with that condition.

(5) Whether the goods were manufactured, altered or adapted at the customer's request.

So, for example, a term would be more likely to be reasonable if:

● the parties were of equal bargaining power; or if the customer could have bought from plenty of other people; or

● if he was given money off to agree to the term; or

● if he could have dealt with someone else who would not have insisted on a similar term; or

● if the term was pointed out to him; or

● if the goods were changed to suit the customer's special needs.

The Unfair Terms in Consumer Contracts Regulations 1999

When the Consumer Rights Act 2015 comes into force the UTCCR 1999 will be repealed, as their provisions will be incorporated into the CRA 2015.

Figure 3.15 gives an overview of the Regulations.

These Regulations were passed to give effect to an EC directive. The Regulations do not replace the Unfair Contracts Terms Act 1977, but run alongside it.

The Regulations apply only to contracts made between a 'seller' or 'supplier' and a 'consumer' (reg. 4(1)). A consumer is defined as a natural person who does not make the contract in the course of a business, trade or profession. (Notice that this test is quite different from the UCTA 1977 test as to whether or not a buyer deals as a consumer.)

In **Evans v Cherry Tree Finance Ltd (2008)** the Court of Appeal held that a loan taken partly for a business purpose and partly for a non-business purpose was covered by the regulations.

A company is not a natural person and so a company can never be a consumer for the purposes of the Regulations. Sellers and suppliers are defined as people who supply goods or services in the course of a business, trade or profession. The Regulations apply to contracts to supply goods or services and are not limited to dealing with exclusion clauses.

Regulation 5(1) provides that:

> A contractual term which has not been individually negotiated shall be regarded as unfair if, contrary to the requirement of good faith, it causes a significant imbalance in the parties' rights and obligations arising under the contract, to the detriment of the consumer.

A term will not have been individually negotiated if the contract was drafted in advance and the consumer had no chance to influence the substance of the term (reg. 5(2)). This is obviously a similar concept to the UCTA 1977 concept of 'written standard terms'. It is for the seller or supplier to prove that a term was individually negotiated (reg. 5(4)). In deciding

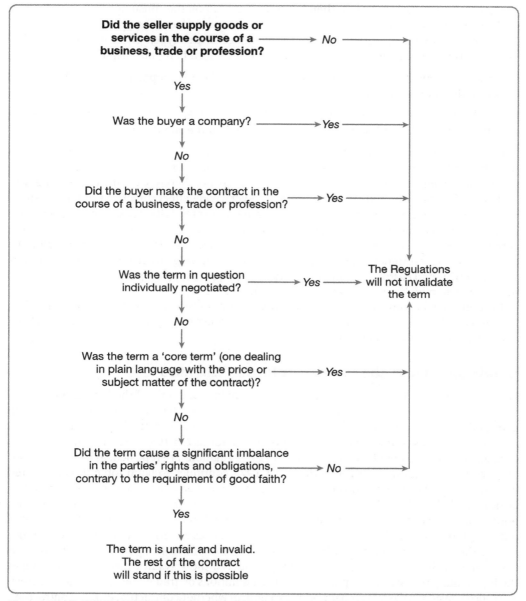

Figure 3.15 Will the UTCC Regulations 1999 invalidate a term?

whether or not the requirement of good faith has been breached, the court will consider all relevant circumstances. In **Director General of Fair Trading *v* First National Bank (2001)** Lord Bingham said that 'the requirement of significant imbalance is met if a term is so weighted in favour of the supplier as to tilt the parties' rights and obligations under the contract significantly in his favour'. Lord Bingham also said that good faith required fair and open dealing, so that there were no hidden traps for the consumer. If terms were disadvantageous to the consumer they should be given prominence, and if the consumer was in a disadvantageous position the supplier should not take advantage of this.

If a term is regarded as unfair, then it is not binding upon the consumer, although the rest of the contact will stand if this is possible without the unfair term (reg. 8).

Schedule 2 to the Regulations sets out examples of the types of terms which may be regarded as unfair. The list is far too long to be reproduced here, but includes:

- making the consumer subject to terms which he had no real opportunity to find out about before the contract was made;
- making a consumer in breach of contract pay too much by way of compensation; and
- making the consumer bound by the agreement when the supplier is not.

The Regulations can consider the effect of any term in a contract except a 'core' term which was written in plain and intelligible language. A 'core' term sets out the contract price or the main subject matter of the contract. The Regulations are not therefore confined to dealing with exclusion clauses. Potentially, they could have a very wide effect. In **Office of Fair Trading v Abbey National and others (2009)** the Supreme Court held that terms which allowed for bank charges to be made when customers overdrew their accounts without permission were core terms, as they set out the price of having a bank account. They could not therefore be assessed for fairness under the Regulations. The price of having an account with the bank was not the same for all customers. Banking services to customers were a package. Customers who overdrew paid a higher price than those who did not.

In addition to making unfair terms not binding upon consumers, the Regulations also allow the Director General of Fair Trading to apply for an injunction to prevent an unfair term from being used in contracts made with consumers.

Unfair terms and the Consumer Rights Act 2015

When the CRA 2015 comes into force it will consolidate and amend the law on unfair contract terms. However, it applies only to 'consumer contracts', that is to say contracts between a 'trader' and a 'consumer', and to 'consumer notices'. Previously, the law relating to unfair contract terms was contained in the Unfair Contract Terms Act 1977 and the Unfair Terms in Consumer Contracts Regulations 1999. The 1999 Regulations are repealed, as their provisions are now to be found in the CRA 2015. UCTA 1977 continues to be in force. It is unaltered insofar as it applies to non-consumer contracts and non-consumer notices. However, it has been amended so that all of the provisions applicable to consumer contracts and consumer notices are repealed. Some of these provisions are now to be found in the CRA 2015. It is important to note that the SGA 1979 concept of 'dealing as a consumer' has become redundant, as the 2015 Act uses a wholly different definition of a consumer. This definition was considered earlier in this chapter when we considered the ways in which the CRA changes the law relating to statutory implied terms. The definitions of 'trader' and 'consumer contract' were also considered. A 'consumer notice' is a notice, whether contractual or non-contractual, which: (a) relates to rights or obligations between a trader and a consumer; or (b) purports to exclude or restrict a trader's liability to a consumer. This is the case even if the notice was not expressed to apply to a consumer as long as it is reasonable to assume that it was intended to be read by a consumer. A consumer notice can take the form of an announcement as well as any other communication or purported communication.

General rules about fairness of contract terms and notices

Section 63(1) and (2) provide that neither an unfair term of a consumer contract, nor an unfair consumer notice, is binding on the consumer. This, however, does not prevent the consumer from relying on the term or notice if he chooses to do so.

Section 63(4) provides that a term of a consumer contract, or a consumer notice, is unfair if, contrary to the requirement of good faith, it causes a significant imbalance in the parties' rights and obligations under the contract to the detriment of the consumer. This replicates reg. 5(1) of the 1999 Regulations, which were considered earlier in this chapter. However, s. 63 applies even if the term was individually negotiated. Whether a term or notice is fair is to be determined for these purposes: (a) by taking into account the nature of the subject matter of the contract; and (b) by reference to all the circumstances existing when the term was agreed and to all of the other terms of the contract or of any other contract on which it depends.

As we saw earlier in this chapter, it is not possible to restrict or exclude liability for breach of any of the implied terms relating to goods, digital content or services.

Section 64 provides that the 20 terms set out in an indicative and non-exhaustive list in Part 1 of Schedule 2 may be regarded as unfair. This list of terms is known as the 'grey list' and is very similar to the grey list in the 1999 Regulations. These terms are not automatically unfair but the court can use them when considering whether a term of a particular contract is unfair. A term in a contract can be unfair even though it is not included in the grey list.

Section 65 excludes from assessment of unfairness the 'core terms' of the contract. These terms specify the main subject matter of the contract or the appropriateness of the price paid by the consumer. However, this is the case only if the term in question is transparent and prominent.

Section 66 reiterates s. 2(1) UCTA 1977 by providing that a trader cannot, by either a consumer contract or a consumer notice, exclude or restrict liability for death or personal injury resulting from negligence. There is no direct equivalent of s. 2(2) UCTA, which deals with the exclusion of loss or damage other than death or personal injury caused by negligence. However, such loss or damage will almost always be caused by a trader when the trader is providing a service to a consumer, and in such a situation s. 58 prevents the trader from contracting out of his s. 50 duty to perform the service with reasonable care and skill. Obviously, a trader who performed the service negligently would breach s. 50. If a consumer suffered loss other than death or personal injury caused by the trader's negligence when a service was not being provided, for example when buying goods in a shop, or when otherwise lawfully visiting a trader's property, then the trader would be liable in the tort of negligence or under the Occupier's Liability Act 1957. Any contract term or consumer notice which attempted to exclude the trader's liability would seem very likely to be unfair and would therefore not be binding upon the consumer by virtue of s. 63.

Where a contract term is not binding on the consumer on account of being unfair, s. 68 provides that the contract continues, as far as practicable, to have effect in every other respect. Section 69 requires a trader to ensure that a written term of a consumer contract, or a consumer notice, is transparent. It also requires any especially onerous or unusual term to be drawn particularly to the consumer's attention. Section 70 provides that if any term or notice is ambiguous the ambiguity must be resolved in the way most favourable to the consumer. Section 72 imposes a duty on a court to consider whether a term in a consumer contract is fair even if neither party intends to raise this issue.

Consumer Rights (Payment Surcharges) Regulations 2012

The Consumer Rights (Payment Surcharges) Regulations 2012 prohibit traders from making consumers pay payment surcharges, unless the surcharges represent the actual processing costs borne by the trader. The Regulations apply to payments made under contracts to provide goods or services. Any provision which requires the consumer to pay more than the trader's actual processing costs is unenforceable, and any excess paid has to be refunded to the consumer.

Essential points

- The terms of a contract define the obligations which the parties to the contract have undertaken.
- A breach of contract occurs whenever a term of the contract is breached.
- Express terms are agreed in words by the parties to the contract.
- Terms may be implied into a contract either by the court or by a statute.
- The Sale of Goods Act 1979 implies five major terms into contracts of sale of goods. The implied terms are:
  - that the seller has the right to sell the goods;
  - that the goods correspond to any description by which they were sold;
  - that goods sold in the course of a business are of satisfactory quality;
  - that goods sold in the course of a business are fit for the buyer's purpose;
  - that, where goods are sold by sample, the bulk of the goods corresponds with the sample in quality.
- A consumer who buys goods which do not conform to the contract is given a hierarchy of rights, these rights being additional to any other rights which the consumer might have.
- When the Consumer Rights Act 2015 comes into force it will change the statutory terms which are implied into consumer contracts. The law will not be changed as regards non-consumer contracts.
- Exclusion clauses are clauses which try to exclude or limit one party's liability for breach of contract or for liability arising in tort.
- The Unfair Contract Terms Act 1977 provides that no contract term can exclude liability for death or personal injury arising from negligence.
- In non-consumer deals, liability for breach of the statutory implied terms as to satisfactory quality, fitness for purpose, correspondence with description and correspondence with sample can be excluded only by a term which is reasonable. When a buyer deals as a consumer these implied terms can never be excluded.
- Only a term which is reasonable can restrict or exclude liability for misrepresentation.
- The Unfair Terms in Consumer Contracts Regulations 1999 apply only to consumer contracts.
- When the Consumer Rights Act 2015 comes into force it will amend the law relating to exclusion clauses in consumer contracts. The law will not be changed as regards non-consumer contracts.

Practice questions

1 Janice, who owns a garden centre, agreed to buy a second-hand tractor from Gerald, a farmer, for £6,500. Janice also agreed to buy 100 sacks of King Edward seed potatoes from Giles, another farmer. Gerald delivered the tractor to Janice. Eighteen months later the police took the tractor away from Janice, explaining that it had been stolen

from Oswald two years ago. Gerald had bought the tractor at an auction and had no idea that it was stolen. At the time when the police took the tractor away it was worth about £2,000 as Janice had used it very extensively. The seed potatoes which Giles delivered were Maris Piper, not King Edwards. Janice was not very bothered about this, as she thought that customers were as likely to buy Maris Piper seed potatoes as they were to buy King Edwards. However, the day after the seed potatoes were delivered, Janice saw a documentary on the television saying that Maris Piper potatoes had been linked to a certain type of cancer. In the light of the documentary Janice does not think that she will be able to sell any of the potatoes once they have been grown. Advise Janice of her legal position as regards both Gerald and Giles.

2 Keith, a market trader, bought ten portable CD players from CDMaker Ltd. The following day Keith sold three of these on his market stall. All three customers have returned the CD players which they bought to Keith's stall and demanded a refund. They claim that the CD players do not work properly as they spring open when being played. Keith finds that this is true, but that the problem can easily be fixed by tightening a screw. The customers refuse to accept this repair and are demanding their money back. Advise Keith of his legal position as regards both his customers and CDMaker Ltd.

3 Manufacturer Ltd pay Service Co £2,000 to service their two boilers. After the service has been completed, Manufacturer Ltd find that neither boiler can be used. The problem with the first boiler was caused by Service Co inserting a replacement valve which did not work properly. Service Co could not have discovered in advance that the valve was faulty because it had been bought as new and looked perfectly all right. The problem with the second boiler was caused by an unknown problem. No parts were supplied or changed and Service Co say that they serviced the boiler while adhering strictly to a code of practice which is widely accepted in the boiler servicing trade. The boiler did not work before the service was carried out and nor did it work afterwards. Advise Manufacturer Ltd of their legal position as regards the defects in the two boilers.

4 A retailer buys a television from a manufacturer. The retailer hires the television to a consumer for a three-month period. The television was badly manufactured, so that its back casing is not tightly fitted together. The retailer could easily have tightened several screws and fixed this defect but did not do so before hiring the television to the consumer. As regards both the sale by the manufacturer and the contract of hire by the retailer, explain which sections of which statutes have been breached and the remedies available.

5 Service Co service a boiler for Buildem Ltd. The contract is made on Service Co's new written standard terms. One term of the contract states that: 'Neither Service Co nor any of its employees can be liable in any way for any loss, injury or damage caused by faulty workmanship.' The Service Co employee who services the boiler forgets to fasten a plate securely. This problem causes the boiler to explode. The explosion badly burns the managing director of Buildem Ltd, completely destroys the boiler and causes extensive damage to Buildem Ltd's factory. Advise Buildem Ltd of their legal position.

6 Satvinder is a keen ballroom dancer and often stays at the Dance Hotel. A prominently displayed notice at the entrance to the Dance Hotel states that: 'All hotel guests are warned that the management cannot be held responsible for the loss of items left in hotel rooms.' Satvinder leaves her handbag in her room while she goes dancing. When she returns she finds that her handbag has been stolen. A chambermaid opened

Satvinder's room but then forgot to lock it. An opportunistic thief then slipped into the room and stole the handbag. Advise Satvinder of her legal position.

7 Explain the protection which the requirement of satisfactory quality, set out in Sale of Goods Act 1979 s. 14(2), gives to buyers of goods. Explain also the remedies available to a buyer of goods if s. 14(2) is breached.

Task 3

A friend of yours who is visiting the country from abroad is thinking of setting up a trading company in the United Kingdom. Your friend is keen to understand English law as it relates to contractual terms, and has asked you to draft a report explaining the following matters:

(a) How the express terms of a contract come to be included in the contract.

(b) The circumstances in which a court will imply terms into a contract.

(c) The terms which are implied into contracts of sale of goods by the Sale of Goods Act 1979.

(d) Other types of contracts into which statutes imply terms similar to those implied by the Sale of Goods Act 1979.

(e) The terms which are implied into a contract to provide services by the Supply of Goods and Services Act 1982.

(f) The effect of the Unfair Contract Terms Act 1977.

(g) The effect of the Unfair Terms in Consumer Contracts Regulations 1999.

mylawchamber

Visit **www.mylawchamber.co.uk/macintyreessentials** to access tools to help you develop and test your knowledge of business law, including interactive multiple choice questions, practice exam questions with guidance, weblinks, glossary, glossary flashcards, legal newsfeed and legal updates.

Use **Case Navigator** to read in full some of the key cases referenced in this chapter with commentary and questions:

Hong Kong Fir Case (1962)

Stevenson v Rogers (1999)

4

Misrepresentation, mistake, duress and illegality

This chapter deals with matters which can invalidate a contract. The first of these matters is misrepresentation. A misrepresentation is made when a statement which is not a part of the contract, but which induced the making of the contract, proves to be false. Remedies are available to the party who was induced by the misrepresentation to make the contract. However, as we shall see, these remedies can easily be lost.

Sometimes the parties make a contract while they are mistaken as to some fundamental fact. Depending upon the nature of the mistake made, it is possible for a contract to be rendered void on account of a mistake having been made.

A contract is made under duress when a party is pushed into it in such a way that he or she did not really consent to it. When a contract is made under duress, or where it is made on account of the undue influence of someone else, the contract can be avoided by the victimised party.

This chapter concludes by examining the grounds on which a contract may be void or illegal.

The difference between terms and representations

A contract is made up of terms and the express terms are inserted into the contract by the parties (see Chapter 3). The offeror proposes a set of terms in the offer. If the offeree accepts the offer, the proposed terms become the terms of the contract. If any term is breached, the injured party will always have a remedy for breach of contract.

Frequently, however, a person is persuaded to make a contract by a statement which is not a part of the contract. Such a statement cannot be a term. If this statement turns out to be untrue, the injured party might or might not have a remedy for misrepresentation. To sue for misrepresentation, however, is not the same as to sue for breach of contract. Not only are the remedies different, but also the whole basis of the action is different. It is therefore necessary to distinguish terms and representations.

Written contracts

In written contracts the express terms will be contained in the written document. Statements which are not contained in the written document cannot be terms but can be representations.

Example

Sarah buys a car from a dealer, and the terms of sale are spelt out in a standard form contract. When both parties sign this contract they expressly agree to all of its terms. If any of the terms are breached, then the injured party will always have a remedy for breach of contract. However, if Sarah was persuaded to sign the standard form contract because the dealer made an untrue statement (perhaps saying that all the cars would be going up in price the following week, when this was not true), then the dealer has not breached a term, but has only made an untrue representation. As no term has been breached, Sarah will not be able to sue for breach of contract. She might, however, have a remedy for misrepresentation.

Similarly, it might have been Sarah who made an untrue statement which caused the dealer to make the contract. A customer who pays with a cheque impliedly makes the statement that the cheque will be honoured. If this implied statement was untrue, because the cheque was stolen and would be dishonoured, the customer would not be breaching a term of the contract. The customer would, however, be making an untrue representation, and the dealer might have a remedy for misrepresentation.

So when both parties have signed a written contract, there is not too much difficulty in telling a term from a representation. Statements included in the written contract will be terms, statements not included can only be representations.

Oral contracts

Where a contract is made orally it is much harder to tell a term from a representation. It is still the case that a term is a part of the contract and a representation is not. However, it can be much harder to tell exactly which statements were included in the contract.

By way of example, let us assume that a farmer, Giles, orally offered to sell his combine harvester to Javed for £1,000. Javed accepted, because shortly before the sale Giles said that the harvester had recently had a new engine fitted. After the contract was made Javed discovered that the harvester had not had a new engine fitted. Was Giles's statement about the new engine a term of the contract, or only a representation?

The courts decide questions such as this by asking whether the reasonable person would have thought that the parties intended the statement to be a term or a representation.

This objective test is necessary because once again there is no point in looking for the opinions of the parties themselves. If the court asks Giles whether he thought that the statement about the new engine was a term or a representation, Giles is likely to say that he thought it was just a representation. If the court asks Javed, he is likely to say that he thought it was a term.

Over the years the courts have devised various tests to decide what the reasonable person would have thought.

Strong statements are likely to be terms

The stronger the statement made, the more likely it is to be a term.

Schawel *v* Reade (1913) (House of Lords)

The claimant was considering buying a horse to be used for stud purposes. The defendant said: 'You need not look for anything; the horse is perfectly sound. If there was anything the matter with the horse I would tell you.' Three weeks later the claimant bought the horse, which turned out to be utterly useless for stud purposes.

Held The defendant's statement was a term. It was so strong that it was the basis on which the offer and acceptance were made.

The weaker the statement, the more likely it is to be a representation.

 Ecay *v* Godfrey (1947)

The claimant bought a boat for £750. Before selling the boat, the defendant said that the boat was sound and capable of going overseas. However, he also advised the claimant to have it surveyed before making the purchase. The claimant bought the boat, without having it surveyed, and soon discovered that it was not at all sound.

Held The statement that the boat was sound was only a representation. It was not a part of the contract because it was a very guarded statement.

The reliance shown to be placed upon the statement

If one of the parties demonstrates that the statement is considered to be vitally important, then the statement is likely to be a term.

 Bannerman *v* White (1861)

The claimant, a merchant who traded in hops, sent around a circular to all the hop farmers with whom he dealt. The circular said that the claimant would no longer buy hops which had been treated with sulphur, because the Burton-upon-Trent brewers would not use them. When later buying a consignment of hops from the defendant, the claimant asked if they had been treated with sulphur, adding that if they had he would not buy them at any price. The defendant said that they had not been treated with sulphur, but in fact some of them had.

Held The defendant's statement was a term. The claimant had demonstrated that he considered the statement to be vitally important.

Comment The defendant's statement was not a term just because the claimant considered it to be vitally important. It was a term because the claimant demonstrated that he considered the term to be vitally important. The reasonable person cannot objectively deduce what the parties are thinking unless the circumstances give some indication of what they are thinking.

The relative knowledge of the parties

A party who has more knowledge about the subject matter of the contract is likely to make terms. A party with less knowledge is likely to make representations. For example, in **Oscar Chess Ltd v Williams (1957)** a customer traded in a car to a car dealer, saying that the car was a 1948 model. In fact, the car was a 1939 model. The customer did not know this because the car's documents said that it was a 1948 model. The customer's statement was only a representation because the dealer was as well placed as the customer to know the true age of the car. By contrast, in **Dick Bentley (Productions) Ltd v Harold Smith (Motors) Ltd (1965)** a motor dealer sold a car to the claimant, saying that the car had only done 20,000 miles since having a new engine fitted. In fact the car had done 100,000 miles. The dealer's statement was a term. The dealer, with his greater knowledge of cars, had much more chance of knowing that the statement was untrue than the claimant had.

It is important to remember that the tests we have used to distinguish terms and representations are useful only to indicate what the parties seemed to have intended. In **Heilbut, Symons & Co v Buckleton (1913)** Lord Moulton said that the various tests were valuable but not decisive. The real test is the apparent intentions of the parties, which can be deduced only by looking at all of the evidence.

Figure 4.1 gives an overview of how terms and representations are distinguished.

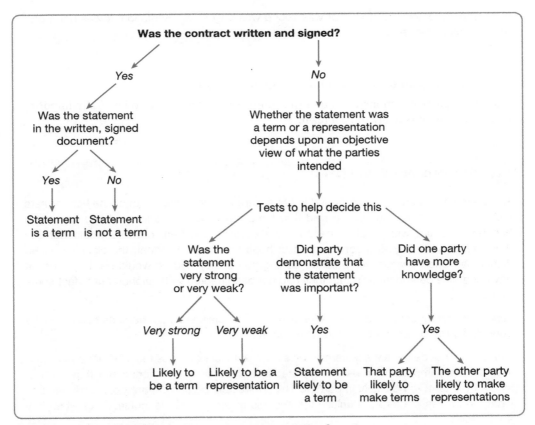

Figure 4.1 Was a statement a term or a representation?

Actionable misrepresentation

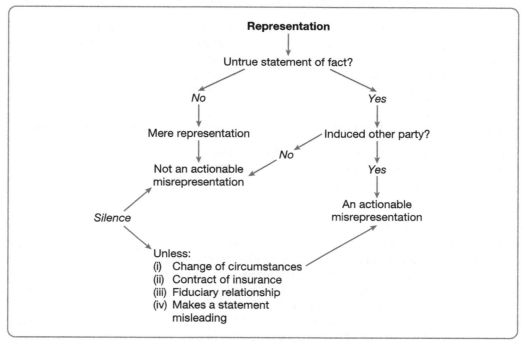

Figure 4.2 How a representation becomes an actionable misrepresentation

A breached term always gives the injured party the right to a remedy for breach of contract. An untrue representation will lead to a remedy if it amounts to an actionable misrepresentation. If, however, the representation does not fit within the definition of an actionable misrepresentation, then it will be a mere representation and no remedy will be available. Figure 4.2 provides an overview of how a representation becomes an actionable misrepresentation.

Definition of a misrepresentation

An actionable misrepresentation is an untrue statement of fact which induced the other party to make the contract.

The statement must be one of fact

Statements of mere opinion are not capable of being misrepresentations.

 Bisset *v* Wilkinson (1927) (Privy Council)

The claimant bought a farm because the defendant told him that the farm would support 2,000 sheep. The claimant knew that the farm had never before been used for sheep farming. In fact the farm, no matter how well managed, could not support anything like 2,000 sheep.

Held The statement was just an opinion and could not therefore amount to a misrepresentation.

However, some statements of opinion imply statements of fact, as the following case shows.

 Smith *v* Land and House Property Corporation (1884) (Court of Appeal)

The claimants offered their hotel for sale, stating that it was occupied by 'Mr Frederick Fleck (a most desirable tenant)'. Before the sale went through, Mr Fleck went bankrupt. The defendants discovered that for some time Mr Fleck had been badly in arrears with his rent. They refused to go ahead with the purchase of the hotel, claiming that the statement that Mr Fleck was a most desirable tenant amounted to a misrepresentation.

Held The statement was a misrepresentation. It sounded like a mere statement of opinion, but it implied facts (such as the fact that the tenant paid the rent) which justified the opinion.

Bowen LJ said: '. . . if the facts are not equally known to both sides, then a statement of opinion by the one who knows the facts best involves very often a statement of a material fact, for he impliedly states that he knows facts which justify his opinion.'

Misrepresentations made without words

In **Spice Girls Ltd *v* Aprilia World Service BV (2000)** a company representing a pop group, the Spice Girls, made an advertisement for another company. All of the Spice Girls took part in the filming of this advertisement. Shortly afterwards, one of the Spice Girls left the group. When the contract for the advertisement was signed, all of the group knew that one of them was about to leave the group. It was held that the act of taking part in the filming amounted to a representation by the company that it did not know at that time, and had no reasonable grounds to believe, that one of the group intended to leave.

The statement must induce the other party to make the contract

A statement can amount to a misrepresentation only if it was one of the reasons why the claimant made the contract. If a person makes a contract without checking the truth of a statement, this suggests that the statement did induce the making of the contract.

 Redgrave *v* Hurd (1881)

The claimant, a solicitor, advertised for a partner who would also buy the solicitor's house and solicitor's practice. The defendant answered the advertisement and was told that the practice made about £300 p.a. The claimant produced papers which he said would prove that his statement about the value of the practice was true, but the defendant did not read the papers. If he had done so, he would have discovered that the practice made only £200 p.a. When the defendant did discover that the practice made only £200 p.a. he refused to go ahead with the purchase.

Held The claimant's statement about the value of the practice was a misrepresentation. It could therefore be used as a defence for not going ahead with the contract. The fact that the defendant did not check the papers showed that the claimant's statement did induce the defendant to make the contract.

A person who checks the truth of a statement cannot later say that the statement induced the making a contract.

Attwood v Small (1838) (Court of Appeal)

The claimant bought a mine because the defendant greatly exaggerated the capacity of the mine. Before buying the mine the claimant got his own experts to check the defendant's statement. The experts mistakenly agreed that the defendant's statement was true.

Held The statement about the mine's capacity was not a misrepresentation because the claimant did not rely on it. By appointing his own experts to check the statement, the claimant proved that he did not rely on it.

Silence as a misrepresentation

Generally, silence cannot be a misrepresentation. The old rule *caveat emptor* (let the buyer beware) applies.

 Fletcher v Krell (1873)

The claimant applied for a job as a governess without revealing that she was divorced. In those days she would have been well aware that she stood no chance of getting the job if her secret had been discovered. The employer did not ask the claimant whether she was divorced, so she did not reveal that she was. The claimant was given a three-year fixed term contract to work in Buenos Aires at a salary of £100 a year. When the employer discovered that the claimant was divorced he ended the contract.

Held The claimant's silence did not amount to a misrepresentation. She was therefore entitled to sue for breach of contract. (The employer had argued that the claimant had made a misrepresentation, and that this gave him a defence to being sued for breach of contract.)

There are, however, four exceptions to the general rule. Silence will amount to a misrepresentation in the following circumstances:

(1) if there has been a change of circumstances;

(2) in contracts of insurance;

(3) if there is a fiduciary relationship between the parties; or

(4) if the silence makes another statement misleading.

These exceptions need to be examined individually.

A change of circumstances

If a person makes a statement which is true, but due to a change of circumstances the statement becomes untrue before the contract is made, then it may be a misrepresentation not to reveal that the circumstances have changed.

 With v O'Flanagan (1936) (Court of Appeal)

A doctor who was selling his practice said that it had a turnover of £2,000 a year. This was true, but when the sale went ahead three months later the practice was virtually worthless because the doctor had been ill.

Held The doctor's failure to reveal the change was a misrepresentation.

Contracts of insurance

Contracts of insurance are contracts *uberrimae fidei* (of the utmost good faith). In such contracts, everything which could affect the price of the premium is a material fact. A person taking out insurance must reveal all material facts, whether asked about the matter or not.

 Lambert *v* Co-op Insurance Society Ltd (1975) (Court of Appeal)

The claimant insured her own and her husband's jewellery. She did not mention that her husband had been convicted of a small theft some years earlier. When the claimant renewed the policy she did not reveal that her husband had recently been sent to prison for 15 months for theft. The insurance company did not ask about convictions so the claimant felt no need to mention them. Over £300-worth of the insured jewellery was later stolen, and the claimant claimed on her insurance.

Held The insurance company did not need to pay on the policy. The convictions were a material fact and the claimant should have revealed them. Not to do so amounted to a misrepresentation.

Where there is a fiduciary relationship between the parties

A fiduciary relationship is a relationship of great trust. When the parties in such a relationship make a contract with each other, everything must be revealed. If this is not done, the silence will amount to a misrepresentation. Promoters and directors of companies owe fiduciary duties to their companies, and partners in a firm owe fiduciary duties to each other.

Silence makes a statement misleading

Even a statement which is literally true can amount to a misrepresentation if the statement conveys a misleading impression.

 Nottingham Patent Brick and Tile Co *v* Butler (1886) (Court of Appeal)

The defendant's solicitor, who was selling land on behalf of the defendant, was asked whether there were any restrictive covenants attached to the land. (The buyer would generally not want restrictive covenants. If there were any, they would be included in documents which the solicitor should have read.) The solicitor replied that he was not aware of any restrictive covenants. This was true, but the reason why the solicitor was not aware of any was that he had not read the documents which he should have read. The claimant agreed to buy the land but pulled out of the contract when he discovered that there were restrictive covenants.

Held The solicitor's statement, although literally true, was a misrepresentation. Therefore the claimant was entitled to withdraw from the contract.

Remedies for misrepresentation

There are three types of actionable misrepresentation. Each type gives rise to different remedies. Table 4.1 shows an outline of the types of actionable misrepresentations and their remedies.

Table 4.1 Types of actionable misrepresentations and their remedies

	Type of misrepresentation		
	Fraudulent	Negligent	Wholly innocent
Definition	Made (i) Knowingly false, or (ii) without belief, or (iii) recklessly, not caring whether it is true or false	Made Honestly, but the maker cannot prove reasonable grounds for believing it was true	Made Honestly, and the maker can prove reasonable grounds for believing it was true
Remedies	Rescind and damages for tort of deceit (time does not run)	Rescind and damages for tort of deceit (time runs from date of contract)	Rescind. Usually no damages (time runs from date of contract)

RESCISSION

Contract is affirmed ◄——— Lost if ———► Cannot be restored to pre-contract position

▼

Third party has rights

Fraudulent misrepresentation (The tort of deceit)

Fraudulent misrepresentation was defined by **Derry v Peek (1889)** as a misrepresentation made either:

(1) knowing that it was untrue; or

(2) not believing that it was true; or

(3) recklessly, not caring whether it was true or false.

> **Example**
>
> Jason sells a lorry to Harjinder and makes a misrepresentation to the effect that the lorry has had a new engine fitted. The misrepresentation will be fraudulent if either: Jason knows that a new engine has not been fitted; or Jason does not think that a new engine has been fitted; or Jason has no idea whether or not a new engine has been fitted.

Remedies for fraudulent misrepresentation

A fraudulent misrepresentation allows the injured party to rescind the contract (call it off) and sue for damages for the tort of deceit. In **Eco3 Capital Ltd v Ludsin Overseas Ltd (2013)** the Court of Appeal, applying **Derry v Peek**, set out the following four requirements of the tort of deceit: (a) the defendant must have made a false representation to the claimant; (b) the defendant must have known the representation was false or have been reckless as to its truth; (c) the defendant must have intended that the claimant should act in reliance on the representation; (d) the claimant must have acted in reliance on the representation and have suffered loss. If the contract is to be rescinded for fraudulent misrepresentation, this must be done within a reasonable time of the innocent party becoming aware of the misrepresentation.

Damages for the tort of deceit are usually much greater than contract damages as a claim can be made for all expenses and losses caused by the deceit, even if these were not reasonably foreseeable.

Negligent misrepresentation

Section 2(1) of the Misrepresentation Act 1967 (MA 1967) defines a negligent misrepresentation as one made by a person who cannot prove that he honestly believed that the facts represented were true and that he had reasonable grounds for this belief.

> ### Example
> Daniel sells a printer to Bill and makes a misrepresentation to the effect that it is a colour printer. Daniel believes this to be true. The misrepresentation will be negligent unless Daniel can prove that he had reasonable grounds for believing that the printer was a colour printer. (Notice that the burden of proof is on Daniel.)

Remedies for negligent misrepresentation

A negligent misrepresentation allows the injured party to rescind the contract and to sue for damages for the tort of deceit. If the contract is to be rescinded for negligent misrepresentation, this must be done within a reasonable time of the misrepresentation having been made.

A person to whom a false statement was made might try to recover damages for negligent misstatement at common law (see Chapter 8). However, if an action for negligent misrepresentation is possible, a claim for negligent misstatement is rarely made. There are three disadvantages to such a claim. First, the claimant will need to prove that there was a 'special relationship' between the parties. Second, the burden of proving negligence will be on the claimant. Third, any damages will be for negligence rather than for the tort of deceit. For these reasons a claim under s. 2(1) MA 1967 is almost always preferable.

Wholly innocent misrepresentation

A wholly innocent misrepresentation is one made by a person who can prove that he honestly believed that the facts represented were true and that he had reasonable grounds for this belief.

> ### Example
> Minoosh sells a computer to Jill and makes a misrepresentation to the effect that it can operate Apple software. Minoosh believed this to be true. If Minoosh can prove that she had reasonable grounds for believing it was true (perhaps because that is what the shop told her when she bought the computer), then she will have made a wholly innocent misrepresentation. If Minoosh cannot prove this, then she will have made a negligent misrepresentation. (Again, notice that the burden of proof is on Minoosh.)

Remedies for wholly innocent misrepresentation

The injured party can rescind but has no right to claim damages. However, as regards both negligent and innocent misrepresentation, s. 2(2) of the Misrepresentation Act 1967 allows the court to award contract damages instead of rescission where the court considers it 'equitable to do so'. It is rare for the courts to use this section to award damages for an innocent misrepresentation, but they sometimes do so when the misrepresentation was so trivial that rescission would be too drastic a remedy.

William Sindall *v* **Cambridgeshire County Council (1994)** provides an example. In 1989 building land was sold for £5 million. The purchasers alleged that there had been a misrepresentation made by the sellers of the land, on account of there being a sewage pipe on the land. By this time the land was worth only £2.5 million because the property market had collapsed. The purchasers claimed that they were rescinding the contract for misrepresentation. The Court of Appeal found that there had been no misrepresentation. However, they said that if there had been a misrepresentation, damages would have been awarded under s. 2(2) instead of rescission. These damages would have compensated for the relatively small cost of removing the sewage pipes. Rescission would have been too drastic a remedy.

The burden of proof

The person who has the burden of proof must prove what he alleges. In civil cases the claimant must prove what he alleges on a balance of probabilities, meaning that he must prove that it is more likely to be true than untrue. In criminal cases all of the elements of the crime must be proved beyond reasonable doubt. However, an exception to the civil standard of proof is made when a claimant alleges fraudulent misrepresentation. A claimant who alleges fraudulent misrepresentation must prove the fraud on a standard approaching the criminal law standard, because in effect the claimant is alleging that a crime has been committed. Almost all fraudulent misrepresentations also amount to a criminal offence.

If a party alleges negligent misrepresentation then he must prove, on the civil standard of proof, that there has been a misrepresentation. The burden of proof is then shifted to the other party, using the civil standard of proof, to prove that he had reasonable grounds for believing that his statement was true. If he cannot do this, the misrepresentation will have been negligent. Because the remedies for fraudulent and negligent misrepresentation are virtually identical, many victims of fraudulent misrepresentation allege negligent rather than fraudulent misrepresentation. All they have to do is prove that there has been a misrepresentation, and this will then be negligent unless the misrepresentor can prove that he had reasonable grounds for believing that his statement was true. This is much easier than proving fraudulent misrepresentation.

Figure 4.3 shows the burden of proof in cases of non-fraudulent misrepresentation.

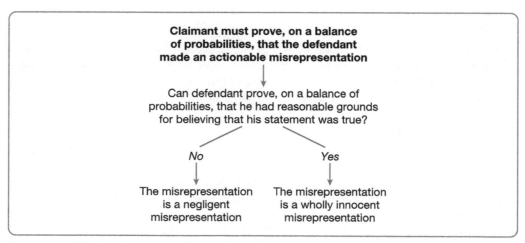

Figure 4.3 The burden of proof in non-fraudulent misrepresentation

Losing the right to rescind

All three types of misrepresentation give the injured party the right to rescind.

Rescission of a contract means that the parties are returned to the position they were in before the contract was made. So the whole of the purchase price will be returned to a purchaser who rescinds. Earlier (see Chapter 3) we saw that s. 48C SGA 1979 allows a secondary remedy of 'rescission' to a consumer who has bought goods which do not conform to the contract. (As explained in Chapter 3, s. 48 SGA 1979 will be replaced by the Consumer Rights Act 2015 when the CRA 2015 comes into force.) A consumer who does rescind under

s. 48C may not get all of the purchase price back as the court may deduct an amount to take account of any use of the goods which the consumer has had. The meaning of rescind under s. 48C is confined to that particular section. In general, a purchaser who rescinds will get all of the purchase price back. A party can rescind merely by letting the other party know that the contract is no longer regarded as binding. Rescission can also be used as a defence to a person who is sued for refusing to perform the contract, as we saw in **Redgrave *v* Hurd**.

The right to rescind can be lost in the following three ways:

(1) if the contract is affirmed;

(2) if a third party acquires rights; or

(3) if the subject matter of the contract no longer exists.

The contract is affirmed

The contract will be affirmed if the claimant decides to carry on with the contract after discovering the misrepresentation. The claimant might indicate affirmation expressly or impliedly. If the claimant does nothing for a considerable period of time, the court might well take the view that the contract has been impliedly affirmed.

 Leaf *v* International Galleries (1950) (Court of Appeal)

The claimant bought a painting from International Galleries because of a non-fraudulent misrepresentation that the painting was by Constable. Five years later the claimant discovered that the painting was not by Constable and he immediately applied to the court for rescission of the contract.

Held The claimant was too late to rescind. He had affirmed the contract by doing nothing for five years.

Comment If the misrepresentation by the gallery had been fraudulent, time would only have started to run against the claimant from the moment when the misrepresentation was discovered. He would therefore have been able to rescind the contract. This is the main difference between the remedies for fraudulent and negligent misrepresentation.

If a third party has acquired rights

A contract which can be rescinded is said to be a voidable contract, because one of the parties has the option to avoid the contract (call it off). Although a misrepresentation makes a contract voidable, it does not prevent ownership of goods sold under the contract from passing to a person who made the misrepresentation. In such a case the person making the misrepresentation will own the goods unless and until the innocent party avoids the contract. The innocent party has no obligation to avoid and may choose to affirm the contract, despite the misrepresentation, and keep what was gained under the contract.

If the misrepresentor sells goods he received under the contract to a third party *before* the contract is avoided, then the third party can keep the goods forever. This is because, at the time when the goods were sold on, the misrepresentor still owned the goods, and therefore still had ownership to pass on. This rule is confirmed by s. 23 of the Sale of Goods Act 1979, which provides that:

> Where the seller of goods has a voidable title to them, but his title has not been avoided at the time of the sale, the buyer acquires a good title to the goods, provided he buys them in good faith and without notice of the seller's defect of title.

If, however, the goods are sold to the innocent third party *after* the contract has been avoided, then the innocent third party will get no ownership of the goods. This is because, when the goods were sold on, the misrepresentor no longer had any ownership to pass on, the contract having been avoided.

Cases on this matter amount to a dispute about who did what first.

 Lewis *v* Averay (1972) (Court of Appeal)

A rogue bought the claimant's car. The rogue paid with a bad cheque, pretending to be a famous actor called Richard Greene. (The rogue therefore made a fraudulent misrepresentation.) At first, the claimant was unwilling to take the rogue's cheque. However, the claimant did take the cheque when the rogue produced a Pinewood Studios pass in the name of Richard Greene, which showed the rogue's photograph. Having got possession of the car, the rogue sold it to the defendant. The defendant paid a reasonable price for the car and believed that the rogue owned it. The claimant later tried to avoid the contract.

Held Although the contract was voidable for fraudulent misrepresentation, the defendant gained complete ownership of it by virtue of s. 23 SGA 1979. Once the car had been resold by the rogue, the claimant was too late to avoid the contract and had lost ownership of the car.

 Car and Universal Finance Co *v* Caldwell (1965) (Court of Appeal)

A rogue bought a car with a bad cheque, knowing that the cheque would not be honoured. The car was later sold to a third party who bought it in good faith. Before this sale the original seller found out about the rogue's fraudulent misrepresentation. He could not find the rogue to tell him that he was avoiding the contract, so he told the police and the AA.

Held Telling the police and the AA was enough to avoid the contract because it was an action which showed a definite intention to avoid the contract. The original seller therefore got the car back from the third party. If the original seller had not told the police and the AA until *after* the rogue had resold the car, s. 23 of the Sale of Goods Act 1979 would have applied and he would never have got the car back.

Comment The misrepresentation in this case was fraudulent. The Court of Appeal raised the question as to whether or not the contract would have been avoided by telling the authorities if the misrepresentation had been either negligent or innocent. Unfortunately, having raised the question, the court said that it did not know the answer. So the case is only an authority where the misrepresentation was fraudulent.

In all of these cases where a rogue buys goods with a stolen cheque, one of two innocent parties is bound to suffer a loss. Either the original owner will get the goods back, in which case the purchaser from the rogue will have paid money to the rogue in return for nothing at all, or the original owner will not get the goods back, and will therefore have been deprived of ownership of the goods in return for a worthless cheque. (It should be noticed that s. 23 SGA 1979 will never operate in favour of a third party who did not act in good faith when buying from the misrepresentor.)

Whichever of the two parties suffers the loss will be left with the right to sue the rogue for damages. However, it should be pointed out that this right is likely to be worth very little. First, the rogue might never be identified. Second, rogues who buy goods with bad cheques rarely have enough money to pay damages.

If it is impossible to put the parties back into their pre-contract positions

When a contract is treated as terminated for breach of a term, future performance of the contract is not required. This is the case whether or not the contract has been partly performed. However, when a contract is avoided, the parties must be put back into the positions they were in before the contract was made. If this cannot be done, then the contract cannot be avoided. In **Clarke v Dickson (1858)** Crompton J gave the example of a butcher who bought live cattle because a farmer had made a fraudulent misrepresentation about them. He said that once the cattle had been slaughtered and butchered rescission would not be possible. (However, damages for the tort of deceit could have been claimed.) Again, it should be noticed that when s. 48C SGA, or the CRA 2015, talks of rescission the word is not used in its usual sense but in a sense which applies only to that section. Under s. 48C, or the CRA 2015, a contract can be rescinded even if the parties cannot be put back into the positions they were in before the contract was made.

Mistake

When the parties make their contract, one or both of them might be mistaken as to some fundamental matter. Here we examine the types of mistake which might be made and the effect of these mistakes upon the validity of the contract. First, we consider the position where both parties make the same mistake. (This is known as common mistake.) Then we consider the position where only one of the parties makes a mistake. (This is known as unilateral mistake.) Figure 4.4 shows an outline of the different types of mistake.

Common mistake

There is said to be a common mistake when both of the parties freely reach agreement, but do so while making the same mistake.

Common mistake as to existence of goods

A common mistake might be made about the existence of the subject matter of the contract. For example, let us assume that X Ltd agrees to buy a second-hand machine from Y Ltd. Let us also assume that at the time of the contract, unknown to both parties, the machine does not exist because it has been destroyed in a fire. Section 6 of the Sale of Goods Act provides that, where there is a contract for the sale of specific goods, and the goods, without the knowledge of the seller, have perished at the time the contract is made, the contract is void. Y Ltd will not therefore be in breach of contract for failure to deliver the machine and X Ltd will not have to pay the contract price. If the contract had been for the sale of unascertained goods, such as 100 tons of wheat, then Y Ltd would have to find another 100 tons of wheat from elsewhere or be in breach of contract. (The difference between specific and unascertained goods is explained in Chapter 7.)

It is important to note here that if specific goods which are sold cease to exist *after* the contract has been made, but before the goods have been delivered to the buyer, the contract will not be void for mistake. Generally, the buyer will have received ownership of the goods

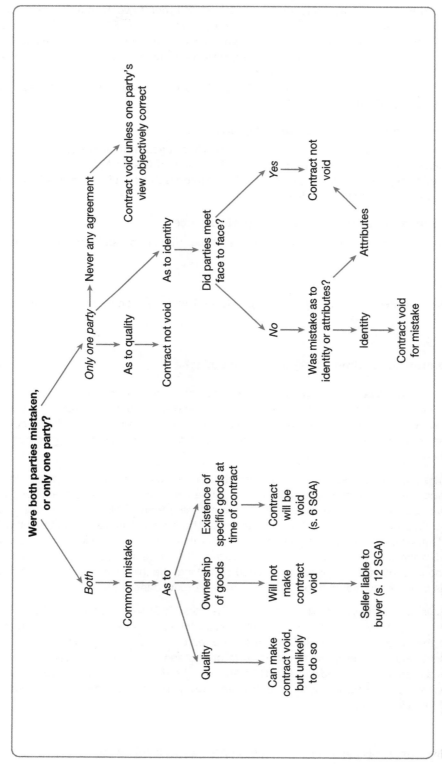

Figure 4.4 An outline of the different types of mistake

as soon as the contract was made and so the goods will then have been at his risk. If this is the case, the buyer will therefore have to pay for the goods. (See SGA 1979 s. 18, rule 1 in Chapter 7.) If, after a contract to sell specific goods was made, the risk had not passed to the buyer at the time when the goods ceased to exist the contract would not be void for mistake; the seller would be in breach of contract.

However, if the goods had perished, s. 7 SGA 1979 would cause the contract to be frustrated (s. 7 is explained in Chapter 7).

Common mistake as to ownership of goods

A common mistake as to the ownership of goods will not generally make the contract void. Earlier (see Chapter 3) we saw that s. 12(1) of the Sale of Goods Act 1979 implies a term that the seller of goods owns the goods. A seller who does not own the goods sold will be in breach of contract, as we saw in **Rowland v Divall**.

Common mistake as to possibility of performance

If the parties agree to make a contract which is, at that time, impossible to perform, then the contract will be void for mistake.

Common mistake as to quality

A common mistake as to the quality of goods sold will not generally make the contract void.

 Bell v Lever Bros (1932) (House of Lords)

A company paid an employee £30,000 in return for him accepting redundancy. Afterwards, it was discovered that the employee could have been dismissed without paying any compensation because he had breached the company's rules. Neither the employee nor the company realised that the employee could have been dismissed without paying compensation when the agreement was made.

Held The agreement was not void for mistake and the employee could keep the money. A common mistake as to quality will make a contract void only if the mistake means that what was being bought was essentially a different thing from what the parties believed it to be. Both parties knew that what was being bought was the right to make the employee redundant. They were mistaken as to how much this was worth, thinking it was worth £30,000 when in fact it was worth nothing. However, they were not mistaken as to what was being bought. Whether it was worth £30,000 or nothing, the thing which was being bought was the same thing, the right to make the employee redundant.

Lord Atkin said: 'A buys B's horse; he thinks the horse is sound and he pays the price of a sound horse; he would certainly not have bought the horse if he had known, as the fact is, that the horse is unsound. If B has made no representation as to soundness and has not contracted that the horse is sound, A is bound and cannot recover back the price. A buys a picture from B; both A and B believe it to be the work of an old master, and a high price is paid. It turns out to be a modern copy. A has no remedy in the absence of a representation or warranty.'

Bell v Lever Bros was applied by the Court of Appeal in the following case.

Great Peace Shipping Ltd *v* Tsavliris Salvage International Ltd (2002) (Court of Appeal)

The defendants offered salvage services to a ship which was in trouble in the Indian Ocean. A reliable third party told the defendants that the claimants' ship, the *Great Peace*, was the closest ship which could provide salvage. So the defendants booked the *Great Peace* for a minimum of five days. When the contract was made, the defendants thought that the *Great Peace* was within 35 miles of the ship in trouble. In fact, the two ships were 410 miles apart and it would have taken the *Great Peace* 39 hours to arrive. The defendants therefore told the claimants that they wanted to cancel the contract, but not until they had found a closer ship. When the defendants did find a closer ship, they cancelled the contract but the claimants refused to accept this. The defendants argued that the contract was void for common mistake because both parties thought that the *Great Peace* was close to the ship which was in trouble.

Held Applying **Bell *v* Lever Bros**, the contract was not void for common mistake. The contract would have been void only if the distance between the ships had meant that the services which the *Great Peace* was to provide were essentially different from what the parties had agreed. The fact that the defendants wanted to keep the contract on unless a closer ship could be found indicated that this was not the case.

Unilateral mistake

Unilateral mistake meaning no agreement was made

If the parties to the contract were at cross purposes when making the offer and acceptance, there may have been no real agreement. If the reasonable person could not objectively say which of the parties' views was obviously correct, then there will be no contract. If the reasonable person could say that the view of one or other of the parties was obviously correct, then there will be a valid contract.

 Raffles *v* Wichelhaus (1864)

A contract was made to buy cotton as soon as it arrived on a ship called *Peerless* which was sailing from Bombay. In fact, two ships called *Peerless* were sailing from Bombay. When the contract was made the defendant was thinking of a ship called *Peerless* which set off in October. The claimant was thinking of a different ship which set off in December.

Held There was no contract because the reasonable person could not say what had been agreed. However, if the reasonable person could have said that one or other of the ships was obviously what the parties seemed to have intended, then there would have been a contract to buy the cotton which arrived on that ship. (This might have happened, for instance, if one of the ships was a world famous carrier of cotton from India, while the other was an unknown ship.)

Unilateral mistake as to the terms of the contract

If one of the parties knows that the other made the contract while making a fundamental mistake as to the terms of the contract, then the contract can be void for mistake. In **Hartog *v* Colin & Shields (1939)**, for example, sellers of a large quantity of animal skins made a slip of the pen and offered to sell them at one-third of their usual price. The buyer accepted, knowing that a mistake had been made. The contract was void for mistake because the buyer knew that the sellers had made a mistake about the terms of their offer. However, if one party knows that the other is making a fundamental mistake about the quality of what is being sold, then the contract will not be void for mistake. For example, in **Smith v Hughes (1871)** a seller of oats showed a potential buyer a sample of the oats. The buyer thought that the oats were old oats and so he bought them. In fact, they were new oats which were no use to him at all. It was held that even if the seller knew of the buyer's mistake the contract was not void for mistake. This situation differs from the examples given by Lord Atkin in **Bell v Lever Bros** because in those examples both parties were mistaken as to the quality of what was being sold.

Mistake as to the identity of the other contracting party

This is the most important type of unilateral mistake and needs to be considered in a little more detail. Most of the cases concern a rogue who buys goods while pretending to be someone else and who pays for the goods with a bad cheque. We have already seen that a rogue who pays with a bad cheque commits a fraudulent misrepresentation which makes the contract capable of being rescinded, which is also known as making the contract **voidable**. So if the person who sells to the rogue avoids the contract before the rogue sells the goods to a third party there will be no need to argue mistake. It is when the person who sells to the rogue does not avoid in time that it becomes necessary to argue that the contract is **void** for mistake. If this argument is successful the person who sells to the rogue will always get the goods back because a void contract is no contract at all. No ownership of the goods ever passes to the rogue under a void contract, or to anyone else to whom the rogue sells the goods.

Figure 4.5 shows the different effect of good, void and voidable contracts. It assumes that A sells goods to B and that B sells the goods on to C, who buys them in good faith. The figure examines the different positions if the contract between A and B was a good contract, a void contract or a voidable contract.

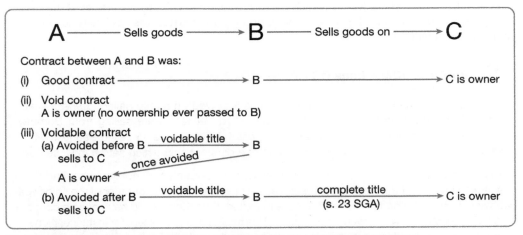

Figure 4.5 The effect of resale after good, void and voidable contracts

Whether or not a mistake as to the identity of the other contracting party will make a contract void depends upon several factors. First, it is necessary that the parties did not meet face to face when making the contract. If the parties did meet face to face, then the contract will not be void for mistake. In **Lewis v Averay**, which we considered earlier in this chapter, the claimant argued that the contract was void for mistake. (If this argument had been successful the claimant would have got the car back.) The Court of Appeal rejected this argument. If the parties meet face to face, then the contract will not be void for mistake.

If the parties did not meet face to face, then it is possible that the contract will be void for mistake. However, this will be the case only where the innocent contracting party was mistaken as to the *identity* of the rogue. If the innocent contracting party was mistaken only as to the rogue's *attributes*, then the contract will not be void for mistake. (Attributes are concerned with a person's qualities or distinguishing features. For example, one of the attributes of Stuart Broad, the cricketer, is that he is a very good fast bowler. This is not the same as his identity. There are other very good fast bowlers.) The following two cases show the difference between being mistaken as to identity and being mistaken as to attributes.

 Cundy *v* Lindsay (1878) (House of Lords)

A rogue ordered a very large quantity of handkerchiefs from the claimants. The rogue pretended to be a reputable firm with whom the claimants had previously dealt. This firm was called Blenkiron & Co of 123 Wood Street, London. The rogue, who was called Blenkarn, disguised his signature to look like Blenkiron & Co, giving his address as 37 Wood Street, where he had hired a room. The trick worked and the claimants sent the handkerchiefs to Blenkiron & Co at 37 Wood Street. The rogue sold 250 dozen of these handkerchiefs to the defendant who bought them in good faith. The claimants sued the defendant to get these handkerchiefs back.

Held The contract was void for mistake because the claimants were mistaken as to the identity of the person with whom they made the contract. Therefore, ownership of the handkerchiefs never moved away from the claimants.

Comment The contract was of course voidable for fraudulent misrepresentation, but the claimants had not avoided it in time. As regards avoiding for misrepresentation, they would therefore have been defeated by s. 23 of the Sale of Goods Act 1979, as explained above.

Kings Norton Metal Co Ltd *v* Edridge, Merrett & Co Ltd (1897) (Court of Appeal)

A rogue ordered goods from the claimants, who were metal manufacturers. The rogue was called Wallis, but he made the letter appear to come from Hallam & Co, Sheffield. No such company ever existed. However, the claimants made the contract and delivered the goods because the rogue's letter was printed on very impressive notepaper. The rogue sold the goods on to the defendants, who bought them in good faith. The claimants sued the defendants to get the goods back.

Held The contract was not void for mistake and so the claimants were not entitled to the goods. The claimants were not mistaken about the identity of the person they were dealing with. (Unlike the claimants in **Cundy *v* Lindsay**, the claimants in this case had no prior knowledge of the person with whom they thought they were dealing.) They were mistaken only about the attributes of that person. They thought that they were dealing with someone who was creditworthy and respectable, whereas in fact they were not.

Comment (i) The contract was voidable for fraudulent misrepresentation but the claimants were defeated by s. 23 of the Sale of Goods Act 1979. (ii) The rogue could have been sued for damages for the tort of deceit. However, this rogue (like most other rogues) would not have had enough money to pay any damages.

In the following case the House of Lords thoroughly reviewed the cases on mistake as to the person.

⚖️ **Shogun Finance Ltd *v* Hudson (FC) (2003) (House of Lords)**

The defendant, Hudson, bought a car from a rogue. The rogue had taken the car on hire-purchase from Shogun Finance Ltd, the claimants. If this contract between the rogue and the claimants was a good contract, then the defendant would become owner of the car under s. 27 of the Hire-Purchase Act 1964. (This is a technical provision with which we need not be concerned here. Its effect is examined in Chapter 7.) If the contract was void, then the defendant could not gain a good title. The question for the House of Lords was therefore whether the contract between the rogue and the claimants was void for mistake. The rogue had not met the claimants face to face but had visited a dealer who was not the claimants' agent. At the dealer's showroom the rogue had produced a driving licence stolen from one Durlabh Patel and had filled in one of the claimants' standard hire-purchase forms in Durlabh Patel's name. A copy of this agreement had been faxed to the claimants who had approved the sale.

Held (3 to 2) The contract between the rogue and the claimants was void for mistake and so the defendant never became owner of the car.

Comment (i) The judges in the majority thought it significant that the contract was a written contract which would not have come into existence until a credit check had been carried out. They indicated that the position might have been different if it had been an oral sale of goods because ownership of the goods could then have already passed to the rogue before the time for payment and identification arose. (The time at which ownership of goods passes to a buyer is considered in Chapter 7.) (ii) All five of the judges thought that **Lewis *v* Averay** was correctly decided. (iii) The two judges in the minority thought that **Cundy *v* Lindsay** should be overruled and that a voidable contract existed between the rogue and the claimants. However, the three judges in the majority confirmed **Cundy *v* Lindsay** as being correct.

The final requirement for a contract to be void on account of a unilateral mistake as to the person is that the mistake must have been a material mistake, that is to say it must have been a mistake which induced the making of the contract. For example, in **Mackie *v* European Assurance Society (1869)** the claimant asked a friend to insure him. The claimant thought that the policy would be taken out with one particular insurance company but in fact it was taken out with another. When the claimant claimed on his insurance policy the insurers refused to pay, arguing mistake as to the person. The contract was not void for mistake. It was true that the parties did not meet face to face and that the claimant was mistaken about the identity of the other contracting party. The contract was not void for mistake, however, because the claimant would not have been bothered which of the two insurance companies made the contract of insurance.

Mistake as to the nature of what is being signed

If a person signs a document while making a complete mistake as to what type of document it is, then the contract can be void for a type of mistake known as *non est factum* (it is not my deed).

Saunders *v* Anglia Building Society (1970) (House of Lords)

An elderly woman intended to leave her house to her nephew after her death. The nephew owed money to one Lee. To pay Lee off the nephew visited the elderly aunt with Lee, who asked the elderly woman to sign a document. Lee told her that this gave the house to the nephew but that she would be allowed to live there for the rest of her life. In fact, the document said that Lee had bought the house and paid for it. The elderly woman did not read the document because her glasses were broken. Lee mortgaged the house to the Anglia Building Society but did not pay any of the mortgage instalments. The building society applied to repossess the house.

Held The contract was not void for *non est factum* because there was not a fundamental difference between what the elderly woman signed and what she thought she was signing. (Either way she was transferring her ownership of the house.) Therefore, the contract was valid and the building society could repossess the house.

Non est factum cannot be claimed by a person who was careless in signing. In **United Dominions Trust Ltd *v* Western (1975)** the Court of Appeal therefore held that it was not available to a person who signed a blank document for the figures to be filled in later.

Foster *v* Mackinnon (1869) provides a rare example of a successful plea of *non est factum*. An old man with very poor eyesight signed a document which he was told was a guarantee. In fact, the document was a cheque. *Non est factum* applied and the old man was not liable on the cheque.

Duress and undue influence

Duress

Traditionally, a contract was voidable for duress only if one of the parties was forced into making it by the threat of illegal physical violence. This common law doctrine was so narrow as to be virtually useless. A person who makes a contract because of such threats is unlikely then to go to court to avoid the contract.

More recently, a doctrine of economic duress has developed. A threat of physical violence is no longer necessary. Now a party who was pushed into a contract in such a way that there was no real consent to the contract can avoid the contract. For example, in **The Universe Sentinel (1982)** shipowners were told that if they did not agree to pay money to a seamen's charity, a trade union would not allow their ship to leave port. The shipowners agreed to the union's demands and their ship was allowed to sail away. The House of Lords held that the shipowners were entitled to recover the money paid to the charity on the grounds of economic duress. They had not freely agreed to pay this money, they were pushed into the contract in such a way that they did not really consent. The following case provides another example.

Atlas Express Ltd *v* Kafco Ltd (1989)

The defendants, a small company, agreed that the claimants would carry their products to Woolworths shops throughout the country. The price of carriage was agreed at £1.10 a carton. The claimants, through their own error, had miscalculated the size of the cartons. The claimants told the defendants that they would not continue to perform the contract unless the defendants agreed to pay a minimum price per load. The defendants could not find another carrier and so they had to agree to this or they would have lost their contract with Woolworths, which was vital to them. After the cartons had been carried, the defendants refused to pay the extra amount.

Held The defendants did not need to pay. The contract was voidable on the grounds of economic duress.

As the law of economic duress has expanded, some of the old cases on consideration might now be differently decided. For example, the ship's captain in **Stilk v Myrick** (which was considered in Chapter 2) was pushed into the contract against his wishes. If the case were to arise today a court might hold that there was a contract but that it was voidable for economic duress.

In **Progress Bulk Carriers Ltd *v* Tube City LLC (2012)** the High Court held, for the first time, that a lawful threat to commit a lawful act amounted to illegitimate pressure so as to make a contract voidable for economic duress. This is unusual, but the more improper and morally wrong the lawful act the more likely it is to be seen as illegitimate pressure.

Undue influence

Undue influence is an equitable doctrine which complements the common law doctrine of duress. It can make a contract voidable if the claimant was unduly influenced by the defendant to make it. If there was a threat, or illegitimate pressure, then the case is likely to be one of duress rather than undue influence.

To establish undue influence the claimant must prove two matters. First, he must prove that there was a relationship of undue influence between himself and the defendant. As regards some types of relationships (such as parent and child, solicitor and client, trustee and beneficiary, and solicitor and client), there is a presumption that the dominant party influenced the weaker party. However, the relationship of husband and wife is not one in which there is a presumption of influence. Where there is no relationship in which influence is presumed, the claimant must prove that he actually was influenced to make the contract by the defendant. The second stage, after influence has been proved one way or another, is that the claimant must show that he entered into a transaction which calls for explanation. This transaction does not need to be a contract with the defendant, it could be a contract with a third party. Once the claimant has done this, the burden of proof shifts to the defendant to show that there was in fact no undue influence. The most effective way to do this is to show that the claimant took independent legal advice before entering into the contract. If the defendant cannot prove that there was in fact no undue influence, then the contract will be voidable by the claimant. As with all contracts which are voidable, the right to rescind can be lost, as we saw earlier in this chapter.

Banks tainted with undue influence

A situation which arises quite commonly is that a husband persuades his wife that they should mortgage the matrimonial home in order to get a loan for the husband's business from a bank. If the loan is not repaid, the bank will want to repossess the matrimonial home. This means that they would sell it to recover the amount which they were owed. In **Royal Bank of Scotland plc v Etridge (No. 2) (1998)** the House of Lords held that the bank should positively inform the wife that she should get independent legal advice before agreeing to the mortgage. If the bank does this, it will be able to enforce the mortgage. If the bank does not do this, and if agreeing to the mortgage could not readily be explained by the relationship of the parties, then the mortgage cannot be enforced. However, in many cases the mortgaging of the matrimonial home can be explained by the relationship of the parties. In many cases it is a reasonable risk to take to secure the husband's business. The principles in this case apply not only to husband and wife, but also whenever the relationship between the debtor and the person guaranteeing the debt is not a commercial relationship.

Illegal contracts

The following types of contracts are illegal at common law and therefore unenforceable.

- *Contracts tending to promote corruption in public life*. An example is provided by **Parkinson v College of Ambulance Ltd (1925)**. The claimant was promised that he would receive a knighthood if he made a donation to a charity. He made the donation but sued for its return when he did not get the knighthood. His action failed because the contract was illegal.

- *Contracts tending to impede the administration of justice*. A contract to make sure that a person is not prosecuted would be illegal and void. However, a contract not to pursue a civil action is perfectly valid. Disputes are often settled in this way and this is known as settling out of court (see Chapter 2).

- *Contracts to trade with enemy nations*. In times of war, certain nations become enemy nations. A contract to trade with a person voluntarily living in an enemy nation is generally void.

- *Contract to commit a tort, fraud or crime*. A strange example is provided by **Everett v Williams (1725)**. One highwayman tried to sue another on an agreement to rob a stage-coach. The highwayman failed in this action. (Both the claimant and the defendant were hanged and the lawyers were fined £50 for bringing the case!)

- *Contracts tending to promote sexual immorality*. An example is provided by **Pearce v Brooks (1866)**, where a prostitute hired a carriage which the owner knew was to be used for immoral purposes. The prostitute refused to pay for the hire of the carriage but the owner was not allowed to recover the agreed payments.

- *Contracts to defraud the Revenue*. In **Miller v Karlinski (1945)** a contract was made to defraud the Revenue. The claimant sued for ten weeks' wages and £21 travelling expenses. Of the travelling expenses, £17 should have been paid as wages. The claimant and the employer agreed to say they were travelling expenses to avoid paying income tax on the £17. The Court of Appeal held that the whole agreement was unenforceable. Therefore, the claimant could not recover anything, not even the proper wages or the £4 genuine travelling expenses.

Many statutes also make certain types of contracts illegal. The contracts concerned are so numerous that it is beyond the scope of this book to attempt to list them.

Contracts which contravene public policy

A contract which contravenes public policy will be void. The most important type of such a contract is a contract in restraint of trade. Contracts in restraint of trade attempt to prevent a person from working or carrying on a business. Such contracts are void unless they can be proved to be reasonable. They tend to arise where a person who sells a business agrees not to compete with the new owner. When considering whether such agreements in **restraint of trade** are reasonable or not, the court will consider the length of time for which the agreement was to last, the extent of the area in which competition was prohibited and the type of competition which was prohibited. Contracts in restraint of trade are also found where an employee agrees not to compete with the employer's line of business after leaving the employment. A contract in restraint of trade which attempts to prevent an ex-employee from working for another employer can be valid only if it was necessary to protect trade secrets, trade connections or confidential information.

Essential points

- A term is part of a contract and if a term is breached this is breach of contract.
- A representation is a statement which persuaded another person to make a contract.
- An actionable misrepresentation is an untrue statement of fact which induced the other party to make the contract.
- Generally, silence cannot amount to an actionable misrepresentation.
- A misrepresentation is fraudulent if it was made either: knowing that it was untrue; or not believing that it was true; or recklessly, not caring whether it was true or false.
- A misrepresentation is made negligently if the person who made it cannot prove that he believed that it was true and that he had reasonable grounds for this belief.
- A misrepresentation is made innocently if the person who made it can prove that he believed that it was true and that he had reasonable grounds for this belief.
- If a contract is rescinded the parties are restored to the positions which they were in before the contract was made.
- The right to rescind can be lost if the contract is affirmed, or if a third party has acquired rights, or if it is impossible to put the parties back into their pre-contract positions.
- There is a common mistake when both of the parties freely reach agreement, but do so while making the same mistake.
- A common mistake might be as to the existence of the subject matter of the contract, or as to the ownership of goods sold or as to the quality of goods sold.
- If one party knows that the other is mistaken as to the terms of the contract, this will make the contract void.
- A mistake as to the identity of the other contracting party can make the contract void if the parties did not meet face to face.
- A contract will be voidable for duress if it was made as a result of actual physical violence or the threat of it.
- A contract may be voidable for economic duress if a person was pushed into it in such a way that there was no real consent to the contract.
- Many types of contracts are made illegal by statute.
- Some contracts are illegal at common law.
- Illegal contracts are void.

Practice questions

1 Two months ago, Samikah bought a small bakery for £1 million. The vendor of the bakery, Bill, told Samikah that the average monthly turnover was about £100,000. Bill offered to show Samikah the business records, which he claimed would have proved that his statement about the turnover was true. Samikah declined this offer, saying that she trusted Bill. The written contract of sale made no mention of the business turnover. Since Samikah bought the business, the turnover has been only £30,000 a month. Samikah has now discovered that the monthly turnover of the business has never exceeded £45,000. Advise Samikah of her legal position.

2 Cedric, a manufacturer of jewellery, received an order from a company called Acme (Superjewellers) Ltd. Cedric sent a small amount of jewellery and received prompt payment. Cedric then received a bigger order from Acme (Superjewellers) Ltd and posted jewellery worth £10,000 to Acme (Superjewellers) Ltd. Cedric did not receive payment for this and has since been informed that Acme (Superjewellers) Ltd is a fictitious company, often used as an alias by Edward, a rogue. Edward has been caught by the police and is likely to be sent to prison. The police have discovered that Frederick now has the jewellery which Cedric sent to Acme (Superjewellers) Ltd. Frederick bought the jewellery from Edward. Advise Cedric of his legal position.

3 Gina, a dealer in antiques, visits the premises of Helen, another dealer. Gina buys a painting for £5,000. Helen does not make any claims about the painting. The painting turns out to be a fake and virtually worthless. Advise Gina of her legal position in the following circumstances.

   (a) Helen, like Gina, believed that the painting was genuine and worth about £5,000.

   (b) Helen had a good idea that the painting was a fake.

4 George is a retired teacher. Fay has agreed to buy George's boat, so that she can sail to the Channel Islands. How would the contract be affected if, unknown to both parties:

   (a) The boat did not belong to George?

   (b) The boat was completely unseaworthy?

   (c) The boat had been destroyed by fire five minutes before the contract was made?

5 Sarah buys a painting from a junk shop for £1,000. What would the effect on the contract be if:

   (a) Sarah discovered that the painting was utterly worthless?

   (b) The shop owner had untruthfully said that the painting was by the minor Edwardian artist, René Dulux, and therefore worth at least £1,000? (In fact the painting is worthless.)

6 Jermaine, a carpenter, put in a tender to do the carpentry work on a development which was being built in North Wales. Jermaine's tender was accepted. The work was to be completed in two months and Jermaine was to be paid £5,000. When Jermaine arrived on the site, he was told that there had been a mistake and another carpenter had been employed instead. Jermaine was told that he could still do the work but that he would only be paid £3,500. Jermaine felt that he had to accept these new terms as he had no other work available and had given up his flat so that he could move to Wales. Jermaine has now finished the job on time. Advise Jermaine of his legal position.

7 Explain any remedies which are available to a person who sells goods to a rogue who buys the goods with a bad cheque whilst using a false identity.

Task 4

A friend of yours who is visiting the country from abroad is considering starting a business in England. Your friend has asked you to write a report, briefly dealing with the following matters:

(a) The difference between a contract term and a representation.

(b) The nature of a misrepresentation.

(c) The remedies for misrepresentation.

(d) The types of mistake which can make a contract void.

(e) The circumstances in which a contract can be voidable for duress or undue influence.

(f) The types of contract which are illegal at common law.

mylawchamber

Visit **www.mylawchamber.co.uk/macintyreessentials** to access tools to help you develop and test your knowledge of business law, including interactive multiple choice questions, practice exam questions with guidance, weblinks, glossary, glossary flashcards, legal newsfeed and legal updates.

mylawchamber
unrivalled support for legal education

5

Discharge of contracts and remedies for breach

Discharge of contractual liability

We have seen (in Chapters 2, 3 and 4) that contractual liability is created when an offer is accepted, and that this liability is to perform the terms agreed upon. When a party's contractual liability is discharged it ceases to exist. This can happen in four ways:

(1) by performance;

(2) by agreement;

(3) by frustration; or

(4) by breach.

In addition, legislation can give a right to conclude certain types of contracts during a 'cooling-off' period. Figure 5.1 gives an overview of how contracts are created and discharged.

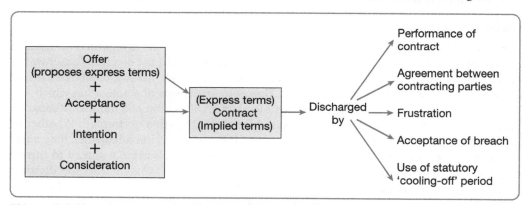

Figure 5.1 How contracts are created and discharged

Discharge by performance of the contract

The Sale of Goods Act 1979, and the Consumer Rights Act 2015 when it comes into force, make special rules about the performance of contracts of sale of goods. These rules are considered later (see Chapter 7). Here we are considering the position as regards contracts other than contracts of sale of goods.

It was seen earlier (in Chapter 2) that a party who makes the offer of a unilateral contract promises to do something if the other party performs an act which has been requested. For example, in **Carlill v The Carbolic Smoke Ball Co (1893)** the company promised to pay any person a £100 reward if they bought a smoke ball, used it properly and caught flu. A party who makes the offer of a unilateral contract needs to keep the promise made only if the other party fully performs the act specified. So if Mrs Carlill had not bought the smoke ball, used it properly and caught flu, there would have been no obligation to pay her any part of the reward.

In bilateral contracts the general rule is that if one party fails to fully perform the contract the other party need not perform the contract at all. The following case demonstrates this general rule.

 Cutter *v* Powell (1795)

Cutter had agreed to be a ship's mate on a voyage from Jamaica to Liverpool. The contract said that Cutter was to be paid £31.50, 'provided he proceeds, continues and does his duty . . . from hence to the port of Liverpool'. The journey took about two months and usually ship mates were paid about £4 a month. Cutter died after three-quarters of the voyage and therefore did not fully perform his contractual obligations. Cutter's widow sued for payment for the work Cutter had performed.

Held The ship's captain had no obligation to pay anything because Cutter had not completely performed his contractual obligations.

There are four exceptions to this general rule:

(1) divisible or severable contracts;
(2) substantial performance;
(3) acceptance of partial performance; and
(4) prevention of performance.

Divisible contracts

Part payment must be made for partial performance if the contract is regarded as divisible or severable. In **Cutter *v* Powell** the wording of the contract, and the fact that Cutter was to be paid an unusually large lump sum for completing the contract, made it plain that Cutter's obligation to act as ship's mate was entire. That is to say, it was one obligation which was either performed or not. If a contract is divisible, then it will consist of a number of separate obligations and part payment will be required for each obligation performed. Whether or not a contract is divisible or entire depends upon what the parties intended when they made the contract. In **Ritchie *v* Atkinson (1808)**, for example, a ship's captain agreed to carry a cargo of hemp at £5 a ton. The captain carried only half the cargo. This contract was divisible because the price was expressed per ton rather than as a lump sum for carrying the whole cargo. The captain was therefore paid for the cargo he did carry (but had to pay damages in respect of the cargo which he failed to carry). If the contract had been entire, then the captain would not have been paid anything at all.

Substantial performance

A second exception to the general rule arises where the partial performance very nearly amounted to total performance. If the partial performance can be regarded as substantial performance, then it will have to be paid for. For example, in **Hoenig *v* Isaacs (1952)** the contract was to decorate and furnish a flat for £750. Defects in the work would have cost £56 to put right. The Court of Appeal held that there had been substantial performance and so the decorator was paid £750, but then had to pay damages of £56. By contrast, in **Bolton *v* Mahadeva (1972)** the contract was to install central heating in a house for £560. Defects in the work would have cost £174 to put right. The Court of Appeal held that there had been no substantial performance and so the installer received no payment at all.

Acceptance of partial performance

A third exception to the general rule arises where partial performance was freely accepted by the other party. However, this acceptance must arise as a matter of choice. For example, in **Sumpter *v* Hedges (1898)** the claimant had agreed to build two houses for the defendant for £565. After doing work to the value of £333 the claimant was forced to stop work because he had run out of money. The defendant finished the work himself. The court held that the defendant did not have to pay the claimant for the work he had done. The defendant's act of finishing the work did not indicate that he had freely accepted the claimant's partial performance.

Prevention of performance

A final exception to the general rule arises where one of the contracting parties prevents the other from fully performing the contract. The party who is prevented from fully performing will be paid the amount deserved for the work done. This is known as a *quantum meruit* payment. In **Planché *v* Colburn (1831)**, for example, the claimant had been commissioned by the defendant to write a book. The book was on costumes and armour, part of a series called the Juvenile Library, and the claimant was to be paid £100 on completion. The defendant cancelled the series when the claimant's book was partly written. The claimant was entitled to a payment of £50 for the work he had done.

Figure 5.2 gives an overview of how contracts other than sales of goods are discharged by performance.

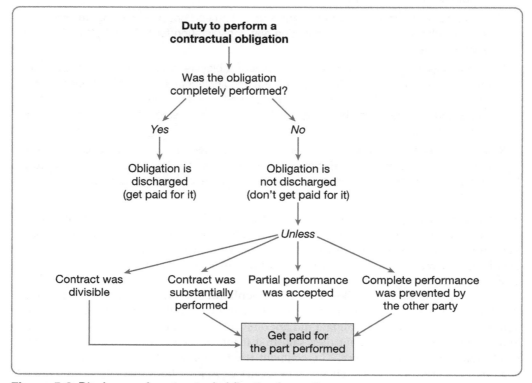

Figure 5.2 Discharge of contractual obligation by performance

Discharge by agreement

Having made a contract, the parties are free to agree to abandon it or to vary it. However, an agreement to do either of these things must amount to another contract. All the requirements of a new contract are therefore necessary. There must be an offer, an acceptance, an intention to create legal relations and consideration moving both ways. As the parties must agree to alter their legal position, there is usually no difficulty in finding the offer and acceptance or an intention to create legal relations. Generally, any problem which arises is caused by the difficulty of showing that consideration has moved from both of the parties. The following extended example shows the possibilities.

> ### Example
>
> John has agreed to service Jim's boiler for £1,000. Several possibilities must be considered.
>
> (1) If both of the parties agree to call the contract off before there has been any performance of it, the contract will be discharged. John has given consideration to Jim by discharging him from the obligation to pay the money. Jim has given consideration to John by discharging him from the obligation to service the boiler.
>
> (2) If John does some of the work, and Jim agrees to pay him a proportion of the money for the work he has done, then the contract is discharged. Jim's consideration is letting John off with finishing the job. John's consideration is letting Jim off with paying the rest of the money.
>
> (3) If John does some of the work and agrees that Jim need not pay him for this work done, then the contract is discharged. John lets Jim off with paying the money. Jim lets John off with finishing the work.
>
> (4) If John finishes the whole job but agrees that Jim need not pay anything, the contract is not discharged. Jim has not provided any consideration for being let off the duty to pay the price.
>
> (5) If John finishes the work and agrees to accept a bicycle instead of the contract price, the contract is discharged. The court will not enquire whether or not the bicycle is worth £1,000. Earlier (in Chapter 2) we saw that consideration must be sufficient (worth something) but need not be adequate (worth the same amount as the other party's consideration).
>
> (6) If John finishes the work but agrees to accept 90 per cent of the contract price, the contract is not discharged. Earlier (in Chapter 2) we saw that (subject to promissory estoppel) a lesser sum of money cannot be consideration for a greater sum owed.

A party may waive (give up) contractual rights by indicating to the other party that the rights will not be insisted upon. If no consideration was given in return for the waiver, the contract is not discharged. However, the rights which were waived can be reintroduced only by giving reasonable notice of this. Until this is done, a party cannot be in breach of contract for failure to perform a waived right.

For example, in **Charles Rickards Ltd v Oppenheim (1950)** the claimant agreed to sell the defendant a specially constructed car. The contract provided that the car was to be delivered on 20 March. The claimant did not deliver on time and the defendant kept asking him for delivery. The defendant then said that if the car was not delivered by 25 July he would refuse to accept delivery. The claimant tried to deliver the car in October, but the defendant refused to accept delivery. The Court of Appeal held that the defendant was entitled to refuse to accept delivery. The defendant had waived his right to receive delivery on 20 March, but had given reasonable notice that delivery had to be made by 25 July. If the claimant had tried to deliver at any time before 25 July the defendant would have been bound to accept the delivery.

Discharge by frustration

A contract may become frustrated if it becomes impossible to perform, illegal to perform or radically different from what the parties contemplated. Before we examine these three grounds on which a contract may be frustrated, it is important to notice that we are talking about a valid contract *becoming* illegal, impossible or radically different. If a contract is impossible to perform when it is made, then it may be void for mistake. If a contract is illegal to perform at the time when it is made then it is an illegal contract and will therefore be void. If the contract was, at the time of making the contract, radically different from what the parties intended then it may be void for mistake. Both mistake and illegal contracts were considered earlier (see Chapter 4).

Impossibility of performance

If a contract becomes impossible to perform then it will be frustrated.

 Taylor *v* Caldwell (1863)

A music hall was hired out for four days. Before these days came around the music hall was accidentally burnt down.

Held The contract was frustrated.

Comment The contract would not have been frustrated if the music hall had been sold, not hired, and had burnt down immediately after the contract. The buyer would have got ownership of the hall and his hall would have burnt down. A contract to sell unascertained goods, such as 100 new DVDs, will not be frustrated if the DVDs which the seller intended to use to perform the contract are destroyed before the DVDs are delivered. If the risk had passed to the buyer, then it would be his loss and if it had not yet passed it would be the seller's loss. Either way, the contract would not be frustrated. If specific goods, such as a particular second-hand machine, are sold then it is possible, but very unlikely, that the contract could be frustrated under s. 7 of the Sale of Goods Act 1979. This would depend upon the goods having perished before the risk had passed. Almost always, however, the contract would not be frustrated. The Sale of Goods Act rules on frustration and risk are considered in an earlier chapter (see Chapter 7). There it will be seen that frustration under the SGA is quite different from common law frustration, which we are considering in this chapter.

If a party who has contracted to perform the contract personally dies or becomes too ill to perform, the contract will be impossible to perform. It will therefore be frustrated.

 Condor *v* The Barron Knights Ltd (1966)

When the claimant was 16 he became a drummer with the defendant band. His five-year contract obliged him to work seven nights a week and sometimes to do two performances in one night. One month after joining the band the claimant collapsed and was taken to a mental hospital. Doctors told the claimant that if he worked more than four nights a week he would have a complete mental breakdown. The band dismissed the claimant because they could not arrange to have the claimant drumming for four nights a week and someone else drumming for three nights a week. The claimant sued the band for wrongful dismissal.

Held The claimant had not been wrongfully dismissed because the contract was frustrated. It had become impossible for the claimant to perform the terms of the contract. If the failure to perform the terms had been for a short time only, then the contract would not have become frustrated. However, since it was long-term impossibility, the contract was frustrated.

Comment In **Cutter v Powell (1795)** (earlier in the chapter), the contract was not frustrated because the doctrine of frustration did not evolve until around the year 1850.

Illegality of performance

Where a contract becomes illegal to perform, it will be frustrated. For example, in the **Fibrosa Case (1943)** the House of Lords held that a contract to supply machinery to Poland was frustrated when Germany occupied Poland. Great Britain was at war with Germany, and it is illegal to supply an enemy-occupied country.

The contract becomes radically different

A contract will be frustrated if it becomes radically different from what the parties intended when they made the contract, so that the foundation of the contract is destroyed.

 Krell v Henry (1903) (Court of Appeal)

King Edward VII was about to be crowned. In celebration, a huge coronation procession was to pass through London on 26 and 27 June. The defendant agreed to hire a room from the claimant for these two days for £75. The written contract did not state the purpose of this. However, both parties understood that the sole purpose was that the defendant and his friends could view the coronation procession from the room. The King was ill and so the coronation procession was cancelled. The claimant sued the defendant for the contract price.

Held The defendant did not have to pay because the contract had become frustrated.

In a similar case, **Herne Bay Steam Boat Co v Hutton (1903)**, the defendant had agreed to hire a steamboat for two days in order to take passengers cruising around the fleet so that they could watch the naval review. The King's illness caused the naval review to be cancelled. The Court of Appeal held that the contract was not frustrated. Performance of the contract was different from what the parties intended, but it was not radically different because the defendant could still have taken passengers cruising around the fleet.

Rules about frustration

Before we examine the effects of a contract becoming frustrated, there are several points about frustration which we should notice.

Performance required in a particular way

If a contract states that it should be performed in a certain way, then it will be frustrated if it becomes impossible to perform in that way. For example, if a contract states that a cargo should be carried on a particular ship then it will be frustrated if that ship sinks. This is the case even if other ships could carry the cargo just as well.

Contract becomes more difficult to perform

A contract will not become frustrated merely because it becomes more difficult to perform. For example, in **Davis Contractors Ltd v Fareham Urban District Council (1956)** the House of Lords held that a contract to build 78 houses in eight months was not frustrated when a shortage of labour and materials meant that the contract took 22 months to perform. The builders should have considered that there might be shortages of labour and materials before agreeing to do the job.

Force majeure clauses

If the parties to the contract foresee that there might be difficulties which they cannot control and set out in the contract what should happen if these difficulties arise, the courts will give effect to what has been agreed. Clauses which make such provisions are known as *force majeure* clauses. For example, in **Davis Contractors Ltd v Fareham UDC** the parties might have included a *force majeure* clause dealing with what the position should be if there turned out to be a shortage of labour and materials. Such a clause might have stated that if there was a shortage of labour and materials, then the contract would be frustrated. Or it might have said that, if there was a shortage of labour and materials, the contract should not be frustrated but the builder should be given more time to do the work and paid more money. Whatever the *force majeure* clause agreed, the court would have enforced the clause.

Frustrating event is foreseen

If only one of the parties knows that the frustrating event might happen (or should have known this), then that party cannot claim frustration. For example, in **Walton Harvey Ltd v Walker & Homfrays Ltd (1931)** a hotel owner who had agreed to let the claimant put advertisements on his hotel could not claim that the contract was frustrated when the hotel was compulsorily demolished. The hotel owner was in breach of contract because he knew that the hotel might be compulsorily demolished and the advertisers did not know this.

One party took the risk

If the interpretation of the contract and the surrounding circumstances indicate that one of the parties took the risk of the 'frustrating' event happening, then the contract will not be frustrated. In **Herne Bay Steam Boat Co v Hutton**, for example, the court thought that the commercial venture of hiring the steamboat was at the defendant's risk and this was a factor in deciding that the contract was not frustrated.

Self-induced frustration

A party to the contract who has brought about a certain event cannot claim that this event frustrates the contract. Self-induced frustration is no frustration.

 Maritime National Fish Ltd v Ocean Trawlers Ltd (1935) (Privy Council)

The claimants chartered a ship with an otter trawl (a certain type of fishing net) to the defendants. Both parties knew that it was illegal for a ship to fish with an otter trawl unless a licence had been gained from the Canadian Government. The defendants applied for five licences because they had four other boats fitted with otter trawls. However, the defendants were granted only three licences. They assigned these licences to three of their own boats and claimed that the contract with the claimants was frustrated because it would be illegal to use the chartered boat for fishing.

Held The contract with the claimants was not frustrated. The defendants were the ones who had caused the chartered boat not to have a licence and so they could not argue that the absence of a licence frustrated the contract.

Leases of land

A lease can be frustrated only in the most exceptional circumstances. A lease is more than a contract; it creates an interest in land.

The legal effect of frustration

As soon as the frustrating event happens, the contract comes to an end. The Law Reform (Frustrated Contracts) Act 1943 (LRFCA 1943) then makes the following rules:

- Money owing under the contract ceases to be payable.
- Money which has already been paid under the contract can be recovered. However, the court has a discretion to allow a party who has incurred expenses to be paid for these expenses. The amount of the expenses cannot be more than the money paid or payable before the contract was frustrated.
- If one of the parties has received a valuable benefit under the contract, the court can order that a fair amount is paid to compensate for this.

Example

X Ltd has agreed to supply Y Ltd with 1,000 toy guns. The contract price was £2,000 and half of this was paid in advance, half was to be paid when all of the goods were delivered. Parliament passes a statute making the sale of toy guns illegal. The contract is therefore frustrated. Y Ltd do not need to pay the £1,000 which has not yet been paid. Y Ltd can recover the £1,000 already paid. However, the court could allow X Ltd to keep some of this money to compensate for expenses incurred. If 100 toy guns had already been delivered, then the court could order that Y Ltd make a payment for these. This payment might be 10 per cent of the contract price (because 10 per cent of the guns have been delivered) but would not necessarily be so. The amount payable, if anything, is at the court's discretion.

Difficulties arise when a valuable benefit conferred is destroyed by the frustrating event. For example, where the contract is to put central heating in a house and shortly before this work is completed the house is burnt down. When is the valuable benefit to be valued? If it is valued immediately before the frustrating event, the contractor might be paid close to the whole contract price. If it is valued immediately after the frustrating event, it is worth nothing. In **BP Exploration Co (Libya) Ltd *v* Hunt (No. 2) (1982)** it was held that the value of any benefit is considered immediately after the frustrating event. So in the example above the contractor would receive nothing for the work already done.

Figure 5.3 gives an overview of frustration.

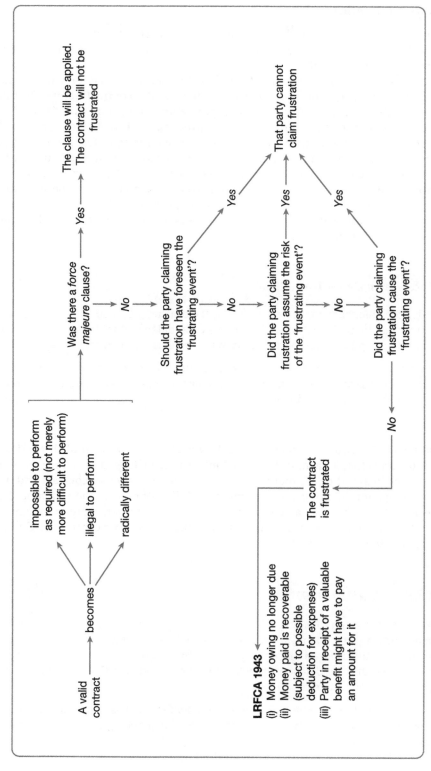

Figure 5.3 An overview of frustration

Discharge by breach

In an earlier chapter we considered the extent to which a party is entitled to treat a contract as discharged on account of the other party's breach of contract. (See conditions, warranties and innominate terms in Chapter 3.)

If a party shows an intention not to be bound by the contract, this is known as a repudiation of the contract. When one of the parties repudiates the contract before the time for performance of the contract is due, this is known as an anticipatory breach. The injured party can either accept the breach or keep the contract open. If the breach is accepted, the injured party can treat the contract as terminated and sue for damages. If the anticipatory breach is not accepted, the contract is still alive. The position then depends upon whether the anticipatory breach becomes an actual breach (because the contract is not performed when performance becomes due). If it does not become an actual breach (because the contract is properly performed in time), then there is no problem. If it does become an actual breach, the injured party can sue for damages for breach of contract. The following case demonstrates these principles.

 Hochster *v* De La Tour (1853)

In April 1852 the defendant contracted to employ the claimant as a courier for a three-month period which was to begin on 1 June. On 11 May the defendant told the claimant that he was not in fact going to employ him. The claimant immediately sued for damages.

Held The claimant was entitled to sue for damages because he had accepted the anticipatory breach. The claimant did not need to wait until the breach became an actual breach (which it would have done on 1 June).

In **Hochster *v* De La Tour** the claimant could have chosen to wait until the anticipatory breach became an actual breach. If the defendant had then changed his mind, and decided to employ the claimant after all, there would have been no breach of contract and no problem. If the defendant did not change his mind, and did not employ the claimant after all, then there would have been an actual breach on 1 June. However, there is a slight risk in waiting until an anticipatory breach becomes an actual breach. The contract might become frustrated, as the following case shows.

 Avery *v* Bowden (1856)

The defendant contracted to supply the claimant's ship with a cargo. The cargo was to be supplied at Odessa within 45 days. When the claimant's ship reached Odessa the defendant repeatedly told the claimant that no cargo would be delivered. The claimant kept his ship in Odessa, hoping that the defendant would change his mind. The Crimean War broke out before the 45 days had expired.

Held The outbreak of war frustrated the contract (because Odessa had become controlled by the enemy and it is illegal to supply an enemy-occupied country) and so the right to sue had been permanently lost.

Figure 5.4 gives an overview of discharge by acceptance of an anticipatory breach.

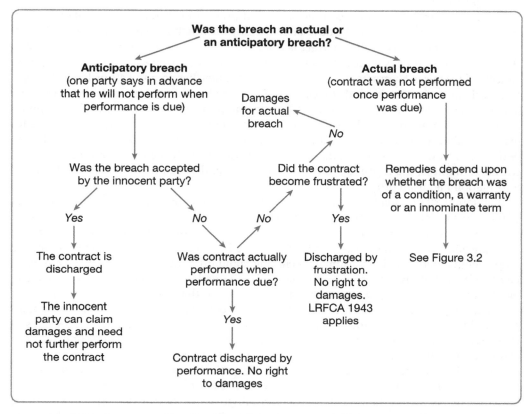

Figure 5.4 Discharge by acceptance of anticipatory breach

Legislation giving right to cancel concluded contracts

Regulation 29 of the Consumer Contracts (Information, Cancellation and Additional Charges) Regulations 2013 gives consumers the right to cancel distance or off-premises contracts within 14 days. No reason needs to be given and the consumer does not incur any liability. The standard EU definition of a consumer is used, so a consumer is an individual acting for purposes which are wholly or mainly outside that individual's trade, business, craft or profession. A distance contract is a contract concluded between a trader and a consumer under an organised distance sales or service-provision scheme without the simultaneous physical presence of the trader and the consumer, with the exclusive use of one or more means of distance communication up to and including the time at which the contract is concluded. An off-premises contract means a contract between a trader and a consumer which is either (a) concluded face-to-face between the consumer and the trader, but off the business premises of the trader; or (b) one where the consumer made an offer face-to-face with the trader, but off the business premises of the trader; or (c) a contract concluded on the business premises of the trader, or through any means of distance communication, immediately after the consumer was personally and individually addressed by the trader off the business premises of the trader or (d) a contract concluded during an excursion organised by the trader with the aim or effect of promoting and selling goods or services to the consumer.

If the contract is a distance contract or an off-premises contract for the sale of goods, the cancellation periods ends 14 days after the day on which the consumer gains physical possession of the goods. If the contract is a service contract, or one to download software, the period ends 14 days after the contract was entered into. However, there is no right to cancel off-premises contracts under which the consumer has to pay £42 or less. The right to cancel does exist as regards distance contracts worth less than this amount. If the contract is a distance or off-premises contract, Schedule 2 requires the trader to give the consumer notice that the right to cancel exists, as well as the conditions, time limit and procedures for exercising that right. If this information is given late, but within 12 months, the cancellation period runs from the date when the information was given. If the information is not given within 12 months, the cancellation period ends 12 months after it would have ended if the information had been properly given.

Regulation 32 provides that the consumer cancels merely by clearly informing the trader of this. No special form needs to be used and the cancellation if posted is effective from the date of posting. However, the burden of proof is on the consumer to show that the contract was cancelled within the period. Once a contract is cancelled the trader must reimburse all payments made by the consumer, including standard delivery costs, within 14 days of being informed of the cancellation. No fee can be charged by the trader, and the reimbursement must be made using the same means of payment as the consumer used. As long as the goods can be returned by post, Regulation 35 provides that it is generally the consumer's responsibility to send the goods back or hand them over to the trader within 14 days of cancellation and to pay the cost of this. If a consumer does withdraw an offer or cancel any contract under the regulations, ancillary contracts are also cancelled.

The trader must not begin to supply a service until the end of the cancellation period, unless the consumer has expressly requested this. If the consumer does expressly request it, but still cancels within the cancellation period, Regulation 36 provides that the consumer must pay a proportionate amount of the total price. Regulation 37 provides that the trader must not supply downloadable software until the end of the cancellation period, unless the consumer has expressly requested this and acknowledged that if the software is supplied the right to cancel will be lost.

As regards distance contracts concluded by electronic means, Regulation 14 provides that a consumer is not bound by a contract or order unless the consumer, when placing the order, explicitly acknowledges that the order implies an obligation to pay. If placing an order entails activating a button or a similar function, the trader must ensure that the button or similar function is labelled in an easily legible manner only with the words 'order with obligation to pay' or a corresponding unambiguous formulation indicating that placing the order entails an obligation to pay the trader. Failure to comply with this will also mean that the consumer is not bound by the contract or order.

Schedule 2 of the Regulations applies to distance and off-premises contracts. It requires the trader to give the consumer detailed information about the main characteristics of the goods or services, the trader's identity and contact details, total costs, delivery details and cancellation rights before the contract is concluded. Where applicable, the following details must also be supplied: that the consumer must bear the cost of returning the goods; details of after-sales assistance and guarantees; details of relevant codes of practice; the minimum duration of the contract; the functionality of digital content; the compatibility of digital content with hardware or software to the extent that the trader is aware of this or can reasonably be expected to have been aware of it; and out-of-court complaint and redress mechanisms. Regulation 16 requires a trader to give a consumer confirmation of a distance contract on a durable medium. The confirmation must include all of the information in Schedule 2 unless this has already been supplied to the consumer on a durable medium prior to the conclusion of the contract. Regulation 10 provides that a consumer is not bound by an off-premises contract until he has been given the information contained in Schedule 2 in a clear and comprehensible manner, along with a cancellation form if there is a right to cancel. Regulation 12 requires the trader to give the consumer a copy of the signed off-premises contract or confirmation of the contract which includes all the information in Schedule 2. The information required by Regulations 10 and 12 must be given on paper or, if the consumer agrees, on another durable medium and must be legible. As regards distance contracts, Regulation 13 provides that if the consumer is not informed of any additional delivery charges or costs, or that the consumer will have to bear the costs of returning the goods, the consumer will not be liable to pay those charges or costs.

As regards on-premises contracts, Regulation 9 requires the trader to give or make available the information in Schedule 1 in a clear and comprehensible manner, if that information is not already apparent from the context. However, this is not the case as regards day-to-day contracts which are performed immediately. Any of the required information is regarded as a term of the contract. Furthermore, the consumer will not be bound by the contract until the information has been given. The information required by Schedule 1 is as follows: the main characteristics of the goods or services; the identity of the trader; his geographical address and telephone number; the total price to be paid; and a reminder that goods supplied must be in conformity with the contract. Where applicable, the following information must also be supplied: total delivery charges; the arrangements for delivery, payment and performance; the trader's complaints policy; the existence and conditions of after-sales services and guarantees; the duration of the contract; the functionality of digital content; and the compatibility of digital content with hardware or software to the extent that the trader is aware of this or can reasonably be expected to have been aware of it.

The Consumer Credit Act 1974 (CCA 1974) allows a debtor or hirer under a regulated consumer credit agreement to cancel the agreement within seven days of making the agreement if oral representations were made before the contract was made. This does not apply if the debtor signed the credit agreement at the creditor's place of business. (This right to cancel is examined in more detail in Chapter 16.) The Consumer Rights Directive, which must be implemented into UK law by December 2013, requires all of the current 7-day statutory cooling-off periods to be replaced with a 14-day cooling-off period.

The Timeshare Act 1992 allows a consumer who has made a timeshare agreement a 14-day cooling-off period.

Remedies for breach of contract

Refusal to perform the contract

We have already seen that in some circumstances one party will be able to refuse to further perform the contract on account of the other party's breach of contract. We have seen that this will be possible if the other party repudiates the contract or breaches a condition of the contract. It will also be possible if the other party breaches an innominate term in such a way that this deprived the injured party of substantially the whole benefit of the contract. (See conditions, warranties and innominate terms in Chapter 3.)

Damages

Any breach of contract always allows the injured party to sue for damages. Contract damages are intended to put the injured party into the same position, as far as money can do this, as if the contract had been performed. It follows that if the injured party has suffered no loss as a result of the breach, only nominal damages will be available. Nominal damages are damages in name only, perhaps 5p or £1. It is also necessary that the defendant's breach of contract caused the loss being claimed for.

Remoteness of damage

When a contract is breached, substantial damages can be claimed only in respect of losses which fall within one of the two rules in **Hadley *v* Baxendale (1854)**. Other losses are regarded as too remote.

Rule 1 allows damages for a loss if the loss arose naturally from the breach of contract, in the usual course of things.

Rule 2 allows damages for a loss if the loss can reasonably be supposed to have been within the contemplation of the parties when they made the contract.

The rules on remoteness of damage provide an important limit on the amount of contract damages. A breach of contract can have many unforeseeable consequences. If there were no rules on remoteness, the person in breach of contract would always be liable for these consequences. This would make people unwilling to make contracts.

The following case shows how the two rules work.

 Victoria Laundry *v* Newman Industries (1949) (Court of Appeal)

The claimants agreed to buy a boiler from the defendants. The defendants knew that the boiler was to be used immediately in the claimants' laundry. They also knew that there was a big demand for general laundry services at this time. The defendants delivered the boiler 20 weeks late. Two claims for damages were made by the claimants. First, they claimed £16 a week, which represented the extra profit they could have made by doing more general laundry work with the new boiler. Second, they claimed £262 a week which had been lost on account of the claimants not being able to use the boiler to fulfil a very profitable contract to dye army uniforms.

Held The claimants were entitled to the £16 a week, under the first rule in **Hadley *v* Baxendale**. The £262 was not available under either rule. (It would have been available under the second rule in **Hadley *v* Baxendale** if the claimants had told the defendants, before the contract was made, that such a very profitable contract would be lost if the boiler was not delivered on time.)

In **Koufos *v* Czarnikow Ltd (The Heron 2) (1967)** Lord Reid held that, under **Hadley *v* Baxendale**, a loss was recoverable because it was 'not unlikely' or 'quite likely' to occur. Damages could be recovered for a loss if the loss was within the reasonable contemplation of the parties when the contract was made.

 In **Transfield Shipping Inc *v* Mercator Shipping Inc (The Achilleas) (2008)**, a case concerning the chartering of a ship, the House of Lords held that there would be no liability for a foreseeable consequence of a breach of contract if both parties would have assumed that the contract breaker would not assume liability for the type of loss in question. The case was an unusual one. It would apply only where the circumstances showed that the parties could not have made the contract on the basis that the defendant was to be liable for a particular kind of loss, even if this loss was reasonably contemplatable or 'not unlikely'.

Having decided that a loss is within one of the two rules in **Hadley _v_ Baxendale**, it must then be decided how much the damages should be.

Amount of damages

If the contract is a sale of goods, the Sale of Goods Act 1979 sets out rules which determine the amount of damages payable. These rules are examined later (see Chapter 7).

In contracts other than contracts of sale of goods, the damages are quantified on the basis that they are intended to put the injured party in the same position, as far as money can do this, as if the contract had been properly performed. Damages will therefore be available for putting right defects caused by the breach of contract. They will also be available for any other losses, such as loss of profits, as long as these were caused by the breach of contract and were within one of the rules in **Hadley _v_ Baxendale**. If the defendant's breach of contract causes the claimant to pay damages to a third party, these damages paid are generally also recoverable.

> ### Example
>
> Jerry agrees to service Z Ltd's oven for £1,000. Jerry knows that Z Ltd need the oven to operate their bakery. Z Ltd tell Jerry that the service must be finished on time because otherwise Z Ltd will be in breach of a very profitable contract to do bakery for Y Ltd. Jerry performs the service so badly that Z Ltd's oven cannot work at all. Jerry cannot fix the problem. Z Ltd hunt around for someone else to fix the oven. The only person they can find is Tom, who fixes the oven one week after Jerry should have fixed it. As Z Ltd could not do the bakery for Y Ltd they are themselves in breach of contract and will have to pay Y Ltd £2,000 damages. Jerry will have to pay damages to Z Ltd as follows: (i) the cost of Tom putting right the fault which Jerry caused; (ii) the amount of ordinary business profit lost by Z Ltd as a consequence of not being able to use the oven for one week; (iii) the profit Z Ltd would have made if they had been able to perform their contract with Y Ltd; (iv) the amount of damages which Z Ltd had to pay to Y Ltd.

Mitigation

In the above example, Z Ltd might have incurred even more losses if they had not hunted around to find someone else to fix the oven. However, if they had not hunted around to find someone else, they could not have claimed more damages. A party who suffers a loss as a result of breach of contract must take all reasonable steps to mitigate (reduce) the loss. No substantial damages can be claimed in respect of a loss which could have been mitigated by taking reasonable steps.

> ### Brace _v_ Calder (1895)
>
> The claimant was employed by a partnership of four people for a fixed two-year period. The partnership was dissolved when two of the partners left. The two remaining partners immediately agreed to employ the claimant on exactly the same terms as he had previously been employed. The claimant refused this offer and sued for breach of contract.
>
> _Held_ There had been a breach of contract because the four partners had not employed the claimant for the full two-year period. However, the claimant was entitled to nominal damages only from the original partners. He should have mitigated his loss by accepting the alternative employment.

Damages are generally not available for injured feelings or disappointment. However, where the contract was to provide the claimant with enjoyment and relaxation (as in the case of a holiday) it is possible that damages can be awarded for disappointment and distress caused by a breach of the contract.

Mitigation and anticipatory breach

Earlier in this chapter we considered anticipatory breach. We saw that a person faced with such a breach can either accept the breach, and regard the contract as terminated, or elect to keep the contract open. A person who accepts an anticipatory breach must mitigate losses in the usual way.

A person who does not accept an anticipatory breach will generally also have to mitigate losses. However, in the following case the anticipatory breach was not accepted, and the injured party who continued to perform the contract had no duty to mitigate. The case was unusual in that the injured party could perform the contract without the co-operation of the party who committed the anticipatory breach.

 White and Carter (Councils) *v* MacGregor (1962) (House of Lords)

The claimants were advertising agents who agreed to advertise the defendants' garage for a three-year period. On the same day that the contract was made the defendants wrote to the claimants asking them to cancel the contract. The claimants did not accept this anticipatory breach but began to advertise the defendants' business as agreed. One of the terms of the contract said that if any of the instalments which the defendants were required to pay became four weeks overdue, then the claimants could sue for the whole contract price. The defendants refused to pay any of the instalments. The claimants advertised the defendants' garage as agreed for the whole three-year period and then sued for the whole contract price.

Held The claimants were entitled to perform the contract and sue for the whole contract price. They were not bound to accept the repudiation and sue for damages. Nor did they have a duty to mitigate their losses.

Comment The principle in this case is unusual and will apply only where: (a) the contract can be performed without the cooperation of the other party; and (b) the injured party has some legitimate interest, other than claiming damages, in carrying the contract on.

Agreed damages

Sometimes, a term of the contract will fix the amount of damages payable in the event of breach of contract. Damages agreed in this way are classified as being either liquidated damages or penalties.

If the amount of damages fixed is the amount which the parties genuinely believed that the loss would be, then the damages agreed are liquidated damages. The amount of damages fixed by the term will then be the amount of damages awarded, no matter what the actual loss turned out to be.

If the amount of damages fixed is not the amount which the parties genuinely believed that the loss would be, but an excessively large amount, then the damages agreed will be a penalty. A penalty is ignored and damages are calculated as if the term setting out the penalty had not existed. Penalties are often put into a contract by the party with the greater bargaining power, to try to terrorise the other party into performing the contract. (Notice that a penalty clause will not amount to economic duress because it is not pushing a person into making a contract: it is saying what the damages will be if the contract is breached.)

> ### Example
>
> John, a builder, agrees to build a new shop which is to be completed by 1 March. A term of the contract states that if the shop is not completed on time, then the damages payable by John will be £500 a week for every week that the shop is not completed. John completes the work ten weeks late. If, when the parties made the contract, they thought that the actual loss to the shop owner would be £500 a week, then the agreed damages are liquidated damages. John would therefore have to pay £5,000 damages, no matter how much his breach of contract actually cost the shop owner. If, when the parties made the contract, they thought that the actual loss in the event of breach would be much less than £500 a week, then the term will be a penalty. The penalty will be ignored and damages will be calculated in the usual way to compensate the shop owner for the actual loss suffered.

Interest on damages

A contract might agree that interest on damages should be paid at a certain rate. If the parties do not make such an agreement, then the court will order that interest is payable from the date when the claim arose.

Figure 5.5 gives an overview of damages for breach of contract.

Suing for the contract price

When a seller sues for the contract price, this is not the same thing as suing for damages. When a claim is made for the payment of a debt, the amount claimed is said to be liquidated. As the claim is not for damages, the rules on remoteness, mitigation and quantification of damages will not apply. For example, let us assume that John agreed to build an office for Tony for £70,000 and completed the job properly. If Tony does not pay the contract price, then John can sue for it. The rules on remoteness, mitigation and quantification of damages will not apply. So there will be no need to consider the rules in **Hadley v Baxendale**, and John does not need to take any steps to reduce his loss. Nor will a court need to make calculations to find the amount being claimed, apart from working out any interest which is payable.

The Sale of Goods Act 1979 lays down the circumstances in which a seller of goods can sue for the contract price. These rules are examined later (see Chapter 7).

The Late Payment of Commercial Debts (Interest) Act 1998 gives all businesses the right to claim interest when a commercial debt arising from the supply of goods and services to another business or to a public sector body is paid late.

As regards business-to-business contracts, invoices must be paid within 60 days of being received unless a longer period is fixed by the contract and this longer period is not grossly unfair to the creditor. (See the Late Payment of Commercial Debts (Interest) Act 1998 in Chapter 16.)

The effect of the Act cannot be avoided by means of a contractual term unless there is a 'substantial' remedy available for the late payment of the debt. It is only possible for a contractual term to postpone the time at which a debt is created to the extent that the term satisfies the UCTA 1977 requirement of reasonableness. (The UCTA requirement of reasonableness was examined in Chapter 3.)

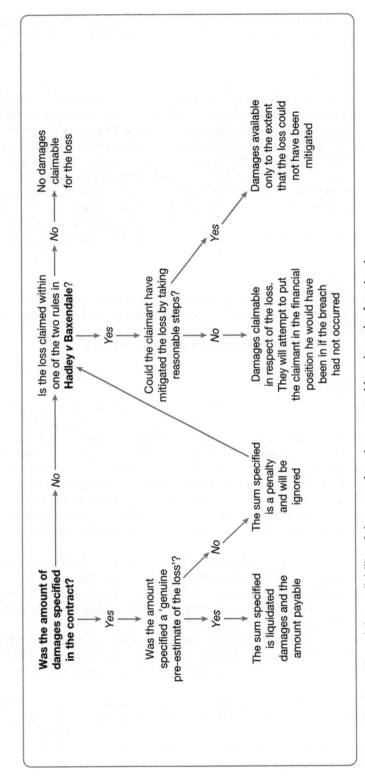

Figure 5.5 An outline of the availability of damages for a loss caused by a breach of contract

Specific performance

Specific performance is an equitable remedy which arises when a court orders a person to actually perform the contractual obligations undertaken. For example, if Mark agreed to sell an antique vase to Asif but then refused to go through with the contract, Asif might ask the court for an order of specific performance. If such an order was made by the court, Mark would be ordered to go through with the contract and to let Asif have the vase. Disobeying such a court order would put Mark in contempt of court and liable to a fine or imprisonment.

Specific performance is rarely ordered by a court. It will not be ordered where damages would provide a good enough remedy. It will not therefore be ordered to make a seller hand over new mass-produced goods which could be obtained from another seller. Specific performance can be ordered where a seller refuses to hand over unique goods (such as an antique vase). All plots of land are regarded as unique and so specific performance will be ordered where a seller of land refuses to perform the contract.

As specific performance is an equitable remedy, it is only available at the court's discretion. The remedy will not be ordered in the following circumstances. First, where the claimant has behaved inequitably (unfairly). This reflects an old saying that: 'He who comes to Equity must come with clean hands.' Second, specific performance will not be ordered to enforce a contract which required personal services to be provided (such as a contract of employment). Third, it will not be ordered where to order it would cause excessive hardship to the defendant. Fourth, it will not be ordered for or against a minor (person under 18).

Injunction

An injunction is a court order which requires a person to do or not to do a certain thing. An injunction can be ordered, as an equitable remedy, to prevent a party from breaching a contract. However, an injunction will not be ordered where an award of damages would give a satisfactory remedy. In cases where specific performance could not be ordered, an injunction will not be ordered if it would have the same effect as an order of specific performance.

 Warner Bros Pictures Inc v Nelson (1936)

An actress, Bette Davis, made a contract with the claimants. She agreed that she would act for the claimants, and not act for anyone else, for a two-year period. The actress intended to act for another company. The defendants sought an injunction to prevent this.

Held An injunction was ordered to prevent the actress from breaching her contract by acting for another company. This did not amount to an order of specific performance of a personal service contract because the claimant was not compelled to act for the defendants. She could have earnt a living in some other way.

Comment An injunction forbidding the defendant from doing any other type of work would not have been ordered. Such an injunction would have forced the defendant to act for the claimants and would therefore have amounted to specific performance of a personal service contract.

Two special types of injunctions may be ordered, but only in very limited circumstances. A freezing order prevents a person from moving assets out of the jurisdiction of the English courts. A search order allows the claimant to take away or photocopy documents which the defendant might destroy. Both of these injunctions are granted only in very exceptional circumstances.

Rectification

Rectification is an equitable remedy which arises when a contract which has been concluded orally is then written down. If what is written down does not accurately reflect what the parties agreed orally, the court can allow the written document to be rectified (put right).

Quantum meruit (as much as he has earned)

A party who receives a *quantum meruit* payment is paid the amount deserved for work done. Such a right can arise in four circumstances:

(1) if the other contracting party prevented further performance of the contract;

(2) if the other contracting party voluntarily accepted partial performance of the contract;

(3) if the contract did not provide how much should be paid; or

(4) if work was done and accepted under a void contract.

Time limits on remedies

The Limitation Act 1980 makes the following rules about the time span within which a remedy for breach of contract must be claimed.

A simple contract (one not made by a deed) must be sued upon within six years of the right to sue arising. The right to sue will arise when the contract is breached. A claim for personal injuries must be made within three years of the right to sue arising. Where a contract is made by a deed, a claim must be made within 12 years of the right to sue arising. Time does not run against minors until they reach the age of 18. Time does not run against a victim of a fraud until the fraud is, or should have been, discovered. Where the claim is for a debt, any written acknowledgement of the debt's existence will cause the time period to begin again.

The time limits set out in the Limitation Act 1980 do not apply to equitable remedies. However, an equitable remedy will not be granted to a party who has delayed unreasonably in asking for the remedy.

Essential points

- Contractual liability can become discharged in four ways: by performance, by agreement, by frustration or by breach.
- The general rule is that if one party fails to fully perform the contract, the other party need not perform the contract at all.
- Contractual obligations can be discharged by agreement, as long as both parties give some consideration to the other in return for being released from their contractual obligations.
- A contract may become frustrated if it becomes impossible to perform, illegal to perform or radically different from what the parties contemplated when they made the contract.
- When one of the parties repudiates the contract before the time for performance of the contract is due, this is known as an anticipatory breach.

- A party will be able to refuse to further perform the contract if a condition is breached.
- A party will not be able to refuse to further perform the contract if a warranty is breached.
- Any breach of contract always allows the injured party to sue for damages.
- Substantial damages can only be claimed in respect of losses which fall within one of the two rules in Hadley *v* Baxendale. Other losses are regarded as too remote.
- Hadley *v* Baxendale rule 1 allows damages for a loss if the loss arose naturally from the breach of contract, in the usual course of things.
- Hadley *v* Baxendale rule 2 allows damages for a loss if the loss can reasonably be supposed to have been within the contemplation of the parties when they made the contract.

Practice questions

1 Giles, a poultry farmer, agreed to supply Export Ltd with 5,000 turkeys. The contract said that the turkeys were for export to Ruritania and had to meet Ruritanian health standards. The contract price was £15,000. £5,000 was paid in advance and £10,000 was to be paid once all the turkeys had been delivered. After 1,000 turkeys had been delivered the exporting of turkeys was made illegal by a statute. Advise Giles of his legal position.

2 TeaSell Ltd, a retailer of high class teas, contracted last year to buy one ton of Darjeeling tea from TeaGrow Ltd. The tea was to be delivered on 1 November. This year the weather in Darjeeling has been very bad and the annual tea crop has been disastrous. TeaGrow Ltd had expected to grow ten tons of Darjeeling but has only managed to harvest one ton. On 1 September TeaGrow Ltd wrote to TeaSell Ltd, saying that it would not be able to supply the ton of Darjeeling tea which it had agreed to sell. The letter explained that TeaGrow Ltd had no other existing contracts to sell the tea to anyone else, but that the price of Darjeeling teas has increased so substantially that it would be able to get a much better price from another buyer. Advise TeaSell Ltd of the following matters:

(a) Whether TeaGrow Ltd has committed a breach of contract.

(b) Whether TeaSell Ltd could prevent the sale of the one ton of Darjeeling tea to another buyer.

(c) Whether TeaGrow Ltd could be ordered to deliver the one ton of Darjeeling tea to TeaSell Ltd, as agreed in the contract.

(d) If TeaGrow Ltd do not deliver the tea, whether a claim for damages could be made in respect of the following losses:

(i) Ordinary business profits lost by TeaSell Ltd as a consequence of their not being able to sell Darjeeling tea to regular customers.

(ii) The loss of a very profitable contract to sell Darjeeling tea to a specialist café.

(iii) Damages which TeaSell Ltd has had to pay because the lack of Darjeeling tea caused TeaSell Ltd to breach a contract to sell tea to a tea shop.

(iv) The managing director of TeaSell Ltd having a heart attack, and spending all of his money on private health care. The heart attack was caused by the stress of TeaGrow Ltd breaching their contract with TeaSell Ltd.

3 With reference to decided cases, explain the circumstances in which a contract may become frustrated. Explain also the legal consequences of a contract being frustrated.

Task 5

A friend of yours from abroad is considering setting up business in England. Your friend would like to know the ways in which contractual liability can be discharged and the remedies available for breach of a contract. Write a report for your friend, briefly explaining the following matters:

(a) How contractual obligations can be discharged by performance.

(b) How a contract can be discharged by agreement between the contracting parties.

(c) The ways in which a contract can become frustrated.

(d) The legal position when a contract is frustrated.

(e) The meaning of an anticipatory breach of contract, and the remedies available to a party faced with an anticipatory breach.

(f) How a court decides whether or not a loss caused by a breach of contract is too remote for damages to be claimed in respect of the loss.

(g) How a court quantifies the amount of damages payable for breach of contract.

(h) What is meant by mitigation of a loss.

(i) Whether the courts will apply a clause in a contract which sets out the amount of damages payable in the event of a breach of contract.

(j) What is meant by specific performance of a contract.

(k) How an injunction can be a remedy for breach of contract.

(l) What is meant by a *quantum meruit* payment, and the circumstances in which a contracting party will be entitled to a *quantum meruit* payment.

(m) The time limits within which a claim for breach of contract must be brought.

mylawchamber

Visit **www.mylawchamber.co.uk/macintyreessentials** to access tools to help you develop and test your knowledge of business law, including interactive multiple choice questions, practice exam questions with guidance, weblinks, glossary, glossary flashcards, legal newsfeed and legal updates.

Use **Case Navigator** to read in full some of the key cases referenced in this chapter with commentary and questions:

Carlill *v* The Carbolic Smoke Ball Co (1893)

Transfield Shipping Inc *v* Mercator Shipping Inc (The Achilleas) (2008)

6

Agency

An agent is a person who has the power to alter the legal position of another person, known as the principal. Generally, an agent has the power to make contracts on the principal's behalf. Once the contract has been made, it is the principal and not the agent who will be bound by it as is shown by Figure 6.1.

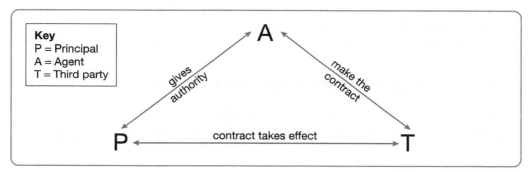

Figure 6.1 Agency

> **Example**
>
> The owner of a painting (the principal) asks an auctioneer (an agent) to sell it at auction. A third party buys the painting for £500. The contract of sale takes effect between the principal and the third party. (The painting which belonged to the principal has been sold to the third party.) But the contract of sale was actually negotiated and concluded by the agent, the auctioneer.

Agency is essential to the business world. If every person making a contract had to do so personally, then the business world would come to a standstill. Without agency, companies and partnerships could not exist. Agency is also far more common that most people think. Shop assistants, for example, are agents. The goods which they sell belong not to themselves but to the owners of the shops in which they work.

As well as having the power to make contracts, agents often also have the power to receive payment on behalf of their principals. For example, shop assistants have the power to receive payment for goods sold on their principal's behalf. If a dishonest shop assistant pockets money paid by a customer, rather than putting it into the till, this is not the concern of the customer. Having paid the price in good faith to the shop assistant, the customer is regarded as having paid the price to the shop owner.

The authority of the agent

An agent cannot act on behalf of a principal unless he has some **authority** to do so. There are different types of authority, which arise in different ways. It is important to know which type of authority an agent has, because the different types have different effects.

Actual authority

The most important type of authority is called **actual authority**. Actual authority arises because the principal agrees with the agent that the agent should have the authority. The principal might agree this using express words, in which case the authority is known as **express actual authority**. Or the principal might agree it impliedly, without express words, in which case it is known as **implied actual authority**. When an agent is appointed to a certain position, then the principal will have impliedly agreed with him that he should do what a person holding that position would usually do. It is important to remember that both types of actual authority arise because the principal has agreed that the agent should have the authority.

  Hely-Hutchinson _v_ Brayhead Ltd (1968) (Court of Appeal)

The board of directors of a company allowed the company chairman to act as if he were the managing director of the company. In fact, the chairman had never been appointed managing director and so had no express authority to bind the company. The chairman made a contract with a third party on the company's behalf.

Held The chairman had implied actual authority to bind the company and so the company was bound by the contract which the chairman had made. The company, by its conduct, had impliedly agreed with the chairman that he should have the same authority as if he had actually been appointed managing director.

Example

In **Hely-Hutchinson _v_ Brayhead Ltd (1968)** Lord Denning MR gave an example of a board of directors of a company passing a resolution authorising two directors to sign cheques. These two directors had been given express actual authority to sign cheques. The example also said that if the board of directors appointed one of the directors to the post of managing director, then they conferred on that director implied actual authority to do what the managing director of such a company would usually do.

Apparent authority

Apparent authority arises in a completely different way. It arises because the principal represents to a third party that the agent has authority. Once the third party has acted on the representation, by agreeing the contract with the agent, the principal is not allowed to deny the truth of what he said. He is estopped from denying it. It is essential that the representation is made by the principal or by someone given actual authority by the principal to make it. It cannot be made by the agent. Nor will apparent authority arise if the third party either knows or ought to know that the agent has no actual authority.

Example

Parveen gives Adrian a job as shop assistant in her shoe shop. Parveen tells Adrian to try to sell one particular pair of red shoes. Adrian has express actual authority to sell this pair of red shoes and implied actual authority to sell all the other pairs of shoes. Both types of authority arose because Parveen agreed with Adrian that they should arise. Adrian also has apparent authority to sell any of the pairs of shoes. This authority arose because Parveen has represented to third parties, the shop's customers, that Adrian has the authority. This representation was made by giving Adrian the job and leaving him in the shop as a shop assistant.

Consequences of different types of authority

We need to tell which type of authority an agent has because the different types of authority have different consequences.

If an agent with actual authority makes a contract with a third party on behalf of a principal, then the consequences are as follows. The contract takes effect between the principal and the third party, just as if the principal had made it personally, and either the principal or the third party can enforce the contract against the other.

If an agent who has *only* apparent authority makes a contract with a third party, then the consequences are not the same. The third party can enforce the contract against the principal, because the principal made a representation which he is estopped from denying. However, the principal cannot enforce the contract against the third party, because the third party did not make any representation. Also, if the agent acts with apparent, but not actual, authority the agent will be liable to the principal if this causes the principal to suffer a foreseeable loss.

Example

Phil, a garage owner, appoints Anjana as a salesperson at his garage. Phil tells Anjana to sell any of the cars except the red Volvo. He also tells her to try to sell the office furniture in the garage. Anjana has implied actual authority to sell any of the cars except the red Volvo. She also has express actual authority to sell the office furniture. If Anjana does sell any of these things, then either Phil or the third party, the buyer, could enforce the contract against the other. Anjana has no actual authority to sell the red Volvo, but she does have apparent authority to sell it (because by putting Anjana in place as a sales person, Phil has represented to outsiders that she can do what a salesperson could usually do, that is to say, sell any of the cars on display). If Anjana does sell the red Volvo to Terry, then Terry can enforce this contract against Phil. However, if Terry changed his mind about buying the car, Phil could not enforce the contract against him. If the red Volvo was sold to Terry, and he knew that Anjana had no actual authority to sell it, then Anjana would have had neither actual nor apparent authority to make the contract. It would not therefore be binding on either Phil or Terry.

The following case shows the difference between actual and apparent authority.

Waugh *v* HB Clifford and Sons Ltd (1982) (Court of Appeal)

The principals, a firm of builders, were being sued by third parties who had bought two houses which had been negligently built. The principals took on agents, a firm of solicitors, to defend the legal proceedings. The third parties suggested a compromise to the solicitors. The solicitors suggested to the builders that they settle the case according to the proposed compromise. The builders told the solicitors not to agree to the compromise with the third parties, but the solicitors agreed to it anyway.

Held The solicitors had no actual authority to make the compromise because they were told not to make it. However, they did have apparent authority to make the compromise because by appointing the solicitors to handle the proceedings the builders had represented to the third parties that the solicitors could agree to a compromise (because solicitors defending legal proceedings could usually do this). So the third parties could enforce the compromise against the builders. The builders could sue the agents for not obeying their instructions.

Example

If Peter gives Andy a job as a salesperson at his car showroom, then Andy will have actual authority to sell the cars on display and will also have apparent authority to do so. Andy will have actual authority because Peter, by giving him the job, agreed with Andy that he should sell the cars. Andy will have apparent authority because Peter, putting Andy in place as a sales person, represented to the showroom's customers that Andy had authority to sell the cars. When an agent has both actual and apparent authority to make the same contract, the apparent authority is not relevant. The agent had actual authority and that is all that matters. For this reason, when considering problem questions on the authority of an agent, actual authority is always considered first. It is when there is no actual authority that apparent authority has to be considered. For example, if Andy told Peter not to sell a particular car, then Peter would not have actual authority to sell that car. However, if Tom bought the car from Andy, not knowing that Andy had been forbidden to sell it, then Andy would have had apparent authority to sell it and Peter would be bound by the contract with Tom.

Ratification

In certain circumstances a principal can ratify a contract made previously by an agent who had no actual authority to make the contract at the time when he did make it. If the principal does ratify the contract, then the agent is regarded as having backdated actual authority.

Example

On Monday Alex buys a car from Tim on Phil's behalf, even though Phil has not asked him to do this. Alex had no actual authority to make the contract, and so Phil cannot enforce it against Tim. Tim would be able to enforce the contract against Phil only if Alex had apparent authority. (If Tim did enforce the contract against Phil, and this caused Phil to suffer a loss,

Phil could sue Alex for acting outside his actual authority.) If Alex had neither actual nor apparent authority, then neither Phil nor Tim could enforce the contract. On Tuesday Phil ratifies the contract. This ratification has retrospective effect and gives Alex actual authority, backdated to the time when he made the contract on Monday. So Phil could enforce the contract against Tim, Tim could enforce the contract against Phil, and Alex would have no liability as he acted with actual authority.

Four conditions must be satisfied for a ratification to be effective:

(1) The agent must have claimed to have acted as an agent, and the third party must have been able to work out who the principal was.

 Keighley Maxted & Co *v* Durant (1901) (House of Lords)

An agent was authorised to buy wheat on behalf of a principal at a certain price. The agent bought wheat at a greater price, by telegram, intending it to be for the principal. The agent did not tell the seller that he was buying the wheat for the principal, but this was always his intention. The principal ratified the contract the following day. Later the principal refused to accept delivery of the wheat.

Held The ratification was not effective, and so the principal could refuse to accept delivery, because the agent made the contract in his own name rather than in the principal's name. The seller could not have worked out that the wheat was intended to be bought for the principal.

(2) The principal must have had full contractual capacity to make the contract both when the agent made the contract and when it was ratified.

(3) At the time of ratification the principal must have either known all of the material facts or intended to ratify no matter what they were.

(4) The contract must be valid; a void contract cannot be ratified.

Ratification must take place within a reasonable time, and will have backdated effect. It will not be allowed where third parties have acquired property rights which would be adversely affected by ratification. A principal can ratify expressly (by saying that he does so) or by some emphatic act (such as suing on the contract) which shows that he is confirming the contract. An example can be seen in **Simpole *v* Chee (2013)**, where a principal ratified the sale of a property by receiving and retaining money paid by the purchaser and by no longer trying to recover rent from the tenant of the property.

Watteau *v* Fenwick authority

The following, difficult, case does not fit within any of the established ways in which agency can be created. However, authority was found to have existed.

 Watteau *v* Fenwick (1893)

A pub owner let a manager (the agent) run a pub. The owner authorised the manager to buy only bottled drinks and expressly forbade him to buy tobacco on credit. Acting against these instructions, the manager did buy tobacco on credit. The tobacco salesman had no idea that the manager was an agent. He thought that the manager owned the pub because he had previously dealt with the manager when the manager used to own the pub and the manager's name was still above the door of the pub. The seller sued the owner, claiming that the owner was liable on the contract.

Held The owner was liable on the contract.

The manager had no express or implied actual authority to buy the cigars. (On the contrary, he had been forbidden to do this.) Nor did the manager have apparent authority because the third party had not relied on a representation that the agent was an agent with such authority. (The third party did not believe the manager to be an agent.) The decision in this case has been doubted in some other cases but it has never been overruled. It is applicable only when:

- the third party did not think that the agent was an agent; and
- the agent made a contract which his position as an agent would usually give him authority to make, but which he had been forbidden by the principal to make.

Agency by operation of law

Agency of necessity

In commercial situations an agent will have authority imposed by the law, on the grounds of necessity, if:

- there was a commercial emergency which made it necessary for the agent to act as he did;
- it was impossible for the agent to obtain the principal's instructions;
- the agent acted in good faith and in the principal's best interests;
- the agent acted reasonably in the circumstances.

Such agency of necessity is usually found in maritime emergencies. Old cases gave the captains of ships the power to sell cargoes which were perishing.

If there is an agency of necessity, then the consequences are the same as if the agent had had actual authority. The principal and third party will be bound by the agent's actions, and the agent will have no liability for acting as he did.

Occasionally, agencies of necessity can be found on dry land.

 Great Northern Railway Co *v* Swaffield (1874)

A horse arrived at a railway station but nobody picked it up. The railway company felt obliged to feed the horse and put it into a stable. When the owner collected the horse he refused to reimburse the railway company.

Held The owner had to pay for the feeding and the stabling as there was an agency of necessity.

As modern communications have improved, agency of necessity is ever less likely to arise.

Statutory agency

Various statutes create agency in very specific situations. These statutory agencies are not of importance outside these specific situations.

No authority

If an agent makes a contract with a third party, claiming to have authority but in fact having no authority, then neither the third party nor the principal will be bound by the contract. If, however, the lack of authority causes loss to the third party, he can sue the agent for breach of warranty of authority, a matter considered later in this chapter. The principal could choose to ratify the contract, in which case the agent would be regarded as having had actual authority when he made the contract. So if the principal did ratify, the agent's liability for breach of warranty of authority would disappear.

Table 6.1 shows the requirements and effects of the different types of authority.

Table 6.1 The types of authority which an agent can have

Type of authority	How created	Effect
Actual (express or implied)	P agreed with A, expressly or impliedly, that A should have the authority.	P can enforce the contract against T. T can enforce the contract against P. A has no liability.
Apparent	(i) P represents to T that A has authority. (ii) T relies on this. (iii) P is estopped from denying it.	T can enforce the contract against P. P cannot enforce the contract against T. P can sue A for acting without actual authority, if A had no actual authority.
Ratification (a form of actual authority)	A, without actual authority, made a contract with T on P's behalf. Later, P ratified (authorised) the contract.	The same as if A had prior actual authority.
Watteau *v* Fenwick	(i) When contract made, T thought it was made with A personally. (ii) A had no actual authority to make the contract. (iii) The contract was a type which an agent such as A could usually have made.	T can enforce the contract against P (in which case P can sue A for acting without actual authority). P cannot enforce the contract against T, and cannot ratify it (because A did not appear to be acting for P).
Necessity	(i) A real emergency. (ii) Impossible to get P's instructions. (iii) A acted in good faith and in P's interests.	The same as if A had prior actual authority.
No authority (but 'the agent' claimed there was)	None of the above types of authority existed. Nor was there authority by operation of law.	P cannot enforce the contract against T (but P might be able to ratify). T cannot enforce the contract against P. T can sue A for breach of warranty of authority.

Figure 6.2 shows how a question on the authority of an agent should be approached.

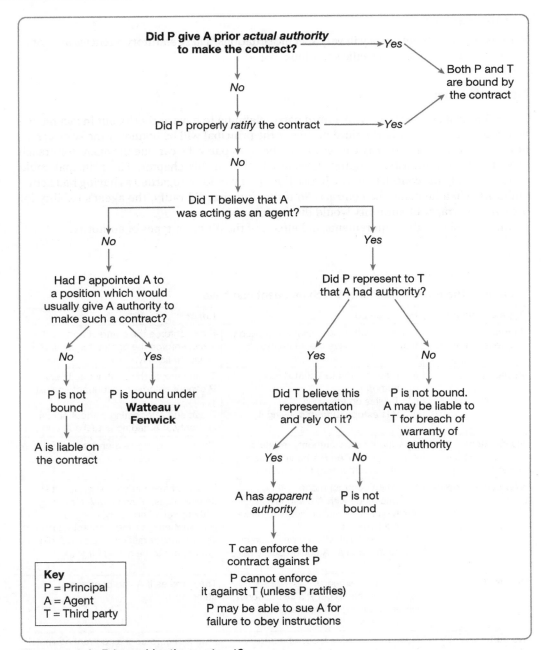

Figure 6.2 Is P bound by the contract?

Liability on contracts made by agents

The rights of a third party to sue on a contract made by an agent differ, depending upon whether the agency was **disclosed** or **undisclosed**.

Disclosed agency

Agency is disclosed when the agent indicates that he is acting as an agent, whether or not the principal for whom he is acting is actually identified.

If an agent makes a contract for a disclosed principal then generally the agent incurs no liability on the contract. By disclosing that he was acting for a principal, the agent will be taken to have shown the third party that he did not intend to become personally liable on the contract. However, an agent who intends to act for a disclosed principal can incur personal liability if the circumstances do not make it clear to the third party that the agent was acting as an agent, rather than for himself.

Undisclosed agency

Agency is undisclosed if the third party did not know that the agent was acting for a principal. In such cases the agent will initially be liable to the third party on the contract. If the agent had actual authority to make the contract the principal is allowed to intervene and enforce the contract against the third party, under the **doctrine of the undisclosed principal** (Figure 6.3). Once the principal has revealed himself, the agent will no longer be able to enforce the contract against the third party. However, both the agent and the principal will now be liable to the third party on the contract. Where such joint liability arises, the third party can choose to sue either the agent or the principal on the contract. However, having made an absolute decision to hold one or other liable on the contract, the third party will not be able to change his mind and then sue the other.

If the agent did not have actual authority to make the contract, then the doctrine of the undisclosed principal cannot take effect to allow the principal to enforce the contract against the third party. The principal cannot even ratify the contract, because ratification is permissible only where the agent purported to act as an agent. Nor will the doctrine make the principal liable on the contract. However, the third party might be able to enforce the contract against the principal, if the unusual conditions set out in **Watteau v Fenwick** are satisfied.

There are four situations where an undisclosed principal cannot sue on the contract, even if the agent did have actual authority to make the contract. These situations are as follows:

(1) Where a term of the contract excluded agency.
(2) Where the third party would have refused to contract with the undisclosed principal, and the personality of either the principal or the agent was so important that it would be inappropriate to allow the principal to intervene. (Such cases are very rare.)
(3) Where the third party made the contract with the agent because he particularly wanted to contract with the agent personally.
(4) Where the agent was asked whether he was acting for an undisclosed principal and told the third party that he was not.

If the principal does enforce the contract against the third party, the third party can use against the principal any defences which he could have used against the agent.

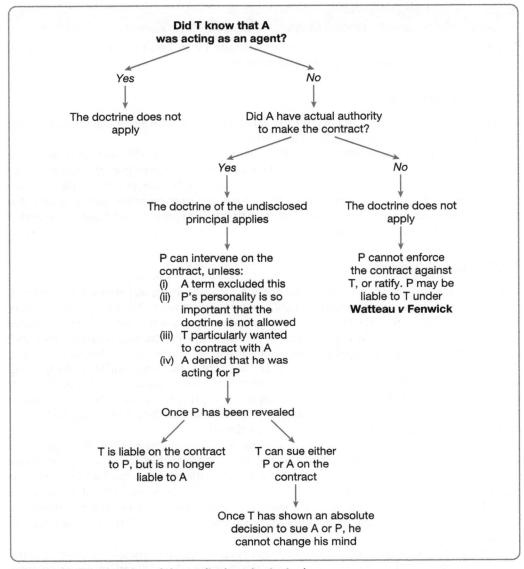

Figure 6.3 The doctrine of the undisclosed principal

The agent's liability for breach of warranty of authority

An agent can be liable to a third party for breach of warranty of authority. This is quite different from being liable on the contract made on the principal's behalf. Liability for breach of warranty of authority arises if:

● an agent makes a representation to a third party, warranting that he has authority to act for a principal;

● the agent does not in fact have such authority; and

● the third party acts on this representation to his detriment.

Usually, the third party will act upon the warranty by making the contract with the principal. An agent can become liable for breach of warranty of authority where he has no authority at all, or where he exceeds the authority which he does have. Liability can arise even if the agent could not have known that his authority had been revoked.

Yonge *v* Toynbee (1910) (Court of Appeal)

A client (the principal) instructed a solicitor (the agent) to defend a case. The principal became certifiably insane and this automatically terminated the agent's authority to act for him. The agent did not know that the principal had become insane and continued to act for him.

Held As soon as the principal was certified insane the agent lost his authority to act for him. All proceedings taken after this date were therefore struck out, and the agent had to pay all the costs of the other party to the litigation which were incurred after this date.

If the principal ratifies the agent's actions, then the agent will not be liable for breach of warranty of authority, because the agent will have acquired back-dated actual authority. Nor will the agent be liable for breach of warranty of authority if the third party knew, or should have known, that the agent did not have the authority warranted. Damages for breach of warranty of authority are calculated by reference to the two rules in **Hadley *v* Baxendale** (see Chapter 5). These damages are therefore designed to put the third party in the position he would have been in if the warranty had not been breached.

Simons *v* Patchett (1857)

An agent bought a ship from a third party, claiming to have authority from the principal. In fact the agent had exceeded his limited authority in doing this. The contract price was £6,000. The principal refused to be bound by the contract. The third party therefore sold the ship to another buyer, X, for £5,500. This was the best price that the third party could get, and was a fair price at the time. The third party sued the agent for breach of warranty of authority.

Held The agent had to pay £500 damages to the third party.

The rights and duties of the agent

Contractual duties

Agents owe both contractual and fiduciary duties to their principals. The three contractual duties are as follows:

(1) the duty to obey the principal's instructions;

(2) the duty to show an appropriate amount of care and skill; and

(3) the duty to perform the agency duties personally.

The duty to obey the principal's instructions

An agent who makes a contract, agreeing to perform certain duties, will be liable in damages if he fails to do what he agreed to do.

The duty to show an appropriate amount of care and skill

The common law requires an agent to show an appropriate degree of care and skill. Where an agent supplies a service in the course of a business, this requirement is set out in s. 13 of the Supply of Goods and Services Act 1982 and, when it is in force, in the Consumer Rights Act 2015. The precise degree of care and skill required of an agent will depend upon several factors, including any expertise which the agent has expressly or impliedly claimed to have. For example, if a professional person, such as a solicitor, is employed as an agent, he should show the degree of care and skill which one could reasonably expect of a solicitor.

A gratuitous (unpaid) agent has no contract with the principal because the principal has given no consideration to the agent. In the following case a gratuitous agent was held liable for failing to show an appropriate amount of care and skill.

 Chaudry *v* Prabhakar (1988) (Court of Appeal)

The principal had just passed her driving test. She asked her friend, the agent, to look out for a car. The principal specified that she did not want any car which had previously been in an accident. The agent had no mechanical expertise and was not being paid for his services. He recommended a car which was being sold by a firm of panel beaters. The principal bought the car, asking the agent whether it had been in an accident. The agent said that it had not. The principal later discovered that it had previously been in an accident and sued both the agent and the panel beaters.

Held The agent was liable for not exercising reasonable care. The standard of care required of an agent is the standard which is reasonable in the light of all the circumstances, whether the agent acted under a contract or not.

The duty to perform the agency duties personally

Delegation of the duties which the agent has undertaken is allowed only if the principal expressly or impliedly authorised it, or if the act delegated required no care and skill.

Fiduciary duties

The relationship of the agent to the principal is a **fiduciary** one, which means that the principal places great faith and trust in the agent. This fiduciary nature of the relationship places extra, fiduciary, duties on the agent. These fiduciary duties are:

- to act in good faith and to avoid any conflict of interest;
- not to make a secret profit;
- not to take a bribe;
- the duty to account; and
- the duty to preserve confidentiality.

To act in good faith and to avoid any conflict of interest

Agents must act in good faith and must not allow their own interests to conflict with the interests of their principals. For example, an agent who is employed to sell the principal's property cannot buy it himself, unless he makes full disclosure of this to the principal. Similarly, an agent employed by the principal to buy cannot perform the contract by selling his own property to the principal.

 Armstrong _v_ Jackson (1917)

An agent, a stockbroker, was asked by a principal to buy 600 shares in a certain company. The agent sold the principal 600 of his own shares in the company, pretending that he had bought the shares in the open market. Some years later the principal discovered what had happened.

Held The principal could have the purchase set aside.

McCardie J said: 'It matters not that the agent sells at the market price, or that he acts without intent to defraud . . . The prohibition of the law is absolute. It will not allow an agent to place himself in a situation which, under ordinary circumstances, would tempt a man to do that which is not the best for his principal.'

In **Rossetti Marketing Ltd _v_ Diamond Sofa Co Ltd (2012)** the Court of Appeal held that an agent can act for two principals with conflicting interests in only two types of case. First, where the principals agree to this, giving consent on a fully informed basis after full disclosure by the agent. Second, in the case of residential estate agents who must be able to act for multiple principals or they would not be able to carry on their businesses.

Not to make a secret profit

Most agents have a contract with their principals, and these contracts generally entitle them to be paid a salary or a commission. There is a strict rule that an agent must not gain any other profit or benefit if it has not been agreed by the principal.

 Boardman _v_ Phipps (1967) (House of Lords)

The agent was a solicitor acting for a trust, the principal. The principal owned shares in a certain company. The agent repeatedly advised the principal's trustees that if they bought more shares in the company they could control it and make huge profits. The trustees repeatedly refused to consider this. The agent therefore bought the extra shares himself. The agent and the principal now controlled the company and this led to both of them making big profits. The principal then sued the agent for the profits he had made.

Held The agent had to hand these profits over to the principal because he held them on trust for the principal. He was in breach of his fiduciary duty because he had used knowledge gained while acting as agent to make a secret profit for himself. In the Court of Appeal, Lord Denning MR said that an agent would have to account to the principal for any benefit made either by using the principal's property, or by using his position as agent, or by using information or knowledge gained as an agent.

Not to take a bribe

Agents must not take bribes. In this context a bribe does not always indicate corruption. Any secret payment to an agent, which is made by a third party dealing with the agent, is likely to be regarded as a bribe. For example, if a firm's buyer is given inducements to favour a particular supplier, this will be regarded as a bribe, whether the agent does in fact favour that supplier or not.

The duty to account

This duty requires that the agent keeps his own property separate from the principal's property. If the agent mixes the two up, the principal will be entitled to all of the property unless the agent can clearly show what property belonged to him. The duty also obliges the agent to keep records which the principal can ask to inspect.

The duty to preserve confidentiality

Agents have a duty to keep the affairs of their principals confidential, and this duty can carry on after the agency has ended.

Remedies for breach of fiduciary duties

The fiduciary duties are very strict indeed. If any of them are breached the principal is given very wide remedies. Potentially, these rights include:

- the right to dismiss the agent without notice;
- the right to refuse to pay the agent's commission;
- the right to recover any secret profit; and
- the right to rescind the contract (see Chapter 3) which the agent made with the third party.

In **FHR European Ventures LLP v Cedar Capital Partners LLC (2014)** the Supreme Court held that if an agent received either a bribe or a secret commission, in breach of his fiduciary duty to his principal, he had to hold the benefit he received on trust for his principal. So if money was received and used to buy other assets the principal could claim these other assets because they would be regarded as all along having been acquired by the agent on the principal's behalf.

Rights of the agent

The agent's contract with the principal may expressly provide that the agent should be paid. If this is not the case, then the agent will not be entitled to payment unless an implied term gives such a right. Such a term will be implied on the same basis as any other term implied by the courts. (The circumstances in which a term will be implied by the courts were examined in Chapter 3.)

 Re Richmond Gate Property Co Ltd (1965)

The articles of association of a company set out the remuneration of the managing director. The relevant article provided that the managing director should receive 'such remuneration (whether by way of salary, commission or participation in profits, or partly in one way and partly in another) as the directors may determine'. The company went into liquidation nine months after incorporation. The managing director had been paid nothing during this time and claimed £400.

Held The managing director was not entitled to any payment. An express term of the contract determined what he should be paid. An implied term could not contradict this, and nor could more be paid on a *quantum meruit* (see Chapter 5) because the express terms of the contract had set out the basis on which he should be paid.

Where a person supplies a service in the course of a business, and the contract or any course of dealings does not fix the price, s. 15 of the Supply of Goods and Services Act 1982 provides that a reasonable price should be paid. This section can apply to agents, but only if the price of the agent's services has not been expressly or impliedly fixed by the contract or by a course of dealings. So s. 15 SGSA would not alter the decision in **Re Richmond Gate Property Co Ltd** if the case were to arise today.

Indemnity

Unless the contract which created the agency provides otherwise, an agent will be entitled to an indemnity from the principal for liability incurred, or money spent, in the performance of the agency. This means that the principal must repay any expenses which the agent has properly incurred while acting within his actual authority.

 Adamson *v* Jarvis (1827)

An auctioneer was asked by a principal to sell goods, and the goods were duly sold for over £6,000. In fact, the principal did not own the goods. After the auctioneer had sold the goods he was sued by the real owner and had to pay damages to him.

Held The auctioneer could recover an indemnity from the principal to cover him for his liability to the true owner.

Lien

A lien is a right to hold on to property until a debt has been paid. An agent to whom the principal owes money may have a lien over the principal's goods. A lien can arise only if the agent has *possession* of the goods. Furthermore, the lien must not be excluded by the contract between the principal and agent.

To exercise the lien, the agent must have lawfully come into possession of the principal's property and have done so in his capacity as an agent. The agent's lien is a particular lien rather than a general lien and can therefore be exercised only over property in respect of which the debt became due. It does not give a right to sell or dispose of the property. An agent may lose a lien by waiving it, or by voluntarily giving up possession of the goods.

Example

Asif is given actual authority to buy jewellery on Phil's behalf. Asif is to be paid a commission of 5 per cent of the purchase price, payable one week after the purchase was made. Asif buys a diamond ring for Phil and takes possession of it from the seller. Three weeks later, Asif has not been paid his commission, despite his asking for it. Asif can keep possession of the ring until he is paid what he is owed. Once he is paid what he is owed, the right will disappear. Asif has no right to sell the jewellery and, if he did so, he would be liable to Phil in the tort of conversion. If Asif surrenders possession of the ring, then he will lose his right to the lien. Similarly, Asif would lose the right to the lien if he waived the right. This would be done by telling Phil, either expressly or impliedly, that he did not want the right to a lien.

Extra rights and duties of self-employed commercial agents

The Commercial Agents (Council Directive) Regulations 1993 are of significance mainly in relation to compensation payable when a self-employed commercial agent ceases to act for a principal. However, the Regulations also set out rights and duties of self-employed commercial agents. The definition of a self-employed commercial agent is fairly narrow, and so relatively few agents are covered by the Regulations.

Definition of a self-employed commercial agent

Regulation 2(1) defines a commercial agent as:

> a self-employed intermediary who has continuing authority to negotiate the sale or purchase of goods on behalf of another person (the 'principal'), or to negotiate and conclude the sale or purchase of goods on behalf of and in the name of that principal.

The following points should be noted:

- A commercial agent must have continuing authority to negotiate the buying or selling of goods on behalf of the principal. An agent who does not negotiate, or who merely negotiates the buying or selling of services, is not included. If the price is fixed by the principal, then this might indicate that the agent did not negotiate.
- The contract must be concluded in the name of the principal.
- A commercial agent must be self-employed, rather than an employee.
- A commercial agent must act in return for payment.
- Limited companies have been held to be commercial agents and there seems no reason why partnerships should not be. Company officers acting on behalf of their companies are excluded. So are insolvency practitioners and individual partners acting on behalf of their firms.
- The Regulations do not apply to a person whose activities as commercial agent are to be considered 'secondary' to the principal's business. Activities are to be considered secondary if: (a) the principal is not in business to sell or buy goods of a certain kind; (b) contracts to buy and sell are not normally negotiated or concluded on a commercial basis; or (c) making one deal is not likely to lead to more deals. The overall idea is that if the agent spends effort, skill and resources in developing a market for the principal's goods, then such activities are in the commercial interests of the principal and the agent should acquire rights.

The Regulations also provide that if customers choose goods themselves, and merely use an agent to place their orders, this would suggest that the agent is not a commercial agent. On the other hand, if the goods are available only through the agent this would suggest that he is a commercial agent. There are four other circumstances in which commercial agency is indicated: first, where the principal was the manufacturer, importer or distributor of the goods; second, where the goods are specifically identified with the principal; third, where the agent devotes substantially the whole of his time to his agency activities; fourth, where the arrangement is described as commercial agency.

Example

Three years ago Peter, an artist, agreed that Alice should try and sell his paintings. Peter is not good at negotiating and agrees that Alice should sell the paintings for as much as she can. Alice is paid 10 per cent commission on paintings sold, and has exclusive rights to sell Peter's paintings. Over the three years Alice has devoted more and more time to selling Peter's paintings and has built up a number of clients who purchase Peter's paintings from her. When paintings are sold, Alice makes it plain that Peter is the seller and cheques are made out to Peter. Alice is a self-employed commercial agent.

Rights given to self-employed commercial agents

The rights given to self-employed commercial agents are as follows:

- to a customary or reasonable amount of remuneration, if no remuneration has been expressly agreed;
- to commission on deals which the agent has set up;
- to have the principal act dutifully and in good faith;
- to be given relevant documentation relating to goods bought or sold;
- to be given information necessary for the agent to perform his contract, and in particular to be warned if the principal expects the level of commercial transactions to fall away;
- to be informed of deals which the principal makes, including a right to inspect the principal's books; and
- to be informed, within a reasonable time, of any acceptance, refusal or non-execution of a commercial transaction which the commercial agent procured for the principal.

Duties which the Regulations impose on the agent

The duties which the Regulations impose on the agent are as follows:

- to look after the interests of his principal;
- to act dutifully; and
- to act in good faith.

To fulfil these duties, the Regulations say that the agent will in particular need to:

- make proper efforts to negotiate and, where appropriate, conclude the transactions he is instructed to take care of;
- communicate to his principal all the necessary information available to him; and
- comply with reasonable instructions given by his principal.

With the exception of the agent's rights to compensation, remuneration and to inspect the principal's books, the rights and duties set out in the Regulations cannot be excluded by agreement between the parties.

Termination of agency

An agent acts for a principal on account of having the principal's actual authority to do so (although an agent can make a principal liable on account of having apparent authority or authority under **Watteau *v* Fenwick**). Apart from some exceptional circumstances which make an agency irrevocable, the principal can withdraw the agent's actual authority at any time. However, unless third parties are informed of this, the agent might still be able to bind the principal on account of having apparent authority.

 Trueman and others *v* Loder (1840)

It was well known that an agent in London represented a certain principal in St Petersburg, and that the agent conducted no business on his own account. The principal withdrew the agent's actual authority, but the agent went on to buy tallow from a third party, who believed that the agent was still acting on behalf of the principal.

Held The principal was bound by the contract. The agent still had apparent authority to act for him.

If the principal does withdraw the agent's authority, then this might or might not be a breach of contract, depending upon what was agreed between principal and agent. Similarly, an agent who terminates the agreement might be liable for breach of contract. If the parties agree to end the agency, there can be no question of breach of contract. If either principal or agent does commit a breach of contract by ending the agency early, damages will be assessed on normal contract principles under the two rules in **Hadley *v* Baxendale**. Specific performance will not be ordered to compel a party to continue to act as agent, as it will not be ordered to enforce personal service contracts. Nor will an injunction be ordered if it would, in effect, amount to specific performance of an agency contract. So in **Warren *v* Mendy (1989)** a professional boxer who had agreed to employ the claimant as his manager, and not to employ any other manager, for a three-year period could not be restrained by injunction from employing another manager before the end of the period. (The remedies mentioned here are explained in Chapter 5.)

A fixed-term agency ends when the term is up. If the agency is not for a fixed term, either party can end it by giving a reasonable amount of notice of his intention to do so, subject to minimum requirements where the Commercial Agents Regulations apply. If the principal unilaterally ends a contract of agency under which the agent was an employee, there may be a claim for unfair dismissal (see Chapter 13), as well as for damages for wrongful dismissal (see Chapter 13).

Agency is **terminated automatically** in the following ways:

- by frustration (this will occur for the usual reasons: that performance of the contract becomes impossible, illegal or radically different – see Chapter 5);
- by the death of either party;
- by the insanity of either party;
- by the bankruptcy of the principal; or
- by bankruptcy of the agent if this would render him unfit to perform his duties.

Termination and the Commercial Agents (Council Directive) Regulations 1993

Minimum notice periods

Where a commercial agency agreement is for an indefinite period, reg. 15 sets out minimum notice periods, as follows. In the first year of the agency contract the minimum period is one month. In the second year it is two months. After two or more years it is three months. The parties cannot agree to shorter notice periods. They can agree to longer periods, as long as the notice to be observed by the principal is not less than that to be observed by the agent. Unless the parties agree otherwise, the notice period must end at the end of a calendar month.

If the agency agreement was for a fixed period but it continues to be performed by both sides after the notice has expired, reg. 14 provides that it is deemed to have been converted into an agreement for an indefinite period. The notice periods set out in reg. 15 will then apply and, in calculating the required notice, the earlier fixed notice period is taken into account.

Regulation 16 provides that the Regulations do not apply if the agency agreement is justifiably terminated immediately on account of one of the parties having failed to carry out all or part of his obligations under the contract, or where exceptional circumstances apply.

Compensation and indemnity payments

Indemnity and compensation are not the same things, and the agent is entitled to be compensated rather than indemnified, unless the agency contract provides otherwise. So compensation is the usual remedy.

Compensation

A commercial agent is entitled to compensation for loss he suffers as a result of the termination of his relations with the principal. There is no requirement that the termination should be the principal's fault.

Loss to the agent is deemed to occur particularly when the termination takes place in either or both of the following two circumstances.

(1) Circumstances which deprive the commercial agent of the commission which proper performance of the agency contract would have gained for him, whilst providing his principal with substantial benefits linked to the activities of the commercial agent.

(2) Circumstances which have not enabled the commercial agent to recover the costs and expenses that he had incurred in the agency contract on the advice of his principal.

In **Lonsdale _v_ Howard & Hallam Ltd (2007)** the House of Lords held that the amount of compensation should be the amount which the agent has lost by not continuing to be agent, that is to say the amount of future commission lost. This can be assessed by asking for how much the agent could have sold the right to be agent to a willing purchaser, assuming that the agency would have continued. If the market was declining, or if earning the commission would have involved expense, then obviously this would reduce the compensation.

Indemnity

The three requirements for an indemnity under the Regulations are as follows:

(1) The contract between the principal and agent provides that the agent should be indemnified rather than compensated.

(2) The agent has brought the principal new customers, or has significantly increased the volume of business with existing customers, and the principal continues to derive substantial benefits from the business with such customers.

(3) The payment of the indemnity is equitable, having regard to all of the circumstances and, in particular, the commission lost by the commercial agent on the business transacted with such customers.

The amount of the indemnity cannot be more than one year's pay, calculated by reference to the agent's actual pay over the previous five years or, if the agent has not worked for five years, by reference to such time as he has worked.

The grant of an indemnity does not prevent the agent from seeking common law damages.

Loss of indemnity and compensation

There are three circumstances in which neither indemnity nor compensation is payable, as follows:

(1) where the principal has justifiably terminated the contract on account of the agent's breach of contract;

(2) where the agent has himself terminated the contract (unless this was justified by circumstances attributable to the principal, or unless the agent had become so old, ill or infirm that he could not reasonably be required to carry on with his activities); or

(3) where the commercial agent, with the agreement of the principal, has signed over his rights to a third party.

Essential points

- An agent is a person who has the power to alter the legal position of another person, known as the principal.
- An agent cannot act on behalf of a principal unless he has some authority to do so.
- Actual authority arises because the principal agrees with the agent that the agent should have the authority.
- Apparent authority arises because the principal represents to a third party that the agent has authority. The principal cannot deny this once the third party has acted on it.
- If a principal ratifies an agent's act, the agent is regarded as having backdated actual authority to perform the act.
- Agents owe both contractual and fiduciary duties to their principals.
- Apart from some exceptional circumstances which make an agency irrevocable, the principal can withdraw the agent's authority at any time.
- An agent may still have apparent authority even after the principal has withdrawn actual authority.
- Agency is terminated automatically by frustration; by the death of either party; by the insanity of either party; by the bankruptcy of the principal; or by bankruptcy of the agent if this would render him unfit to perform his duties.

Practice questions

1 Padraig runs and owns a shop which sells collectable books. When Padraig goes to book fairs he arranges that his friend Arthur should run the shop while he is away. Arthur is told that he can sell any books in stock, as long as he gets at least 75 per cent of the price displayed on them. He is told that under no circumstances should he buy any books.

While Padraig is away Arthur sells a book to Billy for 70 per cent of the price shown on it. Billy thinks that Arthur owns the business. Charlene, who regularly does business with Padraig, buys a book for 60 per cent of the price shown on it. She knows that Padraig usually insists on at least 75 per cent of the price shown, even as regards a trade buyer such as herself. Arthur buys an antique Bible from David, on behalf of Padraig, for £50 because he is sure that it is such a bargain that Padraig would want it. On his return, Padraig discovers that the Bible bought from David is very rare and worth about £2,000. David has also discovered the true value of the Bible and that Arthur had no authority to buy it. David says that the Bible must be returned to him, but Padraig says that he is ratifying the contract.

Advise the parties of their legal positions.

2 Hangpaper Ltd is a company which buys and sells wallpaper and decorating materials. Hangpaper Ltd's articles of association allow for the appointment of a managing director, but none has ever been appointed. Adrian, a director of Hangpaper Ltd, has for the past three years been allowed by the other directors to act as if he had been appointed managing director. Without the authority of his fellow directors, Adrian buys a large consignment of wallpaper paste from Glueit and Co. When the paste ordered is delivered, it is found to be of a type which is unsuitable for Hangpaper's purposes. Hangpaper Ltd phone Glueit to say that Adrian had no authority to buy the paste. Glueit insist that the contract must stand as they believed that, as managing director, Adrian would have had authority. Advise Hangpaper Ltd as to whether or not they will be bound by the contract with Glueit and Co, and of any rights they might have or might acquire against either Adrian or Glueit and Co.

3 Anita works for Pamela as a buyer of second-hand cars. Anita has been expressly forbidden to buy any cars for more than £5,000 each. Acting in contravention of her instructions, Anita buys a car from Tina for £6,250.

(a) Explain the circumstances in which this contract could be ratified by Pamela and how such a ratification would be made.

(b) If there is an effective ratification of the contract, how would this affect the rights of Pamela against Anita and Tina?

4 Alfred is employed by PolishCo Ltd as a buyer of materials at a salary of £26,000 p.a. Alfred's job requires him to visit various manufacturers of solvents and to buy solvents which can be used in the manufacture of polish. Recently, Alfred placed a large order with Madeit Ltd, a company with which PolishCo Ltd had not previously dealt. The solvent delivered by Madeit is slightly more expensive than that delivered by the previous supplier, but Alfred insists that it is definitely of higher quality. Alfred also switched a regular order to SolvCo Ltd, a small company with which PolishCo Ltd had not previously dealt. The solvent delivered by SolvCo is slightly cheaper than that delivered by the previous supplier. It appears to be of exactly the same quality. The managing director of PolishCo Ltd was watching the FA Cup Final on the television when he noticed Alfred sitting in the crowd. The managing director has now discovered that Alfred went to the Cup Final by courtesy of corporate hospitality supplied by Madeit Ltd. The managing director has also discovered that Alfred has a significant shareholding in SolvCo Ltd, and that the solvent supplied by Madeit is of no higher quality than that previously supplied.

Advise PolishCo Ltd of any rights which they may have against either Alfred, Madeit Ltd or SolvCo Ltd.

5 Anne, a self-employed manager of sporting celebrities, agrees to become the manager of Paul Putter, a promising professional boxer. Anne is to arrange bouts for Paul and also to look after his financial affairs. The agreement is for a fixed five-year period, and entitles Anne to an annual fee and 10 per cent commission on all of Paul's earnings.

Fifteen months into the agreement, Paul has become increasingly dissatisfied with Anne's services and would like to be managed by Alice. Advise Paul on the consequences of his ending the contract with Anne, and whether or not Anne could prevent him from employing Alice as his manager.

Explain also how Paul's withdrawal of consent for Anne to act as his agent would affect Anne's ability to make contracts between Paul and third parties.

How would your answer be different if Paul had been a painter, rather than a boxer, and Anne had been employed to negotiate the sale of his paintings under a contract for an indefinite period?

6 With reference to decided cases, explain the different ways in which an agent can acquire authority to bind a principal to a contract with a third party.

Task 6

A friend of yours, who has a business selling and repairing bicycles, is considering getting another friend to help him with the buying and selling side of the business. Your friend has heard of agency but has little idea of the law relating to agency. He has asked you to explain the following matters:

(a) The different types of authority which an agent might have. In particular, your friend wants to know how these types of authority arise and the consequences of their having arisen.

(b) The difference between disclosed and undisclosed agency, and the effect of the doctrine of the undisclosed principal.

(c) The rights and duties which arise between principal and agent.

(d) The ways in which agency can be terminated.

Write a brief report, explaining the legal position.

mylawchamber

Visit **www.mylawchamber.co.uk/macintyreessentials** to access tools to help you develop and test your knowledge of business law, including interactive multiple choice questions, practice exam questions with guidance, weblinks, glossary, glossary flashcards, legal newsfeed and legal updates.

Use **Case Navigator** to read in full some of the key cases referenced in this chapter with commentary and questions:

Hely-Hutchinson v Brayhead Ltd (1968)

7

The Sale of Goods Act 1979

In this chapter important rules laid down by the Sale of Goods Act 1979 are examined. This is not the first time that the Sale of Goods Act has been considered. In an earlier chapter (see Chapter 3) ss. 12–15 of the Act, which imply statutory terms into contracts of sale of goods, were examined. Before examining the nature of the statutory implied terms, the definition of a contract of sale of goods was considered. If you have forgotten this definition you should re-read it. It is necessary to remember the definition of a contract of sale of goods because the rules considered in this chapter apply only to contracts of sale of goods. Similar rules do not apply to other types of contracts.

The passing of ownership and risk

The purpose of a contract of sale of goods is to pass ownership of the goods from the seller to the buyer in return for payment of the price. The SGA 1979 sets out rules which determine exactly when ownership does pass. It can be important to know exactly when ownership passes for two main reasons:

(1) The goods might become lost or damaged. The party who owned the goods at the time of the loss or damage will generally have to bear the loss.

(2) Either the buyer or the seller might become insolvent. The rights of the solvent party will depend upon whether or not ownership had passed at the time of the insolvency.

The goods become lost or damaged

In the SGA 1979 risk means the risk of the goods becoming lost, damaged, stolen or destroyed. Section 20(1), which applies to non-consumer contracts, provides that, unless the buyer and seller have agreed otherwise, the risk of the goods being lost or damaged remains with the seller until ownership of the goods passes to the buyer. Once ownership of the goods has passed to the buyer, then the risk of loss or damage passes to the buyer. The parties might of course agree that the rule set out in s. 20(1) should not apply, but generally they do not do this. So if the goods are accidentally lost or damaged, the loss will usually fall upon the person who has ownership of the goods. It is worth noticing straight away that ownership of the goods is not the same thing as possession of the goods. Section 20(1) provides that the risk passes with ownership whether the goods have been delivered to the buyer or not.

Section 20(4) makes an exception to the rule set out in s. 20(1). It provides that where the buyer deals as a consumer the goods remain at the seller's risk until they are delivered to the consumer. The complex definition of a person who 'deals as a consumer' for purposes of SGA 1979 was explained earlier (see Chapter 3). The ways in which goods can be delivered are considered later in this chapter. As regards consumer contracts only, reg. 43 of the

Consumer Contracts (Information, Cancellation and Additional Charges) (CC(ICA)) Regulations 2013 provides that the goods will be at the trader's risk until they come into the physical possession of the consumer. However, the new rule applies to '**consumer contracts**'. It does not apply to non-consumer contracts. The Regulations' definition of a 'consumer contract' is the same as the definition in the Consumer Rights Act 2015, and is considered in Chapter 3.

If risk has passed from the seller to the buyer at the time when the goods become lost or damaged, the position is straightforward. The loss will fall upon the buyer, who will have to pay the full price of the goods (if the price has not already been paid).

If risk has not passed to the buyer at the time when the goods become lost or damaged, then the loss will fall upon the seller. However, the legal position will then depend upon whether the contract was for the sale of specific or unascertained goods. **Specific goods** are defined by s. 61 of the SGA 1979 as goods which have been identified and agreed upon at the time of sale. For example, if a second-hand car is sold, this is a sale of specific goods because only the particular car identified and agreed upon can be delivered in performance of the contract. **Unascertained goods** are goods which have not been identified and agreed upon at the time of sale. For example, if 100 tons of wheat are sold, and the buyer and seller have not identified any particular 100 tons of wheat as the subject matter of the contract, this is a sale of unascertained goods. The seller's obligation is to deliver any 100 tons of wheat which match the contract description.

If specific goods are lost or damaged before risk has passed to the buyer, the seller is in breach of contract. Obviously, the seller cannot deliver lost goods. Nor can the seller deliver damaged goods because the buyer will be entitled to reject these goods on account of their being of unsatisfactory quality. Therefore, the buyer will not need to pay the price and accept the damaged goods. If the buyer has already paid some of the price of lost or damaged goods, the seller will have to refund the amount paid. The buyer will also be able to sue the seller for damages for non-delivery. In practice, a buyer might choose to accept damaged goods, but at a much reduced price. The strength of the buyer's legal position would put strong pressure on the seller to accept the reduced price.

If unascertained goods are lost or damaged before risk has passed to the buyer, then the legal position will be the same if the seller cannot find replacement goods which match the contract description. However, the seller could still properly perform the contract by acquiring other goods which match the contract description and by delivering these goods to the buyer. A seller who does this will not be in breach of contract. The buyer will therefore have to accept the goods and pay the full price.

Example

Bill agrees to buy a two-year-old lorry (specific goods) from Sajjid for £12,000, and pays a deposit of £2,000. The lorry is damaged by vandals before risk has passed to Bill. Bill need not accept the damaged lorry because it is not of satisfactory quality. Unless the contract is frustrated under s. 7 (considered later in this chapter), Bill has a right to sue Sajjid for damages for non-delivery and need not pay the £10,000 which has not yet been paid. Bill can also recover the £2,000 which has been paid.

Example

Bill agrees to buy 1,000 barrels of oil (unascertained goods) from Sajjid. While Sajjid still has ownership of 1,000 barrels of oil which he intended to supply to Bill, the oil is destroyed in a fire. If Sajjid can acquire another 1,000 barrels of the same type of oil before the date of delivery is due, then Sajjid can deliver this oil to Bill, who must accept it and pay the full contract price. If Sajjid cannot acquire another 1,000 barrels of the same type of oil before delivery is due, then Sajjid is in breach of contract. Bill need not pay the price and can recover any amount of the price already paid. Bill can also sue Sajjid for damages for non-delivery. (This contract cannot be frustrated under s. 7 as the goods were not specific. Nor will it be frustrated at common law because it has not become impossible to perform.)

If the loss of the goods, or the damage to them, was the fault of a particular person the legal position would be the same, except that the party who suffered the loss on account of having the risk at the time of the loss or damage would be able to claim damages from the person who caused the loss or damage. So, if in the second example above it was Cyd's fault that the oil was destroyed, then Sajjid could sue Cyd for damages to compensate for all the loss suffered.

Figure 7.1 shows an outline of the legal position where goods which have been sold have become lost or damaged. It assumes that the loss or damage was not the fault of either party. If the loss or damage is the fault of either the buyer or the seller, the party at fault will have to bear the loss.

Insolvency of the buyer or the seller

A person who has become insolvent has not got enough money to pay his or her debts. If a company becomes insolvent it may be liquidated. This means that a liquidator will be appointed to gather in any assets belonging to the company, and to pay any such assets to creditors, before the company ceases to exist.

If a seller of goods becomes insolvent before the ownership of the goods has passed to the buyer, then the seller's liquidator will have no duty to deliver the goods to the buyer. If the goods have already been delivered to the buyer, then the seller's liquidator will be able to reclaim the goods from the buyer. The buyer will not have to pay for the goods, because ownership has not passed to the buyer. However, a buyer who has paid any or all of the price can only claim against the seller's liquidator as an unsecured creditor. In practice, this means that the buyer will certainly not get back all money which has been paid and may get none of this money back.

If the seller becomes insolvent after the ownership of the goods has passed to the buyer, then the buyer, as owner of the goods, can keep the goods. The seller's liquidator will, however, be able to sue the buyer for any amount of the price which has not yet been paid.

If the buyer becomes insolvent before the ownership of the goods has passed, then the seller need not deliver the goods to the buyer and could reclaim the goods if they had already been delivered. If the buyer has already paid any part of the price, then the buyer's liquidator can reclaim this amount from the seller. However, if the buyer's liquidator chooses to pay the seller the full price, then the seller must deliver the goods. (The contract is not automatically terminated on account of the buyer having become insolvent.)

If the buyer becomes insolvent after the ownership of the goods has passed, then the buyer's liquidator will be entitled to keep the goods. The seller can retain any part of the price which has already been paid, but can sue for any outstanding amount only as an unsecured creditor. (The seller is therefore most unlikely to receive payment in full, if receiving anything at all.)

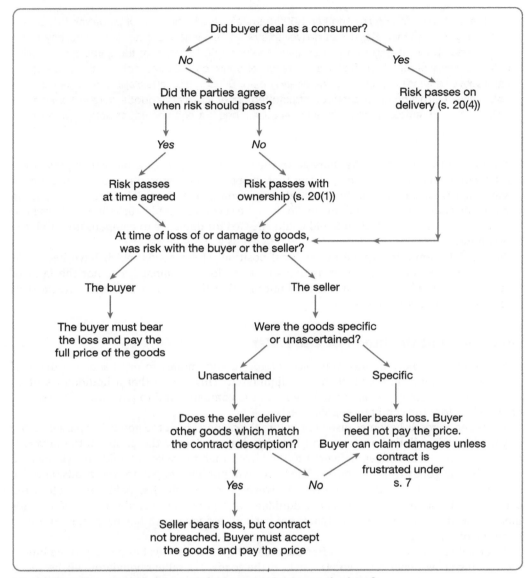

Figure 7.1 The goods are lost or damaged. Who bears the loss?

Example

Steve has sold 100 tons of corn to Bill for £2,000 and Bill has paid £200 in advance. Before ownership has passed to Bill, Steve becomes insolvent. Steve's liquidator has no obligation to deliver the goods and could reclaim the goods if they had already been delivered. Bill has no obligation to pay the £1,800 which has not yet been paid. However, Bill can only reclaim the £200 already paid as an unsecured creditor of Steve.

Example

Steve has sold 100 tons of corn to Bill for £2,000 and Bill has paid £200 in advance. After ownership has passed to Bill, but before the rest of the price has been paid, Bill becomes insolvent. If the goods have been delivered, Steve cannot reclaim the goods from Bill's liquidator as ownership had passed to Bill. If the goods have not been delivered, Steve must deliver them. Steve can keep the £200 already paid and can sue Bill's liquidator for the remainder of the price (£1,800) as an unsecured creditor.

It is important to realise that the rules relating to risk do not apply when the buyer or seller has become insolvent. When the SGA 1979 talks of the risk it means the risk of the goods being lost, damaged or destroyed. It does not mean the risk of one of the parties becoming insolvent.

Figure 7.2 shows an outline of the legal position where either the buyer or the seller has become insolvent.

The Sale of Goods Act rules on the passing of ownership

Sections 16–20 of the Sale of Goods Act 1979 lay down rules which determine exactly when the ownership of goods should pass from the seller to the buyer.

Passing of ownership of specific goods

It has already been explained that specific goods are goods which are identified and agreed upon at the time of sale. It has also been explained that specific goods are contrasted with unascertained goods, which are not identified and agreed upon at the time of sale.

Having decided that the goods sold are specific, the next step is to apply ss. 17 and 18 of the SGA 1979. Section 17, which takes precedence over s. 18, provides that ownership of specific goods passes when the parties intend it to pass. Section 17 also provides that the intention of the parties can be either a term of the contract or inferred from the conduct of the parties or the circumstances of the case.

Example

On 7 July Belle agrees to buy Sam's tractor (specific goods). A written contract is drawn up and one of the terms states that ownership is to pass to Belle on 2 September. Ownership will pass on 2 September, even though an application of s. 18 would have come to a different conclusion. Section 17 takes precedence over s. 18.

If s. 17 does not show when the parties intended the ownership to pass, then the first four rules set out in s. 18 will have to be applied. As we shall see, the rules deal with different types of specific goods.

Rule 1 – Specific goods in a deliverable state

Section 18 Rule 1 provides that where specific goods in a deliverable state are unconditionally sold, ownership passes to the buyer at the time of the contract, even if the times of delivery and payment are postponed.

Goods are in a deliverable state when the seller has nothing more to do to the goods themselves. Goods could be in a deliverable state even if they needed to be packed. Goods would not be in a deliverable state if the seller had to overhaul them before the buyer was to take delivery.

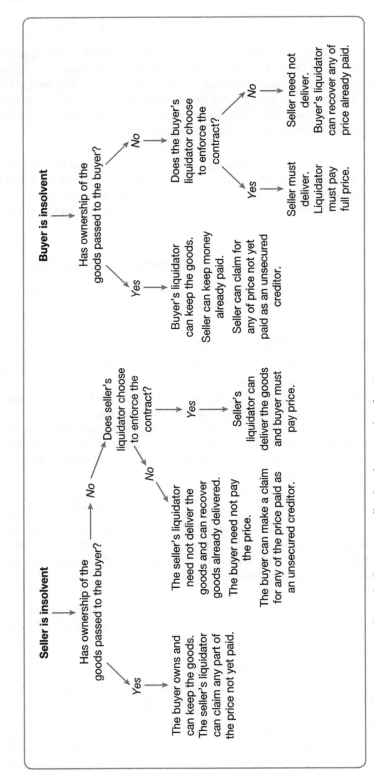

Figure 7.2 The position where the buyer or seller has become insolvent

Tarling _v_ Baxter (1827)

S sold a haystack to B on 6 January. The contract provided that B was to pay the price on 4 February and the haystack was not to be moved until 1 May. The haystack was burned down on 20 January.

Held Ownership had passed to the buyer on 6 January.

Rule 2 – Specific goods which the seller must put into a deliverable state

Section 18 Rule 2 provides that where there is a contract for the sale of specific goods and the seller is bound to do something to the goods to put them into a deliverable state, ownership passes when the seller has done the thing and the buyer has notice that it has been done.

 Underwood Ltd _v_ Burgh Castle Brick and Cement Syndicate (1922) (Court of Appeal)

On 20 February a 30-ton engine was sold. The contract obliged the seller to detach the engine from a concrete casing and to put it on a train. (This would take over two weeks.) While the engine was being loaded on the train it became damaged.

Held Ownership had not passed to the buyer at the time of the damage. The engine was not in a deliverable state at the time of sale. The seller was obliged to free the engine and put it on a train in order to put it into a deliverable state. Ownership would pass to the buyer only when the seller had done these things and had told the buyer that they had been done.

Comment It was not the great weight of the engine which prevented it from being in a deliverable state. A ship which the seller has finished building could be in a deliverable state, even though it might weigh many thousand tons. The goods were not in a deliverable state because when they were sold the seller still had to do something to the goods, that is to free them from the concrete and put them on a train.

Rule 3 – Goods to be weighed, measured or tested by the seller to find the price

Rule 3 applies where the seller has to weigh, measure or test the goods, in order to find the price. It provides that in such a case ownership is not to pass until the goods have been weighed, measured or tested and the buyer has been informed of this.

It is important to notice two things here:

(1) The rule applies only where the weighing etc. has to be done by the seller.

(2) The weighing etc. must be required in order to find the price.

Example

Ben visits Stan's scrap yard and sees a heap of copper. It is agreed that Ben will buy the heap of copper at £4,000 a ton and that Stan will weigh the heap to see how much Ben has to pay. The ownership will pass when Stan has weighed the heap and told Ben that this has been done. (If it had been agreed that Ben would weigh the copper, then Rule 1 would have applied. Ownership would therefore have passed to Ben as soon as the contract was made.)

Rule 4 – Goods delivered on approval, sale or return or other similar terms

Goods are delivered on approval where the buyer has a choice as to whether or not to buy the goods delivered. Goods are delivered on sale or return where it is understood that the buyer is going to try to resell the goods. If the buyer cannot resell the goods, then they will be returned to the seller. Where goods are delivered on approval, sale or return or other similar terms, then the ownership passes to the buyer in the following circumstances:

- when the buyer signifies approval;
- when the buyer does an act which adopts the transaction (an act which would prevent the buyer from returning the goods to the seller, such as selling the goods on to another buyer or consuming the goods);
- when the buyer keeps the goods for longer than a time limit fixed by the contract; or
- if no time limit is fixed by the contract, when the buyer keeps the goods for more than a reasonable time.

> **Example**
>
> Simon delivers goods to Brian, a shopkeeper, on sale or return. Brian sells the goods to a customer. This is an act adopting the transaction. Therefore, the ownership passed to Brian as soon as the goods were sold on. Brian then immediately passed ownership to the customer under s. 18 Rule 1.

Risk, mistake and frustration

We have already seen that in non-consumer contracts s. 20(1) SGA provides that the risk passes to the buyer at the same time as the property, unless the parties have agreed otherwise. We have also seen that reg. 43 of the CC(ICA) Regulations 2013 provides that in consumer contracts risk does not pass until the consumer gains physical possession of the goods.

Section 6 mistake

Section 6 provides that where there is a contract for the sale of specific goods, and the goods without the knowledge of the seller have perished at the time when the contract is made, the contract is void. Goods will have perished if they are stolen, damaged or destroyed. Goods will also be regarded as having perished if they become damaged to the point where they can no longer be regarded as the same thing, in a business sense, as the goods which were sold.

> **Example**
>
> Sally agrees to sell a combine harvester (specific goods) to Bhavesh. Unknown to Sally, the combine harvester had been destroyed in a fire half an hour before the contract was made. The contract is rendered void by s. 6. Therefore, Sally will have no obligation to deliver the goods and will not be in breach of contract for failure to do so. Bhavesh will have no obligation to pay the price and can recover any amount of the price already paid.

Section 7 frustration

Section 7 provides that where there is an agreement to sell specific goods and subsequently the goods, without any fault on the part of the seller or buyer, perish before the risk passes to the buyer, the agreement is avoided.

There are several points to notice about this section:

- The perishing of the goods must not be the fault of the buyer or the seller. If it is the fault of either party, that party will bear the loss.

- The goods must perish after the contract to sell has been made but before the risk has passed. Assuming that the parties have not agreed to separate risk and ownership and that s. 20(4) does not apply, s. 7 cannot therefore operate when s. 18 Rule 1 applies (because risk and ownership will pass to the buyer at the same time, that is to say when the contract is made). Section 7 can operate when s. 18 Rules 2 and 3 apply. When s. 7 does apply, the rules set out in the Law Reform (Frustrated Contracts) Act 1943, which we considered earlier (see Chapter 5), do not apply.

- Both ss. 6 and 7 and can apply only if the goods were sold as specific goods. They can never apply to unascertained goods.

Example

Sid agrees to sell a particular machine to Ben. The contract obliges Sid to overhaul the machine before delivery is made. The contract will be governed by s. 18 Rule 2 because it is a sale of specific goods to be put into a deliverable state by the seller. After the contract has been made, but before Sid has overhauled the machine, the machine is destroyed in a fire. (The fire was not caused by the fault of either Sid or Ben.) Section 7 provides that the contract is frustrated. Therefore, Sid is not in breach of contract for failure to deliver the machine. Ben need not pay the price and can recover any amount of the price which has already been paid. Other losses, such as time spent by Sid on trying to free the machine, lie where they fall. That is to say, no compensation can be claimed in respect of them.

Figure 7.3 shows the rules on the passing of ownership in contracts for the sale of specific goods.

Passing of ownership in unascertained goods

When considering the passing of property in unascertained goods ss. 16, 17 and 18 Rule 5 must be considered, in that order. Section 16 SGA 1979 provides as follows:

> [Subject to section 20A below] Where there is a contract for the sale of unascertained goods no [ownership] in the goods is transferred to the buyer unless and until the goods are ascertained.

The first thing to notice about s. 16 is that it does not tell us when ownership of unascertained goods does pass. It merely says that the ownership cannot pass until the goods have become ascertained. Unascertained goods which have been sold become ascertained when they are identified as the particular goods which are to become the subject matter of the contract. Once the goods have become ascertained, s. 17 will apply and the property will pass when the parties intended it to pass. If s. 17 does not show when the ownership is to pass, then s. 18 Rule 5 will apply.

Section 18 Rule 5 says that the ownership of unascertained goods will pass when goods which match the contract description, and which are in a deliverable state, are unconditionally appropriated to the contract. Goods are unconditionally appropriated to the contract when they are earmarked as the particular goods to be delivered, in such a way that the seller can be taken to have decided that those goods, and no others, were to become the buyer's

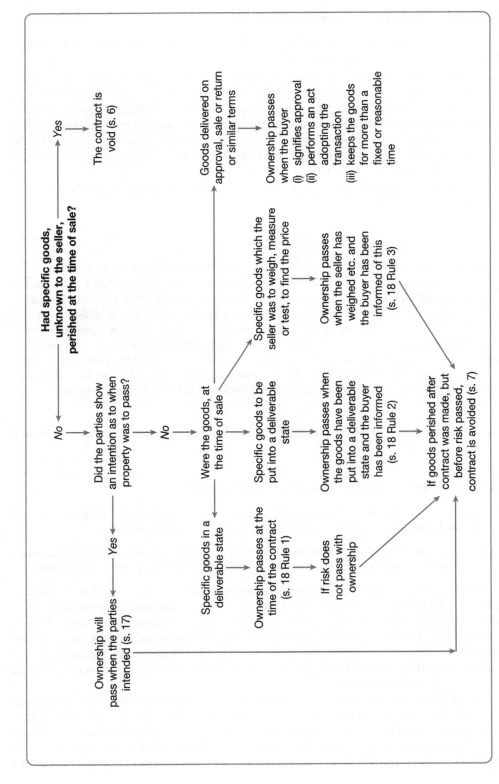

Figure 7.3 The passing of ownership in specific goods

property. If the seller could still substitute other goods, then an unconditional appropriation has not been made.

 Carlos Federspiel & Co SA *v* Charles Twigg & Co Ltd (1957)

A seller who had sold unascertained goods put goods matching the contract description into a crate. The crate was labelled with the buyer's name and the seller intended that the goods in the crate were the ones to be used to fulfil the contract. The seller then became insolvent.

Held Property had not passed. There had been no unconditional appropriation because the seller could have changed his mind and used the goods in the crate to fill other orders.

The unconditional appropriation must be done either by the seller with the buyer's agreement or by the buyer with the seller's agreement. (But a court will generally be fairly willing to infer that either the buyer or the seller agreed to the unconditional appropriation.) It is important to notice that if the goods are unascertained at the time of the contract, then the governing rules are ss. 16, 17 and 18 Rule 5. Once the goods become ascertained you do not switch to s. 17 and s. 18 Rules 1–4. It is also important to realise that the appropriate sections must be applied in the correct order. First s. 16, then s. 17, then s. 18 Rule 5.

Example

Sal sells 100 tons of wheat (unascertained goods) to Baz. The parties did not show any intention as to when ownership was to pass. Sal delivers 100 tons of wheat to an independent carrier to take to Baz. First, s. 16 provides that ownership cannot pass until the goods are ascertained. The goods became ascertained when they were identified as the particular goods to be used in performance of the contract. Second, if the parties had shown an intention as to when the ownership should pass, then this intention would have been given effect by s. 17 (as long as the goods had become ascertained). Third, as the parties did not show an intention as to when ownership was to pass, s. 18 Rule 5 would apply. Ownership would therefore have passed when the 100 tons of wheat were delivered to the carrier to take to Baz. This would have been an unconditional appropriation of the goods to the contract and Baz would be taken to have agreed to it. (The position here is confirmed by s. 32(1) which states that where in pursuance of a contract of sale the seller is authorised or required to send the goods to the buyer, delivery of the goods to a carrier for the purpose of transmission to the buyer is prima facie deemed to be delivery of the goods to the buyer. However, it should be noticed that the rule in s. 32(1) is displaced where the buyer deals as a consumer. Then s. 32(4) provides that delivery of the goods to a carrier is not delivery to the buyer. Delivery will take place when the carrier actually gives possession of the goods to the consumer.) (When the Consumer Rights Act 2015 is in force, the rule in s. 32(4) SGA will be replaced by a similar provision of the CRA 2015. See Chapter 3.)

Appropriation by exhaustion

Section 18, Rule 5(3) allows for unconditional appropriation by exhaustion if the following conditions are satisfied:

- The buyer must have bought a specified quantity of unascertained goods which form part of a bulk. Goods form part of a bulk if they are contained in a defined space or area and all the goods are interchangeable with all the other goods.

- The bulk must have been identified either in the contract or by later agreement between the parties. For example, the sale of 20 tons of the 100 tons of wheat currently stored in the seller's warehouse would be sufficiently identified if it was made plain that the buyer was buying 20 tons out of that particular 100 tons. But if the seller happened to have 100 tons of wheat in his warehouse, an agreement by the seller merely to sell the buyer 20 tons of wheat would not mean that the wheat had been sufficiently identified. (It would have been sufficiently identified if the parties subsequently agreed that the 20 tons was to be taken from the 100 tons in the seller's warehouse.)

- The bulk must have been reduced to the quantity which the buyer bought (or to less than this amount).

- The buyer must be the only buyer to whom goods are due out of that bulk. If all of these conditions are satisfied, the remaining goods will have been ascertained and unconditionally appropriated by exhaustion, and consequently ownership will have passed to the buyer.

Example

Barbara agrees to buy 30 tons of corn from the 100 tons of corn stored in Sid's warehouse. Sid removes 70 tons of corn from the warehouse. The remaining 30 tons are immediately ascertained and unconditionally appropriated by exhaustion. Ownership of these 30 tons therefore immediately passes to Barbara. If Sid had removed 80 tons from the warehouse, the remaining 20 tons would have passed to Barbara. As regards the missing 10 tons, Barbara could have sued Sid for short delivery or have chosen to reject all of the goods on the grounds of short delivery (see later in the chapter).

Undivided shares in unascertained goods which were a specified quantity of an identified bulk

Sections 20A and 20B of the Sale of Goods Act 1979 were introduced into that Act by the Sale of Goods (Amendment) Act 1995. Before ss. 20A and 20B were introduced, the rules on the passing of ownership of unascertained goods could operate very unfairly when a buyer had bought and paid for goods which formed part of an identified bulk. The following case demonstrates this unfairness.

 Re Wait (1927) (Court of Appeal)

The seller owned 1,000 tons of wheat which was on board a certain ship. The seller sold 500 tons of this wheat to a buyer, who paid the price in full. Before the ship arrived in port, the seller became insolvent.

Held The contract was for the sale of unascertained goods because the 500 tons which the buyer had bought had not been identified and agreed upon at the time of sale. (It was just any 500 tons out of the 1,000 tons.) As the sale was of unascertained goods, s. 16 provided that ownership could not pass to the buyer until the goods became ascertained. The goods had not become ascertained at the time of the seller's insolvency and so ownership of the goods could not have passed to the buyer. Therefore, the buyer could only hope to claim his money back from the seller's liquidator as an unsecured creditor.

When we examined s. 16 earlier, we saw that it begins by saying that it is subject to s. 20A. Section 20A allows a buyer who has bought a specified quantity of an identified bulk to become a co-owner of the whole bulk even before his share of the bulk is ascertained. However, the section is limited and will apply only if the following conditions are satisfied:

- The buyer must have bought a specified quantity of unascertained goods which form part of a bulk.
- The bulk must have been identified in the contract or by subsequent agreement between the parties.
- The buyer must have paid some or all of the price. The buyer becomes co-owner of the whole bulk as soon as the price is paid, but only in proportion to the amount of the price of the whole bulk which has been paid.

Example

Re Wait can be used as an example of how s. 20A operates. If the facts of the case were to arise today, s. 20A would apply because the conditions which it sets out have been satisfied. (The buyer bought and paid for a specified quantity of unascertained goods which formed part of a bulk which was identified in the contract.) Therefore, as soon as the buyer paid the price of his 500 tons he would become a half co-owner of the whole bulk of 1,000 tons (because he has paid half of the price of the whole 1,000 tons). If the buyer had paid only half the price of his 500 tons, he would have become a quarter co-owner of the whole bulk of 1,000 tons (because he would have paid a quarter of the price of the whole bulk).

Where several buyers become owners in common of a bulk, through the operation of s. 20A, s. 20B allows the seller to deliver to each buyer the appropriate share of the bulk. Section 20B provides that all the buyers who became co-owners are taken to have agreed to this. When a delivery is made to a buyer under s. 20B, s. 18 Rule 5 operates to pass ownership in the goods delivered to that particular buyer. When ownership passes to this buyer, the other buyers are given an increased percentage ownership of the remaining bulk.

Example

Steve has 100 lawn mowers in his warehouse. Steve sells 50 of these to Bill and 30 to Ben. The conditions set out in s. 20A are satisfied and Bill and Ben both become co-owners of the 100 lawn mowers (Bill has half ownership and Ben has three-tenths ownership). Steve delivers 50 of the lawn mowers to Bill. Bill becomes owner of these 50 lawn mowers (and loses all co-ownership of the other 50) under s. 18 Rule 5 (goods matching the contract description, and in a deliverable state, have been unconditionally appropriated to the contract). Section 20B provides that Ben must assent to this delivery to Bill. As Steve has only 50 lawn mowers left, Ben becomes a three-fifths owner of these 50 lawn mowers.

Sections 6 and 7 have no application to contracts for the sale of unascertained goods. However, s. 20 does apply to such contracts and so the risk will pass with ownership of the goods, unless the parties have agreed otherwise or unless s. 20(4), or the equivalent rule in CRA 2015, applies.

Figure 7.4 shows the rules on the passing of ownership in contracts for the sale of unascertained goods.

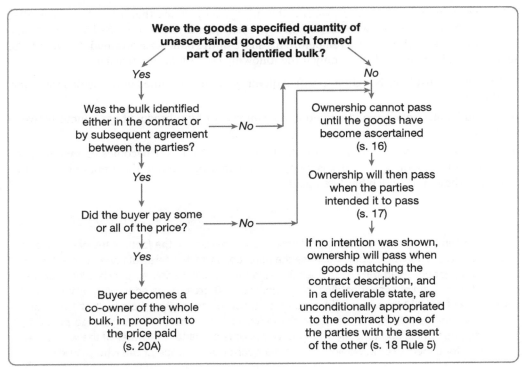

Figure 7.4 The passing of ownership of unascertained goods

Duties of the buyer and the seller

The seller has one duty, to deliver the goods. The buyer has three duties: to accept the goods, to take delivery of them and to pay the price. The seller's duty to deliver the goods and the buyer's duty to pay the price are said by s. 28 to be concurrent conditions, unless the parties agree that they should not be. The effect of s. 28 is that if the seller is not ready and willing to deliver the goods the buyer need not pay the price, and that if the buyer is not ready and willing to pay the price the seller need not deliver the goods. Section 28 is concerned with the parties' willingness to deliver and pay. It does not require that payment and delivery actually take place at the same time.

The seller's duty to deliver

If the contract was for the sale of specific goods, then the seller must deliver those specific goods. If the contract was for the sale of unascertained goods, then the seller can deliver any goods which match the contract description.

Example

Sorab agrees to sell his car (specific goods) to B1 and 10 tons of Basmati rice (unascertained goods) to B2. Sorab must deliver the specific car sold, and no other, to B1. Sorab can deliver any 10 tons of Basmati rice which match the contract description to B2.

The delivery of goods is concerned with passing possession of goods, not with passing ownership. Delivery will usually be made physically. However, delivery to the buyer can also be made in the following ways:

- by delivering a 'document of title' such as a bill of lading to the buyer;
- by delivering the means to control the goods to the buyer – for example, a seller could deliver a car by giving the buyer the keys to the car;
- by getting a third party who has possession of the goods (such as a warehouse keeper) to acknowledge that the goods are now held on behalf of the buyer; or
- where the buyer already has possession of the goods, by allowing the buyer to retain possession.

Section 32(1) provides that where the seller is authorised or required to send the goods to the buyer, delivery of the goods to an independent carrier, for the purpose of transmission to the buyer, is deemed to be delivery to the buyer. However, s. 32(4) provides that this rule does not apply when the buyer deals as a consumer. Then delivery means physical delivery. It is important to note that the rule in s. 32(4) never applies where the carrier is not independent. It would not therefore apply if the carrier was an employee of the seller.

Place of delivery

Section 29 of the SGA 1979 provides that:

(1) Whether it is for the buyer to take possession of the goods or for the seller to send them to the buyer is a question depending in each case on the contract, express or implied, between the parties.

(2) Apart from any such contract, express or implied, the place of delivery is the seller's place of business if he has one, and if not, his residence; except that, if the contract is for the sale of specific goods, which to the knowledge of the parties when the contract is made are in some other place, then that place is the place of delivery.

First, then, s. 29(1) makes it plain that the parties might have agreed either that the seller will take the goods to the buyer, or that the buyer will fetch the goods from the seller. If, however, no such agreement has been made, then s. 29(2) will apply. As regards unascertained goods, s. 29(2) provides that the place of delivery is the seller's place of business or, if the seller has no place of business, the seller's home. This is also true of specific goods – with one exception. If both parties know that the specific goods are in some other place, that place is the place of delivery.

Example

Stan, a garage owner in London, agrees to sell to Bill a Jaguar which is standing on the forecourt of his garage. Stan also agrees to sell a Bentley to Ben. Both Stan and Ben know that the Bentley is standing in a warehouse in Huddersfield. The place of delivery of the Jaguar is Stan's place of business, his garage. The place of delivery of the Bentley is the warehouse in Huddersfield. Bill must therefore come to Stan's garage to collect the Jaguar. Ben must go to the warehouse in Huddersfield to collect the Bentley. Stan fulfils the duty to deliver both cars by making them available for collection by Bill and Ben.

It can be seen that in the Sale of Goods Act the word 'delivery' has a technical sense and is not used in its everyday sense. If I buy a washing machine from a shop, then the shop fulfils its duty to deliver by allowing me to collect the machine. (For this reason, shops can charge extra for physical delivery to the buyer's house.)

Time of delivery

If the contract fixes a time for delivery, then delivery must be made at this time. If no time for delivery is fixed, then delivery must be made within a reasonable time. The amount of time which is reasonable will depend upon all the circumstances of the case.

Earlier (see Chapter 3) it was seen that a breach of warranty entitles the injured party to damages, but not to terminate the contract. It was also seen that a breach of condition allows the injured party to claim damages and/or to terminate the contract. Section 10(2) of the SGA 1979 states that whether late delivery is a breach of condition or a breach of warranty depends upon all the circumstances of the case. In commercial contracts any time fixing delivery is likely to be regarded as a condition.

 Bowes *v* Shand (1877) (House of Lords)

A cargo of rice was sold. The contract stated that the rice was to be put on board a certain ship during March or April 1874. Eighty-seven per cent of the rice was put on board the correct ship in February 1874. The remainder of the rice was put on board in March.

Held The buyers could reject the whole cargo of rice and terminate the contract, even though the value of the rice was unaffected by the early shipment. A condition of the contract had been breached.

When the Consumer Rights Act 2015 comes into force new rules about the time of delivery will apply to consumer contracts, that is to say any type of contracts under which a trader has to deliver goods to a consumer. Section 28 CRA sets out rules which apply if the trader does not need to deliver the goods at the time of the contract. Unless the trader and the consumer agree otherwise, the trader must deliver the goods without undue delay and, in any event, not more than 30 days after the day on which the contract is made. If the trader does not deliver within an agreed period, or without undue delay and within the 30-day time limit, the consumer can require delivery before the end of a further period which is specified by the consumer and which is appropriate in the circumstances. However, the consumer has the right to treat the contract as at an end and gain a full refund of the price under the 'short term right to reject' in three circumstances: (a) if the trader has refused to deliver the goods; (b) if delivery within the agreed time period was essential taking into account all of the circumstances at the time at which the contract was made; or (c) if the consumer told the trader before the contract was made that delivery within the agreed time period or without undue delay and within the 30-day time limit was essential. The consumer does not have to treat the contract as at an end, even if the short term right to reject the goods is claimed. A consumer also has a partial right to reject if only some of the goods are delivered late. The rights conferred under s. 28 SGA do not prevent the consumer from seeking other remedies such as damages.

Delivery of the wrong quantity

If the seller delivers to the buyer a lesser quantity of goods than the contract required, s. 30 of the SGA 1979 gives the buyer a choice: the buyer may either reject the goods (and sue the seller for damages for non-delivery); or accept the goods, pay for them at the contract rate, and sue the seller for damages for non-delivery of the shortfall.

> **Example**
>
> Sid agrees to sell 100 tons of wheat to Bert for £1,500. Sid delivers only 90 tons of wheat. Bert can reject the 90 tons and sue Sid for non-delivery. Alternatively, Bert can accept the 90 tons, pay Sid £1,350 and sue Sid for damages for non-delivery of the 10 tons which were not delivered.

If the seller delivers a quantity of goods which is greater than the contract called for, s. 30 gives the buyer three options. First, the buyer may reject all of the goods and sue the seller for damages for non-delivery; second, the buyer can accept the quantity of goods which should have been delivered and pay the contract price; third, the buyer may accept the whole quantity of goods delivered and pay for them at the contract rate.

> **Example**
>
> Susan agreed to sell Ben 100 tons of wheat for £1,500. Susan delivers 110 tons of wheat. Ben can either: reject the delivery and sue Susan for damages for non-delivery; accept 100 tons and pay the contract price of £1,500; accept all 110 tons and pay £1,650.

Section 30(2A) provides that a buyer who does not deal as a consumer cannot reject on account of the wrong quantity having been delivered if the breach is so slight as to make rejection unreasonable. The buyer could, however, claim damages.

A deviation in the quantity delivered can be ignored if it was so slight that it could be regarded as 'a trifle'. For example, in **Shipton Anderson & Co v Weil Bros (1912)** the buyer tried to reject a delivery of 4,950 tons of wheat because the delivery was 55 pounds over-weight. The buyer could not reject because the deviation was so slight as to be a trifle.

When the Consumer Rights Act 2015 comes into force the s. 30 SGA rules will, as regards consumer contracts only, be set out in s. 25 CRA. The rules will no longer be limited to contracts of sale but will apply to all types of consumer contracts under which a trader has to deliver goods to a consumer.

Delivery by instalments

Section 31 of the SGA 1979 provides that the buyer does not have to accept delivery by instalments unless the contract provided for delivery by instalments. If this were not the case, a seller who delivered less than the contract required could later top the delivery up.

If a contract does provide for delivery by instalments, difficulties arise where the seller breaches a condition by delivering one defective instalment. Can the buyer reject just that one instalment? Or can the buyer terminate the whole contract? Section 31 provides that the answer depends upon whether the seller's breach, in delivering the defective instalment, was a repudiation of the whole contract. If it was a repudiation of the whole contract, the buyer can treat the whole contract as terminated and sue for non-delivery as regards all future instalments. If delivering the defective instalment was not a repudiation of the whole contract, the buyer cannot treat the whole contract as repudiated. The buyer can still refuse to accept the one defective instalment and sue for damages for non-delivery of that particular instalment. In deciding whether or not a defective delivery of one instalment was a repudiation of the whole contract, s. 31 says that regard must be had to the terms of the contract and the circumstances of the case. The two most important circumstances will be:

(1) the percentage of the contract to which the breach related; and

(2) the likelihood of the breach being repeated.

The following two cases provide examples of these tests being applied.

Maple Flock Co Ltd *v* Universal Furniture Products (Wembley) Ltd (1934) (Court of Appeal)

One hundred tons of waste wool was sold, delivery to be made by instalments of one and a half tons each. The first 15 instalments delivered were satisfactory. The sixteenth instalment was defective because it contained eight times more than the legal limit of chlorine. By the time the buyers noticed this defect, two more satisfactory instalments had been delivered.

Held The buyers could not treat the whole contract as terminated. The breach was unlikely to be repeated and affected only a small percentage of the whole contract.

Robert A Munro & Co Ltd *v* Meyer (1930)

Fifteen hundred tons of bone meal were sold, delivery to be by ten instalments. After 600 tons had been delivered, the buyers discovered that all of the meal so far delivered had been deliberately mixed with cocoa husks.

Held The buyers could treat the whole contract as terminated. The breach concerned a large percentage of the contract and indicated that future deliveries might also be defective.

Figure 7.5 gives an overview of the SGA rules about delivery.

When the Consumer Rights Act 2015 comes into force rules very similar to s. 31 SGA 1979 will be found in s. 26 CRA.

The buyer's duty to pay the price

Section 8 sets out the way in which the price of the goods may be fixed.

(1) The price in a contract of sale may be fixed by the contract, or may be left to be fixed in a manner agreed by the contract, or may be determined by the course of dealing between the parties.

(2) When the price is not determined as mentioned in subsection (1) above, the buyer must pay a reasonable price.

(3) What is a reasonable price is a question of fact dependent on the circumstances of each particular case.

If there appears to be a contract of sale of goods but the price cannot be found, then the contract will be void for lack of agreement. However, s. 8 shows that even where the parties do not expressly agree the price, or agree how the price should be fixed, the price usually can be found. First, a course of dealing between the parties might fix the price, under s. 8(1).

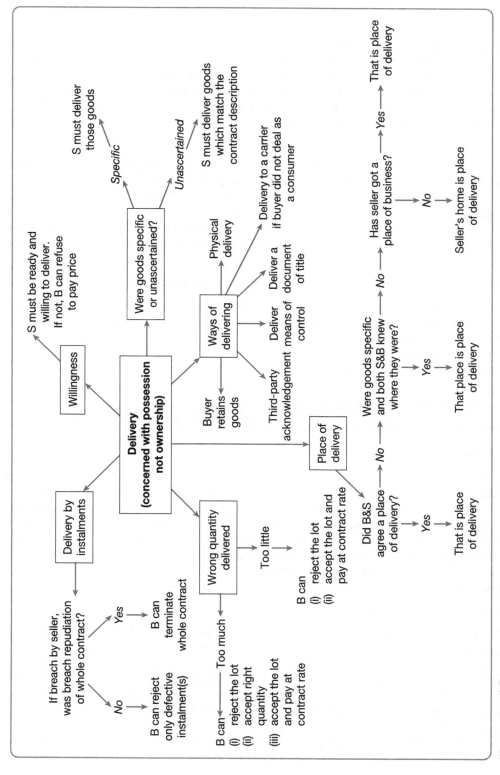

Figure 7.5 SGA rules about delivery

> **Example**
>
> Bob, a plumber, frequently buys a particular type of copper piping from Seema, a plumber's merchant. The first few times Bob makes such purchases the price is agreed at £1 a foot. If Bob rings up and orders another 100 feet of this type of piping, without mentioning the price, then the course of dealing which has taken place between the parties will fix the price at £100. So if Seema has changed the price, this change must be communicated to Bob before it will become effective.

Where the price is not fixed by s. 8(1), s. 8(2) provides that a reasonable price must be paid. So, to extend the example just considered, even if Seema and Bob had never previously dealt with each other, the price would still be fixed. Section 8(2) would require that Bob pay a reasonable price. A court could calculate this price by considering all the circumstances (s. 8(3)). The court would therefore hear evidence as to what a plumber's merchant such as Seema would usually charge a plumber for 100 feet of this type of pipe.

The buyer's duties to accept the goods and take delivery of them

The buyer's duty to accept the goods requires the buyer not to reject the goods without a justifiable reason for doing so. Such a rejection of the goods could be made either before or after the goods had been delivered. If the buyer does wrongfully reject the goods, the seller can sue for damages for non-acceptance. The buyer also has a duty to take physical delivery of the goods if requested to do so by the seller.

Remedies of the buyer and seller

The buyer's remedies

The Sale of Goods Act 1979 gives the buyer the right to sue for damages if the seller fails to deliver the goods or breaches a term of the contract. The term might be a condition or a warranty. If the seller repudiates the contract, or breaches a condition, the buyer will be able to treat the contract as terminated. (This remedy is not available for breach of warranty.) However, once the buyer has 'accepted' the goods, the right to treat the contract as terminated for breach of condition will be lost. The right to damages will, however, remain even after the goods have been accepted. Acceptance is therefore an important matter which needs to be considered in some detail.

Acceptance by the buyer

If the seller has breached a condition, or if the seller has repudiated the contract, then the buyer has a right to reject the goods and to terminate the contract. This right to reject can be exercised even if the buyer has taken delivery of the goods and even if ownership of the goods has passed to the buyer. A buyer who rejects the goods does not need to return the goods physically to the seller. All the buyer has to do is let the seller know that the goods are rejected, and to make them available for collection by the seller. If the buyer does properly reject the goods, then the seller can be sued for damages for non-delivery. A buyer with the right to reject the goods may choose instead to accept the goods and to sue the seller for damages for breach of warranty.

Section 11(4) of the SGA 1979 provides that a buyer who has accepted the goods will no longer be able to treat the contract as terminated and to reject the goods, even if the seller has breached a condition. The buyer's right to damages will remain. The rule in s. 11(4) applies whether the breach of condition was caused by delivering the wrong quantity of goods or by breaching one of the terms implied by ss. 13–15 SGA.

Section 35 SGA 1979 sets out three ways in which the buyer can be deemed to have accepted the goods. These ways are as follows:

(1) The buyer indicates to the seller that the goods are accepted.

(2) After the goods have been delivered to the buyer, the buyer does any act which is inconsistent with the seller still owning the goods. So if the buyer physically altered the goods or consumed them this would be regarded as acceptance, because to do these things would be inconsistent with the seller still owning the goods. If the buyer resells the goods to a sub-buyer, or gets a third party to repair the goods, either of these actions could amount to acceptance (but would not necessarily amount to acceptance). Furthermore, reselling the goods or getting them repaired will not amount to acceptance unless the buyer has had a reasonable opportunity to examine the goods.

(3) The buyer keeps the goods for more than a reasonable time, without letting the seller know that the goods are rejected.

Example

Billy buys a second-hand motorbike from Sarah's garage. The motorbike is not of satisfactory quality and therefore s. 14(2) SGA 1979 has been breached. This breach is a breach of condition and so Billy can reject the motorbike and terminate the contract, as well as claim damages. Billy can reject the motorbike even though it has been delivered to him and even though ownership has passed to him. If Billy told Sarah that he was aware of the defects but was still accepting the motorbike, then he could still claim damages but could not reject the motorbike. Similarly, Billy could not reject the motorbike if he had sprayed it a different colour or if he waited six months before letting Sarah know that he was rejecting it.

When goods are delivered to a buyer who has not already examined them, the buyer cannot lose the right to reject by indicating to the seller that the goods are accepted, unless the buyer has had a reasonable opportunity to examine the goods to see that they conform to the contract. For example, when goods are delivered, buyers often sign a delivery note saying that the goods are in perfect condition and that they are accepted. Signing such a note cannot amount to acceptance until the buyer has had a chance to examine the goods to see if they conform with the contract.

Truk (UK) Ltd *v* Tokmakidis GmbH (2000) held that where the seller knows that the buyer is going to resell the goods, a reasonable time would usually be the time expected to be needed to resell the goods, plus an additional time in which the sub-buyer might inspect the goods and try them out. **Clegg *v* Andersson (2003)** held that time taken by a buyer requesting and agreeing to repairs to complex goods, and time taken for those repairs to be carried out, should not be counted.

Earlier (see Chapter 3) it was seen that s. 15A provides that a buyer who does not deal as a consumer cannot reject the goods on account of a breach of ss. 13, 14 or 15 if the breach is so slight as to make rejection unreasonable. Figure 7.6 gives an overview of how the buyer's right to reject for breach of a condition can be lost.

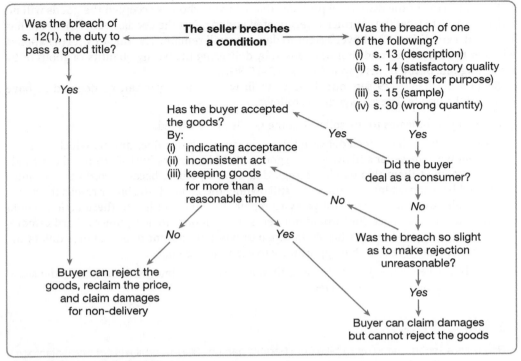

Figure 7.6 The buyer's right to reject

Partial rejection

If goods are delivered to the buyer and some of the goods conform to the contract whilst others do not, s. 35A gives the buyer three options:

(1) The buyer can reject all of the goods and sue the seller for non-delivery.

(2) The buyer can accept only the goods which do conform to the contract. The goods which do not conform to the contract can be rejected and the seller can be sued for non-delivery in respect of these goods.

(3) The buyer can accept all of the goods which do conform to the contract and also accept some of the goods which do not. The seller can be sued for non-delivery in respect of those goods which are rejected. The seller can also be sued for breach of warranty of quality as regards the goods which did not conform to the contract but which were accepted.

However, there is no right of partial rejection where the goods form part of one commercial unit. For example, a buyer who bought a set of encyclopaedias and accepted one volume would not be able to reject later volumes which were badly printed. The buyer would be able to claim damages for breach of warranty of quality.

The buyer's right to damages for non-delivery

The buyer's right to sue for damages for non-delivery arises in the following three circumstances:

(1) where the seller wrongfully neglects to deliver the goods;

(2) where the seller wrongfully refuses to deliver the goods; or

(3) where the seller breaches a condition and the buyer decides to treat the contract as terminated and rejects the goods.

Section 51(2) repeats the first rule in **Hadley v Baxendale** by providing that the measure of damages for non-delivery is the estimated loss directly and naturally arising in the ordinary course of events from the seller's breach of contract.

Where there is an available market for the goods, s. 51(3) provides that the amount of damages is generally to be the difference in price between the contract price and the market price of the goods at the time when the goods should have been delivered. The contract price is deducted from the market price and the difference is generally the measure of damages. If the contract price is the same as, or more than, the market price, then the buyer will only be entitled to nominal damages.

There will be an available market for the goods if the goods were not unique, if a different seller of such goods could be found, and if the price of such goods could be fixed by supply and demand. There is no market price for second-hand cars as they are regarded as unique goods.

A buyer who has a right to claim damages for non-delivery can also refuse to pay the contract price and can recover any amount of the price which has already been paid.

> **Example**
>
> On 6 July Simon agrees to sell Barry 10 tons of coal for £1,000, delivery to be made on 1 December. Barry pays £100 in advance. Simon refuses to deliver on 1 December. Barry can recover the £100 already paid. If there was an available market for coal of this type on 1 December, and the market price for 10 tons of such coal was £1,500, Barry's damages would usually be £500. If on 1 December the market price of this type of coal was either £1,000 or £750, Barry's damages would generally be nominal. That is to say, no substantial damages could be claimed.

If goods are delivered late, but the buyer chooses to accept the goods, damages will be assessed on ordinary contract principles (these were considered in Chapter 5). The buyer might be able to claim for loss of profit or for loss caused by the difference in the price of the goods when they were delivered and the price at the time when the goods should have been delivered.

Damages for breach of warranty

The buyer may claim damages for breach of warranty in the following three circumstances:

(1) where the seller breaches a warranty;

(2) where the seller breaches a condition and the buyer chooses to treat this as a breach of warranty;

(3) where the seller breaches a condition which the buyer is compelled (by reason of having accepted the goods or by s. 15A) to treat as a breach of warranty.

In all three of these circumstances the buyer cannot reject the goods, but can sue for damages for breach of warranty. If the buyer has not already paid the full price, the amount which would be claimable as damages can be deducted from the amount of the price which is still owing.

Section 53(2) provides that the damages for breach of warranty should be calculated using the first rule in **Hadley v Baxendale**. Section 53(3) provides that where the breach is a breach of warranty of quality the buyer's damages are generally to be the difference between the goods in the state they were in at the time of delivery and the amount they would have been worth if the warranty had not been breached.

> ### Example
>
> Basil buys a tea service from a shop for £150. The tea service is not of satisfactory quality because several of the cups are chipped. Basil does nothing about this for six months and is therefore deemed to have accepted the goods. Basil no longer therefore has the right to treat the contract as terminated. Basil then claims damages. If the tea service would have been worth only £50 at the time of delivery, on account of the tea cups being chipped, Basil's damages will generally be £100. If at the time of delivery the tea service was worth £150, or more than £150, Basil's damages would be nominal only.

Figure 7.7 gives an overview of how the buyer's damages are calculated.

Additional rights in consumer cases

Earlier (see Chapter 3) we considered the terms implied by the SGA 1979. We also saw that when these terms are breached a buyer who deals as a consumer is given significant new rights by ss. 48A–48F SGA. These additional rights are to demand repair or replacement of the goods and, possibly, to 'rescind' the contract or have the price reduced. (These important new rights are set out in Chapter 3.)

Specific performance

Section 52 SGA 1979 provides that a buyer might be able to claim specific performance of the contract where the seller breaches an obligation to deliver specific or ascertained goods. Earlier (see Chapter 5) we examined the very limited circumstances in which an order of specific performance will be made.

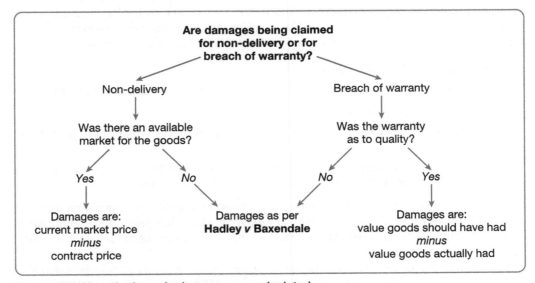

Figure 7.7 How the buyer's damages are calculated

The seller's remedies

If the buyer breaches a contract of sale of goods, the seller will always be entitled to a remedy. The remedies available are classed as either real remedies or personal remedies. The real remedies are taken against the goods, whereas the personal remedies give the seller the right to sue the buyer.

The personal remedies of the seller

The Sale of Goods Act 1979 gives the seller two personal remedies against the buyer. These remedies are:

(1) to sue for the price; or

(2) to sue for damages for non-acceptance.

The right to sue for the price

Section 49 of the SGA 1979 provides that the seller can only sue the buyer for the price if either the contract fixed a definite date for payment, or the ownership of the goods has passed to the buyer.

 Colley *v* Overseas Exporters Ltd (1921)

Unascertained goods were sold. The contract provided that ownership should pass when the goods were loaded on board a ship which the buyer had a duty to nominate. The buyer breached a condition of the contract because he did not nominate an effective ship. This caused the goods to be left lying around on a dockside. The seller sued the buyer for the contract price.

Held The seller was not entitled to the price. The contract had not fixed a definite date for payment and ownership of the goods had not passed to the buyer.

Comment This case is not as harsh on the seller as it might seem. The seller could sue the buyer for damages for non-acceptance.

A seller who sues for the price is suing in debt and so has no duty to mitigate the loss. (See Chapter 5.)

Damages for non-acceptance

The seller can sue for damages for non-acceptance if the buyer wrongfully refuses or neglects to accept the goods. The right to sue for damages for non-acceptance is not affected by whether or not the ownership of the goods has passed to the buyer.

Section 50(2) provides that the amount of damages is generally the loss directly and naturally resulting in the ordinary course of events from the buyer's breach of contract. This restates the first rule in **Hadley *v* Baxendale** and allows the seller to recover damages in respect of matters such as profit lost on account of the buyer not having accepted.

Section 50(3) provides that where there is an available market for the goods, the seller's damages are generally assessed as the difference between the contract price and the market price of the goods when the goods ought to have been accepted or when the buyer refused to accept. The market price is deducted from the contract price and the seller's damages will generally be the difference. If the market price is the same as, or higher than, the contract

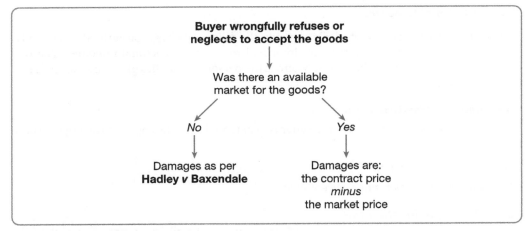

Figure 7.8 The seller's damages for non-acceptance

price, then the seller will be entitled only to nominal damages. Figure 7.8 gives an overview of how the seller's damages for non-acceptance are calculated.

> ### Example
>
> On 1 December Sue agrees to sell 10 tons of coal to Bindi for £1,000, delivery to be made on 1 February. On 1 February Sue tries to deliver but Bindi refuses to accept the coal, saying that it does not match the contract description. In fact, the coal delivered does match the contract description. Bindi has therefore wrongfully refused to accept the goods. Sue can sue for damages for non-acceptance. On 1 February there is an available market for this type of coal. If on 1 February the market price of this type of coal is £90 per ton, Sue's damages will generally be assessed at £100 (10 × £10). If the market price on 1 February is either £110 a ton or £100 a ton, Sue would generally be entitled only to nominal damages.

Section 54 allows the seller to recover additional damages to cover matters such as storing the goods, insuring the goods or the cost of setting up a sale to a different buyer.

Damages for refusing to take delivery on time

Where the buyer does accept the goods, but accepts them late, the seller can sue for damages for refusing to take delivery. Section 37 allows for this where the seller is ready and willing to deliver the goods, and requests the buyer to take delivery, but the buyer refuses to do this. It provides that the seller can sue for any loss caused by the buyer's refusal to take delivery and for a reasonable charge for care and custody of the goods. This section compensates the seller for incidental losses incurred, such as looking after the goods, but not for the loss of the bargain.

Seller's right to terminate the contract

The seller has the right to terminate the contract if the buyer repudiates the contract. A buyer who shows an unwillingness to be bound by the contract will be regarded as having repudiated the contract. A seller who rightfully terminates can sue for damages and (possibly) for the contract price. The circumstances in which a seller can sue for the price were considered earlier.

The real remedies of the unpaid seller

In addition to the personal remedies already explained, an unpaid seller of goods has three real remedies (see Figure 7.9) which allow action to be taken against the goods sold. These remedies are available only to an unpaid seller. Section 36 of the Act defines an unpaid seller as:

(i) a seller who has not been paid, or to whom the buyer has not tendered, the whole of the purchase price; or

(ii) a seller who has received a dishonoured cheque (or other negotiable instrument) as payment for the goods.

The fact that the seller has given the buyer credit will not prevent the seller from being an unpaid seller.

The three remedies which might be available to an unpaid seller of goods are:

(i) a lien over the goods;

(ii) the right to stop the goods in transit; and

(iii) the right to resell the goods.

The unpaid seller's lien

Section 41 provides that the unpaid seller's lien allows an unpaid seller to retain possession of the goods (even if ownership has passed to the buyer or the goods should have been delivered) in the following three circumstances:

(1) where the goods have been sold without any stipulation as to credit; or

(2) where the goods have been sold on credit but the term of credit has expired; or

(3) where the buyer has become insolvent.

By exercising the lien, the unpaid seller is not terminating the contract but merely exercising a self-help remedy. As soon as the price is paid by the buyer, or by the buyer's liquidator, the lien will be lost and the seller will be obliged to hand over possession of the goods. A lien can be particularly useful when a buyer has become insolvent before the goods have been delivered. Notice that a lien cannot be claimed where the buyer has been granted credit, unless the credit term has expired.

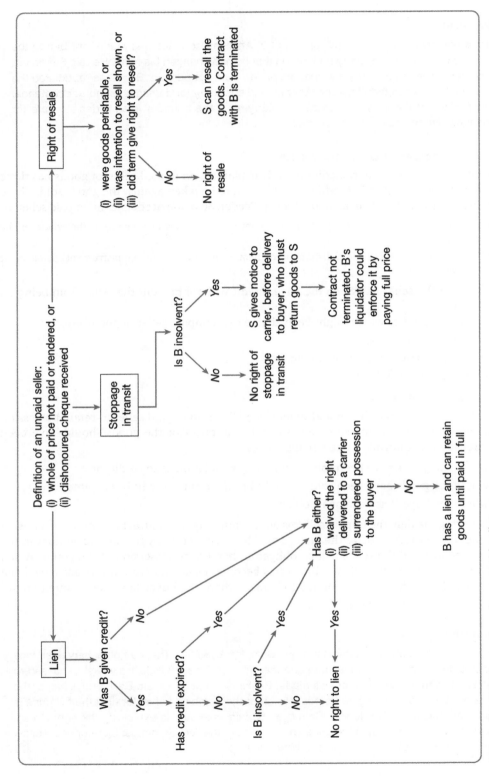

Figure 7.9 Real remedies of an unpaid seller

Section 43 provides that an unpaid seller can lose a lien in three ways:

(1) by waiving the right to the lien, that is to say, by voluntarily surrendering the right to it;

(2) by delivering the goods to a carrier to take to the buyer without reserving the right of disposal of the goods; or

(3) by allowing the buyer to lawfully gain possession of the goods.

The seller's retaining possession of the goods is therefore the key to the lien.

The right of stoppage in transit

The seller's lien is lost once the goods are delivered to a carrier who is to take them to the buyer. If the buyer has become insolvent, and only if the buyer has become insolvent, s. 46 may give an unpaid seller the right to stop the goods in transit. The effect of stoppage in transit is that the seller will recover possession of the goods from the carrier. This is likely to be very important because, if the goods are delivered to the buyer, the buyer's liquidator will be entitled to keep them. The seller would then be reduced to making a claim as an unsecured creditor. If stoppage in transit is achieved, the buyer's liquidator would have the option of enforcing the contract, but the seller would have to be paid the full price of the goods. To achieve stoppage in transit the unpaid seller must let the carrier know that this is being done before the carrier delivers the goods to the buyer. As soon as the goods are delivered to the buyer the right to stoppage in transit will be lost.

Example

Sanjay has sold 12 new cars to B Ltd. The contract price is £90,000. B Ltd has paid a deposit of £9,000. The cars are handed over to a carrier for delivery to B Ltd. Therefore ownership passes to B Ltd by virtue of s. 18 Rule 5. Sanjay then hears on the radio that B Ltd has become insolvent. Sanjay phones the carrier and tells them that he is effecting stoppage in transit. The carrier must return the cars to Sanjay, who must pay the cost of this. B Ltd's liquidator can enforce the contract, and so gain possession of the cars, but only by paying Sanjay the rest of the price (£81,000). If B Ltd's liquidator does not enforce the contract, Sanjay will have to refund to the liquidator the £9,000 already received.

Stoppage in transit is possible only where the carrier is not the agent of either the buyer or the seller. If the carrier is the buyer's agent, then delivery will have been made to the buyer. If the carrier is the seller's agent, stoppage in transit is not necessary, as the agent should anyway obey the seller's instructions to bring the goods back. Stoppage in transit and the right to a lien apply only where the ownership has already passed to the buyer. Where ownership has not already passed, s. 39 gives an unpaid seller a very similar right to withhold delivery until the full price is paid.

The right to resell the goods

In three circumstances s. 48 SGA 1979 gives an unpaid seller the right to resell goods which have already been sold without breaching the contract with the original buyer. The three circumstances in which the right of resale arises are as follows:

(1) where the goods are perishable and the original buyer does not pay the price, or tender the price, within a reasonable time;

(2) where the unpaid seller gives the original buyer notice of an intention to resell the goods and the original buyer does not pay the price within a reasonable time; or

(3) where a term of the contract expressly gives the unpaid seller a right to resell the goods.

It should be noticed that the original buyer's insolvency does not give the unpaid seller the right to resell. The buyer's liquidator might choose to pay the full price and enforce the contract.

Example

Sinead sells a ton of bananas to Barbara for £400. Barbara is not granted credit. Sinead asks for the price but Barbara does not pay it. Sinead exercises a lien over the bananas and refuses to let Barbara have possession of them. Sinead tells Barbara that the bananas must be paid for as they are beginning to over-ripen. Barbara still does not pay the price or tender it. Sinead can resell the bananas to Charlene, without breaching the contract with Barbara.

If the seller exercises the right of resale this terminates the contract with the original buyer. If the seller resells the goods for a higher price than was agreed with the original buyer, then the seller can keep the profit. If the seller resells the goods at a lower price than was agreed with the original buyer, then the original buyer must compensate the seller for this loss. Either way, the seller can sue the original buyer for damages for non-acceptance. If, however, the price of the sale to the second buyer was the same or higher, the damages would be nominal only. The seller must return to the original buyer any part of the price which has been paid.

Reservation of title (ownership) by the seller

Section 19 gives the seller the right to retain ownership of goods sold until some condition (almost always that the buyer has paid the full price) is fulfilled. A clause in a contract which says that the ownership of the goods is not to pass until some condition has been fulfilled is called a reservation of title clause, or a reservation of ownership clause.

Example

Shaun sells his second-hand car to B Ltd, which takes delivery of the car. A term of the contract states that ownership of the car is not to pass to B Ltd until the full price is paid. Normally, ownership would have passed at the time of the contract because the goods were specific goods in a deliverable state (s. 18 Rule 1). However, ownership will not pass to B Ltd until the full price is paid. So if B Ltd becomes insolvent, Shaun will be able to reclaim possession of the car from B Ltd's liquidator because Shaun is still the owner of the car. Shaun would then have to refund to B Ltd's liquidator any part of the price which B Ltd had already paid. If there had been no reservation of title clause, B Ltd's liquidator would have been entitled to keep the car (it would have been B Ltd's property at the time of B Ltd's insolvency) and Shaun could have claimed for the price only as an unsecured creditor. Unsecured creditors are not paid all that they are owed when a company goes into insolvent liquidation and may well be paid nothing (see Chapter 11). So it is far better for a seller to reclaim the goods sold.

There is no doubt that a simple reservation of title (ROT) clause will be effective.

Clough Mill Ltd *v* Geoffrey Martin (1985) (Court of Appeal)

Large quantities of yarn were sold to a manufacturing company. A reservation of title
said that ownership in the yarn was not to pass until it had been paid for in full. Be
yarn had been paid for, the manufacturing company went into liquidation.

Held The seller of the yarn could recover yarn still in the manufacturing company's possession.
The ROT clause was effective and so ownership of this yarn never passed to the manufacturing company.

More complex clauses are less likely to work. Many will be void as unregistered charges.
When a company gives a property interest as security for a debt, that is called a charge
(see Chapter 11). Section 860 of the Companies Act 2006 makes charges void if they are
not registered with the Registrar of Companies. It is impractical to register ROT clauses as
charges.

In **Re Bond Worth Ltd (1980)** Slade J said that a charge would be created:

- whenever a company created an interest in property in order to secure a debt; and
- the property interest would cease to exist if the debt was paid.

This means that the more complex types of ROT clauses might be void as unregistered
charges.

Claims to goods manufactured out of the goods sold

A simple reservation of title clause cannot be effective once the goods sold have been manufactured into other goods, because the goods sold no longer exist. So some clauses state
that if the goods are manufactured into other goods the seller can claim the manufactured
goods.

 Re Peachdart Ltd (1983)

Leather was sold to B Ltd. The contract contained a reservation of title clause which gave
the seller ownership of any goods made from the leather until the price of the leather was
paid in full. B Ltd manufactured the leather into handbags. B Ltd then became insolvent.

Held The seller could not reclaim the leather or the handbags, even though the reservation
of title clause said that the seller could do either of these things. The clause was void as an
unregistered charge. The parties intended that once the leather was made into handbags
it would belong to B Ltd, even if the seller could identify the leather as the leather he had
supplied. So the seller was claiming B Ltd's property as security for a debt, and would cease
to make such a claim if the debt was paid. As the clause was a charge, the seller could make
a claim against B Ltd's liquidator only as an unsecured creditor.

The position where the goods are sold on

Section 25 SGA 1979 gives a buyer who has possession of the goods, but who has not yet
acquired ownership, the power (but not the right) to pass ownership to a sub-buyer who buys
the goods in good faith, and who takes possession of the goods.

> **Example**
>
> Stasia sells 200 tonnes of wheat to B1. The wheat is delivered to B1. A reservation of title clause states that B1 is not to own the wheat until the full price has been paid. B1 sells the wheat to B2, who does not know of the reservation of title clause. B2 takes possession of the wheat. B1 becomes insolvent without having paid any of the price to S. Stasia cannot recover the wheat from B2 or make any claim against B2. Stasia can make a claim against B1's liquidator for the price of the wheat.

Section 25 is considered in slightly more detail in the final part of this chapter.

Claims to proceeds of sale

In the **Romalpa Case (1976)** the Court of Appeal held that the seller could validly claim the proceeds of sale when the buyer sold the goods to a second buyer. The ROT clause said that the buyer had to hold the goods as a fiduciary. The liquidator in the case acknowledged that the goods were held as a fiduciary and paid the proceeds of sale into a separate bank account. Subsequent cases have doubted that a buyer and a seller are in a fiduciary relationship and so it is thought that the case is most unlikely to be followed.

All moneys clauses

An all moneys ROT clause states that ownership of the goods sold is not to pass to the buyer until all sums owing to the seller, whether under the contract in question or under previous contracts, have been paid. If such clauses are effective, they can mean that the buyer will never own any of the goods which he has bought from the seller. For example, let us suppose that a motor manufacturer supplies a car dealer with new cars every six weeks under a contract containing an all moneys reservation of title clause. If the car dealer pays for each delivery of cars two months after delivery, the car dealer will never completely settle his debts to the manufacturer. If the clause is effective, the dealer will not own any of the cars he has ever bought from the manufacturer.

A House of Lords case, **Armour v Thyssen Edelstahlwerke AG (1990)**, held that an all moneys clause did not create a charge and that the clause was therefore valid. The logic was that if the clause was effective, then it prevented any property from ever passing to the buyer company. As the buyer company never owned the property it could not issue a charge in respect of it. However, in this case there was only one contract. It has been argued in many subsequent cases that where an all moneys clause applies to several contracts, as in the example above, a charge must have been created. The seller is claiming goods which have been paid for in order to secure a debt, and if the debt is paid the security will cease to exist.

There is some doubt about the law in this area. If the seller does manage to reclaim goods sold under a previous contract, it seems likely that the buyer can reclaim the price paid under that previous contract on the basis that there has been a total failure of consideration.

Windfall profit

Whenever the seller claims more than the original goods sold, so that a windfall profit would be made if the claim was successful, this is likely to be a charge. The seller is claiming some of the buyer's property as security for a debt, and would cease to claim the security if the debt was paid.

Sale by a person who is not the owner

An old common law rule states that *nemo dat quod non habet* (nobody gives what they do not have). The rule means that a person who does not own goods cannot pass ownership to anyone else.

Let us assume, for example, that Simon, without permission, sells Olive's car to Bill. Simon did not own the car and so cannot pass ownership to Bill. Ownership of the car will remain with Olive.

The rule is reaffirmed by SGA 1979 s. 21. Despite the logic of this rule there are seven exceptions to it:

(1) agency;

(2) estoppel;

(3) mercantile agency;

(4) sale by person with voidable title;

(5) sale by seller in possession;

(6) sale by buyer in possession;

(7) sale of a motor vehicle obtained on hire-purchase.

Agency (s. 21 SGA)

When an agent sells his principal's goods, the whole point of the contract is that the agent (who does not own the goods) passes ownership to the purchaser. However, in some ways agency is not a true exception in that the owner (the principal) is really the one selling the goods. He is just using an agent to create the contract of sale by giving the agent authority to make the sale. Section 21 of the SGA impliedly recognises agency as an exception to the *nemo dat* rule.

All of the following exceptions can apply only if the person claiming to have gained owner-ship acted in good faith and without notice of the seller's lack of ownership.

Estoppel (s. 21 SGA)

A person who is estopped from denying that someone else is the owner of goods is prevented from denying it. Section 21 impliedly recognises estoppel as an exception to the *nemo dat* rule. So an owner of goods who represents that a seller has the right to sell the goods, or who represents that a seller is the owner of the goods, will be estopped (prevented) from denying this later. The following case provides an example of this.

 Eastern Distributors Ltd *v* Goldring (1957) (Court of Appeal)

A car owner wanted to borrow money but could not provide adequate security. As part of a complicated, fraudulent scheme to borrow the money, he gave a car dealer documents which made it seem that the dealer owned the car. The scheme did not work, but, without the owner's knowledge or permission, the dealer sold the car to a finance company.

Held The finance company owned the car. The original owner had given the impression that the car dealer had the right to sell the car, and so he was estopped from denying this later.

Estoppel will not arise merely because an owner is careless with his goods, or because he gives possession of them to someone else. The owner must make a representation that someone else has the right to sell his goods. However, this representation can be made by conduct.

Mercantile agency (s. 2(1) Factors Act 1889)

Section 2(1) of the Factors Act protects a person who buys goods from a mercantile agent. It says that if a mercantile agent sells, pledges or disposes of goods this is as valid as if the owner had expressly authorised him to do so. There are, however, six requirements which need to be fulfilled:

(1) The agent must be a mercantile agent. That is to say, he must be in business and must, at least occasionally, sell or deal with other people's goods.

(2) The agent must be in possession either of the goods or of documents of title to them.

(3) This possession must have been gained with the consent of the owner.

(4) Possession must have been acquired by the agent for some purpose connected with sale.

(5) The sale or disposition of the goods must have been made in the ordinary course of business of a mercantile agent.

(6) The person taking the goods must have done so in good faith, without notice of the agent's lack of authority.

> **Example**
>
> If a customer left a watch with a jeweller, telling him to repair the watch so that it could later be sold, ownership would pass to an innocent party who bought the watch from the jeweller. The customer who left the watch with the jeweller could of course sue the jeweller for damages. This example assumes that the jeweller sometimes sells goods for others.

As long as possession was gained with the consent of the owner, it does not matter that the owner was tricked into giving this consent.

> **Folkes *v* King (1923)**
>
> A mercantile agent gained possession of a car by deception. The owner had given the car to the mercantile agent but had expressly instructed him not to sell it for less than £575. The mercantile agent immediately sold the car to A, who bought it in good faith, for £340. The car passed to several other buyers before passing to K. The original owner sued K to recover the car.
>
> **Held** The original owner could not recover the car. A good title had passed to A under s. 2(1) Factors Act, and this title had passed through the other buyers to K.

Sale by a person with a voidable title (s. 23 SGA)

Earlier (see Chapter 4) we saw that a seller who is induced to make a contract by a misrepresentation has the right to rescind the contract. A contract which is capable of being rescinded is said to be voidable (capable of being made void). So a person who makes a misrepresentation when buying goods does not acquire a complete title to the goods, but only a voidable title, that is one which can be called off by the seller within a reasonable time (see Chapter 4). We also saw that duress might make a contract voidable.

Section 23 provides that if a person with a voidable title sells the goods before the contract was avoided, then a new buyer who acts in good faith will get complete ownership of the goods. This is an exception to the *nemo dat* principle because a seller with a voidable title is giving more than he has got; he is giving a complete title.

⚖ Lewis *v* Averay (1972) (Court of Appeal)

A rogue bought a car with a bad cheque, pretending to be Richard Greene the television actor. As this was a fraudulent misrepresentation, the rogue gained only a voidable title to the car. In the long run this voidable title would have been worth very little to him as the owner would surely have rescinded the contract as soon as he discovered that the cheque was worthless. Before the owner discovered this, the rogue sold the car to the defendant, who bought the car in good faith.

Held The defendant had a complete title to the car as he had bought it before the owner rescinded the contract with the rogue.

In **Car and Universal Finance Co Ltd *v* Caldwell (1965)** the Court of Appeal held that in the case of a contract made voidable by a fraudulent misrepresentation the contract is avoided if the seller does some act which shows a definite intention not to be bound by the contract. In the case this was done by telling the police and the AA to look out for the car obtained by the fraudulent misrepresentation. Unfortunately, the Court of Appeal refused to say whether or not the contract would have been avoided in this way if the misrepresentation had not been fraudulent.

When a contract is voidable but it is avoided before the car is sold on, the final buyer will not get title under s. 23. However, he should then see if s. 25, considered below, might pass title to him.

It should be noticed that if the rogue had been a thief who just stole the car, then he would never have had any title at all, and so could not have passed on any title at all. Therefore, the owner would always get the car back. (See **Rowland *v* Divall**, Chapter 3.)

Figure 7.10 gives an overview of s. 23.

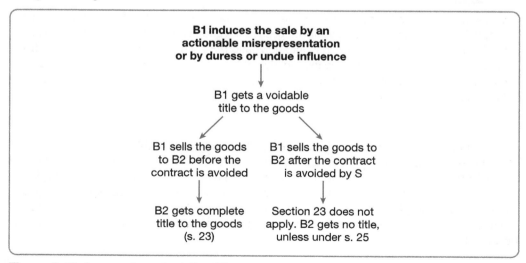

Figure 7.10 An overview of section 23

Sale by a seller in possession (s. 24 SGA)

Section 24 provides that if a seller sells goods to one buyer, but keeps possession of the goods, and then sells the same goods to a second buyer, who takes delivery of the goods, then the second buyer will get ownership of the goods.

This is an exception to the *nemo dat* rule whenever, as is commonly the case, the first buyer would have got ownership of the goods as soon as the contract was made.

The first buyer can of course sue the seller for damages for selling his goods.

> **Example**
>
> A shop has a grand piano in its New Year Sale. Eddie makes a contract to buy the piano. As we have seen earlier in this chapter, this means that Eddie is now owner of the piano by virtue of s. 18 Rule 1. By mistake, another shop assistant sells the same piano to Fred, who takes it away. Fred will get title to the piano. Eddie can sue the shop for selling his property.

This rule seems to be based on convenience. Either Eddie or Fred will get ownership of the piano and the other will be left with the right to sue the shop for damages. Eddie and Fred have behaved identically, and justice does not favour either one of them more than the other. It is more convenient to let Fred keep the piano, as he already has possession of it, than to say that Eddie has ownership of the piano.

Sale by a buyer in possession (s. 25 SGA)

A person might buy goods, or agree to buy them, and take possession of the goods before he owns them. If such a person resells the goods to a second buyer, s. 25 provides that the second buyer will get complete title to the goods as soon as they are delivered to him.

> **Example**
>
> Steve manufactures leather coats and sells 50 coats to a shop. The contract contains a simple ROT clause, so ownership will not pass to the shop until the full price is paid. Before the full price is paid, the shop goes into liquidation. So the shop had agreed to buy the coats but never owned them. Coats already sold by the shop to members of the public cannot be recovered by Steve. Section 25 protects these members of the public because the shop sold the coats as a buyer in possession.

The usefulness of s. 25 was greatly reduced by **Newtons of Wembley v Williams (1965)**. In that case the Court of Appeal took a very restrictive view of the complex wording of s. 25 and held that the section will work only where the buyer sells the goods in business hours and from business premises. This case therefore means that a person who buys goods from a rogue who paid for the goods with a bad cheque is unlikely to gain ownership of the goods under s. 25. Most rogues do not sell the goods on from business premises during business hours.

Motor vehicles on hire-purchase (Hire-Purchase Act 1964 s. 27)

The Hire-Purchase Act 1964 s. 27 provides that if a motor vehicle on hire-purchase is sold to a private purchaser who takes it in good faith, and without notice of the hire-purchase agreement, then a good title will pass to the private purchaser.

> **Example**
>
> Harry has taken a car on hire-purchase. (He does not therefore own the car.) Harry sells the car to Ben, a private purchaser who takes it without knowing about the hire-purchase agreement. Ben will own the car, even though Harry did not.

You should notice the following matters:

- The Act can pass ownership only to a private purchaser. It cannot directly pass ownership to a motor dealer. However, once ownership has been passed to a private purchaser he could of course pass ownership on to a motor dealer.
- The private purchaser must act in good faith and in ignorance of the hire-purchase agreement.
- The protection applies only to motor vehicles on hire-purchase or sold under a conditional sale where the price is payable by instalments. It does not apply to other goods on hire-purchase or sold under a conditional sale.
- There must be a 'disposition' of the vehicle to the third party. This could be by way of a sale, bailment or a hiring under a hire-purchase agreement, but whichever of these three types of disposition occurs it must be in return for money. Part-exchange transactions are covered, as long as the car being acquired is given a genuine price which is greater than that of the one traded in.
- The key to this provision is whether or not the first private purchaser acts in good faith. If he does, then ownership passes to him. If he does not, ownership cannot pass to a subsequent private purchaser acting in good faith.

> **Example**
>
> Henry has taken a car on hire-purchase. He sells this car to Alan, a motor dealer. Alan sells it to Bill, a private purchaser, who sells it to Cindy, another private purchaser, who sells it to David, a motor dealer. Alan cannot gain ownership as he was a motor dealer. Bill is the first private purchaser. If he acted in good faith, then he gains ownership and this ownership is passed on to Cindy and David. If Bill did not act in good faith, neither he, Cindy nor David can gain ownership.

Figure 7.11 gives an overview of the exceptions to the *nemo dat* rule.

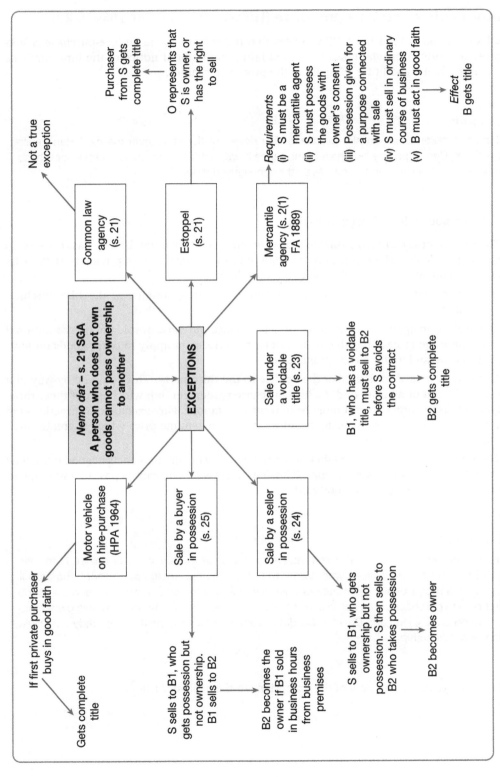

Figure 7.11 An overview of the *nemo dat* rule

- The purpose of a contract of sale of goods is to pass ownership of the goods to the buyer in return for payment of the price.
- Unless the buyer and the seller have agreed otherwise, the risk of the goods becoming lost or damaged remains with the seller until ownership of the goods passes to the buyer. If, however, the buyer deals as a consumer the risk will pass only when the goods are delivered to the buyer.
- The seller has a duty to deliver the goods.
- The buyer has three duties: to accept the goods; to take delivery of the goods; and to pay the price.
- The buyer can claim damages if the seller does not deliver the goods or if the seller breaches a warranty.
- The seller can sue for the contract price only if the contract fixed a definite date for payment or if ownership of the goods has passed to the seller.
- An unpaid seller is given three real remedies. These are to exercise a lien over the goods, to stop the goods in transit or to resell the goods.
- The general rule is that a person who does not own goods cannot pass ownership to anyone else. There are seven exceptions to this rule.
- It is possible for a seller of goods to reserve ownership of the goods until the buyer has paid the full price of the goods. If this is done, ownership remains with the seller even though the buyer may take possession of the goods.

Practice questions

1 Sid, who has owned and run a bicycle shop for many years, has decided to retire. Bryony intends to open a bicycle shop shortly. Sid invites Bryony to his shop to see if she wants to buy any of his stock. Bryony visits Sid's shop on Monday and agrees to buy the following things.

(a) A Super Deluxe Velocipede Mark 2 bicycle, which Sid is repairing. Sid agrees that he will finish the repairs within two days and that this bicycle will then be available for collection by Bryony.

(b) All the paraffin stored in Sid's tank, at a price of £1 a litre. It is not known how much paraffin is in the tank and Sid is to measure the paraffin to discover the price which Bryony must pay.

(c) Three of the six Velocipede Mark 1 bicycles which are stored in Sid's basement.

(d) Sid's computer, on which he keeps track of all his business dealings.

(e) A tricycle, which Bryony is to test ride. If Bryony likes the tricycle she will let Sid know and she will then buy it. If she does not like the tricycle she will return it within two weeks.

Bryony does not take any of the goods with her, except for the tricycle. On Monday night Sid's shop is burnt down by a stray firework and all of the contents of the shop are destroyed. Advise Bryony, who has decided that she does not want to buy the tricycle, of her legal position.

2 On 1 March Bertha agrees to buy 100 bags of potatoes from Susan. The price is £200 and it is agreed that Susan will deliver the potatoes in one month's time, when she has herself bought them from a farmer. Bertha pays £20 of the price in advance. She is given credit as regards the rest of the price, which is to be paid on 1 September.

(a) Where would the place of delivery of the potatoes be?

(b) What would the legal position be if Susan did not deliver the potatoes on time?

(c) What would the legal position be if Susan delivered 120 bags of potatoes, instead of 100 bags?

(d) What would the legal position be if Bertha made it plain that she was not going to take delivery of the potatoes or pay for them?

(e) If delivery was to be made in ten instalments, what would Bertha's position be if the second instalment contained many rotten potatoes?

(f) If no price had been fixed, would there be a contract? If so, how would the price be fixed?

(g) What remedies would be available to Bertha if she took delivery of the potatoes and stored them and, six months later, discovered that they had been rotten at the time of delivery?

(h) What would the legal position be if Bertha took delivery of the potatoes and immediately discovered that they were rotten?

(i) In what circumstances could Susan sue Bertha for the £180 of the price which had not yet been paid?

(j) Is Susan an unpaid seller?

(k) Would Susan have a right to a lien? If Susan did have a right to a lien, what would this right amount to?

(l) In what circumstances would Susan have a right to stop the goods in transit? How would she do this and what would the effect of doing it be?

(m) In what circumstances would Susan have the right to resell the potatoes to a different buyer?

(n) If Susan delivered the potatoes to Bertha, what would be the effect of a reservation of title clause in the contract?

3 Work out who will own the goods in the following examples:

(i) A has agreed that B can borrow his bicycle while A goes on a month's holiday. Without permission or authority, B sells the bicycle to C, who believes that B is the owner of the bicycle. A did not know B well and made no attempt to check whether or not he was honest.

(ii) D buys a car from a garage, deliberately paying with a bad cheque. The following day the garage owner discovers that the cheque has bounced and tells the police and the AA to look out for the car. One week later D sells the car to E, an innocent purchaser who pays a reasonable price for the car.

(iii) F has taken a car on hire-purchase from a finance company. F sells the car to G, a dealer in cars who does not know that the car is the subject of a hire-purchase agreement. G sells the car to H, another dealer in cars. I, a carpenter, buys the car from H in good faith and then sells it on to J.

(iv) An art dealer who often sells paintings on behalf of clients is asked to renovate a painting by K, so that K can sell it at auction. L visits the art dealer's shop while the art dealer is having his lunch and the art dealer's shop assistant sells the painting to L.

(v) N visits an art dealer's shop and examines a painting for some considerable time. Later N phones the shop and makes a definite agreement to buy the painting for £2,000. The dealer is to deliver the painting to N's house the following day. Later, by mistake, a shop assistant sells the same painting to O, who takes it away.

(vi) P buys a machine from Q for £4,000. Ownership is not to pass to P until the full price has been paid. P takes possession of the machine and, without Q's permission or knowledge, sells the machine to R. P has now become insolvent.

4 Explain the circumstances in which a person who does not own goods can nevertheless pass ownership of those goods to a third party.

Task 7

A friend of yours who is visiting the country from abroad is thinking of setting up a trading company in the United Kingdom. Your friend is keen to understand English law as it relates to the sale of goods, and has asked you to draft a report explaining the following matters:

(a) How a contract of sale of goods is defined.

(b) The time at which ownership of the goods sold is transferred from the seller to the buyer.

(c) The duties of the buyer and the seller in a contract of sale of goods.

(d) The remedies available to the buyer and the seller should a contract of sale of goods be breached.

mylawchamber

Visit **www.mylawchamber.co.uk/macintyreessentials** to access tools to help you develop and test your knowledge of business law, including interactive multiple choice questions, practice exam questions with guidance, weblinks, glossary, glossary flashcards, legal newsfeed and legal updates.

8

The tort of negligence

The previous few chapters have considered contractual liability. This chapter and the following one consider a different type of liability: liability in tort. Before considering specific rules about particular torts, it is necessary to consider the differences between liability in contract and liability in tort. Having done this, this chapter examines in some detail the major principles of the tort of negligence. The chapter ends with a consideration of the liability of occupiers of premises and the liability of manufacturers of unsafe products. Both of these types of liability are closely related to the tort of negligence. The following chapter considers torts which are not related to negligence, such as trespass to land and the tort of nuisance.

Contract and tort

A tort can be defined as a civil wrong which is not a breach of contract. This definition makes it plain that civil liability can be broadly classified into two types: liability arising in contract and liability arising in tort. In previous chapters it has been seen that liability under a contract is liability voluntarily undertaken, and that it is undertaken because something (the other party's consideration) is given in return. For example, if Business A makes a contract to buy a computer system from Business B, then both the decision to buy and the decision to sell will have been freely made. In addition, both sides will have made a bargain. That is to say that the liabilities which they assumed under the contract will have been given in exchange for the rights which they gained under the contract.

Liability in tort is not undertaken voluntarily. It is imposed by the courts who have decided that certain types of behaviour give rise to tortious liability. If a person injures someone else by such behaviour the injured person may sue. For example, if a driver runs over a pedestrian, while driving badly, then the injured pedestrian will be able to sue the driver for the tort of negligence. The driver has no choice about whether or not to accept such liability, the courts will impose it. Nor will the driver have received any benefit in return for accepting the liability. It will have arisen not as a result of a bargain, but as a consequence of having committed a tort.

Another difference is that liability in contract is generally strict, whereas liability in tort is almost always based on fault. The tort of nuisance (see Chapter 9) is an exception. For example, s. 14(2) of the Sale of Goods Act 1979 requires that goods sold in the course of a business must be of satisfactory quality (see Chapter 3). This contractual liability is strict. A shop which sells packaged goods which are not of satisfactory quality is liable for breach of contract even though it was not the shopkeeper's fault that the goods were unsatisfactory, and even if the shopkeeper could not have discovered that they were. However, liability in tort is imposed only when a person's conduct does not match up to an objective, reasonable standard. So a driver who runs over a pedestrian will be liable only if he or she drove badly and failed to take reasonable care. If it cannot be shown that the driver drove badly, then there will be no liability, no matter how severe the pedestrian's injuries.

Contract remedies and tort remedies

Both the breaching of a contract and the commission of a tort give rise to liability in damages. However, the purpose of contract damages is not the same as the purpose of tort damages. Both, of course, are designed to compensate. As we saw earlier (Chapter 5), contract damages achieve this by putting the injured party in the position he or she would have been in if the contract had been properly performed, and therefore include damages for loss of the bargain. Tort damages achieve it by putting the injured party in the position he or she would have been in if the tort had never been committed, looking at expenses incurred and injuries suffered.

Example

Business A agreed to deliver a new machine to Business B but delivered the machine one month late. Business B would be entitled to damages for breach of contract. These damages would be calculated by considering how much it had cost Business B that the machine had not been delivered on time. Such damages might include an amount for profit lost as a result of the machine not being available, or for the cost of employing extra workers who were needed to do the work which the machine was meant to do. A pedestrian who was run over by a negligent driver would be awarded tort damages. The purpose of these damages would be to put him or her in the same position as if the tort had not been committed. The damages might include an amount for matters such as pain and suffering, for lost wages and perhaps for damage to clothes. These losses would all be recoverable because if the pedestrian had not been negligently run over none of the losses would have arisen.

It should, however, be pointed out that the two methods of assessing damages will often arrive at much the same result. If an employee loses two months' wages as a result of the contract of employment being breached, the damages awarded would compensate for this loss on the basis that if the contract had been properly performed the employee would have received the wages. If an employee loses two months' wages as a result of being negligently run over by a car driver, the same compensation would be awarded in respect of the lost wages on the basis that if the tort had not been committed the employee would have earned the wages.

Figure 8.1 shows the essential differences between contractual and tortious liability.

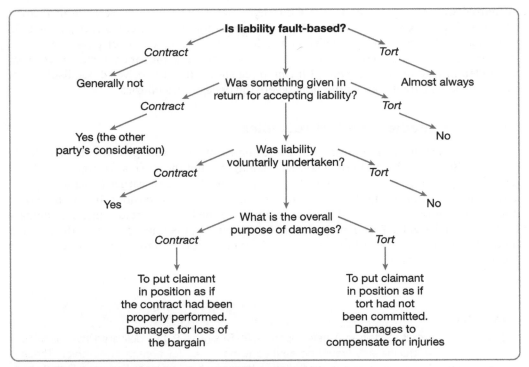

Figure 8.1 **Contractual and tortious liability compared**

Negligence

The tort of negligence is far and away the most important tort. Other torts are narrower and more specific, applying in more limited circumstances. The tort of negligence is very widely defined and can be committed in many ways. In order to establish the tort of negligence the claimant must prove three things, on a balance of probabilities:

(1) that the defendant owed him or her a duty of care;

(2) that the defendant breached that duty; and

(3) that a foreseeable type of damage was caused by the breach.

Each of these requirements needs to be proved, and so each must be considered in detail.

That a duty of care was owed

The following case is the foundation of the modern law of negligence.

 Donoghue *v* Stevenson (1932) (House of Lords)

The claimant and her friend visited a café. The claimant's friend bought some ice cream and a bottle of ginger beer for the claimant. The claimant poured some ginger beer over the ice cream and ate some of this mixture. When the claimant's friend poured out the rest of the ginger beer the remains of a decomposed snail fell out of the bottle. The contamination of the ginger beer caused the claimant to suffer gastroenteritis and the sight of the snail caused her to suffer nervous shock. The claimant could not sue the café which had sold the ginger beer because she had no contract with the café. Instead, she sued the manufacturer of the ginger beer, claiming that the manufacturer owed a duty of care to customers. The manufacturer denied that any such duty was owed.

Held Manufacturers owe a duty of care to see that their customers are not injured by their products.

Lord Atkin said: 'You must take reasonable care to avoid acts and omissions which you can reasonably foresee would be likely to injure your neighbour. Who, then, in law is my neighbour? The answer seems to be – persons who are so closely and directly affected by my act that I ought reasonably have them in contemplation as being so affected when I am directing my mind to the acts or omissions which are called in question.'

Comment (1) If the case were to arise today, the Contracts (Rights of Third Parties) Act 1999 (considered in Chapter 2), would have allowed the claimant to sue the café in contract. (2) As the ginger beer was 'unsafe', the Consumer Protection Act 1987, considered later in this chapter, would now have allowed the claimant to sue the manufacturer of the ginger beer without proving negligence. (3) These new rights to sue do not detract at all from the principles set out in the case, which is considered one of the most important cases in English law.

Using Lord Atkin's famous 'neighbour' speech, the courts have established certain recognised duty situations. For example, it is well established that road users owe a duty of care to other road users and pedestrians. Similarly, manufacturers and repairers owe a duty of care to their customers, and professional advisers owe a duty of care to their clients. The true significance of **Donoghue v Stevenson** is that it allows the tort of negligence to expand to cover new situations. However, when a new situation arises, the courts decide whether or not a duty of care is owed by considering how similar the new situation is to situations where the courts have already decided that duty is or is not owed. This approach is known as an incremental approach.

In **Caparo Industries plc v Dickman (1989)** the House of Lords held that a duty of care would be owed if three conditions were satisfied:

(1) It must have been foreseeable that harm would be caused to the claimant.

(2) There must have been 'proximity' between the claimant and the defendant.

(3) It must be just and reasonable for the court to impose a duty of care.

Proximity can arise only where it was foreseeable that harm would be caused to the claimant, but it is a more complex concept than foreseeability. For example, if a driver ran over a claimant and physically injured him or her, then the necessary proximity would be present just because physical injury was foreseeable. If a second pedestrian, who was not physically injured, suffered nervous shock as a consequence of seeing the accident the necessary proximity might not be present. This would depend upon factors such as the distance the second pedestrian was from the accident and the closeness of the relationship between the two pedestrians. If the second pedestrian was very close to the accident, or if the second pedestrian was a very close relative of the first pedestrian, then it is very likely that the necessary proximity would be present. However, if the second pedestrian was a long way away from the accident and did not know the first pedestrian, then it would be likely that no duty of care would have been owed to the second pedestrian by the defendant. The third step, that it is just and reasonable to impose a duty of care, is much more likely to be satisfied if the claimant has suffered physical injury, rather than economic loss or nervous shock.

Although Lord Atkin's 'neighbour' speech referred to omissions as well as to acts, it is a general principle of English law that a person is not to be made liable for mere failure to act. This is the case even where it is apparent that failure to act will result in another person suffering injury. For example, if I saw a person drowning and made no attempt to save him, this would be very wrong morally, but would not amount to negligence. However, omissions can give rise to a duty of care where the defendant has undertaken to do something which he later fails to do, or where he has led someone else to believe that he has done something which he has not in fact done. So it might well be negligence if a lifeguard did not save someone from drowning or if he wrongfully gave the impression that a person who was drowning was not in danger. The ownership or occupation of land might also create a duty to do something for the benefit of those coming onto the land or for the benefit of neighbours.

Liability for psychiatric injury

A claimant who suffers psychiatric injury as a result of negligence may well be able to claim damages for this. However, the courts have restricted the circumstances in which a duty not to cause psychiatric injury is owed. Damages cannot be claimed in respect of sorrow, grief or short-term anxiety. Many of the older cases classify psychiatric injury caused by a tort as 'nervous shock' and the courts have adopted a cautious approach to finding liability for causing nervous shock. Over the years the courts have made a distinction between 'primary victims', who suffer nervous shock as a result of themselves being physically endangered, and 'secondary victims', who suffer nervous shock as a result of witnessing the death or injury of another person. In **Page v Smith (1995)** the House of Lords held that, as regards primary victims, where physical injury is foreseeable, physical and psychiatric injury should be regarded as the same type of injury.

In the following case the House of Lords considered the position of secondary victims in some detail.

 Alcock v Chief Constable of South Yorkshire Police (1991)

Ninety-five people died, and many more were severely injured, as a consequence of the defendant's negligent policing of a football match. The disaster was seen by a variety of claimants, who were all relatives or friends of those involved. These claimants were not primary victims, as they were never themselves in danger. Some claimants saw the events from the other side of the stadium, others saw them on television or heard them described on the radio. All of the claimants suffered psychiatric illness and claimed in respect of this against the defendant.

Held A duty of care will be owed to a secondary victim who suffers psychiatric illness only if the following conditions are satisfied. First, the relationship between the claimant and those injured would have to be sufficiently proximate. It is not possible to make a closed list of relationships, such as husband and wife or parent and child, which will be regarded as sufficiently proximate. Rather, the necessary proximity will exist if there was a close enough relationship of love and affection to make it reasonably foreseeable that the claimant would suffer nervous shock if they apprehended that the primary victim had been or might be injured. Whether or not such closeness existed would require careful scrutiny in every case.

Second, it is also necessary that the claimant prove closeness to the accident or its aftermath in terms of both time and space. Third, the nervous shock must have been suffered on account of seeing or hearing the accident or its immediate aftermath. Applying these principles, the claims of those who saw the accident on television failed. Two claimants who were inside the football ground failed in their claim because they were not in a sufficiently proximate relationship to the victims of the disaster.

Comment In **Taylor v A Novo UK Ltd (2013)** the Court of Appeal recognised that the principles set out in this case have been criticised as unhelpful because they give little guidance as to where the dividing line between primary and secondary victims should be drawn. However, it was held that the courts should not attempt to substantially develop the principles. That would be a job for Parliament.

Damages will not be awarded for trauma suffered immediately before death by a claimant who is killed by the defendant's breach of duty. It is also the case that the nervous shock must be caused by witnessing a sudden horrific event and not by witnessing a gradual process, such as death from a wasting disease.

Pure economic loss

Earlier (see Chapter 5) we saw that a claim for economic loss is often the basis of a claim for damages for breach of contract. The law of tort is generally concerned with liability for injury to the person and damage to property. However, damages may also be recoverable in respect of economic loss which is a direct consequence of physical injury or damage to the claimant's own property. For example, if a claimant is injured and unable to work, a claim for lost earnings may be made. An example of a business successfully claiming for economic loss can be seen in **British Celanese v A H Hunt Ltd (1969)**. The defendants negligently caused the claimant's factory to suffer a loss of power by allowing foil strips to blow onto a power line. This caused damage to the claimant's machines. The Court of Appeal held that the resulting economic loss of not being able to use the machines was fully recoverable. **Spartan Steel and Alloys Ltd v Martin & Co (contractors) Ltd (1973)** provides a contrast. Here the defendant's power shovel negligently cut a cable belonging to the utility company. This caused the defendant's factory to be without electricity for 14 hours. Damages could be recovered for the reduction in value of metal which had to be removed from a furnace, and for the profit which would have been made on that particular 'melt' of metal. However, the Court of Appeal did not award damages for four other lost 'melts' which would have been produced but for the power cut. This loss was economic loss which did not flow directly from the claimant's own physical loss and so no duty of care was owed in respect of it.

In **Weller v Foot and Mouth Research Institute (1966)** a firm of auctioneers were not able to claim damages in respect of lost profits caused by the defendants negligently allowing foot and mouth disease to escape from their laboratory. The ensuing outbreak caused the claimants to be prevented from holding auctions but the defendants owed them no duty in respect of their lost profits. This principle is necessary to limit the number of persons who might have a claim. If the auctioneers had been able to claim in respect of their economic loss, then a similar claim could have been made by a large number of other businesses, such as pubs and cafés, which had also been caused economic loss. It may, however, be possible for the claimant to succeed in an action for damages for pure economic loss if he can bring himself within one of several exceptions to the general rule. These exceptions would include liability for **negligent misstatement**, which is considered later in the chapter.

In **Commissioners of Customs and Excise v Barclays Bank plc (2006)** the House of Lords held that liability for pure economic loss will arise in only three situations: first, where a person has, or can be taken to have, assumed responsibility for what he said and did in relation to the claimant (see negligent misstatement later in the chapter); second, under the threefold test considered in relation to the general existence of a duty of care (reasonable foreseeability, proximity and whether it is fair, just and reasonable to impose a duty of care); third, under the incremental test as set out in **Caparo** (see earlier in the chapter).

Breaching the duty

Merely owing a duty of care is not enough to give rise to liability for the tort of negligence. Almost everybody owes a duty of care to many people every day. For example, every car driver owes a duty of care to other road users and pedestrians. The driver is not liable to be sued by such people unless he or she injures them by breaching the duty of care which is owed.

A duty of care will be breached if the defendant does not take the care which a reasonable person would take in all the circumstances. This is an objective standard. It is no defence that the defendant was doing his or her incompetent best. In **Nettleship v Weston (1971)** the Court of Appeal held that the duty of care which a learner driver owed to passengers and the public was the same objective and impersonal standard as every other driver owed. Notice the contrast with criminal law here. Most criminal offences demand that the accused deliberately does wrong.

A higher standard of care is expected of professional people and those who claim to have some special competence. Professional people must show the degree of care which a reasonably competent person in that profession would show, and failure to show this standard will amount to breach of duty. In **Bolam v Friern Hospital Management Committee (1957)** McNair J said: 'Where you get a situation which involves the use of some special skill or competence . . . the test is the standard of the ordinary skilled man exercising and professing to have that special skill.' The case concerned a man who had suffered broken bones caused by convulsions experienced when he was given electric shock treatment for depression. There were two schools of thought about whether or not patients undergoing such treatment should be given relaxant drugs. After the case it became accepted that they should. It was held that the hospital did not breach their duty of care by failing to use such drugs. A doctor who acts according to one accepted school of thought is not negligent just because it later turns out to have been wrong.

A duty of care owed will not have been breached unless it could reasonably have been foreseen that the defendant's actions would cause injury.

 Roe v Minister of Health (1954) (Court of Appeal)

In 1947 the claimant was paralysed by an anaesthetic used by a hospital. The anaesthetic was kept in glass ampoules, which were stored in disinfectant. Traces of disinfectant had seeped through the glass ampoules into the anaesthetic and this disinfectant had caused the paralysis.

Held The defendant was not liable because in 1947 no-one knew that fluid could permeate glass. Of course, a hospital would have been liable if a similar accident had occurred after this fact had become known. In the Court of Appeal, Denning LJ said that we: 'must not look at the 1947 accident with 1954 spectacles'.

In deciding whether or not a duty has been breached, the courts tend to attach particular importance to four factors:

(1) the likelihood of the claimant suffering harm;

(2) the potential seriousness of injury which the claimant was likely to suffer;

(3) the cost of making sure that no harm was caused; and

(4) the usefulness of the defendant's actions.

The first two factors are weighed against the second two. If the first two are greater than the second two, then it is likely that the duty will have been breached. If they are smaller it is likely that it will not. These principles are shown in outline in Figure 8.2.

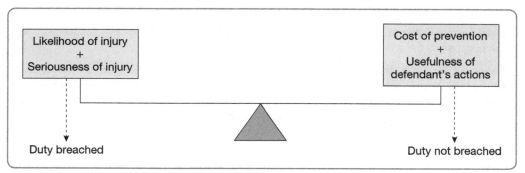

Figure 8.2 Breach of a duty of care: factors to be taken into account

This sounds rather complicated, but the following two cases illustrate that it is relatively straightforward.

 Bolton v Stone (1951) (House of Lords)

A cricket ball was hit right out of a cricket ground and struck and injured the claimant. The ball cleared a 7-foot-high fence built on a 10-foot-high bank. The claimant was 22 yards beyond the fence, about 100 yards from the wicket. About half a dozen balls had been hit out of the ground in the previous 30 years.

Held The duty was not breached. A and B (the likelihood of harm and the potential seriousness of injury) were much smaller than C (the cost of preventing the accident).

Comment The usefulness of playing cricket (D) was not much of a factor in this case. However, it was accepted that people need to take recreation and that cricket is a traditional type of English recreation.

 Paris v Stepney Borough Council (1951) (House of Lords)

The claimant, who had the use of only one eye, was told by his employers to hammer and grind the underneath of a vehicle. He was not given protective goggles and, while hammering, he lost the use of his good eye when this was pierced by a shard of metal.

Held The duty was breached. A and B (the likelihood of harm and the potential seriousness of injury) were much greater than C and D (the cost of preventing the accident and the usefulness of working without goggles).

The usefulness of the defendant's actions tends to be an important factor in cases where the defendant acted in an emergency.

 Watt *v* Hertfordshire County Council (1954) (Court of Appeal)

A fire station received a call that a woman was trapped under a heavy vehicle about 250 yards away from the station. The officer in charge set off immediately, ordering that a lorry should be loaded with heavy lifting gear, which was normally carried on a special vehicle, and that the lorry should follow as soon as possible. The lifting gear was loaded on to the back of the lorry, but it could not be lashed down. When the lorry braked, one of the firemen travelling with the lifting gear was injured.

Held The fire authority was not negligent. The risk to the firemen had to be balanced against the purpose to be achieved.

Denning LJ said: 'If this accident had happened in a commercial enterprise without any emergency, there could be no doubt that the [fireman] would succeed. But the commercial end to make profit is very different from the human end to save life and limb. The saving of life and limb justifies the taking of considerable risk.'

Section 1 of the Compensation Act 2006 has attempted to clarify the standard of care expected, and in particular to counter the 'compensation culture' idea that any activity which involves any degree of danger could lead to liability. It provides that when considering whether a defendant should have taken steps to meet a standard of care, a court should consider two matters: first, whether requiring those steps to be taken would prevent a desirable activity from being undertaken at all, or prevent it from being undertaken to a particular extent or in a particular way; second, whether requiring those steps to be taken would discourage people from doing things connected with a desirable activity. This section does not change the law but codifies it, so that people become aware that some risks are justified. When children play football, for example, there is a risk of injury. But the playing of football is a desirable activity. If a child is injured whilst playing a football match at school, a court will not find that the duty of care which the school owed is breached merely because the school could have banned football and therefore avoided any risk of injury. As the position is now contained in a statute, rather than in case law, it is hoped that fewer unsuitable cases will go to court. It is also hoped that the general public will become aware that the desirability of some activities outweighs the risk involved. Section 1 also applies to statutory duties if they involve a standard of care, as the Occupiers' Liability Acts 1957 and 1984 do. These acts are considered later in this chapter.

Section 2 of the Compensation Act 2006 provides that the mere fact that a person apologises or offers treatment or some other help does not amount to an admission of negligence or breach of a statutory duty.

The thing speaks for itself (previously known as *res ipsa loquitur*)

As negligence is a civil action, the burden of proof is on the claimant to prove his or her case on a balance of probabilities. Sometimes the claimant will not be able to prove in precisely what way the defendant was negligent. In **Donoghue *v* Stevenson**, for instance, the claimant would not have been able to prove exactly how the defendants were negligent in allowing the snail to get into the bottle of ginger beer.

By claiming that the thing speaks for itself, the claimant can reverse the burden of proof, so that the defendant must prove that the damage was not caused by his or her failure to take reasonable care.

The claimant will be able to say that the thing speaks for itself only if the following three conditions are satisfied:

(1) the defendant must have been in control of the thing that caused the damage;

(2) the accident must be the kind of accident which would not normally happen without negligence on the part of some person; and

(3) the cause of the accident must be unknown.

Ward v Tesco Stores (1976) provides an example. A customer in the defendants' supermarket slipped on yogurt which had been left on the floor. The defendants would have breached the duty of care they owed to customers if the yogurt had been on the floor for an unreasonable time, but not otherwise. The claimant did not know how long the yogurt had been on the floor. The defendants were able to prove that they swept the supermarket floor five or six times a day. The Court of Appeal held that the duty of care which the defendants owed to the claimant had been breached. The claimant could not prove that the defendants were at fault. However, the claimant had shown that something had happened which, in the absence of any explanation, made it more likely than not that the defendants were at fault. Once the claimant had proved this, the defendants would be liable unless they could prove that they were not at fault. The defendants could not prove this and so they were liable. **Ward v Tesco Stores** was distinguished by the Court of Appeal in **Tedstone v Bourne Leisure Ltd (2008)**. The claimant was injured when she slipped on a pool of water near a jacuzzi at the defendants' hotel. Water had not gathered in this area before, and had not been there five minutes before the accident. No reasonable system of the defendants could have dealt with the water in such a short time. Therefore the claimant's argument, that the accident would not have happened if the defendants had not been negligent, failed. So no burden of proof passed to the defendants.

A foreseeable type of damage was caused by the breach of duty

In order to recover damages for the tort of negligence the claimant must prove that the defendant's breach of duty caused the loss for which damages are being claimed. Furthermore, the claimant must prove that the loss was a type of loss which would foreseeably follow from the defendant's breach.

Causation

The claimant can recover damages in respect of a loss only if it can be proved that the loss was caused by the defendant's breach of duty. Generally, the courts use a 'but for' test in assessing this. That is to say, they ask whether the claimant would have suffered the loss but for the defendant breaching the duty. If the claimant would not, then this suggests that the defendant's breach of duty caused the loss. If the claimant would have suffered the same loss even if the defendant had not breached the duty, then the defendant will not be liable for the loss. For example, in **Barnett v Chelsea Hospital (1969)** a patient who visited a hospital suffering from vomiting was negligently turned away by a doctor and died from arsenic poisoning. The patient would have died anyway, even if the doctor had given him all possible treatment, and so the hospital was not liable for the patient's death.

In **Hotson *v* East Berkshire Health Authority (1987)** the defendant's negligence had a 25 per cent chance of having caused the claimant's injury. The House of Lords held that to prove causation on a balance of probabilities what was required was at least a 51 per cent probability that the negligence caused the injury. Consequently, the claim failed.

To prove that the defendant caused the loss, the claimant must show that there was a chain of causation between the defendant's breach of duty and the claimant's loss. This chain must not be broken by a new act intervening (previously known as ***novus actus interveniens***).

 The Oropesa (1943) (Court of Appeal)

A ship called the *Oropesa* was negligently navigated and this caused it to damage another ship. The captain of the other ship decided to approach the *Oropesa* in a lifeboat to discuss the best way to save his ship. The lifeboat overturned in the heavy sea and several crew members were drowned. Their relatives sued the owners of the *Oropesa*.

Held The owners of the *Oropesa* were liable. The actions of the captain of the other ship did not break the chain of causation because they were reasonable in all the circumstances.

Comment Unreasonable actions will break the chain. So if one of the lifeboat crew had drowned after deciding to swim to the *Oropesa*, then the chain would have been broken and the owners of the *Oropesa* would not have been liable for his death.

Reflex actions will not break the chain of causation. In **Carmarthenshire County Council *v* Lewis (1955)** a lorry driver was killed when he swerved to avoid running over a 4-year-old boy. A primary school had been negligent in letting the boy get out onto the road. The school was liable for the driver's death. The driver's reflex action of swerving the lorry did not break the chain of causation.

Multiple causes

Difficulties arise where the claimant's loss was caused not only by the defendant's negligence but also by other causes as well.

 McGhee *v* National Coal Board (1972) (House of Lords)

The claimant's employers asked him to clean out brick kilns. No washing facilities were provided, even though the work was hot and dirty and exposed the claimant to clouds of brick dust. The claimant used to ride his bicycle home while caked with sweat and grime. The claimant soon developed dermatitis. This was caused by working in the kiln, but the risk of dermatitis was materially increased by the claimant cycling home without washing.

Held The defendants were liable in negligence. A defendant is liable to a claimant if his breach of duty caused, or materially contributed to, the claimant's injury. This was the case even if there were other factors which contributed to the injury. If the court found that the defendant's breach of duty had materially increased the risk of injury, this amounted to a finding that the breach had materially contributed to the injury (unless the defendant could positively prove otherwise).

Mesothelioma is a type of lung cancer caused by exposure to asbestos. It is invariably fatal. Mesothelioma takes very many years to develop, and so if an employee was exposed to asbestos while working for several different employers it can be impossible to say which exposure caused the disease. So s. 3 of the Compensation Act 2006 provides that if it is impossible to say which defendant caused the mesothelioma, a claimant can claim full damages from any employer who negligently exposed him to asbestos or other causal agent. The employer who is liable can seek a contribution from any other employers who were also negligent. The Mesothelioma Act 2014 allows sufferers to claim up to £123,000 from a government fund if they cannot trace the employer responsible for exposing them to the disease.

Foreseeability

In order for damages to be claimed for a loss, the loss must have been a type of loss or injury which was a foreseeable consequence of the defendant's breach of duty. The extent of the loss does not need to be foreseeable, nor does the precise way in which it arose.

 The Wagon Mound (Overseas Tankship (UK) Ltd *v* Morts Dock & Engineering Co Ltd) (1961) (Privy Council)

The defendants negligently spilt a large quantity of furnace oil into Sydney harbour. The claimants' wharf was about 600 feet away, but the oil soon spread there. The oil was lying on top of the water and so the claimants were advised to stop welding on their wharf. The claimants later carried on welding when they were advised that this was safe. A spark from a welding torch set fire to a large bale of cotton which was floating in the water. This bale ignited the oil and extensive damage was caused to the claimants' wharf. The defendants did not know, and could not have been expected to know, that furnace oil floating on water could be ignited.

Held Even though the defendants had negligently spilt the oil, they were not liable for the damage which the fire caused. Fire was not a foreseeable type of damage. Therefore, the defendants were not liable for any fire damage. If a claim had been made for pollution by oil, then the defendants would have been liable for this, because this was a foreseeable type of damage.

As long as a certain type of damage is foreseeable, then the defendant will be liable for all damage of that type. So the 'eggshell skull' rule holds that if a certain amount of injury to the person was foreseeable, then the defendant will be liable for much greater injury suffered by a particularly sensitive claimant. For example, in **Smith *v* Leech Brain (1962)** the defendants' negligence caused the claimant to suffer injury when a drop of molten metal splashed onto his lip. Unknown to anyone, the claimant was particularly prone to cancer. The injury to his lip caused him to develop cancer, from which he died. The defendants were liable for the claimant's death, even though a burnt lip would not have caused death in many cases.

Damages

It has already been stated that the purpose of tort damages is to put the injured party into the position he or she would have been in if the tort had not been committed.

Where the loss consists of damage to goods the amount of damages will usually be the cost of repairing or replacing the goods. A claim might also be made for not being able to use the goods until they could be repaired or replaced. Such a claim might include an amount for lost profit.

Damages for personal injuries

Whenever damages are claimed in respect of personal injuries, the law makes a distinction between special damages and general damages. This distinction is made whether the personal injury was caused by a breach of contract or by a tort. When a claim is made for special damages, the amount of money claimed in respect of a loss can be calculated exactly because the claimant can itemise the loss and prove that it arose. When a claim for general damages is made, however, the amount of damages claimed in respect of a loss cannot be itemised and proved exactly, but will be assessed by the judge who hears the case.

As special damages can be calculated exactly, they could be claimed for the following matters: loss of earnings before the case came to trial; the cost of private medical care up to the time of the trial; and money lost by other people (such as relatives) who have provided services which became reasonably necessary on account of the injury to the claimant. In most cases, special damages are agreed between the parties, as either allowable or not, before the case comes to court. If this is not agreed, the judge will rule on which claims are to be allowed.

As general damages cannot be calculated exactly, they could be claimed for the following matters: pain and suffering, whether it was endured before the trial or likely to arise in the future; loss of amenities, which means the loss of ability to do things due to physical or mental disability (the younger the claimant the higher these damages are likely to be, especially if they prevented the claimant from pursuing a hobby or a sport which had previously been enjoyed); and loss of future earnings.

Mitigation

A claimant has a duty to take all reasonable steps to mitigate (reduce) the loss suffered. Damages cannot be claimed for a loss which could have been mitigated by taking reasonable steps. However, if a reasonable attempt to mitigate the loss actually increases the loss, the claimant can recover damages to cover this increased loss.

Defences to negligence

Contributory negligence

Contributory negligence is not a complete defence, but reduces the damages payable to the claimant. Individual damages for personal injuries can run to several million pounds, and so any percentage reduction could amount to a great deal of money.

The Law Reform (Contributory Negligence) Act 1945 s. 1 provides that:

> Where any person suffers damage as the result partly of his own fault and partly of the fault of any other person . . . the damages recoverable . . . shall be reduced to such an extent as the court thinks just and equitable having regard to the claimant's share in the responsibility for the damage.

 Froom *v* Butcher (1975) (Court of Appeal)

A motorist was injured by an accident which was not in any way his own fault. He suffered injuries to his head, chest and finger. If he had been wearing a seat belt (which in those days was not compulsory), the injuries to his head and chest would have been avoided altogether.

Held The damages in respect of the head and chest injuries were reduced by 25 per cent. The damages for injury to his finger were not reduced as these would have arisen even if the claimant had been wearing a seat belt.

In **Badger *v* Ministry of Defence (2005)** an award to a widow in respect of her husband's death from lung cancer was reduced by 20 per cent because he had not given up smoking, despite warnings that this was harming his health. The husband had died at 63. Exposure to asbestos at work was the main cause of death but smoking was a contributory factor.

In **Ehrari *v* Curry (2006)** it was held that a child of nearly 14 who walked into a road without first looking for traffic was 70 per cent responsible for the accident. She was hit by a truck driving at 20 mph. The truck driver was negligent in that he had not seen the child at all, even though he knew that children were in the area.

Contributory negligence is concerned with the claimant's contribution to the injury caused by the accident. The claimant's behaviour after the tort has been committed cannot amount to contributory negligence. However, if the claimant unreasonably makes matters worse after the tort has been committed, the damages awarded can be reduced to take account of this. For example, if a claimant suffered moderate injuries because of the defendant's negligence, but suffered much more serious injuries as a consequence of unreasonably failing to get medical treatment, damages would be only in respect of the moderate injuries which should have been suffered. The defendant should have mitigated the loss by seeking medical treatment.

Volenti non fit injuria (to one who volunteers no harm is done)

It is a complete defence to show that the injured person voluntarily assumed the risk which caused the injury. The defence is known by its Latin name, *volenti non fit injuria*. It often defeats employees who are injured as a result of not following safety procedures. The following case provides an example.

 ICI Ltd *v* Shatwell (1965) (House of Lords)

Experienced shot firers were badly injured when they tested detonators without taking the proper safety precautions. They sued their employer, who did not know that the safety precautions had not been adopted.

Held The employer had a complete defence. The injured workers had voluntarily assumed the risk which injured them.

Volenti non fit injuria will not apply if the claimant was injured while reasonably trying to carry out a rescue. For example, in **Haynes *v* Harwood (1935)**, a policeman was injured when he tried to save some children from a runaway horse. The policeman could claim for his injuries, even though they were caused by his decision to try to save the children.

Exclusion of liability for negligence

Earlier (see Chapter 3) the Unfair Contract Terms Act 1977 was examined. It was seen that s. 2(1) of the Act provides that no contract term or notice can exclude or restrict liability for death or personal injury resulting from negligence. It was also seen that s. 2(2) provides that liability for loss or damage other than death or personal injury can be excluded, but only to the extent that this is reasonable.

Negligent misstatement

Negligent misstatement is not a tort in its own right. It is a branch of the tort of negligence. Liability for negligent misstatement was first considered by the House of Lords in the following case.

Hedley Byrne & Co Ltd *v* Heller and Partners Ltd (1963) (House of Lords)

The defendants were merchant bankers. A certain company, E Ltd, banked with the defendants. The claimants were considering giving credit to E Ltd. The claimants asked their own bank to find out whether E Ltd was a good credit risk. The claimants' bank therefore asked the defendants whether E Ltd were a good credit risk. The request was made in confidence. The defendants replied that E Ltd were creditworthy. The letter which said this was headed: 'For your private use and without responsibility on the part of the bank or its officials.' The claimants' bank passed on to the claimants the information that E Ltd were considered creditworthy. Relying on this, the claimants extended credit to E Ltd. However, they lost a great deal of money because E Ltd went into liquidation before repaying this money. The claimants therefore sued the defendants, arguing that the defendants had been negligent in wrongly saying that E Ltd were creditworthy.

Held The defendants were not liable because their letter had made it plain that they gave their advice without responsibility. This prevented a duty of care from arising. If they had not made this plain, the defendants would have been liable for their negligent misstatement.

Hedley Byrne & Co Ltd *v* Heller and Partners Ltd is an important case because the House of Lords made it plain that liability for negligent misstatements could exist, and that this liability could arise in respect of pure economic loss. A claim for pure economic loss caused by a negligent misstatement can be made only if the following four conditions are satisfied. First, there must be a special relationship of trust and confidence between the parties. Second, the party preparing the advice or information must, expressly or impliedly, have voluntarily assumed risk. Third, the claimant must rely on the advice or information. Fourth, this reliance must have been reasonable in all of the circumstances.

In **Caparo Industries plc *v* Dickman (1990)** the House of Lords held that the relationship between individual members of a company and the company auditor was not close enough to amount to a special relationship. The company's auditors said in their auditors' report that the company had made a profit of £1.2 million, whereas in fact it had made a loss of £0.4 million. The claimant was a shareholder in the company and, in reliance on the auditors' report, made a successful takeover bid for the company. The claimant had no claim against the auditors because the auditors owed him no duty of care. However, the auditors do owe a duty of care to the company and to the company members as a whole.

Occupiers' liability

Occupiers of premises owe a duty of care to all lawful visitors, and a separate duty of care to trespassers. Almost all businesses must occupy some premises, and so almost all are potentially liable. Any person with control of the premises can be liable as an occupier. It follows that there might be more than one occupier in respect of the same premises. People who have control of movable structures, such as vehicles or ladders, can also be liable as occupiers.

Lawful visitors

Any person who comes on to premises with either the express or implied permission of the occupier will be a lawful visitor. Express permission is given in words. It can be more difficult to tell when implied permission has been given. It will, however, have been given if the court finds that there was an agreement (not made in words) that the person was allowed to be on the premises. So delivery drivers or service mechanics would be as much lawful visitors on the premises of a business as would invited visitors such as important customers. People who have a statutory right to be on premises, such as meter readers and police officers, are also lawful visitors.

In **Harvey v Plymouth City Council (2010)** the Court of Appeal held that a young man who was running across land owned by the City Council in the early hours of the morning was not a lawful visitor. The man fell five-and-a-half metres down a sheer drop from this land, after tripping on a chain link fence which had been pushed down to a height of about 14 inches. The land had been used for informal recreation for some years. However, the man was not a lawful visitor because the City Council had not impliedly assented to his activities on the land. This was the case even if his activities, or similar activities, could have been foreseen.

The Occupiers' Liability Act 1957 s. 2 requires occupiers of premises to take:

> such care as in all the circumstances of the case is reasonable to see that the visitor will be reasonably safe in using the premises for the purposes for which he is invited or permitted by the occupier to be there.

This standard of care is very similar to the standard required in the tort of negligence. In some ways the statute has just extended the tort of negligence to cover injuries to lawful visitors on premises.

The standard is not an absolute one. It varies with all the circumstances. Some people, such as children, can be expected to be less careful than others, and a higher duty is therefore owed to them. Others, such as contractors, can be expected to look out for themselves rather better than most people, especially if they have been warned of a particular danger. Consequently, they are owed a lower duty. Sections 1 and 2 of the Compensation Act 2006, considered earlier in the chapter, will apply in assessing whether a duty of care has been breached.

Notices which warn of danger might mean that the occupier is not liable, but only if they enable the lawful visitor to be reasonably safe in visiting the premises. Notices which go further than mere warnings, and which try to restrict liability for injury to lawful visitors, will be subject to the Unfair Contract Terms Act 1977. Earlier (in Chapter 3) we saw that s. 2(1) of that Act provides that liability in respect of death or personal injury caused by negligence can never be excluded. We also saw that s. 2(2) provides that liability for damage other than death or personal injury can be excluded, but only by a term or notice which is reasonable. As far as the UCTA 1977 is concerned, liability under the Occupiers' Liability Act 1957 is liability in negligence.

Damages can be claimed only in respect of injuries or losses which were of a reasonably foreseeable type. *Volenti non fit injuria* can be a complete defence and contributory negligence can reduce the amount of damages awarded.

Non-lawful visitors

Any person who enters the premises other than as a lawful visitor will do so as a non-lawful visitor. Frequently, such non-lawful visitors will be trespassing children, and the courts have recognised that even trespassers need considerable protection from inherently dangerous things such as live railway lines.

Section 1(3) of the Occupiers' Liability Act 1984 extends a statutory duty of protection to trespassers. The occupier owes the duty to take such care as is reasonable to see that the trespasser is not injured. The duty arises if three conditions are met:

(1) the occupier knows or ought to know that a danger exists;

(2) the occupier knows or ought to know that the trespasser is in the vicinity of the danger; and

(3) the risk is one against which the occupier could, in all the circumstances of the case, reasonably be expected to offer the trespasser some protection.

Sections 1 and 2 of the Compensation Act 2006, considered earlier in the chapter, will apply in assessing whether a duty of care has been breached.

Liability under the Occupiers' Liability Act 1984 can arise only for personal injuries. The Unfair Contract Terms Act 1977 does not apply to the duty of care created by the 1984 Act. Notices and signs can therefore have the effect of excluding liability, even for death or personal injury. However, notices will have this effect only if they reasonably give notice of the danger concerned or reasonably discourage people from taking the risks which injure them. It seems likely that warning signs cannot protect an occupier who knows that the condition of the land, or the activities of the trespasser, mean that the trespasser is likely to be injured. Nor can liability be excluded for conduct which intentionally or recklessly causes injury.

The Consumer Protection Act 1987 Part I

In 1985 an EU Directive ordered all Member States to pass legislation to introduce the concept of product liability. The United Kingdom passed the Consumer Protection Act 1987 to comply with this Directive.

Under Part I of the Act, a claimant who is injured by an unsafe product will be able to sue the manufacturer of the product, and possibly others, without having to prove the tort of negligence.

When we considered the tort of negligence we saw that manufacturers owe a duty of care to their customers. Earlier in this chapter, when we considered **Donoghue v Stevenson**, we saw that in that case the manufacturers of the ginger beer owed a duty of care to Mrs Donoghue.

However, negligence is a difficult tort to establish. The manufacturers of the ginger beer would not have been liable if they could have proved that they had taken all reasonable care.

Under the Consumer Protection Act, liability is strict. This means that, in the absence of one of the defences listed in the Act, consumers injured by a product will always gain damages from the producer of the product if the product was less safe than could reasonably be expected. The defences available are, as we shall see, narrow and specific.

Who may sue?

The Act gives the right to sue to any person who is injured by a product, the safety of which was 'not such as persons generally are entitled to expect'.

As we have seen, the SGA 1979, requires goods sold in the course of a business to be of satisfactory quality. If a buyer of goods is injured because goods sold by a business were not of satisfactory quality the Sale of Goods Act 1979 will provide the buyer with a remedy. However, privity of contract (see Chapter 2) restricts the remedies offered by the Sale of Goods Act to the buyer of the goods unless the Contracts (Rights of Third Parties) Act 1999 applies. When the Consumer Rights Act 2015 is in force it, rather than the SGA 1979, will imply the requirement of satisfactory quality into consumer contracts. However, privity of contract will still restrict remedies to the consumer who buys the goods. The Consumer Protection Act 1987 gives a similarly high level of protection to anyone injured by unsafe goods. The Consumer Protection Act is not concerned with the general quality of the goods. It applies only where goods are unsafe.

Who is liable?

The Consumer Protection Act 1987 places liability on the 'producer' of the product, and ss. 1 and 2 define the producer as including:

- the manufacturer of the product;
- the extractor of raw materials;
- industrial processors of agricultural produce;
- 'own branders' who add their label to products which they did not produce;
- anyone who imports the product into the EU.

If more than one of these people are liable they are jointly and severally liable. This means that the injured person can sue any or all of them. Retailers who are not own-branders will not be liable under the Act. Retailers who sold an unsafe product would be liable for breach of s. 14(2) SGA 1979.

Defective (unsafe) products

Section 3 says that products can be regarded as defective if their safety is not such as persons generally are entitled to expect. Products include not only finished products but also component parts of another product and raw materials. For example, a new car is a product, but so is the battery in the car and the rubber from which the tyres were made.

The court will consider all the circumstances when deciding whether or not the objective standard which the Act requires has been breached. The Act does, however, mention a number of factors to be considered, including the following:

- the way in which the product was marketed;
- instructions and warnings issued with the product;
- what might reasonably be expected to be done with the product;
- the time at which the product was supplied.

This last factor is designed to give some protection to manufacturers producing new products. These are not to be considered unsafe just because later products were safer. This is linked to the controversial 'development risks' defence, which is considered below.

 Abouzaid v Mothercare (UK) Ltd (2000) (Court of Appeal)

A 12-year-old boy was trying to fit a child's sleeping bag to a pushchair. The defendants had manufactured the sleeping bag, which was designed to be fitted to pushchairs by the use of elastic straps. One of the elastic straps had a metal buckle on the end. The boy let go of the straps while trying to join the straps together. The metal buckle hit the boy in the eye, causing serious injury.

Held The product was defective. The risk of serious injury to the eye meant that the product's safety was not such as persons generally were entitled to expect. The Court of Appeal noted that the way the product was designed allowed such an accident to happen, that the straps did not need to be made of elastic and that instructions could have warned of the danger.

Tesco Stores Ltd *v* Pollard (2006) (Court of Appeal)

A 13-month-old toddler was injured on account of eating dishwasher powder. The Court of Appeal accepted the judge's finding that the toddler's mother had not negligently left the bottle open, but did not seem entirely to believe this. The dishwasher powder had been in a bottle with a child-resistant closure cap, which was more difficult to open than an ordinary screw-top bottle. However, the bottle top did not comply with the British Standard torque measure.

Held The product was not defective. The public would expect the bottle top to be more difficult to open than an ordinary screw top, which it was. Members of the public were unlikely even to know about the existence of the British Standard, never mind what it required. So the product's safety was such as persons generally are entitled to expect.

Comment This decision has been criticised. If the public knew of the existence of the British Standard, they would probably have expected the product to comply with it.

Damage suffered

Section 5 of the Act allows a claimant to claim damages for death or any personal injury caused by the unsafety of the product.

Damage to non-business property is claimable, but only if it causes an individual to suffer a loss of more than £275. The loss may be made up of damage to several items.

Damage to the product itself is not recoverable. Nor is damage to other products supplied with the product. Nor can a claim be made in respect of loss of or damage to business property.

Example

Mr and Mrs Allen are bought a toaster as a wedding present. The toaster catches fire and burns Mr Allen's hand. The kitchen work surface is damaged and the toaster itself is destroyed. Under the Act, damages could be claimed from the manufacturer for the injury to Mr Allen and for all of the damage to the work surface as long as that amounted to more than £275. Damage to the toaster itself could not be claimed under this Act. The buyer of the toaster could claim back from the retailer the price of the toaster under the Sale of Goods Act 1979 (because s. 14(2) of that Act would have been breached) or under the Consumer Rights Act 2015 when it is in force.

Compensation for injury, death and damage to goods must be claimed within three years of the loss becoming apparent. In addition, there is an absolute time limit of ten years after the date when the product was supplied. This means that a person injured by a product more than ten years after buying it will have no remedy.

Defences

Under the Act, liability is strict and this means that the claimant does not need to prove fault. Nor can liability be excluded by any contract term or notice. There are, however, certain defences available, as listed below:

As regards these defences the burden of proof is on the defendant.

- That the defect was caused by complying with EU or UK legislation.

- That the product was not supplied or manufactured in the course of a business. For example, a person who made jam as a hobby would not be liable under this Act if the jam poisoned a person who consumed it. They might of course be liable under the tort of negligence.

- That the defect in the product did not exist when the product was put onto the market.

- A supplier of a component will have a defence if the unsafety arose because the manufacturer of the finished product misused the component.

- The development risks defence gives a defence to a producer if he can show that when he produced it the state of scientific and technical knowledge was 'not such that a producer of products of the same description as the product in question might be expected to have discovered it'.

This last defence is a controversial one. It would have meant that the victims of the drug Thalidomide would not have had a remedy because when the drug was created scientists were not aware of its danger. For the same reason, the drug manufacturers would not have been liable in the tort of negligence. (The drug Thalidomide was widely prescribed to pregnant women in the 1960s and caused very severe disability to their children. The drug had been tested in the usual way and had seemed quite safe.) The Government in power when the Act was passed included the development risks defence because it thought that not to do so would make the manufacture of drugs and certain other products so hazardous as to be economically impractical. Ultimately, the balance to be struck between the interests of drug manufacturers and drug users is a matter of politics.

Contributory negligence on the part of the claimant can reduce the damages.

Figure 8.3 gives an overview of the CPA Part I. If a person is injured by goods which he bought himself, he will not need to use the CPA in order to gain a remedy. The buyer will sue the shop under the Sale of Goods Act 1979 s. 14(2). (See Chapter 3.) A person who did not himself buy the goods which injured him will also be able to sue the shop under SGA 1979 s. 14(2) if the Contracts (Rights of Third Parties) Act 1999 allows him to sue on the contract. The circumstances in which the CRTPA 1999 will allow a person who did not make the contract to sue on the contract were considered in an earlier chapter (see Chapter 2). (When the Consumer Rights Act 2015 is in force, a consumer would sue under that Act, rather than under the SGA 1979 s. 14(2).)

The following examples demonstrate the present-day position as regards product liability.

Example

John buys a toaster from a shop. The toaster explodes, injuring John and damaging his kitchen. John made the contract with the shop. The shop is in breach of s. 14(2) of the Sale of Goods Act 1979, or under the Consumer Rights Act 2015 when it is in force, and will be strictly liable for the damage and the injury. John can sue the shop for breach of contract and will recover damages for his injuries and the damage to his kitchen. John can also recover the price of the toaster from the shop.

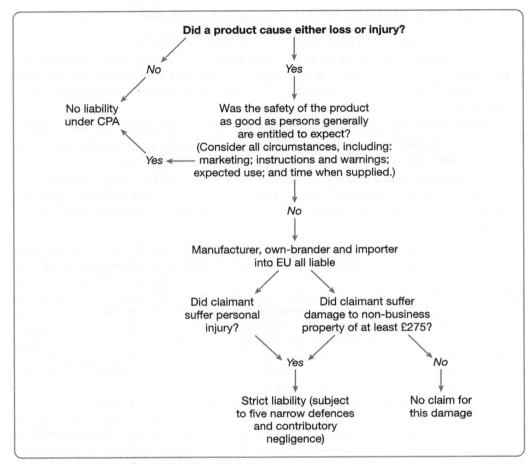

Did a product cause either loss or injury?

No → No liability under CPA

Yes → Was the safety of the product as good as persons generally are entitled to expect? (Consider all circumstances, including: marketing; instructions and warnings; expected use; and time when supplied.)

Yes → No liability under CPA

No → Manufacturer, own-brander and importer into EU all liable

Did claimant suffer personal injury? | Did claimant suffer damage to non-business property of at least £275?

Yes → Strict liability (subject to five narrow defences and contributory negligence)

No → No claim for this damage

Figure 8.3 An overview of the CPA 1987 Part I

Example

John buys a toaster as a Christmas present for Mary. John tells the shop that the toaster is being bought for Mary and asks the shop to deliver it to her house. The toaster explodes, injuring Mary and damaging her kitchen. The Contracts (Rights of Third Parties) Act 1999 allows Mary to sue the shop just as if she made the contract. She will therefore recover damages for her injuries and the damage to her kitchen. John or Mary, but not both of them, can recover the price of the toaster from the shop.

Example

John buys a toaster as a Christmas present for Mary. John does not tell the shop that the toaster is being bought for Mary. The toaster explodes, injuring Mary and damaging her kitchen. Privity will prevent Mary from suing the shop because she has no contract with the shop. The Consumer Protection Act 1987 will allow Mary to sue the manufacturer of the toaster to claim damages for her injuries. Mary will also be able to use the Consumer Protection Act to claim damages for all the damage to her kitchen if this amounts to damage of more than £275. If the damage to Mary's kitchen does not exceed £275, it is possible that Mary could sue the manufacturer of the toaster for the tort of negligence to recover damages. John can recover the price of the toaster from the shop but cannot recover damages on Mary's behalf. If John does not recover the price of the toaster from the shop Mary will have no right to do so or to sue the shop for damages.

Table 8.1 gives an overview of the different types of liability imposed by the SGA 1979, the tort of negligence and the CPA 1987 Part I.

Table 8.1 Liability in contract, in negligence and under CPA 1987

	Contract	Negligence	CPA 1987
Who can sue?	The contracting party or a person within CRTPA 1999	A person suffering loss or injury	A person suffering loss or injury
Who is liable?	Other party to the contract	Person who was negligent	Manufacturer, own-brander or importer into EU
What must be proved?	Breach of any term, express or implied, statutory or common law	(i) Duty of care owed (ii) Duty breached (iii) Causing a foreseeable type of loss/injury	Injury, or property damage over £275, caused by unsafe product
Type of liability	Strict if goods supplied. Fault based if service supplied, unless result guaranteed	Fault-based	Strict
Defences	Term not breached. Exclusion clause, subject to UCTA 1977 or CRA 2015 when it is in force	*Volenti non fit injuria.* Contributory negligence. Exclusion of liability for loss other than personal injury, subject to UCTA 1977 requirement of reasonableness	Contributory negligence. Five narrow, specific statutory defences

Essential points

- Liability in contract is generally strict, liability in tort is almost always based on fault.
- In order to establish the tort of negligence, a claimant must prove that:
  (a) the defendant owed him or her a duty of care;
  (b) the defendant breached this duty; and
  (c) a foreseeable type of loss or damage resulted from the breach of duty.
- Contributory negligence by the claimant can reduce the claimant's damages.
- It is a complete defence for the defendant to prove that the claimant was injured by a risk which he or she freely and voluntarily chose to accept.
- A defendant can become liable for a negligent misstatement which caused the claimant to suffer loss, even if the loss suffered was purely economic loss.
- Occupiers of premises owe a duty of care to all lawful visitors, and a separate duty of care to trespassers.
- The Consumer Protection Act Part I imposes on manufacturers strict civil liability for injuries caused by unsafe products which they manufactured.

Practice questions

1 Alan was walking along the pavement when an HGV lorry reversed out of Bodgit Ltd's premises and ran him over. The lorry was being driven by the managing director of Bodgit Ltd, Billy. Billy did not have a licence to drive HGV vehicles. He was driving the lorry in order to free up a car parking space and did not realise that it was in reverse gear. Alan suffered two broken legs and concussion. His injuries kept him off work for two months. Advise Alan of his legal position.

2 Cathy visits a shop and buys two pre-packed sandwiches. The sandwiches were made by a local company which supplied many local shops with sandwiches. Cathy and her friend Dinah shared the sandwiches. Both Cathy and Dinah were made seriously ill, as the sandwiches were contaminated with rat poison. Advise Cathy and Dinah of their legal positions.

3 The premises of Bodgit Ltd are often in a dangerous state. Last week, two people were injured while on the premises. Edward, an accountant employed by Bodgit Ltd, broke his elbow when he slipped on an oil spillage on some stairs. The oil had been spilt on the stairs four hours earlier. No orders to clear the spillage had been given, although all employees had been warned to take care while using the stairs. Francine, who is 7 years old, was injured while playing on partially completed buildings which are standing on Bodgit Ltd's premises. A friend of hers pushed her over and she fell into an exposed barrel of preservative chemical. The chemical caused severe injuries to Francine's skin. The managing director of Bodgit Ltd knew that children had been breaking in and playing on the building site. Last week he had put up a prominent sign, which read: 'NOTICE. WARNING TO PARENTS. THIS SITE CONTAINS HAZARDOUS BUILDINGS AND DANGEROUS SUBSTANCES. KEEP OUT.' Advise Bodgit Ltd of any liability they might have to Edward or Francine.

4 With reference to decided cases, explain the requirements of the tort of negligence.

Task 8

A friend of yours is contemplating starting a small business manufacturing garden benches to be sold to local garden centres. Your friend has asked you to draw up a report, briefly explaining the following matters:

(a) The matters which need to be proved in order to establish that the tort of negligence has been committed.

(b) The extent to which liability in negligence can be reduced or extinguished.

(c) The extent to which occupiers of premises can incur liability to lawful visitors and to non-lawful visitors who are injured while on the premises.

(d) The circumstances in which the Consumer Protection Act 1987 Part I can impose liability on manufacturers.

(e) The meaning of privity of contract, and the extent to which the Contracts (Rights of Third Parties) Act 1999 has limited the effect of privity.

mylawchamber

Visit **www.mylawchamber.co.uk/macintyreessentials** to access tools to help you develop and test your knowledge of business law, including interactive multiple choice questions, practice exam questions with guidance, weblinks, glossary, glossary flashcards, legal newsfeed and legal updates.

Use **Case Navigator** to read in full some of the key cases referenced in this chapter with commentary and questions:

Caparo Industries plc *v* Dickman (1990)

Abouzaid *v* Mothercare (UK) Ltd (2000)

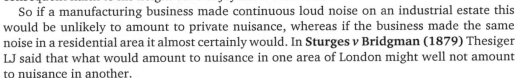

9

Nuisance, trespass, defamation and vicarious liability

Earlier (see Chapter 8) the tort of negligence and the torts closely related to it were considered. In this chapter the torts of nuisance, trespass and defamation are considered. These torts are not closely related to the tort of negligence. At the end of the chapter we examine the circumstances in which an employer can be held liable for torts committed by an employee during the course of his or her employment.

Private nuisance

Private nuisance can be defined as an unreasonable interference with a claimant's land or with a claimant's use or enjoyment of land. The interference must be substantial and unreasonable. Only an owner of land, or a person with a right to be in possession of land, can sue.

Many businesses are at risk of committing private nuisance. Whereas a direct invasion of another person's land, such as dumping rubbish on it, would amount to the tort of trespass to land, an indirect interference with another person's use or enjoyment of land can amount to nuisance. So a business might commit private nuisance by making unreasonable noise or by emitting noxious fumes.

Some businesses are inherently noisy or must emit noxious fumes. This does not mean that such businesses will necessarily commit the tort of nuisance. The key to private nuisance is that the interference with the claimant's use and enjoyment of land must be unreasonable. In **Cambridge Water Co Ltd v Eastern Counties Leather plc (1994)** (House of Lords) Lord Goff said: 'if [the defendant's use of land] is reasonable the defendant will not be liable for consequent harm to his neighbour's enjoyment of his land'.

So if a manufacturing business made continuous loud noise on an industrial estate this would be unlikely to amount to private nuisance, whereas if the business made the same noise in a residential area it almost certainly would. In **Sturges v Bridgman (1879)** Thesiger LJ said that what would amount to nuisance in one area of London might well not amount to nuisance in another.

In **Coventry v Lawrence (2014)** the Supreme Court held that a defendant being sued in nuisance can rely on his own activities as being part of the character of the locality, but only to the extent that those activities do not constitute a nuisance. If the activities could not be carried on without constituting a nuisance then they should be entirely disregarded when the court assesses the character of the neighbourhood.

Leeman *v* Montagu (1936)

The defendant bought a house in a residential area which bordered on open countryside. He kept a flock of 750 cockerels in an orchard about 100 yards from the house. These cockerels crowed from 2 a.m. to 7 a.m., making it impossible for the claimant to sleep. The claimant asked the court for an injunction to prevent the defendant from keeping the cockerels on his land.

Held The defendant had committed a nuisance and so an injunction could be granted.

Liability for nuisance is kept under control by the principle of 'reasonable user', the concept of give and take between neighbouring occupiers of land. This question of reasonableness is to be considered objectively, and not from the point of view of either the claimant or the defendant. In many cases, the location of the claimant's land will be a factor in deciding the way in which he or she can expect to use and enjoy the land. So a farmer who kept noisy cockerels in a completely rural area would be unlikely to commit private nuisance. The length of time for which harm is caused is also relevant in deciding whether an interference is unreasonable. A manufacturer who conducted a noisy cleaning process once a year would be less likely to commit nuisance than a manufacturer who made a similar noise every day. Although one-off events can amount to nuisance, most nuisances involve continuous interference.

As the interference with the claimant's use and enjoyment of land must be unreasonable, abnormally sensitive claimants are not protected.

 Robinson *v* Kilvert (1889) (Court of Appeal)

The claimant occupied the ground floor of the defendant's premises and stored brown paper there. Heat from the defendant's boiler, which was in the basement of the premises, damaged the brown paper. The heat generated would not have damaged ordinary paper, but brown paper is especially sensitive to heat. The claimant wanted an injunction to prevent the defendant from using the boiler.

Held The defendant was not committing a nuisance and so an injunction was not granted.

Lopes LJ said: '. . . a man who carries on an exceptionally delicate trade cannot complain because it is injured by his neighbour doing something lawful on his property, if it is something which would not injure anything but an exceptionally delicate trade.'

If a defendant causes the interference maliciously this is more likely to amount to a nuisance.

 Christie *v* Davey (1893)

Much to the defendant's annoyance, his next-door neighbour gave music lessons and held musical parties. The defendant retaliated by blowing whistles, shrieking, shouting, banging trays and hammering. The claimant asked the court to grant an injunction to prevent the defendant from continuing to make the malicious noises.

Held The defendant's actions amounted to a nuisance because they were done maliciously. Therefore, an injunction was granted.

Any person who has control of premises where the nuisance is caused can be liable, as can an occupier of premises who gives authority for the nuisance to be committed. Landlords are not generally liable for nuisance committed by their tenants. However, they can be liable if they either knew, or should have known, about the nuisance when they let the premises to the tenant.

In order to succeed in an action for nuisance the claimant must prove that the nuisance has caused some damage. This damage might either be to the land itself or to the use and enjoyment of the land. The damage need not be physical and might include loss of sleep or inability to sit in the garden. However, a claim of damage to property is much more likely to be successful than a claim of interference with leisure. In **Hunter v Canary Wharf Ltd (1997)** the House of Lords held that clouds of dust raised when Canary Wharf was being built could be nuisance if they reduced the value of neighbouring properties but could not be nuisance if they merely interfered with television reception. However, the court was not prepared to hold that interference with television reception could never be nuisance.

Remedies

Damages

In **Cambridge Water Co Ltd v Eastern Counties Leather plc** the House of Lords held that a defendant would not be liable in nuisance unless the damage suffered was a type of damage which the defendant could reasonably foresee. (The **Wagon Mound** test was applicable – see Chapter 8.) However, as long as the type of damage was reasonably foreseeable, even a defendant who had taken all reasonable care could be liable. So liability is strict but not absolute.

Damages will be quantified using the same principles as for the quantification of damages for negligence. (See Chapter 8.) If the land is damaged, the damages will generally be the amount by which the value of the land was reduced. If the use and enjoyment of land was interfered with, the damages will generally be the amount by which the land had a reduced value while the interference was happening. Consequential losses, such as loss of business, or the cost of moving, are recoverable.

Mitigation

The defendant must take reasonable steps to mitigate any loss and so will not be able to claim damages for losses which could have been mitigated by taking reasonable steps.

Injunction

An injunction is a court order requiring a person to behave in a certain way. In nuisance cases the injunction will order the defendant to stop committing the nuisance. A defendant who disobeys the court order will be liable to punishment for contempt of court.

The issuing of an injunction could cause a business to shut down. For example, if a business needs to make excessive noise in order to manufacture its products, and an injunction is issued forbidding the business to make the noise in the area where it currently operates, the business will be compelled either to move or to stop manufacturing.

An injunction is generally the most sought-after remedy for private nuisance. Usually all the claimant wants is that the defendant stops committing the nuisance.

Abatement

Abatement allows a claimant to remove the nuisance in an emergency or if this can be done without entering onto the defendant's land. In **Lemmon v Webb (1895)**, for example, the Court of Appeal held that a land owner had the right to trim branches of mature trees which hung over his land. In **Burton v Winters (1993)** the Court of Appeal held that abatement was a right which could arise only if legal proceedings were inappropriate or if it was obviously necessary to take urgent action.

Defences

Statutory authority

A defendant will not be liable for a nuisance which was necessarily committed in order to comply with a statute.

 Allen v Gulf Oil Refining Ltd (1981) (House of Lords)

An Act of Parliament gave Gulf Oil the right to compulsorily purchase land and build an oil refinery on it. Once the refinery was running, a nearby resident said that its noise, smell and vibrations amounted to a nuisance.

Held It was Parliament's intention that the oil refinery should be built and should operate on the site. As the noise, smells and vibrations were an inevitable consequence of the operation of a refinery, the defendant had a complete defence.

In **Coventry v Lawrence (2014)** the Supreme Court held that the mere fact that planning permission had been granted for an activity was not a defence to a defendant being sued in nuisance.

Prescription

Prescription is a property right which can give a right to continue committing what would otherwise be a nuisance. In order to establish such a right a person must show that he has enjoyed the right, uninterrupted, as of right, for 20 years. The act which would otherwise be a nuisance must have been committed without force, openly and without permission.

Consent of claimant

It is a complete defence that the claimant consented to the nuisance being committed. (The defence of consent was considered in relation to negligence. See *volenti non fit injuria* in Chapter 8.) In **Coventry v Lawrence (2014)** the Supreme Court reaffirmed that it is no defence to nuisance to show that the claimant acquired property or started to occupy property after the nuisance had started. This is consistent with nuisance being a property-based tort. However, the court left open the question whether it would be a defence to show that a pre-existing activity of the defendant had become a nuisance only because the claimant had changed the use of the property, or built on it.

Contributory negligence

This might be a defence where the nuisance was committed by negligent conduct.

Figure 9.1 gives an overview of private nuisance.

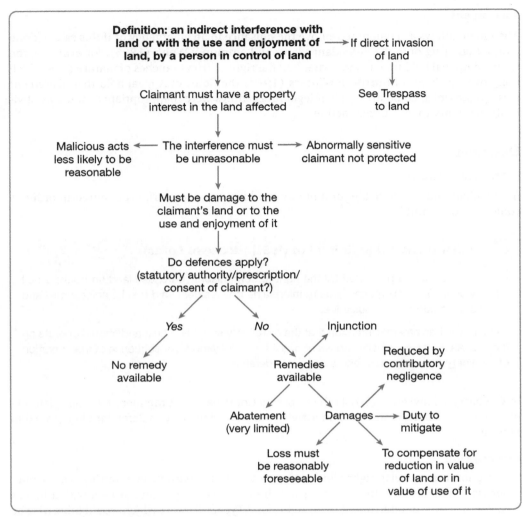

Figure 9.1 An overview of private nuisance

Public nuisance

Public nuisance is both a crime and a tort. It can be defined as any act or omission which endangers the health, property or comfort of the public, or which prevents the public from exercising rights which all citizens enjoy. Although public nuisance is primarily a criminal offence, it is possible for a private citizen to sue. However, in order to be able to bring an action the claimant must show that the nuisance has caused more damage to him or her than to the public generally. Only a person who has some control over the nuisance can be liable for public nuisance.

Many actions for public nuisance concern obstructing a highway. In such cases the particular damage which the claimant must prove might consist of lost business. However, no claim will succeed if others have also lost business, even if the claimant has lost more than they have. The claimant must show a particular kind of loss, over and above the kind of loss suffered by others. Other recent examples of public nuisance include organising a rave and picketing by trade unionists.

An obstruction of the highway which is both temporary and reasonable will not be a public nuisance. However, a badly parked car which partially blocks a highway has been held to be a public nuisance.

Earlier in this chapter we saw that only a person with some kind of interest in property can sue for private nuisance. Public nuisance has no such requirement. Furthermore, prescription is not a defence to public nuisance.

Remedies

Injunction

A person not suffering special damage may apply for an injunction to prevent the continuation of a public nuisance, although the permission of the Attorney-General may be necessary. Local authorities can also seek an injunction to gain relief from a public nuisance if this would promote and protect the interests of people living in the area.

Damages

Damages can be claimed only in respect of a type of loss which causes 'special damage', that is to say damage which is of a more severe type than that suffered by others who are affected by the nuisance. The loss must also be reasonably foreseeable under the **Wagon Mound** test. Damages for pure economic loss (see Chapter 8) can be claimed in an action for public nuisance. It is probably the case that such damages cannot be claimed in an action for private nuisance. Damages might be claimed in respect of lost business, personal injury or damage to property.

Defences

Statutory authority, contributory negligence and consent are available as defences.

The rule in Rylands *v* Fletcher

The rule in **Rylands *v* Fletcher** is the name given to a tort of strict liability. The requirements of the tort are:

- the defendant must either bring something onto his land or let it accumulate there;
- this must be a non-natural use of the land;
- the thing must be likely to do mischief if it escapes;
- the thing must escape and cause damage.

The rule applies only if the defendant's use of the land is 'non-natural'. So it would not apply if land became covered in weeds, or flooded by water which was not deliberately accumulated.

> ⚖️ **Rylands *v* Fletcher (1866) (House of Lords)**
>
> The defendants took on reputable engineers as independent contractors (see later in this chapter) to build a reservoir on their land. The defendants took all reasonable care but the engineers did not, as they failed to seal some disused mine shafts. This failure caused the claimant's mine to be flooded.
>
> *Held* The defendants were liable, even though they had not been negligent and were not vicariously liable (see later in this chapter) for the actions of the engineers.

As we have seen, the tort would not apply as regards things, such as rainfall or weeds, which are on the land without any action on the defendant's part. In **Transco plc *v* Stockport Metropolitan Borough Council (2003)** it was held that the gradual and invisible saturation of the adjacent ground by a water pipe which was not known to be burst could not be described as an accumulation made by human design and so the conditions for strict liability had not been fulfilled. By contrast, in **Rylands *v* Fletcher (1866)**, the case that created the tort, a defendant was liable when water escaped from a reservoir which he had planned, constructed and started to fill. Following **Transco**, the tort is likely to apply only to activities which can be regarded as ultra-hazardous.

In **Stannard *v* Gore (2012)** the Court of Appeal considered liability under **Rylands *v* Fletcher** for damage caused by fire. The defendant operated a tyre-fitting and supply business on an industrial trading estate. An electrical fault caused a fire which ignited some 3,000 tyres, and the fire spread to the claimant's adjoining premises. The Court of Appeal unanimously held that there was no liability under **Rylands *v* Fletcher**. The tort requires that a dangerous thing must be brought onto the defendant's land, that it must escape, and that it must cause damage. Although the defendant had brought the tyres onto his land, it was not the tyres which had escaped but the fire. The defendant had not brought the fire onto his land. Furthermore, the tyres were not an especially dangerous or mischievous thing to bring onto premises such as the defendant's. The defendant's use of the land was not 'non-natural', as **Rylands *v* Fletcher** requires, because it was a perfectly reasonable and normal type of business to carry on in premises such as his.

Only an owner of land, or a person with a right to be in possession of land, can sue.

Remedies

Damages are available to the defendant. **Cambridge Water Co Ltd *v* Eastern Counties Leather plc** established that the **Wagon Mound** test on foreseeability applies. So a claim can be made only in respect of a type of damage which was reasonably foreseeable. However, the tort is one of strict liability in that a defendant can be liable even if he or she has taken all reasonable care to prevent the thing escaping.

Defences

Statutory authority and contributory negligence are available as defences. Both of these were considered earlier in this chapter, in relation to the tort of nuisance.

Consent of the claimant

The consent of the claimant, whether express or implied, to the thing being accumulated on the defendant's land is a defence.

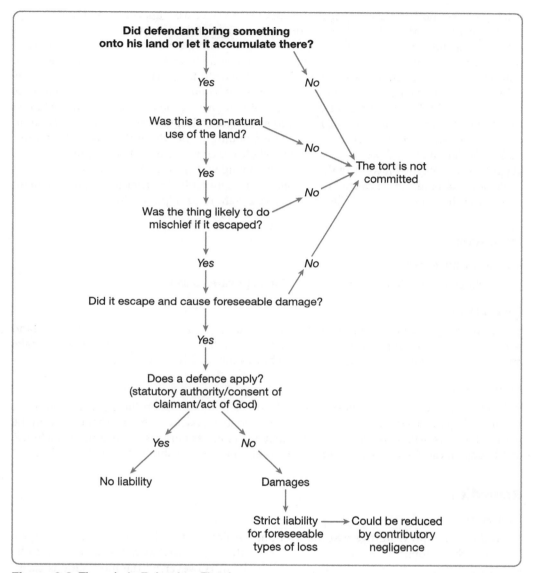

Figure 9.2 The rule in **Rylands v Fletcher**

Act of God

This defence would apply where natural forces, rather than human intervention, caused the escape in circumstances which no human foresight could provide against. The defence might apply if the escape was caused by an earthquake or a tornado.

Figure 9.2 gives an overview of the rule in **Rylands v Fletcher**.

Trespass to land

Trespass to land is committed by a direct, unauthorised interference with another person's land. Only a person in possession of land can sue. A business might commit trespass by driving across another's land, by allowing animals to walk across another's land or by dumping rubbish on another's land. It is not only the surface of the land which is protected. If it were not for the defence of statutory authority, coal mining companies would commit trespass when mining under land and aeroplanes would commit trespass when flying over land. For example, in **Star Energy UK Onshore Ltd *v* Bocardo SA (2010)** an owner of land was able to sue an oil company which had built oil wells at a depth of 800 to 2,900 feet below his land. It was held that the owner of the surface of land owned the land beneath it, including the minerals, unless rights had been granted to someone else, either by a conveyance, or at common law or by statute. There would be a stopping point where the physical features, such as temperature and pressure, made the whole concept of the land belonging to anyone absurd. However, the oil wells in the case were a long way from such a stopping point.

Trespass to land can be caused intentionally or negligently. In order to sue, the claimant must either be in possession of the land or have a right to be in possession of the land.

Defences

Statutory authority

This defence was explained above, in relation to private nuisance.

Justification

There are many circumstances in which a person has legal authority to enter another's land without committing trespass. For example, the police have the right to enter land to make an arrest and the general public have the right to walk the highway.

Permission

If the claimant expressly or impliedly gives the defendant permission (licence) to enter his or her land, then the defendant cannot commit trespass to land while adhering to the terms of the permission. It is usually taken for granted that a person has permission to approach a house and knock on the door, unless that person has already been prohibited from doing this.

Remedies

Damages

In **Stadium Capital Holdings *v* St Marylebone Properties Co (2010)** the Court of Appeal held that the amount of damages should generally be assessed as a reasonable fee to be paid by the trespasser for the occupation of the land. However, in the most serious cases, damages could be assessed on the basis of what the trespasser had gained by using the land. Damages might also cover matters such as damage to land or buildings, loss of profits or the cost of repairs. Even if no loss or damage is suffered the claimant may be awarded nominal damages.

Injunction

An injunction can be awarded to prevent a continuing trespass.

The relationship between nuisance, Rylands *v* Fletcher and trespass to land

These torts have developed over many years and there is some overlap between them. In outline, we can say that trespass to land involves a direct physical invasion of land; that private nuisance is not a direct physical invasion but an unreasonable interference with the

Table 9.1 Comparison of private nuisance, public nuisance, **Rylands v Fletcher** and trespass to land

The tort	Private nuisance	Public nuisance	Rylands v Fletcher	Trespass to land
Essence of the tort	Indirect interference with land or use and enjoyment of it	Act which endangers public or prevents public from exercising a right	Bringing dangerous thing onto land and allowing it to escape	Directly invading another's land
Examples	Making unreasonable noise/emitting fumes unreasonably	Blocking the highway	Allowing chemicals to escape from land	Driving on land/depositing waste on land
Who can sue?	Person with a property right in affected land	Person suffering loss over and above that suffered by public	Injured person with a property interest. Possibly injured person without property interest	Person in possession of the affected land
Who can be sued?	Person in control of land where nuisance committed	Person who has control over the nuisance	Occupiers of land	Anyone committing the trespass
Strict liability?	Yes	Yes	Yes	Need intention to invade land
Remedies	Damages, injunction, abatement	Damages, injunction	Damages	Damages, injunction
Defences	Statutory authority, Prescription, Consent of claimant, Contributory negligence	Contributory negligence, Consent of claimant, Statutory authority	Statutory authority, Contributory negligence, Consent of claimant, Act of God	Statutory authority, Justification, Permission granted

use and enjoyment of land; that public nuisance is an act or omission which endangers the public or prevents the public from exercising rights; and that the rule in **Rylands v Fletcher** arises when any non-natural thing brought onto the land (or allowed to accumulate there) causes mischief when it escapes.

Table 9.1 compares nuisance, public nuisance, **Rylands v Fletcher** and trespass to land.

Trespass to the person

There are three torts of trespass to the person: battery, assault and false imprisonment.

Battery

Battery is committed by any direct and intentional physical contact with the claimant's body without the claimant's consent. Often, the defendant will have intended to harm the claimant but this is not necessary. The touching of others which is part of accepted everyday conduct is not battery.

If there is a dispute as to whether or not battery was consented to, the burden of proof is on the claimant to show that it was not consented to. A claimant can sue for battery (or assault) without proving physical harm or financial loss.

Assault

Assault is committed by any act which directly and intentionally causes the claimant to reasonably fear that he or she is immediately about to suffer battery. Examples would include pointing a gun at a person or threatening to punch them. It is not assault to photograph a person against his or her will, because there is no fear of an immediate battery; mere words can amount to assault, however. They can also prevent actions from being assault, as in **Tuberville v Savage (1669)**, in which case the defendant's placing his hand on his sword was not assault because the defendant said: 'If it were not assize time, I would not take such words from you.'

False imprisonment

False imprisonment is committed by directly and intentionally depriving the claimant of his or her liberty. A business might commit false imprisonment by wrongfully detaining a person suspected of shoplifting. The deprivation of the claimant's liberty must be total but there is no need to actually put someone in prison. Preventing a person from leaving a car, by driving so fast that he could not get out, has been held to be false imprisonment.

Damages for false imprisonment can compensate for injured feelings or for loss of reputation. In **Thompson v Metropolitan Police Commissioner (1998)** the Court of Appeal gave some rough guidelines indicating that £500 might be payable for the first hour of false imprisonment, about £3,000 for the first 24 hours and that the amount should diminish progressively for each subsequent day.

Defences to trespass to the person

Consent

It is a defence to trespass to the person that the claimant consented to what the defendant did. This defence would apply, for example, in relation to sports such as boxing or football. As we have seen, the burden of proof falls on the claimant to show that there was no consent. In **Co-operative Group (CWS) Ltd v Pritchard (2011)** the Court of Appeal held that contributory negligence cannot be a defence to the intentional torts, such as assault and battery.

Self-defence

There is no specific defence of self-defence, but at common law a person can use reasonable force to prevent injury or the threat of it. Also, s. 3 of the Criminal Law Act 1967 allows a person to use such force as is reasonable in the prevention of a crime.

Statutory authority

The Police and Criminal Evidence Act 1984 gives the police the power to arrest and search people in certain circumstances. Similarly, judges and magistrates acting in good faith are protected from claims of false imprisonment.

Trespass to goods

The tort of conversion is the main form of trespass to goods. It is committed if the defendant deals with goods in a manner which is inconsistent with the right of another person to possess the goods. Conversion can be committed by a person who does not know that he or she is denying somebody else the right to possess the goods. However, a defendant cannot be liable in conversion unless he fully intended to deal with the goods. Earlier (see Chapter 3) we examined **Rowland v Divall (1923)**, a case in which a thief stole a car and sold it on. The thief and all of the subsequent buyers of the car could have been liable to the owner in conversion.

Conversion can be committed by destroying goods, by damaging them, by wrongfully taking possession of them, or by wrongfully refusing to give possession to someone entitled to possession. In **Vine v Waltham Forest LBC (2000)** the Court of Appeal held that it could be conversion to wheel-clamp a car if the owner of the car had not consented to the risk of this or willingly assumed the risk.

Where the goods are destroyed, the damages for conversion are generally the market value of the goods. Where the goods are returned to the person entitled to possession, the damages are generally the loss caused by not having had possession of the goods.

Defamation

Defamation occurs when a defendant publishes a statement which either lowers the claimant in the estimation of right-thinking people generally or causes the claimant to be shunned and avoided. The Defamation Act 2013 (DA 2013) s. 1(1) states that a statement is not defamatory unless its publication has caused or is likely to cause serious harm to the reputation of the claimant. In the case of businesses, harm is not 'serious harm' unless it has caused or is likely to cause the business serious financial loss.

If the publication is in some permanent form, such as writing, the defamation will be libel. If the publication has no permanent form, as in the case of mere spoken words, the defamation will be slander. In **Monson v Tussauds Ltd (1894)** Lopes LJ said: 'Libels are generally in writing or printing, but this is not necessary; the defamatory matter may be conveyed in some other permanent form. For instance, a statue, a caricature, an effigy, chalk marks on a wall, signs or pictures may constitute a libel'.

Statements of opinion can amount to defamation. Both trading companies and living people can be defamed. A statement which does not directly cause people to think less of the claimant can be defamatory if reasonable people would infer something against the claimant. Sometimes the claimant can establish that the statement, although not defamatory to most reasonable people, was defamatory to those with special knowledge. When the claimant pleads this type of special knowledge this is known as innuendo. The drawback to pleading innuendo is that the damages are likely to be reduced because the claimant has been defamed only as regards people who understood the innuendo.

In defamation cases in which there is a jury, the judge first decides whether or not the defendant's statement is capable of being defamatory and the jury then decide whether or not it actually is defamatory. However, s. 11 of the DA 2013 provides that trial should be without a jury unless the court orders otherwise, and so generally it is a judge who will decide whether or not a statement is defamatory. In defamation proceedings Legal Aid is not available to either defendant or claimant.

The defendant does not need to intend to defame or even know that his statement is defamatory. Although the claimant does not need to be mentioned in the statement, words can be defamatory only if they are understood to be published about the claimant. A statement cannot be defamatory unless it was published. However, in this context, publishing merely means making the statement known to one person other than the claimant. This could be done, for example, by dictating a letter to a typist. As regards the creator of the statement, liability is strict and neither a worthy motive nor a belief that the statement was true are relevant.

Libel is the more serious form of defamation and is always actionable without proof of actual damage (actionable *per se*). Slander is generally not actionable unless actual damage can be proved. However, slander is actionable *per se* in two circumstances: where it clearly and unambiguously imputes that the claimant has committed an imprisonable crime; or if it disparages (damages the reputation of) the claimant in any office, profession, calling, trade or business held by the claimant at the time of publication. Where it is necessary to prove actual damage the **Wagon Mound** test on remoteness of damage applies. Therefore, the claimant can claim only for a type of loss which was a reasonably foreseeable consequence of the defendant's act.

Defences

Consent of the claimant

A claimant who consented to the publication, expressly or impliedly, cannot sue for defamation.

Truth (section 2)

Section 2(1) DA 2013 provides that it is a defence for the defendant to show that the imputation conveyed by the statement complained of is substantially true. However, truth (or justification as it was known before the DA 2013 came into force) can be a risky defence. If the defence is unsuccessful then the claimant's damages can be increased if the plea of truth extends the period during which damage was caused by the defamation.

Honest opinion (section 3)

Section 3 DA 2013 sets out a defence of honest opinion if the following conditions are satisfied. First, the statement complained of was a statement of opinion. Second, the statement complained of indicated, whether in general or specific terms, the basis of the opinion. Third, an honest person could have held the opinion on the basis of: (a) any fact which existed at the time the statement complained of was published; or (b) anything asserted to be a fact in a privileged statement published before the statement complained of. The defence is defeated if the claimant shows that the defendant did not hold the opinion. But this does not apply in a case where the statement complained of was published by the defendant but made by another person ('the author'). In such a case the defence is defeated if the claimant shows that the defendant knew or ought to have known that the author did not hold the opinion.

Publication on matter of public interest (section 4)

Section 4 DA 2013 provides that it is a defence for the defendant to show that: (a) the statement complained of was, or formed part of, a statement on a matter of public interest; and (b) the defendant reasonably believed that publishing the statement complained of was in the public interest. The defence is available whether the statement complained of is a statement of fact or a statement of opinion. In determining whether it was reasonable for the defendant to believe that publishing the statement complained of was in the public interest, the court must make such allowance for editorial judgement as it considers appropriate.

Operators of websites (section 5)

Section 5 provides that it is a defence for an operator of a website to show that it was not the operator who posted the statement on the website. However, the defence is defeated if the claimant shows that: (a) it was not possible for the claimant to identify the person who posted the statement; (b) the claimant gave the operator a notice of complaint in relation to the statement; and (c) the operator failed to respond to the notice of complaint in accordance with any provision contained in regulations (which have yet to be passed). It is possible for a claimant to 'identify' a person only if the claimant has sufficient information to bring proceedings against the person. This defence is defeated if the claimant shows that the operator of the website has acted with malice in relation to the posting of the statement concerned. The defence is not defeated merely because the operator of the website moderates the statements posted on it by others.

Peer reviewed statement in scientific or academic journal etc. (section 6)

The publication of a statement in a scientific or academic journal (whether published in electronic form or otherwise) is privileged if the following conditions are met. First, the statement relates to a scientific or academic matter. Second, before the statement was published in the journal an independent review of the statement's scientific or academic merit was carried out by (a) the editor of the journal, and (b) one or more persons with expertise in the scientific or academic matter concerned.

Reports protected by privilege (section 7)

Section 7 protects court reporting of proceedings in any court in the UK and several other countries, as well as proceedings of the legislature of any country in the world.

Single publication rule (section 8)

Section 8 deals with the one-year limitation period, during which an action must for defamation must be brought. (This time limit is set out in s. 4A Limitation Act 1980.) It provides that if a person publishes a statement to the public ('the first publication'), and later publishes (whether or not to the public) that statement or a statement which is substantially the same, the time limit for a defamation action is to be treated as having started on the date of the first publication. However, this does not apply in relation to the subsequent publication if the manner of that publication is materially different from the manner of the first publication. In deciding whether or not a subsequent publication is materially different the court may consider (amongst other matters) the level of prominence that a statement is given, and the extent of the subsequent publication.

Action against a person not domiciled in UK, EU etc. (section 9)

Section 9 applies where an action for defamation is bought against a person who is not domiciled in the UK, the EU, Iceland, Norway or Switzerland. A court will not have jurisdiction to hear a case unless it is satisfied that, of all the places in which the statement complained of has been published, England and Wales is clearly the most appropriate place in which to bring an action in respect of the statement. This defence attempts to prevent 'libel tourism', where cases were inappropriately brought to court in the UK in order to gain greater damages.

Action against a person who was not the author, editor etc. (section 10)

Section 10 provides that a court does not have jurisdiction to hear an action for defamation brought against a person who was not the author, editor or publisher of the statement complained of unless the court is satisfied that it is not reasonably practicable for an action to be brought against the author, editor or publisher.

Offer of amends

Sections 2–4 of the Defamation Act 1996 allow a defendant who did not know, and had no reason to believe, that his statement referred to the claimant and defamed him to offer to make amends. There are four requirements:

(a) the offer must be in writing;

(b) it must correct and apologise for the original statement;

(c) it must offer to publish the correction and apology; and

(d) it must also offer to compensate the claimant and pay his legal expenses.

If the claimant accepts the offer of amends he is entitled to compensation and an apology or correction but no action can later be brought in respect of the defamatory statement. If the parties cannot agree on the amount of compensation then this must be decided by the court.

Remedies

Damages

Damages for defamation must compensate a successful claimant for damage to his reputation. They must also vindicate the claimant's name and take account of the distress, hurt and humiliation caused to him. Although these three features apply in all cases, the emphasis which should be placed on each one varies from case to case. In every case the court has to ask how much loss and damage the publication of the defamation caused to the claimant and how this is to be reflected in monetary terms.

Injunction

A defendant may seek an injunction to prevent further publication of a defamatory statement.

Power of court to order its judgment to be published (section 12)

Where a court gives judgment for the claimant in an action for defamation s. 12 DA 2013 allows the court to order the defendant to publish a summary of the judgment. The wording of any summary and the time, manner, form and place of its publication are for the parties to agree. If the parties cannot agree on the wording, the wording is to be settled by the court. If the parties cannot agree on the time, manner, form or place of publication, the court may give such directions as to those matters as it considers reasonable and practicable in the circumstances.

Order to remove statement or cease distribution etc. (section 13)

Where a court gives judgment for the claimant in an action for defamation s. 13 DA 2013 allows the court to order: (a) the operator of a website on which the defamatory statement is posted to remove the statement; or (b) any person who was not the author, editor or publisher of the defamatory statement to stop distributing, selling or exhibiting material containing the statement.

Passing-off

The tort of passing-off prevents one trader from representing that his goods or services are those of another. Passing-off has three requirements: reputation or goodwill, misrepresentation and damage. The tort is committed if a trader makes a misrepresentation to prospective customers, which is calculated to injure the business or goodwill of the claimant, and which causes actual or prospective damage to the business or goodwill of the claimant.

The misrepresentation must be to the effect that the defendant's goods or services emanate from the claimant and must be likely to cause confusion in a substantial section of the minds of the purchasing public. This could be done in various ways: by marketing a product as that of the claimant; by using the claimant's name, trade mark or trade name; by imitating the physical appearance of the claimant's goods or packaging; by registering Internet domain names which are very close to those of well-known companies and threatening to use them to block or divert trade; or by false advertising. However, mere confusion by prospective customers is not enough. The defendant must misrepresent his goods in such a way that it is a reasonably foreseeable consequence of the misrepresentation that the claimant's business or goodwill will be damaged. The misrepresentation must be more than transitory. It must continue until some material step is taken by a purchaser. A substantial number of members of the public, relative to the product and the market in question, must be misled. Dishonesty is not a requirement of the tort. However, if a trader alters his name or intended to deceive by use of his name then it is much more likely that he will be liable. Generally, the tort will not be committed if the claimant and defendant are in completely different lines of business.

The tort protects goodwill, the concept of which is explained in relationship to partnership in Chapter 12. Generally, the tort would be committed by a defendant misrepresenting to customers that his products were those of the claimant. There is no need for the claimant to prove that actual damage has occurred, prospective damage is enough. The damage would usually be a diversion of the claimant's sales but damage might also be to the claimant's reputation. Generally, words which merely describe a product, such as 'vacuum cleaner' will not be protected. But, exceptionally, descriptive words may become so associated with one trader that they become regarded as synonymous with the goods of a particular trader. A claimant might have goodwill in only one particular locality. However, the mere fact of his not trading in a locality will not necessarily mean that he has not got goodwill there.

The remedies are either an injunction or damages. Generally, the damages will be for loss of profit caused by customers being diverted. But damages can be claimed for any damage to goodwill, such as loss of business reputation. As an alternative to damages the claimant might claim an account of the profits which the defendant made from the passing-off. As a defence a defendant might raise acquiescence, delay or estoppel.

Vicarious liability

Employers are vicariously liable for torts committed by their employees during the course of their employment. For example, if a lorry driver, while employed by a company, negligently caused a crash which injured another motorist, the company would be liable to the other motorist in the tort of negligence. The lorry driver would also be personally liable but the injured motorist would generally prefer to sue the employer as the employer is more likely to be able to pay damages and should be insured. Although this example is straightforward, this is not always the case. It can be difficult to decide whether a worker is an employee or an independent contractor. If a worker is an independent contractor, the person using his services will not be vicariously liable for his torts. It can also be difficult to decide exactly when an employee was acting in the course of his or her employment.

Employees contrasted with independent contractors

Employees are said to work under a contract of service whereas independent contractors work under a contract for services. A person who works for another may do so either as an employee or as an independent contractor. For example, an hourly-paid bricklayer working full-time for a local authority will be an employee, whereas a bricklayer building a wall in my garden for £500 will be an independent contractor. Sometimes, as in this example, the distinction is obvious. However, in many cases it can be very difficult to say whether a worker is an employee or an independent contractor.

The Employment Rights Act 1996 (ERA 1996) s. 230(1) says that an employee works under a contract of employment. Section 230(2) states that a contract of employment, for the purposes of ERA 1996: 'means a contract of service or apprenticeship whether express or implied, and whether oral or in writing'. This definition has two problems for our purposes. First, the definition applies only for the purposes of ERA 1996, which does not impose vicarious liability on employers. Second, the definition does not help in determining exactly what a contract of service is.

Over the years, the courts developed several tests to distinguish employees from independent contractors. One of these tests held that if the boss had control not only of what work was done but also of how the work was done, then the worker was an employee. If there was no such control the worker was an independent contractor. Under another test Lord Denning said that employees were 'part and parcel of the organisation', whereas independent contractors were not.

The modern approach is that there is no single test which can always provide the right answer. In **Ready Mixed Concrete (South East) Ltd v MPNI (1968)** Mackenna J created the multiple test. Under this test a worker will be an employee if three conditions are satisfied:

(1) The worker agrees to provide his own work and skill in return for a wage or other payment. A worker who can send a substitute to do his work is most unlikely to be an employee.

(2) The worker agrees, expressly or impliedly, that he will be under the control of the person paying for his work.

(3) The rest of the terms of the contract are consistent with a contract of employment. This would include matters such as who paid the worker's tax, what type of national insurance contributions were paid and who provided equipment.

In **Lee v Chung (1990)** the Privy Council held the appropriate question to be 'Is the person who has engaged himself to perform these services performing them as a person in business on his own account?' If the answer is yes, as in the example of the bricklayer building the wall in my garden, then the person providing the services is an independent contractor. If the answer is no, as in the example of the bricklayer working for the local authority, then the person providing the services is an employee. The Privy Council also accepted that no absolute test or strict rules could ever decide the matter conclusively. It recognised that control of the work would always have to be considered. However, this would have to be considered along with other matters such as:

- whether the worker provided his own equipment;
- whether the worker hired those who helped him;
- the amount of financial risk the worker took;
- how much responsibility the worker took for investment and management; and
- the extent to which the worker had an opportunity to profit from performing a service well.

In **Hall v Lorimer (1994)** the Court of Appeal indicated that every case needed to be decided on its own particular facts and that 'mechanical tests' should be avoided.

It can be very difficult to say whether casual workers are employees. The 'mutuality of obligation' test looks at whether the employer has a duty to provide work, and whether the worker has a corresponding duty to accept the work. If there are no such obligations going both ways, then it is likely that the worker is not an employee.

 Carmichael v National Power (1999) (House of Lords)

Two married women worked at a power station as hourly-paid casual guides. They had begun working in 1990, doing less than four hours a week, and by 1995 they were working up to 25 hours a week. They were paid by the hour. The women claimed that because they were employees they were entitled to written particulars of the terms of their employment. (See Chapter 13.) The women were on the payroll for PAYE purposes but they worked only when they were available and chose to work. The question for the court was whether the women had a contract of employment when they were not working.

Held There was no contract of employment when the women were not working because the power station had no contractual obligation to provide work and the women had no contractual duty to accept it. The parties did not intend there to be a contract. This could be deduced mainly from the fact that the women chose whether to work or not. There had been no question of disciplining them when they had chosen not to work. Other matters which indicated that the parties did not intend there to be a contract were that the women were not part of the full-time employees' sickness, holiday or pension schemes and that the usual grievance and disciplinary procedures did not apply to them.

Comment In this case the House of Lords also made it plain that they were not considering whether the women were employees when they actually were working as guides. They were deciding whether or not the women had a contract of employment.

Sometimes workers who are in fact employees agree to be called self-employed. This does not mean that they are independent contractors. The courts will consider the reality of the situation rather than what was agreed.

 Ferguson v John Dawson Ltd (1976) (Court of Appeal)

The claimant was paid an hourly rate for working as a casual labourer on the defendants' building site. The claimant was told that no cards were required because he was an independent contractor. No tax or national insurance was deducted from the claimant's pay because the work was 'off the cards'. The claimant did what the foreman told him and tools were provided for him. The claimant was injured at work and wanted to sue the defendants. This would only have been possible if he was an employee.

Held The terms of the contract indicated that the claimant was an employee. This intention could be found by looking at all of the circumstances.

Massey *v* Crown Life Insurance Co (1978) (Court of Appeal)

From 1971 to 1973 the claimant was an employee of the defendant insurance company, working as branch manager. In 1973, for tax purposes, he and the employer agreed that he should work exactly as before but on a self-employed basis. When the defendant ended the relationship in 1975, the claimant claimed unfair dismissal (see Chapter 13). This claim could only succeed if the claimant was an employee.

Held The claimant was an independent contractor and so he could not claim unfair dismissal. The parties had genuinely intended that the claimant should become an independent contractor.

These two Court of Appeal cases do not disagree with each other. There were important differences which enabled the court in **Massey *v* Crown Life Insurance Co** to distinguish **Ferguson *v* John Dawson Ltd**. First, Massey had asked to become an independent contractor, whereas Ferguson had little choice but to be called an independent contractor. Second, Ferguson was unskilled, whereas Massey was skilled. Third, Ferguson's claim was for personal injury and in such cases the courts are more willing to find employment because they want to make sure that workers are compensated for their injuries.

The status of agency workers has recently caused difficulty.

Johnson Underwood Ltd *v* Montgomery (2001) (Court of Appeal)

The claimant was registered with the defendants' employment agency. The defendants sent the claimant to a local firm where she worked as a telephonist for two and a half years. The defendants paid the claimant's wages. The local firm asked the defendants to get rid of the claimant as they were dissatisfied with her. The defendants therefore withdrew the claimant from the local firm and sent her to work for a different firm. The claimant refused to accept this and sued both the defendants and the firm where she had worked for unfair dismissal.

Held Neither of the claims succeeded. The claimant was clearly not an employee of the firm where she had worked. Nor was she an employee of the defendants, because the defendants had no control over her work.

Comment The logical consequence of this case would seem to be that if the claimant had injured somebody whilst working for the local firm, she, and she alone, would have been liable. As she would have been highly unlikely to have thought of herself as self-employed, she would also have been highly unlikely to have carried insurance against such a risk.

Dacas *v* Brook Street Bureau (UK) Ltd (2004)

Mrs Dacas was registered with the defendants' employment agency and they sent her to Wandsworth Council, where she worked for six years. Wandsworth Council exercised day-to-day control over the claimant but the defendants also exercised considerable control in that they paid her wages, could discipline her and could terminate her contract. However, the claimant's contract with the defendants stated that she was not employed by them.

Held The claimant was employed by the defendants. They had considerable control of her, there was mutuality of obligation as required by **Carmichael v National Power** and it was obviously not correct to regard her as in business on her own account. The fact that her contract said that she was not an employee could not be the determining factor in deciding whether in fact she was.

Comment (1) This decision of the Employment Appeal Tribunal in **Dacas v Brook Street Bureau** is somewhat at odds with the Court of Appeal decision in **Johnson Underwood Ltd v Montgomery**. In that case the Court of Appeal thought that perhaps the claimant was neither an employee nor an independent contractor but had a special type of contract somewhere between the two.

(2) In **Cable and Wireless plc v Muscat (2006)** the Court of Appeal approved the decision in **Dacas**. In the typical triangular arrangement, such as the one in **Dacas**, there was not necessarily an implied contract between the end-user and the worker but there could be if this is what all of the circumstances indicated. The **Carmichael v National Power** test could be satisfied where the end-user was indirectly paying the worker's wages.

(3) Both **Dacas** and **Muscat** were reviewed by the Court of Appeal in **James v London Borough of Greenwich (2008)**. The court stressed that **Dacas** was not an authority that long-term agency workers were always employees of the end-user. This was merely a possibility, which depended upon whether, on the facts of the case, a contract could be implied. **Muscat** correctly stated that in order to imply a contract of employment this must be *necessary* to give effect to the business reality of the relationship between the worker and the end-user. The point was also made that, in some very extreme cases, a sham arrangement could be exposed as a contract of employment.

The Agency Workers Regulations 2010 are considered in Chapter 13. The regulations give rights to equal treatment over matters such as pay, but do not deal with the question as to whether or not an agency worker is an employee or an independent contractor.

Sometimes one employer lends an employee to another employer. In **Mersey Docks & Harbour Board v Coggins and Griffiths (Liverpool) Ltd (1947)** the House of Lords held that when this happens it is strongly presumed that the employer who lent the employee out retains liability. However, if it can be proved that the borrowing employer had sufficient control of the employee, then it is possible to displace this presumption.

Finally, it should be noted that, although the higher courts decide the basis on which employees should be distinguished from independent contractors, the question is in every case one of fact not law. Therefore, the decision will be made by the trial court and an appeal court will reverse the decision only if the trial court took a view of the facts which could not reasonably be entertained. Figure 9.3 gives an overview of the main tests used to distinguish employees from independent contractors.

When is an employee acting in the course of his or her employment?

Earlier in this chapter, it was seen that employers are liable for the torts of their employees only if these torts were committed during the course of the employee's employment. So if a teacher negligently injured a student while teaching during school hours the teacher's employer would be liable to the student in the tort of negligence. If the same teacher,

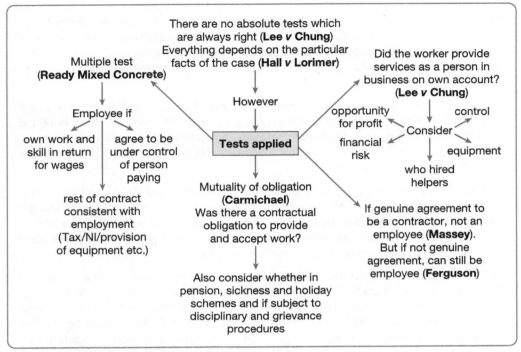

Figure 9.3 Employee or independent contractor?

when on holiday, accidentally ran over a pedestrian the employer would not be liable to the pedestrian. This example is straightforward. However, it is not always so easy to say whether or not an employee was acting in the course of his or her employment when the tort was committed. The courts have therefore devised various tests.

● An employee will be acting in the course of employment when doing what he or she was expressly or impliedly authorised to do.

⚖ Poland *v* John Parr & Sons (1927) (Court of Appeal)

An employee wrongly believed that a boy was tampering with a bag of sugar on one of the employer's wagons. To protect the sugar, the employee slapped the boy, who fell under the wagon. The boy suffered injuries which resulted in the amputation of his leg.

Held The employer was vicariously liable. The employee had implied authorisation to protect the employer's property.

● If an employee is authorised to do an act properly, then the employer will be liable if the employee performs the act negligently.

If all employees performed their work properly, then vicarious liability would be unlikely ever to arise. So if employers could escape liability on the grounds that the employee had been acting negligently the concept of vicarious liability would all but disappear.

Century Insurance Co Ltd *v* Northern Ireland Road Transport Board (1942) (House of Lords)

A petrol tanker driver, while emptying his tanker, lit a cigarette and threw away the match. This caused a huge explosion.

Held The employer was liable. The driver was employed to empty his tanker and that was what he was doing, albeit negligently, when he caused the explosion.

- If an employee commits a tort while doing an act which is designed to help the employer, then the employer will be liable.

 Kay *v* ITW (1967) (Court of Appeal)

The assistant manager of a warehouse was employed to drive small vans and cars. In order to make a space in the warehouse, he moved a large diesel truck belonging to another firm. He did not notice that the truck was in reverse, and when he started it up he ran over the claimant.

Held The employer was liable. The employee moved the truck so that he could get on with his work. Moving the truck was within the scope of his contract of employment.

- If an employee does something entirely for his own benefit, he is said to be 'on a frolic of his own', and the employer will not be liable.

 Hilton *v* Thomas Burton (Rhodes) Ltd (1961)

In the middle of the afternoon employees of a demolition contractor drove from their place of work to visit a café. The men were working 30 miles away from the employer's main business premises and the café was seven miles from the site at which they were working. On the way back, the driver crashed the firm's van and the foreman was killed. The employer did not mind the men using the firm's van to fetch refreshments.

Held The employer was not liable. The men were acting entirely for their own benefit and were therefore 'on a frolic of their own'.

Liability for prohibited acts

An employer who absolutely prohibits an employee from performing certain acts will generally not be liable if the employee ignores the prohibition. However, an employer who only prohibits the manner in which an authorised act should be performed will remain liable. The following two cases illustrate this distinction.

 Iqbal *v* London Transport Executive (1973)

A bus conductor had been expressly prohibited from driving buses. The bus on which he worked was parked in such a way that it was causing an obstruction. The conductor was ordered to fetch an engineer to move the bus. He attempted to move the bus himself and caused an accident.

> *Held* The employer was not liable. The conductor was acting outside the course of his employment because the thing he had been expressly forbidden to do (drive buses) was never part of his job.

 Limpus *v* London General Omnibus Co Ltd (1862)

The defendants' bus driver obstructed the claimant's bus in order to prevent it passing. This caused injury to one of the claimant's horses and damage to the claimant's bus. The defendants had specifically ordered their drivers not to race with or obstruct other firms' buses.

Held The defendants were liable. The driver had been in the course of his employment when he caused the accident. He had express authorisation to drive buses. The prohibition was only as to the manner of doing this.

Until recently, it was thought that employers would not be vicariously liable for serious criminal acts committed by their employees. However, in **Lister *v* Hesley Hall (2001)** the House of Lords held a school liable for a warden who sexually abused children with emotional and behavioural difficulties while they were in his care. The abuse had been so closely connected with what the warden was employed to do that it was fair, just and reasonable to hold the employers vicariously liable.

Defences

Consent of the victim and contributory negligence (both considered earlier in this chapter) are both available as defences to an employer sued on the grounds of vicarious liability.

The Civil Liability (Contribution) Act 1978 allows an employer who has been found liable to get a contribution from the employee who caused the accident. However, employers rarely use the Act because generally they will carry insurance.

Liability for independent contractors

In general, a person who uses the services of an independent contractor will not be liable for any torts committed by the contractor. However, liability can arise if the 'employer' authorises the contractor to commit the tort or if the tort is one which can be committed without negligence. We saw an example of such liability earlier in this chapter in the case of **Rylands *v* Fletcher (1866)**. As regards torts where negligence does need to be proved, the 'employer' of an independent contractor will not be liable unless he is himself negligent, for example by appointing an obviously incompetent contractor, or unless the duty delegated was a kind of duty where responsibility cannot be delegated. Statute creates several non-delegable duties which are generally rather technical.

In **Biffa Waste Services Ltd *v* Machinenfabrik Ernst Hese GmbH (2008)** the Court of Appeal held that a person who employs an independent contractor will be liable for the negligence of that independent contractor where the independent contractor is engaged to carry out 'extra-hazardous or dangerous operations'. These operations, by their very nature, involve special danger to others, for example removing support from adjoining houses, doing dangerous work on the highway, or creating fire or explosion. Because these operations are inherently dangerous, the 'employer' is under a non-delegable duty to see that all reasonable precautions are observed. If he does not he will be responsible for the consequences, even if he has stipulated that all reasonable precautions should be taken by the independent contractor.

Breach of statutory duty

In some cases a statute may impose duties without mentioning civil sanctions. In such a situation a person who has suffered harm as a result of a breach of the statutory duty might try to sue in tort. To succeed, he must show that Parliament intended liability in tort to ensue, despite its not having mentioned such liability in the statute.

It is essential that the legislation in question imposes an obligation upon the defendant. The claimant must also show that he was within a class which was intended to benefit from the statute, and that the statute indicates that Parliament intended to give a right to sue if the statute was breached.

Time limits for tort remedies

A claim under the Consumer Protection Act 1987 Part I must be brought within three years of the loss becoming apparent. There is also an absolute time limit of ten years from the date when the product was supplied.

As regards the common law torts considered in this and the earlier chapter (see Chapter 8), the following rules apply. An action which is not for personal injuries must be brought within six years of the date when the right to sue arose (s. 2 of the Limitation Act 1980). However, in cases where the damage does not become apparent for some time after it was caused, there may be an alternative period of three years from the date when the claimant knew about the damage, with a long-stop period of 15 years from the commission of the tort (s. 14 of the Limitation Act 1980). In cases of defamation the time limit is one year unless the court grants an extension.

A claim for personal injuries must be brought within three years of either the date of the commission of the tort or the date when the claimant knew of the injury and that it was caused by a defendant who could be identified (s. 11 of the Limitation Act 1980). However, in cases of battery where the injury was deliberately inflicted the period is six years.

Time does not run against people under the age of 18 until they reach the age of 18. Time does not run against people with mental disorders (within the meaning of the Mental Health Act 1983) who are incapable of managing their affairs.

In the case of claims based on fraud, or where the defendant deliberately conceals the claimant's right to sue, time does not run against the claimant until the fraud is discovered or should have been discovered.

Essential points

- Private nuisance is an unreasonable interference with a claimant's land or with a claimant's use or enjoyment of land.
- Only an owner of land, or a person with a right to be in possession of land, can sue in private nuisance.
- The rule in Rylands *v* Fletcher imposes strict liability if a person brings a non-natural thing onto his or her land and that thing escapes and causes damage.
- Trespass to land is a direct, unauthorised interference with another person's land.
- Trespass to the person can consist of battery, assault or false imprisonment.
- Trespass to goods is committed by dealing with goods in a manner which is inconsistent with the right of someone else to possess the goods.
- Defamation is committed by publishing a statement which lowers the claimant in the estimation of right-thinking people generally or causes the claimant to be shunned and avoided.
- Employers are vicariously liable for torts committed by their employees during the course of their employment.

Practice questions

1 A manufacturer of chemicals has committed the following torts.

Tort 1 – The manufacturer left an uncovered pool of lethal chemical near a broken down fence. Young children broke through the fence and were killed by exposure to the chemical.

Tort 2 – The manufacturer deposited large quantities of stones and soil on the land of a neighbouring manufacturer.

Tort 3 – The manufacturer's premises emitted noxious fumes which caused injury to a local farmer's sheep.

Tort 4 – One of the manufacturer's lorry drivers spilt oil on a main road, whilst driving badly, causing a car following behind to crash.

Tort 5 – Several barrels of highly toxic chemicals rolled downhill out of the manufacturer's premises and onto a farmer's field, causing damage to crops.

Tort 6 – The manufacturer blocked the highway leading to a remote farm so that the farmer was unable to deliver his milk to his main customer.

Decide which tort has been committed in each case and outline the essential requirements of the torts in question. (You may need to look at the torts covered in the previous chapter.)

2 Parveen, a chemistry teacher, is employed by her local authority. Would the local authority be liable for the following?

(a) During a laboratory experiment, Parveen overheats some chemicals and causes a small explosion which injures several students.

(b) Parveen injures a pedestrian when reversing out of the school car park to visit a student on work experience.

(c) Parveen injures a pedestrian when reversing out of a city-centre car park on Saturday afternoon.

(d) Noticing that there is no electricity in the laboratory, Parveen switches on the supply at the main fuse box. This causes injury to an electrician, who had cut off the supply so that he could check the wiring. All of the teachers had been warned that the electrician would need to disconnect the electricity but Parveen had forgotten.

3 John, a building labourer, is employed by a building company. Would the company be liable for the following? In each case, use a decided court case to back up your opinion.

(a) John moves a JCB, which he is not authorised to drive, so that he can continue digging a trench. He does not notice that the JCB is in reverse and injures a colleague.

(b) John habitually drives a van on site, even though the foreman knows that he has no driving licence. While driving the van, John knocks over a colleague.

(c) John is authorised to drive a tractor on site to pull trailers. When driving tractors in this way, John and his colleagues sometimes play a game whereby they deliberately drive as close to each other as they can. While doing this John injures a workmate.

(d) On his birthday John drives the JCB down the main road to the pub. On the way he crashes into a car, severely injuring its occupants.

4 The Smalltown Sports Centre was taken over by new owners two years ago. The new owners have considerably expanded the Centre's activities and the Centre now has three times the number of members it used to have. The Centre's car park is not sufficiently large to cater for all the cars of the new members and so they park around the local streets (where parking is permitted). For the past 12 months the Centre has run a monthly football competition which has proved remarkably popular. Generally, about 16 teams take part in these competitions, which run from midday until 11 p.m. on a Saturday. Local residents have complained about the noise of these competitions, as several of the teams bring large numbers of rowdy supporters. The buses of these teams have often parked in such a way that they cut off vehicular access to a small group of shops. One of these shops, a small builders' merchant, claims that their trade is well down on days when football competitions are held as customers cannot drive into their car park and the builders' merchants' delivery vans have been prevented from making deliveries. Advise the owners of the Sports Centre as to any liability they might have in respect of these facts.

5 Dirty Ltd manufactures pesticides. Six months ago Clean Ltd, a manufacturer of wholefood products, moved to premises adjacent to those of Dirty Ltd. Clean Ltd have encountered the following two problems. First, a barrel containing a toxic chemical rolled downhill from the premises of Dirty Ltd onto the premises of Clean Ltd. The chemical has contaminated a consignment of wholemeal flour. Dirty Ltd claim that they were not negligent in allowing the chemical to escape from their premises, as the accident was caused by a squirrel chewing through a cable which secured the barrel in place. Second, Clean Ltd claim that fumes from Dirty Ltd's furnace are being blown

towards the warehouse in which they store their raw materials and that if their customers discovered this they might not buy their products. Dirty Ltd reply that they have been emitting the same fumes for 30 years and that any contamination would be so slight as to be incapable of being detected, even by chemical analysis. Advise Clean Ltd of any rights which they might have in respect of these facts.

6 Jim works as a security guard for X Ltd. One night, whilst guarding X Ltd's premises, Jim comes across an intruder. The intruder says that he has accidentally walked on to the premises and offers to leave. Jim is convinced that the intruder is the person who stole X Ltd's safe three months ago. Jim threatens to attack the intruder with a crowbar if he tries to leave. This frightens the intruder, who runs away. Jim rugby tackles the intruder and punches him several times. Jim then locks him in a storeroom while the police are summoned. When the police arrive, an hour later, it is established that the intruder had been acting innocently throughout. The intruder has suffered a broken nose and his clothes are ripped. What torts might Jim have committed? (You should explain the essential requirements of these torts.) Will Jim's employer be vicariously liable for any torts committed?

7 At the Christmas Dinner of Office Ltd, Jan is asked to give a speech celebrating the career of the managing director, Keith, who is retiring. Halfway through the speech, Jan breaks into speaking Dutch, a language which the managing director speaks fluently, and says that any success which the managing director has enjoyed has been achieved by personal meanness and by spying on the activities of competing firms. Later that day Keith posts an article on the Internet which says that Jan is incapable of telling the truth and that this condition has been brought about because he is suffering from AIDS. Jan's friend, Lenny, tells Jan about this article. Jan contacts the Internet service provider on whose news server this article appeared and the provider immediately removes the article. Advise the parties of any torts which might have been committed in respect of the above facts.

8 With reference to decided cases, explain the concept of vicarious liability.

Task 9

Try to think of ways in which local businesses might commit the following torts:

(a) private nuisance

(b) public nuisance

(c) strict liability under **Rylands v Fletcher**

(d) trespass to land

(e) trespass to the person

(f) trespass to goods

(g) defamation.

For example, you might decide that a local supermarket could commit trespass to the person by wrongly arresting a suspected shoplifter. Try to think of realistic examples of all the other torts. What steps might the businesses take to ensure that they do not incur liability?

mylaw*chamber*

Visit **www.mylawchamber.co.uk/macintyreessentials** to access tools to help you develop and test your knowledge of business law, including interactive multiple choice questions, practice exam questions with guidance, weblinks, glossary, glossary flashcards, legal newsfeed and legal updates.

Use **Case Navigator** to read in full some of the key cases referenced in this chapter with commentary and questions:

Cambridge Water Co Ltd *v* Eastern Counties Leather plc (1994)

Hunter *v* Canary Wharf Ltd (1997)

10

Companies (1): Characteristics and formation

This is the first of two chapters which consider the law relating to companies. This chapter considers the characteristics of companies and the way in which companies are formed. The following chapter considers the rights of shareholders, how companies are managed and how they are wound up. The shareholders in a company are known as the members of the company.

There are around 3 million active registered companies in the UK. The law regards each of these as a legal person, with its own legal rights and obligations. All companies are now governed by the Companies Act 2006 which has replaced earlier Companies Acts. However, many sections of the 2006 Act are identical to sections of earlier Companies Acts. Therefore, in many areas of company law, cases decided under the earlier Acts still apply to the 2006 Act.

The Companies Act 2006

The Companies Act 2006 was introduced to improve the UK's competitiveness in the twenty-first century. It aims to do this by providing a sound, flexible framework for UK company law.

The 2006 Act has four main objectives:

(1) to enhance shareholder engagement and to foster a long-term approach to investment

(2) to adopt a 'Think Small First' approach and ensure that companies are better regulated

(3) to make it easier to create and run a company

(4) to provide flexibility for the future.

Enhancing shareholder engagement and fostering a long-term approach to investment

As we shall see, the directors of a company are elected by the shareholders (the members) to run the company. One of the main objectives of the 2006 Act is to create a good understanding between directors and shareholders. The Act aims to ensure that their roles are clearly defined and that they should find it easy to communicate with each other.

The Act encourages companies to communicate with shareholders electronically. It is hoped that this will not only save money but also encourage more shareholders to be involved in a dialogue with the company. The Act also intends to make directors more accountable to their companies. To achieve this aim, it has introduced a new 'derivative claim' which allows members to sue, on the company's behalf, if the directors breach their duties.

The 'Think Small First' approach and better regulation

Ninety per cent of companies have five or fewer shareholders. However, the earlier Companies Acts were written mainly with large companies in mind. The 2006 Act takes a new approach with its 'Think Small First' approach. All companies must have articles of association which set out the internal rules of the company. Three sets of model articles have been designed for use by the three most common types of companies.

The members of a company have always been able to make decisions by passing resolutions. The 2006 Act envisages that most resolutions of private companies will be passed as written resolutions. A written resolution allows shareholders to vote in favour of a resolution merely by signing it, rather than by having to attend a company meeting and vote at the meeting.

The Act has removed the rule that private companies must have a company secretary. So it is now possible for one person to be the sole shareholder and the sole director, and to run a company without help from any other person.

The 2006 Act envisages three tiers of companies: private companies; public companies which are not quoted on a stock exchange; and public companies which are quoted. Private companies are presumed to be small. In many areas they will have minimal regulation imposed on them if they do not positively introduce more extensive rules. If a private company is large, as many are, it can opt for its own more extensive regulation.

Ease of formation and flexibility

As we shall see later in this chapter, the Act has made it easy and quick to register a new company. In the following chapter we shall see that it has also become easier to run a small company.

The 2006 Act has been written in such a way that it will be relatively easy to amend in the light of changing circumstances, thus allowing for flexibility in the future.

The characteristics of companies

A company is created by registration under the 2006 Act. The process of registration is considered later in this chapter. Here it is enough to say that the people who want to create the company, the promoters of the company, must send certain documents to the Registrar of Companies. The Registrar is the head of a Government agency called Companies House. If the documents are in order, the Registrar will issue a certificate of incorporation and the company will then exist as a corporate body.

Incorporation has several important consequences. To some extent these are interconnected, but they are easier to understand if considered separately.

The company is a separate legal entity

The most important consequence of incorporation is that a company is regarded as being a legal person in its own right. This means that a company has a legal identity of its own which is quite separate from the legal identity of its owners. If a wrong is done to a company, it is the company, and not its owners, which has the right to sue. Conversely, if a company injures a person, that person can sue the company but cannot sue the owners. This well-established principle was laid down in the following case.

⚖️ Salomon *v* Salomon & Co Ltd (1897) (House of Lords)

For several years Mr Salomon had carried on a business as a boot repairer and manufacturer. He formed a limited company and sold his business to the company for £39,000. The company paid the purchase price in three ways, as follows: first, by issuing Salomon with 20,000 £1 shares; second, by regarding him as having loaned the company £10,000; and third by paying him £9,000 in cash as money came into the company. Salomon took all of the company's assets as security for the loan which had been made by him. Unsecured creditors lent the company a further £8,000. Shortly after its incorporation, the company got into financial difficulty and was wound up. The assets of the company amounted to about £6,000. Creditors who have been given security for their loan are entitled to be repaid before unsecured creditors. Salomon therefore took all of the £6,000. The unsecured creditors claimed that Salomon should repay their loans personally because he was the same person as the company.

Held The company had been formed properly and without any fraud. Although Salomon owned all but seven of the issued shares, he was one person and the company was another. Salomon therefore had no more obligation to pay the company's debts than he had to pay his next-door neighbour's debts.

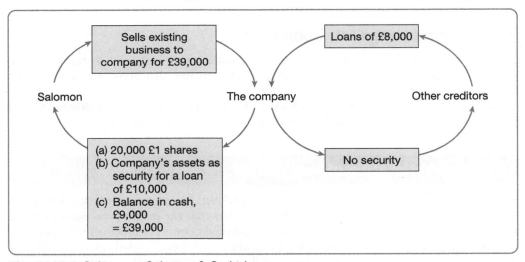

Figure 10.1 Salomon *v* Salomon & Co Ltd

Salomon's case is regarded as one of the most important in English law, mainly because of the protection which it offers to the owners of limited companies. However, the decision that a company has a legal identity of its own has many other consequences, as the following two cases show.

⚖️ Macaura *v* Northern Assurance Ltd (1925) (House of Lords)

Macaura owned almost all of the shares in a timber company. The company owed money to Macaura but not to anyone else. Macaura insured the company's timber in his own name. Two weeks later, the timber was destroyed by fire and Macaura claimed on his insurance.

Held Macaura could not claim on the insurance policy because he did not own the timber. The company owned the timber, and it is a rule of insurance law that only the owner of goods can insure them.

 Tunstall *v* Steigmann (1962) (Court of Appeal)

Mrs Steigmann ran a pork butcher's shop and leased the shop next door to Mrs Tunstall. Mrs Steigmann wanted to end the lease. As the law stood at that time, Mrs Steigmann could order Mrs Tunstall to leave the shop only if she intended to occupy the building herself, to carry on a business there. Mrs Steigmann did intend to occupy the shop herself, to carry on her butchery business. But before the case came to court she turned her business into a company. Mrs Steigmann claimed that as she owned all but two of the shares in the company she was still the person who wanted to take over the premises.

Held It was not Mrs Steigmann who wanted to take over the business, her company wanted to take it over. Willmer LJ said: 'There is no escape from the fact that a company is a legal entity entirely separate from its corporators – see **Salomon *v* Salomon & Co**. Here the landlord and her company are entirely separate entities. This is no matter of form; it is a matter of substance and reality. Each can sue and be sued in his own right; indeed, there is nothing to prevent the one suing the other. Even the holder of 100% of the shares in a company does not by such holding become so identified with the company that he or she can be said to carry on the business of the company.'

However, the principle of a company's separate legal identity will not allow a person to benefit from his own wrongdoing. In **Brumder *v* Motornet Service and Repairs Ltd (2013)** the sole director and sole shareholder of a company was injured at work and sued the company for breach of the Provision and Use of Work Regulations 1998, which imposed absolute liability on the company to ensure that equipment at work was safe. It was only through the claimant that the company could have ensured this. The Court of Appeal unanimously held that the claimant could not succeed. He could not argue that the company had failed to do all that it could to ensure compliance with the Regulations when it was only through his own actions that it could have done so.

Although a company is regarded as a legal person, it does not have human characteristics. For example, in **Richmond London Borough Council *v* Pinn and Wheeler Ltd (1989)** the Divisional Court held that a company cannot drive a lorry. Pill J said: 'The act of driving a lorry is a physical act which can be performed only by natural persons.'

Limited liability

In **Salomon's case** we saw that Salomon was not personally liable for the debts of the company. When people buy shares in a limited company, the only commitment they make is that they agree to pay the price of their shares. Often, they do not pay the full price immediately. When the public utilities were privatised, for example, investors generally paid half of the share price when subscribing for the shares and remained liable for the other half. If one of these privatised companies had gone into liquidation before shareholders had paid this second instalment, the shareholders would have been liable to pay the amount outstanding.

However, beyond this they would not have been liable to contribute any more money. A shareholder who has already paid the full price of the shares held has no liability to pay any more.

It must, of course, be emphasised that it is the shareholders who have limited liability, and not the company. If a company has debts it must pay these debts, even if this means selling all of its assets and going into liquidation.

Creditors of limited companies can protect themselves in two ways. First, they can make sure that the company gives them adequate security for the loan (see company charges in Chapter 11). Second, they can insist that the owners of the company personally guarantee that the loan will be repaid.

Perpetual succession

A company can be liquidated at any time if the members of the company pass a special resolution that it should be liquidated. (A special resolution is passed if at least three-quarters of company members who vote on the resolution are in favour of passing it.) If a company is liquidated, then the company will cease to exist. However, companies can continue in existence indefinitely, and therefore they are said to have perpetual succession.

Shareholders, of course, must die. But even if all the shareholders in a company die, their shares will be inherited by others and the company will continue in existence. For example, the Hudson's Bay Company has been in existence since 2 May 1670. Generations of its shareholders have died, but the company still exists.

As we shall see later (in Chapter 12), the death of a partner ends a partnership. The existing partners might agree to carry the partnership on but, technically at least, the firm will be dissolved when a partner dies.

Ownership of property

A company can own property, and this property will continue to be owned by the company regardless of who owns the shares in the company. This can be important when a company is trying to borrow money, because the company can give its own property, both present and future assets, as security for a loan.

Contractual capacity

A company has the power to make contracts and can sue and be sued on these contracts. This power must be delegated to human agents, and it is the company directors and other agents who actually go through the process of forming the contracts. But the important point is that it is the company itself which assumes the rights and liabilities which contracts create.

A company can also sue and be sued in tort. (A tort is a civil wrong other than a breach of contract, for example negligence, trespass or defamation. See Chapter 8.)

Criminal liability

To commit a crime a defendant must generally commit a guilty act while having a guilty mind. At first sight it would seem that companies cannot commit crimes because they have not got minds of their own. However, the courts are sometimes prepared to regard the controllers of the company as the minds of the company.

In **Tesco Supermarkets Ltd** *v* **Nattrass (1971)** the House of Lords held that a person who was sufficiently senior in a company could be regarded as the mind of the company. If a person senior enough to be regarded as the mind of a company had a guilty mind, then the company could be regarded as having a guilty mind. Persons who were not senior enough could be regarded only as the hands of the company. If such a person had a guilty mind, then this could not be regarded as the guilty mind of the company. In the case it was held that a supermarket manager employed by Tesco Ltd was not senior enough to be regarded as the mind of the company, whereas a very senior manager might have been.

The Corporate Manslaughter and Corporate Homicide Act 2007

The Corporate Manslaughter and Corporate Homicide Act 2007 has created a new offence of corporate manslaughter (corporate homicide in Scotland). The offence can be committed by companies and by other incorporated bodies, such as LLPs, as well as by some types of unincorporated associations, such as partnerships. The Director of Public Prosecutions must consent to a prosecution being brought.

Section 1(1) provides that the offence of corporate manslaughter is committed by a relevant organisation if the way in which its activities are managed and organised:

- causes a person's death; and
- amounts to a gross breach of a relevant duty of care owed by the organisation to the deceased.

Section 1(3) provides that an organisation is guilty of the s. 1(1) offence only if the way in which its activities are managed or organised by its senior management is a substantial element in the breach to which s. 1(1) refers. Section 1(4)(b) provides that a breach is a 'gross breach' only if it falls far below what can reasonably be expected of the organisation in the circumstances.

Section 1(4)(c) defines 'senior management', in relation to an organisation, as the persons who play significant roles in:

- the making of decisions about how the whole or a substantial part of its activities are to be managed or organised; or
- the actual managing or organising of the whole or a substantial part of those activities.

The penalty for commission of the offence is a fine.

Section 2(1) provides that a 'relevant duty of care' is a duty of care owed under the law of negligence. (See Chapter 8.)

Whether or not a duty of care was owed is a question of law for the judge, not a question of fact for the jury. Whether there was a gross breach of that duty is a question for the jury. In deciding this the jury should consider all relevant matters. However, s. 8 highlights several matters. Section 8(2) provides that the jury must consider whether the evidence shows that the organisation failed to comply with any health and safety legislation that relates to the alleged breach, and if so (a) how serious that failure was; and (b) how much of a risk of death it posed. Section 8(3) provides that the jury may also (a) consider the extent to which the evidence shows that there were attitudes, policies, systems or accepted practices within the organisation that were likely to have encouraged any such failure as is mentioned in s. 8(2), or to have produced tolerance of it; and (b) have regard to any health and safety guidance that relates to the alleged breach.

Section 9 allows a court to make a remedial order requiring a breach of s. 1(1) to be remedied. Section 10 allows a court to order a convicted organisation to publicise the conviction in a specified manner.

The corporate veil

We have seen that a company has a legal identity of its own. A natural consequence of this is that only the company can be liable in respect of a wrong done by the company. The owners of the company will normally be free of any liability. They are said to be protected by the 'veil of incorporation'. This image regards the company's artificial legal personality as a veil, which hangs between the company and the members of the company.

As we have already seen, the idea that the members of a company are not liable for the company's wrongdoings is very well established. But there are circumstances in which a court or a statute will lift the corporate veil so that the members of the company are not protected by the company's artificial legal personality.

In **Prest v Petrodel Resources Ltd (2013)** a seven-justice Supreme Court thoroughly examined whether the corporate veil could ever be pierced (disregarded), reviewing the leading cases in considerable detail. This case must now be regarded as the only authoritative decision on piercing of the corporate veil.

Four of the justices thought that there was a difference between concealment cases and evasion cases. In cases of concealment a company receives money or property as the company controller's agent rather than receiving it in the company's own right. The controller is therefore liable to account for the money or property, just as he would be if the agent company had been a human agent rather than a company. In such cases there is no piercing of the corporate veil. The evasion principle applies only if a controller has deliberately used the company's separate legal personality to evade an existing personal liability which he otherwise would have had. In such cases the corporate veil can be pierced. Where the corporate veil is pierced this is a true exception to **Salomon's case** because a person who owns and controls a company is identified with the company by virtue of that ownership and control. The following two, well-known, cases were used to demonstrate the difference between concealment and evasion.

In **Gilford Motor Co Ltd v Horne (1933)** Horne's contract of employment prevented him from competing with his employer after leaving his employment. To evade this, Horne formed a company and offered his services through the company. The Court of Appeal granted an injunction against both Horne and the company because the company was 'a mere cloak or sham'. The order was made against the company to ensure that Horne was deprived of the benefit which he would otherwise have derived from the company's separate legal personality. The order against the company was a genuine case of piercing the corporate veil. In **Jones v Lipman (1962)** Lipman sold a property and then did not want to go through with the sale. He therefore bought an off the shelf company and transferred the property to it, so that specific performance of the sale could not be ordered. The court ordered specific performance against Lipman and against the company. The order of specific performance against Lipman personally was an example of the concealment principle and did not involve piercing the corporate veil. It merely involved identifying Lipman as the man in control of the company. As regards the order of specific performance against the company, there was disagreement amongst the justices. Some thought the order against the company was justified on the evasion principle and did involve piercing the veil. Others thought that the order against the company was unnecessary because the court could have ordered Lipman to do everything in his power to see that the property was conveyed to the purchaser, without any piercing of the corporate veil. The four judges who thought the cases could be divided into concealment and evasion cases all agreed that there is a limited principle of piercing the corporate veil, which applies when a person is under an existing legal obligation or liability or subject to an existing legal restriction which he deliberately evades or whose enforcement he deliberately frustrates by using a company under his control.

Two of the justices did not think that all of the old cases where the separate legal personality of the company was disregarded could neatly be divided into concealment and evasion. The cases might simply be examples of the principle that those who control companies should not be able to take unfair advantage of those with whom they do business. One justice thought that piercing the corporate veil was not a doctrine at all or a rule of law. It was simply a label attached to the disparate occasions on which some rule of law produced an apparent exception to the principle of separate legal personality which was reaffirmed in **Salomon's case**.

On the facts of **Prest v Petrodel Resources Ltd**, all seven justices agreed that it was not necessary to pierce the corporate veil. Yasmin Prest had obtained a divorce from her husband Michael. Michael owned and controlled several companies, the Petrodel Group, which owned seven properties. The court had to decide whether these seven properties could be transferred to Yasmin. The Supreme Court held that the properties were held on trust for Michael by the companies, and that the companies could therefore be ordered to transfer them to Yasmin. This did not involve piercing the corporate veil.

It should be remembered that there are several statutes which override the effect of a company's separate legal personality, but these are not regarded as piercing the corporate veil. For example, in divorce cases, the Matrimonial Causes Act 1973 allows a court to set aside dispositions of property which were designed to frustrate the exercise of the court's powers. Also, s. 15 of the Company Directors Disqualification Act 1986 imposes personal liability on a disqualified director who manages a company which incurs debts while he is disqualified.

Classification of companies

Companies can be classified in several different ways, but from a business perspective only four classifications are useful.

Public companies and private companies

Public companies can offer shares and debentures for sale to the public. The articles of private companies usually restrict the sale of the company's shares. The most common restrictions

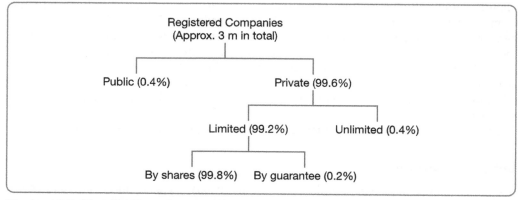

Figure 10.2 Classification of companies

are either that the shares must first be offered to other members of the company, or that the shares can be sold only to persons of whom the directors approve. No matter what the articles of association say, it is a criminal offence for a private company to offer its shares for sale to members of the public.

Although public limited companies (plcs) make up less than 1 per cent of all companies, they tend to be very much larger than most private companies. The assets of all public companies would far outweigh the assets of all private companies.

Although plcs can be listed on the London Stock Market, most are not. Only about 2,000 plcs are listed. The shares of many more plcs are traded on the Alternative Investment Market.

It is possible for a private company to re-register as a public company and vice versa. If this is done, a new certificate of incorporation is issued. Most plcs began as private companies and made the change after they had become very successful. A special resolution is needed to change from a private company to a plc or to change from a plc to a private company. (The different types of resolutions, and how they are passed, are considered in Chapter 11.) Table 10.1 shows the main differences between public and private companies.

Table 10.1 Differences between public and private companies

Public companies	Private companies
Name must end with the words 'Public Limited Company' or 'plc'	Name must end with 'Limited' or 'Ltd' (unless the company is unlimited)
Must have £50,000 allotted share capital, one-quarter of which must be paid up	No limit on share capital
Shares can be listed on stock exchange (no requirement that they should be listed)	Shares cannot be listed on stock exchange, or advertised for sale
Must have at least two directors	Need have only one director
Shares allotted by the company must be paid for in cash (or qualified auditor must value assets given as payment)	Shares can be given away by the company
Must have a company secretary, who must be suitably qualified	No need to have a company secretary. If there is one, does not need to be qualified
Must hold AGM every calendar year	No AGM unless positive decision taken to hold one
Cannot pass written resolutions	Can pass written resolutions

Unlimited companies

Slightly under half of 1 per cent of registered companies are unlimited companies. These companies do have a legal personality of their own, distinct from that of the company members, but the members have agreed that they will assume unlimited liability for the debts of the company. Public companies may not register as unlimited companies.

Unlimited companies enjoy some advantages over limited companies. For example, their accounts need not be published or delivered to the Registrar of Companies. However, these advantages are generally considered to be far outweighed by the unlimited liability of the members.

The names of unlimited companies must not contain the words 'limited' or 'Ltd'.

Limited companies

Limited companies can themselves be classified into two types: companies limited by shares and companies limited by guarantee.

Companies limited by shares

The vast majority of companies are limited by shares. As we have seen, this means that in the event of liquidation of the company a member's liability is limited to paying off any amount unpaid on his or her shares. (When any reference to a company is made it should be assumed that the company is limited by shares unless there is an indication to the contrary.)

Companies limited by guarantee

The liability of members of companies limited by guarantee is restricted to paying an amount which they have agreed to pay in the event of the company going into liquidation. This amount is usually small, typically £5, and is spelt out in the application for registration, a document which must be registered with the Registrar of Companies when the company is formed.

Before the Companies Act 1980 a company could register itself as limited by shares and by guarantee, in which case the members were liable to pay both the amount guaranteed and the amount unpaid on their shares. Some such companies, formed before 1980, continue to exist. However, since the Companies Act 1980 a company must either be limited by shares or be limited by guarantee.

Public companies have never been allowed to be limited by guarantee: they must be limited by shares. Most companies limited by guarantee are educational or charitable. Guarantee companies are not a suitable medium for trading companies. Figure 10.2 gives an overview of the main ways in which companies can be classified.

Method of creation

Companies are created by registration under the Companies Act, a procedure which is examined later in this chapter. Some very few companies have been created by Royal Charter or by statute. However, these methods of creation are not significant in a business context. Almost all companies currently in existence were created by registration under the Companies Act. The process is quick and cheap, and it is generally understood that when people speak of a company this is the type of company which they mean.

Size of company

Single-member companies

It is possible for any company, public or private, to have only one member. New companies can be created with only one subscriber to the memorandum, or an existing private company can allow its membership to fall to one.

Small and medium-sized companies

Companies which can be classified as small can submit abbreviated accounts to the Registrar of Companies, although full accounts will still have to be delivered to the members.

A company is regarded as a small company if it meets two out of the following three requirements:

(1) the company's annual turnover is £6.5m or less;

(2) the total assets of the company are £3.26m or less;

(3) the company has 50 or fewer employees.

Medium-sized companies can omit certain matters from the business review which directors have to submit for each financial year. A company is regarded as a medium-size company if it meets two out of the three following requirements:

(1) the company's annual turnover is £25.9m or less;

(2) the total assets of the company are £12.9m or less;

(3) the company has 250 or fewer employees.

Formation of registered companies

Registration under the Companies Act 2006

A registered company is formed by promoters, who must pay a fee and register certain documents with the Registrar of Companies. If the Registrar is satisfied with the documents, he will issue a certificate of incorporation, and the company will then exist as a corporate body.

The 2006 Act has changed the process of registering a company. Companies which were registered before the 2006 Act came into force will have been registered under the old procedure. They will not need to re-register. Most companies currently in existence were registered under the old procedure. It is therefore necessary to describe that old procedure to some extent. First, the new registration procedure is described.

Registration documents

Section 9(1) of the 2006 Act provides that in order to register a new company the following must be sent to the Registrar, along with a £20 fee:

- a new-style memorandum of association;
- an application for registration of the company;
- the documents which s. 9 requires the application to contain; and
- a statement of compliance.

A company may not be formed for an unlawful purpose.

The new style of memorandum of association

The new style of memorandum is quite different from the old style of memorandum, which existed before the 2006 Act came into force. A new style of memorandum merely states that the subscribers, the people who sign it, wish to form a company under the Act and that they agree to become members of the company by taking at least one share each. This memorandum will not be capable of being changed later. It gives a 'historical snapshot' of the company members on formation of the company.

The application for registration

Section 9(2) requires that the application for registration must state:

- the company's proposed name;
- whether the company's registered office is to be situated in England and Wales (or in Wales), in Scotland or in Northern Ireland;
- whether the liability of the members of the company is to be limited, and if so whether it is to be limited by shares or guarantee; and
- whether the company is to be a public company or a private company.

The documents which the application must contain

The documents which s. 9 requires the application to contain are set out in ss. 9(4) and (5). These are:

- a statement of share capital and initial shareholdings, or a statement of guarantee if the company is to be limited by guarantee;
- a statement of the company's proposed officers;
- a statement of the intended address of the company's registered office; and
- a statement of any proposed articles of association, to the extent that model articles are not being used.

The **statement of capital and initial shareholdings** is required by s. 10(2) to state the following:

- the total number of shares to be taken on formation by the subscribers to the memorandum;
- the total nominal value of those shares;
- for each class of shares:
  - particulars of the rights attached to the shares,
  - the total number of shares of that class, and
  - the total nominal value of shares of that class;
- the amount to be paid up and the amount, if any, to be unpaid on each share.

If the company has more than one class of shares, then this information must be given in respect of each class of shares. The nominal value of a share represents the face value which the company has agreed that the share should have. This amount can be expressed in sterling, euros or any other currency. Different classes of shares can have nominal values in different currencies. The total nominal value of shares to be taken by subscribers to the memorandum means the total amount stated to be payable to the company for all of the shares which the subscribers to the memorandum take. So, for example, let us assume that the four subscribers to the memorandum of Acme Ltd each agree to take 250 shares. The nominal value of each share is agreed to be £1 and so the aggregate nominal value of shares taken by the subscribers would be £1,000. It is not possible to agree that the members will pay less than the nominal value of a share. They might, however, pay more because the nominal value of a share does not represent its true value. If more is paid, the extra amount is regarded as a share premium and must be kept in a share premium account. Such an account cannot be used to pay dividends to members.

A **statement of guarantee** is necessary only if the company is limited by guarantee. It must identify the guarantors, who subscribe to the memorandum, and state what contribution they have each agreed to make. These contributions are payable if the company is wound up while a guarantor is a member or within a year of his ceasing to be a member.

The **statement of proposed officers** must give the names and addresses of the first directors and the first company secretary (if the company is to have a company secretary). The statement must also include such information as would be required to be in the register of directors, the register of directors' residential addresses and in the register of company secretaries. (See Chapter 11.) The residential addresses of directors need not be disclosed. Directors can give a service address, which can be the address of the company's registered office.

The statement must also contain consent by each person named as a director or secretary to act in the relevant capacity. Once the company is registered they are deemed to have been appointed.

The statement of compliance

The **statement of compliance** merely states that the Act's requirements as to registration have been complied with.

If the Registrar is satisfied that the requirements of the Act have been complied with he registers the documents delivered to him and issues a certificate of incorporation.

The effect of registration

A **certificate of incorporation** is conclusive evidence that the requirements of registration have been complied with and that the company has been duly registered under the Act. Once the certificate is issued the company has a legal personality of its own.

Section 15(2) provides that the certificate must state:

- the name and registered number of the company;
- the date of its incorporation;
- whether it is a limited or unlimited company, and if it is limited whether it is limited by shares or limited by guarantee;
- whether it is a private or a public company; and
- whether the company's registered office is situated in England and Wales (or in Wales), in Scotland or in Northern Ireland.

From the date of incorporation the company is capable of exercising all the powers of a registered company. The subscribers to the memorandum become members of the company and become holders of the shares to the extent set out in the statement of capital and initial shareholdings. The proposed directors and secretary are deemed to have been appointed.

Old-style registration

Companies which registered before the 2006 Act came into force do not need to re-register. Obviously, for some years to come most companies will have completed an old-style registration. This has important consequences for the constitution of those companies. Therefore it is necessary to know the procedure required for an old-style registration.

Under the old-style registration the documents which had to be sent to the Registrar were:

- the company's memorandum of association;
- the company's articles of association;
- a statement giving the names of the company's first directors and of the company secretary; and
- a statement that all the statutory requirements of registration had been complied with.

Old-style memorandum of association

An old-style memorandum of association was of considerable importance. The constitution of a company registered before the 2006 Act came into force used to be contained in its memorandum and articles of association. The memorandum set out the structure of the company, whereas the articles were the internal rules.

Section 2 of the Companies Act 1985 stated that the memorandum of a company limited by shares had to contain five obligatory clauses. The only one of lasting significance is the objects clause. This stated the purposes for which the company was being formed and set out the contracts which the company could validly make. The problems caused by objects clauses, and the extent to which these problems have been resolved, are considered more fully later (see Chapter 11).

As well as the five compulsory clauses there could be additional clauses. If an additional clause was stated to be unalterable, then it could not be altered by the members. This is no longer the case. Section 28(1) of the 2006 Act provides that all provisions of an old-style memorandum, except the basic provisions which would need to be contained in a new-style memorandum, are to be treated as provisions of the company's articles. The articles of a company can generally be altered by a special resolution of the members. However, some articles may be entrenched. Such articles can be altered only by a specified procedure which is more onerous than the passing of a special resolution, as we shall see later in the chapter. However, entrenched articles cannot be made unalterable. So it is no longer possible for a company to have an unalterable provision in its constitution.

The constitution of a company

Section 17 of the 2006 Act provides that a company's constitution includes the company's articles of association and certain types of resolutions. Other matters can be included in the constitution. For example, a company's incorporation certificate will state whether the company is public or private and will therefore be constitutionally relevant.

Constitutionally relevant articles

Section 29 sets out the types of resolutions which are constitutionally relevant. Broadly speaking, these are special resolutions, or other resolutions or agreements agreed to by all the members of the company, which would not have been effective unless they had been passed as a special resolution. Special resolutions are passed only if a majority of at least 75 per cent of members who vote on the resolution vote in favour of it. The 2006 Act requires some matters to be passed by special resolution (see Table 11.1). Section 30 requires that copies of these constitutionally relevant resolutions must be sent to the Registrar within 15 days of their being passed. Section 32 requires an up-to-date copy of the constitutional documents to be sent to members on request.

The articles of association

The articles of association are the rules of the company and they bind both the company and the members of the company. Before the 2006 Act came into force, the rules of the company could be found in the old-style memorandum and the articles. The articles were the internal rules of the company whereas the old-style memorandum set out the structure of the company. As we have seen, as regards companies formed under the 2006 Act, the new-style memorandum is a mere historical snapshot giving information about the company when it was formed. The rules of the company are set out in the articles. As regards companies formed before the 2006 Act came into force, s. 28(1) provides that provisions of an old-style memorandum are to be treated as provisions of the company's articles. This is the case with all provisions of an old-style memorandum except those minimal provisions which would be found in a new-style memorandum. So, again, the articles of pre-2006 companies are the rules of the company.

Section 18 provides that a company must have articles of association and that these must be contained in a single document which is divided into consecutively numbered paragraphs. Different types of model articles, suitable for different types of companies, have been written by the Secretary of State. Section 20(1) provides that these articles will apply by default when a company is formed, if other articles are not registered. It also provides that if other articles are registered the model articles will still apply to the extent that they are not excluded or changed by the articles which are registered. The model articles are designed to allow companies to be formed and do business even if they have not created suitable articles. Existing companies will not be subject to the application of model articles by default, although they will be able to adopt them either wholly or partially. If a company was registered using the old Table A model articles, which could be adopted before the 2006 Act came into force, they will continue to be governed by Table A.

Section 25 provides that an alteration of the articles which increases the liability of a member since he became a member is invalid against that member unless he has given express written consent to it.

Amendment of articles

Section 21(1) provides that a company's articles may generally be amended by special resolution. However, s. 22(1) allows the articles to contain entrenched articles. Something more than a special resolution is required to change or remove an entrenched article. The Act does not say exactly what is required. However, since a special resolution can be passed only by a 75 per cent majority of those voting on it, the requirement might be, for example, a unanimous vote or a vote passed by a 90 per cent majority of all company members. Section 22(2) provides that an article can become entrenched only if the company's articles say so when the company is formed, or if all of the members of the company agree to the articles being amended.

It is not possible to make entrenched articles unalterable. Section 22(3) provides that entrenched articles can always be altered by an agreement of all the members of a company or by a court order.

Where a company's articles are amended so as to include or remove an entrenched article, s. 23 requires the company to give notice of this to the Registrar. A document showing the amendment also has to be sent to the Registrar along with a statement of compliance. This statement will certify that the amendment has been made in accordance with the company's articles. So both the Registrar and any person searching the public register of companies will be able to see whether or not any articles are entrenched and, if they are, how they can be altered.

Before the 2006 Act came into force there was no such concept as entrenched articles. The articles could always be altered by special resolution. However, provisions which might have been in the articles could be made unalterable by putting them in an old-style memorandum and stating that they were unalterable. This practice is now redundant as the new-style memorandum now gives only basic information about the company when it was created. Any other matters will be found in the articles.

Whenever a company's articles are amended, whether there is provision for any articles to be entrenched or not, s. 26(1) provides that the company must send the Registrar a copy of the amended articles within 15 days of the amendment taking effect.

If something cannot be done by a company unless the articles authorise it, then a special resolution authorising the thing will not be effective because the articles will not be impliedly changed. However, if the resolution states that it is doing the thing 'notwithstanding anything in the articles', then the thing will be validly done.

When the members do alter the articles they must exercise this power *bona fide* for the benefit of the members of the company as a whole, that is to say for the benefit of the company in its capacity as a separate legal person.

The legal effect of the constitution

Section 33(1) of the 2006 Act provides that the constitution makes a contract between every shareholder and the company and between every shareholder and every other shareholder.

The constitution as a contract between the company and the members

The constitution forms a contract between a company and its members, in respect of their ordinary rights as members. So the company can insist that the members abide by the articles.

 Hickman *v* Kent or Romney Marsh Sheep-Breeders' Association (1915)

The Sheep-Breeders' Association was registered as a non-profit making company. One of the association's articles provided that any dispute between the association and a member should be referred to arbitration. One member tried to sue the association.

Held The member had no right to sue the association. He should have referred the dispute to arbitration.

Equally, the members can insist that the company sticks to the articles.

 Pender *v* Lushington (1877)

The articles of a company provided that every ten shares commanded one vote, but that no member should be entitled to more than 100 votes. A shareholder who held more than 1,000 shares transferred some of these to Pender, so that the shares could use their full voting power. The chairman of the company, Lushington, refused to accept the votes of Pender's shares.

Held The shares had been properly transferred and so not to accept Pender's votes was a breach of his rights as a member of the company.

It is important to realise that members are bound to the company only in their capacity as members, and that the company is bound to members only in their capacity as members. For example, in **Beattie *v* E and F Beattie Ltd (1938)** a director, who was also a member of the company, tried to rely on one of the articles when he was sued by the company for the return of money which had been improperly paid to him as a director. The defendant was not able to rely on the article. He was not attempting to rely on the article in his capacity as a member of the company but in his capacity as a director.

The constitution as a contract between the members

Section 33(1) tells us that the constitution creates a contract between each member and all the other members. However, this is only true in relation to matters which concern membership of the company.

Rayfield v Hands (1960)

An article of the company provided that if any member intended to transfer shares in the company he should inform the directors who 'will take the said shares equally between them at a fair price'. The claimant informed the directors that he intended to transfer some shares and they refused to buy them, arguing that the articles imposed no such liability upon them.

Held The directors were bound by the article and therefore had to take the shares at a fair price. The article in question was concerned with the relationship between the claimant as a member and the defendants as members of the company.

The constitution does not make any contract with outsiders.

Shareholder agreements

As we have seen, a company must have articles of association and these will be binding upon all company members. In addition, some or all of a company's members might enter into a shareholder agreement. Such an agreement would not be a part of a company's constitution. A shareholder agreement would form a binding contract between those who enter into it, but would not need to be registered with the Registrar of Companies. Outsiders could not therefore discover what had been agreed. Caution has to be exercised because new members of a company would not be bound by a pre-existing shareholder agreement unless they agreed to be bound by it. Furthermore, if the agreement did not set out the way in which it could be altered, then only a unanimous agreement of all contracting parties could alter the agreement. A company can itself be a party to a shareholder agreement. However, in **Russell v Northern Bank Development Corporation Ltd (1992)** the House of Lords held that any agreement by a company that it would not use its statutory power to alter its articles would be unenforceable.

Off-the-shelf companies

An alternative to the promoters themselves forming a company is for them to buy an 'off the shelf' company. Some businesses form companies in large numbers, in the hope that customers will wish to buy the companies. A person who forms such a company registers himself as the company's first director and takes one share. Then, when a customer wishes to buy an off-the-shelf company, the share is transferred to the customer. The original director resigns, having appointed the customer the new director, and notifies Companies House of this change. Before the 2006 Act came into force, the risk involved in this could be substantial, because a company's articles must be suitable for that particular company. Many businesses, in too much of a hurry to become incorporated, adopted unsuitable articles, either by buying an off-the-shelf company or by adopting the old Table A model articles without considering their effect. Of course, it is always possible to alter these articles while the promoters or the creators of the company hold all the shares in it. However, all too often the members were in too much haste to set the company up to realise the importance of ensuring that the articles suited their needs. Promoters of off-the-shelf companies are now likely to use the new model default articles. These are far more likely to be suitable for the company than the old Table A articles. However, the purchasers of the company should still ensure that the articles are tailored to their needs.

Contracts made before the company is formed

A company does not come into existence until the registrar issues its certificate of incorporation. It follows that until the certificate is issued the company has no capacity to make contracts.

However, those who wish to form the company, the promoters, might want to make contracts on the company's behalf in advance of incorporation. For example, if a shop intended to begin trading as a company on 1 October, then the promoters would need to buy stock in advance of that date.

Section 51(1) of the Act provides that:

> A contract which purports to be made by or on behalf of a company when the company has not been formed has effect, subject to any agreement to the contrary, as one made with the person purporting to act for the company or as agent for it, and he is personally liable on the contract accordingly.

It will be noticed this section applies 'subject to any agreement to the contrary'. It is therefore possible for the promoter to disclaim personal liability when making the contract on the company's behalf. However, it would be inadvisable for others to deal with the promoters on this basis. In effect they would be making contracts which could be enforced against themselves but which they might not be able to enforce against anyone.

Suppliers to the company might do well to insist that the company is actually formed before they make any contract. Another way around the problem would be for the supplier to make two contracts. The first draft contract would be with the company, stating that it will pay as soon as it is formed. The second contract would be made with the promoters, who would agree that they would pay in the event that the company does not.

Promoters are fiduciaries and therefore owe duties of loyalty and good faith to the company. So a promoter will be liable to the company for any profit made by selling his own property to the company unless this is disclosed to the company directors or to its prospective shareholders. In addition, the company will be able to avoid the contract.

The company name

The name of every public company must end with the words 'public limited company' or the abbreviation 'plc'. The name of every private limited company must end with the word 'limited' or the abbreviation 'Ltd'. (If the company's registered office is in Wales, then the Welsh equivalents of these names may be used.) So the word 'limited' must appear in the names of both types of companies, although of course it is not the company's liability which is limited, but the liability of its members.

Unlimited companies may not include the word 'limited' in their names.

The word 'company' is not often included in the names of companies. Strangely, the word appears in the names of partnerships more frequently than in the names of companies. For example, a business called 'Brown & Co' could not be a company unless it was an unlimited company. Almost always, a business with such a name would be a partnership. (Partnership names are considered in Chapter 12.)

Prohibited names

The Act prohibits the use of certain names:

- The words 'limited' or 'unlimited' or 'public limited company' can be used only at the end of the name.
- The Registrar will refuse to register a name which is identical to the name of another company already on the register.
- The Registrar will refuse to register a name the use of which would, in the opinion of the Secretary of State, constitute a criminal offence or be offensive.
- Regulations made by the Secretary of State prohibit the use of certain words without permission. These words suggest a connection with Government or with local authorities. Other Regulations prohibit the use of certain words unless permission is granted by an appropriate body. Currently about 100 words are listed, including 'Building Society', 'Chamber of Commerce', 'English', 'Insurance', 'National', 'Prince', 'Queen', 'Royal', 'Trade Union', 'Trust', and 'Windsor'.

The Regulations explain from whom permission to use the words must be gained. For example, the words which suggest a royal connection can be used only if the Home Office gives permission.

Objection to a company name

Section 69(1) allows any person to object to a company's registered name on the ground:

- that it is the same as a name associated with the applicant in which he has goodwill, or
- that it is sufficiently similar to such a name that its use in the United Kingdom would be likely to mislead by suggesting a connection between the company and the applicant.

The applicant must make the objection to a company names adjudicator, who can order that a name be changed. A right of appeal lies to the courts.

Before the 2006 Act came into force a business would bring a passing-off action to prevent a company registering a name which was so similar as to be likely to divert trade away from the business. The 2006 Act has not removed the common-law right to bring a passing-off action. Such an action would be appropriate if damages were being sought. A passing-off action will be successful only if the use of the name is likely to divert customers away from the established business or cause confusion between the two businesses (see Chapter 12).

Publication of name and address

All companies must publish their names:

- outside the registered office and all places of business;
- on all letters, invoices, notices, cheques and receipts;
- on the company seal, if the company has a seal; and
- on the company's websites.

If the company does not publish its name as required, then all of its officers, all the directors and the company secretary, are liable to be fined. Furthermore, a person who signs company letters or cheques which do not publish the company name will be personally liable to any creditor who relies on the document and loses money. This liability will also be imposed if the company name is incorrectly stated.

For example, in **Penrose _v_ Martyr (1858)**, a company secretary signed a cheque on the company's behalf and was held personally liable because the word 'limited' was omitted from the company name.

Change of name

Section 77 provides that a company may change its name by special resolution, or by an ordinary resolution following a direction from the Secretary of State or a decision from the company names adjudicator, or by other means provided for by the company's articles. Where a name is changed, the company must give notice to the Registrar.

The same prohibitions will apply to a change of name as applied to the use of a name on formation of a company. The Registrar must register the changed name and has the same powers to refuse.

The Registrar of Companies

The Registrar of Companies is an official of the Department of Trade and Industry and is the head of an agency known as Companies House. The Registrar has many other duties besides registering newly formed companies. The main duties of the Registrar are:

- to issue a certificate of incorporation when a company is first registered – this is conclusive evidence that the company has been formed and, if appropriate, that it is limited;
- to issue a certificate of incorporation on change of company name – although a new certificate is issued the company remains the same legal person and its registered number remains the same;
- to keep a list of the names of all UK registered companies, limited partnerships and limited liability partnerships;
- to issue certificates of re-registration when a private company changes to a public one, or vice versa, or from unlimited to limited, or vice versa;
- to receive the annual return and the annual financial statements of companies;
- to register and keep safe the documents which statutes require him to hold;
- to issue certificates which register mortgages and charges granted by companies;
- to strike companies off the register when they are dissolved;
- to allow any member of the public to see the file of a particular company;
- to register special and extraordinary resolutions;
- to publish in the _London Gazette_ the fact of receipt of various documents.

Section 107(5) gives the Registrar the power to correct a document informally, if it appears incomplete or inconsistent with itself. However, the company must consent and give instructions in response to an enquiry from the Registrar. Section 108(1) allows the Registrar to make certain annotations to registers, showing such things as the date a document was received, corrections which were made to it or materials which were removed from it.

Essential points

- A company is a legal person, with a legal identity of its own.
- The members of a limited company have limited liability for the debts of the company.
- Public limited companies (plcs) can offer their shares for sale to members of the public. It is a criminal offence for a private company to offer its shares for sale to the public.
- Plcs must have at least two directors. Private companies need have only one director.
- Private companies can pass written resolutions and do not need to hold annual general meetings.
- Companies are created by registration with the Registrar of Companies. Once registered, a company will be given a certificate of incorporation and will exist as a legal person.
- A company is formed under the 2006 Act by sending a memorandum of association to the Registrar together with an application for registration of the company, the documents which s. 9 requires and a statement of compliance.
- The articles of association are the internal rules of the company. They bind the company and all of the members as if they had been signed by all of the members.
- The names of public companies must end with 'public limited company' or 'plc'.
- The names of private limited companies must end with the word 'limited' or the abbreviation 'Ltd'.

Practice questions

1   It is now possible for a person to own all of the shares in a company. If X owned all of the shares in X Co Ltd, and X Co Ltd owed no money to any creditors:

   (a) Could X steal from the company?

   (b) Could X sue the company?

   (c) Could X be employed by the company?

2   In **Lee v Lee's Air Farming Ltd (1961)**, Mr Lee owned 2,999 of the 3,000 shares in a crop-spraying company. While at work Lee crashed his plane and was killed. His widow sued under a statute which required employers to pay compensation if an employee was killed at work. The company's insurers refused to pay, arguing that Lee was employed by himself, and could not therefore be an employee of the company. Did the insurers have to pay up?

3   The decision in **Salomon's case** means that investors in a limited company do not have to pay the company's debts. They may lose the value of their shares, but they can lose no more. Why is this regarded as such an important rule in a capitalist society? In what way would society be different if members of companies could not enjoy limited liability?

4 A business is registered under the name Acme Trading Ltd. Which one of the following might the company be?

(a) A public limited company.

(b) A partnership.

(c) A private limited company.

(d) Either a limited private company or an unlimited private company.

5 Arthur owns 100 shares in a private limited company which has gone into liquidation with heavy debts. Arthur has paid half the price of his shares. Which one of the following statements would be true?

(a) As the company is limited it need not pay its debts.

(b) Limited liability will mean that Arthur has to pay nothing towards the company's debts.

(c) Arthur must pay the amount unpaid on his shares. Beyond that he need pay no more.

(d) The amount of the company's debts must be paid by all shareholders in proportion to their shareholding.

6 Which one of the following statements is true?

(a) A public company need have only one director.

(b) A public company cannot be unlimited.

(c) A public company's shares must be quoted on the Stock Exchange.

(d) A public company's shares must be offered for sale to the public.

7 Which one of the following statements is not true of a private limited company?

(a) The company will continue in existence indefinitely unless it is liquidated.

(b) The company can sue on contracts made in its name.

(c) The company can employ the person who owns all the shares in the company.

(d) A major shareholder in the company cannot hold shares in a rival company.

8 Explain the characteristics of a limited company.

Task 10

A friend of yours from France is considering setting up a business in England. Your friend has asked you to draw up a report briefly explaining the following matters:

(a) The characteristics of a company.

(b) The distinction between a public company and a private company.

(c) The names which a company may use and the places in which the company name must be displayed.

(d) How a company is formed.

mylawchamber

Visit **www.mylawchamber.co.uk/macintyreessentials** to access tools to help you develop and test your knowledge of business law, including interactive multiple choice questions, practice exam questions with guidance, weblinks, glossary, glossary flashcards, legal newsfeed and legal updates.

Use **Case Navigator** to read in full some of the key cases referenced in this chapter with commentary and questions:

Salomon *v* Salomon & Co Ltd (1897)

11

Companies (2): Management, control and winding up

In this chapter we consider the management and control of companies and the ways in which companies can be wound up.

Management and control of companies

In the previous chapter we saw that a company limited by shares must have shareholders, who are known as the company's members. We also saw that a company's articles of association are part of its constitution, and that the constitution of a company binds both the members and the company. A company's articles will provide that its board of directors should manage the company. They will also set out rules relating to the appointment and removal of directors.

Executive directors devote substantially the whole of their working time to performing their duties and derive most of their income from their connection with the company. They are usually employees of the company. Non-executive directors do not devote their whole time to performing their duties. They are generally paid a small fee for their services.

Appointment and removal of directors

The first directors of a company agree to become directors when the company is registered. Unless the articles provide otherwise, subsequent directors are appointed by an ordinary resolution of the members. Articles often provide that directors may be appointed in other ways. For example, the articles of many large companies allow the board of directors to appoint directors to fill casual vacancies which have arisen.

Public companies must have two directors but private companies only need to have one. Usually the directors of a company also own shares in the company. In small companies they often own a majority of the shares. However, there is no requirement that a director should also be a member of the company.

The articles of association usually set out how a director can be removed. Sometimes, for example, the articles of public companies provide that directors should retire by rotation. If this is the case, the directors who have held office for the longest would retire at the company's annual general meeting. The retiring directors could usually offer themselves for re-election and could be automatically re-elected if no-one else stood to fill the vacancies.

No matter what the articles might say, s. 168 of the Companies Act 1985 provides that a director can always be removed by an ordinary resolution of which the company has been given special notice. This means that the company has been given 28 days' notice of the resolution and the members have been given 14 days' notice. A director whose removal is proposed in this way has a right to speak at the meeting at which his or her removal is proposed. For this reason a written resolution cannot be used to remove a director by means of s. 168.

On a resolution to remove a director the shares of the director whose removal is proposed might have enhanced voting power.

 Bushell v Faith (1970) (House of Lords)

The 300 shares in a company were owned equally by a brother and two sisters. All three shareholders were also directors. The articles provided that on any resolution to remove a director that director's shares should carry three votes per share. The two sisters proposed a resolution to remove their brother as a director. At a general meeting the sisters voted for removal, the brother voted against. The sisters claimed that the resolution had been passed by 200 votes to 100. The brother claimed that it had been defeated by 200 votes to 300.

Held The article giving the enhanced voting rights was perfectly valid. Therefore the resolution to remove the brother from the board of directors had been defeated by 200 votes to 300.

The powers of directors

The powers of the directors will be contained in the articles of association. In the previous chapter we saw that companies can adopt model articles. Article 3 of the model articles for both public and private companies provides that:

3 Directors' general authority
  Subject to the articles, the directors are responsible for the management of the company's business, for which purpose they may exercise all the powers of the company.

The board of directors then are usually given very wide powers to manage the company. They might exercise these powers to employ people to work for the company and might delegate some powers of management to these employees. The model articles for both public and private companies allow the members to pass a special resolution requiring the directors to do or not to do something. However, as long as the directors stay within their powers, they need not obey ordinary resolutions (see later in the chapter) passed by the members.

 Automatic Self-Cleansing Filter Syndicate Co Ltd v Cuninghame (1906) (Court of Appeal)

One of the company's articles gave the directors the power to sell the company property on whatever terms they thought fit. At a general meeting of the company an ordinary resolution was passed, ordering the directors to sell company property to a new company. The directors did not approve of the terms of the contract and refused to sell.

Held The directors were within their rights. Whether or not to sell was a question for them and not for the shareholders.

The members of a company can ratify unauthorised acts committed by the directors. If this is done, the authority which was lacking is supplied with back-dated effect and the act in question is adopted as an act of the company. An ordinary resolution is needed, unless the act was outside the company's objects clause, in which case a special resolution is needed.

This special resolution would confer retrospective authority on the directors, but a separate special resolution would be needed to prevent the directors from incurring personal liability. However, neither a special nor an ordinary resolution could validate an act which amounted to a breach of a director's fiduciary duties. (See later in the chapter.)

Directors as agents

The directors are given the power to act as the agents of the company, and a company can act only through its agents. Sometimes those who manage a company call themselves something other than directors. Section 250 of the 2006 Act provides that anyone who occupies the position of a director is to be regarded as a director, whatever name they give to their position. Such people are called shadow directors, and in **McKillen v Misland (Cyprus) Investments Ltd (2012)** it was held that a person could be a shadow director if a majority, but not necessarily all, of the directors were accustomed to acting in accordance with his directions.

When the directors act collectively they act as the board of directors. Directors must attend board meetings (which are quite different from general meetings of the company members). Unless the articles provide otherwise, any director may call a board meeting. A resolution of the board of directors is not passed unless more directors vote in favour of it than vote against it. However, many articles allow the chairman of the board of directors to have the casting vote where the votes of the directors are equally split. (The model articles for both private and public companies do this.) Section 248(1) requires that minutes of board meetings be kept, although the failure to keep minutes does not invalidate decisions taken. The minutes do not need to be registered with the Registrar of Companies.

The articles of some companies allow a managing director to be appointed. Such a managing director acts as an executive officer in charge of the day-to-day administration of the company. However, the title managing director has become somewhat outdated and to some extent has been replaced by the title Chief Executive Officer or CEO.

The objects clause

An objects clause is a clause in a company's articles which sets out the types of contracts which a company can make. Section 31(1) of the 2006 Act provides that, 'Unless a company's articles specifically restrict the objects of the company, its articles are unrestricted.' So it is no longer necessary for a company to have an objects clause, although most companies will have one in their articles.

Before the 2006 Act came into force all companies had to have an objects clause in their memorandum of association. (Such clauses have now been transferred to the company's articles.) However, since 1985 a company could state that its objects were to carry on business as a general commercial company. This meant that the company could carry on any trade or business whatsoever. So even before the 2006 Act came into force companies could, in effect, do away with an effective objects clause.

When a company acts for a purpose outside its objects clause the contract is said to be *ultra vires*. If this contract causes loss to the company the director who made the contract is personally liable to reimburse the company for the money lost, as the director will have breached the s. 171(a) duty to act within the company's constitution. The members can excuse the director from making this payment by passing an ordinary resolution.

Before the law was reformed in 1972 an *ultra vires* contract would be void. The current law is set out in s. 39(1) of the 2006 Act, which states:

> The validity of an act done by a company shall not be called into question on the ground of lack of capacity by reason of anything in the company's constitution.

Section 39(1) therefore means that when the act done on the company's behalf is done by a person who had authority to do it, then the *ultra vires* rule cannot be used by anyone to argue that the contract is invalid, even if the act was outside the objects clause.

A contract will not be binding upon the company if the person making the contract on the company's behalf had no actual or apparent authority to do so. This is the case whether or not the contract was within the company's objects clause. Even if the person making the contract has been given authority to do so, it is possible that the contract might contravene the company's constitution. Section 40(1) of the 2006 Act, which replaced s. 35A of the 1985 Act, protects third parties by providing that:

> In favour of a person dealing with a company in good faith, the power of the directors to bind the company, or authorise others to do so, is deemed to be free of any limitation under the company's constitution.

We have seen that s. 39(1) provides protection where the contract made was a type of contract which the company had no capacity to make, because the contract was outside the company's objects clause. Section 40(1) provides protection where the person who bound the company otherwise contravened the company's constitution by making the contract.

Section 40 does not prevent the company members from getting an injunction to prevent the directors from doing an *ultra vires* act, but if the directors have made a binding contract the members cannot undo it. Nor does s. 40 prevent the directors from being liable to the company for having exceeded their powers.

Different rules apply when an *ultra vires* contract is made between the company and a director. Section 41 provides that an *ultra vires* transaction entered into by the company with the directors of the company is voidable by the company despite s. 40. (For the meaning of voidable see Chapter 4.) Whether the contract is avoided or not, the directors who made the contract would then have to account to the company for any gain they have made and compensate the company for any loss it has suffered. The contract ceases to be voidable if the company affirms the transaction.

Holding out as a director

If a company represents that a person has the authority to make a transaction on the company's behalf, then the company will be bound by such a transaction, whether or not the person who made it really did have such authority. This is known as holding out. The company is said to have held out that the person had authority, and will not be allowed later to deny this.

 Freeman & Lockyer *v* Buckhurst Park Properties Ltd (1964) (Court of Appeal)

A company was formed to buy and resell an estate. The directors had the power to appoint a managing director but they never did so. One of the directors, Mr Kapoor, acted as if he had been appointed managing director. The other directors knew this but did nothing about it. Kapoor asked architects to do work on behalf of the company. When the architects sued the company for their fees the company argued that Kapoor had no authority to employ architects and therefore the contract was not binding on the company.

Held A managing director would usually have authority to employ architects. The company had represented that Kapoor was managing director. Therefore, as regards people dealing with the company in good faith, Kapoor had the authority to bind the company as if he really was managing director. The company had held him out to have such powers to bind the company, so it could not deny that he did have such powers. In agency terms, Kapoor had apparent authority to bind the company and the company would be 'estopped' from denying this later.

Remuneration of directors

Directors are not automatically entitled to any salary. However, if, as is usual, directors have a contract which gives them a salary, then they will be able to sue for compensation if the contract is breached. The directors can be paid even if the company does not make any profit.

Directors' duties

Sections 171–177 set out seven general duties which all directors owe to their companies. Generally, it would be the company which would sue if one of these duties was breached. If the company was unwilling to do this, a member of the company could bring a **derivative claim** under s. 260. (Derivative claims are considered later in this chapter.)

The new statutory duties codified the common law. So when the courts interpret and develop them they will bear in mind the principles of law which existed before the 2006 Act came into force. It should be remembered that, in addition to the general duties, the 2006 Act imposes many administrative duties on directors, such as the duty to file accounts.

The seven general statutory duties are as follows:

- the duty to act within powers (Section 171)
- the duty to promote the success of the company (Section 172)
- the duty to exercise independent judgment (Section 173)
- the duty to exercise reasonable care, skill and diligence (Section 174)
- the duty to avoid conflicts of interest (Section 175)
- the duty not to accept benefits from third parties (Section 176)
- the duty to declare an interest in a proposed transaction or arrangement (Section 177).

More than one of the general duties may apply in any given case.

The duty to act within powers

Section 171 states that a director of a company must:

(a) act in accordance with the company's constitution, and

(b) only exercise powers for the purposes for which they are conferred.

Before the 2006 Act came into force, this duty would have been regarded as two separate duties. The meaning of a company's constitution was set out in the previous chapter. However, in this context the company's constitution also includes unanimous informal decisions taken by the company members, even if these concern a matter which would not have needed to be passed as a special resolution.

The duty to promote the success of the company

Section 172(1) states that:

A director of a company must act in the way he considers, in good faith, would be most likely to promote the success of the company for the benefit of its members as a whole, and in doing so have regard (amongst other matters) to:

(a) the likely consequences of any decision in the long term

(b) the interests of the company's employees

(c) the need to foster the company's business relationships with suppliers, customers and others

(d) the impact of the company's operations on the community and the environment

(e) the desirability of the company maintaining a reputation for high standards of business conduct, and

(f) the need to act fairly as between members of the company.

This section is intended to promote the concept of 'enlightened shareholder value'. The directors are expected to act in good faith to promote the success of the company. As long as they do this they will not become liable merely because a decision turns out to have been a bad one. However, this section needs to be read in conjunction with s. 174, which imposes a duty to exercise reasonable care, skill and diligence.

The duty to exercise independent judgment

Section 173 provides that:

(1) A director of a company must exercise independent judgment.

(2) This duty is not infringed by his acting

(a) in accordance with an agreement duly entered into by the company that restricts the future exercise of discretion by its directors, or

(b) in a way authorised by the company's constitution.

The constitution of the company may allow a director to delegate some of his duties. Alternatively, an agreement with the company may prevent the director from acting in a certain way. These matters aside, s. 173 requires a director to exercise independent judgement and not merely to obey instructions from other people, such as fellow directors.

The duty to exercise reasonable care, skill and diligence

Section 174 states that:

(1) A director of a company must exercise reasonable care, skill and diligence.

(2) This means the care, skill and diligence that would be exercised by a reasonably diligent person with

(a) the general knowledge, skill and experience that may reasonably be expected of a person carrying out the functions carried out by the director in relation to the company, and

(b) the general knowledge, skill and experience that the director has.

A director must exercise the standard of care, skill and diligence which could objectively be expected of a director, but if he has any extra skill, knowledge or experience this will raise the standard expected of him.

The duty to avoid conflicts of interest

Section 175 sets out the duty to avoid a conflict between a director's own interests and those of the company. It states that:

(1) A director of a company must avoid a situation in which he has, or can have, a direct or indirect interest that conflicts, or possibly may conflict, with the interests of the company.

(2) This applies in particular to the exploitation of any property, information or opportunity (and it is immaterial whether the company could take advantage of the property, information or opportunity).

Section 175(3) provides that this duty does not apply to a conflict of interest which arises in relation to a transaction or arrangement with the company. This is because s. 177 deals with this situation.

Section 175(4) provides that this duty is not breached if the conflict has been authorised by the directors. In a private company such authorisation is allowed if nothing in the constitution prevents it. In a public company the constitution must positively allow for the authorisation. As regards both public and private companies, s. 175(6) provides that the director in question does not count towards the quorum of the meeting which gives authorisation. Nor can that director's vote count in favour of authorisation.

A person who ceases to be a director continues to be subject to the duty to avoid a conflict of interest as regards the exploitation of any property, information or opportunity of which he became aware at a time when he was a director.

The duty not to accept benefits from third parties

Section 176(1) provides that:

A director of a company must not accept a benefit from a third party conferred by reason of

(a) his being a director, or
(b) his doing (or not doing) anything as director.

However, s. 176(4) provides that this duty is not breached if the acceptance of the benefit cannot reasonably be regarded as likely to give rise to a conflict of interest.

Whereas s. 175 is primarily concerned with a director using company property to his own advantage, s. 176 is concerned with a director receiving a benefit from a person other than the company. Section 176 will overlap with s. 175 where a director receives a benefit, such as a bribe, as an inducement to bring about a conflict of interest.

A person who ceases to be a director continues to be subject to the duty not to accept benefits from third parties as regards things done or omitted by him before he ceased to be a director.

The duty to declare an interest in a proposed transaction or arrangement

Section 177(1) provides that:

If a director of a company is in any way, directly or indirectly, interested in a proposed transaction or arrangement with the company, he must declare the nature and extent of that interest to the other directors.

Section 182(1), considered below, requires a director to declare an interest in any **existing** transaction with the company. Criminal liability is imposed if the section is not complied with. Section 177 by contrast is a general duty, imposing civil liability, which requires a director to declare any interest in a **proposed** transaction with the company. If a declaration made under s. 177 is, or becomes, incomplete or inaccurate a further declaration has to be made.

There are four situations in which a director does not need to declare a conflict of interest. First, where he is not aware of the interest or transaction in question. However, the director is treated as being aware of matters of which he ought reasonably to be aware. Second, in relation to matters which cannot reasonably be regarded as likely to give rise to a conflict of interest. Third, if the other directors are, or ought reasonably to be, aware of the interest. So there is no duty to disclose where a company has only one director. Fourth, if the interest concerns the director's service contract and this has been approved by the directors.

Civil consequences of breach of one of the general duties

The remedy for a breach of s. 174 is damages. The other general duties are fiduciary. The possible remedies for breach of one of the fiduciary duties would include damages, avoiding a contract, the restitution of property, an order to account for profits or an injunction.

The director's duties will generally be enforceable only by the company. This means by the board of directors or by the members in general meeting. However, an individual member might be able to bring a statutory derivative claim on behalf of the company. Derivative claims are considered later in this chapter.

Declaration of interest in existing transaction or arrangement

Section 182 sets out a further duty of a director to declare to the other directors any interest in a transaction with a company. It is not regarded as one of the general duties, as it imposes criminal liability. If the duty is breached the director will have breached a fiduciary duty and so the company will be able to avoid the contract.

This duty is similar to the s. 177 duty. However, it applies when the transaction or arrangement is already existing. If a declaration has been made under s. 177, then a further declaration does not need to be made under s. 182.

If a company has only one director, then s. 182 is generally inapplicable. However, s. 231 applies where a single-member company makes a contract with the sole member if he is also a director and the contract is not entered into in the ordinary course of the company's business. It requires the contract to be in writing, in a written memorandum, or recorded in the minutes of the next directors' meeting. Failure to comply with this section is also a criminal offence but does not invalidate the contract.

Transactions with directors requiring approval of members

The following four types of transactions with directors must be approved by the members:

(1) long-term service contracts;

(2) substantial property transactions;

(3) loans to directors; and

(4) payments of over £200 for loss of office.

Failure to gain the members' approval will have civil consequences but will not cause a criminal offence to have been committed.

Protecting directors from liability

The company's constitution might contain provisions which protect directors from liability. Alternatively, the members might ratify wrongful acts of directors.

Section 180(4)(a) allows the members of the company (not the directors) to authorise any breach of duty which is yet to be committed, including a conflict of interest. This authorisation may be given specifically or generally but is subject to common law rules. Section 180(4)(b) provides that the general duty to avoid a conflict of interest is not breached by anything done or not done by the directors in accordance with the company's articles.

Section 232(1) provides that any provision that purports to exempt a director of a company (to any extent) from any liability that would otherwise attach to him in connection with any negligence, default, breach of duty or breach of trust in relation to the company is void. However, s. 239 retains the common law right of the members to pass an ordinary resolution saying that the company is ratifying such conduct if it has already occurred. The director in question, and any person associated with him, cannot vote on the resolution (s. 239(4)). However, the director can count towards the quorum of any meeting and can speak at the meeting. An ordinary resolution of the members is all that is required unless the company's articles require a higher majority or unanimity.

Under the common law, some types of acts can be ratified by ordinary resolution, some by special resolution and some cannot be ratified at all. Generally the position is that if the directors do exceed their powers or use them irregularly or negligently, the shareholders may still ratify their acts at a general meeting, as long as the directors did not act fraudulently, illegally or in bad faith.

 Bamford v Bamford (1970) (Court of Appeal)

The company was in danger of being taken over. To avoid this the directors issued an extra 500,000 shares to a business which distributed the company's products. This might have been contrary to the company's articles. This point was never decided. The shareholders approved the issue of the shares by passing an ordinary resolution at a general meeting.

Held Even if the directors had irregularly exercised their powers, the ratification by the shareholders made the contract a good one, and absolved the directors from all liability.

Harman LJ declared: *'Directors can, by making a full and frank disclosure and calling together the general body of the shareholders, obtain . . . forgiveness of their sins; and . . . everything will go on as if it had been done right from the beginning. I cannot believe that this is not a commonplace of company law. It is done every day. Of course, if the majority of the general meeting will not forgive and approve, the directors must pay for it.'*

A director will not be liable to the company for the acts of other co-directors if he or she did not know of the act and should not have suspected it. This is because directors do not employ each other and are not each other's agents.

If directors are liable together, they are jointly and severally liable. This means that a single director who is sued can be ordered to pay all of the damages which the directors who are jointly and severally liable owe. However, the director who pays will be entitled to a contribution from the other directors.

Relief from the court

Section 1157 allows the court to grant relief to a director (or company secretary or auditor) in breach of his duty if the director 'acted honestly and reasonably and ought fairly to be excused'.

Disqualification of directors

In certain circumstances a person will be disqualified from directing or managing a company. A person who is disqualified automatically ceases to hold office as a director.

First, it is a criminal offence for an undischarged bankrupt to be concerned in the management of a company, without permission from the court which made the bankruptcy order. So bankrupts are disqualified.

A separate matter is that a person may be made the subject of a disqualification order, made under the Company Directors Disqualification Act 1986. A person who has been disqualified may not take part in the management of a company, or promote a company, or act as an insolvency practitioner. Not only is it a criminal offence to ignore such an order, but a person who does ignore it can be made personally liable for all debts and liabilities incurred while acting in contravention.

Disqualification orders may be made on the following grounds:

- conviction of serious offences in connection with a company;
- persistently not sending documents which have to be filed with the Registrar of Companies;
- fraud or breach of duty committed while an officer of a company which has become insolvent;
- conduct in relation to an insolvent company which makes a person unfit to be concerned with the management of a company;
- if the Trade Secretary concludes from an inspector's report that a person's conduct makes him unfit to be concerned in the management of a company, or that a disqualification order should be made in the public interest;
- if the person has been held by a court to be responsible to contribute to the assets of a liquidated company on the grounds of either fraudulent or wrongful trading, both of which are considered at the end of this chapter.

A register of disqualification orders is kept at Companies House and members of the public may inspect this free of charge.

The register of directors

Section 162(1) of the Act requires every company to keep a register of its directors. The register must give the following information about each director who is an individual:

- his full name and any former name;
- a service address, that is to say an address at which documents may be effectively served on him;
- the country or state (or part of the UK, England, Scotland, etc.) in which he is usually resident;
- his nationality;
- his business occupation (if any); and
- his date of birth.

Section 163(5) allows the service address to be stated to be 'The company's registered office'. However, the company must also keep a register of directors' residential addresses.

The register of directors must be kept available for inspection at the company's registered office or at another place notified to the Registrar of Companies. The members of the company are entitled to inspect the register of directors free of charge. Non-members are entitled to inspect it upon payment of a small fee. The Registrar of Companies must be informed of any change in the register within 14 days.

Section 240 provides that a director's residential address is 'protected information', even after he has left the company. Section 241 prevents the company from using or disclosing this protected information unless it does so for one of three purposes:

(1) communicating with the director in question; or

(2) sending required particulars to the Registrar of Companies; or

(3) complying with a court order.

However, the protected information can be used or disclosed in other circumstances if the director in question consents.

Control of the company

The directors have the power to manage the company while they hold office. However, the long-term control of the company lies in the hands of the company members. The members exercise this power by passing resolutions at company meetings. As we have seen, a company's directors can always be removed by an ordinary resolution of which special notice has been given.

Types of shares

A company's articles may allow for the creation of different types of shares, with each class enjoying different rights. If there is only one class of share, then each share will carry the same right to vote. However, different classes of shares might carry different voting rights. For example, in **Holt *v* Holt (1986)** a company had 999 class B shares, which carried 1 vote per share, and 1 class A share, which carried 10,000 votes.

Generally, ordinary shares will carry the right to vote at company meetings, the right to a dividend if one is declared and the right to share in the company's surplus assets if the company is wound up. (The surplus assets would consist of any money left once all of the company's property had been sold and all of its debts paid.) Members with these ordinary shares are known as ordinary members. The dividend paid to any ordinary member is paid as a certain amount per share held. For example, a company which has ordinary shares with a nominal value of £1 might declare a dividend of 5p per share. (We saw in the previous chapter that the nominal value of a share represents the face value which the company has agreed that the share should have.)

The paid-up share capital of a company is the total amount of the nominal share value which has been actually paid by the members. The called-up share capital consists of the paid-up share capital and additional amounts which have become due to be paid towards the nominal value by the members. A public company cannot return capital to the members, because the creditors of the company are entitled to expect that the capital will be available to pay them, unless it has been lost in the course of the company's business. A private company can reduce its capital if it passes a special resolution and adheres to statutory procedures.

Preference shares

The most common type of shares which are not ordinary shares are preference shares. The term 'preference share' is not strictly defined and any rights might possibly attach to preference shares. The articles of association will spell out the rights attaching. However, in general preference shares have the following characteristics. The dividend paid to preference shareholders is usually expressed as a certain rate per annum. For example, the articles might state that the preference shares are to receive interest at 8 per cent per annum. A shareholder with 1,000 £1 preference shares would therefore receive a yearly dividend of £80, if a dividend is declared. Preference shareholders, like ordinary shareholders, have no right to a dividend. However, if a dividend is not paid to preference shareholders in any particular year, then all dividends not paid must be paid before ordinary shareholders can receive any dividend. Unless it is agreed otherwise, preference shares will carry the same right to vote as ordinary shares. However, it is often agreed in the articles that preference shares carry no right to vote. When a company is wound up the nominal value of the preference shares is usually repaid in full before that of the ordinary shares is repaid at all. This is an advantage where the company is insolvent, as preference shareholders are more likely to get their capital returned. However, it is a disadvantage where a company is wound up with large surplus assets. As the preference shares are repaid at face value, the preference shareholders will have no right to share in these assets.

> **Example**
>
> X Co Ltd has two classes of shares: 1,000 preference shares and 1,000 ordinary shares. Both types of shares have a nominal value of £1. X Co Ltd is wound up. After all costs of winding up and outside creditors have been paid, the realised assets amount to £800. Each preference share will be repaid at 80p in the pound. The ordinary shareholders will not be repaid any of their capital. If the surplus assets had amounted to £101,000, the preference shareholders would have had their capital repaid and would therefore have received £1 per share. The ordinary shareholders would have shared in the surplus assets, each ordinary shareholder receiving £1,000 per share.

Some companies issue non-voting shares. These shares carry no right to vote at company meetings, but do allow the shareholders to receive a dividend, if one is declared, and to share in surplus assets when the company is wound up.

Company meetings

Company resolutions are passed by the company members either at company meetings or, in the case of private companies only, by means of a written resolution.

A public company must hold an **annual general meeting** (AGM) within six months of the end of its financial year. A private company is not required to hold an AGM but may nevertheless choose to do so.

The AGM of a public company gives the company members the chance to question the way in which the company is being run. The directors would set the agenda for the AGM, and typically this would include laying the accounts before the members, the appointment of the auditors and the presentation of the directors' report. The directors' report is significant because it reports upon the general position of the company and because it sets out what dividend, if any, the directors are recommending. Shareholders invest money in a commercial company because they expect a dividend to be paid. This dividend can be paid only out of company profits. It can also be paid only if the directors recommend that it should be paid. The directors might instead recommend that profits be retained in the company. Generally, the articles of most companies provide that the members would have no power to increase the dividend which the directors recommend. They can approve the dividend recommended or reduce it. If the members are unhappy with the dividend recommended, they might consider removing the directors at a future meeting.

Section 302 provides that the directors have the power to call a general meeting of the company. Generally, it will be the directors who do call meetings. However, the members may require the directors to call a general meeting of the company under s. 303. Section 303(2) provides that the directors are required to call a general meeting once they have received requests to do so from members holding at least 10 per cent of paid-up shares which carry voting rights. As regards private companies only, this figure is reduced to 5 per cent. The members' request, which can be made electronically, must state the general nature of the business to be dealt with at the meeting and may include the text of a resolution to be proposed and voted upon at the meeting.

If the directors are required to hold a meeting under s. 303, then s. 304 requires them to call the meeting within 21 days of receiving the request. The meeting must actually be held within 28 days of the notice convening the meeting. If the request for the meeting contained a proposed resolution, notice of the meeting must contain notice of the resolution.

If the directors are requested under s. 303 to call a meeting, but do not do so in accordance with s. 304, then s. 305 allows the members who requested the meeting, or any of them holding at least half of the relevant voting rights, to call a meeting at the company's expense.

Conduct of meetings

A member who does not attend a meeting can ask a proxy to attend and vote instead. The proxy does not need to be a company member. A meeting must have a quorum (set minimum number) of members. In all but single-member companies the quorum will be set at two members, unless the articles provide otherwise. This means that if only one member turns up to the meeting it will be inquorate and therefore invalid. Proxies do count towards a quorum. A meeting needs to be quorate only at its commencement. Once the meeting has begun the number present may fall below the quorum. There must be a chairman to preside over the meeting. The chairman's job is to ensure that the meeting follows the procedure set out in the agenda. Often the articles, like the model articles for both public and private companies, give the chairman the casting vote if the votes of the members are tied.

Voting

Usually a vote is taken by a show of hands. Each member has one vote, regardless of how many shares he or she holds. However, any member has the right to demand a poll. If this is done, each voting share will carry the voting rights conferred on it by the articles. Generally, matters which are not contentious are voted on by a show of hands. When a matter is contentious some members are likely to insist on a poll. A member can insist on a poll either before the vote on a show of hands or when the outcome of the vote on a show of hands is declared.

Example

Ace Ltd has one class of shares, each share carrying one vote. X holds 55 of these shares, Y holds 30 and Z holds 15. An ordinary resolution is proposed at the AGM of Ace Ltd. On a show of hands X votes in favour of the resolution. Y and Z vote against it. X was outvoted on the show of hands, but can demand a poll where all of the shares will carry one vote each. X then outvotes Y and Z by 55 votes to 45 and so the resolution is passed.

Notice of meetings

At least 14 days' notice must be given of a company meeting unless the meeting is the AGM of a public company, in which case at least 21 days' notice must be given. Notice of a general meeting may be given in hard copy, electronically or by means of a website, or by a combination of these methods. The company's articles might require longer periods of notice. The members can require a shorter period of notice but this must be agreed by a majority of at least 90 per cent if the company is private and of at least 95 per cent if it is a public company.

The written notice of a meeting must explain the nature of any business which is not ordinary business, as well as the date, the place and the time of the meeting. If a special resolution is proposed, the text of the resolution must be specified in full. Minutes of company meetings must be kept and must be available for inspection by members.

Resolutions

As we have seen, it is the directors who manage a company. But to appoint directors, or remove them, or to do other acts which can be done only by the members themselves, a resolution must be passed at a company meeting.

Resolutions may be ordinary or special. Table 11.1 shows the differences between the two types of resolutions.

Table 11.1 Company resolutions

	Ordinary resolutions	Special resolutions
Proposed by	The directors. Members holding 5 per cent of eligible shares if resolution is to be moved at AGM of plc. Members holding 5 per cent of eligible shares if it is a written resolution.	The directors. Members holding 5 per cent of eligible shares if resolution is to be moved at AGM of plc. Members holding 5 per cent of eligible shares if it is a written resolution.
Can be written?	Only if co. is private.	Only if co. is private.
Majority needed	If at meeting, over 50 per cent of voting shares cast. If written, must be signed by members representing over 50 per cent of voting rights.	If at meeting, at least 75 per cent of voting shares cast. If written, must be signed by members representing at least 75 per cent of voting rights.
Formalities required	Minutes kept. No need to register.	Minutes kept. Must be registered with Registrar of Companies within 15 days.
Type of business	To remove directors. (Special notice of 28 days required if done under s. 168.) To resolve not to sue directors for breach of duty. To appoint auditors. Any business for which special resolution not required.	To alter unentrenched articles. To alter company name. To change from public co. to private, or vice versa. To petition for winding up of the company. To require directors to take or not to take some action. (If model articles for public or private companies are adopted.)
Notice requirements if moved at a meeting	14 days, unless moved at AGM of plc when 21 days. 28 days if to remove a director under s. 168.	14 days, unless moved at AGM of plc when 21 days.

Resolutions at company meetings

It is envisaged by the 2006 Act that private companies will generally pass resolutions as written resolutions. However, private companies may choose to hold company meetings to vote on resolutions. Public companies cannot pass written resolutions. They can pass resolutions only at company meetings.

Generally, the directors propose resolutions to be moved at company meetings. However, s. 338 allows the members of a public company to propose a resolution to be moved at the AGM and to require the directors to give notice of the resolution to all company members. The directors must do this either if members holding at least 5 per cent of the total voting rights request it, or if at least 100 members holding voting shares, which have an average sum paid up of £100 each, request it. The expenses of complying with this are paid for by the company, as long as the members requested the circulation of the resolution before the end of the company's previous financial year.

We have already seen that s. 303 gives members of any type of company, if they hold at least 5 per cent of the voting shares, the power to require the directors to hold a general meeting. We also saw that when requesting this meeting the members can include the text of a resolution to be proposed and voted upon at the meeting.

Section 314 provides that the members of any type of company may require the company to circulate a statement of not more than 1,000 words with respect to a matter referred to in a proposed resolution to be dealt with at a company meeting, or with respect to other business to be dealt with at a company meeting. This statement must be circulated to all members entitled to receive notice of the meeting. The company is required to circulate a statement either if members holding at least 5 per cent of the total voting rights request it, or if at least 100 members holding voting shares, which have an average sum paid up of £100 each, request it. The request may be in hard copy or in electronic form and must be received by the company at least one week before the meeting to which it relates.

Section 316 provides that the expenses of the company in complying with s. 315 do not need to be paid for by the members who requested the circulation if the meeting in question is the AGM of a public company and the request is given to the company before the end of the company's previous financial year. Otherwise, the expenses must be paid by the members who made the request, unless the company passes a resolution excusing them.

Written resolutions

Written resolutions may be passed only by *private companies*. Both ordinary and special resolutions can be passed as written resolutions. However, as we have seen, a written resolution cannot be used to remove a director under s. 168 of the 2006 Act. On a written resolution, each share carries one vote and members cast their votes by signing the resolution. A written ordinary resolution is passed if it is signed by members representing over 50 per cent of the shares entitled to vote. A special resolution is passed if it is signed by members representing 75 per cent of the shares entitled to vote.

Written resolutions are generally proposed by the directors. When the directors propose a resolution as a written resolution, s. 291(2) requires the company to send a copy of the resolution to every eligible member. A single copy, or several copies, of the resolution might be sent around for the members to sign. Alternatively, copies can be sent electronically or by means of a website. So an email could be sent from member to member.

Section 292(1) allows the members of a private company who hold at least 5 per cent of the voting shares to require the company to circulate a written resolution, along with a statement of not more than 1,000 words on the subject matter of the resolution. A lower percentage can be specified in the company's articles. Section 294 provides that the expenses of the company in complying with the request must be paid by the members who requested the circulation of the resolution, unless the company passes a resolution to excuse them. In addition, the company can demand a deposit of a reasonable sum to meet these expenses, unless the company resolves otherwise. If this deposit is not paid, the company has no obligation to circulate the resolution.

The company's articles might specify the time period within which a proposed written resolution must be passed. If the articles do not do this, a proposed written resolution will lapse after 28 days, beginning with the date on which it was circulated.

Unanimous informal consent

Unanimous consent of the members can be substituted for ordinary resolutions and for some types of special resolutions. In **Re Duomatic Ltd (1969)** Buckley J said: 'where it can be shown that all shareholders who have a right to attend and vote at a general meeting of the company assent to some matter which a general meeting of the company could carry into effect, that assent is as binding as a resolution in general meeting would be.' However, unanimous consent could not be used to dismiss a director or auditor before the end of his term of office because the director or auditor would have the right to address the meeting at which his dismissal was proposed.

The position of minority shareholders

The voting shareholders control a company. A shareholder with more than 50 per cent of the voting shares can pass an ordinary resolution and could therefore elect and remove the directors of the company. A shareholder with at least 75 per cent of the shares can pass a special resolution. Similarly, shareholders who between them can muster over 50 per cent, or at least 75 per cent, can exercise the different types of control.

These percentages can be vitally important when a person is considering investing in a company. Let us look at an example. If Bill invites Alan to form a company with him, and Alan takes 49 per cent of the shares while Bill takes 51 per cent, then their ownership of the company is almost equal. However, their control of the company is very far from equal, and Alan should be very wary about accepting such a proposition. Alan would at least have some degree of 'negative control,' in the sense that he could block a special resolution. If Alan was offered only 25 per cent of the shares, he would have very little control, although he could at least prevent an entrenched article from being altered.

If two shareholders each have 50 per cent of the shares, then they will both have negative control. Neither will be able to force through any resolution without the consent of the other. This might sound an ideal way to run a company owned by two people, and while the shareholders get on with each other it probably is. However, if complete deadlock is reached, then the court may well wind the company up (if either party so requests) on the grounds that this is just and equitable.

The position of minority shareholders is not improved by the rule in **Foss v Harbottle (1843)**. This states that if a wrong is done to a company, then only the company has the right to take action in respect of that wrong. It also states that a court will not interfere with the internal management of a company while the company is acting within its powers.

The case itself illustrates the problems which this can cause for minority shareholders.

 Foss v Harbottle (1843)

Two members of a company sued five directors who had sold land to the company for more than it was worth.

Held The shareholders had no right to sue. If the directors had wronged the company, then only the company could sue in respect of that wrong. (The company was most unlikely to do this because it was controlled by the very directors who had cheated it!)

The rule in **Foss v Harbottle** is a logical extension of **Salomon v Salomon and Co Ltd**. That case decided that a company is a separate legal person. It follows that if a company is wronged it alone has the power to sue.

The rule has the advantage of preventing multiple actions. If every shareholder in every company was able to sue for any perceived wrong to the company, then there would be an enormous number of potential court cases. However, the rule could obviously be very unfair to minority shareholders, and now both the courts and statute offer protection to the minority.

Statutory protection of minority shareholders

Statutory derivative claims

Section 260(1) of the 2006 Act has introduced a new derivative claim. Such a claim is brought by a member of the company on behalf of the company in respect of a right to sue which the company has. So any remedy which is ordered will be a remedy in favour of the company.

Section 261(1) provides that a member of a company who brings a derivative claim must apply to the court for permission to continue it. At this stage the defendant takes no part in the proceedings. The court must dismiss the application if it appears to the court that the application, and the evidence filed by the claimant in support of it, do not disclose a *prima facie* case for giving permission. On hearing the application, s. 261(4) gives the court three options:

(1) to give permission for the claim to be continued on such terms as it thinks fit;

(2) to refuse permission and dismiss the claim; or

(3) to adjourn the proceedings and give such directions as it thinks fit.

So if the court does not dismiss the claim, it has considerable power to impose requirements on either side.

Section 260(2) and (3) provide that a derivative claim may be brought only in respect of two matters. First, in respect of negligence, default, breach of duty or breach of trust by a director of the company. Second, in pursuance of a court order in proceedings under s. 994 for protection for relief from 'unfair prejudice'. (Unfair prejudice is considered in the section below.) The first category is the more important and would allow a claim to be brought whenever a director breached any of the general statutory duties set out ss. 171–177. A person who becomes a member of a company will be able to bring a claim in respect of acts which the directors have already committed.

Section 262(3) allows a member of a company to apply to the court for permission to continue a claim brought by the company as a derivative claim. This section is necessary because otherwise directors in breach of duty might cause the company to bring a claim with the intention that the claim could later be abandoned or deliberately made unsuccessful.

The court *must* refuse permission to continue a derivative claim brought in respect of a director's breach of duty in two circumstances:

(1) if a person acting in accordance with section 172 (duty to promote the success of the company) would not seek to continue the claim; or

(2) the members of the company have voted to authorise or ratify the act or omission complained of. (Earlier in this chapter we saw that the members can pass an ordinary resolution authorising any breach of duty which is yet to be committed, including a conflict of interest. We also saw that s. 239 allows the members to pass an ordinary resolution which ratifies a breach of duty by a director, but that the director in question cannot vote on the resolution.)

Section 263(3) lists six matters which the court should take into account in particular in considering whether to give permission to continue a derivative claim brought in respect of a director's breach of duty. These matters are:

(1) whether the member is acting in good faith in seeking to continue the claim;

(2) the importance that a person acting in accordance with s. 172 (the duty to promote the success of the company) would attach to continuing the claim;

(3) where the cause of action results from an act or omission that is yet to occur, whether the act or omission could be, and in the circumstances would be likely to be, either authorised by the company before it occurs or ratified by the company after it has occurred;

(4) where the cause of action arises from an act or omission that has already occurred, whether the act or omission could be, and in the circumstances would be likely to be, ratified by the company;

(5) whether the company has decided not to pursue the claim; and

(6) whether the act or omission in respect of which the claim is brought gives rise to a cause of action that the member could pursue in his own right rather than on behalf of the company.

Section 263(4) provides that the court should have particular regard to the views of members of the company who have no personal interest, direct or indirect, in the matter.

Section 264 allows a second member to continue a derivative claim originally brought by another member.

Lewison J in **Iesini v Westrip Holdings Ltd (2009)** considered some of the factors which a director acting in accordance with s. 172 would take into account in deciding whether or not to continue a claim. He said:

> They include: the size of the claim; the strength of the claim; the cost of the proceedings; the company's ability to fund the proceedings; the ability of the potential defendants to satisfy a judgment; the impact on the company if it lost the claim and had to pay not only its own costs but the defendant's as well; any disruption to the company's activities while the claim is pursued; whether the prosecution of the claim would damage the company in other ways (e.g. by losing the services of a valuable employee or alienating a key supplier or customer) and so on. The weighing of all these considerations is essentially a commercial decision, which the court is ill-equipped to take, except in a clear case.

This statement has subsequently been approved by several courts.

Section 994 of the Companies Act 2006

Any member may petition the court on the grounds that the affairs of the company are being, or have been, or will be, conducted in a manner which is **unfairly prejudicial** to the members generally or to particular members.

If the court agrees that the conduct is unfairly prejudicial, it can make any order it sees fit. In particular it may:

● order the company to behave in a certain way in the future;

● require the company to do or not to do certain acts;

● authorise a person to sue in the company name on behalf of the company;

● order the company not to alter its articles without the court's permission;

● order the company, or certain members of the company, to buy the shares of any members.

Re HR Harmer Ltd (1958) (Court of Appeal)

Harmer had a successful business dealing in postage stamps. He formed a company to take the business over. His two sons were, like him, life directors. Harmer retained voting control of the company although his sons held most of the shares. When Harmer was 88 his sons asked the court for relief on the grounds that he completely ignored their wishes, running the company as if he still owned all of it. He had made bad business decisions, employed private detectives to watch the staff and countermanded resolutions passed by the board.

Held The court ordered that Harmer should be made president of the company for life (without any special powers) and be paid a salary. They also ordered him not to interfere in the company's business otherwise than in accordance with the valid decisions of the board of directors.

In **O'Neill *v* Phillips (1999)** Lord Hoffmann gave the only judgment of the House of Lords and considered unfair prejudice in considerable detail. He made the following points:

(1) Although fairness was the criterion on which relief under s. 994 might be granted, and although the court has a wide power to do whatever it considers just and equitable, the concept must be applied rationally and upon judicial principles.

(2) In deciding what is fair, the context and background will be extremely important.

(3) Generally, members will be bound by the articles, as these were the terms on which they agreed that the company's affairs should be conducted. However, equitable principles might make it unfair to rely strictly on the articles in a way which equity would regard as contrary to good faith.

(4) The way in which equitable principles are applied is reasonably well settled. These should not be abandoned in favour of some uncertain notion of fairness.

(5) Conduct can be unfair under s. 994 even if it would not be sufficient to wind the company up.

(6) In deciding whether conduct is unfair, it should be asked whether the exercise of the power complained of is contrary to what the parties agreed, either by words or conduct.

(7) In quasi-partnership companies what was agreed will usually be found in the understandings between the members when they entered into association. Promises exchanged in quasi-partnership companies should be binding as a matter of equity even if they are not binding as a matter of law.

(8) Breaching a promise or undertaking is not the only ground on which unfair prejudice may be founded. An analogy could be made with frustration of a contract (see Chapter 5). The majority might use their powers in a way which the minority can reasonably say that they did not agree to. This might allow winding up of the company or it might afford a remedy for unfair prejudice.

(9) The majority must not use their powers, in breach of equitable considerations, when the articles do not contain the fundamental expectations of the shareholders. For example, if members have entered the company on the understanding that they have all put in capital and will all manage the company, equitable considerations would require that

this agreement would be honoured or that a member would be able to withdraw from the company on reasonable terms. A minority shareholder expectation will not give rise to a right to petition merely because the shareholder reasonably and legitimately thought something likely to happen. In fairness or equity the minority shareholder must have a right to expect the thing to happen.

(10) There would be no unfair prejudice if the majority offered to buy the minority's shares at a reasonable price. This price should not be at a discount on account of the shareholding being a minority shareholding, it should amount to the value of the equivalent proportion of the share capital. (In special circumstances a discounted valuation might be appropriate.) An independent expert should usually make this valuation. Both sides should have access to all company information which would affect the value of the shares.

(11) The majority shareholders should be given a reasonable time in which to make the offer to buy out the minority.

In **Re Guidezone Ltd (2000)** Parker J said that **O'Neill v Phillips** had established that: 'unfairness [for the purposes of s. 994] is not to be judged by reference to subjective notions of fairness, but rather by testing whether, applying established equitable principles, the majority has acted, or is proposing to act, in a manner which equity would regard as contrary to good faith.' This statement has since received considerable judicial approval.

The Insolvency Act 1986

A court can wind a company up under ss. 122–124 of the Insolvency Act 1986 on the grounds that it is just and equitable to do so. Even a single shareholder can petition the court to do this.

Protection from the courts

The courts will protect a minority shareholder in three situations: fraud on the minority; if the personal rights of a member have been infringed; or as regards an act which is *ultra vires*.

Fraud on the minority

At common law, minority shareholders who have been defrauded by a decision of the majority have the right to have the decision overturned. Since the coming into force of the Companies Act 2006, there is no longer much need for an action for fraud on the minority. First, in cases in which the company itself was defrauded, usually by transferring the company's assets to the directors, an aggrieved shareholder could now bring a derivative claim. Second, in cases in which the controlling shareholders and directors defrauded only the minority shareholders, and then passed a resolution to ratify this decision, s. 239(4) will allow the ratification to be effective only if it could be achieved without the votes of the director in question. Nor can this provision be evaded by the board of directors voting to ratify the matter at a board meeting rather than at a company meeting. Section 175(5) will allow the board of directors to approve a director's conflict of interest only if the vote to approve can be passed without the votes of the errant directors. It is still possible that the minority could be defrauded despite these safeguards, particularly because s. 184(4) allows the members of a company to authorise a breach of duty in advance, with no rule that any members are barred from voting on the resolution. So directors who were also majority shareholders could vote in advance to authorise a breach of duty by themselves. However, the common law does not allow ratification or authorisation of any misappropriation of company property, and the rules on unfair prejudice might also provide protection.

Where the personal rights of a member have been infringed

In the previous chapter we saw an example of a court holding that a member's personal rights had been infringed in **Pender v Lushington**. It might be remembered that the company chairman refused to accept the votes of Pender's shares, as the articles required him to do, and the court held that this was a breach of Pender's rights as a member. However, this is not a true exception to the rule in **Foss v Harbottle**. A member whose rights have been infringed will have a contractual right to sue on account of the articles forming a contract between himself and the company and between himself and the other members.

Actions which are *ultra vires*

Any member of a company has the right to prevent the company from entering into an *ultra vires* transaction, that is to say a transaction which is outside the company's objects clause. But if the transaction has already been concluded a member has no power to undo it. The members will not have the power to prevent the company entering into an *ultra vires* transaction if the transaction has been approved by special resolution.

The company secretary

Every public company must have a company secretary, who might also be one of the directors. Private companies do not need to have a company secretary but might choose to have one. The company secretary of a plc must be suitably qualified (generally, as a lawyer or an accountant). The company secretary of a private company does not need to hold any qualifications.

The secretary's duties are to look after the administration of the company. This would include matters such as keeping the company registers up to date, sending information to the Registrar of Companies, arranging meetings, sending notice of meetings and resolutions to members and keeping up to date with legislation which affects the company.

The company secretary has a limited power to make contracts which bind the company, but only as regards the type of administrative contracts which a company secretary could be expected to make.

 Panorama Developments (Guildford) Ltd *v* Fidelis Furnishing Fabrics Ltd (1971) (Court of Appeal)

A company secretary hired cars in the company name. It appeared to the hirers that the cars were being used to meet the customers of the company. In fact the secretary was using the cars for his own purposes. The hirers sued the company for the hire charges.

Held The company was liable. The secretary had been held out as having authority to hire the cars on behalf of the company and so he had apparent authority to do so.

Section 275(1) requires every company to keep a register of its secretaries at its registered office or at a place specified in regulations under s. 1136. The register must give the following details of the company secretary: his full name, any former name and his address. The address required to be stated is a service address and can be 'The company's registered office'. If the company secretary is changed, notification must be sent to the Registrar within 14 days, along with signed consent by the new secretary appointed. If the details on the register change, the Registrar must be informed within 14 days. Members can inspect the register of directors and secretaries free of charge, and non-members can be charged a small fee. If the register is not open to inspection, the company and its officers may be fined and the court may order immediate inspection to be allowed.

Company registers

A company is obliged to keep the following registers at its registered office. Most of these registers can be inspected by members of the public, although some can only be inspected by company members.

- The register of directors and the register of secretaries. (For details, see elsewhere in the chapter.)
- The register of members. This register must give the names and addresses of all the members, the dates on which they became or ceased to be a member, the number of shares held and the amount paid up on each share. If the company is a single-member company the register of members must state this, as well as giving the name and address of the member.
- The register of directors' interests. This lists any interest which the directors, or their immediate family, have in the company's shares or debentures.
- A register of charges. (Charges are explained later in the chapter.)
- A copy of every contract under which a public company bought its own shares within the last ten years.
- A public company must keep a register of people who hold more than a specified number of the voting rights of its shares.

Annual return

Section 854 requires every company to submit an annual return to Companies House. This gives basic information about the company on a particular date, its return date, every year. A company which fails to submit an annual return within 28 days of the return date commits a criminal offence.

The following information must be given in the annual return.

- The address of the company's registered office.
- The type of company and its principal business activities.
- The names of the directors; their service addresses; their countries of residence; their nationalities; their usual business occupations; and their dates of birth.
- The name and address of the company secretary, if the company has one. The address can be a service address.
- If either the register of members or the register of debenture holders is not kept at the company's registered office, the address of the place where these registers are kept.
- A statement of share capital. This must give the total number of shares in the company; the aggregate nominal value of those shares; and the amounts paid up and unpaid on each share.
- Details of every member of the company or of every person who has ceased to be a member since the previous annual return was submitted.

- The number of shares of each class held by each member.
- The number of shares of each class transferred by each member or former member since the previous annual return was submitted, and the dates of transfer.

A £30 annual fee is charged for registration of the annual return. This fee is reduced to £15 if the return is filed electronically. The Registrar operates a shuttle system. This involves sending the company the information contained in the previous year's annual return and asking that changes are notified, or that the company indicates that no changes have been made. The return must be signed by a director or the company secretary. The annual return can be inspected at Companies House without this fact being revealed to the company.

Accounts and accounting records

Companies are under a duty to keep accounting records, and to prepare annual accounts.

Accounting records

Section 386 of the Act requires every company to keep accounting records for inspection by the officers of the company. These are not the same as the accounts, but are the documents which enable the accounts to be prepared, e.g. ledger, order forms, cash books, receipts, etc. They must show with reasonable accuracy the financial position of the company at any particular moment.

The annual accounts

A company's accounts consist of a balance sheet, a profit and loss account, the director's report and the auditor's report.

Every company will have an accounting reference period and an accounting reference date. The period from one accounting reference date to the next makes up the company's financial year and is its accounting reference period.

Section 415 requires the directors to prepare a **directors' report** for each financial year. This should contain a fair view of the development of the company's business and of the company's position at the end of the financial year. If the directors are recommending a dividend this must be stated in the report. The directors' report is therefore of considerable interest to shareholders. Either the company secretary or any director may sign the directors' report, but it must be approved by the board of directors.

The **profit and loss account** shows the income and expenses of the company over the financial year. If the income exceeds the expenditure, the company will have made a profit; if it is less than the expenditure, the company will have made a loss. Capital profits, which arise when the company sells a fixed asset such as land, are generally included as an exceptional item.

The **balance sheet** shows the assets and liabilities of the company on a particular date. The *auditor's report* must certify that in the auditor's opinion the books give a true and fair reflection of the company's financial position and have been properly prepared in accordance with the Companies Act 2006.

A copy of the annual accounts must be sent to every member of the company, whether the company is public or private. The directors of a public company must lay the annual accounts before a general meeting of the members. The annual accounts must also be registered with the Registrar of Companies. Public companies have six months from their accounting reference date in which to do this, and private companies have nine months.

Abbreviated accounts

Small and medium-sized companies can submit abbreviated accounts to the Registrar, although full accounts will still have to be delivered to the members. (For the definition of small and medium-sized companies see Chapter 10.) Outsiders examining small company abbreviated accounts would not be able to see how much the directors were paid, or the amount paid to the auditors, or the amount of the dividend recommended.

Medium-sized companies can file 'modified' accounts. These are full accounts except that certain matters can be omitted.

The auditor

Except as regards very small companies, companies will generally need to employ an accountant to prepare the accounts which must be given to members of the company and submitted to Companies House. The accountant will be appointed by the directors of the company. The auditor is not the company accountant, but a different accountant who keeps an eye on the company's accounts and accounting procedures. The auditor is appointed by the members of the company and reports to the members.

The need to have an auditor

Companies which are not small or dormant must have an auditor. A company is dormant in a period during which no significant accounting transaction occurs.

The auditor is neither a manager nor an employee of the company. Unlike the directors and the secretary, the auditor is an independent contractor.

Appointment and leaving office

Officers and employees of the company are prohibited from being appointed as the company auditor. With a few minor exceptions, a person can be appointed as an auditor only if he is a chartered or certified accountant.

The first auditor of a company is appointed by the directors. Subsequent auditors are appointed by ordinary resolution of the company members. In private companies the auditor can be automatically reappointed without a resolution of the members. However, members holding at least 5 per cent of voting shares can prevent automatic reappointment. In public companies the auditor must be appointed before the end of the general meeting at which the accounts are considered. The auditors appointed at the meeting then hold office until the next such meeting.

An auditor can be removed from office at any time. This can be achieved by an ordinary resolution of which special (28 days') notice has been given. The auditor must be given a copy of the resolution, and has the right to compel the company to circulate written representations of reasonable length to all the members entitled to vote at the meeting. The auditor also has a right to speak to the meeting. A written resolution cannot therefore be used to dismiss an auditor. If an auditor is removed, the Registrar of Companies must be informed within 14 days.

An auditor can resign by delivering written notice of the fact to the company's registered office. To be effective, the resignation notice must either contain a statement that there are no circumstances connected with the resignation which ought to be brought to the attention of the members of the company or the creditors, or state what those circumstances are.

Auditor's duties

The auditor has two duties: to audit the accounts and to prepare an auditor's report. Auditing of the accounts involves carrying out a series of checks and tests to see that they are fair and accurate. In the auditor's report the auditor must certify that in his opinion the books give a true and fair reflection of the company's financial position and have been properly prepared in accordance with the Companies Act 2006.

Lopes LJ described the care and skill required of an auditor in **Re Kingston Cotton Mill Co (No. 2) (1896)**:

> An auditor is not bound to be a detective, or, as was said, to approach his work with suspicion or with a foregone conclusion that there is something wrong. He is a watch-dog, but not a bloodhound. He is justified in believing tried servants of the company in whom confidence is placed by the company. He is entitled to assume that they are honest, and to rely upon their representations, provided he takes reasonable care. If there is anything calculated to excite suspicion he should probe it to the bottom; but in the absence of anything of that kind he is only bound to be reasonably cautious and careful.

The auditor owes his duty of care and skill to the company and to the membership as whole. However, the duty is not owed to members of the public nor to individual members of the company.

 Caparo Industries plc v Dickman (1990) (House of Lords)

The claimants owned shares in F plc. After receiving the audited accounts of F plc, the claimants bought more shares in the company and later made a successful take-over bid for the company. Later they sued the auditors of F plc because the accounts had shown a pre-tax profit of £1.2 million and the claimants alleged that it should have shown a loss of £0.4 million. The claimants alleged that the auditors had owed them a duty of care, which they had breached.

Held The auditors owed no duty of care to the claimants.

Liability limitation agreements

Section 534 allows for liability limitation agreements between companies and their auditors. Such an agreement would limit the amount of a liability owed to a company by its auditor in respect of any negligence, default, breach of duty or breach of trust, occurring in the course of the audit of accounts, of which the auditor may be guilty in relation to the company. The agreement, which can be in respect of only one financial year at a time, must be authorised by an ordinary resolution of the company members.

Section 537(1) limits the effect of a liability limitation agreement by providing that the auditor's liability cannot be limited to less than such amount as is fair and reasonable in all the circumstances, having particular regard to the auditor's responsibilities, the nature and purpose of the auditor's contractual obligations to the company, and the professional standards expected of him.

Figure 11.1 shows, in very broad terms, the essential roles of the board of directors, the shareholders, the company secretary and the auditors.

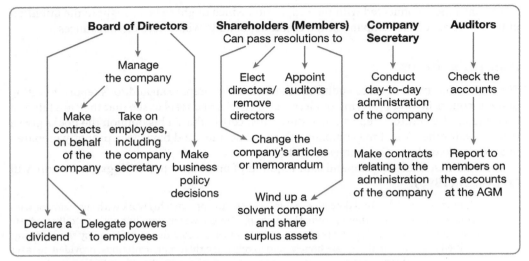

Figure 11.1 What is their role?

Loans to the company

It is possible that the members of the company will contribute all the capital which the company needs. However, most companies also borrow money, either as a loan or by buying goods on credit.

A **debenture** is a document issued by the company which acknowledges that the company owes a debt. It will state the date on which the debt is to be repaid and the rate of interest which is payable. Debenture holders are not members of the company; they are creditors of the company. Debenture holders will want security for their debts in the form of a company charge.

A company can give security to any creditor by granting a charge over some or all of the company's assets. If the debt is not repaid, the lender will be able to sell the charged assets and take what is owed. Companies can give two types of charges: fixed charges and floating charges.

Fixed charges

A company can provide security for a loan by granting a fixed charge on certain assets. In effect this means that it mortgages those assets to the creditor. Consequently, the company will not be able to dispose of, or change the nature of, the property charged without the permission of the charge holder.

For example, Dash Ltd wants to borrow £400,000 from the bank. The bank lends the money but takes a fixed charge on the company's factory. As long as the company is repaying the loan as agreed, it will retain possession of the factory and can use it in the ordinary way. The company cannot, however, sell the factory without the bank's permission. Furthermore, if the company fails to repay the debt, the bank can sell the factory and deduct what it is owed from the proceeds of sale.

Floating charges

A company may grant more than one fixed charge on any particular asset.

Let us assume that a few years ago Runner Ltd borrowed £90,000 from the bank and granted a fixed charge over the company factory, currently worth £2,000,000. If the company now wanted to borrow a further £60,000 from a different creditor, then that creditor would be quite happy to register a second fixed charge on the company factory. If the company does not repay its debts, then the factory could be sold by the creditors. The bank would be entitled to its £90,000 first because it was the first charge registered. But the sale of the factory would easily realise enough to repay the second charge holder.

If, however, there were no assets on which a fixed charge could be secured, the creditor might be prepared to accept a floating charge. This means that the creditor would take a class of, or all of, the company's property, both present and future assets, as security.

A floating charge does not attach to any particular items of property until it crystallises, because it is recognised that the class of assets charged will change from time to time in the ordinary course of the company's business. It is also recognised that a floating charge does not prevent the company from selling the assets over which it is granted. It is particularly useful then when a company has a good deal of money tied up in raw materials, stock in trade or book debts. A book debt is a debt owing to the company.

> **Example**
>
> Let us assume that Speedy Ltd, which manufactures televisions, has already granted a fixed charge over all those assets, such as its factory, which it does not need to sell. Let us further assume that the company has a warehouse stocked with televisions ready for sale, that it is owed money by various creditors and that it has a large stock of materials with which it makes the televisions. None of these remaining assets could be the subject of a fixed charge without crippling the company's activities. The company would not be able to sell the televisions already manufactured, or work the raw materials into televisions, without the permission of the fixed charge holder. If such permission was granted, the charge holders would then lose their security.
>
> But the finished televisions, the money owed and the raw materials are worth a great deal. A creditor might well therefore take a floating charge over these assets, secure in the knowledge that if the company did not repay him he could recoup his loan by calling in the charge, selling the assets charged, and deducting what he was owed from the proceeds.
>
> If more than one floating charge is issued, the charges take priority in the order in which they were created. Like a fixed charge, a floating charge must be registered with the Registrar of Companies.

Crystallisation of floating charges

A company can continue to sell assets over which a floating charge has been granted up until the time of 'crystallisation'. So in the example just considered, Speedy Ltd could still sell the finished televisions, even though they were the subject of a floating charge. But when crystallisation occurs, the floating charge will become a fixed charge attaching to the assets of the company charged at that time. This, of course, will mean that the company is no longer free to dispose of the assets.

Crystallisation occurs automatically:

- when a receiver is appointed;
- when the company goes into liquidation;
- when the company ceases to carry on business; or
- on the occurrence of an event which the contract stipulated would lead to automatic crystallisation.

Crystallisation may also occur when the debenture holder gives notice that he is converting the floating charge into a fixed charge. This can only be done if the contract which created the charge allows for it. If the assets which were the subject of the charge are sold after crystallisation, then the charge holder can recover them from the party to whom they were sold.

Registration of charges

Section 860(1) requires companies to register charges with the Registrar of Companies within 21 days of their creation. This registration is necessary so that others who might wish to do business with the company can see what charges exist over the company's property. If a charge is not registered it will be invalid, although the creditor will still be able to sue as an unsecured creditor.

Priority of charges

As regards properly registered charges, the order of priority is as follows.

(1) A fixed charge has immediate effect from the moment it was created. It ranks higher than existing floating charges unless the floating charge expressly prohibits the creation of another charge over the same property and the person taking the later fixed charge knew that this was the case. (Registration is not enough on its own to amount to actual notice of the prohibition.)

(2) Floating charges attach to property only from the moment of crystallisation.

(3) Floating charges generally rank amongst themselves in order of priority of creation. This is not the case where the contract creating the first floating charge provides that a later floating charge may have priority.

Winding up of companies

The legal personality of a company is ended by a process known as liquidation or winding up. The terms mean the same thing. After the company is wound up it will cease to exist. A liquidation may either be ordered by the court or brought about by the members of the company. A liquidation ordered by the court is called a compulsory liquidation. A liquidation brought about by the members is known as a voluntary liquidation.

Liquidation by court order

A court can order the compulsory liquidation of a company on several grounds. The two most important grounds are that the company cannot pay its debts, or that it would be just and equitable to wind the company up.

A company will be regarded as unable to pay its debts if it does not satisfy a court judgment in favour of a creditor. For example, if Alec is awarded damages of £2,000 against X Ltd, the company will be regarded as unable to pay its debts if it does not pay the £2,000 damages to Alec. A company is also regarded as unable to pay its debts if a creditor who is owed more than £750 serves a written demand for payment at the company's registered office and is not paid within three weeks. For example, if X Ltd owed Billy £800 and Billy served a written demand for payment at X Ltd's registered office, X Ltd would be regarded as unable to pay its debts if it did not pay Billy within three weeks.

Even if a court is satisfied that a company cannot pay its debts, it does not have to wind the company up. If the majority of the company's creditors think that the best thing would be to let the company keep trading, then the court can allow this. Once a court makes a winding up order the liquidator takes over the directors' powers. The employees of the company are regarded as dismissed unless the liquidator decides to re-employ them until the winding up is finished.

A court can order the liquidation of a company on the grounds that it would be just and equitable to wind the company up. Over the years the courts have used this power to wind companies up for reasons such as that there is deadlock in the management of a small company, or that there is a justifiable lack of confidence in the management or that the company was formed for a fraudulent purpose.

Voluntary liquidation

A voluntary liquidation takes place without a court order. A members' voluntary liquidation can be made only while the company is solvent. The members of the company might decide that they would like to end the company, and then share the money generated by the sale of any assets which remained after all creditors had been paid. In order to start a member's voluntary liquidation the members must pass a special resolution that the company be wound up. A liquidator will be needed to wind the company up, but the company members choose who the liquidator should be. A member's voluntary liquidation is only possible if the directors of the company can make a declaration of solvency. This declaration states that the company will be able to pay all of its debts within a period which may not be longer than 12 months.

If no declaration of solvency can be made, the company members might start a creditors' voluntary liquidation. In order to do this the members would need to pass a special resolution. A meeting of all creditors would then be called and the creditors would have the choice of who the liquidator should be.

When either type of voluntary winding up is made, the company must cease trading as soon as the special resolution is passed, except as so far as may be required to bring about a beneficial winding up. The liquidator will take over the directors' powers. Employees would be dismissed unless the liquidator decided to re-employ them.

As regards any type of winding up, the order in which the company's creditors are paid is the same. First, those with a fixed charge over any of the company's property can sell that property and take what they are owed. Any remaining money goes into the pool of assets. Then the liquidator sells all the company's assets for as much as possible and gathers in all money owing to the company. The assets gained in this way are now distributed in the following order:

(1) the liquidator's remuneration and the costs and expenses of winding up;

(2) the preferential creditors at the time of winding up; (There are several types of preferential creditors. The most important categories are wages (up to £800 per employee) and holiday pay owing to employees, loans made specifically to pay employee's wages and contributions to occupational pension schemes. If director's fees are due under a contract of employment, they will be preferential up to the £800 limit.)

(3) floating charges created before 15 September 2003;

(4) top-sliced assets for distribution to the unsecured creditors (see immediately below);

(5) floating charges created on or after 15 September 2003;

(6) the unsecured creditors;

(7) sums due to members but not yet paid: for example, dividends declared but not yet paid;

(8) the members of the company, as set out in the articles of association.

If there are not enough assets to pay each class of creditors in full then each member of the relevant class is paid the same percentage of the money owing to them.

Top slicing

The charge holders will be paid what they are owed, if enough money is generated, after the costs of realising these assets have been paid. If the assets are sold for more than the amount of the charge, any surplus goes into the general pool of assets. However, as regards floating charges created after 15 September 2003, 'top-slicing' applies. This means that the liquidator must set aside a certain percentage of the assets which would otherwise be payable to floating charge holders, so that this amount can be paid to the unsecured creditors. The amount which must be set aside for the unsecured creditors is 50 per cent if the company's net property does not exceed £10,000 in value. If the company's net property exceeds £10,000, then the amount to be set aside is 50 per cent of the first £10,000, then 20 per cent of the remainder, the fund having a ceiling of £600,000. However, if the value of the company's net property is less than £10,000, the liquidator does not have to distribute the funds to the unsecured creditors if he considers that this would be disproportionate to the costs of doing so.

Liability arising from insolvency

In general, a liquidator will not be able to claim assets which do not belong to the company or which are not owed to the company. However, there are certain exceptions to this principle, which are considered below.

Wrongful trading

Section 214 of the Insolvency Act allows a liquidator to apply to the court to declare that a person who is, or has been, a director should be liable to make such contribution to the company's assets as the court thinks proper. The court may declare a person liable to make a contribution if:

- the company has gone into liquidation; and
- at some time before the commencement of the winding up of the company, that person knew or should have known that there was no reasonable prospect that the company would avoid going into insolvent liquidation; and
- that person was a director or shadow director of the company at that time.

However, a person will not be liable for wrongful trading if the court is satisfied that he took every step which he ought to have taken to minimise the potential loss to the company's creditors.

Fraudulent trading

Section 213 of the Insolvency Act 1986 provides that if it appears to a liquidator that any business of the company has been carried on with the intention of defrauding creditors, or for any fraudulent purpose, the person who acted fraudulently should make such contributions to the company's assets as the court thinks proper. In addition, a disqualification order could be made under s. 10 of the Company Directors Disqualification Act 1986. In order to be liable under s. 213, a person must have deliberately been dishonest by the standards of ordinary business people.

Transactions at undervalue and preferences

Section 238 of the Insolvency Act 1986 provides that where the company has gone into liquidation, the liquidator may apply to the court to set aside the transaction and claim back the assets if the company has, within two years of the onset of insolvency, entered into a transaction with any person at an undervalue. The section is intended to prevent the defrauding of creditors and members by giving away the company's assets, or selling them too cheaply, prior to liquidation.

Section 239 of the Insolvency Act allows the court, upon an application by a liquidator, to make an order where the company has given a preference to a creditor. A company gives a preference to a creditor if it does anything which has the effect of putting the creditor into a position which, in the event of the company going into insolvent liquidation, will be better than the position he would have been in if the thing had not been done: for example, paying one creditor in full shortly before going into liquidation with massive debts. Another example would be paying personal debts to themselves or their relatives whilst not paying other creditors.

Administration

Administration is a measure short of liquidation under which the administrator, who must be a qualified insolvency practitioner, attempts to rescue an ailing company. So administration may well not lead to the winding up of the company. In recent years several professional football clubs have gone into administration but have escaped liquidation.

The administrator must perform his functions in the interests of the company's creditors as a whole and has three hierarchical objects. First, to rescue the company as a going concern (the primary purpose). Second, to achieve a better result for the company's creditors than would be achieved if the company was wound up. Third, to sell property to make a distribution to one or more secured or preferential creditors.

A court will appoint an administrator only if it is satisfied that the company cannot pay its debts. A floating charge holder can appoint an administrator, but only if his charge or charges relate to substantially the whole of the company's property. The company or the directors can appoint an administrator.

Administration lasts for one year unless a court order extends it or unless the creditors agree to extend it. Once a company is in administration any petition to wind the company up will either be dismissed or suspended until the period of administration is over. No steps can be taken to enforce a charge without the consent of the administrator or the permission of the court. All business documents (invoices, orders for goods or services and business letters) issued by or on behalf of the company must state the name of the administrator and that he is managing the company's affairs. All creditors must be informed that the administrator has been appointed.

The administrator may do anything necessary or expedient for the management of the affairs, business and property of the company, including removing or appointing directors. He takes control of all the property to which he thinks the company is entitled and may pay off creditors. He can sell off property which is subject to a floating charge but the charge holder gets the same priority in respect of any property then acquired. In effect, this reverses the crystallisation of the charge. By court order he can sell off property subject to a fixed charge, but only if the charge holder has made available to him the net proceeds of sale and any other sum which the court thinks would bring the amount up to the market value of the charged property.

Company voluntary arrangement (CVA)

The directors of an insolvent company can propose a scheme of arrangement to be supervised by an insolvency practitioner. Under such an arrangement, which must be agreed by a three-quarters majority of the company's unsecured creditors, all unsecured creditors are paid a proportion of their debts over a period of time. This can be done even if the company is in liquidation or administration.

Meetings of all company creditors and all members must be called. These meetings can approve the proposal or a modification of it. However, the meetings cannot deprive a floating charge holder of the right to enforce his security without that creditor's approval. Nor can the priority of preferential debts be changed without the approval of the preferential creditors who would be affected. If a proposal is approved at the meetings, notice must be given to all the members and creditors who were invited to the meetings and to the court. All members and creditors are then bound by the agreement. If the meetings come to different results, the meeting of the creditors prevails. However, any member then has 28 days to apply to the court to have the decision of the creditors' meeting changed or overruled.

Within 28 days of receiving notice of the proposal, any creditor or member can apply to the court to have the proposal set aside on the grounds that it unfairly prejudices the interests of a creditor or member, or that there was a material irregularity at the meeting. The court then has the power to approve, revoke or suspend the approval and to direct that revised proposals be put to another meeting.

Voluntary arrangement is an insolvency procedure but not a liquidation procedure. It is generally hoped that the company can survive it. Individuals may enter into a similar procedure, known as an individual voluntary arrangement or IVA.

Essential points

Directors

- The board of directors of a company have all the power to manage the company.
- The members of a company have the power to elect the directors, but do not have the power to manage the company.
- A director of a company can always be removed by an ordinary resolution of the members, of which special notice has been given.
- Directors have seven statutory general duties.

Shares, meetings and resolutions

- Companies may issue different classes of shares, with different rights attaching to the various classes.
- A public company must hold an annual general meeting (AGM) of the members within six months of the end of its financial year.
- At company meetings, ordinary resolutions are passed by a simple majority of members who vote; special resolutions are passed by a 75 per cent majority of those who vote.
- A private company may pass any type of resolution as a written resolution, without the need to hold a company meeting.

Protection of minority shareholders

- A member alleging breach of director's duties or unfair prejudice can bring a derivative claim on the company's behalf.
- A member can petition the court for relief from unfair prejudice.
- A member can petition the court to wind the company up under the Insolvency Act 1986.
- The courts will protect a minority shareholder in three situations: fraud on the minority; if the personal rights of a member have been infringed; or as regards an act which is *ultra vires*.

The company secretary

- Every plc must have a company secretary. Private companies may choose to have one.
- The company secretary deals with the administration of the company and can make contracts which bind the company, as long as the contracts were concerned with the administration of the company.

Winding up of companies

- When a company is wound up (or liquidated) it will cease to exist.
- If a company cannot pay its debts (which has a technical meaning) the court may order that it be compulsorily wound up.
- The company members may themselves wind the company up. A special resolution will be needed to do this.
- When a company is wound up the assets of the company are gathered in and then distributed in a certain order.

Practice questions

1 Consider the following case.

 Regal (Hastings) Ltd *v* Gulliver (1942) (House of Lords)

Regal Ltd owned a cinema. It wanted to acquire two more cinemas so that it could sell all three as a going concern. A subsidiary company was formed to make the purchase. The sellers of the cinemas would not go ahead with the deal unless the subsidiary company had at least £5,000 paid-up share capital. Regal could only provide £2,000 of the money which the subsidiary needed. The directors of Regal therefore personally subscribed for a further 3,000 £1 shares in the subsidiary. At the conclusion of the whole business the shares in the subsidiary were sold for £3.80 each. Both Regal and its directors had therefore made a handsome profit.

Held The directors had to account to Regal for the profit they had made. It was only because they were directors of Regal that they gained the opportunity to make the profit.

If the case were to come to court today, which of the statutory duties in ss. 171–177 might the directors of Regal have breached? What might the consequences of any breach be?

2 Ace Ltd has three shareholders; Arthur, Cherie and Edward. Each of the shareholders holds 100 ordinary shares. For the past five years Arthur and Cherie have been elected as the company directors. Arthur has been the company secretary for six years. Edward considers that the affairs of the company are not being run as well as they might be. Edward thinks that the company should pass a special resolution to alter the articles to make each of the three shareholders company directors for life. Arthur and Cherie have not commented on this suggestion. Advise Edward of the following matters:

   (a) Whether he can propose a resolution that the articles be altered in the way which he wants.

   (b) The support he would need in order for the resolution to be passed.

   (c) The extent to which he can influence the way in which the company is run.

3 (a) Complete Table 11.2 to show the rights which usually attach to shares and debentures.

   Table 11.2

	Ordinary shareholders	Preference shareholders	Debenture holders
On dissolution, will they own any surplus assets of the company? (yes/no/maybe)			
Entitled to vote at company meetings? (yes/no/maybe)			
Are they paid interest? (yes/no)			
Relative priority of payment on dissolution? (Paid 1st/2nd/3rd)			

   (b) Compare the rights of ordinary shareholders, preference shareholders and debenture holders. Are preference shares more similar to ordinary shares or to debentures?

4 For several years Fred and George were the sole partners in a successful building firm. Ten years ago they formed a limited company. Fred and George were the only two directors. The company had an authorised share capital of 100 £1 ordinary shares, and George and Fred each took fifty of these. Two years ago George's son, Tony, was appointed a director of the company and George and Fred each transferred ten shares to Tony. Last year Fred discovered that the company had sold building materials to another company in which George and Tony are the only shareholders. Fred brought this matter up at a board meeting. Since this time Tony and George have passed two ordinary resolutions. The first removed Fred as a director. The second ratified the sale of the building materials.

   Advise Fred of any rights which he might have.

5 A medium-sized company which manufactures furniture wants to borrow money. To do this it will need to issue debentures.

(a) Over what types of assets might it issue a fixed charge?

(b) Over what type of assets might it issue a floating charge?

(c) Which type of charge would give the lender the greater security?

(d) What precautions should be taken by (i) the manufacturer and (ii) the lender?

6 A friend of yours runs a small company and is in need of capital. The company is prepared to raise the capital by issuing ordinary shares, preference shares or debentures. In which way would you be most willing to contribute if:

(a) You were sure that the company would prove to be extremely successful?

(b) You thought that the company might face severe difficulties?

7 'The rule in **Foss** v **Harbottle** can operate very unfairly against minority shareholders. However, there are many legal safeguards to make sure that this does not happen.' Explain the protection given to minority shareholders to prevent the majority from abusing their positions.

Task 11

Five friends of yours are considering going into business together as painters and decorators. Your friends have asked you to draw up a report, dealing briefly with the following matters.

● How limited companies are controlled and managed.

● The different roles of directors, the company secretary and auditors.

● The powers that can be exercised by a company's shareholders.

● How minority shareholders in a company are protected against abuse by the majority.

● How companies and partnerships are wound up.

mylawchamber

Visit **www.mylawchamber.co.uk/macintyreessentials** to access tools to help you develop and test your knowledge of business law, including interactive multiple choice questions, practice exam questions with guidance, weblinks, glossary, glossary flashcards, legal newsfeed and legal updates.

Use **Case Navigator** to read in full some of the key cases referenced in this chapter with commentary and questions:

Freeman & Lockyer v Buckhurst Park Properties Ltd (1964)

Salomon v Salomon and Co Ltd (1897)

O'Neill v Phillips (1999)

Caparo Industries plc v Dickman (1990)

Regal (Hastings) Ltd v Gulliver (1942)

12

Partnership, limited liability partnership and choice of legal status

In this chapter trading as a partnership and trading as a limited liability partnership (LLP) are considered. These are quite distinct ways of trading, with quite separate legal regimes. People have traded as partners for hundreds of years. The law relating to partnership was codified by the Partnership Act 1890 (PA 1890). This Act is still in force and it is backed up by a wealth of case law. The Limited Liability Partnerships Act 2000 introduced the concept of the LLP, and as yet there is little case law to expand the Act. However, as LLPs combine many of the features of both partnerships and companies, some case law on companies and partnerships may be applicable to LLPs.

At the end of the chapter the advantages and disadvantages of trading as either a company, a partnership or an LLP are considered.

Partnership

Definition of a partnership

Partnership is defined by s. 1(1) of the Partnership Act 1890, which states:

> Partnership is the relation which subsists between persons carrying on a business in common with a view of profit.

This definition is deceptively complex. It is best understood if broken down into smaller parts.

'Partnership is the relation which subsists between persons . . .'

This opening phrase is revealing. A partnership is not a separate entity with a legal personality of its own, as a company is. A partnership is merely a relationship between persons. Such a relationship gives rise to legal rights and liabilities, but it does not create a new legal person. Although a company cannot be a partnership, a company can be a partner in a partnership.

'Business'

'Business' is defined by s. 45 of the Partnership Act as including 'every trade, occupation or profession'.

Mann v D'Arcy (1968) held that even if the business is only to make one deal (in this case to buy and sell 350 tons of potatoes), this can be enough to create a partnership.

'In common'

'In common' means not only that all of the partners carry on the business, but also that the business is carried on for the benefit of all of them. Most partnerships employ workers. These employees are not partners. They may help to carry the business on, but it is not carried on for their benefit.

Many firms have so-called 'salaried partners', who may or may not in fact be partners. It is impossible to say, as a matter of law, whether or not a salaried partner really is a partner in a firm. This will depend upon the substance of the relationship, rather than the label attached to it. A partner in a firm might take his share of the profits by drawing a salary and this will not prevent him from being a partner. On the other hand, some people who are plainly employees rather than partners are called 'salaried partners'. Even employees who are called 'salaried partners' might become liable to outsiders under s. 14 PA 1890 on account of having been knowingly held out as partners. Despite this liability they would not in fact be partners. Section 14 is considered later in this chapter.

'View of profit'

'View of profit' does not mean that the business must make a profit, but rather that the partners should intend to make a profit. This intention to make a profit distinguishes partnerships from non-profit making members' clubs, such as social clubs.

Despite the statutory definition provided by s. 1(1) of the Partnership Act, it is often difficult to tell whether a business is, or is not, a partnership. Some slight help is provided by s. 1(2) of the Act, which states that a company cannot be a partnership. Section 2(1) says that the sharing of gross takings does not necessarily make the people who share them partners. Section 2(2) tells us that the mere fact that people own property together does not necessarily make them partners, even if they share any profits made from the property. However, s. 2(3) says that if a person receives a share of the profits of a business this is strong evidence, although not conclusive evidence, that he is a partner in the business. So sharing gross takings is not a strong indication of partnership, whereas sharing profits is. Gross takings consist of all the money which a business takes in. Gross profits are made up of any surplus which remains once all the business liabilities have been taken away from gross takings.

In **Khan v Mia (2000)** the House of Lords decided that persons who were intending to trade as a partnership could be partners even before the business actually began to trade. Merely agreeing to be partners was not enough. However, as soon as contracts were made on behalf of the business a partnership was formed even if the business (a restaurant) had not started to trade.

Characteristics of a partnership

The two most important characteristics of a partnership are the unlimited liability of the partners and the power of partners to act as agents of their fellow partners.

Unlimited liability

Partners are not protected by limited liability because a partnership is not a legal person with a legal identity of its own. Every partner is liable for the firm's (partnership's) debts to the full extent of his or her personal wealth.

These concepts of agency and unlimited liability can have extremely serious consequences, as is demonstrated by the classic quotation from James LJ in **Baird's Case (1870)**:

> Ordinary partnerships are by the law assumed to be based on the mutual trust and confidence of each partner in the skill, knowledge and integrity of every other partner. As between the partners and the outside world (whatever may be their private arrangements between themselves), each partner is the unlimited agent of every other in every matter connected with the partnership business . . . A partner who may not have a farthing of capital left may take money or assets of the partnership to

the value of millions, may bind the partnership by contracts to any amount . . . and may even – as has been shewn in many painful instances in this court – involve his innocent partners in unlimited amounts for frauds which he has carefully concealed from them.

It is possible for one or more partners to limit their liability under the Limited Partnerships Act 1907. This act is considered at the end of this chapter. It is of little practical importance because a partner who has limited his liability is not allowed to manage the firm. It should of course be remembered that a limited liability partnership (LLP) is quite different. LLPs are considered later in this chapter.

Agency

Partners are the agents of their fellow partners and of the firm. This means that contracts made by individual partners can become binding on all of the partners. Furthermore, if an individual partner commits a tort, other partners can become liable for this. To understand the way in which one partner can make fellow partners liable, it is best to separate liability in contract from liability in tort.

The firm's liability in contract

Section 5 of the Partnership Act explains the partnership's liability under contracts made by individual partners on behalf of the firm. This section takes the form of one very long sentence, and if it is is read as a whole it can be difficult to understand. However, if the section is broken down into its component parts it becomes relatively straightforward. First, though, it is necessary to reproduce s. 5 in its entirety:

> Every partner is an agent of the firm and his other partners for the purpose of the business of the partnership; and the acts of every partner who does any act for carrying on in the usual way business of the kind carried on by the firm of which he is a member bind the firm and his partners, unless the partner so acting has in fact no authority to act for the firm in the particular matter, and the person with whom he is dealing either knows that he has no authority, or does not know or believe him to be a partner.

Now we break s. 5 down into its component parts.

> Every partner is an agent of the firm and his other partners for the purpose of the business of the partnership . . .

An agent has the power to make contracts on behalf of a third party, his or her principal, as we saw earlier (see Chapter 6). Shop assistants, for example, are agents. They sell goods which belong not to themselves, but to the shop owners for whom they work. Once a contract with a customer has been made it is binding on the shop owner, not on the shop assistant. Similarly, purchasing clerks and salespeople are agents. It is not their own goods which they buy and sell.

So when the opening part of s. 5 states that partners are agents of the firm and of their other partners, this is of enormous significance. It means that, no matter how disastrous a contract one partner makes on behalf of the firm, all fellow partners will be completely bound by the contract. If there are not enough partnership assets to honour the contract, then this liability will extend to each partner personally.

This agency of the partner only applies to contracts made '. . . for carrying on in the usual way business of the kind carried on by the firm of which he is a member . . .'

This is a very important limitation. The firm will not be bound by all contracts made by a partner on behalf of the firm. It will only be bound if the contract appeared to be the type of contract which the firm would usually make in the course of its business, and if the contract appeared to be made in the usual way one would expect such a contract to be made.

For example, if a partner in a firm of accountants ordered office furniture or a new computer for the firm, these contracts would be binding on the firm. If, however, the partner ordered a new yacht for the firm, this contract would not; it is not in the usual way of business for a firm of accountants to order yachts. In **JJ Coughlan Ltd *v* Ruparelia (2003)** a dishonest partner in a solicitor's firm persuaded a third party to give him £500,000 to invest, by promising a return of 6,000 per cent a year. The dishonest partner stole the money and the third party claimed it back from another partner in the firm. The Court of Appeal held that the partner of the dishonest solicitor was not liable under s. 5 because the scheme was so unbelievable that a reasonable third party would have thought that it was not the kind of transaction which was within the usual business of a solicitor.

The final part of s. 5 allows for situations where a partner will not be the agent of the firm, even as regards goods which were ordered in the usual way of the firm's business.

> . . . unless the partner so acting has in fact no authority to act for the firm in the particular matter, and the person with whom he is dealing either knows that he has no authority, or does not know or believe him to be a partner.

It can be seen that there are two requirements here. First, the partner must have had no authority to act for the firm in the way that he did. Second, the person with whom the partner dealt must either have known this, or must have thought that the partner was not in fact a partner in the firm.

For example, let us assume that the partnership deed of firm ABC says that partner C has no authority to buy supplies on the firm's behalf. If C does buy the type of goods which the firm usually needs, on the firm's behalf, the firm will be bound by the contract unless:

- the supplier knows that C has no authority to buy; or
- the supplier does not know or believe C to be a partner in the firm.

Section 7 deals with contracts which are not made in the ordinary course of the firm's business:

> Where one partner pledges the credit of the firm for a purpose apparently not connected with the firm's ordinary course of business, the firm is not bound, unless he is in fact specially authorised by the other partners; but this section does not affect any personal liability incurred by any individual partner.

Again, it is helpful to break this section down. Section 7 begins:

> Where one partner pledges the credit of the firm for a purpose apparently not connected with the firm's ordinary course of business, the firm is not bound . . .

For example, in a firm of accountants, DEF, partner D orders a new snooker table for the firm, saying that the firm would pay for it later. D has therefore pledged the firm's credit because he has arranged for the firm to be given credit. Under s. 7 this contract would not be binding on the firm because it is not in the ordinary course of business for a firm of accountants to need a snooker table. Section 7 continues:

> . . . unless he is in fact specially authorised by the other partners . . .

So the contract to buy the snooker table would be binding on the firm if E and F had authorised D to order it. The final part of s. 7 says:

> . . . but this section does not affect any personal liability incurred by any individual partner.

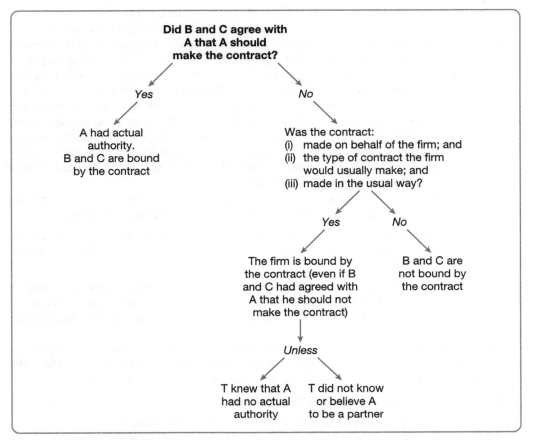

Figure 12.1 The liability of fellow partners (B and C) on a contract which a partner (A) made with T

This merely means that the one who made the contract (in this case D, who ordered the snooker table) will be personally liable whether the other partners are liable or not.

Figure 12.1 gives an outline of the extent to which one partner is liable on a contract made by another partner.

The firm's liability for a partner's torts

Here we consider whether the partnership as a whole is liable if one partner commits a tort. (The nature of a tort was explained in Chapter 8.) Let us assume, for example, that partner G in the firm GHI accidentally crashes his car into a bus, injuring several passengers. Can the injured passengers sue H and I as partners of G? Or are they restricted to suing G alone?

Section 10 provides the answer:

> Where, by any [tort] . . . of any partner acting in the ordinary course of the business of the firm, or with the authority of his co-partners, loss or injury is caused to any person not being a partner in the firm . . . the firm is liable therefore to the same extent as the partner [who committed the tort] . . .

It can be seen that the partnership is only liable for another partner's torts if either:

- the tort was committed in the ordinary course of the firm's business; or
- the other partners authorised the tort.

So a firm of accountants would be liable for a partner who stole money which he or she had been given to invest for a client. Investing money would be in the ordinary course of the firm's business, and stealing money would amount to the tort of conversion. However, the firm would not be liable for a partner who lost his or her temper and battered a client (unless the other partners had authorised the battery!).

If we have another look at the case of partner G, who crashed into the bus, we can now decide whether or not the other partners would be liable. They would be liable if G was driving on the firm's business. So they would be liable if G was going to see one of the firm's clients but would not be liable if G was driving otherwise than on the firm's business. So they would not be liable if G was going home after work or driving to visit friends.

 Dubai Aluminium Co Ltd _v_ Salaam and others (2002) (House of Lords)

A dishonest solicitor committed a tort by setting up fake contracts which defrauded a third party out of $50 million. The dishonest solicitor was acting for other fraudsters. He did not receive any of the $50 million, but was paid his usual fees for his work.

Held The innocent co-partners of the dishonest partner were liable to the third party under s. 10. The fraudulent acts of the dishonest partner were so closely connected with the type of acts which he was meant to do that they could fairly and properly be regarded as having been done in the ordinary course of the firm's business.

Comment In JJ Coughlan Ltd _v_ Ruparelia (2003) it was held that the words 'in the ordinary course of the business' in s. 10 meant the same as the words 'in the usual way of the business carried on' in s. 5. As regards both sections, the question was whether the act of the partner (in making the contract or committing the tort) appeared to be the type of act which the firm would usually make in the course of its business, and if the act appeared to be done in the usual way one would expect such an act to be done.

Liability by 'holding out'

A person 'holds himself out' to be a partner if he leads third parties to believe that he is a partner. If a third party gives credit to the firm as a consequence of a person holding himself out as a partner, then the person who held himself out to be a partner will be liable as if he really was a partner.

Section 14 states that:

Every one who by words spoken or written or by conduct represents himself, or who knowingly suffers (allows) himself to be represented, as a partner in a particular firm, is liable as a partner to anyone who has on the faith of any such representation given credit to the firm . . .

Note that the person can hold himself out as a partner by 'words spoken or written or by conduct'.

If the representation is made by a third party, the person represented as a partner will not be liable unless he 'knowingly suffers himself to be represented as a partner'.

⚖ Tower Cabinet Co Ltd *v* Ingram (1949)

Christmas and Ingram were partners in a firm of furnishers called Merry's. After Ingram's retirement, Christmas ordered goods using old partnership notepaper. This notepaper contained the names of both Ingram and Christmas. Ingram did not know that Christmas had used the notepaper and the supplier of the goods had never dealt with the firm when Ingram was a partner. The suppliers were not paid for their goods. Having sued the firm and won, they claimed the money from Ingram.

Held Ingram was not liable under s. 14 because he had not knowingly allowed himself to be represented as a partner. If he had known that Christmas had used the notepaper, then Ingram would have been liable.

To avoid any possibility of continuing liability, it is prudent for partners who leave a firm to inform existing customers that they have left.

Figure 12.2 gives an outline of the extent to which one partner is liable for a tort committed by another partner.

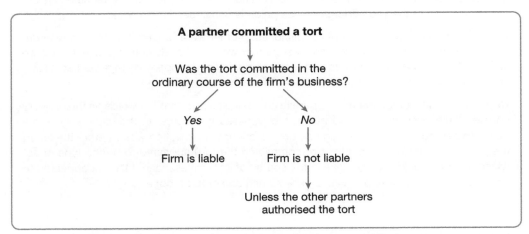

Figure 12.2 The firm's liability for the tort of an individual partner

Partnership agreements

Earlier in this chapter we saw that a partnership is formed merely by the fact of people carrying on a business in common with the intention of making a profit. Partners might or might not enter into a written partnership agreement, usually called a partnership deed.

If a partnership deed is signed by the partners, then this will govern the partners' relationship with each other. The deed will also state the date at which the partnership commenced. Firms carrying on a professional business, such as firms of accountants or solicitors, would almost certainly regulate their relations with a detailed partnership deed. Other firms, such as firms of window cleaners or market traders, might not have a written agreement. This would not prevent them from being partnerships.

The partnership deed

A very simple partnership deed is reproduced on page 348. It should be stressed that such a deed is very brief and is only a model. In its current form it is unlikely to be ideal for many firms. The partners should ensure that changes are made to suit their particular circumstances.

More complicated partnership deeds can run to several thousand words. These deeds cover the same matters as the simple deed in very much more detail. In addition, they might contain articles dealing with matters such as leasing premises, payment of private debts, negative covenants, banking arrangements, retirement provisions, expulsion of partners, provisions for retiring partners, options to purchase the share of outgoing partners, income tax and retirement annuities.

Section 19 provides that the partnership deed can be altered only by unanimous consent of the partners and this consent can be inferred from the conduct of the partners. In **Const *v* Harris (1824)** Lord Eldon gave the following example of how this might happen:

> If in a common partnership, the parties agree that no one of them shall draw or accept a bill of exchange in his own name, without the concurrence of all the others, yet, if they afterwards slide into a habit of permitting one of them to draw or accept bills, without the concurrence of the others, this Court will hold that they have varied the terms of the original agreement in that respect.

Absence of written partnership agreement

If there is no written partnership agreement, then it may be very difficult to state whether or not there is a partnership. Many people who are partners do not realise that they are.

The decision as to whether or not a partnership exists is based on ss. 1 and 2 of the Partnership Act 1890.

As we have seen, s. 1 provides the classic definition of a partnership as: 'the relation which subsists between persons carrying on a business in common with a view of profit'.

Partnership is a contractual relationship. Ultimately, the question is whether those who carried on the business made a contract with each other, expressly or impliedly, that they should carry on a business with each other to try and make a profit. It should be noticed that the question is not whether they made a contract with each other agreeing that they would be partners.

Management of partnerships

Usually, a partnership agreement will state that most disputes between partners can be resolved by a simple vote. If this is the case, then each partner will have one vote and the majority will get their way. Of course, many partnership agreements do not say this; they might state that one partner's vote is to count more than another's, or that certain partners are to have a veto over certain issues.

Implied rules of partnerships

Partners do not need to make any formal agreement. Indeed, those trading as partners may not come to any agreement at all about important matters. Section 24 of the Partnership Act 1890 therefore lays down a number of rules about the management of a partnership. These rules will apply only if no agreement has been made, or if the agreement made does not cover the situation in question; they are therefore known as default provisions. Section 19 provides that the rules in s. 24 can be changed only by the express or implied agreement of all of the partners. The rules contained in s. 24 are as follows.

Model Partnership Deed

This partnership agreement is made on *(date)* ....

between *(name 1)* .... of *(address 1)* ....

and *(name 2)* .... of *(address 2)* ....

and *(name 3)* .... of *(address 3)* ....

It is agreed as follows:

1) The partners shall carry on business in partnership as *(business)* .... under the firm name of *(partnership name)* .... of *(partnership address)* ....

2) The partnership will commence on the date of this agreement and shall continue in existence for five years.

3) The partners shall be entitled to the profits arising from the partnership in equal shares.

4) The bankers of the firm shall be *(name)* .... of *(address)* .... Cheques drawn in the name of the firm must be signed by all of the partners.

5) Each partner shall devote his or her whole time to the business of the partnership.

6) Each partner shall be entitled to *(number)* .... weeks' holiday each year.

7) None of the partners shall without the consent of the other: engage in any business other than partnership business; or employ or dismiss any partnership employee.

8) Each partner shall be entitled to draw *(amount)* .... as salary from the partnership bank account each month.

9) All matters relating to the management of the affairs of the partnership shall be decided by votes taken at a meeting of the partners. At such meetings each partner shall be entitled to one vote and resolutions shall be passed by a simple majority vote.

10) If any disputes should arise as to the meaning of this partnership deed or as to the rights and liabilities of the partners under it, such disputes shall be referred to an arbitrator to be appointed by the President of the Chartered Institute of Arbitrators. The decision of the arbitrator shall be binding on all of the partners.

Signed as a deed by *(name 1)* .... in the presence of *(witness)* ....

Signed as a deed by *(name 2)* .... in the presence of *(witness)* ....
Signed as a deed by *(name 3)* .... in the presence of *(witness)* ....

Capital and profits

Section 24(1) states that all partners are entitled to share equally in the firm's capital and profits and all must contribute equally to losses of capital.

So if A and B go into partnership together and do not agree anything about profits and losses, then they will share these equally, even if they are doing different amounts of work for the firm. In most partnerships profits and losses will not be shared equally because there will be an agreement to the contrary.

Indemnity

Section 24(2) states that if a partner incurs any expense in the ordinary and proper conduct of the firm's business, the firm must indemnify that partner in respect of the liability incurred.

For example, if partner A in firm ABC suddenly has to travel abroad on the firm's business, then the firm must pay the expenses which A incurs.

Interest on capital and advances

Section 24(4) tells us that a partner is not entitled to any interest on capital contributed to the partnership.

But if a partner advances any money beyond the amount of capital he or she agreed to contribute, this is treated as a loan to the partnership. Section 24(3) provides that interest on such loans should be paid at a rate of 5 per cent per annum. It is, of course, quite likely that partnership agreements will make other rules, particularly about the rate of interest.

Management

Section 24(5) provides that every partner may take part in the management of the firm. The partnership deed might, however, state that partners do not have an equal right to manage. If the deed went further and excluded one partner from management altogether, that partner could apply to have the firm wound up on the just and equitable ground (see later in the chapter). Such an exclusion of the right to manage would run contrary to the very definition of a partner as a person who 'carries on a business in common . . .'. We have seen that partners will be liable for the firm's debts. It would not be fair to make them liable if they did not have a right to manage the firm.

Remuneration

Section 24(6) says that no partner is entitled to any salary for taking part in the business of the partnership. It is very common for partnership agreements to provide that partners should be paid salaries. If salaries are paid, this is really just a way of distributing the profits. Salary paid to one partner will obviously reduce the amount of profit available to be shared by the partners.

Admitting a new partner

Section 24(7) provides that unanimous agreement is needed to admit a new partner. However, the partners might give this consent in advance when signing the partnership deed. It is not unusual for a partnership deed to state that a relative of one of the partners may later be introduced as a partner.

Disputes about ordinary matters

Section 24(8) makes two provisions. First, it states that the nature of the partnership business may not be changed without the consent of all of the partners. Second, it states that differences about ordinary matters connected with the partnership business can be resolved by a simple majority.

So a majority of the partners in a firm of car dealers could take the decision to move to new premises. The decision to move into a new type of business, such as selling videos, would have to be unanimous.

Partnership books

Section 24(9) says that the partnership books are to be kept at the firm's place of business, and that every partner may have access to them, when he or she thinks fit, and inspect and copy any of them. A partner may also appoint an agent to inspect the books on his or her behalf.

Expulsion of partners

Section 25 provides that: 'No majority of the partners can expel any partner unless a power to do so has been conferred by express agreement between the partners.'

This express agreement may well be contained in the partnership agreement. It is fairly common for an article in a partnership deed to lay down that a partner can be expelled for breaking the partnership rules. Even if this is the case, the expelling partners must exercise the article in good faith. They cannot use the article to unjustifiably expel a partner. The default provisions in s. 24 can be changed by express or implied agreement between the partners. The provision in s. 25 can be changed only by express agreement. So an agreement to change it could not be implied from the conduct of the partners.

Figure 12.3 shows the effect of ss. 24 and 25.

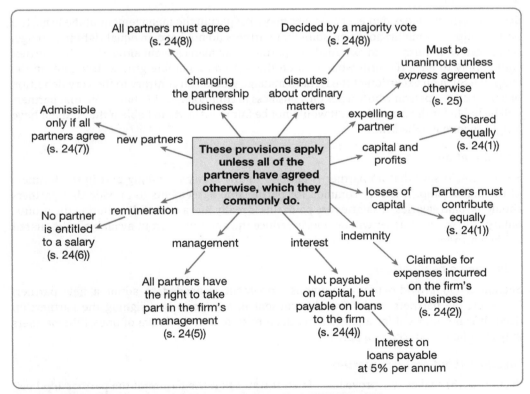

Figure 12.3 The default provisions in sections 24 and 25 PA 1890

Numbers of partners

Until recently, most firms were not allowed to have more than 20 partners. This prohibition has now been lifted, so that there is no upper limit on the number of members a firm may have.

Illegal partnerships

A partnership formed for an illegal purpose will be void. The purpose will be illegal if either statute or the common law prohibits it. So many statutes prohibit so many types of behaviour that it would be pointless to try to list them all. As we earlier (in Chapter 4), the common law makes several different types of contract illegal, including contracts to commit a crime, tort or fraud.

 Everett *v* Williams (1725)

Two highwaymen robbed a coach, intending to share the proceeds. One highwayman sued the other for his share, claiming that he was entitled to this as a partner.

Held No partnership existed as the business carried on was illegal. (Both of the highwaymen were hanged and the claimant's lawyer was fined for bringing the case!)

If a partnership is declared illegal, the courts will refuse to recognise its existence and will not order one partner to pay towards losses suffered by another.

The partnership name

Partnerships do not need to register the names under which they trade. Apart from the prohibition as to using the word 'limited', 'LLP' or 'Ltd.', partners can trade under any name they like, as long as they comply with the Companies Act 2006, and as long as the name is not designed to confuse the public.

The Companies Act 2006

The Companies Act requires partnerships to comply with certain rules if they carry on business in a name other than the surnames of all the partners. If the partners merely add their first names, or their initials, to their surnames they will not be subject to the Act. However, if anything else is added, even the words '& Co.', the name must comply with the Act.

Section 1193 makes it a criminal offence to use names which would suggest a connection with Government or local authorities. The Secretary of State can grant permission for such names to be used. Section 1194 makes it a criminal offence to use 100 or so sensitive words, which are listed in the Companies and Business Names Regulations 1981.

Sections 1202 and 1204 apply where a firm uses a business name. A business name is one which consists of anything other than all of the partners' surnames, or all of their surnames along with their first names or initials. Section 1202 requires firms to display the names of all partners, and an address at which documents can be served, on all business documents. Section 1204 requires firms to display the same information on all business premises to which the customers or suppliers have access. Business documents include all business letters, written orders for goods or services, invoices, receipts and written demands for payment of a debt. However, firms with 20 or more partners do not have to give the names of all the partners on business documents if three conditions are satisfied. First, the firm keeps a list of the names and addresses of all the partners at the firm's main place of business. Second, business documents state the address of the firm's main place of business, and that a list of all the partners' names is open for inspection there. Third, the list is available for inspection during office hours.

If the requirements of ss. 1202 or 1204 are not complied with, a criminal offence is committed and, in some circumstances, contracts made by the firm may be unenforceable by the partners.

Confusion with other names

If a company registers a name which is too similar to that of a partnership, a complaint can be made to the Company Names Adjudicator. (See Chapter 10.)

A **passing off** action can be brought to prevent partners from trading under a name which is likely to cause confusion with another business.

In **Levy v Walker (1879)** James LJ explained the nature of a passing off action:

> . . . it should never be forgotten in these cases that the sole right to restrain anybody from using any name that he likes in the course of any business that he chooses to carry on is a right in the nature of a trade mark, that is to say, a man has a right to say 'you must not use a name whether fictitious or real, you must not use a description, whether true or not, which is intended to represent, or is calculated to represent to the world that your business is my business, and so by a fraudulent misstatement deprive me of the profits of the business which would otherwise come to me'.

 Croft v Day (1843)

A well-known firm of boot polish manufacturers, Day and Martin, carried on business in Holborn. Two people called 'Day' and 'Martin' set up as partners making boot polish with the intention of diverting business from the well-known firm. The established firm applied for an injunction to prevent Day and Martin from trading in boot polish in their real names.

Held The injunction was granted. Although 'Day' and 'Martin' were the real names of the defendants, the intention of the partnership was to deceive the public.

Fiduciary duties

Partners are in a fiduciary position to each other and therefore owe each other fiduciary duties. They cannot agree to generally do away with these duties, although if any particular breach of duty was consented to by the other partners, those partners will not be able to claim in respect of that particular breach. The fiduciary duties are broad and cannot be precisely defined. However, ss. 28–30 of the Partnership Act 1890 spell out three specific duties: that partners must render true accounts and information, that they must account for profits, and that they must not compete with the firm.

Rendering true accounts and information

Section 28 provides: 'Partners are bound to render true accounts and full information of all things affecting the partnership to any partner or his legal representatives.'

Law _v_ Law (1905)

Two brothers, W and J, were partners in a manufacturing business in Halifax. J ran the firm while W lived in London and took little part in the firm's affairs. J bought W out for £21,000, but later W discovered that the business was worth far more than J had led him to believe.

Held The court set aside W's agreement to sell his share of the partnership. J had not put W in possession of all material facts relating to the partnership's assets.

Accounting for profits

Section 29 provides:

> Every partner must account to the firm for any benefit derived by him without the consent of the other partners from any transaction concerning the partnership, or from any use by him of the partnership property name or business connection.

If a partner makes any personal profit as a consequence of his being a partner, he must hand this profit over to the firm.

 Bentley _v_ Craven (1853)

Bentley and Craven were in partnership together in a firm which bought and sold sugar. Craven was the firm's buyer and on account of his business skill was occasionally able to buy sugar at a greatly reduced price. On one occasion he was offered a consignment of sugar at well below the wholesale price. He bought this sugar himself and then sold it to the firm at the going wholesale rate.

Held Craven had to account to the firm for this secret profit. That is to say, he had to pay the profit he had made to the firm. He had used a partnership asset (his position in the firm) to make the profit.

Competing with the firm

Section 30 provides:

> If a partner, without the consent of the other partners, carries on any business of the same nature as and competing with that of the firm, he must account for and pay over to the firm all profits made by him in that business.

This section is similar to s. 29. The difference is that under s. 30 the partner is liable merely as a result of competing with the firm. He or she does not need to use partnership property or assets. Under s. 29, a partner is liable for misusing partnership property or assets. He or she does not need to be competing with the firm.

Note that it is permissible for partners to compete with the firm or use the firm's assets to make a profit as long as the other partners consent to this. In **Bentley _v_ Craven**, one partner, Craven, also carried on a business as a sugar buyer in his own right. This did not breach his duty not to compete with the firm because the other partners knew about it and agreed that he should be able to do this.

Partnership property

When a firm is wound up, the partnership property will be used to pay the debts and liabilities of the firm. Partnership property does not belong to individual partners; it belongs to all of the partners, who hold it on trust for each other. Property is partnership property if:

- it was brought into the firm as partnership property; or
- if it was bought with the firm's money as partnership property; or
- it was acquired for the purposes of the firm and in the usual course of the firm's business.

Partnership property must be distinguished from property belonging to the individual partners for three main reasons. First, if the property increases in value, this increase will belong to the firm rather than to any individual partner. Second, partnership property should be used exclusively for the purposes of the partnership, as defined by the partnership agreement. Third, on dissolution of the firm creditors are first paid out of partnership property.

The goodwill

The goodwill of the firm might be one of the firm's most valuable assets. Accountants might define the goodwill as the excess of the market value of a business over the value of its individual assets. Various legal definitions have been put forward.

In **Trego v Hunt (1896)** Lord McNaughton defined goodwill as:

> the whole advantage, whatever it may be, of the reputation and connection of the firm, which may have been built up by years of honest work or gained by lavish expenditure of money.

In **Hill v Fearis (1905)** Warrington J said that the goodwill was:

> the advantage, whatever it may be, which a person gets by continuing to carry on, and being entitled to represent to the outside world that he is carrying on, a business which has been carried on for some time previously.

Once the goodwill has been sold for the benefit of all of the partners, those partners will not be able to use the firm's name or solicit its customers. There is no reason why they should not otherwise carry on a rival business, unless a valid restraint of trade clause forbids this. (Restraint of trade clauses were considered in Chapter 4.) Lord McNaughton, in **Trego v Hunt** explained the position in this way:

> A person who has sold the goodwill of his business is under no obligation to retire altogether from the field. Trade he undoubtedly may, and in the very same line of business. If he has not bound himself by special stipulation . . . he is free to set up business wherever he chooses. But, then, how far may he go? He may do everything that a stranger to the business, in ordinary course, would be in a position to do. He may set up where he will. He may push his wares as much as he pleases. He may thus interfere with the custom of his neighbour as a stranger and outsider might do; but he must not, I think, avail himself of his special knowledge of the old customers to regain, without consideration, that which he has parted with for value. He must not make his approaches from the vantage ground of his former position. He may not sell the custom and steal away the customers.

Winding up of partnerships

A partnership may be dissolved either by the partners themselves or by the court. A dissolution by the partners themselves might be allowed for by the partnership deed. For example, the deed might state that the firm is to run for a fixed period. If this is the case, the partnership will be dissolved when that period expires or if all the partners agree to dissolve it before the fixed time has expired. If a partnership is not for a fixed time, it is known as a partnership at will, and any partner may dissolve it by giving reasonable notice of an intention to leave the firm. The death or bankruptcy of a partner will also cause the firm to be dissolved. A partnership will be dissolved by the court in several circumstances, the two most important of which are that the firm can only be carried on at a loss, or that the court considers it just and equitable to wind the firm up.

Sometimes, a dissolution of a partnership is little more than a technicality and does not lead to a full-scale winding up. For example, when a partner leaves a large firm of solicitors, the firm is technically dissolved and a set of accounts will need to be drawn up. However, the other partners will generally then carry the business on much as before. When a firm is wound up it is permanently finished. After a winding up, the authority of the partners to bind the firm remains only in so far as this is necessary to effect the most beneficial winding up. The firm's assets will be gathered in, and the goodwill of the firm may well be a valuable asset.

A firm is solvent if it can pay all of its debts. The mere fact that the firm has made a loss, and therefore lost some of the capital contributed by the partners, will not necessarily make the firm insolvent. If the firm is solvent when it is liquidated, payments are made in the following order:

- First, all outsiders will be fully paid what they are owed.
- Second, loans made by partners will be repaid.
- Third, the partners will be repaid the capital which they contributed to the firm. If there is not enough capital to repay all of the partners, the partners must contribute to the lost capital in the same proportion as they were to share profits (unless they had agreed otherwise).
- Finally, any surplus will be paid to the partners in the ratio in which they were to share profits.

Example

Firm RST is wound up. The three partners, R, S and T were to share profits equally. R contributed £30,000 capital, S contributed £20,000 and Z contributed £10,000. (Total £60,000.) The partners made no loans to the firm. If, after all the creditors had been paid, there was a loss of capital of £12,000, each partner would have to contribute to this equally. They would all therefore contribute £4,000. R would therefore receive £26,000 (£30,000 − £4,000); S would receive £16,000 (£20,000 − £4,000); T would receive £6,000 (£10,000 − £4,000.) If after all the creditors had been paid, there was enough to repay all of the capital and £66,000 was left over, each partner would receive £22,000 and full repayment of their capital.

The firm will be insolvent if it does not have enough assets to pay its debts. Section 44(a) of the Partnership Act 1890 provides that losses must be paid first out of profits, next out of capital and lastly, if necessary, by the partners individually in the proportion in which they were to share profits. When a firm is insolvent, it may well be that one or more of the partners remain solvent. If more than one partner is solvent, the solvent partners have to repay the firm's debts in the proportion in which they were going to share profits. If some partners are personally insolvent, and so cannot pay their share, the other partners will take over liability to pay the insolvent partners' share. Partners may be made bankrupt if they cannot pay their share. Creditors of the firm can apply to the court to have a firm wound up.

Example

In firm PQR the three partners, P, Q and R, share profits equally. The firm is wound up and the assets realised amount to £20,000. Outside creditors are owed £95,000. The £20,000 is used to pay the creditors and each partner must personally contribute another £25,000 (because profits were to be shared equally).

   If partner P was insolvent, and could contribute nothing, Q and R would each have to contribute £37,500. If both P and Q were insolvent, and could contribute nothing, R would have to pay all £75,000. If R could not do this, but could contribute only £20,000, the £40,000 raised would be divided amongst the creditors, each creditor being paid the same percentage of what he was owed. Each insolvent partner could be made bankrupt if he had not paid all that he was meant to pay.

Suing a partnership

It is possible to sue a partnership in the firm's name. This is merely a rule of convenience and does not detract from the principle that a partnership has no legal personality of its own. A writ can be served on any of the partners or it can be sent to the firm's principal place of business.

Limited partners

It is not possible for all of the partners in a firm to have limited liability in the same way that all the shareholders in a limited company have limited liability.

   It is, however, possible for one or more of the partners to have limited liability under the Limited Partnerships Act 1907. However, there must always be at least one general partner who has unlimited liability.

   Every limited partnership must register with the Registrar of Companies, giving the following information:

- the firm name; (As regards firms registered on or after 1 October 2009, the name must end with the words 'limited partnership' or the abbreviation 'LP'. Capital letters or lower case letters may be used, or any combination of the two.)
- the general nature of the business;
- the principal place of business;
- the full name of each of the partners;
- the date of commencement and the length of time for which the business is entered into;
- a statement that the partnership is limited, and the description of every limited partner;
- the sum contributed by every limited partner, and whether paid in cash or otherwise.

There must then be two classes of partner in a limited partnership. General partners, who manage the business and have unlimited liability; and limited partners, who contribute a certain amount of capital and are not liable beyond this amount. Limited partners are not allowed to take part in the management of the business and are not agents of the firm. If a limited partner does take part in management, he or she will lose his or her limited liability. In practice, the Limited Partnerships Act is of very little significance.

Limited liability partnerships

Since April 2000, two or more persons have been able to trade together as a limited liability partnership (LLP). An LLP is quite different from an ordinary partnership, being a separate legal entity in its own right.

An LLP can carry on trade in any kind of business. Those who participate in an LLP are known as members of the LLP and not as partners. LLPs have some of the features of an ordinary partnership but are closer to limited companies. The main similarity with a limited company is that an LLP is a corporate body and so, in general, only the LLP itself will be liable for the debts of the LLP. Other similarities with limited companies are that LLPs have perpetual succession, can own property and can make contracts. However, LLPs do not pay corporation tax, as companies do, but rather the members are taxed individually on their share of the profits.

Formation of LLPs

LLPs are incorporated by registration with the Registrar of Companies. The process of incorporation is very similar to the process of incorporating a limited company. There is, however, one main difference in that there must be at least two members of an LLP. It is not possible to have a single person LLP. Once registration is completed a certificate of incorporation is issued.

The rules relating to prohibited names, the places in which a name must be displayed and the way in which the LLP name can be changed are identical to the rules which apply to limited companies.

Members and designated members

LLPs do not have directors and shareholders. Instead they have members and designated members. Being a member of an LLP is similar to being a partner in an ordinary partnership. However, every LLP must always have at least two designated members. The designated members have duties similar to those imposed on the officers (the directors and the secretary) of a limited company. So, for example, they must sign the accounts and the annual return and inform the Registrar of Companies of the names of the designated members.

A register of members and designated members is kept at Companies House. Each year an LLP must submit an annual return, giving basic details about the LLP, and a £30 fee.

Members as agents

Section 6 of the Limited Liability Partnerships Act 2000 is very similar to s. 5 of the Partnership Act 1890 (see earlier in the chapter). Every member is an agent of the LLP and can therefore make contracts on behalf of it. However, the LLP is not bound if the member in fact had no authority to make the particular contract and the third party either knew this or did not believe that the member was a member of the LLP. There are, however, two differences. First, it is the LLP which will be bound by the contract, not each of the members. Second, there is no requirement that the contract should have been the type of contract which the LLP would usually make.

Section 4(4) of the Limited Liability Partnership Act 2000 is similar to s. 10 of the Partnership Act 1890 (see earlier in the chapter). It makes an LLP liable for the torts of its members if these were committed during the course of the business of the LLP or with the authority of the LLP.

Members' relationship with each other

The Limited Liability Partnerships Act 2000 has been expanded by the Limited Liability Partnerships Regulations 2001. Regulation 7 sets out default provisions, which will govern the members' relationship with each other. The members can choose to make their own provisions instead, but if they do not the default provisions will apply.

There are ten default provisions in Regulation 7. The first seven are virtually identical to the first seven provisions made by s. 24 of the Partnership Act 1890. However, it should be noted that the members of an LLP do not have to share in the losses of the LLP, because the LLP is a corporate body with a legal identity of its own. The final three default provisions are very similar to ss. 28–30 of the Partnership Act 1890. (Sections 24, 28, 29 and 30 of the Partnership Act 1890 were considered earlier in this chapter.)

Regulation 8 is virtually identical to s. 25 of the Partnership Act. It states that no majority of members of an LLP can expel a member unless a power to do so has been conferred by express agreement between the members.

Members of an LLP owe a fiduciary duty to the LLP.

Accounts and accounting records

The rules relating to accounts and accounting records are similar to those relating to limited companies (see Chapter 11). The financial boundaries of being a small LLP or a medium-sized one are the same as for small and medium-sized companies. The accounts of LLPs have to be audited, unless the LLP is small enough to be exempt. The auditor is appointed annually by the members of the LLP.

Minority protection

Any member of an LLP can petition the court to wind the LLP up under s. 122 of the Insolvency Act 1986. Any member also has the right to petition the court, claiming unfair prejudice under s. 994 of the Companies Act 2006. Both of these provisions were considered earlier (see Chapter 11) in relation to limited companies. There is no right to bring a statutory derivative claim.

The Company Directors Disqualification Act 1986 (considered in the previous chapter) applies to both members and designated members.

Winding up of limited liability partnerships

LLPs are wound up in the same way as companies. They can issue charges over their property which must be registered with Companies House. (Charges are explained in relation to companies in Chapter 11.) The assets of the LLP are applied in the same order as the assets of a company would be. Members and designated members can be liable for wrongful or fraudulent trading, both of which were considered earlier (see Chapter 11) in relation to limited companies. In addition, members of an LLP can agree with the other members or with the LLP that they will be personally liable for the LLP's debts up to a certain amount. However, this rule, which is contained in s. 74 of the Insolvency Act 1986, applies only if a member agrees to become liable to contribute in this way.

Are LLPs more like companies or partnerships?

Limited liability partnerships share some of the characteristics of limited companies and some of the characteristics of ordinary partnerships.

Like shareholders in limited companies, the members of LLPs have limited liability for the debts of the business and, like companies, LLPs can also give the LLP's assets as security for a loan by way of a floating charge. However, capital cannot be raised by selling shares to people who have no desire to manage the business. Other similarities are that LLPs have perpetual succession, are formed by registration with the Registrar of Companies and have to submit an annual return.

However, LLPs are similar to partnerships in that the members of the LLP manage the business, and are the agents of it, and the members pay income tax rather than the business paying corporation tax.

Members of an LLP can always leave the business by giving notice. However, as this does not automatically dissolve the LLP, the member who leaves will have no automatic right to share in the assets of the LLP. Members who want to leave could therefore find themselves in a vulnerable position unless the LLP agreement or the rules on minority protection give them help.

Company, partnership or limited liability partnership? Choice of legal status

A person wishing to go into business with other people must trade either as a company, a partnership or a limited liability partnership. People going into business together must therefore choose what sort of business organisation they wish to form. Often they might have very clear views. They might be quite sure that they want to trade either as a company, a partnership or an LLP. In many other cases, however, the choice may not be so clear-cut.

When a business is being set up, there are often many matters requiring urgent attention. Perhaps staff must be employed, money borrowed or premises leased. It is easy to regard the decision as to the legal status of the business as less pressing. However, the choice is a very important one. Prospective business people should consider the advantages and disadvantages of companies, partnerships and LLPs in some detail.

Limited liability

Earlier (see Chapter 10) we examined **Salomon v Salomon & Co Ltd (1897)** and saw that shareholders in a limited company cannot be required to pay the debts of the company. In a similar way, the members of an LLP are not liable to pay the debts of the LLP. Partners, on the other hand, are completely liable for the firm's debts to the full extent of their personal fortune. This is, perhaps, the principal disadvantage of a partnership.

There is another side to limited liability, though, and that is that creditors may be much less willing to extend credit to a small company, or to an LLP, than they would be to a partnership. Suppliers dealing with a partnership need not have any worries about getting paid as long as they know that some, or all, of the partners are financially sound. However, suppliers dealing with a small company or an LLP should be very careful. If the business fails, suppliers who are owed money are likely to be unsecured creditors and to find themselves at the back of the queue. When a company or LLP is insolvent, the unsecured creditors will not receive full payment of their debts and may well be paid nothing.

The right to manage

As we have seen in this chapter, all partners have a right to manage the partnership's affairs, and all partners are agents of the firm as regards contracts made in the ordinary course of the firm's business. The members of an LLP are in essentially the same position.

Shareholders, no matter how large their percentage holding, do not have a right to manage a company. This right is vested in the board of directors, the directors being elected by a simple majority vote of the shareholders at a general meeting. Therefore, a shareholder with over 50 per cent of the shares has the power to change the directors. It must be emphasised, however, that until the shareholder exercises this right the directors who are in office have the right to manage the company's affairs.

A shareholder with less than 50 per cent of the votes can be outvoted on a resolution to appoint or change the directors. So minority shareholders are in the unfortunate position of having no right to manage the company's affairs, and no power to change this situation. However, we saw earlier (in Chapter 11) that an entrenched article, or a **Bushell v Faith** clause in the articles, might allow a minority shareholder to remain a director and, so, with careful planning, the vulnerability of minority shareholders in small companies can be reduced.

A person going into business with one other might therefore be very unwilling to form a company unless he or she was to own 50 per cent of the shares. Similar problems arise when there are several shareholders. If a group of majority shareholders have a closer relationship with each other than they have with the minority shareholder, then a minority shareholding can again be a very precarious position.

 Irvine _v_ Irvine (2006)

Two shareholders (P and T) between them held 49.96 per cent of the shares in a company. The rest of the shares were held by one other shareholder, I. The company was a family company, which had been owned equally by two brothers, I and M. M died and in his will he left one share to I. He left the rest of his holding to P, his wife, and to T, a trust set up for the benefit of his children. When I gained the majority shareholding he elected himself as director and paid profits to himself, in the form of a salary, rather than awarding proper dividends.

Held Unfair prejudice was established under what is now s. 994 of the Companies Act 2006 and I was ordered to buy the shares of P and T. However, because the company could not be regarded as a quasi-partnership, the price of these shares should be based on the basis that they were a minority shareholding. The court ordered that a valuation be made by a valuer.

Comment Having heard the views of two valuers, the court later ordered that I buy the shares of P and T at a 30 per cent discount. So the shares, which were worth £2.5 million, were bought for £1.75 million. The discount would have been much greater if the shareholding of P and T combined had been so small that they could not have prevented I from passing a special resolution. The court also ordered that I should account to P and T for the excessive amount of profit which he had taken in salary. However, this excessive amount was also subject to the 30 per cent discount.

Quasi-partnership companies are small companies in which the shareholders have a personal relationship, trust each other and expect each other to remain as directors (see also Chapter 11 on **O'Neill _v_ Phillips**). When a buyout of shares in a quasi-partnership is ordered, the shares should be valued as a pro rata share of the overall company.

The rights of partners to manage the firm and of LLP members to manage the LLP will usually be regulated by a formal agreement. Such an agreement can be changed only by unanimous consent and so individual partners and individual members of LLPs are much better protected than company members.

Agency

The board of directors are the agents of a company, and this means that they can make binding contracts on the company's behalf. The shareholders, no matter how large their shareholding, are not the company's agents and cannot make contracts on its behalf.

Every partner is an agent of the firm in respect of contracts made in the ordinary course of the firm's business. It is therefore absolutely vital that partners trust each other implicitly. A dishonest partner can bankrupt fellow partners and there have been countless cases where this has happened. A dishonest partner can order goods in the firm's name and take possession of the goods. If he or she then steals the goods, the other partners are absolutely liable to the suppliers for the price of the goods.

It is possible to have some safeguards over matters such as signing cheques, but liability to outsiders dealing with the partner in good faith cannot be excluded. Of course, it is not a good idea to form a company with a rogue, but at least limited liability restricts the amount which can be lost. Nor is it only a dishonest partner who can bankrupt fellow partners. An incompetent partner may be just as bad. If he or she makes disastrous contracts on the firm's behalf the firm will be bound to honour them.

LLP members are the agents of the LLP in the same way that partners are agents of the firm. So they too can make disastrous contracts. However, these contracts bind the LLP, not the members of the LLP. So the LLP could be made insolvent, but limited liability would protect the members from personal liability. Even so, members could lose all of the money which they had contributed.

Withdrawal from the business

Partnerships may be entered into for a fixed period of time, in which case the partners cannot leave before that time has expired (unless all of the partners agree). If partnerships are not entered into for a fixed time they are partnerships at will. Any partner can leave a partnership at will by giving reasonable notice of an intention to do so. If a partner does withdraw, the firm will then be dissolved, and each partner will recover a share of any surplus assets. If a partnership is for a fixed term, a partner wishing to withdraw must wait until the end of that term. Even so, an end is in sight.

Members of an LLP have a right to leave the LLP by giving notice or by agreement with the other LLP members. However, a member who is leaving will not have a right to share in the assets of the LLP, unless an agreement has been made giving him such rights. Ordinarily, there should be such an agreement, but if there was not, it might be impractical for a member to leave.

In the case of companies, shareholders may or may not have a right to transfer their shares to whoever they wish. It all depends on the articles of association, and these might well say that the board of directors can refuse a transfer to persons of whom they disapprove. It is even possible for the articles to say that the board of directors has an absolute veto over any transfer of shares. If this is the case, then the shareholders will be locked into the company. No matter how much they dislike the way the company is run they cannot, short of there being a fraud on the minority or unfair prejudice, sell their shares.

Potential shareholders who are worried about this happening might do well to insist that they will not buy the shares unless the articles do allow them to be freely transferred. Whether or not the controllers of the company would agree to such an article might well depend on how badly they wanted the shareholder's investment.

Business property

Company property belongs to the company and not to the shareholders, just as LLP property belongs to the LLP. An important consequence of this can be that a company or an LLP can give its assets as security by way of a floating charge and yet remain free to deal with the assets as it sees fit. We saw earlier (see Chapter 11), that a floating charge will be created if a creditor takes the company's assets as security for a loan, while leaving the company free to deal with the assets.

Partnership property cannot belong to the partnership, because a partnership has no separate legal existence of its own. Despite its name, partnership property belongs to all the partners jointly. A partnership is not allowed to offer a floating charge over partnership property. The partners can, of course, offer a mortgage, but this would restrict the use of the property over which the charge is granted.

Borrowing power

If sole traders want to borrow money from a commercial lender, then they will need to provide security for the loan. There are several ways in which they might do this, but generally they will need either to find a guarantor, who agrees to repay the loan if the trader defaults, or to mortgage their property. Banks tend to demand very solid security for any money advanced.

Partners are in the same position as sole traders, except that since there are more of them they might well find it easier to find guarantors, or might have more property to mortgage. Creditors who are to be repaid out of partnership profits should make it very clear that they do not intend that this should make them partners.

Members of companies or LLPs can raise money in the same way as partners or sole traders, but companies and LLPs also have additional options.

First, companies (but not LLPs) can sell shares to people who wish to invest in the company but who have no desire to manage it. Shares in a private limited company cannot be offered to the general public but, subject to the articles of association, they can be offered to individuals. An investor who is convinced that the company will be a commercial success might be more than willing to pay for shares. Some small companies achieve spectacular success and eventually change into plcs with enormous assets. If an investor had contributed capital into a company such as Body Shop International plc when it was first formed as a private company for, say, 10 per cent of the shares, this would have been an outstandingly good bargain. The converse, of course, is that very many small companies go to the wall, in which case the shares become worthless.

Second, companies and LLPs can raise capital by granting floating charges over their assets. This means that the company or LLP gives its assets as security for a loan while still maintaining the right to use those assets. As long as the sale of the assets would be guaranteed to raise more than the amount loaned, then the creditor has cast-iron security. Many lenders, though, take a particularly jaundiced view of the value of business assets. They value them on the basis that everything which could possibly reduce their value will in fact do so. This can make it difficult for companies or LLPs without substantial assets to raise much money by means of floating charges.

Formation

A business which wants to trade immediately will have to do so as a partnership rather than as a company or an LLP. A partnership can be created without any formalities. As soon as two people carry on a business in common with a view to profit they will be a partnership, whether they realise this or not. It is, however, quite likely that partners will want to have a deed of partnership drawn up by a lawyer. If so, then this too is bound to involve some expense and delay.

Companies and LLPs are formed by registration with the Registrar of Companies. This process generally takes about one week. However, if an extra fee is paid, they can be registered within one day. This means that any advantage partnerships once had in respect of speed of formation is very much diminished.

Formalities

Partners do not need to adhere to any formalities. There is no need for them to hold formal meetings. This used to represent a significant advantage over companies. However, since the Companies Act 2006 came into force, private companies are not required to hold formal meetings. Small private companies and small LLPs do not have to have their accounts audited.

Publicity

The affairs of a partnership are completely private. Like anyone else, the partners will of course need to declare their earnings to HMRC. Beyond this there is no need to reveal their accounts to anyone.

The affairs of companies and LLPs are much more public. Any member of the public can inspect the annual return, the registered accounts, registers held by the Registrar of Companies, and most of the registers which must be held at the registered office. Until relatively recently, all companies had to publish full accounts. Small companies and LLPs can now publish abbreviated accounts. The members are still entitled to full accounts. These abbreviated accounts would deliver very little meaningful information to an outsider, and so the advantage which partnerships used to enjoy in respect of keeping their financial affairs private has been considerably diminished.

Companies and LLPs are defined as small if they have two out of three of the following qualifications:

(1) The company's annual turnover is £6.5 million or less.

(2) The total assets of the company are £3.26 million or less.

(3) The company has 50 or fewer employees.

As can be seen, these qualifications are fairly generous.

Tax

There can be tax advantages in trading as a company and taking dividends from the company, rather than taking a salary as a director. It is beyond the scope of this book to consider these advantages in any detail. In recent years HMRC has very often argued that persons who supply services through a company to one other person are in fact employees and should be taxed accordingly. The fact that HMRC takes this line, and that the taxpayers vigorously oppose it, indicates that tax advantages can be enjoyed by trading as a company. Partners and LLP members do not receive dividends. They receive a share of the profits and pay income tax on the share received.

Even so, they probably pay less tax than they would if they were employees. From April 2014 salaried partners in LLPs are taxed as employees. Previously, as is the case with ordinary partners, they were taxed as self-employed. The Chancellor of the Exchequer had suggested that LLPs were disguising employees (some salaried partners) as partners so that they would pay less tax.

Perpetual succession

Companies and LLPs continue in existence until they are wound up. The death of a shareholder or even of all the shareholders will not end the company. This can be useful when a family company is passed down from one generation to the next. LLPs stay in existence indefinitely in the same way as companies.

In contrast, the death of a partner will end the partnership. However, the partnership deed might well provide that the surviving partners should carry on the business (in which case they must pay an appropriate amount to the estate of the deceased partner). If the surviving partners do carry the business on, then the dissolution of the partnership will amount only to a technical dissolution.

Sole traders

By definition, a sole trader is in business alone. However, a sole trader should consider the benefits of forming a company. In effect, he or she can trade as a company and still be in business on his or her own. This is especially true now that it is possible to have private limited companies with only one shareholder and one director.

Essential points

- Partnership is the relationship which exists between persons who carry on a business with each other with the intention of making a profit.
- A partnership does not have a separate legal identity of its own. It is merely a relationship between the partners.
- A person who is not a partner but who allows outsiders to believe that he or she is a partner can become liable to those outsiders as if he or she really was a partner.
- A partnership agreement can be altered by the express or implied consent of all of the partners.
- The court will order a partnership to be wound up if it can only be carried on at a loss.
- The partners themselves may wind up a partnership. Any partner can dissolve the partnership by giving notice unless the partnership was for a fixed time.
- A partnership for a fixed time will be dissolved when the time has expired, or if all the partners agree to terminate it before the time has expired.
- Limited liability partnerships (LLPs) are not the same as ordinary partnerships.
- LLPs are corporate bodies with a legal personality of their own. They are formed by registration with the Registrar of Companies.
- Every LLP must have at least two designated members. Designated members have duties similar to those of company directors and the company secretary.
- LLPs are wound up in the same way as companies.

Practice questions

1 Alan, Bernie and Charles are in partnership as landscape gardeners. They do not have a formal partnership agreement and have not fixed a definite period for which they should be in partnership. Alan frequently disagrees with Bernie and Charles as to how the firm should be run. In particular, Alan is concerned that Bernie and Charles want to expand the business to start acting as interior designers. Advise Alan of the following matters:

   (a) Whether Bernie and Charles can outvote him as to the ordinary way in which the business is run.

   (b) Whether he could prevent the firm from working as interior designers.

   (c) Whether he could terminate the partnership.

2 Alice, Belinda and Cherry run a shop as partners. The partnership deed states that only Alice can buy goods on behalf of the firm. Yesterday, in contradiction of this, Belinda bought a large quantity of new stock from Duncan. Alice and Cherry think that Belinda paid far too much for the stock and that it will be very difficult to sell. Two days ago, Alice negligently spilt some oil on the shop floor and failed to clean it up. A customer slipped on the oil and badly injured herself. The partnership had failed to renew its insurance policy and so there was no insurance in place at the time of the accident. It seems likely that the firm has not got enough money to pay the likely damages to the injured customer and to pay Duncan's bill. Advise the three partners of their legal position in respect of the above facts.

3 Andy and Brendan are intending to go into partnership as market traders. Andy is to work full-time in the business, actually standing behind the market stall, and take 75 per cent of the profits. Brendan, who has a full-time job as a sales representative, is to work ten hours a week and receive 25 per cent of the profits. Brendan is also to act as the firm's buyer and look after the paperwork. Andy's father, an accountant, is prepared to check the books free of charge on a regular basis.

   If Brendan spots a bargain he often has to buy it immediately. Andy is happy to let Brendan write cheques for up to £100 on the firm's behalf. Brendan has an ambition to work in Australia but would not travel there without a definite job offer. Occasionally, he writes to Australian firms, asking for jobs. He realises that he has very little chance of getting a job in this way, but if he was offered one he would want to leave for Australia immediately.

   Andy and Brendan want a partnership deed. They think that the model partnership deed is a suitable model but realise that changes would have to be made if the deed was to suit their needs.

   (a) List the articles which you think should be changed.

   (b) Write alternative articles to replace those which you consider unsuitable.

4 Firm XYZ has been wound up. The assets of the firm amounted to £100,000. Partner X contributed capital of £20,000, Y contributed £10,000 and Z contributed £5,000. The three partners were to share profits equally.

   (a) How would the loss of capital be borne if after all outside creditors had been fully paid the capital had been reduced from £35,000 to £20,000?

   (b) What would be the position if outside creditors were owed £210,000?

5 Keith, Lorna and Mary are the only members of an LLP, which deals in antiques. Before forming the LLP, the members had considered forming a limited company or trading as

a partnership. In what ways is their LLP similar to a limited company and in what ways is it similar to a partnership?

6   Three years ago, Martha finished a college course in Health and Beauty Therapy. After a year working in a salon, she spent three months in the United States. On a trip to California, Martha was extremely impressed by some of the alternative beauty treatments available there.

Martha now wants to market some of the Californian ideas in England, and is worried that if she waits too long others will beat her to it.

Martha's grandfather, Charles, has recently retired from the board of a multinational company. He has a variety of interests but, seeing Martha as a 'chip off the old block', he is prepared to invest in her proposed business and help her in the running of it.

Martha is very fond of her grandfather but thinks that he is too cautious, not realising that in the modern age opportunities must be seized immediately before it becomes too late. Charles is very proud of Martha but feels that, expert though she might be in the field of beauty therapy, she has a great deal to learn as far as business goes.

Charles has agreed to invest £50,000 in the business and put in three or four hours' work a week. Martha is putting in her savings of £7,000 and will devote all of her time to the business.

(a) Do you think that Charles would prefer that the business was a company or a partnership?

(b) Which do you think Martha would prefer?

(c) As an objective outsider, which type of business organisation do you think they should become? Might an LLP be the most suitable type of business to form?

(It should be pointed out that there are no absolutely right or wrong answers to questions such as these. Both types of business organisation have considerable advantages and disadvantages. However, at least five of the matters considered in the chapter will have a bearing on the decisions. Try and identify these five and then decide how important each one is.)

7   Explain the circumstances in which one member of a partnership can make fellow members liable in contract or in tort.

Task 12

A group of French students visiting your college are keen to understand the risks which a partner assumes under English law.

Using a partnership of solicitors as an example, write a report indicating:

(a) The extent to which one partner can be liable for goods ordered by another partner.

(b) The extent to which a partner can be liable for another partner's torts.

(c) What duties the partners will owe to each other.

(d) How a partnership is formed.

(e) The order in which the assets of a partnership are applied when a partnership is wound up.

Explain also how your answers would be different if an LLP, rather than a partnership, had been formed.

mylawchamber

Visit **www.mylawchamber.co.uk/macintyreessentials** to access tools to help you develop and test your knowledge of business law, including interactive multiple choice questions, practice exam questions with guidance, weblinks, glossary, glossary flashcards, legal newsfeed and legal updates. **mylaw**chamber
unrivalled support for legal education

Use **Case Navigator** to read in full some of the key cases referenced in this chapter with commentary and questions:

Salomon *v* Salomon & Co Ltd (1897)

13

Employment (1): The contract of employment, employment rights and dismissal

This is the first of two chapters on employment law. This chapter begins by considering how a contract of employment is formed and the terms such a contract might contain. It then considers several statutory employment rights, before concluding by considering rights which arise when an employee is dismissed or made redundant.

The following chapter considers discrimination in employment and health and safety at work.

The contract of employment

In an earlier chapter (see Chapter 9) vicarious liability was explained and the ways in which the courts decide whether a contract of employment exists were considered. Like other contracts, a contract of employment can be created orally or in writing, and will contain both express and implied terms. The express terms would be agreed by the parties, the implied terms would be implied by the courts.

Written statement of employment particulars

Section 1 of the Employment Rights Act 1996 (ERA 1996) requires an employer to provide all employees with a written statement of employment particulars. The statement, which has to be provided within two months of the employment beginning, must contain the following particulars:

- the names of the employer and the employee;
- the date on which the employment began;
- the date on which the employee's period of continuous employment began, taking into account whether any previous employment is to count as continuous employment; (Continuous employment is important in relation to dismissal and redundancy, as we see later in this chapter.)
- the scale or rate of pay and the method of calculation;
- the intervals at which payment is made (weekly, monthly, etc.);
- any terms and conditions relating to hours of work;
- any terms and conditions relating to holiday entitlement, sick pay or pensions;
- the length of notice which either party needs to give to end the employment;

- the job title of the employee, or a brief description of his duties;
- where the employment is not intended to be permanent, the period for which it is expected to continue or, of it is for a fixed term, the date on which the term is to end;
- the place of work;
- any trade union agreements which directly affect the terms and conditions of the employment;
- where the employee is required to work outside the UK for a period of more than one month, the period for which he is to work outside the UK, the currency in which he is to be paid while working outside the UK and any additional salary or benefits to be paid on account of his being required to work outside the UK.

The written particulars are very strong evidence of the terms of the contract of employment. However, they are not the contract itself as this will already have been formed by the time the statement is provided. An employee who has not been given the particulars within the specified time period may complain to an employment tribunal. The tribunal will make a minimum award of two weeks' pay and a maximum award of four weeks' pay and order that particulars are given. For these purposes, the week's pay is capped at the limit of £464 which applies when calculating a redundancy payment.

Itemised pay statements

Section 8(1) ERA 1996 requires employers to provide a written itemised pay statement when wages or salary are paid. Section 8(2) provides that this statement must contain particulars of:

- the gross amount of the wages or salary;
- the amount of any deductions from the gross amount and the purposes for which they are made;
- the net amount of wages or salary payable; and
- where different parts of the net amount are paid in different ways, the amount and method of payment of each part-payment.

Implied obligations of the parties

Certain terms are implied into contracts of employment. Some of these impose obligations on the employee and some impose obligations on the employer.

Obligations imposed on the employee

The obligations imposed on the employee are as follows:

- to show mutual respect to the employer;
- to faithfully serve the employer;
- to obey lawful and reasonable orders;
- to use reasonable care and skill;
- not to accept bribes;
- not to reveal confidential information.

However, as regards the duty not to disclose confidential information, the Public Interest Disclosure Act 1998 protects 'whistleblower' employees who disclose certain information, such as that a crime is being committed or health and safety procedures are being ignored.

Such whistleblower employees must not suffer a detriment because of what they have done, and any dismissal in consequence of what they have done will be automatically unfair. Employees do not have a duty to disclose their own shortcomings. However, some employees, particularly those who are responsible for others, may have a duty to disclose the shortcomings of others.

Implied obligations of the employer

The implied obligations of the employer are as follows:

- to show mutual respect to the employee;
- to provide work, or pay the employee if there is no work;
- to pay wages;
- not to reveal confidential information;
- to indemnify employees for expenses and costs reasonably incurred;
- to insure the employee;
- to take reasonable care and skill in preparing a reference. (However, an employer has no duty to provide a reference.)

It is possible that terms can be implied into a contract of employment by custom and practice, as long as the terms in question are well known, certain and reasonable. Rule books at some places of employment are sometimes agreed by the parties to be included as terms of the contract of employment. In other cases, the rules in the workbook are imposed by the employer. If this is the case, then failure to obey the rules may be a breach of the duty to obey instructions.

Variation of the terms of the contract

Earlier (see Chapter 5) we examined the ways in which a contract can be discharged by agreement. We saw that one party cannot unilaterally alter the terms of a contract but that both parties must agree to the alteration. If an employer unilaterally imposes a significant change in an employee's terms and conditions, then this will amount to a repudiation of the contract and the employee can either accept the variation or not. An employee who does not accept the variation can regard the contract as terminated and himself as dismissed. (In technical terms, the employee accepts that the employer's repudiation has ended the contract.) However, the employee might accept the variation. If so, the old contract will have been discharged and the new one substituted. If an employee refuses to accept the new terms but continues working under protest, then, for a short time at least, the employee can still leave and claim to have been dismissed. An employee who continues to work without protesting will generally be taken to have accepted the unilateral change.

Figure 13.1 shows the employee's options.

Statutory rights of the employee

Maternity rights

Unless the contract terms give a more generous entitlement, all female employees have a statutory right to 26 weeks' ordinary maternity leave and 26 weeks' additional maternity leave. This right, which is set out in the Maternity and Parental Leave Regulations 1999, applies no matter how long the employee has worked for the employer.

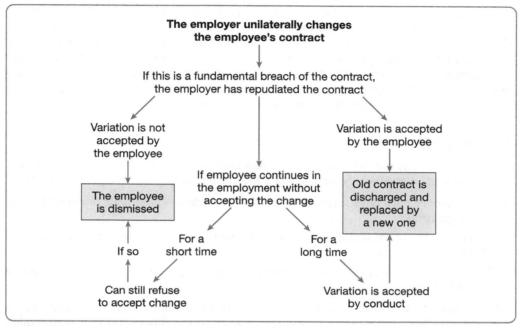

Figure 13.1 The effect of responses to a unilateral change of employment terms

A female employee will qualify for statutory maternity pay if she meets three conditions:

(1) She must have 26 weeks' continuous employment at a point 14 weeks before the expected week of childbirth.
(2) She must have stopped work due to the pregnancy.
(3) She must have average earnings of at least £111 a week.

Statutory maternity pay

An employee is entitled to statutory maternity pay for 39 weeks, beginning when she goes on ordinary maternity leave. However, this period must begin between 11 weeks and one week before the baby is due. The employee has to give 28 days' notice of an intention to go on leave or, if this is not possible, as much notice as is possible. The employer can ask for a medical certificate which confirms that the employee is pregnant and the date when the birth is due. Pregnant women are also allowed time off work to receive ante-natal care.

During the first six weeks of ordinary maternity leave the employee is entitled to 90 per cent of her normal weekly pay, which is calculated by looking at the weekly pay in the 12 weeks before the maternity leave began. For the next 33 weeks, the employee is entitled to a minimum of £138.18 a week or 90 per cent of her normal weekly pay, whichever is lower. However, if the employee does not qualify for statutory maternity pay, she may be entitled to a maternity allowance. Statutory maternity pay is subject to the usual deductions, such as tax and national insurance, and is paid at the same time as the employee would normally have been paid.

It is not only pay that the employee is entitled to, but also other contractual benefits of the job which she would normally have enjoyed.

Women who do not qualify for statutory maternity pay may be entitled to a Statutory Maternity Allowance of £138.18 per week, or of 90 per cent of their average weekly earnings, whichever is lower, for 39 weeks. To qualify the woman must have worked, either in employment or as self-employed, for at least 26 of the 66 weeks before the baby is due, and must have earned at least £30 for 13 of those 66 weeks. Statutory Maternity Allowance is paid by the Government. Employers can reclaim from the Government about 90 per cent of the amount which they have paid in statutory maternity leave.

Paternity leave and pay

Part II of the Paternity and Adoption Leave Regulations 2002 gives rights to paternity leave and paternity pay. In order to qualify for paternity leave, the employee must satisfy three conditions:

(1) The employee must have responsibility for the new child's upbringing or expect to have this responsibility.

(2) He must either be the biological father of the child or he must be the husband or partner of the child's mother.

(3) He must have at least 26 weeks' continuous employment 15 weeks before the baby is due to be born.

Paternity leave can either be for one week or for two consecutive weeks. It cannot be for parts of a week but it can begin midweek. The leave can begin either at the date of the child's birth or at some later date, but it must be completed 56 days after the child was born. If the mother gives birth to twins, no extra paternity leave is available. The rate of statutory paternity pay is currently either £138.18 a week or, if the average weekly earnings are less than £138.18, 90 per cent of average weekly earnings. Other contractual benefits must also be received. Employees who do not earn enough to pay any national insurance contributions are not entitled to statutory paternity pay.

Employees intending to take statutory paternity leave must inform their employers at least 15 weeks before the baby is expected. They must say when the baby is due, when they want the leave to start, and whether they want one week's leave or two weeks' leave. Employees are obliged to give the employer a completed self certificate which provides evidence of their entitlement to statutory paternity pay. A model certificate can be found on the DTI website: www.dti.gov.uk. Employees who take statutory paternity leave are entitled to return to work afterwards and must not be discriminated against for having taken the leave. Employers can reclaim from the Government about 90 per cent of the amount which they have paid in statutory paternity pay.

Shared parental leave and pay

As we have seen, employed mothers can be entitled to 52 weeks of Maternity Leave and 39 weeks of statutory maternity pay. However, mothers who are entitled to this can choose to end their maternity leave early and opt for Shared Parental Leave. This leave can be shared with their partner or the child's father, as long as they have been employed or self-employed for 26 of the 66 weeks before the child is due or due to be adopted. Statutory Parental Leave is paid at £138.18 per week or 90% of the employee's weekly pay, whichever is lower.

Adoption leave and pay

When a couple adopt a child, Part III of the Paternity and Adoption Leave Regulations 2002 entitles one member of the couple to time off work with statutory adoption pay. In addition, the other member of the couple, or a partner of an individual who adopts, may be entitled to paternity leave and pay.

In order to claim adoption leave, the employee must have worked continuously for the employer for 26 weeks and be newly matched with a child by an adoption agency. Such employees are entitled to 26 weeks' ordinary adoption leave, during which they are entitled to statutory adoption pay, and an additional 26 weeks' adoption leave. The leave can start either on the date of the child's placement or 14 days before the expected date of the placement. The rate of statutory adoption pay, which is payable for 39 weeks, is £138.18 a week or 90 per cent of the normal weekly wage if this is less than £138.18. Adopters have to give notice of their intention to take adoption leave. Employers can also ask for a matching certificate from the adoption agency. Those taking time off are entitled to contractual benefits other than pay which they would normally receive, and have a right to return to work after the adoption leave. Employers can reclaim about 90 per cent of money paid in adoption leave from the Government. The statutory rates of maternity pay, paternity pay and adoption pay increase periodically.

Parental leave and time off for dependants

An employee with at least one year's continuous employment is entitled to take up to 13 weeks' unpaid parental leave, in respect of each child, to look after his or her child or to make arrangements for the child's welfare. In the case of disabled children, 18 weeks' leave per child can be taken. In the case of twins, both parents can have 13 weeks' leave for each child. The leave must be taken before the child's fifth birthday and can be taken in either long blocks or short blocks.

All employees are entitled under s. 57A ERA 1996 to take time off work to look after dependants in an emergency. The right can arise in the following circumstances:

- if assistance is needed when a dependant gives birth, is injured or assaulted;
- to provide care for a dependant who is ill or injured;
- when a dependant dies;
- when there is an unexpected disruption or ending of arrangements for the care of a dependant; or
- when an incident involving the employee's child arises unexpectedly during school hours.

Dependants include spouses, children, parents and people who live in the same house as the employee. It also includes people who reasonably rely on the employee. There is no entitlement to pay during the time off.

Flexible working for parents and carers

Section 80F of the Employment Rights Act 1996 allows all employees to make a request for flexible working. Employers have a statutory duty to consider these applications seriously within three months, but there is no automatic right to work flexibly. However, an employer should refuse an application only if there are good business reasons for doing so. Only employees with at least 26 weeks' continuous employment can apply.

The application can ask for a change of hours, a change to the times of work or to work from home. If the application is accepted, then the change will be permanent unless the parties agree otherwise. As a change in working pattern might involve a drop in pay, applicants need to think things through carefully before applying. Once the employer receives a written application, a meeting with the employee must be arranged within 28 days. At this meeting the application, and other possible solutions, are considered. Within 14 days of the meeting, the employer has to write to the employee, either agreeing to a new date on which a new work pattern starts or giving reasons why the application has been refused.

Transfer of employees

The Transfer of Undertakings (Protection of Employment) Regulations 2006 (TUPE) provide that when a business is transferred from one employer to another as a going concern the contracts of employment of all the employees are also transferred. These contracts then take effect as if made between the individual employees and the new employer.

If an employee refuses to accept the transfer, this ends the employment without a dismissal having taken place. (So the employee will have no remedy.) However, an employee can claim unfair dismissal if his refusal to be transferred was because the transfer would result in significant and detrimental change. Any dismissal made because of the transfer is automatically unfair unless it is made on account of the employee refusing to accept the transfer.

National minimum wage

The National Minimum Wage Act 1998 introduced new rights to a national minimum wage. The amount of the minimum wage depends upon the employee's age. The rate at the time of writing is £6.50 per hour for workers aged 21 or over, £5.13 per hour for workers aged between 18 and 21, and £3.79 per hour for those aged 16 or 17. These limits are increased periodically, roughly in line with inflation.

Employers must keep records relating to pay, and individual workers have a right to inspect, examine and copy their records. If this right is denied, an employment tribunal can award 80 hours' pay at the national minimum wage rate. However, the right to have access to records applies only if the employee has reasonable grounds to believe that there has been a breach of the Act's requirements and if it is necessary to see the records to establish whether this is the case.

A 'worker' is defined by the Act so as to include both employees, agency workers, Crown workers and home workers. The armed forces, prisoners, voluntary workers, the self-employed, some community workers and employees who live as part of a family, such as au pairs, are not protected. Nor are apprentices under the age of 19. The worker's hourly rate is calculated by looking at a 'relevant pay period'. This period is usually one month, and bonuses and performance-related pay count when calculating how much the worker has been paid. However, overtime and shift allowances do not count.

Example

Jane, aged 26, is paid £6 an hour basic pay plus a 20 per cent shift allowance. Her pay is below the minimum, even though it is £7.20 an hour. John is an 18-year-old salesman, who is paid £4.20 an hour basic rate. Every month he earns £400 additional commission. The Act has not been breached. When the commission is included, John's wage is well above the £5.13 minimum.

HMRC can enforce the Act on behalf of workers. It can also issue penalty notices. Employers in breach of the Act can be fined on a daily basis.

The Working Time Regulations 1998

These Regulations provide that no worker's working time should be more than 48 hours, including overtime, in each seven-day period when calculated over any 17-week period. It is the employer's duty to see that the limit is not exceeded. Any days which are taken off as annual holiday, sick leave or maternity leave are regarded as excluded days. When assessing the hours worked in a seven-day period, these excluded days are not counted and an appropriate number of days are added on to cater for them.

> **Example**
>
> Fred worked in a factory for 52 hours a week for 15 consecutive weeks. Fred then took two weeks' annual leave. Fred then worked 35 hours a week for two weeks. The annual leave is excluded. So Fred has worked 780 hours plus 70 hours = 850 hours in a 17-week period. The regulations have been breached because this averages out at 50 hours per week.

It is possible for a worker to agree that the 48-hour limit should not apply. However, such an agreement must be in writing to be effective.

Young workers (those who are under 18) cannot be made to work more than eight hours in any one day, or more than 40 hours in any one week.

Night workers

A night worker works a period of at least seven hours, at least three hours of which are between the hours of 11 p.m. and 6 a.m. No worker should be given night work unless the employer has first made sure that the worker has the opportunity of a free health assessment. Night workers must also be given regular opportunities to have a free health assessment. Over any 17-week period, with rest periods not counting, night workers should not work more than an average of eight hours in every 24 hours. If the night work involves special hazards, or heavy physical or mental strain, there is no averaging out over a 17-week period. These workers should never work more than eight hours in any 24-hour period.

Daily and weekly rest periods

If a pattern of work is likely to put a worker's health and safety at risk, the worker is entitled to a rest period of at least 11 consecutive hours in each 24-hour period of work. Workers under 18 (young workers) are entitled to 12 consecutive hours' rest. Work which is monotonous, or where the work rate is predetermined, is particularly likely to be such a pattern of work. Young workers are entitled to a 48-hour uninterrupted rest period in each seven-day period of work. Adult workers are entitled to a 24-hour uninterrupted rest period in each seven-day period of work, although the employer can insist that this is taken as one uninterrupted 48-hour period in each 14-day period of work. Adult workers are entitled to a rest break of at least 20 minutes if their daily working time is more than six hours. Young workers have an entitlement to a rest break of 30 minutes if their daily working time is more than four-and-a-half hours.

Annual leave

Workers are entitled to at least 5.6 weeks' paid leave every year (28 days for those who work a five-day week), or the appropriate proportion of this if less than a year is worked. Where the employment ends before the leave has been taken, the employer can make a payment in lieu. Generally, a worker can take leave whenever he wants by giving the employer notice. However, the employer is entitled to give notice that leave must be taken on particular days.

Enforcement

In these Regulations, 'workers' are defined in much the same way as they are in the National Minimum Wage Act 1998. The Regulations are enforced by the Health and Safety Executive and by local authority inspectors. Employers can be prosecuted for breaching the Regulations. Employees can enforce their rights before an employment tribunal and must not be victimised for having done so. A dismissal in connection with the Regulations will be automatically unfair.

ACAS grievance procedure

When an employee raises a concern, problem or complaint with his employer, the ACAS Code of Practice should be followed. The Code advises that employers and employees should try to resolve disciplinary and grievance matters informally in the workplace, and should consider using independent third parties to help if necessary. However, where this is not possible the Code sets out procedures which aim to ensure fairness and a standard of reasonable behaviour.

First, the employee should formally raise the grievance with the employer, via a manager who is not the subject of the grievance. This should be done in writing and without unnecessary delay.

Second, the employer should hold a formal meeting with the employee, without unreasonable delay, to discuss the nature of the grievance. The employer and the employee should make every effort to attend the meeting. The employee should be given a chance to explain the grievance and how he thinks it should be resolved. The employer should consider adjourning the meeting to conduct any necessary investigation. The employer should allow the employee to be accompanied at the meeting by a companion, such as a fellow worker or a trade union representative.

Third, the employer should decide on appropriate action and communicate this to the employee in writing. The employee should also be told of the right to appeal against the decision.

Finally, the employer should allow the employee to appeal against the decision if he does not think that the grievance has been satisfactorily resolved. Appeals must be submitted in writing and without unreasonable delay. An appeal should be heard without unreasonable delay, preferably by a manager who has not previously been involved. The employee has the right to be accompanied at the appeal. The outcome of the appeal should be communicated in writing without unreasonable delay.

The grievance procedure does not apply when a recognised trade union, or other appropriate workplace representative, raises a grievance on behalf of two or more employees. In such cases the organisation's collective grievance procedures will apply. If an employee raises a grievance during a disciplinary process, the disciplinary process can be suspended until the grievance has been dealt with. However, where the disciplinary and grievance cases are related, both can be dealt with in the same proceedings. An ACAS Guide provides sample grievance procedures and sample letters which might be used by the employer.

The Code is not legally binding but is admissible as evidence and can be taken into account by the employment tribunal. A tribunal, if it considers it just and equitable, can increase any award to an employee by up to 25 per cent if it appears to the tribunal that the employer has unreasonably failed to comply with the Code. A corresponding power to reduce the award by up to 25 per cent exists where it is the employee who has unreasonably failed to comply with the Code.

Unfair and wrongful dismissal

A dismissed employee may be able to sue the employer for either unfair or wrongful dismissal. These are quite separate matters.

Unfair dismissal is a statutory remedy which gives the dismissed employee a right to a fixed payment.

An employee who sues for wrongful dismissal is simply suing for breach of contract. All contracts of employment give the employee an entitlement to a certain amount of notice after one month in the job. If an employee is wrongfully dismissed, without having been given this notice, the contract will have been breached and the employee will therefore be entitled to damages. In theory, an employer could sue an employee who left the employment without giving the required amount of notice but in practice this hardly ever happens.

Unfair dismissal

Figure 13.2 shows an overview of **unfair dismissal**.

Who can claim?

Section 94(1) of the Employment Rights Act 1996 gives an employee who has at least two years' continuous employment the right not to be unfairly dismissed. Section 212(1) ERA 1996 defines the weeks which count towards continuous employment:

> Any week during the whole or part of which an employee's relations with his employer are governed by a contract of employment counts in computing the employee's period of employment.

What is important then is not the kind of work done, but merely whether the employee continuously worked for an employer. It should be noticed that only employees are entitled to claim unfair dismissal. Independent contractors cannot claim unfair dismissal. (In Chapter 9 we examined the ways in which the courts distinguish between employees and independent contractors.)

Section 212(3) ERA 1996 allows a week to count towards continuous employment, up to a maximum of 26 weeks, even if the employee was absent due to illness, or a temporary cessation of work, or absent by arrangement or custom. Weeks lost through industrial action do not break the continuity of employment, although they do not count as weeks of continuous employment either (s. 216 ERA 1996). If a business is taken over by a new employer as a going concern, weeks worked for the old employer count as weeks worked for the new employer (s. 218 ERA 1996).

Since September 2013 employees have the choice of giving up their rights in relation to unfair dismissal and statutory redundancy pay in return for shares in the employer company worth at least £2,000. However, even such employee shareholders will retain the right not to be unfairly dismissed for an automatically unfair reason or on the grounds of discrimination.

What is a dismissal?

There can be a claim for unfair dismissal only if the employee is dismissed. Section 95 ERA 1996 provides that an employee is dismissed if:

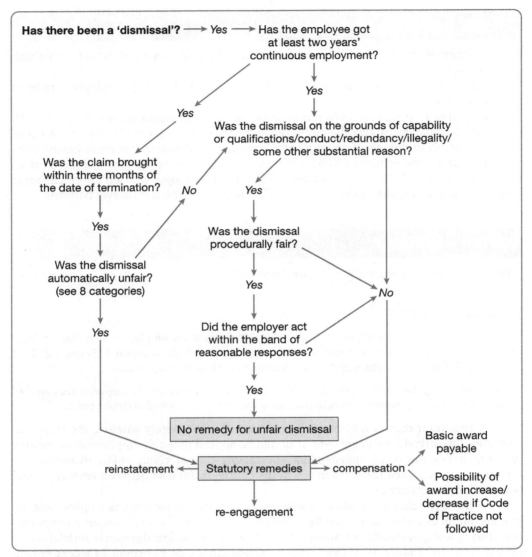

Figure 13.2 An overview of unfair dismissal

- the employer terminates the contract, with or without notice;
- a fixed term contract ends and is not renewed; or
- the employee terminates the contract on the grounds of the employer's unreasonable conduct (this is known as **constructive dismissal**).

In **Western Excavating v Sharp (1978)** Lord Denning explained the meaning of constructive dismissal:

> If the employer is guilty of conduct which is a significant breach going to the root of the contract . . . then the employee is entitled to regard himself as discharged from any further performance . . . He is constructively dismissed. The employee is entitled in those circumstances to leave at the instant

without giving any notice at all, or, alternatively, he may give notice and say that he is leaving at the end of the notice.

If a contract is frustrated there will be no dismissal. The meaning of frustration, in relation to contracts of employment, is considered later in the chapter in relation to wrongful dismissal.

When is a dismissal unfair?

'Unfair' has a technical meaning here. Section 98 ERA 1996 provides that all dismissals are unfair unless the employer can justify the dismissal on one of following six grounds:

(1) The employee's capability or qualifications to do the job. (Dismissal for lack of qualifications is very unusual. Dismissal for lack of capability often arises because the employee is ill.)

(2) The employee's conduct, inside or outside the employment. (If the conduct is outside the employment, then it must be serious enough to have a detrimental effect on the employer's business.)

(3) That the employee was made redundant. (Redundancy is considered later in this chapter.)

(4) That it would be illegal to keep the employee on in the job.

(5) Some other substantial reason which would justify the employee's dismissal.

The last category is necessary to prevent the list of reasons from becoming too rigid. Usually the reason is a commercial one.

 Wilson v Underhill House School Ltd (1977)

Teachers were awarded a national pay rise. The school where the applicant was employed was in financial difficulties and could not meet the award in full. All the other teachers agreed to forgo some of their pay rise. The applicant would not agree to this and so she was dismissed.

Held The dismissal was fair.

Was the dismissal actually fair?

If the employer can show that the dismissal was for one of the six reasons which can be fair, then the tribunal will have to decide whether the dismissal actually was fair. The courts have adopted a test known as the band of reasonable responses. Under this test the tribunal will ask whether a reasonable employer could have acted in the same way as the employer who dismissed the employee. If the tribunal objectively considers that a reasonable employer could have acted in the same way, the dismissal will not be unfair. This test seems very favourable to the employer but it was affirmed by the Court of Appeal in **Post Office v Foley (2000)**.

In **British Home Stores Ltd v Burchell (1980)** the Employment Appeal Tribunal held that an employment tribunal should decide whether an employer had acted reasonably by establishing the following matters:

- The employer should believe in the employee's guilt or misconduct. Only the facts known to the employer at that time could be relevant here, not facts discovered later.

- The employer should have had reasonable grounds to believe in the employee's guilt or misconduct.
- The employer should have carried out as much investigation as was reasonable in all the circumstances. An employer who followed these three steps would have acted reasonably.

Disciplinary and dismissal procedure

Earlier in this chapter the new grievance procedures contained in the ACAS Code of Practice were considered. The Code also introduced new disciplinary and dismissal procedures. As is the case with grievances, both employers and employees should attempt to settle disciplinary matters informally, using outside third parties if necessary. They should also attempt to deal with matters promptly, without undue delay. The Code does not apply to dismissals by way of redundancy or to dismissals which occur when a fixed term contract is not renewed. The following five stages should be followed when a disciplinary issue cannot be resolved informally.

(1) The employer should establish the facts of the case. This should be done without undue delay and will involve carrying out necessary investigations. A preliminary investigative meeting with the employee may be required to achieve this but no disciplinary action should be taken at this preliminary meeting.

(2) The employer should inform the employee of the problem. If there is a disciplinary case to answer, the employee should be given details of the case in writing. The details should give the employee enough information for him to prepare an answer, and copies of any written evidence should be provided. As well as receiving written notice of the time and place of the disciplinary meeting, the employee should be informed of his right to be accompanied at the meeting.

(3) The employer should hold a meeting with the employee to discuss the problem. The employee must be given time to prepare his case but the meeting should otherwise be held without unreasonable delay. At the meeting the evidence against the employee should be explained and gone over. The employee should be given a chance to set out his own case and answer allegations and should also be given a reasonable opportunity to ask questions, present evidence and call witnesses. If either side intends to call witnesses, they should give advance notice of this.

(4) If the meeting could result in a formal warning being issued, or some other disciplinary action being taken, the employer must allow the employee to be accompanied by a companion at the meeting. The companion could be a fellow worker, a trade union representative or an official employed by a trade union. The companion would have no right to answer questions on the employee's behalf. However, the companion would have the right to address the meeting in order to put and sum up the employee's case, to respond on the employee's behalf to any views expressed at the meeting and to confer with the employee during the meeting.

(5) The employer must decide upon appropriate action and inform the employee of this decision in writing. As regards most cases of misconduct or unsatisfactory performance, a first written warning would be the usual action taken, with the threat of a final written warning if there was further misconduct or a failure to improve performance. If the misconduct or unsatisfactory performance is sufficiently serious, a final written warning might be appropriate. A written warning should set out the employee's poor performance or misconduct, the change in behaviour or improvement required and the timescale for this.

The employee should also be told for how long the warning remains in force and what the consequences of further misconduct or failure to improve might be. Even if there is gross misconduct which would justify dismissal without a warning, the disciplinary process should always be followed. Disciplinary rules should set out examples of gross misconduct. If the employee is persistently unwilling or unable to attend a meeting, without a good reason, the employer should make a decision on the evidence available.

(6) The employer should provide the employee with an opportunity to appeal. Appeals should be heard without unreasonable delay, preferably by a manager who has not previously been involved. The employee has the right to be accompanied at the appeal. The outcome of the appeal should be communicated in writing without unreasonable delay.

The Code is not legally binding but is admissible as evidence and can be taken into account by the employment tribunal. A tribunal, if it considers it just and equitable, can increase any award to an employee by up to 25 per cent if it appears to the tribunal that the employer has unreasonably failed to comply with the Code. There is a corresponding power to reduce the award by up to 25 per cent where it is the employee who has unreasonably failed to comply with the Code.

Under **Polkey v A E Dayton Services Ltd (1988)** a dismissal might be unfair, even if for one of the fair reasons specified and even if the employer acted within the band of reasonable responses, purely because the correct dismissal procedure was not complied with. In such cases the tribunal should reduce or eliminate the compensation payable, other than the basic award (see later in the chapter), to reflect any likelihood that the employee would have been dismissed even if the correct procedures had been complied with. Despite the **Polkey** ruling, there will have been no unfair dismissal if the tribunal concludes that the employer acted as a reasonable employer would have acted in taking the view that, in the exceptional circumstances of the particular case, the normal procedural steps would have been futile and were dispensed with because they could not have altered the decision to dismiss.

Automatically unfair dismissals

A dismissal is automatically unfair if it was:

- on the grounds of the employee trying to enforce a relevant statutory right;
- on the grounds of pregnancy;
- for being a member of a trade union;
- for being on strike, if the dismissal occurred in the first eight weeks of the strike;
- for being a union representative;
- for carrying out health and safety duties;
- for refusing to work on Sundays (some workers do not have this protection);
- in connection with a transfer of undertakings from one employer to another.

The effective date of termination

A claim must be brought before the employment tribunal within three months of the effective date of termination of the employment. The effective date of termination can also be important for calculating the amount of compensation. Section 97 ERA 1996 defines the effective date of termination as:

- Where the contract is terminated by notice, the date on which the notice ends. It does not matter whether the notice is given by the employer or the employee.
- Where the contract is terminated otherwise than by notice, the date on which the termination takes effect.
- Where the employee is employed under a contract for a fixed term, which expires without being renewed under the same contract, the date on which the fixed term expires.

A new system of fees for bringing a tribunal case was introduced in 2013. As regards a claim for unfair dismissal the fee for issuing a claim is £250 and the tribunal hearing fee is £950. The tribunal has the power to order the employer to reimburse the fees of successful claimants. Since these fees have been introduced there has been a very substantial drop in the number of employment tribunal cases.

Remedies for unfair dismissal

The three possible remedies for unfair dismissal are: reinstatement, re-engagement and compensation.

Reinstatement

If the employment tribunal orders reinstatement, then the employee must be treated as if he had never been dismissed. He will therefore get his old job back and recover back pay for any time that he has not been allowed to work. The employment tribunal will set the amount of back pay. Orders of reinstatement are rarely made.

Re-engagement

Here the employee is not given his old job back, but the employer is ordered to give him a similar job. The employment tribunal will set out the terms of the employment.

Like reinstatement, re-engagement is not awarded very often. If an employee takes the employer to the employment tribunal for unfair dismissal, this generally means that the implied term of mutual trust and respect has been permanently breached.

Compensation

The basic award is calculated in the same way as a redundancy payment. First, the relevant number of complete years of continuous employment is calculated. Then this figure is multiplied by the normal weekly wage:

- For years worked while under the age of 22, each year of continuous employment entitles the employee to half a week's pay.
- For years worked while over 22 and under 41 years old, each year of continuous employment entitles the employee to one week's pay.
- For years worked while the employee was over 41, each year of continuous employment entitles the employee to one and a half week's pay.

The week's pay is the gross pay which the employee normally earns, excluding overtime. However, there are two limits on the size of the award. First, the employee can only claim for up to 20 years' continuous employment. Second, the week's pay is capped at £464. (This amount is increased periodically to keep up with inflation.) There is no duty to mitigate loss because the basic award is not an award of damages. However, the award can be reduced if the tribunal considers that the employee's behaviour makes this equitable.

Example

Asif and Bill are both unfairly dismissed. Asif is 28 and has ten years' continuous employment. His normal weekly wage is £200 and the continuous employment started on his 18th birthday. The four years worked while under the age of 22 entitle Asif to two weeks' pay. The six years worked since becoming 22 entitle Asif to six weeks' pay. Asif is therefore entitled to eight weeks' pay, at £200 per week, which equals £1,600. Bill is 63. He has 40 years' continuous employment and earns £600 a week. Bill can count only 20 years' continuous employment. As his best 20 years were all worked while over the age of 41, this entitles Bill to 30 weeks' pay. Bill's normal weekly pay is capped at £464. Bill therefore gets the maximum basic award possible of £13,920.

There can also be a compensatory award of up to £76,574. In cases where discrimination has occurred, the amount of damages which can be awarded is unlimited. The compensatory award takes account of matters such as immediate and future loss of earnings, with no upper limit on the weekly pay, loss of statutory rights, loss of pension rights and a supplementary amount which can be awarded if the employer failed to go through an established appeals procedure. However, here the employee has a duty to mitigate any losses and so would have to take another suitable job if one arose. The award will also be reduced by the amount of jobseeker's allowance which the applicant has received. Section 123(6) ERA 1996 allows the award to be reduced on the grounds of contributory negligence. For the purposes of the compensatory award, the weekly pay received is the net pay rather than gross pay and there is no upper limit.

An additional award of between 13 and 26 weeks' pay can be made if the employer refuses to comply with a re-engagement or reinstatement order. If the dismissal was on the grounds of discrimination, the additional award is of between 26 and 52 weeks' pay. As regards these awards, the week's pay is still subject to the statutory maximum of £464.

An employee who has been made redundant but who has refused an offer of suitable alternative employment will be entitled to an award of two weeks' pay.

Wrongful dismissal

An employee is summarily dismissed when he is dismissed without notice. The employee's behaviour might justify such a dismissal, in which case he will have no remedy. If an employee is summarily dismissed without a justifiable reason, however, then his contract of employment, which will entitle him to a period of notice, will have been broken. The employee can then sue the employer for breach of contract, and such an action is known as an action for wrongful dismissal. Of course, it is possible that the employer may lawfully dismiss the employee without notice. This would be the case if the employee had behaved so badly that he had committed a repudiation of the contract. The employer could accept the repudiation and dismiss the employee without committing a breach of contract. It is difficult to generalise from the cases, but employees have been held to repudiate the contract by refusing to obey lawful orders, by gross misconduct, neglect or serious breach of duty. However, it must be stressed that each of these matters will not necessarily amount to a repudiation which justifies dismissal. In each case the employment tribunal must consider the facts and come to a decision.

In general, an employer can escape liability for wrongful dismissal, but not for unfair dismissal, by giving the employee wages in lieu of notice.

Constructive dismissal

If the employer's behaviour is so bad as to amount to a repudiation of the contract, then the employee can resign, without giving notice, and sue for wrongful dismissal. (As we saw when considering unfair dismissal, the employee accepts the repudiation and this ends the contract.) This is known as constructive dismissal.

How much notice?

The contract of employment will usually state the amount of notice required. In addition, every employee is entitled to a reasonable period of notice, the length of which will depend upon a variety of factors, such as the nature of the position and the length of service with the employer.

ERA 1996 s. 86 lays down that employees are entitled to a minimum of one week's notice after they have been continuously employed for between one month and two years. After being continuously employed for two years or more, employees are entitled to one week's notice for every year of continuous employment (up to a maximum of 12 weeks). The effect of s. 86 is shown in Table 13.1.

There will be no right to sue for wrongful dismissal if the employer and employee agree to terminate the contract without notice. However, the employment tribunal would need to be satisfied that the agreement was genuine and that the employee was not pushed into it against his or her will.

Nor will there be a right to sue for wrongful dismissal if the contract was frustrated. Earlier (see Chapter 5) we saw that a contract will be frustrated if it becomes impossible to perform, illegal to perform or radically different from what the parties contemplated when they made the contract. A contract of employment can become frustrated by the imprisonment of the employee or by long-term illness. In **Egg Stores (Stamford Hill) Ltd v Leibovici (1977)** an employee of 15 years' standing was off work for five months after a car crash. After paying the employee's wages for two months, the employer stopped doing so when another employee was taken on. The Employment Appeal Tribunal held that, as regards a long-term employee, the employer should ask whether the time had arrived when the employer could no longer reasonably be expected to keep the employee's job open for him. This would require examination of matters such as: the length of employment, the nature of the job, the length and nature of the illness, the need for the job to be done, whether wages continued to be paid and whether the employer could reasonably be expected to wait any longer.

A person on a fixed-term contract who is dismissed when the contract ends is not wrongfully dismissed. (He could, however, have been unfairly dismissed.)

Wrongful dismissal is not a great deal of use to many employees because their notice entitlement is not long enough to result in large damages. It can be very useful to those who are highly paid and who are entitled to long periods of notice.

Table 13.1 The minimum periods of notice to terminate a contract of employment

Length of continuous employment	Notice entitlement
Less than 1 month	None
1 month–2 years	1 week
2–12 years	1 week per year worked
Over 12 years	12 weeks

Earlier (see Chapter 5) we saw that the purpose of contract damages is to put the injured party in the position he would have been in if the contract had been performed as agreed. The injured party will be able to claim for any foreseeable loss which resulted from the breach of contract. Damages can only be claimed for matters which would have arisen if the employer had not breached the contract. So if the employee was contractually entitled to a bonus, damages could be claimed in respect of this. If, however, the bonus was discretionary, damages could not be claimed. The claimant must take all reasonable steps to mitigate the loss. If the dismissed employee receives jobseeker's allowance, this will be deducted from the damages.

The employment tribunal can award £25,000 damages for wrongful dismissal. If the wrongful dismissal claim is for more than £25,000, it must be pursued through the ordinary courts. Figure 13.3 gives an overview of wrongful dismissal.

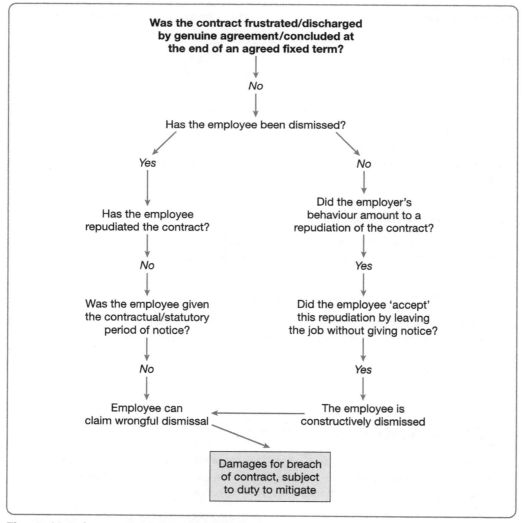

Figure 13.3 An overview of wrongful dismissal

Redundancy

Section 139(1) of the ERA 1996 explains that an employee has been made redundant if he was dismissed wholly or mainly because:

- the employer ceased, or intended to cease, to carry on the business; or
- the employer ceased, or intended to cease, to carry on the business in the place where the employee was employed; or
- the need for work of a particular kind to be carried on, or to be carried on in the place where the employee worked, had either ceased or diminished or was expected to do so.

Where the employer moves the place of business, whether or not the employees have been made redundant will depend upon how far the business moved and the amount of inconvenience caused to the employees by the move.

The meaning of the words 'work of a particular kind' have caused difficulty. In **Safeway Stores plc v Burrell (1997)** it was held that s. 139(1) involved a three-stage process:

(1) It should be asked if the employee has been dismissed.

(2) It should be asked whether the requirements of the employer's business for employees to carry out work of a particular kind had ceased or diminished or were expected to do so.

(3) It should be asked whether the dismissal of the employee was caused wholly or mainly by the state of affairs identified at stage two.

If the answer to the questions posed in the three stages was in each case 'yes', then the employee had been made redundant. This test was approved by the House of Lords in **Murray v Foyle Meats (1999)**.

Who can claim redundancy?

In order to claim redundancy, an employee must have at least two years' continuous employment. People who are ordinarily employed outside Great Britain cannot claim.

Offer of suitable alternative employment

If the employer offers the employee suitable alternative employment, and the employee unreasonably refuses to accept this, then the employee cannot claim to have been made redundant. The offer must be made within four weeks of the expiry of the employment and must be reasonable in all the circumstances.

 Taylor v Kent County Council (1969)

A 53-year-old, who had been headmaster of a school for ten years, was made redundant when his school was merged with another school. He was offered alternative employment as a supply teacher at his headmaster's salary. He declined the offer.

Held He was made redundant. The alternative employment was not suitable.

Redundancy payments

A redundancy payment is calculated in the same way as the basic award for unfair dismissal. (See earlier in this chapter.) However, a redundancy payment cannot be reduced on account of the employee's conduct.

It is important to remember that what is being considered here is the right to a statutory redundancy payment. The terms of many contracts of employment agree that more generous payments should be made in the event of redundancy. Figure 13.4 gives an overview of redundancy.

Procedure for large-scale redundancies

In **Williams v Compair Maxam Ltd (1982)** five principles were laid out to be followed when a large number of people are to be made redundant:

(1) The employer should give the employees as much warning as possible.

(2) The employer should consult the trade union in order to be fair, and to cause as little hardship as possible.

(3) Subjective criteria should not be used. The process should be objective and matters such as attendance records and length of service should be considered.

(4) Union representatives should be consulted as to the appropriate criteria to be used.

(5) The employer should try to offer alternative employment instead of just making employees redundant.

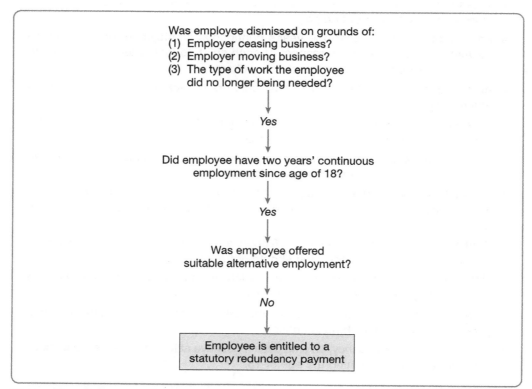

Figure 13.4 An overview of redundancy

If the employer does not follow these procedures, then it seems likely that the employees will not have been made redundant but will have been unfairly dismissed. This will be beneficial to the employees, as the tribunal may make a compensatory award. As we have seen, the basic award for unfair dismissal will be the same as a statutory redundancy payment.

Consultation on redundancies

An employer who intends to make 20 or more employees at one establishment redundant must consult with trade unions with a view to reaching agreement with them. If it is proposed to make at least 100 employees redundant at one establishment, the Secretary of State must be notified in writing.

Essential points

- Contracts of employment can be created orally or in writing and contain both express and implied terms.
- As a matter of law, implied terms of the contract of employment place obligations on both the employer and the employee.
- All female employees have a statutory right to 52 weeks' maternity leave.
- Mothers who qualify for maternity pay and leave can opt to end their maternity leave early and share parental leave with their partner or the father of the child.
- When a couple adopt a child, one member of the couple is entitled to time off work with statutory adoption pay.
- An employee with at least one year's continuous employment can take up to 13 weeks' parental leave, in respect of each child, to look after his or her child or to make arrangements for the child's welfare.
- All employees are entitled to take time off work to look after dependants in an emergency.
- Parents with children under 16 years old have the right to apply for flexible working. However, the employer need not grant this.
- When a business is transferred from one employer to another, the contracts of employment of all the employees are also transferred.
- All employees are entitled to be paid at least the national minimum wage. There is a minimum rate for workers aged 20 or over and lower rates for workers aged under 20.
- Workers should not work more than 48 hours a week. However, individual workers can agree in writing that this limit should not apply.
- Unfair dismissal is a statutory remedy which gives a dismissed employee with at least two years' continuous employment a right to a fixed payment.
- An employee is wrongfully dismissed when he is dismissed without having been given the notice to which he is entitled.
- In order to claim redundancy, an employee must have at least two years' continuous employment since reaching the age of 18.

Practice questions

1 Jane works for Ace Supplies Ltd. She has four years' continuous service and earns £20,000 a year. Jane has recently discovered that she is pregnant and that the baby is due in six months' time. Advise Jane of her rights to take maternity leave and the amount of any maternity pay which she will receive.

2 Jane's partner, Harry, wants to take paternity leave when Jane's baby is born. Explain the requirements which he will need to satisfy. Explain also the length of time which he will be able to take off and the amount of paternity pay which he will receive. Harry has worked for Ace Supplies Ltd for five years and earns £20,000 a year.

3 Explain the main differences between unfair dismissal and wrongful dismissal. Which remedy would be likely to be more useful to: (a) a very highly paid football manager; and (b) a long-serving factory worker if they were both wrongfully and unfairly dismissed?

4 On what six grounds can an employer justify a dismissal, so that the dismissal may not amount to unfair dismissal?

5 An employee is dismissed for the following reasons. Which of the reasons would mean that the employee was made redundant?

   (a) Because the employer is going out of business.

   (b) Because the employee was convicted of drinking and driving.

   (c) Because the employee became too ill to do the job properly.

   (d) Because the employer no longer did the type of work which the employee was employed to do.

   (e) Because the employer is transferring his business to a new site several hundred miles away.

6 Calculate the amount of the basic award for unfair dismissal in the following cases.

   (a) Farzana, a 21-year-old waitress with four years' continuous employment, who earns £220 a week.

   (b) Gerry, a 42-year-old painter with one year's continuous employment, who earns £280 a week.

   (c) Kevin, a 58-year-old football club manager with ten years' continuous employment, who earns £5,000 a week.

   (d) Alex, a 40-year-old doorman with 18 years' continuous employment, who earns a basic weekly wage of £300 and earns an average of £100 a week in overtime.

Task 13

A group of students from China are visiting England on a cultural exchange visit. Prepare notes for a presentation to be made to the visiting students. The presentation should cover, briefly, the following matters:

(a) The way in which a contract of employment is formed and the terms which are usually implied into such contracts.

(b) The way in which a contract of employment can be varied.

(c) The statutory procedure which must be followed when an employee brings a grievance against his or her employer.

(d) The essential differences between claims for unfair dismissal, wrongful dismissal and redundancy.

(e) The statutory procedure which must be followed when an employee is dismissed or disciplined.

mylawchamber

Visit **www.mylawchamber.co.uk/macintyreessentials** to access tools to help you develop and test your knowledge of business law, including interactive multiple choice questions, practice exam questions with guidance, weblinks, glossary, glossary flashcards, legal newsfeed and legal updates.

Use **Case Navigator** to read in full some of the key cases referenced in this chapter with commentary and questions:

Western Excavating *v* **Sharp (1978)**

Post Office *v* **Foley (2000)**

British Home Stores Ltd *v* **Burchell (1980)**

14

Employment (2): Discrimination and health and safety

Introduction

This chapter first considers discrimination in employment and then health and safety at work. The Equality Act 2010 has consolidated the law on discrimination. Before the Act came into force the law was contained in a large number of different regulations and statutes. Legislation which prevents discrimination on account of the type of contract on which an employee works, for example on a part-time contract or on a fixed-term contract, has not been consolidated. However, the Equality Act has replaced all of the previous legislation which outlawed discrimination on account of an employee's personal characteristics. It has therefore replaced statutes such as the Equal Pay Act 1970 and the Race Relations Act 1976.

The Equality Act 2010

The Equality Act aims to harmonise discrimination law and strengthen progress on equality. It adopts a common approach to outlawing discrimination at work where the discrimination is based on a person's personal characteristics, such as being female, black or disabled. It also allows positive discrimination to overcome or minimise disadvantage suffered on account of personal characteristics. In addition, certain public bodies are required to consider socio-economic disadvantage when making strategic decisions.

The protected characteristics

Section 4 of the Act lists nine protected characteristics. Discrimination on the grounds of one or more of these characteristics is outlawed. The protected characteristics are:

- age;
- disability;
- gender reassignment;
- marriage and civil partnership;
- pregnancy and maternity;
- race;
- religion or belief;
- sex; and
- sexual orientation.

As regards each of the protected characteristics, the Act protects those who have the particular characteristic and those who belong to a group which shares the same characteristic.

The **protected characteristic of age** means belonging to a particular age group, such as being under 18 or over 50. Where people belong to the same age group, they share the protected characteristics of age. For example, both 18-year-olds and 50-year-olds share the characteristic of being in the 'under 60' age group.

Discrimination on the grounds of age is allowed if it is a proportionate means of achieving a legitimate aim. In **Seldon v Clarkson Wright and Jacques (2012)** the Supreme Court considered this in relation to compulsory retirement. The partnership deed of a firm of solicitors stated that partners should retire at the age of 65. A partner who was retired at this age claimed discrimination on the grounds of age. The Supreme Court recognised 'inter-generational fairness', which would involve matters such as sharing opportunities to work between the generations, as a legitimate aim. But even if such an aim was capable of being a legitimate aim it would still be necessary to show that it was in fact the aim being pursued in the case before the court and that the aim was legitimate in the circumstances of the particular business. Also, the means chosen to bring about the aim would have to be both appropriate and necessary, so that a less discriminatory measure would not be possible. The Supreme Court referred the case back to the employment tribunal to decide, as a matter of fact, whether the firm's retirement policy at the age of 65 was proportionate, appropriate and necessary. The decision in this case has meant that businesses which have a policy of compulsory retirement at a certain age might need to review the policy.

Schedule 9 exempts the different national minimum wages. Redundancy schemes are also exempted as long as all employees' redundancy payments are calculated on the same basis. So a person with more years of continuous employment can be given a greater redundancy payment than a person with fewer years.

A person has the **protected characteristic of disability**, and is known as a disabled person, if he has a physical or mental impairment and the impairment has a substantial and long-term adverse effect on his ability to carry out normal day-to-day activities. An impairment is long-term if it has lasted for at least 12 months, or is likely to do so, or is likely to last for the rest of a person's life. If an impairment has ceased to have a substantial adverse effect on a person's ability to carry out normal day-to-day activities it will still be regarded as a disability if it is likely to recur. Severe disfigurement is regarded as having a substantial adverse effect on a person's ability to carry out normal day-to-day activities. Cancer, HIV infection and multiple sclerosis are each regarded as a disability.

A person has the **protected characteristic of gender reassignment** if he or she is a transsexual person. A transsexual person is a person who is proposing to undergo a process to change sex, or has started or completed such a process.

A person has the **protected characteristic of marriage or civil partnership** if he or she is either married or a civil partner. People who are not married and not in a civil partnership do not have this protected characteristic and are not protected by the Act.

The **protected characteristic of race** includes colour, nationality or ethnic or national origins. People who share the same colour, nationality or ethnic or national origins share the same racial group, and one racial group can comprise two or more distinct racial groups. For example, 'black Britons' are a racial group comprising the racial group 'black' and the national group 'British'. Caste is currently not an aspect of race, but s. 9 allows a Government minister to amend the Act so that caste becomes an aspect of race. The following case considered the meaning of 'ethnic'.

Mandla *v* Dowell Lee (1983) (House of Lords)

A school refused to admit a Sikh boy because he would not cut his hair and stop wearing a turban. The trial judge held that no claim could be brought under the Act because Sikhs are not a racial group.

Held Sikhs are a racial group defined by ethnic origins. So the boy succeeded in his claim that he had been indirectly discriminated against.

In this case, when considering the meaning of ethnic group, the House of Lords held that two characteristics were essential and another five characteristics would commonly be found.

The two essential characteristics of ethnic groups are:

(1) that the group has a long shared history of which it is conscious as distinguishing it from other groups and the memory of which it keeps alive; and

(2) that the group has a cultural tradition of its own, including family and social customs and manners, which is often but not necessarily associated with religious observance.

The five non-essential characteristics are:

(1) common origin from one geographical area or descent from a small number of ancestors;

(2) a common language, even though others might speak it;

(3) a common literature which is peculiar to the group;

(4) a common religion which is different from that of neighbouring groups or that of the general surrounding community;

(5) being a minority or being an oppressed or dominant group within a larger community.

The **protected characteristic of religion** applies to any religion as well as to a lack of religion. The **protected characteristic of belief** applies to any religious or philosophical belief, including a lack of belief.

References to the **protected characteristic of sex** are references to being either a man or a woman.

The **protected characteristic of sexual orientation** is defined as a sexual orientation towards persons of the same sex, persons of the opposite sex or persons of either sex.

Direct discrimination

Direct discrimination, indirect discrimination, harassment and victimisation all amount to prohibited conduct. Each of these needs to be considered in turn.

Section 13(1) sets out the meaning of direct discrimination. It says that a person (A) discriminates against another (B) if, because of a protected characteristic, A treats B less favourably that A treats or would treat others. So it would be direct discrimination, for example, to refuse to employ a person either because he was a Hindu, or because he associated with Hindus or because he was wrongly thought to be a Hindu. It makes no difference that A has the same characteristic. So a woman can be liable for discriminating against another woman. Section 13 then goes on to make five specific rules which relate to direct discrimination on five of the protected characteristics.

Section 13(2) states that if the protected characteristic is age, A does not discriminate against B if A can show A's treatment of B to be a proportionate means of achieving a legitimate aim.

Section 13(3) states that if the protected characteristic is disability, it is not discrimination to treat a disabled person more favourably than a non-disabled person.

Section 13(4) states that if the protected characteristic is marriage and civil partnership, it is only a person who is married or in a civil partnership who can be the victim of dicrimination.

Section 13(5) states that if the protected characteristic is race, less favourable treatment includes segregating B from others.

Section 13(6) states that if the protected characteristic is sex:

(a) less favourable treatment of a woman includes less favourable treatment of her because she is breast-feeding (but this does not apply for the purposes of employment);

(b) a man cannot claim discrimination on account of not being given the special treatment afforded to a woman in connection with pregnancy or childbirth.

Section 14 provides that direct discrimination can be committed by discriminating against a person on account of their having two of the relevant protected characteristics, for example being an Asian woman. For example, an employer might prohibit Asian women from going on a certain training scheme, even though he allows non-Asian women and Asian men to go on the scheme. This would amount to dual discrimination.

Direct discrimination against disabled persons

Section 15 provides that it is discrimination to treat a disabled person unfavourably not just because he is disabled but because of something which arises in connection with his disability. For example, it would be discriminatory to dismiss a visually impaired person because he could not read as quickly as a normally sighted person or because he needed to attend a large number of hospital appointments. However, it will not be discrimination if the employer can show that his treatment of the disabled person was a proportionate means of achieving a legitimate aim. Nor will it be discriminatory if A shows that A did not know, and could not reasonably have been expected to know, that B had the disability.

Direct discrimination in pregnancy and maternity cases

Section 18 makes it discriminatory for an employer to treat a woman less favourably because of her pregnancy or because of an illness connected with her pregnancy. It is also discrimination to treat a woman less favourably because she is on maternity leave or is exercising her right to maternity leave or additional maternity leave.

Indirect discrimination

Section 19(1) provides that a person (A) discriminates against another (B) if A applies to B a provision, criterion or practice which is discriminatory in relation to a relevant protected characteristic of B's (except pregnancy and maternity).

A provision, criterion or practice is discriminatory in relation to a relevant protected characteristic of B's if:

- A applies, or would apply, it to persons with whom B does not share the characteristic;
- it puts, or would put, persons with whom B shares the characteristic at a particular disadvantage when compared with persons with whom B does not share it;
- it puts, or would put, B at that disadvantage; and
- A cannot show it to be a proportionate means of achieving a legitimate aim.

An example might help to show the meaning of this. Let us assume that an employer, A, imposes a pattern of shift working on all employees, and that this pattern would prevent women with young children from continuing in the job. The new shift pattern applies to men as well as women (s. 19(1)(a)). It puts some women at a particular disadvantage (s. 19(1)(b)). One particular woman shows that she is put at a disadvantage because she cannot keep the job if the pattern is imposed (s. 19(1)(c)). This will be indirect discrimination unless the employer can show that imposing the new shift pattern is a proportionate means of achieving a legitimate aim (s. 19(1)(d)).

Section 20 requires employers to make reasonable adjustments to see that disabled employees are not disadvantaged by work practices or by physical features of the workplace. If necessary, the employer must also provide auxiliary aids. If the employer fails to comply with this duty, then this amounts to discrimination.

Need for a comparator

Section 23 requires that a person claiming direct, dual or indirect discrimination does so by reference to a comparator. The comparator can be a real or a hypothetical person whose circumstances are the same as the claimant's, except that the comparator does not share the claimant's protected characteristic. So, for example, an employee who claimed to be discriminated against on account of being a woman would have to do so by reference to a male comparator whose circumstances were the same as her own. When considering cases of direct or dual discrimination on grounds of disability, the circumstances can include the abilities of the claimant and the comparator to do the job.

Harassment

Section 26(1) provides that a person (A) harasses another (B) if:

- A engages in unwanted conduct related to a relevant protected characteristic, or of a sexual nature; and
- the conduct has the purpose or effect of –
  - violating B's dignity; or
  - creating an intimidating, hostile, degrading, humiliating or offensive environment for B.

Examples of harassment might include an employer putting up a topless calendar which some employees, male or female, found offensive or a manager making an employee listen to racially offensive jokes. When considering whether or not the conduct has the effect referred to in s. 20(1)(b), three matters have to be taken into account. These matters are: the perception of B; the other circumstances of the case; and whether it is reasonable for the conduct to have that effect.

Victimisation

Section 27(1) provides that a person (A) victimises another person (B) if A subjects B to a detriment because:

- B does a protected act; or
- A believes that B has done, or may do, a protected act.

Section 27(2) states that each of the following is a protected act:

- bringing proceedings under the Act;
- giving evidence or information in connection with proceedings under the Act;

- doing any other thing for the purposes of or in connection with the Act;
- making an allegation (whether or not express) that A or another person has contravened the Act.

So if a black employee was not promoted because he had complained about discrimination, this would amount to victimisation.

Victimisation can occur after the employment has ended, as in **Jessemey v Rowstock Ltd (2014)**, where an employee who had brought tribunal proceedings against his employer was held to have been victimised when he was later given a bad reference for having brought the proceedings.

Discrimination against employees and applicants for employment

Section 39 states that when selecting employees it is unlawful to discriminate against a person or victimise a person in the following ways:

- by making discriminatory arrangements for the purposes of determining who should be offered employment; or
- by offering discriminatory terms of employment; or
- by refusing or deliberately omitting to offer employment.

As regards existing employees, it is unlawful to discriminate against a person or victimise a person:

- in the terms of the employment;
- in the way access to opportunities for promotion, transfer or training, or to any other benefits are given; or by refusing or deliberately omitting to allow access to these things; or
- by dismissing the employee or subjecting him or her to any other detriment.

Schedule 9 to the Act provides that, as regards not offering a person a job, not offering access to promotion, etc. or dismissing a person, the employer might have the defence of **occupational requirement**. The employer will have to show that, having regard to the nature or context of the work, a requirement imposed by the employer is an occupational requirement which the employee or applicant does not have. The employer will also need to show that the application of the requirement is a proportionate means of achieving a legitimate aim. So, for example, an employer making a film about Nelson Mandela could insist that the actor who was to play Mandela should be both a man and black.

Section 40 requires employees not to harass employees or applicants for employment. Employers also have a duty to make sure, as far as is reasonably practicable, that third parties do not harass either.

Section 60 prevents employers from asking applicants for jobs about their health, except in so far as this is to do with the applicant's ability to do the job or for the purpose of monitoring diversity.

Remedies and burden of proof

If discrimination is proved then a tribunal may:

(a) make a declaration of the complainant's rights;

(b) award compensation;

(c) recommend that the defendant takes certain action within a specified time.

There is no limit on the amount of damages in discrimination cases. Damages can take account of injury to feelings, injury to health, loss of earnings, other provable losses and interest. Aggravated damages, which rarely exceed £5,000, can be awarded if the employer has been cruel, oppressive, malicious or insulting and this has injured the claimant's feelings. Psychiatric injury does not need to have been foreseeable. Recommendations might require the employer to: introduce an equal opportunities policy; ensure the better implementation of a harassment policy; set up a panel to deal with equal opportunities; retrain staff; or publicise the criteria used for selection or promotion.

A claimant who alleges discrimination under the Equality Act must first prove his or her case. Once the claimant has proved, in the absence of any other explanation, that a breach of the Act occurred, the burden of proof then shifts onto the employer to show that there was no breach of the Act.

Under the new fees regime it costs £250 to issue a claim in a discrimination case and the tribunal hearing fee is £950.

Equal pay and conditions for women

The Equality Act requires that men and women working for the same employer should be treated equally as regards pay and other benefits. It is convenient to talk of a woman bringing a claim under the Act but there is no reason why a man should not bring a claim. Section 65 allows a woman to bring a claim on three grounds:

(1) that she does 'like work' to that of a male comparator;

(2) that the work is rated as equivalent; or

(3) that the work is of equal value.

Article 157 of the Treaty on the Functioning of the European Union requires Member States of the EU to ensure the principle of equal pay for male and female workers if they do equal work, or work of equal value. In **Pickstone v Freemans plc (1988)** the House of Lords indicated that national courts should try to interpret UK legislation so as to give effect to Article 157.

The Equality Act 2010 has the same effect as the Equal Pay Act 1970 in this area. Therefore, cases decided under the Equal Pay Act will continue to apply.

The need for a male comparator

A woman can bring a claim under the Act only if she can show that she has been treated less favourably than a male working for the same employer or for an associated employer. An employer is associated if one person or company controls both employers. It is therefore necessary to find a real, not hypothetical, comparator of the opposite sex. It does not matter that the comparator works in a different place, as long as common terms and conditions are observed at both places.

In **British Coal Corporation v Smith (1996)** female canteen workers and cleaners, working at 47 different places, were allowed to compare themselves with male surface workers and clerical staff, working at four different establishments. The House of Lords held that the terms and conditions did not have to be identical, rather they had to be substantially comparable on a broad basis. It is for the woman bringing a claim to choose the comparator, to prevent the employer choosing a token male who is paid less, and it is possible to choose a previous employee. In **North v Dumfries and Galloway Council (2013)** the Supreme Court firmly rejected an argument that there had to be a real possibility that a comparator in an equal pay claim could actually be transferred to the same workplace as the claimant. The correct approach is first for the court to imagine that the comparator is transferred to do his present job in a different location. Then it should ask whether in that event, however unlikely it might be, he would remain employed on the same or broadly similar terms and conditions to those applicable in his current place of work. If he would, he could be used as a comparator. The object of the Act was to allow comparison between people who never had and never would work in the same workplace.

Once it has been shown that the woman does like work, work rated as equivalent or work which is of equal value to that of a man, s. 66(1) provides that the woman's contract of employment should be deemed to include an **equality clause**. Such a clause would require the terms of the woman's contract to be changed so that they became no less favourable than similar terms in the male comparator's contract.

Like work

Section 65(1) provides that a woman does like work with that of a man only if her work is the same or of a broadly similar nature to that of the man. Any differences between what she does and what the man does must not be of practical importance in relation to the terms and conditions of employment. Both the frequency with which any differences occur in practice, as well as the extent and nature of the differences, should be considered.

 Capper Pass *v* Lawton (1976) (House of Lords)

A woman who cooked 10–20 lunches for directors wished to be compared to two male assistant chefs who cooked 350 lunches for the general work force. The directors ate in one sitting, whereas the male assistants had to prepare six sittings a day, two at breakfast, two at lunch and two at tea. The woman worked alone in the kitchen for 40 hours a week. The two male assistants worked 45 hours a week and were supervised by a head chef.

Held The woman's work was broadly similar to that of the male assistants and so it was like work. The woman was therefore entitled to the same rate of pay as the men.

Differences in the work of the woman and the male comparator must be practical rather than merely theoretical.

 Shields *v* E Coombes Ltd (Holdings) (1978) (Court of Appeal)

A female betting-shop counterhand was paid 92p per hour, whereas the male comparator counterhand, working in the same shop, was paid £1.06 per hour. The employer argued that their work was not broadly similar because the betting shop was in a rough area and the male had the responsibility of sorting out any trouble.

Held The employer's argument failed. The male's additional duties were of no practical importance because, in the previous three years, there had been no trouble for the male to sort out. So the woman was entitled to equal pay and conditions.

Basic pay should not differ merely because the men do different hours, such as working shifts. If men work shifts they can be paid extra by means of a shift allowance. But if both men and women work different hours, such as shifts, the basic pay of shift workers can be higher than that of non-shift workers.

Work rated as equivalent

Work will be rated as equivalent only if a properly conducted job evaluation scheme has found that the work is equivalent (s. 65(2)).

Work of equal value

Work done by a woman is of equal value to that of a male comparator if the demands made on the woman are comparable with the demands made on the male. Matters such as effort, skill and decision-making are taken into account (s. 65(6)).

 Hayward v Cammell Laird Shipbuilders Ltd (1988) (House of Lords)

A female caterer wished to be compared to male painters and joiners working at the same shipyard. As apprentices the caterers, painters, thermal insulation engineers and joiners had all been paid the same rate. After the apprenticeship the caterer was paid a lower hourly wage, although she had better conditions on holidays, meal breaks and sick pay. She applied to be paid the same hourly wage as the men.

Held The applicant won, even though her contract of employment, when viewed overall, was already as favourable as that of the men. As the woman's work was broadly similar to that of the men she was entitled to an equal rate of pay.

Comment The House of Lords indicated that the men would be able to bring a claim to gain the better conditions on holidays, meal breaks and sick pay which the woman enjoyed. So there was bound to be some degree of leap-frogging.

Defence of material factor

Section 69 gives an employer a defence if he can prove that the different treatment of the woman was due to a material factor which does not directly or indirectly discriminate against the claimant because of her sex. If this can be proved, the equality clause will not take effect. If the claimant can show that the factor upon which the employer relies is indirectly discriminatory, the equality clause will apply unless the employer can also show that the factor is a proportionate means of achieving a legitimate aim. A long-term objective of reducing inequality between men's and women's terms of work is always to be regarded as a legitimate aim. Where a man had been downgraded and his pay protected by being 'red-circled' this could be a genuine material factor as long as the **red-circling** was not done in a discriminatory way.

Discussions about pay and publishing information

Section 77 applies where a term of the contract of employment tries to prevent employees from discussing their pay with others, where the purpose of the discussions is to discover a connection between a difference in pay and a protected characteristic. If an employer takes any action against a person who is protected by this section, then this would amount to victimisation. So if a woman thought she was being paid less than a man doing the same type of work, and asked him what he was paid, it would be victimisation of the man if the employer took any action against him for having discussed his pay.

Employers of 250 or more employees may be required by future regulations to publish information relating to differences in the pay of male and female employees.

Remedies under the Act

A claimant must bring a case before an employment tribunal while still in the employment or within three months of leaving it. However, in **Birmingham City Council v Abdulla (2012)**, a judgment of huge practical significance, the Supreme Court held that a claim for equal pay could also be brought in the county court. The time limit for bringing a claim, other than one for personal injury, in the county court is six years and so this decision has enabled many women who appeared to be out of time to issue claims for equal pay.

The tribunal has several powers. It can make a declaration as to the parties' rights, or make a recommendation to an employer that it reduces or eliminates discrimination. Damages can be awarded for financial losses, such as loss of earnings, and for injury to feelings. There is no upper limit on the amount of damages. As regards equal pay and conditions claims, it is not only 'pay' in respect of which a claim can be made. Each term of the woman's contract must be no less beneficial than that of the male comparator. Therefore claims can be made in respect of matters such as lower redundancy payments, lower travel benefits for retired employees and lower rates of sick pay.

Figure 14.1 shows an overview of the equal pay provisions.

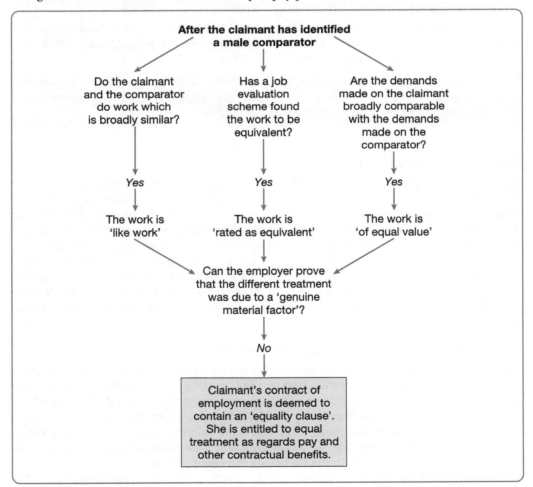

Figure 14.1 An overview of the equal pay provisions

Burden of proof under the Act

Section 136 provides that a claimant who alleges discrimination, harassment of victimisation under the Act must initially prove his or her case. Once the claimant has proved, in the absence of any other explanation, that a breach of the Act occurred, the burden of proof then shifts on to the employer to show that there was no breach of the Act.

Public sector equality duty

Section 149(1) requires public authorities, in the exercise of their functions, to have due regard to the need to:

- eliminate discrimination, harassment, victimisation and any other conduct that is prohibited by or under the Act;
- advance equality of opportunity between persons who share a relevant protected characteristic and persons who do not share it; and
- foster good relations between persons who share a relevant protected characteristic and persons who do not share it.

When a major public authority, such as a local authority, makes a decision of a strategic nature about how to exercise its functions, it must have due regard to trying to exercise them in such a way that is designed to reduce the inequalities which result from socio-economic disadvantage. This might involve matters such as publicising access to health or educational programmes more widely in disadvantaged areas.

Positive action

Section 158 allows an employer to discriminate in favour of people who are disadvantaged on account of having a protected characteristic. So particular disadvantaged groups could be targeted for extra training or education. Any such action must be a proportionate means of achieving a positive aim.

Discrimination against part-time workers

The Part-time Workers (Prevention of Less Favourable Treatment) Regulations 2000 outlaw discrimination against part-time workers. However, this is the case only if the part-time worker is employed under the 'same type of contract' as a full-time comparator, and if the work done is the 'same or broadly similar'. The House of Lords held in **Mathews and others v Kent and Medway Towns Fire Authority (2006)** that part-time fire-fighters were entitled to equal treatment as regards full-time fire-fighters. This was because the work which they did was broadly similar to that done by full-time fire-fighters, and differences in treatment could not be justified on objective grounds. The correct approach under the Regulations is, first, to establish whether the two groups were employed on the same type of contract, and then to concentrate on similarities between the work done by both groups. It did not matter that the full-timers had additional duties unless these additional duties were doing the more important work. The approach is not the same as the one used under the Equality Act 2010 because it is inevitable that part-time work is in some ways different from full-time work.

Regulation 5(1) provides that:

A part-time worker has the right not to be treated by his employer less favourably than the employer treats a full-time worker –

(a) as regards the terms of his contract; or

(b) by being subjected to any other detriment by any act, or deliberate failure to act, of his employer.

This Regulation applies only if the unfavourable treatment of the part-time worker was on the grounds that he is a part-time worker. These rights conferred do not apply if the treatment is justified by the employer on objective grounds. The **pro rata** principle is used to assess whether or not a part-time worker has been treated less favourably. Under this principle a part-time worker should receive the appropriate proportion of pay and other benefits enjoyed by a full-time worker with whom he compares himself. These benefits include sick pay, maternity pay, access to pension schemes, training, career breaks and holiday entitlement. A part-timer is not entitled to overtime rates until working longer than full-time hours.

Regulation 6 entitles a part-time worker who is being treated less favourably to a written statement which explains why this is happening. If a worker is dismissed for bringing proceedings under the Regulations, this is automatically unfair dismissal. Complaints under the Regulations are made, in the usual way, to the employment tribunal. The tribunal can declare the claimant's rights, order the payment of damages or recommend that action be taken to get rid of or reduce the discrimination within a certain time. However, the employee has a duty to mitigate any loss, and damages cannot be awarded in respect of injured feelings. Figure 14.2 shows the effect in outline of the Part-time Workers Regulations 2000.

Fixed-term workers

The Fixed-term Employees (Prevention of Less Favourable Treatment) Regulations 2002 provide that workers on fixed-term contracts should not be treated less favourably than other workers, unless there is a justifiable reason for the less favourable treatment. A contract is a fixed-term contract if it is agreed at the outset to be in existence for a fixed time, rather than being a contract which can be ended by giving notice. In order to claim, a comparator working for the same employer must be found.

A fixed-term employee can request a written statement asking the employer to explain the reasons why he is being treated less favourably. In addition, after four years have been worked on consecutive fixed-term contracts, the contract is renewed as a permanent contract.

Persons with criminal records

The Rehabilitation of Offenders Act 1974 allows people whose convictions have become spent to deny that they have ever been convicted. Furthermore, if a person is dismissed because of a spent conviction, this will amount to unfair dismissal. The Act was passed to help people with criminal records back into employment. If such people are discriminated against by being refused employment, they are more likely to continue to commit criminal offences.

Some criminal offences involving children are never spent. Otherwise, a conviction becomes spent after a length of time which varies with the severity of the sentence passed. The times are shown in Table 14.1.

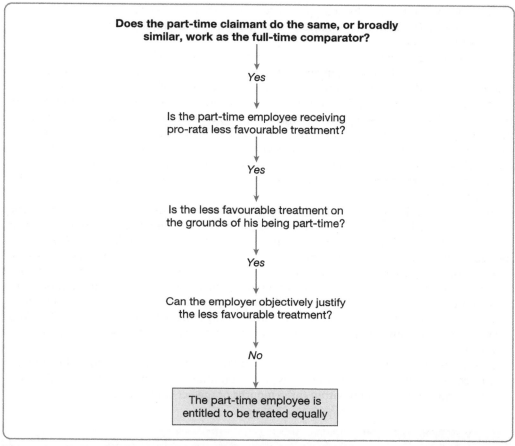

Figure 14.2 The Part-Time Workers Regulations 2000

Table 14.1

Over 2.5 years' imprisonment	Never spent
6 months–2.5 years	Spent after 10 years
Less than 6 months	Spent after 7 years
Youth custody	Spent after 7 years
Fined/community service order	Spent after 5 years
Detention centre	Spent after 3 years
Probation	Spent after 5 years
Curfew orders	Spent after 5 years
Absolute discharge	Spent after 6 months

The Agency Workers Regulations 2010

These regulations protect agency workers. Regulation 3 defines an agency worker as an individual who is supplied by a temporary work agency to work temporarily for and under the direct supervision of a hirer. The individual must also either have a contract of employment with the agency or have a different type of contract to perform work and services personally for the agency. The definition does not cover genuinely self-employed people who provide services for an agency.

Regulation 5 gives an agency worker the right to the same basic working and employment conditions as he would have been entitled to if he had been employed directly by the hirer. There is no need for a comparator. However, reg. 6(1) restricts the 'relevant terms and conditions' to the following six matters: pay; the duration of working time; night work; rest periods; rest breaks and annual leave. Regulation 6(3) specifically excludes sick pay, pensions, maternity, paternity or adoption leave, redundancy payments and certain other matters. Regulation 7 sets out a qualifying period which must have been worked before reg. 5 can apply. This period is 12 continuous calendar weeks, during which the worker must work in the same role for the same hirer during one or more assignments. Any part of a week worked counts as a calendar week.

Regulation 12(1) provides that as from the first day of working for a hirer an agency worker is entitled to be treated no less favourably than a comparable worker in relation to the collective facilities and amenities provided by the hirer. Regulation 13(1) requires an agency worker to be informed of any relevant vacant posts with the hirer, to give the agency worker the same opportunity as a comparable worker to find permanent employment with the hirer. Regulation 16 gives agency workers the right to request written information from the employer so that they can see if their rights have been infringed. If an agency worker is dismissed on account of bringing proceedings under the regulations, or for doing anything else in connection with the regulations, this is regarded as automatically unfair dismissal.

The rights are enforced through the employment tribunal, which can award compensation to cover the worker's loss. Generally, the minimum award will be two week's pay. A complaint must be presented within three months of the act complained of.

Health and safety

Health and Safety at Work Act 1974

The Health and Safety at Work Act 1974 (HSWA 1974) imposes various duties on employers. It is a criminal offence for an employer to breach one of these duties.

Enforcement of the Act

The Health and Safety Executive (HSE) aims to protect against risks to health or safety which arise out of work activities. It conducts its own research and sponsors research by other people, as well as providing training and information. It operates an information and advisory service and proposes new regulations and codes of practice, or the revision of existing ones.

The HSE has a network of advisory committees dealing with particular hazards, such as genetic modification, nuclear safety and hazards found in industries such as the textile and railway industries. The members of these committees are nominated by employers, trade unions and public interest representatives.

The HSE has the task of making sure that risks to people's health and safety arising out of work activities are properly controlled. Various directorates deal with matters such as corporate science, hazardous installations and nuclear safety. Advisory groups also exist in relation to specific industries such as the chemical industry and underground mining.

Inspectors can be appointed by the HSE or by local authorities. They have very wide powers to enforce health and safety legislation, including the powers to do the following:

- enter premises at any reasonable time, taking with them any duly authorised person or any necessary equipment;
- examine and investigate any matter to the extent that this is necessary;
- order that premises be left undisturbed so that they can be examined or investigated;
- take measurements, photographs or samples of articles or substances;
- cause articles or substances to be dismantled, taken away for examination or subjected to any test;
- require a person to give information and sign a declaration of the truth of his answers;
- inspect, take copies of or require the production of any documents;
- require any person to facilitate and assist them in respect of their duties;
- take any necessary action to enforce relevant statutory provisions.

Inspectors can also issue **improvement notices** requiring employers to stop contravening health and safety legislation within 21 days. If the employer is carrying on an activity which involves a risk of serious personal injury, inspectors can issue **prohibition notices** requiring the activity to cease with immediate effect. Inspectors also have the power to deal with a cause of imminent danger by seizing and rendering harmless any article or substance found on any premises.

Duties of the employer

Section 2 of the HSWA 1974 states that it is the duty of every employer to ensure, so far as is reasonably practicable, the health, safety and welfare at work of all his employees. In particular, this means:

- providing and maintaining safe plant and systems;
- ensuring safe use, handling, storage and transport of articles and substances;
- providing necessary information, instruction, training and supervision;
- maintaining the condition of the workplace so that it is safe and without risk to health;
- providing safe access and a safe way out; and
- providing a safe working environment.

Section 3 requires that the self-employed should not be exposed to risks to their health and safety and should be allowed to conduct their work in a safe way.

Employers with more than five employees also have a duty to prepare and keep up to date a written statement of general policy with respect to the health and safety at work of employees and the arrangements for carrying out that policy. They must bring the statement to the notice of all employees. They may also be required to consult with recognised trade unions to promote and develop health and safety measures.

Section 4 of the Act imposes a duty on controllers of premises to take such steps as are reasonable to ensure that non-employees are safe.

Duty in relation to articles and substances

Section 6 imposes a duty on any person who designs, manufactures, imports or supplies any article for use at work. The designer etc. must ensure that the article is designed and constructed so as to be safe. This may involve carrying out tests and examinations. There is also a duty to see that people provided with the article have been given adequate information about it and that this information is updated.

Duties of other persons

Section 7 imposes a general duty on employees to take reasonable care of the health and safety of themselves and of others who might be affected by their acts or omissions. There is also a duty to co-operate with the employer so that he can perform or comply with his statutory obligations.

Section 8 imposes a duty on any person not to interfere with or misuse things provided in pursuance of health and safety legislation. Section 9 prevents employers from charging for things done to maintain health and safety legislation.

Section 36 provides that where one person commits an offence under the Act, but this is due to the fault of some other person, then the other person can be charged with and convicted of the offence. So a person who was not an employer could be charged with a breach of s. 2 of the Act, which sets out the duties of an employer.

Section 37 provides that where a company commits an offence under the Act, if the offence was committed with the consent or connivance of, or was attributable to, any director or manager, both he and the company should be guilty of an offence. Where a company commits an offence under the Act, it will often be the case that a manager or director consented to the offence being committed.

Common law health and safety

The requirements of the tort of negligence were set out earlier (see Chapter 8). Employers owe a duty of care to their employees. If this duty is breached, and this breach causes the claimant to suffer a foreseeable type of injury, then the employee can sue in the tort of negligence. Employers owe three particular duties of care to their employees:

(1) They owe a duty to provide safe plant and equipment.

(2) They owe a duty to provide a safe system of work.

(3) They owe a duty to provide reasonably competent fellow employees.

In each case the duty owed is to take such care as an ordinary prudent employer would take in all the circumstances and cannot be delegated.

As the duty is owed to employees personally, if an employer knows that an employee has a particular weakness, account must be taken of this. For example, in **Paris v Stepney BC (1951)** an employee who had only one good eye was asked to work on the underneath of a vehicle and was not given protective goggles. He was blinded because when he hammered a bolt this caused a shard of metal to fly into his good eye. The House of Lords held that the employer was liable in the tort of negligence, and the fact that the employee was known to have only one good eye was a relevant factor.

As we have studied the requirements of the tort of negligence already, we need say only a little about the three particular duties owed to employees.

Safe plant and equipment

An example of an employer being liable for breach of this duty can be seen in the following case.

Bradford _v_ Robinson Rentals (1967)

A 57-year-old radio service engineer generally had to travel only short distances between customers' houses. In January 1963, during an exceptionally cold spell of weather, he was asked to drive for 20 hours on a 500-mile journey to change a colleague's van. The vans were unheated and the employee said he thought he should not go on the journey as it would be hazardous. He was ordered to go, and suffered frostbite.

Held The employer was liable in the tort of negligence.

Safe system of work

An employer has a duty to provide a safe system of work. This duty embraces all matters relating to the way the work is done, including the provision of training and safety equipment.

Duty to provide reasonably competent fellow employees

If an employer knows that the incompetence of one employee is endangering another, then he must take reasonable precautions to prevent this. If necessary, the incompetent employee should be dismissed.

Both contributory negligence and consent can provide a defence to the employer. These matters were considered earlier (see Chapter 8). An example of the defence of consent can be seen in **ICI Ltd _v_ Shatwell (1965)**, where experienced shot-firers ignored safety procedures when testing detonators. One of the shot-firers was badly injured as a consequence. However, the House of Lords held that the employer had a complete defence because the employee was deemed to have consented to the risk.

Control of Substances Hazardous to Health Regulations 2002

Regulation 4 prohibits the importation or supply for use at work of certain substances. These substances include benzene, sand containing free silica, ground flint or quartz, white phosphorus and certain types of oil.

Regulation 6 requires employers to carry out an assessment of the risk to health created by work involving any substances hazardous to health. Such a risk assessment requires consideration of:

- the hazardous nature of the substance;
- how long the employees are exposed to it;
- the effect of preventative measures; and
- the results of health surveillance.

Assessments have to be reviewed regularly and, if the employer employs five or more employees, they must be recorded.

Regulation 7 requires every employer to make sure that the exposure of his employees to substances hazardous to health is prevented or, if this is not possible, adequately controlled. In general, hazardous substances must be replaced with non-hazardous substances, so far as this is reasonably practicable. Regulation 7 also provides measures which an employer must take when exposure to a biological agent cannot be prevented. These measures include:

- posting warnings;
- specifying decontamination procedures;
- arranging safe collection and storage;
- testing to see if the agent has escaped;
- setting out procedures for working with the agent;
- vaccinating employees, if appropriate; and
- putting in place hygiene measures to prevent the accidental release of the agent.

Appropriate washing facilities must also be supplied and eating and drinking prohibited, if this is appropriate.

Regulation 8 requires employers to take all reasonable steps to ensure that any control measures are properly used and applied. Employee users have a duty to use control measures and to report any defects in them to the employer immediately.

Regulation 9 requires that control measures are kept in an effective state. It also requires that personal protective equipment, such as protective clothing, must be properly stored, checked regularly and repaired or replaced as soon as it becomes defective.

Regulation 10 requires employers to monitor the exposure of employees to hazardous substances if the risk assessment has indicated that this is necessary. This monitoring must be done at regular intervals and records must be kept. Employees can insist on access to their personal monitoring records.

Regulation 11 provides that, if appropriate for the protection of employees' health, the employer must ensure that employees liable to be exposed to hazardous substances are placed under suitable health surveillance.

Regulation 12 requires every employer who undertakes work which is liable to expose an employee to a hazardous substance to provide that employee with suitable and sufficient information, instruction and training.

Regulation 13 requires the employer to ensure that appropriate procedures, information and warnings are provided to deal with accidents, incidents and emergencies.

Regulation 14 requires an employer using certain fumigants to inform in advance the police and health and safety inspectors.

Under reg. 15 the Health and Safety Executive can grant exemption from the requirements of regs. 4, 8, 9 and 14. However, this will not be done unless the HSE is satisfied that it will not affect or prejudice the health and safety of any persons. The Secretary of State for Defence is allowed to exempt the armed forces from some aspects of the Regulations.

The 'six pack' Regulations

Article 153 of the Treaty on the Functioning of the European Union gives the power to pass directives which will improve the working environment so as to protect the health and safety of workers and their working conditions. Six sets of Regulations, known as the 'six pack', set out the steps which employers must actively take.

The Management of Health and Safety at Work Regulations 2003

These are the most important of the six pack Regulations. Regulation 3 requires every employer to make a suitable and sufficient assessment of the risks to health and safety of employees while they are at work. There must also be an assessment of the risks to persons other than employees. Such assessments must be reviewed if there is any reason to suspect that they are no longer valid or if there have been significant changes in the matters to which they relate. Employers of more than five people must keep written records. These records must show any significant finds of the assessment and any group of employees identified as being at special risk.

Regulation 5 requires every employer to make and give effect to appropriate health and safety arrangements. The employer must also ensure that his employees are provided with appropriate health surveillance, having regard to the risks to health and safety which are identified by the assessment.

Regulation 7 requires the employer to take on competent persons to assist him to comply with statutory health and safety requirements.

If there is likely to be serious and imminent danger, or a danger area, reg. 8 requires the employer to establish and give effect to appropriate procedures. Regulation 9 requires the employer to ensure that there are necessary contacts with external services providing first aid, emergency medical care and rescue work.

Regulation 10 requires the employer to provide all employees with comprehensible and relevant information on the risks to their health and the preventative and protective measures being taken. Where two or more employers share a workplace, reg. 11 imposes a duty to cooperate and coordinate on statutory safety requirements.

Regulation 13 requires the employer to take into account an employee's capabilities as regards health and safety before giving him a particular task.

Regulation 14 requires employees to work in accordance with training procedures and to inform the employer of any situation which presents a danger.

Regulations 15–19 require special measures for temporary workers, expectant mothers and young persons.

The Workplace (Health, Safety and Welfare) Regulations 1992

These Regulations require employers to maintain equipment, devices and systems in an efficient state. They must be in efficient working order and in good repair.

The employer must provide sufficient ventilation, ensure that during working hours the temperature in all workplaces is reasonable and that every workplace has suitable and sufficient lighting. The workplace must be kept sufficiently clean and waste materials should not be allowed to accumulate.

Each employee should have at least 11 cubic metres of space and suitable workstations and seating if appropriate. The floors and traffic routes must be kept in good condition and measures taken to prevent falling objects or employees falling such a distance that they are likely to be injured. Windows, doors, gates and walls should be made of safe materials. Windows and skylights should be designed so that they can be cleaned safely.

Sanitary conveniences, washing facilities and drinking water should be provided for all employees. If an employee's own clothes are not worn at work, suitable accommodation for clothing, and facilities for changing, should be provided. There should be suitable facilities for rest and to eat meals.

The Provision and Use of Work Equipment Regulations 1998

These Regulations require every employer to ensure that work equipment is so constructed or adapted as to be suitable for the purpose for which it is used or provided. They also impose duties to maintain and inspect equipment. Where the use of equipment is likely to provide specific risk, every employer must ensure that the equipment is used only by people who are meant to use it. 'Work equipment' is interpreted broadly. In **Spencer-Franks v Kellogg Brown and Root Ltd (2008)** the House of Lords held that a device which ensured that a control room door on an oil rig stayed closed was 'work equipment' within the Regulations. So a mechanic who was injured while repairing the device could claim under the Regulations.

Employees must be given information instructions and training on how to use equipment. If there are any special hazards, such as a high or very low temperature, the employer must take measures to ensure that a person using work equipment is not unnecessarily exposed to the hazard. Where appropriate, all work equipment must be provided with emergency stop controls. The employer must ensure suitable lighting and provide suitable warnings.

The Personal Protective Equipment at Work Regulations 1992

These Regulations require every employer to ensure that suitable personal protective equipment is provided to employees who may be exposed to a risk to their health or safety while at work. The employer must carry out an assessment to ensure that the personal protective equipment he intends to supply is suitable. The protective equipment must be adequately maintained and replaced if necessary. There must be accommodation in which the equipment can be stored. Employees must be given information, instruction and training on the use of the equipment and employers must ensure that it is properly used. If an employee finds any defect in the equipment, he has a duty to report it immediately.

The Health and Safety (Display Screen Equipment) Regulations 1992

These Regulations require every employer to perform a suitable and sufficient analysis of workstations which comprise display screen equipment. The activities of workers using such workstations must be periodically interrupted by breaks or changes of activity to reduce their workload at the equipment. Employees using data screen equipment can demand eye and eyesight tests to be carried out by appropriate persons. The employer must ensure that employees using display screen equipment are provided with adequate training and information.

The Manual Handling Operations Regulations 1992

These Regulations require every employer to avoid, so far as is reasonably practicable, the need for employees to undertake any manual handling operations at work if these involve a risk of their being injured. If it is not reasonably practicable to avoid the need for employees to undertake manual handling operations, the employer must make a suitable and sufficient assessment of such operations. He must also take appropriate steps to reduce the risk of injury and, so far as is reasonably practicable, give precise information on the weight of each load and how this weight is distributed. Employees have a duty to make full and proper use of any system of work provided.

Building Regulations

The Building Act 1984, and Regulations made under the Act, impose requirements for building design and construction. These requirements try to make sure that people in and around buildings are safe. They also aim to conserve energy and cater for the needs of disabled people.

The Building Regulations 2000 set out the circumstances in which building controls apply as well as the procedures which must be followed. They also regulate individual aspects of building design and construction. Approved documents deal with matters such as structure, fire safety, resistance to passage of sound, ventilation, hygiene, glazing and drainage.

The Health and Safety Executive issues guidance on workplace fire safety. This guidance deals with matters such as alarms, fire doors, use of suitable materials, access for fire engines and stability of buildings when exposed to fire.

Ergonomics

The Health and Safety Executive has reported that musculoskeletal disorders affect over a million workers and that repetitive strain injury costs £3 billion a year. Employers can be liable in the tort of negligence, if they satisfy the requirements of that tort. (See Chapter 8 and the section on common law health and safety set out earlier in this chapter.) Employers can also be liable criminally if they breach one of the 'six pack' Regulations considered earlier in this chapter.

The Health and Safety Executive has conducted research into ergonomic risks in over 20 specific situations. The HSE has produced reports on matters such as occupational noise exposure, manual handling, disorders in fruit pickers and injuries caused by deboning meat.

Pest control

The Biocidal Products Regulations 2001, as amended, regulate the marketing and use of biocidal products. Such products contain at least one active substance which kills or controls living organisms. These products are used extensively, for example to control rats and fungi which attack wood. Further details of the Regulations can be obtained from the Health and Safety Executive's website: www.hse.gov.uk.

Certain animals introduced into the wild, often to control other animals which were perceived to be pests, have got out of control and caused much harm. The Wildlife and Countryside Act 1981 prohibits the release into the wild of any animal not native to the United Kingdom. It also prohibits the release of certain other animals, plants and algae which are listed in the Act. The Plant Protection Products Regulations 1995 regulate the use of pesticides and chemicals in agriculture.

Food hygiene

The Food Hygiene (England) Regulations 2006 require all food businesses to train their staff on hygiene matters, identify and control food hazards and audit their hygiene procedures. A hazard analysis and critical control points system should be put in place to identify and control food hazards.

Essential points

- The Equality Act 2010 outlaws direct discrimination, indirect discrimination, victimisation or harassment on the protected characteristics of age; disability; gender reassignment; marriage and civil partnership; pregnancy and maternity; race; religion or belief; sex; and sexual orientation.

- The Part-time Workers (Prevention of Less Favourable Treatment) Regulations 2000 outlaw discrimination against part-time workers.

- The Fixed-term Employees (Prevention of Less Favourable Treatment) Regulations 2002 provide that fixed-term workers should not be treated less favourably than other workers.

- The Rehabilitation of Offenders Act 1974 allows people whose convictions have become spent to deny that they have ever been convicted.

- The Health and Safety at Work Act 1974 allows delegated legislation on health and safety matters to be passed. It also provides a framework of the law and sets out various enforcement procedures.

- Employers owe a duty of care to their employees. If this duty is breached, and this breach causes the claimant to suffer a foreseeable type of injury, then the employee can sue in the tort of negligence.

Practice questions

1 Alicia works as a computer operator for Cheapco Ltd in Nottingham. She is paid £6.80 an hour. Bert, who has worked in the same office as a computer operator for ten years, is paid £7.80 an hour. If any of the computer operators experience a problem, Bert is required to provide assistance, although such assistance is very rarely in fact needed. Alicia has heard that computer technicians employed by Cheapco Ltd in London earn £10 an hour and that female computer operators employed by a subsidiary company of Cheapco Ltd earn £7.90 an hour.

   Advise Alicia as to whether or not there are grounds on which she might bring a claim for equal pay and of any defences which Cheapco Ltd might have.

2 Benjamin is a Rastafarian. Three years ago, Benjamin was injured in a car crash and this has confined him to a wheelchair. Benjamin works as an accounts clerk at a local college. As part of a major reorganisation, the college is moving the accounts department onto the third floor from the ground floor where it is currently situated. The college does not have a lift. Benjamin tells his office manager that he will not be able to work on the third floor as he will not be able to negotiate the stairs. The manager says that if Benjamin cannot get to the third floor, he will have to leave the job. Benjamin was considering applying for a job advertised by a different employer. However, the advertisement said: 'Must be of smart appearance, no Rastas, ear-rings etc.' Benjamin applied for the job anyway. He was invited for an interview but when the employer saw his dreadlocks he refused to interview him.

   Advise Benjamin as to any rights he might have against his current employer or against the employer who refused to interview him.

3 Unsafe Ltd is a manufacturer of furniture. It has recently come to light that guards have been removed from electric saws and that workers have been continuously exposed to leather dust. The office typist has developed a bad back after typing while sitting on a dining-room chair provided by the company. No risk assessment has ever been carried out and individual workers in the despatch area are expected to lift sofas onto lorries without any assistance. Explain the criminal offences which might have been committed and the powers of health and safety inspectors to investigate and make Unsafe Ltd's premises safe.

4 Charlie has worked in a bakery for seven years. The work is somewhat monotonous and Charlie seeks to enlighten the atmosphere by playing practical jokes. Charlie climbed into one of the mixing machines so that he could leap out and give a fellow employee, David, a surprise. Charlie has done this type of thing fairly frequently over the years. The foreman has often told him not to, but rather lightheartedly as he too seems to

enjoy Charlie's antics. David is not working on the particular morning when Charlie hides in the mixing machine. Eric, a worker transferred from the cake department, turns on the mixing machine and Charlie is killed. All of the employees in Charlie's department know of the rule that the mixing machines must never be turned on unless they have been checked to see that no-one is cleaning them or otherwise too near them. The transferred employee had not been told this. As a result of the accident, the transferred employee suffers nervous shock and depression which keep him off work for eight months.

Advise the employers of any civil or criminal liability which they might have incurred.

5 Outline the way in which the Equality Act 2010 seeks to prevent discrimination in employment.

Task 14

A group of students from Japan are visiting your college. Using decided cases where possible, prepare notes for a presentation to be made to the Japanese students. The presentation should show an example of the workings of:

(a) The Equality Act 2010.

(b) The Fixed-term Employees (Prevention of Less Favourable Treatment) Regulations 2002.

(c) The Rehabilitation of Offenders Act 1974.

mylawchamber

Visit **www.mylawchamber.co.uk/macintyreessentials** to access tools to help you develop and test your knowledge of business law, including interactive multiple choice questions, practice exam questions with guidance, weblinks, glossary, glossary flashcards, legal newsfeed and legal updates.

mylaw**chamber**
unrivalled support for legal education

15

Regulation of business by the criminal law

We begin this chapter by considering the nature of criminal liability. We then consider several areas in which the law regulates business by the imposition of criminal liability.

The nature of criminal liability

Generally, criminal offences are made up of two elements, an *actus reus* and a *mens rea*. The *actus reus* is often defined as the guilty act, whereas the *mens rea* is defined as the guilty mind. The prosecution must prove both the *actus reus* of an offence and the *mens rea* beyond a reasonable doubt.

Homicide provides an easily understood example of what is meant by *actus reus* and *mens rea*. The *actus reus* of both murder and manslaughter is the same. For both crimes, the accused must voluntarily and unlawfully cause the death of another human being. It is the different *mens rea* of the two crimes which distinguishes them. The *mens rea* of murder is that the accused either intended to kill or intended to cause grievous bodily harm. The *mens rea* of manslaughter is that the death was caused by the accused acting in a grossly negligent or reckless manner, but without the *mens rea* necessary for murder. (There are also several defences which reduce murder to voluntary manslaughter.)

Most *mens rea* consist of intention or recklessness. However, Parliament has created a number of offences of **strict liability**, where the prosecution do not need to prove *mens rea* in respect of one or more elements of the *actus reus*. As we shall see, the main offence created by the Consumer Protection from Unfair Trading Regulations 2008 is an offence of strict liability.

The Consumer Protection from Unfair Trading Regulations 2008

These Regulations, which implement an EU Directive, make it an offence to engage in an unfair commercial practice. They represent a huge change in the criminal law relating to commercial consumer practices. Forty statutes have been repealed or amended, as have thirty-five statutory instruments.

Before considering the regulations in detail, it is important to note that they are limited in two ways. First, they create criminal offences but they do not directly give a consumer any right of action, nor do they invalidate any contract which a consumer might have made. Second, the regulations do not cover unfair business-to-business commercial practices.

However, this second matter is dealt with by the Misleading Marketing Regulations 2008 which impose criminal liability in relation to unfair business-to-business advertising.

The structure of the Regulations

The Regulations are set out in four parts. Part 1 deals with definitions within the Regulations. Part 2 describes the acts and omissions which the Regulations prohibit. Part 3 sets out the criminal offences which the Regulations create, as well as the defences available. Part 4 deals with enforcement.

The prohibitions under the Regulations

Regulation 3(1) states that unfair commercial practices are prohibited. Regulations 3(3) and 3(4) then describe what is meant by an unfair commercial practice. Regulation 3(3) sets out a general definition of an unfair commercial practice, whereas Regulation 3(4) deals with four, more specific, types of unfair commercial practices.

The reg. 3(3) definition of unfair commercial practices

Regulation 3(3) states that:

> A commercial practice is unfair if –
>
> (a) it contravenes the requirements of professional diligence; and
>
> (b) it materially distorts or is likely to materially distort the economic behaviour of the average consumer with regard to the product.

A 'commercial practice' is defined by reg. 2(1) as any act, omission, course of conduct, representation or commercial communication (including advertising or marketing) by a trader, which is directly connected with the promotion, sale or supply of a product to or from consumers, whether occurring before, during or after a commercial transaction (any) in relation to a product.

This definition makes it plain that a commercial practice can have occurred even if no commercial transaction has occurred. So if a manufacturer advertised his product to consumers, this would be a commercial practice even if no consumers bought the product or entered into any other commercial transaction. However, as noted above, if one trader merely misdescribed a product to another trader, there would have been no commercial practice. Nor can a commercial practice be engaged in by a consumer. Only a trader can engage in a commercial practice. The width of the definition of a commercial practice is also noteworthy. 'Any act, omission, course of conduct, representation or commercial communication' would encompass just about anything done or not done by a trader. However, the thing done or not done would have to be 'directly connected with the promotion, sale or supply of a product' to or from a consumer. Even the provision of an after-sales service or the collection of a debt would be included. It is plainly the case that a commercial practice could be committed by a trader who buys from a consumer.

'Professional diligence' is defined as:

> the standard of special skill and care which a trader may reasonably be expected to exercise towards consumers which is commensurate with either –
>
> (a) honest market practice in the trader's field of activity, or
>
> (b) the general principle of good faith in the trader's field of activity.

'Consumer' means an individual acting for purposes that are wholly or mainly outside that individual's business. However, a trader can commit an unfair commercial practice without dealing directly with a consumer as long as a consumer will be involved later. This could happen, for example, when a manufacturer attached misleading descriptions to a product which would eventually be sold to a consumer. The definition of an 'average consumer' is complex. Generally, the average consumer is regarded as reasonably well informed, observant and cautious. However, if a commercial practice is aimed at a particular group of consumers, the average consumer is an average member of that group. So if a commercial practice is aimed at consumers who are physically or mentally disabled, or old or very gullible, this will be taken into account in assessing the impact on the average consumer.

A 'trader' is defined as a person acting (personally or through an agent) for purposes relating to that person's business. So employees, such as shop assistants, are regarded as traders for the purposes of this offence.

A 'product' includes goods, services and digital content.

Regulation 3(3)(b) requires that the commercial practice must materially distort, or be likely to materially distort, the economic behaviour of the average consumer with regard to the product. Generally, this would mean that it would have to persuade, or be likely to persuade, a consumer to buy the product. It might also mean that it persuaded, or would be likely to persuade, a consumer to sell a product.

Commercial codes of practice have been drawn up. These indicate whether or not a trader is behaving in a professionally diligent manner. However, the mere fact of compliance with such a code will not automatically mean that a trader has been professionally diligent.

The reg. 3(4) definitions of unfair commercial practices

Regulation 3(4) states that a commercial practice is also unfair in four other, more specifically defined, circumstances:

(1) if it is a misleading action, as defined by reg. 5;

(2) if it is a misleading omission, as defined by reg. 6;

(3) if it is aggressive under reg. 7; or

(4) if it is listed in Schedule 1.

Misleading actions under reg. 5

Regulation 5(2) states that a commercial activity is misleading:

(a) if it contains false information and is therefore untruthful in relation to any of the matters in paragraph 5(4) (see immediately below) or if it or its overall presentation in any way deceives or is likely to deceive the average consumer in relation to any of the matters in paragraph 5(4), even if the information is factually correct; and

(b) it causes or is likely to cause the average consumer to take a transactional decision he would not have taken otherwise.

The matters set out in reg. 5(4) are very specific, being as follows:

(a) the existence or nature of the product;

(b) the main characteristics of the product (as defined in paragraph 5);

(c) the extent of the trader's commitments;

(d) the motives for the commercial practice;

(e) the nature of the sales process;

    (f) any statement or symbol relating to direct or indirect sponsorship or approval of the trader or the product;

    (g) the price or the manner in which the price is calculated;

    (h) the existence of a specific price advantage;

    (i) the need for a service, part, replacement or repair;

    (j) the nature, attributes and rights of the trader (as defined in paragraph 6);

    (k) the consumer's rights or the risks he may face.

In reg. 5(4)(b), the 'main characteristics of the product' include:

    (a) availability of the product;

    (b) benefits of the product;

    (c) risks of the product;

    (d) execution of the product;

    (e) composition of the product;

    (f) accessories of the product;

    (g) after-sale customer assistance concerning the product;

    (h) the handling of complaints about the product;

    (i) the method and date of manufacture of the product;

    (j) the method and date of provision of the product;

    (k) delivery of the product;

    (l) fitness for purpose of the product;

    (m) usage of the product;

    (n) quantity of the product;

    (o) specification of the product;

    (p) geographical or commercial origin of the product;

    (q) results to be expected from use of the product; and

    (r) results and material features of tests or checks carried out on the product.

In reg. 5(4)(j), the 'nature, attributes and rights' as far as concern the trader include the trader's –

    (a) identity;

    (b) assets;

    (c) qualifications;

    (d) status;

    (e) approval;

    (f) affiliations or connections;

    (g) ownership of industrial, commercial or intellectual property rights; and

    (h) awards and distinctions.

Regulation 5(3) provides that a commercial practice is also misleading if:

    (a) it concerns any marketing of a product (including comparative advertising) which creates confusion with any products, trade marks, trade names or other distinguishing marks of a competitor; or

    (b) it concerns any failure by a trader to comply with a commitment contained in a code of conduct which the trader has undertaken to comply with, if –

    (i) the trader indicates in a commercial practice that he is bound by that code of conduct, and

    (ii) the commitment is firm and capable of being verified and is not aspirational, and it causes or is likely to cause the average consumer to take a transactional decision he would not have taken otherwise, taking account of its factual context and of all its features and circumstances.

The approach to reg. 5 is to first find a commercial practice which contains false information. Next, to consider as to which of the matters in reg. 5(4) it is untruthful or deceptive. Case law on the Trade Descriptions Act 1968 suggests that it will always be necessary to specify precisely which matters are appropriate. Finally, to show that it caused, or was likely to cause, the average consumer to make a transaction he would not have taken otherwise.

Example

Mrs Smith bought a pair of shoes from Badtrade's shop because she was told by a salesman that the shoes were made of leather. In fact, the shoes were largely made of synthetic materials. Badtrade's commercial practice of describing the shoes as leather contains false information. The information is untruthful in relation to reg. 5(4)(b), as defined by reg. 5(5)(e). This caused an average consumer to buy the shoes. Therefore Badtrade's description of the shoes was a misleading action and an unfair commercial practice.

Misleading omissions under reg. 6

Regulation 6 provides that:

(1) A commercial practice is a misleading omission if, in its factual context, taking account of the matters in paragraph (2) –

    (a) the commercial practice omits material information,

    (b) the commercial practice hides material information,

    (c) the commercial practice provides material information in a manner which is unclear, unintelligible, ambiguous or untimely, or

    (d) the commercial practice fails to identify its commercial intent, unless this is already apparent from the context,

and as a result it causes or is likely to cause the average consumer to take a transactional decision he would not have taken otherwise.

(2) The matters referred to in paragraph (1) are –

    (a) all the features and circumstances of the commercial practice;

    (b) the limitations of the medium used to communicate the commercial practice (including limitations of space or time); and

    (c) where the medium used to communicate the commercial practice imposes limitations of space or time, any measures taken by the trader to make the information available to consumers by other means.

(3) In paragraph (1) 'material information' means –

    (a) the information which the average consumer needs, according to the context, to take an informed transactional decision; and

    (b) any information requirement which applies in relation to a commercial communication as a result of a Community obligation.

(4) Where a commercial practice is an invitation to purchase, the following information will be material if not already apparent from the context in addition to any other information which is material information under paragraph (3) –

(a) the main characteristics of the product, to the extent appropriate to the medium by which the invitation to purchase is communicated and the product;

(b) the identity of the trader, such as his trading name, and the identity of any other trader on whose behalf the trader is acting;

(c) the geographical address of the trader and the geographical address of any other trader on whose behalf the trader is acting;

(d) either –

    (i) the price, including any taxes; or

    (ii) where the nature of the product is such that the price cannot reasonably be calculated in advance, the manner in which the price is calculated;

(e) where appropriate, either –

    (i) all additional freight, delivery or postal charges; or

    (ii) where such charges cannot reasonably be calculated in advance, the fact that such charges may be payable;

(f) the following matters where they depart from the requirements of professional diligence –

    (i) arrangements for payment,

    (ii) arrangements for delivery,

    (iii) arrangements for performance,

    (iv) complaint handling policy;

(g) for products and transactions involving a right of withdrawal or cancellation, the existence of such a right.

The approach to reg. 6 is first to decide which of reg. 6(1)(a)–(d) is applicable. Next, to find which of the reg. 6(2) matters is appropriate. Finally, to show that the commercial practice caused, or was likely to cause, the average consumer to make a transaction he would not have taken otherwise.

Example

Mr Hussein buys a new lamp from Ripoff Ltd. He pays by credit card and is charged more than he expected because the price displayed in the shop did not include VAT. Regulation 6(1)(a) is applicable because Ripoff Ltd have omitted material information, taking account of reg. 6(2)(a). The fact that the price did not include VAT was material information within reg. 6(3) and, since there was an invitation to purchase, also within reg. 6(4)(d)(i). This caused an average consumer to buy the lamp. Therefore Ripoff Ltd's description of the price of the lamp was a misleading action and an unfair commercial practice.

Aggressive commercial practices under reg. 7

Regulation 7 provides that:

(1) A commercial practice is aggressive if, in its factual context, taking account of all of its features and circumstances –

    (a) it significantly impairs or is likely significantly to impair the average consumer's freedom of choice or conduct in relation to the product concerned through the use of harassment, coercion or undue influence; and

    (b) it thereby causes or is likely to cause him to take a transactional decision he would not have taken otherwise.

(2) In determining whether a commercial practice uses harassment, coercion or undue influence account shall be taken of –

   (a) its timing, location, nature or persistence;

   (b) the use of threatening or abusive language or behaviour;

   (c) the exploitation by the trader of any specific misfortune or circumstance of such gravity as to impair the consumer's judgement, of which the trader is aware, to influence the consumer's decision with regard to the product;

   (d) any onerous or disproportionate non-contractual barrier imposed by the trader where a consumer wishes to exercise rights under the contract, including rights to terminate a contract or to switch to another product or another trader; and

   (e) any threat to take any action which cannot legally be taken.

(3) In this regulation –

   (a) 'coercion' includes the use of physical force; and

   (b) 'undue influence' means exploiting a position of power in relation to the consumer so as to apply pressure, even without using or threatening to use physical force, in a way which significantly limits the consumer's ability to make an informed decision.

Example

Pressure Ltd invite people who responded to an advertisement to a hotel. Once inside, the customers are told that they cannot leave until they sign a contract to book a holiday. Mr Jones did not book a holiday although he was very frightened to leave without doing so. Pressure Ltd's commercial practice is aggressive within reg. 7(1), taking account of reg. 7(2)(a), (b), (c), (d) and (e). This was likely to cause an average consumer to book a holiday. Therefore Ripoff Ltd's commercial practice was aggressive and an unfair commercial practice.

The unfair commercial practices listed in Schedule 1

Schedule 1 sets out the following 31 commercial practices which are always to be considered unfair. Unlike the other offences, there is here no requirement that a consumer might have been induced to behave differently.

1. Claiming to be a signatory to a code of conduct when the trader is not.

2. Displaying a trust mark, quality mark or equivalent without having obtained the necessary authorisation.

3. Claiming that a code of conduct has an endorsement from a public or other body which it does not have.

4. Claiming that a trader (including his commercial practices) or a product has been approved, endorsed or authorised by a public or private body when the trader, the commercial practices or the product have not or making such a claim without complying with the terms of the approval, endorsement or authorisation.

5. Making an invitation to purchase products at a specified price without disclosing the existence of any reasonable grounds the trader may have for believing that he will not be able to offer for supply, or to procure another trader to supply, those products or equivalent products at that price for a period that is, and in quantities that are, reasonable having regard to the product, the scale of advertising of the product and the price offered (bait advertising).

6. Making an invitation to purchase products at a specified price and then –

    (a) refusing to show the advertised item to consumers,

    (b) refusing to take orders for it or deliver it within a reasonable time, or

    (c) demonstrating a defective sample of it,

with the intention of promoting a different product (bait and switch).

7. Falsely stating that a product will only be available for a very limited time, or that it will only be available on particular terms for a very limited time, in order to elicit an immediate decision and deprive consumers of sufficient opportunity or time to make an informed choice.

8. Undertaking to provide after-sales service to consumers with whom the trader has communicated prior to a transaction in a language which is not an official language of the EEA State where the trader is located and then making such service available only in another language without clearly disclosing this to the consumer before the consumer is committed to the transaction.

9. Stating or otherwise creating the impression that a product can legally be sold when it cannot.

10. Presenting rights given to consumers in law as a distinctive feature of the trader's offer.

11. Using editorial content in the media to promote a product where a trader has paid for the promotion without making that clear in the content or by images or sounds clearly identifiable by the consumer (advertorial).

12. Making a materially inaccurate claim concerning the nature and extent of the risk to the personal security of the consumer or his family if the consumer does not purchase the product.

13. Promoting a product similar to a product made by a particular manufacturer in such a manner as deliberately to mislead the consumer into believing that the product is made by that same manufacturer when it is not.

14. Establishing, operating or promoting a pyramid promotional scheme where a consumer gives consideration for the opportunity to receive compensation that is derived primarily from the introduction of other consumers into the scheme rather than from the sale or consumption of products.

15. Claiming that the trader is about to cease trading or move premises when he is not.

16. Claiming that products are able to facilitate winning in games of chance.

17. Falsely claiming that a product is able to cure illnesses, dysfunction or malformations.

18. Passing on materially inaccurate information on market conditions or on the possibility of finding the product with the intention of inducing the consumer to acquire the product at conditions less favourable than normal market conditions.

19. Claiming in a commercial practice to offer a competition or prize promotion without awarding the prizes described or a reasonable equivalent.

20. Describing a product as 'gratis', 'free', 'without charge' or similar if the consumer has to pay anything other than the unavoidable cost of responding to the commercial practice and collecting or paying for delivery of the item.

21. Including in marketing material an invoice or similar document seeking payment which gives the consumer the impression that he has already ordered the marketed product when he has not.

22. Falsely claiming or creating the impression that the trader is not acting for purposes relating to his trade, business, craft or profession, or falsely representing oneself as a consumer.

23. Creating the false impression that after-sales service in relation to a product is available in an EEA State other than the one in which the product is sold.

24. Creating the impression that the consumer cannot leave the premises until a contract is formed.

25. Conducting personal visits to the consumer's home ignoring the consumer's request to leave or not to return, except in circumstances and to the extent justified to enforce a contractual obligation.

26. Making persistent and unwanted solicitations by telephone, fax, e-mail or other remote media except in circumstances and to the extent justified to enforce a contractual obligation.

27. Requiring a consumer who wishes to claim on an insurance policy to produce documents which could not reasonably be considered relevant as to whether the claim was valid, or failing systematically to respond to pertinent correspondence, in order to dissuade a consumer from exercising his contractual rights.

28. Including in an advertisement a direct exhortation to children to buy advertised products or persuade their parents or other adults to buy advertised products for them.

29. Demanding immediate or deferred payment for or the return or safekeeping of products supplied by the trader, but not solicited by the consumer, except where the product is a substitute supplied in accordance with reg. 19(7) of the Consumer Protection (Distance Selling) Regulations 2000 (inertia selling)(11).

30. Explicitly informing a consumer that if he does not buy the product or service, the trader's job or livelihood will be in jeopardy.

31. Creating the false impression that the consumer has already won, will win, or will on doing a particular act win, a prize or other equivalent benefit, when in fact either –

    (a) there is no prize or other equivalent benefit, or

    (b) taking any action in relation to claiming the prize or other equivalent benefit is subject to the consumer paying money or incurring a cost.

The approach to Schedule 1 is merely to find which of the paragraphs is applicable.

The offences which the Regulations create

The reg. 8 offence

Regulation 8 sets out the most serious offence, for which *mens rea* is required. It states:

8. (1) A trader is guilty of an offence if –

    (a) he knowingly or recklessly engages in a commercial practice which contravenes the requirements of professional diligence under Regulation 3(3)(a); and

    (b) the practice materially distorts or is likely to materially distort the economic behaviour of the average consumer with regard to the product under Regulation 3(3)(b).

If reg. 3(3) has been mastered this offence becomes relatively easy to understand. Only a trader can commit the reg. 8 offence. The definition of a trader was considered earlier in relation to reg. 3(3), as were the requirements of professional diligence. It is important to notice that reg. 8(1)(b) requires the commercial practice to materially distort, or be likely to materially distort, the economic behaviour of the average consumer with regard to the product. Generally, this would mean that it persuades a consumer to buy a product or to be more likely to do so.

Mens rea is required for this offence. The trader must knowingly or recklessly engage in the relevant commercial practice. Regulation 8(2) deals with the meaning of 'recklessly'. It states that:

A trader who engages in a commercial practice without regard to whether the practice contravenes the requirements of professional diligence shall be deemed recklessly to engage in the practice, whether or not the trader has reason for believing that the practice might contravene those requirements.

Case law on the Trade Descriptions Act 1968 would suggest that a trader will have behaved recklessly unless he first positively asks himself whether or not a practice contravenes the requirements of professional diligence, and then decides that it does not.

> **Example**
>
> Harry, a garage owner, advertises a car as never having been in an accident when he knows that it has been in a serious accident. First, Harry is a trader, the car is a product and the advertisement is aimed at consumers. Therefore, the advertisement is a commercial practice, as defined by reg. 2(1). Second, the commercial practice was unfair, as defined by reg. 3(3) because (a) the advertisement contravened the requirements of professional diligence and (b) it was likely to materially distort the economic behaviour of the average consumer with regard to the product. Third, Harry acted knowingly and therefore committed the reg. 8 offence.

The reg. 9 offence

The strict liability reg. 9 offence is committed by engaging in a commercial practice which is misleading under reg. 5.

The reg. 10 offence

The strict liability reg. 10 offence is committed by engaging in a commercial practice which is a misleading omission under reg. 6.

The reg. 11 offence

The reg. 11 offence is committed by engaging in a commercial practice which is agressive under reg. 7.

The reg. 12 offence

The reg. 12 strict liability offence is committed by engaging in a commercial practice which is set out in Schedule 1. However, it is not an offence to engage in the commercial practices set out in paragraphs 11 or 28 of Schedule 1.

Companies can commit any of the offences and if a company is found guilty its officers can also be found personally guilty if they connived in the commission of the offence. Prosecutions for all of the offences must be brought within three years of the commission of the offence or within one year of its discovery, whichever is earlier. The maximum penalty is two years' imprisonment.

Defences

The Regulations set out defences which can apply to the reg. 9, 10, 11 or 12 offences, but not to the reg. 8 offence.

Due diligence defence

Regulation 17(1) provides that it is a defence for the person charged under reg. 9, 10, 11 or 12 to prove:

- that the commission of the offence was due to
  - a mistake, or to
  - reliance on information supplied to him by another person, or to
  - the act or default of another person, or to
  - an accident, or
  - some other cause beyond his control; and
- that he took all reasonable precautions and exercised all due diligence to avoid the commission of the offence.

The defendant needs to prove both elements of the defence on a balance of probabilities. If the defence is that the offence was committed due to a mistake, then the mistake must be one made by the person charged, not by any other person.

In **Tesco Supermarkets v Nattrass (1971)**, an important Trade Descriptions Act case which will apply here, the House of Lords held that the very senior managers of a company might be regarded as the controlling mind and will of the company, and therefore as the company. A mere supermarket manager could not be regarded as the company and was therefore 'another person'.

Whichever of the aspects of the reg. 17 defence is being relied upon, the defendant will always need to prove that he took all reasonable precautions and exercised all due diligence to prevent the commission of the offence. Whether or not this has been done will be an objective question of fact, to be decided by examining all the circumstances of the case. In **Tesco Supermarkets Ltd v Nattrass** it was held that a company would have satisfied the requirement if it had created a system which could be rationally said to be designed to prevent offences from being committed.

Regulation 18 gives a defence to an advertiser who receives an advertisement in the ordinary course of business and did not know, and had no reason to suspect, that the publication of the advertisement would amount to an offence under the Act.

The by-pass provision

Regulation 16 deals with the situation where the offence was committed due to the act or default of another person. If the defendant uses that as a reg. 17 defence, he must give the name of the person at fault to the prosecution. Regulation 16 provides that the person at fault can then be guilty of an offence, even if he is not a trader. For example, in **Olgeirsson v Kitching (1986)** a private motorist sold a car to a garage saying that it had done 38,000 miles, even though he knew that this was not true. The owner of the garage sold the car on, applying the 38,000 mile description. The purchaser found out that the description was false. The private motorist was guilty of an offence under the by-pass provision in the TDA 1968, even though he could not have been guilty of any other offence under that Act because he was not in business.

The Act is enforceable by the Office of Fair Trading and local authority trading standards departments. They are given wide powers to make test purchases, enter premises, carry out investigations and seize goods or documents. They also have a duty to enforce the regulations. This does not necessarily mean bringing prosecutions, but rather to ensure compliance through the most appropriate methods.

Consumer rights of redress

The Consumer Protection (Amendment) Regulations 2014 have amended the 2008 Regulations to give consumers rights of redress in respect of misleading practices and aggressive commercial practices. The rights of redress are available under reg. 27A if three conditions are met. First, the consumer must have contracted to buy goods or services from a trader or must have made a payment to the trader. Second, the trader must have engaged in a misleading or aggressive practice in relation to a product. Third, the prohibited practice must have been a significant factor in the consumer's decision to enter the contract or make the payment.

The rights to redress are first to 'unwind' the contract, which means to cancel it within 90 days of delivery or first performance and claim back any money paid. If the product was goods or digital content it must not have been fully consumed, and must be returned to the trader; if it was services it must not have been fully performed. Alternatively, a consumer might get a discount off the price. As regards products with a market value of £5,000 or less, the discount is 25 per cent if the prohibited practice is minor, 50 per cent if it is significant, 75 per cent if it is serious and 100 per cent if it is very serious. If the product has a market value greater than £5,000, and that value is clearly lower than the amount payable under the contract, the fixed rate discounts are not applied. Instead, the discount is such discount as is appropriate, having regard to the difference between the market value and the amount payable and the seriousness of the prohibited practice. Whichever remedy is gained, damages can also be claimed in respect of additional financial losses, alarm, distress, physical discomfort and inconvenience caused by the prohibited practice.

Product safety

Criminal liability as regards unsafe products is imposed by the General Product Safety Regulations 2005.

The general safety requirement

Regulation 5 sets out the general safety requirement:

(1) No producer shall place a product on the market unless the product is a safe product.

(2) No producer shall offer or agree to place a product on the market or expose or possess a product for placing on the market unless the product is a safe product.

(3) No producer shall offer or agree to supply a product or expose or possess a product for supply unless the product is a safe product.

(4) No producer shall supply a product unless the product is a safe product.

Regulation 2, the interpretation regulation, defines a 'producer' as including the manufacturer, own branders and people who import products into the European Union. Retailers are not included in this definition unless their activities affect the safety properties of a product. However, distributors can commit two separate offences under reg. 8, as we shall see.

Regulation 2 defines a 'product' as a product which is intended for consumers or likely, under reasonably foreseeable conditions, to be used by consumers, even if not intended for them. The product must be supplied in the course of a commercial activity but there is no requirement that the consumer pays for it. Both new and used goods are included. However, equipment used by service providers themselves to provide a service is not included. Transport services provided by suppliers, such as buses and trains, are specifically excluded.

Regulation 2 also defines a 'safe product':

'safe product' means any product which, under normal or reasonably foreseeable conditions of use including duration, . . . does not present any risk or only the minimum risks compatible with the product's use, considered to be acceptable and consistent with a high level of protection for the safety and health of persons. In determining the foregoing, the following shall be taken into account in particular –

(a) the characteristics of the product, including its composition, packaging, instructions for assembly and, where applicable, instructions for installation and maintenance,

(b) the effect of the product on other products, where it is reasonably foreseeable that it will be used with other products,

(c) the presentation of the product, the labelling, any warnings and instructions for its use and disposal and any other indication or information regarding the product, and

(d) the categories of consumers at risk when using the product, in particular children and the elderly.

A product is not to be considered dangerous just because it would be possible to make it safer, nor just because other products are safer.

The Regulations do not apply to antiques, or to second-hand products supplied for repair or reconditioning before use, provided the supplier clearly informs the person to whom he supplies the product to that effect.

Regulation 7(1) requires a producer, within the limits of his activity, to provide consumers with the relevant information to enable them to assess the risks inherent in a product throughout the normal or reasonably foreseeable period of its use, where such risks are not immediately obvious without adequate warnings, and to take precautions against those risks.

Regulation 8 requires that distributors act with due care in order to help ensure compliance with the applicable safety requirements. (A distributor is defined as any professional in the supply chain whose activity does not affect the safety properties of a product. It would generally therefore include retailers.)

Regulation 9 requires producers and distributors who know that they have placed an unsafe product on the market or supplied an unsafe product to notify the authorities in writing. If the risk is serious they must identify the product, fully describe the risk, give all information needed to trace the product and describe the action they have taken to prevent risks to the consumer.

Regulation 29 sets out the standard defence of due diligence. Regulation 31 sets out a by-pass procedure.

Local authority enforcement authorities are given very wide powers, including issuing suspension notices, withdrawal notices and recall notices. They can require that products are marked or warnings are issued. Products can be forfeited and test purchases can be made. Authorities are also given the power to enter premises and carry out searches.

The Computer Misuse Act 1990

The Computer Misuse Act 1990 was passed to deal with computer hacking. Since 1968, the Theft Act could deal adequately with computer crime where money was stolen or where property was obtained by deception. However, no statute dealt with computer hacking, that is to say with merely accessing another's computer system without that person's express or implied permission. The need for a new statute was made plain by the House of Lords' decision in **R v Gold (1988)**. In that case two journalists gained access to BT's computer network and altered some data. One of the journalists also gained access to the Duke of Edinburgh's PC and left the message: 'GOOD AFTERNOON, HRH DUKE OF EDINBURGH.' The journalists, who claimed to have acted to demonstrate how easy hacking was, were charged with an offence under the Forgery and Counterfeiting Act 1981. The House of Lords held that the defendants had committed no offence under this Act and so the need for new legislation was made apparent.

The unauthorised access offence

Section 1(1) of the Computer Misuse Act makes hacking a criminal offence. The offence does not require that the defendant succeeds in securing unauthorised access, it is enough that he intends to do this. The maximum prison sentence is six months.

Intent to commit a further offence

The more serious s. 2 offence is committed by committing the s. 1 offence with the intention of committing, or facilitating the commission of murder or a further offence which carries a sentence of at least five years' imprisonment.

There is no requirement that the further offence should be committed at the same time as the s. 1 offence. Indeed, the s. 2 offence can be committed even though it was impossible to commit the further offence. The sentence for the s. 2 offence is five years' imprisonment. So the s. 2 offence will not generally be used where the defendant succeeds in committing the further offence, because the defendant could anyway be sentenced to at least five years for having committed that offence. The s. 2 offence is therefore useful when the defendant does not succeed in committing the further offence. For example, it would be useful where a defendant hacked into a computer to try and commit blackmail, but failed so abysmally that he could not be convicted of blackmail or attempted blackmail.

Unauthorised modification of computer material

Section 3 makes it an offence to modify computer material without authorisation. The following points should be noted.

There is a need for an intent to cause a modification of the contents of any computer program and by so doing:

- impair the operation of any computer; or
- prevent or impair access to any program or data held on any computer;
- impair the operation of any such program or reliability of such data.

Section 17(7) defines modification as using any computer so as to alter, add to or erase any program or data. Therefore, sending computer viruses is clearly within s. 3. The maximum sentence is five years.

In **DPP v Lennon (2006)** the Divisional Court considered whether 'mail-bombing' a computer amounted to an unauthorised modification of its contents. The defendant, a 16-year-old who had been sacked after three months' employment, used an Avalanche V3.6 programme to send half a million emails to his former employer. The emails, which were sent from different email addresses to try and prevent the employer from stopping them, were made to seem to come from the employer's Human Resources Manager. The defendant was found guilty of the s. 3 offence. It would generally be implied that a computer owner would consent to receiving emails. However, an owner did not impliedly consent to emails which were designed to interrupt the proper operation and functioning of his system. Therefore the modification was unauthorised.

Competition law

It is generally accepted that competition amongst businesses produces better results than monopoly. Free competition leads to lower prices, better goods and services and more choice for consumers as producers are forced to work with ever greater efficiency to maintain their position. Consequently, a body of competition law has been created. This body of law aims to protect consumers and businesses and to ensure that no one producer can take advantage of its dominant position in the market place. Small producers are given some protection from their most powerful competitors and mergers may be forbidden. In the UK there are three main sources of competition law: Articles 101–102 of the Treaty on the Functioning of the European Union, the Competition Act 1998 and the Enterprise Act 2002. It is not possible in a book of this nature to examine these matters in any depth.

Articles 101–102 of the Treaty on the Functioning of the European Union

Article 101 renders void the following:

- all agreements between organisations; or
- decisions by associations of organisations; or
- concerted practices which may affect trade between Member States of the EU;

if they try to prevent, restrict or distort competition within the EU.

This would include matters such as fixing prices, controlling production, sharing markets and selectively applying disadvantageous terms of trade. Any agreement or decision prohibited under Art. 101 is automatically void. (There are some very technical exceptions.)

An example of the effect of Art. 101 can be seen in **ICI v EC Commission (Dyestuffs) (1972)**. Leading producers of dye introduced identical price increases at identical times for the three years 1964, 1965 and 1967. It was held that the businesses had colluded amongst themselves so that the prices were increased at the same time. Customers therefore had no choice but to pay the increased prices. The businesses were 'substituting co-operation for the risks of competition'.

Article 102 outlaws any abuse by one or more organisations of a dominant position within the EU.

An example of Art. 102 can be seen in **United Brands Co v EC Commission (1978)**. United Brands, an American undertaking, was dominant with respect to production, distribution and retailing of bananas within the EU. They were found to be in breach of Art. 102 as a result of abusing their dominant position on a number of counts, including refusal to supply to an individual wholesaler and operating discriminatory pricing between customers.

It is crucial to recognise that an undertaking will not breach Art. 102 simply by being dominant in a particular product market. It is only where an undertaking abuses its dominant position (i.e. takes advantage of the fact) that it will be in breach of Art. 102.

The Competition Act 1998

The Competition Act 1998 is composed of four parts. Part I is divided into five chapters. Chapter I contains prohibitions which are similar to Art. 101 of the TFEU. Chapter II contains prohibitions which are similar to Art. 102. However, the provisions of the Competition Act apply to practices affecting competition within the UK, rather than within Member States of the EU.

The Enterprise Act 2002

The Enterprise Act 2002 is mainly concerned with enforcement of competition law. It does, however, create cartel offences relating to price-fixing, limiting or controlling supply, market sharing and bid rigging.

Organisations which breach competition law can be fined very heavily.

The Bribery Act 2010

The Bribery Act 2010 has reformed the law by creating new offences relating to bribery. The previous law was contained in several statutes which were over 100 years old. These statutes no longer adequately dealt with modern business practices.

The offences

The Bribery Act 2010 has created four new offences relating to bribery.

Section 1 creates the offence of bribing another person. This offence can be committed in two different ways, known as Case 1 and Case 2. The *actus reus* of both Case 1 and Case 2 is committed by offering, promising or giving a financial or other advantage to another person. The *mens rea* of the Case 1 offence requires that the accused intends the advantage given (i) to induce a person to perform improperly a relevant activity or function, or (ii) to reward a person for the improper performance of such a function or activity. It does not matter whether the person bribed is the same person as the person who is to improperly perform the activity or function. For example, the offence would be committed by paying a firm's manager to make sure that a buying clerk placed an order for goods with a particular supplier. The *actus reus* of the Case 2 offence has already been set out: offering, promising or giving a financial or other advantage to another person. The *mens rea* is that the accused knows or believes that the acceptance of the advantage would itself constitute the improper performance of a relevant function or activity. As regards both Case 1 and Case 2, it does not matter whether the advantage is offered, promised or given by the accused directly or through a third party.

Section 2 creates several offences relating to being bribed. These offences are called Case 3, Case 4, Case 5 and Case 6. The Case 3 offence is committed by an accused who requests, agrees to receive or accepts a financial or other advantage, intending that, in consequence, a relevant function or activity should be performed improperly. The improper performance can be by the accused or by another person. The Case 4 offence is committed by an accused who requests, agrees to receive or accepts a financial or other advantage, and the request, agreement or acceptance itself constitutes the improper performance by the accused of a relevant function or activity. The Case 5 offence is committed by an accused who requests, agrees to receive or accepts a financial or other advantage as a reward for the improper performance (by the accused or by another person) of a relevant function or activity. The Case 6 offence is committed where, in anticipation of or in consequence of the accused requesting, agreeing to receive or accepting a financial or other advantage, a relevant function or activity is performed improperly. The improper performance can be either by the accused or by another person with the accused's assent or acquiescence. As regards Cases 3–6, it does not matter whether the accused requests, agrees to receive or accepts the advantage directly or through a third party. Nor does it matter whether the advantage is for the benefit of the accused or for the benefit of another person. As regards Cases 4–6, it does not matter whether the accused knew or believed that the performance of the function or activity was improper. In Case 6, where a person other than the accused is performing the function or activity, it does not matter whether the person knows or believes that the performance of the function or activity is improper.

Section 6 makes it an offence to bribe foreign officials. The accused must intend to influence the foreign official in his capacity as a foreign official. The accused must also intend to obtain or retain business, or intend to obtain or retain an advantage in the conduct of business.

Furthermore, the offence is committed only if the accused, directly or through a third party, promises or gives any financial or other advantage to the foreign official or gives it to another person at the foreign official's request or with his assent or acquiescence.

Section 7 makes it an offence for a commercial organisation to fail to prevent bribery. This offence is committed by a commercial organisation (C) if a person connected with C bribes another person intending to obtain or retain business for C, or intending to obtain or retain an advantage in the conduct of business for C. However, it is a defence for C to prove that C had in place adequate protection procedures to prevent persons connected with (C) from undertaking such conduct.

A relevant function or activity

A relevant function or activity is defined by s. 3 as one which is either:

- of a public nature;
- any activity connected with a business;
- any activity performed in the course of a person's employment; or
- any activity performed by or on behalf of a body of persons such as a company or a partnership.

However, a function can be a relevant function only if the person performing it is expected to perform it in good faith, or impartially or if the person performing it is in a position of trust by virtue of performing it. The function or activity does not need to be performed in the UK or to have a connection with the UK.

Improper performance to which the bribe relates

Section 4 provides that a relevant function or activity is performed improperly if it is performed in breach of a relevant expectation, or if there is a failure to perform the function or activity and that failure is itself a breach of a relevant expectation. Section 5 sets out an expectation test. For the purposes of ss. 3 and 4, the test of what is expected is a test of what a reasonable person in the United Kingdom would expect in relation to the performance of the type of function or activity concerned. For example, it would be expected that a police officer should not take money to overlook a crime. Where the function or activity is not subject to the law of the United Kingdom, any local custom or practice is to be disregarded unless it is permitted or required by the written law of the country concerned.

Defences and penalties

It is a defence for an accused to prove that his conduct was required by the armed forces or the intelligence services. The maximum penalty for offences under ss. 1, 2 or 6 is ten years' imprisonment or a fine. The s. 7 offence is punishable only by a fine.

Essential points

- The *actus reus* of an offence is the guilty act. The *mens rea* is the guilty mind.
- A crime of strict liability is one which does not require the prosecution to prove *mens rea* in respect of one or more elements of the *actus reus*.
- The Consumer Protection from Unfair Trading Regulations 2008 prohibit unfair commercial practices.
- A commercial practice is generally unfair if –
  - (a) it contravenes the requirements of professional diligence; and
  - (b) it materially distorts or is likely to materially distort the economic behaviour of the average consumer with regard to the product.
- It is an offence to knowingly or recklessly engage in a commercial practice which is generally unfair.
- A commercial practice is also unfair: if it is a misleading action; if it is a misleading omission; or if it is listed in Schedule 1 of the regulations. It is an offence of strict liability to commit a commercial practice which is unfair in one of these ways.
- The Bribery Act 2010 creates four offences in relation to bribery. These are bribing another person; requesting, agreeing to receive or requesting a bribe; bribing a foreign official; and failure by a commercial organisation to prevent a bribe.

Practice questions

1 Consider whether or not an offence has been committed under the Consumer Protection from Unfair Trading Regulations 2008 in the following circumstances.

   (a) A representative from a holiday company drives consumers to a remote area of Dartmoor and refuses to bring them back until they agree to take out extra holiday insurance.

   (b) A trader increases his prices by more than the rate of inflation.

   (c) A debt collector threatens a debtor with imprisonment for debt if he does not settle the debt immediately. (It is not possible to be imprisoned for debt.)

   (d) A car dealer reduces the allowance on a car which a consumer is trading in by untruthfully saying that the car has no chance of passing its MOT.

   (e) A postman sells potatoes which he has grown in his garden, describing them as organically grown, which they are not.

   (f) A manufacturer of furniture, who never sells direct to consumers, falsely describes his beds as made from oak in a newspaper advertisement.

   (g) A holiday company advertises that a hotel has a swimming pool when it does not.

   (h) A trader advertises televisions for sale without revealing that they have been reconditioned.

   (i) An estate agent describes a house as having three double bedrooms when the third 'bedroom' is too small to fit a bed in.

2 Explain the offences created by the Consumer Protection from Unfair Trading Regulations 2008.

Task 15

Your employer has asked you to draft a report briefly outlining the following matters:

(a) The main effect of the Consumer Protection from Unfair Trading Regulations 2008.

(b) How a business can become criminally liable on account of producing an unsafe product.

(c) How a business might commit a criminal offence by misusing a computer.

(d) How a partner in a firm might commit an offence under the Bribery Act 2010.

mylawchamber

Visit **www.mylawchamber.co.uk/macintyreessentials** to access tools to help you develop and test your knowledge of business law, including interactive multiple choice questions, practice exam questions with guidance, weblinks, glossary, glossary flashcards, legal newsfeed and legal updates.

mylawchamber
unrivalled support for legal education

16

Credit transactions and intellectual property rights

In this chapter we consider credit transactions and intellectual property rights. The subjects are not closely connected, but neither merits a whole chapter on its own and so the two are considered together here.

Types of credit transactions

When a loan is made, one person lends money to another. The person who has taken the loan is known as a debtor because he is in debt and must repay the debt. The person who has given the loan has provided credit and is therefore known as a creditor. Credit is given not only when a loan is made, but also whenever the payment of a debt is agreed to be postponed. So if Business A supplies goods or services to Business B, and does not require payment for 30 days, Business B will have been given 30 days' credit. Until the contract price is paid, Business A will be a creditor and Business B will be a debtor.

We have considered the essential nature of a loan but now we need to consider loans in more detail, as well as other ways in which businesses might be granted credit.

Loans

A loan is the most fundamental form of credit. If a loan is made, a creditor lends money to a debtor so that the debtor can buy goods or services. The debtor agrees to repay the money, with interest, over a period of time.

The creditor is generally not connected with the transaction he is financing. A bank, for example, may lend money to enable a business to buy new machinery. The contract between the business and the supplier of the machinery is nothing to do with the bank. The bank merely lends the money.

Creditors are, however, likely to want security for the money they lend. In this context, security means something given, or promised, to ensure that the debt is repaid.

If the debtor is a company or an LLP, the creditor will probably register a charge over the company's assets. The effects of this are considered in detail in an earlier chapter (see Chapter 11). Essentially a charge is a mortgage over some of the company's property. If the charge is a floating charge, the company will be free to continue to use the property but if it does not repay the debt as agreed, the bank can order the sale of the assets over which it has a charge and take what it is owed. To preserve the rights granted, a charge holder should register the charge with the Registrar of Companies.

If the debtor is a partnership or a sole trader, the creditor may take a mortgage of property. The property mortgaged does not need to be business property; it might well be the house of the sole trader or of one of the partners. If the loan is not repaid, the creditor will be able to repossess the property (sell it and take the amount still owed). Where an individual or a partnership gives goods as security for a loan, but retains possession of the goods, the security interest must be registered under the Bills of Sale Act 1878. If the documents relating to the security interest are not attested and registered, within seven days, the security becomes unenforceable. Registration requires a detailed inventory of the goods given as security. For this reason individuals and partnerships cannot grant the equivalent of a floating charge where a class of assets, both present and future, are given as security for a loan.

Future rights can be given as security. David Bowie famously gave future earnings from all of his songs as security for a very large loan.

Alternatively, the creditor may be willing to accept a third-party guarantee of the loan. The guarantor would then be liable to repay the loan if the debtor defaulted. Such guarantees are effective as long as they are evidenced in writing.

Security for a loan is not always necessary. Sometimes, a bank will allow an overdraft without requiring security. An overdraft is a form of loan whereby customers can overdraw their bank accounts (take more money out of the account than has been deposited into it) on the understanding that money will be deposited later. There will be a limit above which the customer may not overdraw. The rate of interest on an overdraft is usually higher than on a bank loan. However, the customer can clear his overdraft as soon as he wishes, and if the account is overdrawn for only a short time he might not pay much interest. Large overdrafts are a risky way for a small business to borrow money, as the bank can insist that they be repaid at any time.

The Consumer Credit Act 1974, which is considered later in this chapter, applies to loans as long as they fit within the Act's definition of a regulated agreement.

Hire-purchase

Under a hire-purchase agreement a creditor hires goods for a fixed period, and has an option to buy the goods for a token sum at the end of that period.

Example

A butcher is acquiring a van on hire-purchase from a finance company. He agrees to pay 36 monthly instalments of £350 each. For the duration of the agreement, the butcher is paying the money to hire the van, which remains the finance company's property. With the 36th payment, the butcher buys the van, which then becomes his property. At no stage does the butcher make a commitment to continue with the agreement for the full 36 months. However, if the agreement is a regulated agreement the Consumer Credit Act 1974 will require the butcher to pay at least half of the total amount due under all of the instalments.

A person who takes goods on hire-purchase has been given credit. The credit consists of the difference between what the customer would have had to pay to buy the goods, and the amount he actually paid by way of deposit. For example, John takes a car with a purchase price of £10,000 on hire-purchase. He pays a £1,000 deposit and agrees to pay £300 a month for 36 months. John has been given £9,000 credit. The extra amount paid by way of interest is ignored in calculating the amount of credit.

Usually, a third party finances the deal, although the customer might not be aware of this. If the finance is provided by a third party, the hire-purchase agreement takes the form of a triangular transaction, as shown in Figure 16.1.

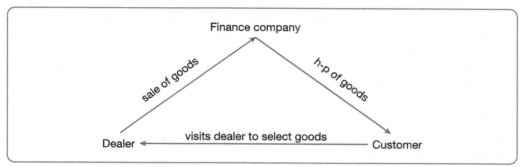

Figure 16.1 A triangular transaction in hire-purchase

- The dealer sells the goods to the finance company.
- The finance company makes the hire-purchase agreement with the customer.
- The dealer may be regarded as the agent of the finance company, as explained below.

Hire-purchase presents difficulties when the goods do not match the description given to them by the dealer. It would seem that the customer has no rights. His contract was not with the dealer but with the finance company, which did not make the description. However, as long as the hire-purchase agreement is a regulated agreement, s. 56 of the Consumer Credit Act will make the dealer the agent of the finance company. This agency relates only to mis-representations and breach of descriptive terms made by the dealer before the hire-purchase agreement was made. The effect of this will be that the finance company is liable for any misrepresentation or breach of term as to description even though these were made by the dealer (see s. 56 of the Consumer Credit Act 1974, considered later in this chapter).

If the car is not of satisfactory quality, Then s. 10 SGITA 1973, or the Consumer Rights Act 2015 when it comes into force, will give the customer rights against the finance company (see Chapter 3).

Conditional sales

A conditional sale is an agreement to sell under which ownership of the goods stays with the seller until the buyer has paid the full price for the goods. The buyer usually takes immediate possession of the goods.

> **Example**
>
> A garage makes a conditional sale of a delivery van to a florist. The terms of the contract might provide that the florist is to pay for the van in 36 monthly instalments. The florist will take immediate possession of the van, but the van will remain the property of the garage until all the instalments have been paid.

Conditional sales often involve a triangular transaction. So, in our example, the garage might sell the car to a finance company and the finance company then make a conditional sale to the florist.

Where the goods are to be paid for by instalments, a conditional sale is very similar to hire-purchase. The essential difference is that in hire-purchase the buyer does not commit himself to completing the payments.

One difference between a conditional sale and hire-purchase is that it is SGA 1979, rather than SGITA 1973, which applies the term as to satisfactory quality. However, this is of no practical importance as the term implied by both statutes is identical. Furthermore, when the CRA 2015 comes into force it will imply the terms, as regards consumer contracts, in both conditional sales and hire-purchase. The Consumer Credit Act applies to conditional sales if the agreement is a regulated agreement.

Credit sales

Under a credit sale, ownership of the goods passes to the buyer immediately, and the seller extends credit to the buyer.

Example

A mail-order catalogue firm sells a coat to a customer under a credit sale. The coat becomes the customer's property as soon as the coat is posted. The mail-order firm gives the customer credit, without taking any security, and the customer is obliged to pay the price of the coat under the credit terms specified in the contract.

Credit sales are commonly used where the goods supplied have a low second-hand value, there being no point in the seller retaining ownership if the goods are worth very little.

The Sale of Goods Act, and the CRA 2015 when it is in force, apply to credit sales. The Consumer Credit Act will apply to credit sales if the agreement is a regulated agreement.

Hire and rental agreements

A person who rents goods to another gives possession of the goods in return for regular payments. He does not sell or agree to sell the goods. Hire is very similar, but is usually for a shorter period.

SGA 1979 does not apply to rental agreements, but SGSA 1982 does (see Chapter 3). When the CRA 2015 is in force it will imply terms into consumer contracts of hire.

The Consumer Credit Act applies to both hire and rental agreements if the agreement is a regulated agreement.

Pledge

Goods are pledged when possession of them is given to a lender as security for a loan. When the debtor repays the loan, he is given the goods back. If the debtor does not repay, the creditor can eventually sell the goods and take what he is owed from the proceeds.

Easily transportable goods of high value are suitable to pledge, often to a pawnbroker.

Example

Sally wants to borrow £100, so she pledges her camera, worth £1,000, to a pawnbroker. As long as Sally repays the £100 with interest within a certain time, the pawnbroker will return the camera. If Sally does not repay the debt, then eventually the pawnbroker will be able to sell the camera and take what he is owed from the proceeds.

Neither the Sale of Goods Act nor the Supply of Goods and Services Act apply to pledges, but the Consumer Credit Act does apply if the agreement is a regulated agreement.

Table 16.1 gives an overview of the different types of credit transactions.

Table 16.1 Rights of ownership and statutory provisions governing credit transactions

	Loan to buy goods	Goods on HP (triangular transaction)	Conditional sale (if not triangular transaction)	Credit sale of goods	Hire/rent of goods
Creditor and supplier the same person?	No	No	Yes	Yes	Yes
Does customer get immediate ownership of the goods?	Not applicable	No	No	Yes	No
Which statute implies term as to satisfactory quality?	Not applicable	SGITA 1973 CRA 2015 when it is in force	SGA 1979 CRA 2015 when it is in force	SGA 1979 CRA 2015 when it is in force	SGSA 1982 CRA 2015 when it is in force
Does Consumer Credit Act apply?	Yes, if the agreement is a regulated agreement				

The Consumer Credit Acts 1974 and 2006

The Consumer Credit Act 1974 (CCA), as amended by the Consumer Credit Act 2006, gives important rights to creditors, but only if the credit is given under a regulated agreement. In 2011 several new sets of regulations came into force. These regulations implement the 2008 Consumer Credit Directive, which requires maximum harmonisation of credit laws throughout the EU. As well as giving rights directly to creditors, the CCA creates criminal offences relating to advertising and canvassing credit. Businesses which provide consumer credit need to be licenced by the Financial Conduct Authority which regulates the consumer credit industry.

The definition of a regulated agreement

Figure 16.2 shows how to decide whether or not a credit agreement is a regulated agreement. As the diagram shows, a contract of hire can be a regulated agreement.

There are several points to make about the diagram:

- The parties might make a regulated agreement without intending to do so. In **Dimond v Lovell (2000)** the House of Lords held that a form of short-term car hire, which was available to motorists whose cars had been damaged by the fault of another, was a consumer credit agreement because the hirer did not have to pay anything when the period of hire ended. The hirer had been given credit because she had been given the hire of the car, and if there had been no credit she would have been required to pay for it during the contract of hire or at the end of that contract. The House of Lords held that, generally, credit will have been provided whenever a contract gives a debtor the right, or the option, to pay at a later time than would have otherwise been the case. However, in commercial contracts payment

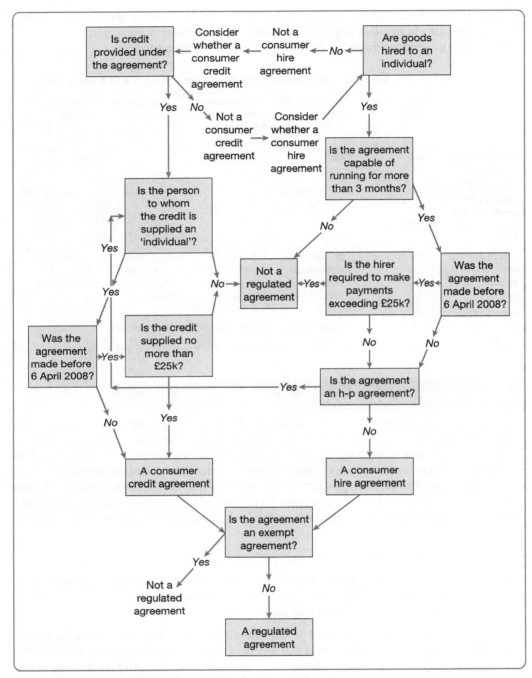

Figure 16.2 The definition of a regulated agreement

might be deferred for reasons other than providing credit, for example as security for the performance of some other obligation by the creditor.

- Living people and partnerships with two or three partners are regarded as individuals, but companies, LLPs and partnerships with four or more partners are not. So when a company is given credit the agreement cannot be a regulated agreement.

- An agreement can be a regulated agreement no matter how much credit is provided. However, if credit of more than £25,000 is given to an individual for business purposes then the agreement will be an exempt agreement. As regards agreements made before 6 April 2008 an agreement will not be a regulated agreement if credit of over £25,000 was given to anyone.

- To qualify as a consumer hire agreement the agreement must be capable of running for more than three months. However, there is no minimum time for which the agreement must actually run.

- Hire-purchase agreements are not consumer hire agreements because they are consumer credit agreements.

- Exempt agreements include the following types of agreements:
  - Mortgages given on land, provided that they are given by a local authority or by a non-profit making organisation, such as a building society rather than a bank.
  - Some low-interest agreements if they are offered to a limited class of people, such as employees, rather than to the general public.
  - Some agreements, other than conditional sale or hire-purchase agreements, where all the payments must be made within 12 months of the date of the agreement and the number of payments is four or fewer.
  - Purchases made on a credit card which require the debtor to settle the account in full with one payment within a certain time. A purchase with an American Express credit card would therefore be exempt, as this is the way that American Express cards operate. However, a purchase made with an Access card or a Barclaycard would not be an exempt agreement because the holders of Access cards and Barclaycards do not have an obligation to settle the account with one payment within a given period.

High net worth debtors and business exemptions

As regards agreements created after 6 April 2008, agreements made by high net worth debtors and agreements relating to businesses can be exempted from all of the provisions of the Act, except those relating to unfair relationships between creditors and debtors.

Section 16A(1) provides that, as regards agreements created after 6 April 2008, a consumer credit agreement or a consumer hire agreement will not be regulated by the Act where:

- the debtor is a natural person (not a partnership or company);
- the agreement includes a declaration made by him to the effect that he agrees to forgo the protection and remedies that would be available under the Act if the agreement were a regulated agreement;
- a statement of high net worth has been made in relation to him; and
- that statement is current in relation to the agreement and a copy of it was sent to the creditor or owner before the agreement was made.

The statement of high net worth cannot be made by the person to whom it relates. It must be made by the creditor or an accountant. A statement of high net worth will state that, in the opinion of the person making it, the natural person in relation to whom it is made either:

- had income totalling £150,000 in the previous financial year; or
- throughout the previous financial year had net assets of a specified description with a total value of not less than £500,000.

If there are two or more debtors or hirers, then a statement of high net worth must be made in relation to each of them.

> **Example**
>
> The following example illustrates how s. 16A might apply. John, who has retired early in May 2012, owns a house worth £2 million. John has little income until he claims his pension in September 2014 when he reaches the age of 60. John wants to borrow £8,000 to live on. A local business will lend John the money, at a favourable rate of interest, but does not want the agreement to be regulated by the CCA 1974. So the business agrees to lend the money if a high net worth exemption is made. John makes a declaration in the specified way that he is giving up the protection and remedies afforded by the Act. A specified person (maybe John's accountant) makes a statement that John's relevant net assets were in the previous financial year worth more than £500,000. The money is lent, probably secured against John's house. John will have to repay it on the terms agreed and will have no rights or remedies under the Act, except those relating to unfair relationships between creditor and debtor.

Section 16B makes a separate exemption in relation to business borrowing. It provides that as regards agreements entered into on or after 6 April 2008 the Act does not regulate:

- a consumer credit agreement by which the creditor provides the debtor with credit exceeding £25,000; or
- a consumer hire agreement that requires the hirer to make payments exceeding £25,000

if the agreement is entered into by the debtor or hirer wholly or predominantly for the purposes of a business carried on, or intended to be carried on, by him.

Formalities which must be complied with

If an agreement is a regulated agreement, then certain formalities must be complied with when the agreement is entered into. If these formalities are not complied with, the agreement will be improperly executed and enforceable only by a court order.

The main requirement is that a document containing all the terms of the agreement must be signed by both the debtor and the creditor. In addition, the debtor must be given a copy of the agreement and written notice of the statutory right to cancel the agreement within a specified period.

Cancellation rights

A regulated agreement may be cancelled by the debtor or hirer if negotiations which took place before the agreement was signed included oral (spoken) representations made in the presence of the debtor or hirer. Negotiations will not be made in the presence of the debtor or hirer if they are made entirely by telephone. There will be no cancellation rights if the agreement is signed by the debtor or hirer at the business premises of either the creditor or hirer. It is where the debtor signed, rather than where the negotiations took place, that is important here.

If a debtor or hirer wishes to cancel a cancellable agreement, he must serve notice of cancellation within a time period which cannot be longer than 12 days from the time when the agreement was made.

A new section, s. 66A, allows a debtor to withdraw from a credit agreement within 14 days of making it. Any credit accrued must be repaid with interest. The right to withdraw does not allow the debtor to cancel contracts for goods or services which were to be financed by the credit. Section 66A does not apply if the credit was more than £60,260 or if the agreement was secured on land.

Creditor regarded as agent of the supplier

Often a creditor deals directly with a debtor, for example where a business directly gives credit to a customer. However, credit is sometimes given without the creditor meeting the debtor. This happens, for example, when a customer uses a credit card in a shop or when a shop arranges a hire-purchase contract for the customer. Section 56 CCA 1974 provides that if there is a connection between the supplier and the creditor, the supplier of the goods is regarded as the agent of the creditor. The consequence of this will be that the creditor will be liable for what the supplier says when negotiating. The creditor is therefore liable for statements of the supplier which amount to misrepresentations or to terms of the contract, and money paid to the supplier is regarded as having been paid to the creditor. There is a connection between supplier and creditor when a credit card is used by the customer, because the supplier will have agreed with the creditor that he will accept this type of credit card. There is a also a connection when goods are taken on hire-purchase, because the supplier first sells the goods to the creditor who then makes the hire-purchase agreement with the customer. (See triangular transactions, explained in Figure 16.1.)

Example

Salman visits a car dealer and buys a second-hand car because the dealer says that it will do 50 miles to the gallon. He pays with his credit card. In fact, the car does only 30 miles to the gallon. The dealer has made a misrepresentation and Salman will be able to rescind the contract. However, the dealer has gone into liquidation. Section 56 regards the misrepresentation as having been made by the credit card company, as well as by the dealer. Salman can therefore regard the company as having made the misrepresentation and insist that they re-credit his account in return for his giving back the car.

Creditor responsible for dealer's misrepresentations and breaches of contract

Section 75 CCA 1974 protects a customer who uses credit supplied by someone other than the supplier of the goods or services being bought. It provides that the creditor is liable for any misrepresentation or breach of contract made by the supplier if:

- the contract was a commercial transaction relating to the supply of a single item with a cash price between £100 and £30,000; and

- the credit is given either under a credit card or where there is a connection between the supplier and the creditor.

This section is particularly useful when the supplier has become insolvent before the contract has been performed. When Laker Airways went into liquidation, customers who had paid cash for their tickets were left with no remedy. Those who had paid any amount of the ticket price with their credit cards could sue the credit card companies for the whole of their ticket price.

Notice that s. 75 will apply only if the cash price of any single item was more than £100. If a customer bought five different items at £90 each from the same supplier, the provider of credit would not assume any liability under s. 75. However, if the cash price of any single item is between £100 and £30,000, then the creditor is fully liable in respect of that particular item, no matter how small the credit advanced.

Notice also that s. 75 does not apply where the customer has arranged his own credit in advance. It would apply to purchases with a credit card but would not apply where a customer overdraws his bank account to make the purchase.

In limited circumstances, a new s. 75A gives a debtor the right to pursue a creditor where a supplier has breached a contract to supply goods or services with a cash value of over £30,000, if a regulated consumer credit agreement was used specifically to finance the contract. (Generally, it will not therefore apply where a credit card is used.) Section 75A can apply only if:

- the supplier cannot be traced,
- the debtor has contacted the supplier but the supplier has not responded,
- the supplier is insolvent, or
- the debtor has taken reasonable steps to pursue his claim against the supplier but has not obtained satisfaction for his claim.

Cooling-off period

A debtor who makes a regulated agreement anywhere other than at the creditor's place of business is given a cooling-off period by ss. 67–74 CCA 1974. During this period, the debtor can cancel the whole deal, giving back what he gained and escaping from all liability. For example, if a salesman calls at Mrs Stone's house and persuades her to make a credit deal to have the house double glazed, then she has the right to cancel the agreement. If Mrs Stone had made the deal at the double glazing firm's place of business, then she would not have such a right.

This cooling-off period lasts for five days after the customer has received his second copy of the credit agreement. (This second copy must be delivered to the customer within seven days of his making the deal.)

Early settlement

Section 97 gives the debtor a right to require the creditor to say how much would have to be paid to clear the debt. Section 94 gives the debtor a right to clear the debt at any time, and save some interest on future payments. This right cannot be excluded.

Repossession of the goods

Section 90 requires the seller to get a court order to repossess goods if the buyer has paid at least one-third of the total purchase price of the goods. This prevents the creditor from 'snatching back' the goods from the debtor.

Unfair relationships

A court can declare an agreement void because there was an unfair relationship between creditor and debtor. In deciding whether or not this was the case, the court can consider all of the circumstances, but particularly the terms of the agreement and the way in which the creditor exercised or enforced his rights. If an unfair relationship is found, the court has wide powers to alter the agreement or to order repayment of some or all of the money due or paid under it. These provisions apply whenever credit is provided. There is no requirement that the credit was provided under a regulated agreement. In **Plevin v Paragon Personal Finance Ltd [2014]** the Supreme Court held that an agreement could be unfair within s. 140A without any breach of duty on the part of the creditor. Whether or not a relationship between a creditor and a debtor was unfair involved a good deal of judicial discretion.

Misuse of credit cards

Sections 83 and 84 CCA 1974, along with the Lending Code 2011, protect credit card holders if their cards are misused by another person.

As long as the card holder was not fraudulent or grossly negligent, his maximum loss for misuse of the card is £50. As soon as the credit card company is informed of the situation the holder is not liable for further loss. If a stolen card is used to make a distance contract, then the Consumer Contracts (Information, Cancellation and Additional Charges) Regulations 2013 allow the card holder to cancel any payment. (See Chapter 5.)

Interest on trade debts

Businesses which supply goods and services on credit might insist that a term is included in the contract making interest payable on the money owed. However, many suppliers are reluctant to do this for fear of losing future contracts with the person to whom credit is provided. Small businesses which supply large businesses have in the past been particularly vulnerable to late payment of debts.

The Late Payment of Commercial Debts (Interest) Act 1998 provides that business-to-business contract invoices must be paid within 60 days of being received unless a longer period is fixed by the contract and this longer period is not grossly unfair to the creditor. Where the debtor is a public authority the 60-day period is reduced to 30 days. Interest becomes payable once the 60 or 30 day period has expired. The rate of interest is set at 8 per cent above the base rate. Once statutory interest begins to run in relation to a qualifying debt, the creditor is also entitled to a fixed-sum. This sum is £40 if the debt is less than £1,000, £70 if the debt is between £1,000 and £10,000, and £100 if the debt is more than £10,000.

Business property

Legal concepts of property

The common law categorises all property as either real property or personal property. Real property is made up of all freehold interests in land. Personal property is made up of all other property, including leases of land. Although leases of land are classed as personal property rather than as real property, the reasons for this are historical. Most businesses would regard freehold and leasehold interests in land as much the same type of property.

Personal property is classed as either chattels real or chattels personal. Chattels real consist of leases of land. Chattels personal consist of all the remaining types of personal property. Chattels personal are divided into things in possession, things in action and intellectual property rights. Things in possession are movable things of which physical possession can be taken, for example machines or books. Things in action are intangible rights which can be enforced only by taking legal action, for example debts. Intellectual property rights, such as copyright or patents, are a separate class of intangible property rights.

The different types of property can be seen in Figure 16.3.

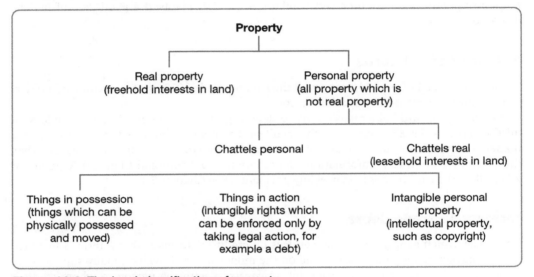

Figure 16.3 The legal classification of property

Most people are familiar with the nature of land and goods, so we need investigate only the nature of intellectual property rights.

Copyright

The law relating to copyright is governed by the Copyright, Designs and Patents Act 1988.
Section 1(1) CDPA 1988 defines copyright as a property right in either:

- original literary, dramatic, musical or artistic works;
- sound recordings, films, broadcasts or cable programmes; or
- the typographical arrangements of published editions.

Typography is the art of planning and setting out type so that a work can be printed. Most readers of a book would recognise that the author or publisher had copyright in the words. However, they might not realise that copyright also exists in the typographical arrangement of the book, that is to say in the way in which the words appear on the page.

Copyright protects the way in which ideas are expressed, rather than the ideas themselves. In **University of London Press Ltd *v* University Tutorial Press Ltd (1916)** it was decided that mathematics exams which drew on the stock of knowledge common to mathematicians were literary works. The ideas were not new, but the precise way in which they were expressed was new.

It is not essential that the work must have taken a long time to complete, but very small numbers of words will not be governed by copyright.

A street directory has been held to be a literary work, because it presented information in an original way. It is therefore plain that a literary work does not have to be what most people would regard as a work of literature.

A musical work is defined as a work consisting of music, exclusive of any words or action intended to be sung, spoken or performed with the music. A dramatic work is not defined, but includes a work of dance or mime as well as the more obvious example of a script for a play.

Acquiring copyright

Section 3(2) CDPA 1988 provides that copyright does not exist in a literary, dramatic or musical work until it is recorded, in writing or otherwise. As soon as it is recorded, it does exist without the need for any formal application process. The recording of the work does not need to be done by the author or with the author's permission.

Authorship and ownership of copyright

The Act defines the author of a work as the person who created it. However, where a literary, dramatic, musical or artistic work, or a film, is made by an employee in the course of his employment, the employer is the first owner of any copyright in the work subject to any agreement to the contrary.

Duration of copyright

Copyright exists for different lengths of time, depending upon the type of work concerned. As regards the copyright in literary, dramatic, musical or artistic works, the copyright finishes at the end of 70 years from the end of the calendar year in which the author dies.

Copyright in a sound recording finishes 70 years from the end of the calendar year in which it is released.

The copyright in films expires 70 years from the end of the calendar year in which the death occurs of the last to die of:

- the principal director;
- the author of the screenplay;
- the author of the dialogue; or
- the composer of music specially created for and used in the film.

Copyright in broadcast or cable programmes expires at the end of the period of 50 years from the end of the calendar year in which the broadcast was made or the programme was included in a cable programme service.

Copyright in typographical arrangements of published editions expires at the end of 25 years from the end of the calendar year in which the edition was first published.

Special rules apply to Crown and parliamentary copyright. As regards literary, dramatic, musical or artistic work, Crown or parliamentary copyright does not expire until 125 years from the end of the calendar year in which the work was created or for 50 years after the end of the year in which the work was first commercially published, if the work was commercially published within 75 years of its creation. As regards Acts of Parliament, copyright expires 50 years after the end of the year in which the Act was given the Royal Assent.

Rights of copyright owners

Section 16(1) CDPA 1988 gives the copyright owner the exclusive right to:

- copy the work;
- issue copies of the work to the public;
- rent or lend the work to the public;
- perform, show or play the work in public;
- broadcast the work or include it in a cable programme service;
- make an adaptation of the work or do any of the above in relation to an adaptation.

If any person does any of the acts listed above, without the permission of the copyright holder, or authorises anyone else to do this, copyright in the work is infringed. It is important to remember that what is protected is not an idea, but the way in which an idea is expressed. It is also important to realise that infringement does not need to be intentional and can be committed unknowingly.

Copying the work can be done by storing the work electronically, for example by downloading material onto a computer. Making a video recording of a film would infringe copyright. Copyright can be infringed by renting the work for commercial gain. Lending of the work to the public can also infringe copyright, even if no commercial advantage is gained.

Secondary infringement is committed not by copying the work, but by exploiting it commercially.

Fair dealing with a literary work (other than a database), or a dramatic, musical or artistic work for the purposes of research or private study does not infringe copyright. Special exemptions also apply as regards:

- things done for the purpose of education;
- libraries and archives; and
- things done for the purposes of parliamentary or court proceedings.

If the copyright is transferred by the author to another by way of assignment, then the transferee takes over from the author all rights in respect of infringement.

The Digital Economy Act 2010 places obligations on Internet Service Providers (ISPs) to monitor and report upon online copyright infringement by subscribers (such as illegal peer-to-peer file sharing and illegal downloading of copyright material). Sanctions, such as reducing the quality of a subscriber's Internet connection, can then be taken against subscribers to deter copyright infringement.

Remedies for infringement

Damages and an injunction to prevent future breaches of copyright are the usual remedies for infringement. An owner of copyright may also apply for a court order that a person hands over an infringing copy of a work in his possession. An infringer may also be ordered to hand over profits made from exploiting the copyright.

Moral rights

Authors are given several moral rights in respect of their works. These are not economic rights, but if these rights are infringed, then a remedy for breach of statutory duty will be available. Damages are therefore available. An injunction will be the appropriate remedy to prevent derogatory treatment of the work.

There are five moral rights.

First, an author who asserts his right to be identified as the author of a literary, dramatic, musical or artistic work has the moral right to be identified as the author of the work whenever the work is performed commercially or performed in public. (The paternity right.)

Regardless of whether or not the author asserted any rights, he is also given a second moral right to object to any derogatory treatment of the work, and a third right not to have literary, dramatic, musical or artistic works falsely attributed to him as author. (This particular right subsists only for 20 years after the author's death; the other moral rights subsist for as long as the copyright itself subsists.)

A fourth moral right gives a person who commissions the taking of a photograph or the making of a film for private purposes not to have the work, or copies of it, exhibited, broadcast or shown in public.

A fifth and final moral right, the artist's resale right or *droit de suite*, gives artists the right to a commission of 3 per cent or 4 per cent whenever their art is resold. However, the right applies only to works of graphic or plastic art, such as paintings, sculptures, ceramics, glassware etc.

Criminal offences

Various criminal offences are created in relation to articles which are, and which the defendant knows or has reason to believe are, infringements of copyright. These offences relate to:

- making copies of the work for sale or hire;
- importing them for business purposes;
- possessing them for business purposes with a view to committing a copyright infringement; and
- selling, exhibiting or distributing them.

Patents

Patents can be taken out only in respect of inventions which are capable of having an industrial application. A patent must be applied for and is not easily granted. Patent law is governed by the Patents Act 1977 as amended by the Patents Act 2004.

Patents have two purposes: they encourage innovation by granting monopoly rights in respect of inventions, while at the same time making technological advances public.

Patentable inventions

Section 1(1) of the Patents Act 1977 provides that a patent can only be granted for an invention if:

- the invention is new; and
- it involves an inventive step; and
- it is capable of industrial application.

PA 1977 does not define what an invention is, but s. 1(2) provides that the following matters are not inventions and that there can therefore be no patenting of them:

- discoveries, scientific theories or mathematical methods;
- aesthetic creations and literary, dramatic, musical or artistic work (because these are covered by copyright);
- ways of performing a mental act, playing a game, or doing business,
- a program for a computer; or
- the presentation of information.

An invention can be regarded as new only if it does not form part of the state of prior knowledge, which includes all matters that have at any time before the date of the invention been made available to the public in any way.

A step can be regarded as an inventive step only if it was not obvious to a person who was skilled in the relevant field.

An invention is capable of having industrial application if it can be made or used in any kind of industry, including agriculture. Almost every new invention will be regarded as having an industrial application. There is no requirement that it can be put to an immediate industrial use. New methods of surgery, therapy or diagnosis which are to be practised on humans or animals cannot be taken to be of industrial application.

Patents can apply not only to new items, but also to the way an existing item is used, or to the way in which an existing item is produced. For example, a new way of manufacturing paper could be patentable.

Making an application

Applications for a patent are made to the UK Patent Office, to whom a fee must be paid. The application must contain a description of the invention, as well as a claim for the patent.

Property in patents

The owner of a patent has a monopoly right to exploit it. This is the case even if it could be shown that someone else had independently reached the same inventive step. A patent can be licensed to another person, who may then exploit the patent without infringing the rights of the owner. Rights are commonly granted in this way.

Infringement of patents

Once a product has been patented, infringement is committed by:

- making the product;
- disposing of it;
- offering to dispose of it;
- using or importing it; or
- keeping it.

If a process, rather than a product, has been patented, infringement consists of using it with knowledge that this is infringement.

However, private, non-commercial use or use as an experiment will not constitute infringement.

An injunction, damages, an order to hand over profits made from exploiting the product, or to hand over the product itself are the usual remedies.

Trade marks

Meaning of trade marks and registration of trade marks

The Trade Marks Act 1994 (TMA 1994) governs the law on trade marks. A trade mark is given a wide definition as a 'sign', and can consist of almost any visual representation, including a letter, word, drawing or shape. The only two requirements are that the sign should be capable of being reproduced graphically and that it should be capable of distinguishing one person's products from another person's. A mark which has no distinctive character cannot be registered as a trade mark, but it is possible to register a shape.

The rights given by TMA 1994 are only conferred once the trade mark, which is a property right, is registered. As regards an unregistered trade mark an action for passing off may lie, but TMA 1994 will provide no remedies.

Effect of registered trade mark

The proprietor of a registered trade mark is given exclusive rights in the trade mark. If the trade mark is used in the United Kingdom without his consent, these rights are infringed.

A sign can be used in various ways, including by:

- fixing it onto a package;
- putting goods under the sign;
- importing or exporting under the sign; or
- using the sign on business paper or in advertising.

Trade marks are not infringed by a person using his own name and address, as long as the use is in accordance with honest practices in industrial or commercial matters. This is an objective test and is not the same as asking whether or not the defendant acted honestly.

An action for infringement is brought by the owner of the trade mark, and all remedies which would be available in respect of any other property right are available. In addition the court may:

- order offending signs to be erased or removed;
- order infringing goods, materials or articles to be delivered up to the owner; and
- order that these may be destroyed or forfeited to such person as the court thinks fit.

If a groundless threat of infringement proceedings is made, the victim may apply to a court for a declaration that the threats are unjustifiable, or for damages or for an injunction.

A registered trade mark is personal property which can be co-owned or assigned to another. Licences permitting their use may be granted to others.

Procedure for registration

An application for registration of a UK trade mark has to include a statement of the goods or services to which the trade mark is to apply, and a representation of the trade mark itself.

A system of classification exists under which the applicant applies for registration into one of more than 42 classes of goods and services. Where the registrar decides that the application for registration has been accepted, he publishes this in the *Trade Marks Journal*. Initially, trade marks are registered for a ten-year period from the date of registration. Registration may be renewed for further periods of ten years if the proprietor pays the appropriate fee. Many trade mark owners prefer to register an EU-wide mark known as a CTM or Community Trade Mark. This is done by registering the mark with the Office for Harmonisation in the Internal Market. A CTM is valid in all of the signatory countries of the EU, including the UK. There is therefore no need for a separate UK registration.

Damages or an injunction are the usual remedies for infringement, but destruction of offending goods or erasure of offending signs can also be ordered.

Breach of confidence

Article 8 of the European Convention on Human Rights gives the right to respect for a person's private and family life, home and correspondence. The Human Rights Act 1998 came into force in 2000. It did not create a new tort of invasion of privacy but it did strengthen the law of breach of confidence. However, Art. 10 of the Convention gives the right to freedom of expression, and so freedom of the press has to be weighed against the right to privacy.

Suing for breach of privacy

A person bringing a claim for breach of privacy will need to prove three things:

(1) that the information disclosed was confidential;

(2) that there was an obligation of confidence; and

(3) that there was unauthorised use of the information.

That the information disclosed was confidential

Any type of information, either commercial, Government or personal secrets, can be confidential. However, very trivial information is not protected, nor is information which is widely known.

That there was an obligation of confidence

A statute or a contract might impose an obligation of confidence. Or an obligation might arise from a relationship, such as an employment, commercial or professional relationship.

That there was unauthorised use of the information

To be an unauthorised use of the information, it must actually be used or there must be a threat to use it. Whether or not there was unauthorised use of the information is an objective test. It is no defence that the unauthorised use was made honestly.

Defences

It is a defence to show that the information was in the public domain; that is to say that it was not confidential. It is also a defence to show that the public had a legitimate interest to know the information. An action for breach of confidence is equitable and so it must be brought reasonably quickly or it will defeated by lapse of time.

Remedies

The usual remedies are damages or an injunction. In addition, the claimant can sue for profits made from unauthorised use of the information. Also, a defendant who put the information in the public domain can be prevented from using the information for a certain time, even though it is in the public domain.

Essential points

- A regulated agreement is a consumer credit agreement, or consumer hire agreement, other than an exempt agreement.
- The definition of a regulated agreement is significant because most of the provisions of the Consumer Credit Act 1974 apply only to regulated agreements.
- Section 56 CCA 1974 can make a supplier of goods the agent of the creditor in some circumstances.
- Section 75 CCA 1974 makes a creditor liable for a misrepresentation or breach of contract made by a supplier in some circumstances.
- Copyright is concerned with protecting the expression of ideas, rather than with protecting ideas themselves.
- An invention can only be patented if it is new, involves an inventive step and is capable of industrial application.
- A trade mark is a sign capable of being represented graphically which is capable of distinguishing the goods or services of one business from those of another.

Practice questions

1 In the transactions described below, company A has agreed to supply machinery to company B. The six transactions described provide one example of each of the following types of credit: a loan; hire-purchase; a conditional sale; a contract of hire; a credit sale; and an overdraft. Match the transactions to the various types of credit.

(a) Company B takes possession of the machinery, but ownership is not to pass to company B until it has paid all 36 instalments of the price. At the outset, company B commits itself to making all 36 payments.

(b) Company B takes possession of the machinery, but ownership is not to pass to company B until it has paid all 36 instalments of the price. Company B does not commit itself to making all 36 payments.

(c) Company B has agreed to pay £1,000 a month for the use of the machinery until it has filled an order. After that, the machinery will be returned to company A.

(d) Company B's bank has agreed that company B can pay for the machinery by writing a cheque for £10,000. The company bank balance stands at £2,300.

(e) Company B's bank has credited the company account with £10,000 so that the machinery can be bought. Company B is to repay this money by paying £560 a month for two years.

(f) Company B takes immediate possession of the machinery and gets immediate ownership of it. The contract of sale says that the price is to be paid by 12 monthly instalments of £1,000 each.

2 Are the following regulated agreements, made last month, within CCA 1974?

   (a) A company borrows £12,000 from its bank to buy a new computer system.

   (b) Mrs Allwood buys a new car for £26,000. She is to pay the price by instalments over two years. The car dealer allows Mrs Allwood £5,000 for her old car. The total amount of interest to be paid is £5,000.

   (c) A builder buys a new van on hire-purchase on behalf of his firm, which has six partners. The builder traded in the firm's old van and under the hire-purchase agreement has to pay £320 a month for 36 months. The APR is 18 per cent.

   (d) Mr Callow borrows £1,000 from a bank, at 21 per cent APR, to pay for an exotic holiday.

3 Explain the ways in which the Consumer Credit Act 1974 can directly protect creditors.

Task 16

Your employer has asked you to write a report, dealing briefly with the following matters:

(a) The different ways in which a business might acquire goods without immediately paying the full price.

(b) How the Consumer Credit Act 1974 can help a person who is given credit.

(c) The essential nature of copyright, a patent and a trade mark.

mylawchamber

Visit **www.mylawchamber.co.uk/macintyreessentials** to access tools to help you develop and test your knowledge of business law, including interactive multiple choice questions, practice exam questions with guidance, weblinks, glossary, glossary flashcards, legal newsfeed and legal updates.

mylawchamber
unrivalled support for legal education

17

The resolution of business disputes

Throughout this book, we have studied rights and obligations. Ultimately, these rights and obligations can be enforced only by taking a case to court. For all business organisations this is a last resort. The process is lengthy and expensive, and it is also likely to cause ill will. If a business sues a customer then, win or lose, the customer is unlikely to deal with the business again.

The vast majority of legal disputes do not go to court. They are settled between the parties themselves. This saves time and money and perhaps keeps a business relationship alive. If a civil dispute does reach the stage of going to court, then it will begin either in the county court or in the High Court.

Jurisdiction of the County Court

The national County Court deals with civil cases. The county court system was restructured in 2014. Before the changes England and Wales had around 200 county courts. Now there is one national County Court, and the old county court buildings have been renamed County Court hearing centres. One of these, based in Northampton, is called the County Court Business Centre. The Centre has 170 staff and deals with over half of all claims, electronically or by post. At the CCBC claims are issued, and defences received, and then the case is transferred to the appropriate hearing centre.

The County Court no longer deals with family proceedings, which have been transferred to the new Family Court. The most important change from a practical point of view is that the County Court now hears almost all civil disputes below £100,000. However, personal injury claims of more than £50,000 can still be started in the High Court. In Equity disputes, such as those involving wills, trusts or mortgages, the County Court hears all disputes below £350,000. Another important change is that some nominated County Court judges can now issue injunctions known as freezing orders, which prevent a person from moving assets out of the jurisdiction of the English courts. Before the County Court was restructured it heard 90 per cent of civil cases, with the other 10 per cent being heard in the High Court. Now it is likely to hear more cases. There are three main reasons why a case would be heard in the High Court rather than in the county court. First, the case may be very complex. Second, the amount of damages claimed might be so large that the High Court is more appropriate. Third, the case might be likely to set an important precedent. This last reason reflects the fact that High Court decisions have force as legal precedents, whereas county court decisions do not. (The system of precedent is explained in Chapter 1.)

Each hearing centre has at least one circuit judge and at least one district judge. Appeals from district judges go to circuit judges and a second appeal goes to the Court of Appeal. Appeals from a circuit judge go to a High Court judge unless they are against a final decision in a multi-track case, in which case they go to the Court of Appeal.

County Court judgments are registered with the Registry of County Court Judgments and can remain on the register for six years. However, if the judgment is satisfied (complied with) within one month, then the judgment debtor's name is altogether removed from the register. Unsatisfied judgments remain on the register. If the judgment is satisfied more than one month after the judgment is given, the judgment debtor's name remains on the register, along with a note stating that the judgment has been satisfied. Those who have judgments registered against them are unlikely to be granted credit by a commercial lender. The county court does not directly enforce its judgments, although it does provide the machinery by which judgments can be enforced.

Jurisdiction of the High Court

The High Court sits in London and several provincial towns. It has jurisdiction to hear financial claims of over £100,000 and personal injury claims of over £50,000. However, many claims which are above these financial limits are heard in the national County Court in order to reduce costs.

The High Court is divided into three Divisions. The largest of these is the Queen's Bench Division and it is in this Division that contract and tort cases are heard. Currently, there are 108 High Court judges, 70 of whom sit in the Queen's Bench Division. These judges are assisted by Masters, who hear cases which are slightly less complex. Disputes concerning companies and partnerships are generally heard in the Chancery Division, which currently has 18 judges.

Appeals from the High Court are normally made to the Court of Appeal and from there to the Supreme Court. It is, however, possible to appeal straight from the High Court to the Supreme Court, under the 'leapfrog' procedure. This is most unusual, only being possible if the case involves a point of law of public importance, and if the Supreme Court gives permission for the appeal. Figure 17.1 shows the civil court structure.

Any court can refer a dispute to the Court of Justice of the European Union (CJEU) to get an authoritative opinion on a matter of EU law. The court then waits for the CJEU to give the ruling. When this has been done, the court then applies the ruling. The Supreme Court must refer a question of EU law to the CJEU where a relevant point of EC law is at issue and where the CJEU has not previously ruled on the matter.

Earlier (see Chapter 16) we saw that businesses can be prosecuted for criminal offences. Figures 17.2 and 17.3 show the structure of the criminal courts. Indictable offences are serious offences, tried with a jury; summary offences are less serious and tried without a jury in the magistrates' court.

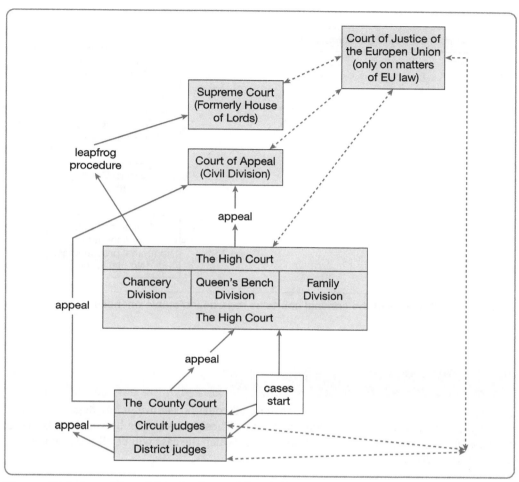

Figure 17.1 An outline of the structure of the civil courts

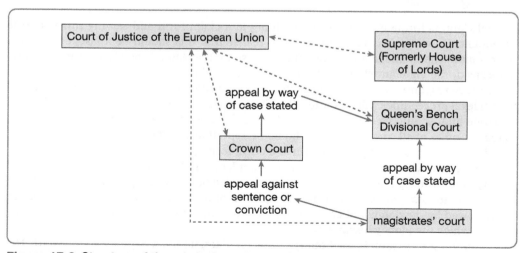

Figure 17.2 Structure of the criminal courts as regards summary offences

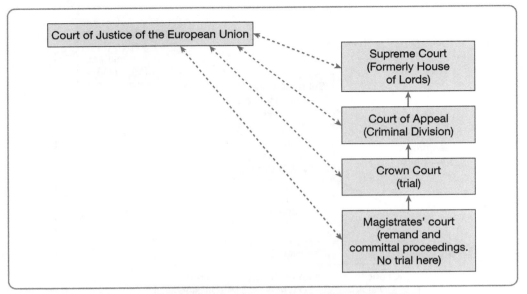

Figure 17.3 Structure of the criminal courts as regards indictable offences

Civil procedure

It is not appropriate for this book to consider civil court procedure in any degree of detail. However, three matters are dealt with in outline. These matters are: how a claim is made; the possible responses to a claim; and the track to which the case will be allocated if the case proceeds to court.

Making a claim

A legal claim is formally commenced by filling in a claim form and serving this upon the defendant. However, it is very important to realise that this should be a last resort. First, the claimant should make a genuine attempt to settle the claim. If no satisfactory response is received, the claimant should send a final letter to the other party, explaining that if a satisfactory response is not received within a certain time, then a claim will be made and formal legal proceedings will be started. This letter should not be too unreasonable or hostile. The time limit should be definite but should give the defendant a reasonable time in which to reply. Copies of all correspondence should be kept. If no satisfactory response is received, then it will be necessary to fill in and serve a claim form.

Claim forms, which are relatively easy to complete, can be collected free from any local County Court hearing centre or they can be downloaded online. County Court staff or Citizens' Advice Bureaux staff will give advice on completion of the form if this is needed. Interest on money owed by the defendant can be claimed at the rate of 8 per cent per annum from the date on which the money became owed.

In order to start a claim in the County Court, the claimant must pay a fee to the court. The amount of the fee is between £25 and £815, depending upon the size of the claim.

Claims made electronically are about 10 per cent cheaper than those made by post. If the case is actually heard by the court then a further hearing fee must be paid. This fee ranges from £25 for a small claim of less than £300 to £1,090 for a multi-track case.

Once the claim form has been completed, the claimant should photocopy it twice. The form and a copy of it are given to the court. The court will keep the form and send the copy to the defendant along with a 'response pack', which outlines the various responses which the defendant might make. The claimant should keep one copy of the claim. As an alternative to getting the court to serve the documents on the defendant, the claimant may serve them personally. This involves giving the documents to the defendant and explaining what they are. If the defendant refuses to take the documents, the claimant serves them by dropping them at the defendant's feet. If the defendant is a partnership the documents may be personally served upon any partner. If the defendant is a company the documents may be personally served upon any director of the company or upon the company secretary.

The claimant will need to indicate on the claim form the full name and address of the defendant. If the defendant is in trade as a sole trader, the claimant should give the defendant's name and add any name under which the defendant is trading. For example, 'Jane Smith trading as Smith's Florists'. If a partnership is sued, the claimant should give the firm name and add the words 'a firm'. For example, 'Smith & Co, Florists – a firm'. When either an individual or a firm is sued, the claimant should give as the address for service of the documents either the individual's residential address or the principal place of business conducted by the individual or the firm. When a company is sued, the claimant should give the full name of the company, and the address given should be either the company's registered office or any other place where the company carries on business if this has a real connection with the case. For example, in a case in which the claimant claims to have been injured by faulty goods sold by Acme Ltd, a retailer, the address might either be Acme Ltd's registered office or the address of the shop where the faulty goods were bought.

Responses to a claim

The defendant must respond to the claim form within 14 days of receiving it. If the defendant offers no response, then judgment can be entered against him or her. This means that the claimant will have won the case. The various responses which the defendant can make are illustrated by Figure 17.4.

In order to make a counterclaim against the claimant, the defendant will need to pay a court fee. This fee will be calculated according to the size of the counterclaim. The fee payable is the same amount as if the defendant was making an original claim. If an acknowledgement of service is made, this is done on a form which is sent to the defendant in the response pack.

Allocation to a track

Once the defendant has responded to the claim (other than to admit all of the claim), then the case will be allocated to one of three tracks.

Small claims track

Claims for £10,000 or less, which are straightforward, will be allocated to the small claims track. However, if the claim includes a claim of £1,000 or more for personal injuries, then it is not allocated to the small claims track. If both parties agree, cases which are outside these financial limits can be heard on the small claims track. One obvious advantage of this would be that the costs would be reduced.

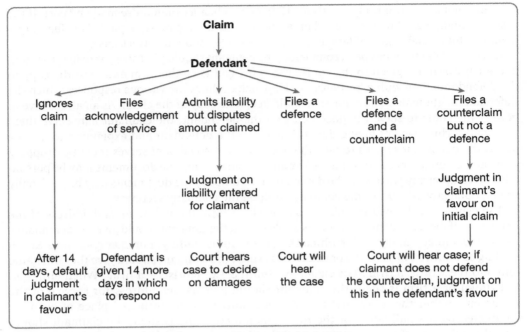

Figure 17.4 The possible responses to a claim which has been served

Small claims track cases are heard by a district judge. Although the proceedings are conducted informally, a small claims track case will generally be open to the public. Documents to be used during the case must be deposited with the court 14 days before the case is heard. Expert witnesses can be allowed only if the district judge agrees that they should be. A claimant who wins the case will be able to recover the court fees paid to start the case, as well as up to £90 per day expenses for attending the court, travelling and accommodation. Apart from these matters, the parties generally pay their own costs and so a claim for the costs of using lawyers cannot be made. This is because the system is designed to be usable without legal representation. When the case is heard the parties explain their positions and the judge applies the law on their behalf. However, the court can allow up to £750 costs for an expert witness whom the court has allowed to give evidence. The hearing of the case will be relatively informal and an appeal can only be made with the judge's permission.

Fast track

Claims which are outside the financial limits for the small claims track will be allocated to the fast track if the claim is for not more than £25,000. Fast track cases will be heard by a circuit judge. It is anticipated that judgment will be given within 30 weeks of allocation to the fast track. The parties to a fast track will almost always be legally represented by a barrister or a solicitor. The winner of the case will almost always be able to claim the cost of legal representation from the other party. This means that the loser will have to pay both sides' costs, including the cost of expert witnesses used by both sides and the court fees. The actual hearing of a fast track case will usually take five hours and be conducted on one day.

Multi-track

Cases are allocated to the multi-track if they are not suitable for the small claims track or the fast track.

The three main reasons for an allocation to the multi-track are that the amount claimed is over £25,000, or that there is likely to be considerable expert evidence, or that the hearing of the case is likely to take more than one day in court. There is no standard procedure for a multi-track case. The judge actively manages the case and sets the most appropriate procedure. The judge may hold case management conferences in advance of the trial. These meetings resemble business meetings and are designed both to make the parties cooperate on certain issues and to identify precisely what issues are in dispute. In a particularly complex case the judge might order a pre-trial review to consider both preliminary issues and the way in which the trial should be run. At the end of the case, the loser will generally be ordered to pay the costs of both parties. As the parties will generally be represented by barristers, these costs are likely to be very considerable. The legal costs will include all the pre-trial work done by the parties' solicitors and might include very considerable costs of expert witnesses.

Payment into court and offers to settle

When a big civil case is looming, the costs of the litigation are likely to be very large. It is in everybody's interests that a settlement is made before the trial, as the costs of the trial may be very substantial. A defendant faced with a claim for a debt or damages might pay a sum of money into court in settlement of the dispute. This can be an important tactic. If the claimant is not awarded more than the sum which the defendant paid into court, then the claimant will normally have to pay all costs incurred 21 days after the money was paid into court. This is because the claimant has 21 days in which to take the money paid into court in settlement of the dispute. If the claimant is awarded more than the sum paid into court, then costs will be calculated in the usual way.

Similarly, the claimant might make a written offer, stating the sum of money which he or she would take in order to settle the dispute. If the defendant does not accept this, and if the claimant is awarded more than the amount he or she offered to accept, then the defendant will (as the loser of the case) have to pay all the costs of both parties. In addition, the defendant will normally be penalised in that the court will order him or her to pay interest on the sum for which the claimant offered to settle at a rate of interest which can be as high as 10 per cent above the base rate. The judge who tries the case must not be told that a payment into court or an offer to settle has been made until he or she has decided on liability and awarded a sum as damages.

Example

John has been badly injured by David's negligence. The amount of damages is likely to be high and the case is allocated to the multi-track. After a few months of negotiations, both John and David have each incurred legal costs of £5,000. David then pays the sum of £100,000 into court. John responds immediately by offering to settle the matter for a payment of £170,000. The parties do not settle the case, which goes to court. John's legal fees incurred after the offer to settle amount to £43,000. David's legal fees after the payment into court was made amount to £46,000.

➡

(a) At the trial John is awarded damages of £100,000 or less. John must pay all of his own costs of £48,000 (£5,000 + £43,000) and David's costs incurred after David's payment into court (£46,000). If John was awarded damages of less than £94,000 he would therefore have all of his damages eaten up and might still owe money.

(b) John is awarded damages of more than £100,000 but less than £170,000. David, as the loser of the case, will have to pay the costs of both sides.

(c) John is awarded damages of more than £170,000. David, as the loser of the case, will have to pay the costs of both sides. In addition, the court can order that David pays interest on the £170,000 for which John offered to settle, at a rate which must not be more than 10 per cent above the base rate.

Tribunals

Various Acts of Parliament have established tribunals to hear certain types of cases. These tribunals hear more cases than are heard by the County Court or the High Court.

It is not possible to take a dispute to a tribunal unless the dispute concerns the particular type of matter with which the tribunal deals. If the dispute does concern such a matter, then a dispute cannot be taken before the ordinary courts but must be dealt with by the relevant tribunal. In the study of business law the only tribunals of real significance are the employment tribunals and the Employment Appeal Tribunal.

Several advantages are claimed for tribunals. They are likely to hear a case more quickly than the County Court, with lower costs, as the parties can represent themselves. The proceedings are often informal and tribunal members have considerable experience in their fields.

Alternative dispute resolution

As mentioned earlier, litigation should always be a last resort. We have seen that if a case does reach the stage of going to court, then the loser will generally have to pay the costs of both sides. We have also seen that these costs can be very substantial. In many cases the costs are greater than the amount being claimed. As well as the costs which are claimable by the winner, other hidden costs (such as the cost of time spent instructing solicitors) are likely to be incurred. The winner of the case will not be able to claim anything in respect of these hidden costs. Furthermore, there is the risk that the loser will become insolvent. If this happens, then the winner of the case is likely to have to pay all the legal costs which he or she has incurred, even though the winner does not normally have to pay costs.

A further disadvantage of litigation is that it is a very stressful experience. The worry involved can take a toll on health. One factor which makes this particularly true is that litigation takes time, particularly when a case is allocated to the multi-track. Another disadvantage is that a court case is heard in public and this publicity can be very harmful if the other side makes allegations about the business. Furthermore, litigation is almost certain to mean that the parties do not deal with each other again.

In the light of all these disadvantages, many legal disputes are settled by alternative dispute resolution. That is to say, they are settled without a court case. The simplest way in which this can happen is that the parties, usually through their lawyers, voluntarily agree to a settlement. As we saw in an earlier chapter (in Chapter 2), if the parties agree to settle out of court this agreement is a binding contract. There are various other methods of alternative dispute resolution, which are considered below.

Arbitration

Business disputes are often settled by arbitration. If a dispute is settled in this way, then it is resolved by an impartial referee, an arbitrator, who takes over the role of the court. Once the parties have agreed to arbitration, they will not be able to change their minds and take the dispute to court. If one party does try to take the dispute to court, the other party will be able to get any court proceedings stayed (discontinued).

Advantages of arbitration

The main advantage of arbitration is that the proceedings are conducted privately, whereas court proceedings are held in public. Privacy can be a very important factor in business disputes. Let us assume, for example, that a dispute has arisen between Acme Ltd and Bill's Bakery Co. Acme Ltd supplied a new boiler to Bill's Bakery Co and are suing for the price. Bill's Bakery Co are refusing to pay the price because they say that the boiler supplied was not of satisfactory quality. Neither of the parties would want the publicity which might arise if this dispute were to be heard in open court. Acme Ltd would not want it to be publicly claimed that their boilers were not of satisfactory quality. Bill's Bakery Co would not want it to be publicly claimed that the business does not pay its debts. If the dispute is referred to arbitration this adverse publicity will be avoided.

A second advantage of arbitration is that an arbitrator with specialist knowledge can be chosen. Eventually, the dispute between Acme Ltd and Bill's Bakery Co would depend upon whether or not the boiler supplied was of satisfactory quality. If the case went to court, the judge would make this decision, probably after listening to expert witnesses from both sides. It is highly unlikely that the judge would know much about boilers. The side which loses the case would be likely to feel that the judge got it wrong. Both Acme and Bill's Bakery Co might have more faith in the decision if it was taken by an expert in the field, perhaps by the chairman of the local Boilermakers' Federation.

Arbitration might also be cheaper than going to court. However, this is by no means certain. Arbitrators can demand good money for their skills and the lawyers arguing the case in front of an arbitrator will often charge the client the same rate as they would for going to court. It is also the case that in large commercial disputes the arbitrators are often High Court judges or Masters. Often the procedures followed by such arbitrators are very similar to High Court procedures. The advantage of privacy is retained, but the proceedings are unlikely to be substantially cheaper than High Court proceedings. Of course, the parties have the choice of arbitrator and might choose less formal and cheaper proceedings if they were satisfied that these would not prejudice their interests.

A dispute sent to arbitration is likely to be resolved relatively quickly. It takes a long time for a case to get to court, whereas arbitration can be quickly arranged. Delays in arbitration are usually caused because the parties cannot agree who the arbitrator should be. The Arbitration Act 1996 has considerably reduced the delays which used to arise.

A final advantage of arbitration is that the right to appeal is severely restricted. The parties know that once the arbitrator has made the award that is the end of the dispute. If a dispute is taken to court, an appeal, or the threat of one, can hang over the winner for some considerable time.

Reference to arbitration

A dispute can only be referred to arbitration if both sides agree that it should be. If the dispute is a contractual one, then a term of the contract may provide for arbitration. Such terms are common in contracts made in the context of certain industries, including the insurance industry and the building industry. But arbitration clauses are by no means restricted to contracts made in those industries. It is quite possible that a contract between a boilermaker and a business customer, such as the example used in relation to Acme Ltd and Bill's Bakery Co, might have contained a clause stating that any dispute arising under the contract should be resolved by arbitration.

Alternatively, the parties might agree to arbitration once the dispute has arisen and both sides have made their positions clear. Perhaps the arrival of Acme Ltd's claim form would be enough to convince Bill's Bakery Co that the dispute was serious, and lead them to suggest arbitration.

Whether the agreement is made in the contract itself or later, the important thing is that once the parties have agreed to arbitration neither of the sides will be able to unilaterally change their minds. If a party who has agreed to an arbitration clause tries to take the dispute to a court instead of to the arbitrator, the court will stay (discontinue) the proceedings.

It is a principle of contract law that no clause in a contract may prevent matters of law from being decided by the ordinary courts of the land. Arbitration is the only exception to this principle.

In addition to the parties in dispute agreeing to arbitration, many trade associations provide that particular types of disputes should be referred to arbitration. These schemes do not take away a customer's rights or prevent a customer from taking a dispute to court, but do provide a cheap way of resolving a dispute without going to court. These arbitration schemes try to ensure that members of the particular trade association stick to the association's Codes of Practice. These Codes of Practice are generally agreed to voluntarily as a condition of membership of the trade association. Generally the Codes of Practice will set out the standards which customers are entitled to expect. Perhaps the best known of these arbitration schemes is the scheme run by the Association of British Travel Agents, which attempts to resolve disputes arising in connection with the travel industry. Other schemes apply to very many trades, including double glazing, laundry services, electrical repairs and the processing of photographs. These schemes may well give a remedy to a customer where the law would not do so. They also have the advantage that the arbitrators will be closely connected with the trade in question and will be able to apply this knowledge in settlement of any dispute. Disadvantages are that the Codes of Practice are not always enthusiastically enforced and that customers might feel that the arbitrator is not truly independent. It is also the case that those who do not belong to the trade association in question are outside the Codes of Practice altogether.

The Arbitration Act 1996 provides that the purpose of arbitration is to obtain a fair resolution of disputes by an impartial tribunal without unnecessary delay or expense. The Act also requires the arbitrator to deal fairly with the parties and to allow them to present their case and deal with their opponent's case. Under the Act the parties to the arbitration must do everything necessary to allow the arbitration to proceed properly and quickly. Before the Act came into force, it was common for some parties to arbitration to delay matters by every possible means in the hope that this would force the other side to either give up or settle the case.

Figure 17.5 shows an overview of arbitration.

Mediation

When a dispute is referred to mediation, a mediator tries to help the parties to settle their dispute. There are no set rules about how this should be done. The most common method would probably be that the mediator asks the parties to put their case to each other in his or her presence. The mediator might then get the parties to agree what the essential matters in

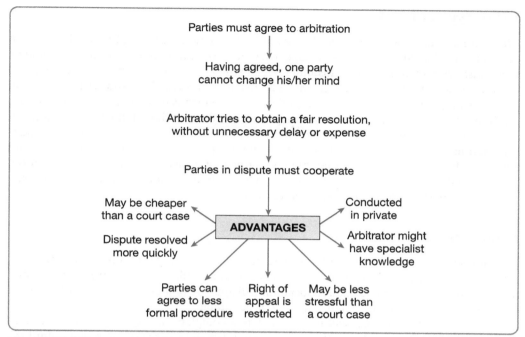

Figure 17.5 An overview of arbitration

dispute were. Then the parties in dispute might go to different rooms and be visited in turn by the mediator. The mediator would put forward the points of view of one party to the other and suggest various compromises. Eventually, the parties might manage to reach agreement with each other and settle the dispute. Many disputes which are not settled during the mediation are settled soon afterwards.

The Civil Mediation Council has set up a National Mediation Helpline to give civil court users advice and information about mediation. The Helpline does not itself provide mediation but, after having asked about the dispute, can pass the details on to a mediation provider who has been approved by the Civil Mediation Council. Such a mediator will provide services for a set fee and for a set time.

Often solicitors act as mediators. When this is the case they are bound by a Law Society Code of Conduct and a high standard of service is therefore ensured. One disadvantage of mediation is that the parties might enter into it without any intention of settling the case, merely to find out more about the other party's case.

Conciliation

Conciliation involves a conciliator bringing the parties together and suggesting a compromise which they might agree to. It is therefore similar to mediation, except that the conciliator takes a more active approach, not merely passing on the other side's point of view but also actively suggesting the basis on which the dispute might be settled. In employment cases conciliation has been around for a long time. An official from ACAS attempts to conciliate before an employment dispute is taken to an employment tribunal. Mediation and conciliation are not strictly defined, and not everyone agrees that mediators do not suggest the basis of agreement whereas conciliators do.

Other types of ADR

There are several other widely used types of ADR. **Early neutral evaluation** involves an expert telling the parties, at an early stage, what he or she thinks that the outcome would be if the case were to go to court. This might well cause one or more of the parties to change their approach and enable a settlement to be reached. **Neutral fact finding** is similar. An expert gives a non-binding view of a technical matter which is in dispute. Again, the parties might be more prepared to settle once they have heard the finding. **Expert determination** involves an expert giving a binding decision on a particular matter, usually a technical matter. **Med-arb** is a combination of mediation and arbitration. The parties agree to try and settle the dispute through mediation but also agree that if this fails it will go to arbitration. If the mediator and the arbitrator are agreed to be the same person, this may encourage settlement before the stage of arbitration is reached.

Ombudsmen

Ombudsman is the Swedish word for a representative. As regards certain types of disputes, ombudsmen exist to investigate complaints which arise within a certain trade or industry. The British and Irish Ombudsman Association will approve ombudsmen only if it is satisfied that they are independent, effective, fair and accountable.

Generally, an ombudsman will not investigate a complaint if the complaint is currently the subject of legal proceedings. Nor will the ombudsman investigate a complaint until the complainant has completely exhausted any internal complaints procedure which might exist.

Ombudsmen may be limited in the amount which they can award, but generally this amount is fairly generous. As well as investigating a particular complaint, an ombudsman might make recommendations to improve matters generally within the area concerned. It is often the case that the awards of ombudsmen cannot be legally enforced. However, most traders will comply with any award because the publicity attached to not doing so would be very undesirable. In England and Wales the following ombudsmen operate in the private sector: the Legal Services Ombudsman, the Housing Ombudsman, the Financial Services Ombudsman, the Estate Agents Ombudsman, the Funeral Ombudsman, the Investment Ombudsman and the Pensions Ombudsman. There are also ombudsmen operating in the public sector, including: the Parliamentary Ombudsman, the Health Service Ombudsman, the Local Government Ombudsman and the Independent Police Complaints Commission.

Complaint-handling bodies which do not involve an ombudsman exist in relation to complaints about HMRC, Social Security, the Child Support Agency, barristers, prisons, subsidence and waterways.

Essential points

- Civil disputes are first heard in either the County Court or the High Court.
- Any UK court can refer a matter of EU law to the Court of Justice of the European Union to get an authoritative opinion on the matter.
- Litigation in court has many disadvantages: the costs of litigation can be very high; litigation is very stressful; it can take a long time; it can destroy business relationships; and the public nature of hearings can lead to bad publicity.
- Alternative dispute resolution can avoid some or all of the disadvantages of litigation.
- The simplest form of alternative dispute resolution occurs when the parties agree to settle their case out of court.
- Arbitration involves an impartial third party, an arbitrator, making a binding resolution of a dispute.
- A mediator tries to help the parties settle a dispute by seeking agreement on certain matters and by communicating to the parties the position of the other party.
- A conciliator attempts to resolve a dispute by suggesting a compromise to which both parties might agree.
- Ombudsmen investigate complaints arising within certain trades or industries.

Practice questions

1 For many years a wholesaler has supplied a garden centre with flower seeds. The wholesaler and retailer have always enjoyed good relations, but a serious dispute has now arisen over the quality of seeds delivered last year. The garden centre say that many of the seeds did not produce flowers and that customers have been complaining. The wholesaler has not received any similar complaints from other retailers supplied from the same batch of seeds.

(a) List, in order of importance, the reasons why the parties might prefer to resolve this dispute through arbitration rather than through the courts.

(b) Explain how the dispute might be settled by mediation or conciliation.

(c) If the dispute eventually did lead to a court case, on which track would the case be likely to be heard if the damages claimed were:

  (i) £800?

  (ii) £12,000?

  (iii) £63,000?

(d) To which court could the loser appeal if the case was first heard:

  (i) By a circuit judge in the County Court?

  (ii) In the High Court?

Task 17

Explain the different ways in which a legal dispute might be settled without going to court.

mylawchamber

Visit **www.mylawchamber.co.uk/macintyreessentials** to access tools to help you develop and test your knowledge of business law, including interactive multiple choice questions, practice exam questions with guidance, weblinks, glossary, glossary flashcards, legal newsfeed and legal updates.

mylawchamber
unrivalled support for legal education

Glossary

Abatement A self-help remedy in the tort of nuisance.

Acceptance (of goods) Once goods have been accepted, or are deemed to have been accepted, they can no longer be rejected for breach of condition. The right to damages remains.

Acceptance (of an offer) Agreement to the terms proposed in the offer. The point at which a contract is formed.

Account for profits Hand profits over to the person to whom they belong.

Accounting records The documents (such as ledger, order forms, cash books, receipts, etc.) which enable accounts to be prepared. Every company must keep accounting records for inspection by the company officers.

Acquittal A decision by a court that a defendant is not guilty of the crime of which he was accused.

Act (of Parliament) A statute.

Act of God A defence in tort, which applies where natural forces, rather than human intervention, caused the act complained of in circumstances which no human foresight could provide against.

Actual authority An agent's power to act on behalf of a principal which arises on account of the agent and principal agreeing that the agent should have the power.

Actus reus The guilty act which needs to be proved before a person can be convicted of a crime.

Adequacy (of consideration) Consideration is adequate if it is of the same value as the other party's consideration for which it is exchanged. There is no legal requirement that consideration should be adequate. (See also **sufficiency**.)

Administration (of a company) A measure short of liquidation under which

an administrator, who must be a qualified insolvency practitioner, attempts to rescue an ailing company.

Adversarial system of trial A system under which the parties to a trial are adversaries. They try to prove their case, and the facts upon which it depends. The judge does not actively investigate the facts.

Affirmation Declaration of an intention to proceed with a contract despite knowing that it could be avoided, thus losing the right to avoid. Can be done expressly or impliedly and lapse of time may indicate affirmation.

Agent A person with authority to alter the legal position of another person, the principal. Such an alteration is usually achieved by making a contract for the principal.

Alternative dispute resolution (ADR) Various methods by which legal disputes can be settled without going to court.

Amending Act A statute which changes some of the provisions of another statute which is already in force.

Annual accounts (company) A company's annual accounts consist of a balance sheet, a profit and loss account, the directors' report and the auditor's report.

Annual general meeting (AGM) A meeting of company members which is held once every calendar year. Public companies must hold an AGM; private companies might choose to do so.

Annual return Basic information about a company which must be submitted to the Registrar of Companies once a year.

Anticipatory breach A breach of contract which is committed by repudiating the contract before performance of the contract becomes due.

Apparent authority The power to act on a principal's behalf which an agent appears to have. It is created when the principal represents to a third party that the power exists.

Appellate court A court which hears appeals from other courts.

Arbitration A method of settling civil disputes whereby the parties agree that an arbitrator should hear the case and award an appropriate remedy.

Arbitrator A disinterested person chosen by parties in dispute to settle the dispute.

Articles of association The rules of a company, which bind both the company and the members of the company.

Assault A tort, committed by any act which directly and intentionally causes the claimant to reasonably fear that he or she is immediately about to suffer battery.

Auditor An accountant who checks a company's accounts and reports to the members of the company regarding the accounts.

Avoid (a contract) To call off future performance of a contract on account of misrepresentation, duress or undue influence. (See also **Rescission**.)

Balance sheet Part of a company's accounts which show the assets and liabilities of the company on a particular date.

Bankrupt An individual (not a company) can be declared bankrupt by a court on account of not being able to pay his or her debts.

Base rate An official rate of interest to be paid on credit. The base rate is set by the Bank of England once a month. Many creditors set the rates of interest which they charge by reference to the base rate.

Basic award An amount of money to which employees who have been unfairly dismissed are entitled.

Battery A tort committed by a direct and intentional physical contact with the claimant's body without the claimant's consent.

Beneficiary A person entitled to the benefit of property which is held on trust.

Bilateral contract A contract in which the consideration of both parties consists of a promise. (Almost all contracts are bilateral.)

Bill A proposed Act of Parliament before it has received the Royal Assent.

Bill of exchange A cheque, or other unconditional order in writing requiring one person to pay another.

Board of directors Directors of a company acting collectively. The board can exercise all the powers of the company.

Board meeting A meeting of the board of directors.

Bona fide In good faith or honestly.

Breach (of term/contract) Breaking the contract by not performing a contractual obligation.

Bulk (in sale of goods) Goods form part of a bulk if they are contained in a defined space or area and all the goods are interchangeable with all the other goods.

Burden of proof The obligation to prove facts or to prove a legal case.

Cab-rank rule The rule that a barrister, like a taxi, should provide his services to anyone willing to pay for them.

Capacity (in contract) The power to make a contract.

Capital Money or wealth.

Causation The relationship between cause and effect.

Cause of action The factual situation which gives a person a right to a legal remedy.

Certificate of incorporation Certificate issued by the Registrar of Companies which shows that a company has come into existence.

Chambers (i) The rooms from which self-employed barristers work. (ii) Rooms attached to a court in which a judge conducts business which does not need to be done in open court.

Charge (in relation to companies) A property interest given by a company to secure a debt, which will cease to exist if the debt is repaid. Charges are void if not registered with Companies House.

Chattel (personal) A physical thing which can be touched and moved.

Cheque A bill of exchange which orders a bank to pay money.

Circuit judge A judge attached to a County Court hearing centre who hears claims allocated to the multi-track or the fast track.

Code of practice A code which is produced alongside some statutes, such as the Consumer Protection Act 1987 to illustrate how the statute is intended to work.

Codifying Act A statute which puts all of the existing case law and statute law into one new statute (e.g. Partnership Act 1890).

Commercial agent A self-employed commercial agent is defined by the Commercial Agents (Council Directive) Regulations 1993 as a self-employed intermediary who has continuing authority to negotiate the sale or purchase of goods on behalf of another person (the principal), or to negotiate and conclude the sale or purchase of goods on behalf of and in the name of that principal. The Regulations give such agents rights, particularly in relation to termination of their agency. The Regulations also impose duties on such agents.

Common law (1) The body of law made by the courts, rather than by Parliament. (2) The body of law which did not originate in the Court of Chancery.

Companies House A Government department which deals with the administration of companies and LLPs. Its main functions are incorporating and dissolving companies, storing information about companies and LLPs, and making this information available to the public.

Company An incorporated body which has a legal personality of its own.

Company secretary An officer of a company who deals with the company's administration.

Comparator In employment law, a person with whom a person claiming discrimination wishes to compare himself or herself.

Competition law A body of law which tries to ensure that businesses compete with each other freely.

Conciliation A form of ADR under which a conciliator tries to find middle ground on which the parties might agree to settle their dispute.

Condition (of a contract) An important type of contract term, breach of which allows the injured party to terminate the contract and/or claim damages. A term is a condition if, when the contract was made, it was considered to go to the root of the contract. Some statutory terms are also labelled conditions. Contrasted with a warranty.

Conditional sale A sale of goods whereby the buyer gets possession of the goods but ownership remains with the seller until the full price is paid.

Consideration The promise (or in cases of unilateral contracts, the act) which a party to a contract gives in return for the other party's consideration. This requirement of a contract distinguishes contracts from gifts.

Consideration (total failure of) A total failure to perform one's contractual obligations.

Consolidating Act A statute which replaces one or more existing statutes on a particular subject.

Constitution (of company) The rules of a company, consisting of its articles of association and special resolutions or unanimous resolutions which could have been passed only as special resolutions.

Constructive dismissal A dismissal which occurs when an employee leaves the job, justifiably, on the grounds of the employer's conduct.

Consumer As regards most consumer protection legislation, a natural person (and therefore not a company) who is acting for purposes which are outside his business. However, the Sale of Goods Act definition of a person who 'deals as a consumer' is quite different.

Contributory negligence A defence whereby a claimant's damages are reduced by the extent to which his own fault contributed to his loss.

Conversion A tort giving the owner of goods the right to sue a person who wrongfully possesses, damages or destroys the goods. The tort is committed by intentionally dealing with goods in a way which is inconsistent with another's right to possess the goods.

Conviction (1) A decision by a court that a defendant is guilty of the crime of which he was accused. (2) A record of a person having been found guilty of a crime.

Cooling-off period A short period of time during which a concluded contract can, in some circumstances, be terminated.

Copyright A right which protects the way in which ideas are expressed.

Corporate veil The idea that a company is a legal person separate from its members. It is based on an image of a veil hanging between the company and its members.

Counter offer The rejection of an offer, made by proposing a different set of terms.

Court of Appeal The second highest court in the English legal system. The court sits as either a criminal division or a civil division and only hears appeals. No cases begin in the Court of Appeal.

Court of Chancery A medieval court, presided over by the Lord Chancellor, which dealt with defects in the common law and with matters of conscience. Ceased to exist in 1873 when the Chancery Division of the High Court was created.

Court of Human Rights A court in Strasbourg which hears cases involving breach of the European Convention on Human Rights.

Court of Justice of the European Union (CJEU) The highest court in relation to matters of EU law. It sits in Luxembourg.

Credit The right to have payment of a debt postponed.

Creditor A person who is owed money.

Credit sale A sale of goods whereby the buyer gets ownership and possession of the goods before payment of the price.

Crown Court Court which tries serious criminal cases in front of a judge and jury.

Crystallisation (of a charge) The turning of a floating charge into a fixed charge.

Damages A payment of a sum of money to compensate for a loss suffered as a result of a tort or a breach of contract.

Debenture A document which shows that a loan has been given by a company.

Debtor A person who owes money.

Decisions (i.e. of EU Council) Minor EU legislation, addressed to an individual or Member State.

Declaration of incompatibility A declaration by a precedent-making court that a piece of legislation is incompatible with rights contained in the European Convention on Human Rights.

Deed A written contract which is signed by the makers and also signed by people who witness the makers' signatures. The document must make it clear that it is intended to be a deed.

Defamation A tort, committed by publishing a statement which either lowers the claimant in the estimation of right-thinking people generally or causes the claimant to be shunned and avoided.

Default position The position which will apply if no action is taken to change it.

Default provisions Provisions in the Partnership Act 1890, or the Limited Liability Partnerships Act 2000, which regulate the members' or partners' relationship with each other, but only if they do not substitute their own arrangements.

Delegated legislation Legislation delegated by Parliament to some other body to make.

De minimis An abbreviation of the rule *de minimis non curat lex*, the law is not concerned with trifles (very trivial matters).

Derivative claim A legal action brought by a company member on behalf of the company.

Designated member (of an LLP) A member of an LLP who has duties which are similar to the duties of company directors and the company secretary.

Direct applicability EU law which is directly applicable automatically forms part of the law of Member States, such as the UK.

Directive A form of EU secondary legislation, which must be implemented into the law of Member States before a certain date.

Director A person who manages a company.

Directors' report Part of a company's accounts which gives a fair view of the development of the company's business and of the company's position at the end of a financial year.

Discharge (of contract) When a contract is discharged, the obligations it created cease to exist.

Disclosed agency Agency which exists when the third party with whom the agent deals knows that the agent is acting as an agent.

Disqualification order A court order disqualifying a person from being a company director for a certain time.

Dissolution (of a partnership) The ending of a partnership, which may be little more than a formality. (Contrast **winding up**.)

Distance contract A contract concluded solely by means of distance communications, without the consumer and the supplier actually meeting each other.

Distinguishing Occurs when a lower court refuses to follow an apparently binding precedent, on the grounds that it is materially different from the facts of the case in front of it.

District judge A judge attached to a County Court hearing centre who hears claims allocated to the small claims track.

Divisible contract A contract which can be divided into several, independent obligations. Also known as a severable contract. Contrasted with an entire contract.

Document of title A document, such as a bill of lading, which indicates that the holder can treat the goods as if he owned them.

Duress Improper pressure, pushing a party into a contract in such a way that he did not really agree to it. Makes the contract voidable.

Duty of care (in tort of negligence) A duty to take care not to injure people whom you can reasonably foresee might be injured by your actions.

EC The European Community. Now known as the EU or European Union.

Economic loss A loss which is not connected to injury to the person or damage to property, but which is purely financial, e.g. lost profits.

Ejusdem generis rule A rule of statutory interpretation that general words which follow specific words must be given the same type of meaning as the specific words.

Employee A person who works under a contract of employment.

Employer Person who employs an employee under a contract of employment.

Employment tribunal A court which hears only employment cases.

Entire contract A contract consisting of one single obligation. Contrasted with a **divisible contract**.

Equality and Human Rights Commission A new body which will take action against those who discriminate unlawfully or who breach human rights.

Equality clause A clause, deemed by the Equality Act 2010 to be in a woman's contract of employment, to the effect that her terms and conditions should be no less favourable than those of a man doing the same type of work for the same employer.

Equity The body of law which originated in the Court of Chancery. It is contrasted with **common law**, which did not originate in this way.

Estoppel A rule that a person who has made a representation to another cannot deny the truth of the representation once it has been acted upon.

Ethnic group A group of people with a shared history and culture.

EU The European Union.

European Commission A permanent EU body which makes broad EU policies and proposes EU legislation.

European Convention on Human Rights A Treaty setting out human rights. The Treaty was created in 1950 and the United Kingdom ratified it in 1951.

European Council A temporary body, made up of Ministers from EU States, which makes policy on particular matters.

European Parliament The elected Parliament of the EU, which approves the EU budget and can veto some EU legislation.

European Union A union of 27 States which aims to enhance political, economic and social co-operation. It was previously known as the European Community (EC) and before that as the European Economic Community (EEC).

Exclusion clause A term of a contract which attempts to limit or exclude liability for breach of the contract.

Executed consideration Consideration which occurs when one of the parties makes the offer or the acceptance in such a way that he has completely fulfilled his liability under the contract.

Executory consideration Consideration which consists of a promise to do something in the future.

Express actual authority Actual authority of an agent which is created by express words, written or spoken.

Express term A term of a contract which was agreed by the parties in express words (written or spoken).

Expressio unius est exclusio alterius A rule of statutory interpretation that if there is a list of specific words, not followed by any general words, then the statute applies only to the specific words mentioned.

Extraordinary general meeting (EGM) A meeting of company members which is not the AGM.

Factor (Also known as a **mercantile agent**.) An agent in business to buy or sell goods who can, in certain circumstances, pass ownership of another person's goods even when acting without authority to do so.

Fair comment A defence to defamation which is available to a person who acted without malice when commenting on a matter of public interest.

False imprisonment A tort, committed by directly and intentionally depriving the claimant of his or her liberty.

Fiduciary Involving great trust or confidence.

Firm A partnership.

First instance (court of) A court which first hears a case.

Fixed charge A company charge which mortgages specific property belonging to the company.

Fixed-term contract A contract which is agreed at the outset to be in existence for a fixed time, rather than being a contract which can be ended by giving notice.

Floating charge A company charge under which a creditor takes a class of, or all of, the company's property, both present and future assets, as security for a debt.

Force majeure **clause** A term of a contract which might excuse non-performance of the contract if this was caused by matters beyond the control of the parties, such as a tsunami.

Foreseeability The extent to which damage or loss was foreseeable.

Freezing injunction An injunction which prevents a person from moving assets out of the jurisdiction of the English courts. Previously known as a Mareva injunction.

Frustration (1) Discharge of a contract on the grounds that it has become impossible to perform, illegal to perform or radically different from what the parties contemplated. (2) Discharge of a contract of sale of specific goods which perish after they have been sold but before the risk has passed to the buyer.

Goods Property which can be touched and moved. (Not interests in land, money or things in action.)

Goodwill The amount by which the market value of a business is worth more than the value of its individual assets.

Gratuitous agent An agent who acts for no reward or payment.

Gross pay The amount of pay made to an employee before any deductions, such as tax, have been made. (Compare **net pay**.)

Gross profits Any pre-tax profits which remain once all the business liabilities have been taken away from gross takings. (Compare **net profits**.)

Gross takings All the money which a business takes in.

Harassment In employment law, harassment means unwanted conduct which is intended to have, or has, the effect of violating a person's dignity or creating an intimidating, hostile, degrading, humiliating or offensive environment for that person.

Hire (contract of) A contract under which possession, but not ownership, of goods is given in return for payment.

Hire-purchase (contract of) A contract under which goods are hired for a fixed time in return for regular payments, with the hirer given an option to buy the goods for a nominal sum when the agreement ends.

HMRC HM Revenue and Customs which was formed in 2005, following the merger of the Inland Revenue and HM Customs and Excise Departments.

Holding out A person who holds something out represents that that thing is true and will be prevented from denying the truth of the representation as regards a person who has relied on it.

Horizontal effect EU law which can be relied upon by one individual to sue another individual. (Contrast **vertical effect**.)

House of Lords (1) Formerly, the highest court in the English legal system. (2) A law-making house of Parliament in which Members of the House of Lords sit.

Hybrid (or either way) offence A criminal offence which is neither particularly serious nor particularly minor, and which may be tried either by the Crown Court or by the magistrates' court.

Illegal contract A contract which cannot be enforced because its purpose is illegal.

Implied actual authority Actual authority of an agent which is created by conduct rather than by words.

Implied term A term which was not expressly agreed by the parties but which was implied by the courts or by a statute.

Indemnity A payment to compensate for expenses properly incurred.

Independent contractor A person who works in a self-employed capacity, rather than as an employee.

Indictable offence A serious criminal offence, which will be tried in the Crown Court in front of a judge and jury.

Injunction A court order requiring a person to do or not to do some act.

Innocent publication A defence to defamation which is available only to a distributor.

Innominate term A term of a contract which is not a **condition** or a **warranty**. If such a term is breached the injured party will be entitled to damages but will not be entitled to treat the contract as terminated unless the breach deprived him/her of substantially the whole benefit of the contract.

Innuendo In **defamation**, a meaning which would be known only to those with special knowledge.

Inquisitorial system of trial A system under which the judge sets out to discover the facts.

Insolvent Unable to pay existing debts. Individuals who are insolvent may be made bankrupt. Companies which are insolvent may be liquidated.

Intellectual property right An intangible property right such as copyright, patent or trade mark.

Intention to create legal relations One of the four main requirements of a contract. Even if there is an offer, an acceptance and an exchange of consideration, there will be no contract unless it appears that the parties intended to create legal relations.

Interest Money charged in return for the use of other money.

Invitation to treat In contract, an invitation to make an offer. Its main significance is that it is not itself an offer.

Invoice A document which a seller of goods or services sends to a buyer, describing what has been sold and showing the price and how much money is due.

Joint and several liability People who have the same liability so that any of them can be sued in respect of it. The person sued may receive a contribution from others who were liable.

Judicature Acts 1873–1875 Statutes which merged the administration of common law and equity.

Judicial precedent The system which operates in England whereby the decisions (*ratio decidendi*) of higher courts can be binding on lower courts.

Judicial review A procedure by which the Administrative Court can declare decisions of public law bodies to be illegal.

Judiciary All of the judges in the country make up the judiciary.

Jurisdiction The power of a court to hear a legal case.

Jury A group of persons who take an oath to decide questions of fact in judicial proceedings. Juries of 12 sit in the Crown Court. Indictable offences are tried by jury; summary offences cannot be. Hybrid offences are sometimes tried by jury. Juries used to sit in civil cases but generally do not do so any more.

Justification (1) In defamation, a defence that the allegedly defamatory statement was true. (2) A defence to trespass to land, that the defendant has legal authority to enter the land.

Law Lord A judge who used to sit in the House of Lords, e.g. Lord Hoffmann, before the Supreme Court replaced the House of Lords.

Law reports Records containing the full decisions of certain cases made by precedent-making courts.

Lay magistrate A magistrate who is not trained as a lawyer.

Lay person A person who is not trained as a lawyer.

Legislation Law made or approved by Parliament in the form of statutes or delegated legislation.

Libel Defamation in a permanent medium, such as writing.

Licence Permission granted by an occupier of land to enter onto the land.

Lien A right to keep possession of another's goods until a debt is paid.

Lieu (in lieu) Instead of.

Limited company A company in which the liability of the members is limited to paying fully for their shares. Beyond this, the members have no liability to pay the debts of the company. Most companies are limited.

Limited liability partnership A business organisation, with two or more members, which shares some of the features of a partnership and some of a limited company.

Liquidated damages clause A term in a contract which sets out the amount of damages to be paid if the contract is breached, the amount specified being the amount which the parties genuinely thought that the loss would be in the event of breach. The amount specified will be the amount payable, no matter what the actual loss turned out to be. Contrasted with a **penalty**.

Liquidation The ending of a company's existence, or an LLP's existence, when its debts are paid and any surplus assets are divided amongst the shareholders or members. Also known as winding up.

Liquidator A person appointed by a court to liquidate a company or an LLP.

LLP See **limited liability partnership**.

Loan Money lent, usually in return for the payment of interest.

Lord Justice of Appeal A judge who sits in the Court of Appeal, e.g. Laws LJ.

Magistrates' court Court which tries less serious criminal cases.

Mediation A form of ADR under which a mediator tries to bring the parties together to settle their dispute.

Member of a company A shareholder in a company.

Member States States which are members of the EU.

Memorandum of association A document needed to register a company which gives basic information about the company. This is a 'historical snapshot' which cannot later be altered.

Mens rea The guilty state of mind which needs to be proved before a person can be convicted of a crime.

Mercantile agent (Also known as a **factor**.) An agent in business to buy or sell goods who can, in certain circumstances, pass ownership of another person's goods even when acting without authority to do so.

Minor A person under 18 years of age. Minors do not have full capacity to make contracts.

Minority shareholder A shareholder in a company with less than 50 per cent of the shares which carry voting rights.

Mischief rule A rule of statutory interpretation which allows a court to consider what mischief or problem a statute sought to rectify.

Misrepresentation (actionable) An untrue statement of fact which induced the making of a contract. An actionable misrepresentation makes a contract voidable.

Mistake (common) A mistake made by both of the parties to a contract.

Mistake (unilateral) A mistake made by only one of the parties to a contract.

Mitigation The duty to take reasonable steps to reduce a loss caused by a tort or a breach of contract.

Mortgage A form of security whereby property is given as security for a debt. If the debt is not repaid the property can be sold by the creditor who can take what he is owed from the proceeds.

Negligence (tort of) The most important tort. Liability in negligence arises when a defendant who owes a duty of care breaches that duty in such a way that this causes a foreseeable type of damage.

Negligent misstatement A form of the tort of negligence whereby a person in a special relationship with another person can be liable on account of statements made to that other person.

Nemo dat **rule** (*Nemo dat quod non habet*) The general rule that a person who does not

own goods cannot pass ownership of those goods to another person.

Net pay The amount of money which an employee actually receives as pay, after deductions such as tax have been made.

Net profits The profit which remains after all tax and other lawful deductions have been made.

Nominal damages Damages in name only. Token damages, often 5p or £1.

Nominal sum A token (very small) sum of money.

Non est factum A kind of mistake which makes a contract void because a person, who was not careless, was completely mistaken about the nature of what it was he or she signed.

Notice (1) Notification of a fact. (2) In employment, the amount of time needed to notify either an employer or an employee that the contract is to be unilaterally ended.

Novus actus interveniens A new act intervening, which breaks the chain of causation in tort.

Nuisance A tort. See **public nuisance** and **private nuisance**.

Obiter dicta (Literally, other things said.) A legal principle which is part of a precedent-making court's decision but which cannot be binding as a judicial precedent because it was not the **ratio decidendi**.

Objects clause A part of a company's old-style **memorandum of association** which sets out the contracts which the company has the capacity to make. Since the Companies Act 2006 came into force, newly formed companies no longer need to register an objects clause.

Occupiers' liability The liability of occupiers of premises owed both to lawful visitors to those premises and to trespassers.

Offence A crime.

Offer A proposal of a set of terms by which the offeror is willing to be contractually bound.

Offer to settle A formal offer to settle a civil claim for a certain amount.

Offeree A person to whom an offer is made.

Offeror A person who makes an offer.

Off-the-shelf company A company formed in advance so that it can be sold to people who do not want to form their own company.

Office of Legal Complaints A new body which will investigate complaints against solicitors and barristers.

Ombudsman A person empowered to investigate disputes which arise within a certain trade or industry.

Oral contract A contract made by spoken words (i.e. not made in writing or by conduct).

Ordinary resolution A company resolution which is passed if a majority of eligible members (who actually vote) vote in favour of the resolution.

Overdraft Credit given by a bank in allowing a customer to take more money out of his or her account than is in the account.

Overrule A higher court overrules a *ratio decidendi* of a lower court by declaring it to be invalid and overturned.

Parent Act A statute which gives the power to make delegated legislation.

Parliament The supreme governing body of the United Kingdom which can pass legislation. It is made up of the Queen, the House of Lords and the House of Commons.

Partnership Two or more persons carrying on a business together, with the intention of making a profit, and without operating as a company or an LLP.

Partnership agreement A written agreement setting out the rights of partners as regards each other. Can be in the form of a deed, but does not need to be.

Partnership property Property which belongs to all of the partners in a firm, rather than to individual partners.

Party A person.

Passing off A tort committed by deceiving the public so that they believe that a business is in fact a different business.

Past consideration A promise to perform an act which has already been performed (cannot be good consideration in law of contract).

Patent A right to exploit a new inventive step which has been registered as a patent.

Payment into court A formal offer to settle a civil claim for a certain amount.

Penalty A term in a contract which sets out the amount of damages to be paid if the contract is breached, the amount specified being a large sum to terrorise the other party into performance, rather than a genuine pre-estimate of what the loss would be. Penalties are ignored by the courts, which assess damages as if the penalty did not exist. Contrasted with **liquidated damages clauses**.

Perpetual succession The idea that a company or an LLP can stay in existence permanently.

Plc See **public company**.

Pledge (or pawn) Handing over possession of goods as security for a loan, on the understanding that the goods can be sold if necessary to recoup any part of the debt which is not repaid.

Pledge credit Gain credit by promising that the debt will be repaid.

Poll A vote on a company resolution where each voting share carries one vote. Contrast **show of hands**.

Postal rule The rule that acceptance of an offer by letter or telegram is effective when it is posted. The rule applies only if acceptance by letter or telegram is asked for or reasonably expected.

Preference (in relation to companies) An act by a company which puts a creditor of the company into a better position if the company should go into insolvent liquidation than he otherwise would have been. A court can order that a preference be repaid to the company.

Preference shares A class of shares which have rights which are not the same as the rights attaching to ordinary shares.

Preferential creditor A creditor of a company who has taken security for the debt and is therefore allowed to take payment out of the sums realised by the security ahead of unsecured creditors. However, this right can be subject to 'top-slicing'.

Prescription A property right which can give a right to continue committing what would otherwise be a nuisance. The right is acquired by continuously doing the act which causes the nuisance for 20 years.

Presumption A state of affairs which a court will presume to exist unless evidence rebuts the presumption. (See also **rebut**.) A few presumptions are irrebuttable, in which case no evidence will be allowed to contradict them.

Principal A person on whose behalf an agent acts.

Private company A company which is not allowed to offer its shares and debentures to the public.

Private nuisance A tort consisting of an unreasonable interference with a claimant's land or with a claimant's use or enjoyment of land.

Privilege (in defamation) Absolute and qualified privilege are defences to defamation.

Privity of contract The common law rule that a person who did not make a contract can neither sue on it nor be sued on it. The rule has been modified to some extent by the Contracts (Rights of Third Parties) Act 1999.

Privy Council The Supreme Court justices when they sit to hear an appeal from certain Commonwealth countries.

Pro rata In the same proportion, or at the same rate.

Procedure The rules applying to the bringing of a court case. The way in which a civil or criminal court case must be conducted.

Proceeds of sale The amount of money received when property is sold.

Product liability An area of law concerned with making sure that manufacturers and importers into the EU do not put unsafe products on to the market.

Profit and loss account Part of a company's accounts which show the income and expenses of the company over the financial year.

Promoter Person who forms a company.

Protocol An agreement between States which is less formal than a Treaty.

Proxy A person entitled to vote in place of a company member, who authorised him to do so, at a company meeting.

Public company (plc) A company which is allowed to offer its shares and debentures to the public. Also known as a public limited company.

Public nuisance A crime and a tort, which is committed by any act or omission which endangers the health, property or comfort of the public, or which prevents the public from exercising rights which all citizens enjoy.

QC (Queen's Counsel) A senior barrister who has been declared a QC by a selection panel. Such a barrister usually acts in court with an assistant barrister and can usually charge higher fees.

Quantum meruit A claim to be paid on a proportional basis for work completed. Literally, 'As much as he has earned'.

Ratification (in agency) A principal's act of conferring actual authority on an agent who has already acted for the principal at a time when he did not have actual authority.

Ratification (of a Treaty) Agreeing to be bound by a Treaty.

Ratio decidendi A legal principle which is part of a court's decision and which can be binding as a judicial precedent. (Literally, the reason for the decision.)

Real remedy (sale of goods) A remedy taken by an unpaid seller against the goods, rather than against the buyer. (See **lien, stoppage in transit** and **right of resale**.)

Realisation (of security) Selling an asset or property right given as security for a debt, so that the amount owing can be deducted from the proceeds of sale.

Rebut To contradict or to provide an answer to an argument or to a presumption.

Rectification An equitable remedy which allows a written document to be corrected to reflect what was agreed orally.

Red-circling Allowing workers who have been demoted in a reorganisation to remain on their previous rates of pay.

Redundancy A dismissal of an employee on the grounds of the employer going out of business, moving the business, or not needing work of the type which the employee performed.

Re-engagement A remedy for unfair dismissal, rarely awarded, in which an employer is ordered to give an unfairly dismissed person another job similar to the one from which he or she was dismissed.

Registrar of Companies An official who deals with the administration of companies. The head of Companies House.

Regulation A form of directly applicable EU secondary legislation.

Regulations A form of UK delegated legislation.

Reinstatement A remedy for unfair dismissal, rarely awarded, in which an employer is ordered to re-employ an unfairly dismissed person on the same conditions as he or she held before the dismissal.

Rejection (of goods) Refusal to accept goods.

Representation A statement which induces the making of a contract and which is not a term of the contract.

Repudiation An indication by a contracting party that he does not intend to perform the contract.

Resale (right of) A right which can give an unpaid seller of goods the right to resell the goods to a second buyer.

Rescission (1) The calling off of future performance of a contract on account of misrepresentation, duress or undue influence. (See also **avoiding the contract**.) (2) Terminating a contract under ss. 48A–48F of the Sale of Goods Act 1979.

Resolution A decision passed by a vote of company members. See **ordinary**, **special** and **written resolutions**.

Restraint of trade clause A term of a contract which tries to prevent a person from working or carrying on a business. Void unless reasonable.

Retention of title clause A term in a contract which stipulates that ownership of goods which have been agreed to be sold will remain with the seller until the price is paid, even though the buyer may take possession of the goods.

Reversing In the same case, an appeal court changes (reverses) the decision of the lower court so that the person making the appeal wins in the appeal court.

Revocation (of an offer) Calling an offer off, so that it can no longer be accepted.

Right of resale A right of an unpaid seller to resell goods to a second buyer after they have already been sold to the first buyer.

Risk (in sale of goods) Risk passes from the seller of goods to the buyer, with ownership unless agreed otherwise. The party with the risk bears the loss if the goods are lost, stolen, damaged or destroyed.

Rogue Dishonest person.

ROT clause (1) A retention of title clause. (2) A restraint of trade clause.

Royal Assent The final stage in the passing of a statute. At this point a Bill becomes a statute.

Rylands *v* Fletcher A tort of strict liability.

s. An abbreviation for section. So s. 1 SGA 1979 means section 1 of the Sale of Goods Act 1979.

Sample (sale by) A small quantity of goods to be examined by a buyer on the understanding that the bulk of the goods, when they are delivered, will correspond with the sample in quality.

Satisfactory quality A requirement that goods sold or supplied in the course of a business meet the standard that a reasonable person would regard as satisfactory, taking account of the price, description and other relevant circumstances.

Search order An injunction which allows the claimant access to premises to make sure that evidence is not destroyed. (Previously known as an Anton Pillar order.)

Secured creditor A creditor who has taken some security for a debt.

Security An asset or property right which can be sold, in order to take what is owing, if a debt is not repaid.

Self-employed A person who works for himself rather than for an employer.

Set off An amount of money which a claimant owes to a defendant, and which the defendant uses as a total or partial defence to a claim by the claimant.

Shares The interest of a member in a company, measured by a sum of money.

Show of hands A vote on a company resolution where each member has one vote, regardless of his or her shareholding.

Single member company A company which has only one member.

Slander Defamation in a temporary medium, such as speech.

Sole trader A person who is in business on his own, not as a company, an LLP or a partnership.

Special resolution A company resolution which is passed if 75 per cent of eligible members who actually vote vote in favour of the resolution.

Specific goods Goods which are identified and agreed upon at the time a contract of sale of goods is made. Contrasted with **unascertained goods**.

Specific performance A court order, rarely granted, ordering a party to perform his contractual obligations.

Standard of proof The extent to which a burden of proof must be satisfied. In civil cases this is generally on a balance of probabilities. In criminal cases the prosecution must prove all elements of the case beyond reasonable doubt.

State A sovereign country.

Statute An Act of Parliament.

Statutory authority A defence to various torts, that the act complained of was authorised by a statute.

Statutory duty (breach of) Liability in tort which can arise on account of breaching the provisions of a statute, even though the statute did not specifically spell out civil liability.

Stoppage in transit A right of an unpaid seller to recover goods being delivered by a carrier to an insolvent buyer.

Strict liability (1) In civil law, liability which can arise without fault. (2) In criminal law, an offence which can be committed without the prosecution needing to prove *mens rea* in respect of all aspects of the *actus reus*.

Subject to contract A willingness to accept an offer subject to contract indicates that no contract will be created until the parties have completed further formalities.

Subpoena A court order, requiring a person to attend court and give evidence.

Substantial performance Performance of a contract which is sufficiently complete to enable a claim for the price to be made. Damages may be payable in respect of the part of the contract which was not performed.

Sufficiency (of consideration) Consideration is sufficient if it is of some recognisable value, no matter how small, in relation to the consideration for which it is exchanged. If a party's consideration is not sufficient, then no contract will be formed. (See also **adequacy**.)

Summary dismissal Dismissal of an employee without notice.

Summary offence A minor criminal offence which will be heard by the magistrates' court.

Supreme Court The highest court in the English legal system, formerly the House of Lords.

Supreme Court justice A judge who sits in the Supreme Court.

Surplus assets Assets of a company or an LLP which are left over after the company or LLP has been wound up and all creditors paid.

Tender An offer to buy or sell goods, made in response to an invitation for tenders.

Tender of performance A demonstrated willingness to perform an obligation.

Tender of the price An offer to pay the price.

Term (of a contract) An agreement within a contract which gives rise to contractual liabilities.

Thing in action An intangible property right, such as a patent, which can be enforced only by taking legal action.

Third party A person other than the parties to a contract.

Title (in goods) Ownership of the goods.

Top-slicing In relation to floating charges created on or after 15 September 2003, top-slicing requires a liquidator of an insolvent company to set aside a certain percentage of the company's assets for payment to the unsecured creditors. This amount is paid to the unsecured creditors ahead of any amount paid to the floating charge holders.

Tort A civil wrong other than a breach of contract.

Track Civil cases will be allocated to one of three tracks: the small claims track, the fast track or the multi-track, depending upon the size and complexity of the claim.

Trade mark An image which distinguishes the products of one business from those of other businesses.

Treaty A binding agreement made between different States.

Treaty of Rome The Treaty which founded what is now the EU in 1957.

Trespass to land A direct, unauthorised interference with another person's land.

Trespass to the person Either assault, battery or false imprisonment.

Tribunal A specialist court which hears disputes of a certain type, e.g. the employment tribunal hears employment cases.

Trifle A matter so trivial that it can be ignored.

Trust An equitable obligation under which a trustee holds ownership of property for the benefit of one or more beneficiaries.

Trustee A person who holds property on trust for a beneficiary.

Uberrimae fidei Of the utmost good faith.

Ultra vires An act which a company's objects clause did not permit the company to do.

Unascertained goods Goods which are not identified and agreed upon at the time a contract of sale is made. Contrasted with **specific goods**.

Undisclosed agency Agency which arises when an agent with actual authority acts on behalf of a principal, and the third party dealing with the agent does not know that the agent is acting for a principal.

Undue influence Improper influence which persuades a person to make a contract. A contract made because of undue influence is voidable.

Unfair dismissal A statutory remedy available to employees who are unfairly dismissed.

Unilateral contract A contract in which the offeror promises to be bound if the offeree performs a specified act, and the offeree accepts by performing the act.

Unlimited company A private company in which the liability of the members for the debts of the company is not limited.

Unpaid seller A seller of goods who has not been paid or offered the whole of the purchase price of the goods.

Unsecured creditor A creditor who has taken no security for a debt.

Vertical effect EU law which can be relied upon by an individual only to sue the State, or an emanation of the State. It cannot be relied upon to sue another individual. See also **horizontal effect**.

Vicarious liability The liability of employers for torts committed by their employees during the course of their employment.

Void A void contract is a contract which never comes into existence, even though the parties have tried to form a contract. Contracts can be rendered void if their purpose is illegal, or if the parties make certain types of mistake when forming the contract.

Voidable A voidable contract is one which can be avoided or rescinded. Until the contract is avoided it has legal effect.

Volenti non fit injuria A defence to an action in tort, whereby the defendant shows that the claimant voluntarily assumed the risk which caused his injury.

Voting rights In relation to company shares, shares which carry the right to vote at a meeting of company members. Non-voting shares have no such right.

Waiver The voluntarily giving up of a right, which then becomes lost.

Warranty A term of a contract, breach of which gives a right to damages but no right to terminate the contract. A term is a warranty if, when the contract was made, it was considered not to go to the root of the contract. Some statutory terms are also labelled warranties. Contrasted with **conditions**.

Warranty of authority In agency, an untrue representation made by an agent to a third party, to the effect that the agent has authority to act for a principal.

Winding up (of a company, LLP or partnership) The ending of the existence of a company, an LLP or a partnership, when its debts are paid and any surplus assets are divided amongst the owners of the business. In the case of companies and LLPs, also known as **liquidation**.

Written resolution A resolution of a private company which is passed by the required majority of shareholders signing it, rather than by a vote at a company meeting.

Wrongful dismissal A claim in contract by an employee who has been dismissed without having been given the period of notice to which his contract entitled him.

Index